International Politics

INTERNATIONAL POLITICS

Enduring Concepts and Contemporary Issues

THIRD EDITION

ROBERT J. ART
Brandeis University

ROBERT JERVIS
Columbia University

HarperCollins*Publishers*

Sponsoring Editor: Catherine Woods
Project Coordination, Cover Design, and Cover Illustration: York Production Services
Production Manager: Michael Weinstein
Compositor: York Production Services
Printer and Binder: R.R. Donnelley & Sons Company
Cover Printer: New England Book Components

International Politics, Third Edition
Copyright © 1992 by HarperCollins Publishers Inc.

Library of Congress Cataloging-in-Publication Data
International politics : enduring concepts and contemporary issues /
  [edited by] Robert J. Art, Robert Jervis.—3rd ed.
      p.   cm.
  Includes bibliographical references.
  ISBN 0-673-52161-3
    1. International relations.   I. Art, Robert J.   II. Jervis,
Robert, 1940–   .
JX1395.I576   1992
327—dc20   91-24190
                                                          CIP

91 92 93 94 9 8 7 6 5 4 3 2 1

Brief Contents

Detailed Contents

Preface

The first edition of *International Politics* appeared in 1973. Since then, the field of international relations has experienced a dramatic enrichment in the subjects studied and in the quality of works published. Political economy came into its own as an important subfield in the 1970s. New and important works in the field of security studies appeared. The literature on cooperation among states flourished in the early 1980s, and important studies about the environment appeared in the mid-1980s. The growing diversity of the field has closely mirrored the actual developments in international relations. Now, as the third edition appears, the Cold War is over, but the outlines of what will replace it have not yet emerged.

In fashioning the third edition, we have kept in mind both the new developments in world politics and the literature that has accompanied them. But we have tried to put them both in the context of the patterns that still remain valid for understanding how international relations differs from domestic politics. The theme for the third edition therefore revolves around "enduring concepts and contemporary issues" in world politics.

Consequently, we have retained the four major divisions that existed in the second edition—the meaning of anarchy, the uses of force, the nature of political economy, and the nature of decisionmaking within a state—and have added a fifth on justice, human rights, and the environment. Only Part Four of this third edition remains the same as in the second, and only eight other selections from the second edition have been retained. The third edition of *International Politics* is, therefore, essentially a new reader because nearly two-thirds of the selections are new.

In the third edition, we have continued to follow the four principles that guided us in putting together the first two editions:

1. A selection of subjects that, even though they do not exhaustively cover the field of international politics, nevertheless encompasses most of the essential topics that we teach in our introductory courses.
2. Individual readings that are mainly analytical in content, that take issue with one another, and that thereby introduce the student to the fundamental debates and points of view in the field.
3. Editors' introductions to each part that summarize the central concepts the student must master, that organize the central themes of each part, and that relate the readings to one another.
4. A reader that can be used either as the core around which to design an introductory course or as the primary supplement to enrich an assigned text.

Finally, in putting together the third edition, we received excellent advice from the following colleagues, whom we would like to thank for the time and care they took: Henri J. Barkey, Lehigh University; Steven R. David, Johns Hopkins University; Robert Gilpin, Princeton University; Henry A. Shockley, Boston University; Jack Snyder, Columbia University; and Stephen M. Walt, University of Chicago.

Robert J. Art
Robert Jervis

International Politics

ANARCHY AND ITS CONSEQUENCES

*U*nlike domestic politics, international politics takes place in an arena that has no central governing body. No agency exists above the individual states with authority and power to make laws and settle disputes. States can make commitments and treaties, but no sovereign power ensures compliance and punishes deviations. This—the absence of a supreme power—is what is meant by the anarchic environment of international politics. Anarchy is therefore said to constitute a *state of war:* When all else fails, force is the *ultima ratio*—the final and legitimate arbiter of disputes among states.

The state of war does not mean that every nation is constantly at the brink of war or actually at war with other nations. Most countries, though, do feel threatened by some states at some time, and every state has experienced periods of intense insecurity. No two contiguous states, moreover, have had a history of close, friendly relations uninterrupted by severe tension if not outright war. Because a nation cannot look to a supreme body to enforce laws, nor count on other nations for constant aid and support, it must rely on its own efforts, particularly for defense against attack. Coexistence in an anarchic environment thus requires *self-help*. The psychological outlook that self-help breeds is best described by a saying common among British statesmen since Palmerston: "Great Britain has no permanent enemies or permanent friends, she has only permanent interests."

Although states must provide the wherewithal to achieve their own ends, they do not always reach their foreign policy goals. The goals may be grandiose; the means available, meager. The goals may be attainable; the means selected, inappropriate. But even if the goals are realistic and the means both available and appropriate, a state can be frustrated in pursuit of its ends. The reason is simple, but fundamental to an understanding of inter-

1

national politics: What one state does will inevitably impinge on some other states—on some beneficially, but on others adversely. What one state desires another may covet. What one thinks its just due another may find threatening. Steps that a state takes to achieve its goals may be rendered useless by the countersteps others take. No state, therefore, can afford to disregard the effects its actions will have on other nations' behavior. In this sense state behavior is contingent: What one state does is dependent in part upon what others do. Mutual dependence means that each must take the others into account. Kenneth Waltz explores this point more fully and shows why "in anarchy there is no automatic harmony."

Mutual dependence affects nothing more powerfully than it does security—the measures states take to protect their territory. Like other foreign-policy goals, the security of one state is contingent upon the behavior of other states. Herein lies the *security dilemma* to which each state is subject: In its efforts to preserve or enhance its own security, one state can take measures that decrease the security of other states and cause them to take countermeasures that neutralize the actions of the first state and that may even menace it. The first state may feel impelled to take additional actions that will provoke additional countermeasures . . . and so forth. The security dilemma means that an action-reaction spiral can occur between two states or among several of them so that each is forced to spend even larger sums on arms and be no more secure than before. All will run faster merely to stay where they were.

At the heart of the security dilemma are these two constraints: the inherent difficulty in distinguishing between offensive and defensive postures and the inability of one state to bank on the fact that another state's present pacific intentions will remain so. The capability to defend can also provide the capability to attack. In adding to its arms, state A may know that its aim is defensive, that its intentions are peaceful, and therefore that it has no aggressive designs on state B. In a world where states must look to themselves for protection, however, B will examine A's actions carefully and suspiciously. B may think that A will attack him when A's arms become powerful enough and that A's protestations of friendship are designed to lull him into lowering his guard. But even if B believes A's actions are not directed against him, B cannot assume that A's intentions will remain peaceful. B must allow for the possibility that what A can do to him, A sometime might do. The need to assess capabilities along with intentions, or, the equivalent, to allow for a change in intentions, makes statesmen profoundly conservative. They prefer to err on the side of safety, to have too much rather than too little. Because security is the basis of existence and the prerequisite for the achievement of all other goals, statesmen must be acutely sensitive to the security actions of others. The security dilemma thus means that statesmen cannot risk *not* reacting to the security actions of other states, but that in so reacting they can produce circumstances that leave them worse off than before.

The anarchic environment of international politics, then, allows every state to be the final judge of its own interests, but requires that each provide the means to attain them. Because the absence of a central authority permits wars to occur, security considerations become paramount. Because of the effects of the security dilemma, efforts of statesmen to protect their peoples can lead to severe tension and war even when all parties sincerely desire peace. Two states, or two groups of states, each satisfied with the status quo and seeking only security, may not be able to achieve it. Conflicts and wars with no economic or ideological basis can occur. The outbreak of war, there-fore, does not necessarily mean that some or all states seek expansion, or that men have an innate drive for power. That states go to war when none of them wants to, however, does not imply that they never seek war. The secu-rity dilemma may explain some wars; it does not explain all wars. States often do experience conflicts of interest over trade, real estate, ideology, and prestige. For example, when someone asked Francis I what differences led to his constant wars with Charles V, he replied: "None whatever. We agree perfectly. We both want control of Italy!" (Cited in Frederick L. Schuman, *International Politics*, 7th ed., New York, 1953, p. 283.) If states cannot ob-tain what they want by blackmail, bribery, or threats, they may resort to war. Wars can occur when no one wants them; wars do occur when someone wants them.

In an anarchic condition the better question to ask is not "Why does war occur?" but "Why does war not occur more frequently than it does?" Instead of asking "Why do states not cooperate more to achieve common interests?" we should ask "Given anarchy and the security dilemma, how is it that states are able to cooperate at all?" This perspective, generally labeled *Realism*, is not without its critics. As Milner notes, the absence of a formal international authority and world government may mean that international politics is tech-nically anarchic, but it does not mean that the contrast to domestic politics is as extreme as Realists claim. States are tied together by a complex web of interests and values. Attacking or even menacing others often is not a pru-dent policy, even for a state that is more powerful than its neighbors. We should not exaggerate either the insecurities or the opportunities created by the international system.

Summarizing a great deal of recent research, Kenneth Oye shows that even if anarchy and the security dilemma inhibit cooperation, they do not prevent it. A number of conditions and national strategies can make it easier for states to achieve common ends. Cooperation is usually easier if there are a small number of actors. Not only can each more carefully observe the others, but all actors know that their impact on the system is great enough so that if they fail to cooperate with others, joint enterprises are likely to fail. Furthermore, when the number of actors is large, there may be mechanisms and institutions that group them together, thereby reproducing some of the advantages of small numbers. The conditions actors face also influence their fates. The barriers of anarchy are more likely to be overcome when actors have long time horizons, when even successfully exploiting others produces an outcome that is only a little better than mutual cooperation, when being exploited by others is only slightly worse than mutual noncooperation, and when mutual cooperation is much better than unrestricted competition. Under such circumstances, states are particularly likely to undertake contingent strategies such as tit-for-tat. That is, they will cooperate with others if others do likewise and refuse to cooperate if others have refused to cooperate with them.

But even under propitious circumstances, cooperation is far from ensured, Realists argue. Joseph Grieco points out that in anarchy, states are often more concerned with relative advantages than with absolute gains. That is, because international politics is a self-help system in which each state must be prepared to rely on its own resources and strength to further its interests, statesmen often seek to become more powerful than their potential adversaries. Cooperation is then made difficult not only by the fear that others will cheat and fail to live up to their agreements, but also by the felt need to gain a superior position. The reason is not that statesmen are concerned with status, but that they fear that arrangements which benefit all, but provide greater benefits to others than to them, will render their country vulnerable to pressure and coercion in the future.

COPING WITH ANARCHY

Even Realists note that conflict and warfare is not a constant characteristic of international politics. Most states remain at peace with most others most of the time. Statesmen have developed a number of ways of coping with anarchy, of gaining more than a modicum of security, of regulating their competition with other states, and of developing patterns that contain, although not eliminate, the dangers of aggression. Most strikingly, it appears that democracies have never gone to war against each other. This is not to say, as Woodrow Wilson did, that democracies are inherently peaceful. They seem to fight as many wars as do dictatorships. But, as Michael Doyle shows, they do not fight each other. If this is correct—and, of course, both the evidence and the reasons are open to dispute—it implies that anarchy and the security dilemma do not prevent peaceful and even harmonious relations among states that share certain common values and beliefs.

Democracies are relatively recent developments. For a longer period of time, two specific devices—international law and diplomacy—have proven useful in resolving conflicts among states. Although not enforced by a world government, international law can provide norms for behavior and mechanisms for settling disputes. The effectiveness of international law derives from the willingness of states to observe it. Its power extends no further than the disposition of states "to agree to agree." Where less than vital interests are at stake, statesmen may accept settlements that are not entirely satis-

factory because they think the precedents or principles justify the compromises made. Much of international law reflects a consensus among states on
what is of equal benefit to all, as, for example, the rules regulating international communications. Diplomacy, too, can facilitate cooperation and resolve
disputes. Particularly if diplomacy is skillful, that is, if the legitimate interests of the parties in dispute are taken into account, understandings can often be reached on issues that might otherwise lead to war. These points and
others are explored more fully by Stanley Hoffmann and Hans Morgenthau.

Statesmen use these two traditional tools within a balance-of-power system. Much maligned by President Wilson and his followers and often misunderstood by many others, balance of power refers to the manner in which
stability can be the outcome of the efforts of individual states, whether or
not any or all of them deliberately pursue that goal. Just as Adam Smith
argued that if every individual pursued his or her own self-interest, the interaction of individual egoisms would enhance national wealth, so international
relations theorists have argued that even if every state seeks power at the
expense of the others, no one state will likely dominate. In both cases a
general good can be the unintended product of selfish individual actions.
Moreover, even if most states desire only to keep what they have, their own
interests dictate that they band together in order to resist any state or coalition of states that threatens to dominate them.

The balance-of-power system is likely to prevent any one state's acquiring hegemony. It will not, however, benefit all states equally nor maintain
the peace permanently. Rewards will be unequal because of inequalities in
power and expertise. Wars will occur because they are one of the means by
which states can preserve what they have or acquire what they covet. Small
states may even be eliminated by their more powerful neighbors. The international system will be unstable, however, only if states flock to what they
think is the strongest side. What is called *bandwagoning* or the *domino
theory* argues that the international system is precarious because successful
aggression will attract many followers, either out of fear or out of a desire to
share the spoils of victory. Stephen Walt disagrees, drawing on balance-of-
power theory and historical evidence to argue that rather than bandwagoning, under most conditions states balance against emerging threats.
They do not throw in their lot with the stronger side. Instead, they join with
others to prevent any state from becoming so strong that it could dominate
the system.

Power balancing is a strategy followed by individual states acting on their
own. Other ways of coping with anarchy, which may supplement or exist
alongside this impulse, are more explicitly collective. Regimes and institutions can help overcome anarchy and facilitate cooperation. When states
agree on the principles, rules, and norms that should govern behavior, they
can often ameliorate the security dilemma and increase the scope for cooperation. Institutions may not only embody common understandings but, as Robert Keohane argues, they can also help states work toward mutually desired

outcomes by providing a framework for long-run agreements, making it easier for each state to see whether others are living up to their promises, and increasing the costs the state will pay if it cheats. In the security area, the United Nations has the potential to be an especially important institution.

As Bruce Russett and James Sutterlin note, the end of the Cold War opens up new possibilities for the internationalization of deterrence and force in the service of common security.

Conflict and Cooperation in Anarchy

The Anarchic Structure of World Politics

Kenneth N. Waltz

POLITICAL STRUCTURES

Only through some sort of systems theory can international politics be understood. To be a success, such a theory has to show how international politics can be conceived of as a domain distinct from the economic, social, and other international domains that one may conceive of. To mark international-political systems off from other international systems, and to distinguish systems-level from unit-level forces, requires showing how political structures are generated and how they affect, and are affected by, the units of the system. How can we conceive of international politics as a distinct system? What is it that intervenes between interacting units and the results that their acts and interactions produce? To answer these questions, this chapter first examines the concept of social structure and then defines structure as a concept appropriate for national and for international politics.

A system is composed of a structure and of interacting units. The structure is the system-wide component that makes it possible to think of the system as a whole. The problem is . . . to contrive a definition of structure free of the attributes and the interactions of units. Definitions of structure must leave aside, or abstract from, the characteristics of units, their behavior, and their interactions. Why must those obviously important matters be omitted? They must be omitted so that we can distinguish between variables at the level of the units and variables at the level of the system. The problem is to develop theoretically useful concepts to replace the vague and varying systemic notions that are customarily employed—notions such as environment, situation, con-

---

From Kenneth N. Waltz, *Theory of International Politics*, © 1979, Addison-Wesley, Reading, Massachusetts, pp. 79–106. Reprinted with permission. Portions of the text and some footnotes have been omitted.

text, and milieu. Structure is a useful concept if it gives clear and fixed meaning to such vague and varying terms.

We know what we have to omit from any definition of structure if the definition is to be useful theoretically. Abstracting from the attributes of units means leaving aside questions about the kinds of political leaders, social and economic institutions, and ideological commitments states may have. Abstracting from relations means leaving aside questions about the cultural, economic, political, and military interactions of states. To say what is to be left out does not indicate what is to be put in. The negative point is important nevertheless because the instruction to omit attributes is often violated and the instruction to omit interactions almost always goes unobserved. But if attributes and interactions are omitted, what is left? The question is answered by considering the double meaning of the term "relation." As S. F. Nadel points out, ordinary language obscures a distinction that is important in theory. "Relation" is used to mean both the interaction of units and the positions they occupy vis-à-vis each other.[1] To define a structure requires ignoring how units relate with one another (how they interact) and concentrating on how they stand in relation to one another (how they are arranged or positioned). Interactions, as I have insisted, take place at the level of the units. How units stand in relation to one another, the way they are arranged or positioned, is not a property of the units. The arrangement of units is a property of the system.

By leaving aside the personality of actors, their behavior, and their interactions, one arrives at a purely positional picture of society. Three propositions follow from this. First, structures may endure while personality, behavior, and interactions vary widely. Structure is sharply distinguished from actions and interactions. Second, a structural definition applies to realms of widely different substance so long as the arrangement of parts is similar.[2] Third, because this is so, theories developed for one realm may with some modification be applicable to other realms as well. . . .

The concept of structure is based on the fact that units differently juxtaposed and combined behave differently and in interacting produce different outcomes. I first want to show how internal political structure can be defined. In a book on international-political theory, domestic political structure has to be examined in order to draw a distinction between expectations about behavior and outcomes in the internal and external realms. Moreover, considering domestic political structure now will make the elusive international-political structure easier to catch later on.

Structure defines the arrangement, or the ordering, of the parts of a system. Structure is not a collection of political institutions but rather the arrangement of them. How is the arrangement defined? The constitution of a state describes some parts of the arrangement, but political structures as they develop are not identical with formal constitutions. In defining structures, the first question to answer is this: What is the principle by which the parts are arranged?

Domestic politics is hierarchically ordered. The units—institutions and agencies—stand vis à vis each other in relations of super- and subordination. The ordering principle of a system gives the first, and basic, bit of information about how the parts of a realm are related to each other. In a polity the hierarchy of offices is by no means completely articulated, nor are all ambiguities about relations of super- and subordination removed. Nevertheless, political actors are formally differentiated according to the degrees of their authority, and their distinct functions are specified. By "specified" I do not mean that the law of the land fully describes the duties that different agencies perform, but only that broad agreement prevails on the tasks that various parts of a government are to undertake and on the extent of the power they legitimately wield. Thus Congress supplies the military forces; the President commands them. Congress makes the laws; the executive branch enforces them; agencies administer laws; judges interpret them. Such specification of roles and differentiation of functions is found in any state, the more fully so as the state is more highly developed. The specification of functions of formally differentiated parts gives the second bit of structural information. This second part of the definition adds some content to the structure, but only enough to say more fully how the units stand in relation to one another. The roles and the functions of the British Prime Minister and Parliament, for example, differ from those of the American President and Congress. When offices are juxtaposed and functions are combined in different ways, different behaviors and outcomes result, as I shall shortly show.

The placement of units in relation to one another is not fully defined by a system's ordering principle and by the formal differentiation of its parts. The standing of the units also changes with changes in their relative capabilities. In the performance of their functions, agencies may gain capabilities or lose them. The relation of Prime Minister to Parliament and of President to Congress depends on, and varies with, their relative capabilities. The third part of the definition of structure acknowledges that even while specified functions remain unchanged, units come to stand in different relation to each other through changes in relative capability.

A domestic political structure is thus defined: first, according to the principle by which it is ordered; second, by specification of the functions of formally differentiated units; and third, by the distribution of capabilities across those units. Structure is a highly abstract notion, but the definition of structure does not abstract from everything. To do so would be to leave everything aside and to include nothing at all. The three-part definition of structure includes only what is required to show how the units of the system are positioned or arranged. Everything else is omitted. Concern for tradition and culture, analysis of the character and personality of political actors, consideration of the conflictive and accommodative processes of politics, description of the making and execution of policy—all such matters are left aside. Their omission does not imply their unimportance. They are omitted because we want to figure out the expected effects of structure on process and of process on structure. That can be done only if structure and process are distinctly defined.

I defined domestic political structures first by the principle according to which they are organized or ordered, second by the differentiation of units and the specification of their functions, and third by the distribution of capabilities across units. Let us see how the three terms of the definition apply to international politics.

1. Ordering Principles

Structural questions are questions about the arrangement of the parts of a system. The parts of domestic political systems stand in relations of super- and subordination. Some are entitled to command; others are required to obey. Domestic systems are centralized and hierarchic. The parts of international-political systems stand in relations of coordination. Formally, each is the equal of all the others. None is entitled to command; none is required to obey. International systems are decentralized and anarchic. The ordering principles of the two structures are distinctly different, indeed, contrary to each other. Domestic political structures have governmental institutions and offices as their concrete counterparts. International politics, in contrast, has been called "politics in the absence of government."[3] International organizations do exist, and in ever-growing numbers. Supranational agents able to act effectively, however, either themselves acquire some of the attributes and capabilities of states, as did the medieval papacy in the era of Innocent III, or they soon reveal their inability to act in important ways except with the support, or at least the acquiescence, of the principal states concerned with the matters at hand. Whatever elements of authority emerge internationally are barely once removed from the capability that provides the foundation for the appearance of those elements. Authority quickly reduces to a particular expression of capability. In the absence of agents with system-wide authority, formal relations of super- and subordination fail to develop.

The first term of a structural definition states the principle by which the system is ordered. Structure is an organizational concept. The prominent characteristic of international politics, however, seems to be the lack of order and of organization. How can one think of international politics as being any kind of an order at all? The anarchy of politics internationally is often referred to. If structure is an organizational concept, the terms "structure" and "anarchy" seem to be in contradiction. If international politics is "politics in the absence of government," what are we in the presence of? In looking for international structure, one is brought face to face with the invisible, an uncomfortable position to be in.

The problem is this: how to conceive of an order without an orderer and of organizational effects where formal organization is lacking. Because these are difficult questions, I shall answer them through analogy with microeconomic theory. Reasoning by analogy is helpful where one can move from a domain for which theory is well developed to one where it is not. Reasoning by analogy is permissible where different domains are structurally similar.

Classical economic theory, developed by Adam Smith and his followers, is microtheory. Political scientists tend to think that microtheory is theory about small-scale matters, a usage that ill accords with its established meaning. The term "micro" in economic theory indicates the way in which the theory is constructed rather than the scope of the matters it pertains to. Microeconomic theory describes how an order is spontaneously formed from the self-interested acts and interactions of individual units—in this case, persons and firms. The theory then turns upon the two central concepts of the economic units and of the market. Economic units and economic markets are concepts, not descriptive realities or concrete entities. This must be emphasized since from the early eighteenth century to the present, from the sociologist Auguste Comte to the psychologist George Katona, economic theory has been faulted because its assumptions fail to correspond with realities.[4] Unrealistically, economic theorists conceive of an economy operating in isolation from its society and polity. Unrealistically, economists assume that the economic world is the world of the world. Unrealistically, economists think of the acting unit, the famous "economic man," as a single-minded profit maximizer. They single out one aspect of man and leave aside the wondrous variety of human life. As any moderately sensible economist knows, "economic man" does not exist. Anyone who asks businessmen how they make their decisions will find that the assumption that men are economic maximizers grossly distorts their characters. The assumption that men behave as economic men, which is known to be false as a descriptive statement, turns out to be useful in the construction of theory.

Markets are the second major concept invented by microeconomic theorists. Two general questions must be asked about markets: How are they formed? How do they work? The answer to the first question is this: The market of a decentralized economy is individualist in origin, spontaneously generated, and unintended. The market arises out of the activities of separate units—persons and firms—whose aims and efforts are directed not toward creating an order but rather toward fulfilling their own internally defined interests by whatever means they can muster. The individual unit acts for itself. From the coaction of like units emerges a structure that affects and constrains all of them. Once formed, a market becomes a force in itself, and a force that the constitutive units acting singly or in small numbers cannot control. Instead, in lesser or greater degree as market conditions vary, the creators become the creatures of the market that their activity gave rise to. Adam Smith's great achievement was to show how self-interested, greed-driven actions may produce good social outcomes if only political and social conditions permit free competition. If a laissez-faire economy is harmonious, it is so because the intentions of actors do *not* correspond with the outcomes their actions produce. What intervenes between the actors and the objects of their action in order to thwart their purposes? To account for the unexpectedly favorable outcomes of selfish acts, the concept of a market is brought into play. Each unit seeks its own good; the result of a number of units simultaneously doing so transcends the motives and the aims of the separate units. Each would like to work less hard and price his product higher. Taken together, all have to work harder and price their products lower. Each firm seeks to increase its profit; the result of many firms doing so drives the profit rate downward. Each man seeks his own end, and, in doing so, produces a result that was no part of his intention. Out of the mean ambition of its members, the greater good of society is produced.

The market is a cause interposed between the economic actors and the results they produce. It conditions their calculations, their behaviors, and their interactions. It is not an agent in the sense of A being the agent that produces outcome X. Rather it is a structural cause. A market constrains the units that comprise it from taking certain actions and disposes them toward taking others. The market, created by self-directed interacting economic units, selects behaviors according to their consequences. The market rewards some with high profits and assigns others to bankruptcy. Since a market is not an institution or an agent in any concrete or palpable sense, such statements become impressive only if they can be reliably inferred from a theory as part of a set of more elaborate expectations. They can be. Microeconomic theory explains how an economy operates and why certain effects are to be expected. . . .

International-political systems, like economic markets, are formed by the coaction of self-regarding units. International structures are defined in terms of the primary political units of an era, be they city states, empires, or nations. Structures emerge from the coexistence of states. No state intends to participate in the formation of a structure by which it and others will be constrained. International-political systems, like economic markets, are individualist in origin, spontaneously generated, and unintended. In both systems, structures are formed by the coaction of their units. Whether those units live, prosper, or die depends on their own efforts. Both systems are formed and maintained on a principle of self-help that applies to the units. . . .

In a microtheory, whether of international politics or of economics, the motivation of the actors is assumed rather than realistically described. I assume that states seek to ensure their survival. The assumption is a radical simplification made for the sake of constructing theory. The question to ask of the assumption, as ever, is not whether it is true but whether it is the most sensible and useful one that can be made. Whether it is a useful assumption depends on whether a theory based on the assumption can be contrived, a theory from which important consequences not otherwise obvious can be inferred. Whether it is a sensible assumption can be directly discussed.

Beyond the survival motive, the aims of states may be endlessly varied; they may range from the ambition to conquer the world to the desire merely to be left alone. Survival is a prerequisite to achieving any goals that states may have, other than the goal of promoting their own disappearance as political entities. The survival motive is taken as the ground of action in a world where the security of states is not assured, rather than as a realistic description of the impulse that lies behind every act of state. The assumption allows for the fact that no state always acts exclusively to ensure its survival. It allows for the fact that some states may persistently seeks goals that they value more highly than survival; they may, for example, prefer amalgamation with other states to their own survival in form. It allows for the fact that in pursuit of its security no state will act with perfect knowledge and wisdom—if indeed we could know what those terms might mean. . . .

Actors may perceive the structure that constrains them and understand how it serves to reward some kinds of behavior and to penalize others. But then again they either may not see it or, seeing it, may for any of many reasons fail to conform their actions to the patterns that are most often rewarded and least often punished. To say that "the structure selects" means simply that those who conform to accepted and successful practices more often rise to the top and are likelier to stay there. The game one has to win is defined by the structure that determines the kind of player who is likely to prosper. . . .

2. The Character of the Units

The second term in the definition of domestic political structure specifies the functions performed by differentiated units. Hierarchy entails relations of super- and subordination among a system's parts, and that implies their differentiation. In defining domestic political structure the second term, like the first and third, is needed because each term points to a possible source of structural variation. The states that are the units of international-political systems are not formally differentiated by the functions they perform. Anarchy entails relations of coordination among a system's units, and that implies their sameness. The second term is not needed in defining international-political structure, because, so long as anarchy endures, states remain like units. International structures vary only through a change of organizing principle or, failing that, through variations in the capabilities of units. Nevertheless I shall discuss these like units here, because it is by their interactions that international-politics structures are generated.

Two questions arise: Why should states be taken as the units of the system? Given a wide variety of states, how can one call them "like units"? Questioning the choice of states as the primary units of international-political systems became popular in the 1960s and 1970s as it was at the turn of the century. Once one understands what is logically involved, the issue is easily resolved. Those who question the state-centric view do so for two main reasons. First, states are not the only actors of importance on the international scene. Second, states are declining in importance, and other actors are gaining, or so it is said. Neither reason is cogent, as the following discussion shows.

States are not and never have been the only international actors. But then structures are defined not by all of the actors that flourish within them but by the major ones. In defining a system's structure one chooses one or some of the infinitely many objects comprising the system and defines its structure in terms of them. For international-political systems, as for any system, one must first decide which units to take as being the parts of the system. Here the economic analogy will help again. The structure of a market is defined by the number of firms competing. If many roughly equal firms contend, a condition of perfect competition is approximated. If a few firms dominate the market, competition is said to be oligopolistic even though many smaller firms may also be in the field. But we are told that definitions of this sort cannot be applied to international politics because of the interpenetration of states, because of their inability to control the environment of their action, and because rising multinational corporations and other nonstate actors are difficult to regulate and may rival some states in influence. The importance of nonstate actors and the extent of transnational activities are obvious. The conclusion that the state-centric conception of international politics is made obsolete by them does not follow. That economists and economically minded politics scientists have thought that it does is ironic. The irony lies in the fact that all of the reasons given for scrapping the state-centric concept can be related more strongly and applied to firms. Firms competing with numerous others have no hope of controlling their market, and oligopolistic firms constantly struggle with imperfect success to do so. Firms interpenetrate, merge, and buy each up at a merry pace. Moreover, firms are constantly threatened and regulated by, shall we say, "nonfirm" actors. Some governments encourage concentration; others work to prevent it. The market structure of parts of an economy may move from a wider to a narrower competition or may move in the opposite direction, but whatever the extent and the frequency of change, market structures, generated by the interaction of firms, are defined in terms of them.

Just as economists define markets in terms of firms, so I define international-political structures in terms of states. If Charles P. Kindleberger were right in saying that "the nation-state is just about through as an economic unit,"[5] then the structure of international politics would have to be redefined. That would be necessary because economic capabilities cannot be separated from the other capabilities of states. The distinction frequently drawn between matters of high and low politics is misplaced. States use economic means for military and political ends; and military and political means for the achievement of economic interests.

An amended version of Kindleberger's statement may hold: Some states may be nearly washed up as economic entities, and others not. That poses no problem for international-political theory since international politics is mostly about inequalities anyway. So long as the major states are the major actors, the structure of international politics is defined in terms of them. That theoretical statement is of course borne out in practice. States set the scene in which they, along with nonstate actors, state their dramas or carry on their humdrum affairs. Though they may choose to interfere little in the affairs of nonstate actors for long periods of time, states nevertheless set the terms of intercourse, whether by passively permitting informal rules to develop or by actively intervening to change rules that no longer suit them. When the crunch comes, states remake the rules by which other actors operate. Indeed, one may be struck by the ability of weak states to impede the operation of strong international corporations and by the attention the latter pay to the wishes of the former.

It is important to consider the nature of transnational movements, the extent of their penetration, and the conditions that make it harder or easier for states to control them. But the adequate study of these matters, like others, requires finding or developing an adequate approach to the study of international politics. Two points should be made about latter-day transnational studies. First, students of transnational phenomena have developed no distinct theory of their subject matter or of international politics in general. They have drawn on existing theories, whether economic or political. Second, that they have developed no distinct theory is quite proper, for a theory that denies the central role of states will be needed only if nonstate actors develop to the point of rivaling or surpassing the great powers, not just a few of the minor ones. They show no sign of doing that. . . .

States are the units whose interactions form the structure of international-political systems. They will long remain so. The death rate among states is remarkably low. Few states die; many firms do. . . . To call states "like units" is to say that each state is like all other states in being an autonomous political unit. It is another way of saying that states are sovereign. But sovereignty is also a bothersome concept. Many believe, as the anthropologist M. G. Smith has said, that "in a system of sovereign states no state is sovereign."[6] The error lies in identifying the sovereignty of states with their ability to do as they wish. To say that states are sovereign is not to say that they can do as they please, that they are free of others' influence, that they are able to get what they want. Sovereign states may be hardpressed all around, constrained to act in ways they would like to avoid, and able to do hardly anything just as they would like to. The sovereignty of states has never entailed their insulation from the effects of other states' actions. To be sovereign and to be dependent are not contradictory conditions. Sovereign states have seldom led free and easy lives. What then is sovereignty? To say that a state is sovereign means that it decides for itself how it will cope with its internal and external problems, including whether or not to seek assistance from others and in doing so to limit its freedom by making commitments to them. States develop their own strategies, chart their own courses, make their own decisions about how to meet whatever needs they experience and whatever desires they develop. It is no more contradictory to say that sovereign states are always constrained and often tightly so than it is to say that free individuals often make decisions under the heavy pressure of events.

Each state, like every other state, is a sovereign political entity. And yet the differences across states, from Costa Rica to the Soviet Union, from Gambia to the United States, are immense. States are alike, and they are also different. So are corporations, apples, universities, and people. Whenever we put two or more objects in the same category, we are saying that they are alike not in all respects but in some. No two objects in this world are identical, yet they can often be usefully compared and combined. "You can't add apples and oranges" is an old saying that seems to be especially popular among salesmen who do not want you to compare their wares with others. But we all know that the trick of adding dissimilar objects is to express the result in terms of a category that comprises them. Three apples plus four oranges equals seven pieces of fruit. The only interesting question is whether the category that classifies objects according to their common qualities is useful. One can add up a large number of widely varied objects and say that one has eight million things, but seldom need one do that.

States vary widely in size, wealth, power, and form. And yet variations in these and in other respects are variations among like units. In what way are they like units? How can they be placed in a single category? States are alike in the tasks that they face, though not in their abilities to perform them. The differences are of capability, not of function. States perform or try to perform tasks, most of which are common to all of them; the ends they aspire to are similar. Each state duplicates the activities of other states at least to a considerable extent. Each state has its agencies for making, executing, and interpreting laws and regulations, for raising revenues, and for defending itself. Each state supplies out of its own resources and by its own means most of the food, clothing, housing, transportation, and amenities consumed and used by its citizens. All states, except the smallest ones, do much more of their business at home than abroad. One has to be impressed with the functional similarity of states and, now more than ever before, with the similar lines their development follows. From the rich to the poor states, from the old to the new ones, nearly all of them take a larger hand in matters of economic regulation, of education, health, and housing, of culture and the arts, and so on almost endlessly. The increase of the activities of states is a strong and strikingly uniform international trend. The functions of states are similar, and distinctions among them arise principally from their varied capabilities. International politics consists of like units duplicating one another's activities.

3. The Distribution of Capabilities

The parts of a hierarchic system are related to one another in ways that are determined both by their functional differentiation and by the extent of their capabilities. The units of an anarchic system are functionally undifferentiated. The units of such an order are then distinguished primarily by their greater or lesser capabilities for performing similar tasks. This states formally what students of international politics have long noticed. The great powers of an era have always been marked off from others by practitioners and theorists alike. Students of national government make such distinctions as that between parliamentary and presidential systems; governmental systems differ in form. Students of international politics make distinctions between international-political systems only according to the number of their great powers. The structure of a system changes with changes in the distribution of capabilities across the system's units. And changes in structure change expectations about how the units of the system will behave and about the outcomes their interactions will produce. Domestically, the differentiated parts of a system may perform similar tasks. We know from observing the American government that executives sometimes legislate and legislatures sometimes execute. Internationally, like units sometimes perform different tasks . . . but two problems should be considered.

The first problem is this: Capability tells us something about units. Defining structure partly in terms of the distribution of capabilities seems to violate my instruction to keep unit attributes out of structural definitions. As I remarked earlier, structure is a highly but not entirely abstract concept. The maximum of abstraction allows a minimum of content, and that minimum is what is needed to enable one to say how the units stand in relation to one another. States are differently placed by their power. And yet one may wonder why only *capability* is included in the third part of the definition, and not such characteristics as ideology, form of government, peacefulness, bellicosity, or whatever. The answer is this: Power is estimated by comparing the capabilities of a number of units. Although capabilities are attributes of units, the distribution of capabilities across units is not. The distribution of capabilities is not a unit attribute, but rather a system-wide concept. . . .

The second problem is this: Though relations defined in terms of interactions must be excluded from structural definitions, relations defined in terms of grouping of states do seem to tell us something about how states are placed in the system. Why not specify how states stand in relation to one another by considering the alliances they form? Would doing so not be comparable to defining national political structures partly in terms of how presidents and prime ministers are related to other political agents? It would not be. Nationally as internationally, structural definitions deal with the relation of agents and agencies in terms of the organization of realms and not in terms of the accommodations and conflicts that may occur within them or the groupings that may now and then form. Parts of a government may draw together or pull apart, may oppose each other or cooperate in greater or lesser degree. These are the relations that form and dissolve within a system rather than structural alterations that mark a change from one system to another. This is made clear by the example that runs nicely parallel to the case of alliances. Distinguishing systems of political parties according to their number is common. A multiparty system changes if, say, eight parties become two, but not if two groupings of the eight form merely for the occasion of fighting an election. By the same logic, an international-political system in which three or more great powers have split into two alliances remains a multipolar system—structurally distinct from a bipolar system, a system in which no third power is able to challenge the top two. . . .

In defining international-political structures we take states with whatever traditions, habits, objectives, desires, and forms of government they may have. We do not ask whether states are revolutionary or legitimate, authoritarian or democratic, ideological or pragmatic. We abstract from every attribute of states except their capabilities. Nor in thinking about structure do we ask about the relations of states—their feelings of friendship and hostility, their diplomatic exchanges, the alliances they form, and the extent of the contacts and exchanges among them. We ask what range of expectations arises merely from looking at the type of order that prevails among them and at the distribution of capabilities within that order. We abstract from any particular qualities of states and from all of their concrete connections. What emerges is a positional picture, a general description of the ordered overall arrangement of a society written in terms of the placement of units rather than in terms of their qualities. . . .

ANARCHIC STRUCTURES AND BALANCES OF POWER

[We must now] examine the characteristics of anarchy and the expectations about outcomes associated with anarchic realms. . . . [This] is best accomplished by drawing some comparisons between behavior and outcomes in anarchic and hierarchic realms.

4. Violence at Home and Abroad

The state among states, it is often said, conducts its affairs in the brooding shadow of violence. Because some states may at any time use force, all states must be prepared to do so—or live at the mercy of their militarily more vigorous neighbors. Among states, the state of nature is a state of war. This is meant not in the sense that war constantly occurs but in the sense that, with each state deciding for itself whether or not to use force, war may at any time break out. Whether in the family, the community, or the world at large, contact without at least occasional conflict is inconceivable; and the hope that in the absence of an agent to manage or to manipulate conflicting parties the use of force will always be avoided cannot be realistically entertained. Among men as among states, anarchy, or the absence of government, is associated with the occurrence of violence.

The threat of violence and the recurrent use of force are said to distinguish international from national affairs. But in the history of the world surely most rulers have had to bear in mind that their subjects might use force to resist or overthrow them. If the absence of government is associated with the threat of violence, so also is its presence. A haphazard list of national tragedies illustrates the point all too well. The most destructive wars of the hundred years following the defeat of Napoleon took place not among states but *within* them. Estimates of deaths in China's Taiping Rebellion, which began in 1851 and lasted 13 years, range as high as 20 million. In the American Civil War some 600 thousand people lost their lives. In more recent history, forced collectivation and Stalin's purges eliminated 5 million Russians, and Hitler exterminated 6 million Jews. In some Latin American countries, coups d'états and rebellions have been normal features of national life. Between 1948 and 1957, for example, 200 thousand Colombians were killed in civil strife. In the middle 1970s most inhabitants of Idi Amin's Uganda must have felt their lives becoming nasty, brutish, and short, quite as in Thomas Hobbes's state of nature. If such cases constitute aberrations, they are uncomfortably common ones. We easily lose sight of the fact that struggles to achieve and maintain power, to establish order, and to contrive a kind of justice within states may be bloodier than wars among them.

If anarchy is identified with chaos, destruction, and death, then the distinction between anarchy and government does not tell us much. Which is more precarious: the life of a state among states, or of a government in relation to its subjects? The answer varies with time and place. Among some states at some times, the actual or expected occurrence of violence is low. Within some states at some times, the actual or expected occurrence of violence is high. The use of force, or the constant fear of its use, are not sufficient grounds for distinguishing international from domestic affairs. If the possible and the actual use of force mark both national and international orders, then no durable distinction between the two realms can be drawn in terms of the use or the nonuse of force. No human order is proof against violence.

To discover qualitative differences between internal and external affairs one must look for a criterion other than the occurrence of violence. The distinction between international and national realms of politics is not found in the use or the nonuse of force but in their different structures. But if the dangers of being violently attacked are greater, say, in taking an evening stroll through downtown Detroit than they are in picnicking along the French and German border, what practical difference does the difference of structure make? Nationally as internationally, contact generates conflict and at times issues in violence. The difference between national and international politics lies not in the use of force but in the different modes of organization for doing something about it. A government, ruling by some standard of legitimacy, arrogates to itself the right to use force—that is, to apply a variety of sanctions to control the use of force by its subjects. If some use private force, others may appeal to the government. A government has no monopoly on the use of force, as is all too evident. An effective government, however, has a monopoly on the *legitimate* use of force, and legitimate here means that public agents are organized to prevent and to counter the private use of force. Citizens need not prepare to defend themselves. Public agencies do that. A national system is not one of self-help. The international system is.

5. Interdependence and Integration

The political significance of interdependence varies depending on whether a realm is organized, with relations of authority specified and established, or remains formally unorganized. Insofar as a realm is formally organized, its units are free to specialize, to pursue their own interests without concern for developing the means of maintaining their identity and preserving their security in the presence of others. They are free to specialize because they have no reason to fear the increased interdependence that goes with specialization. If those who specialize most benefit most, then competition in specialization ensues. Goods are manufactured, grain is produced, law and order are maintained, commerce is conducted, and financial services are provided by people who ever more narrowly specialize. In simple economic terms, the cobbler depends on the tailor for his pants and the tailor on the cobbler for his shoes, and each would be ill-clad without the services of the other. In simple political terms, Kansas depends on Washington for protection and regulation and Washington depends on Kansas for beef and wheat. In saying that in such situations interdependence is close, one need not maintain that the one part could not learn to live without the other. One need only say that the cost of breaking the interdependent relation would be high. Persons and institutions depend heavily on one another because of the different tasks they perform and the different goods they produce and exchange. The parts of a polity bind themselves together by their differences.[7]

Differences between national and international structures are reflected in the ways the units of each system define their ends and develop the means for reaching them. In anarchic realms, like units coact. In hierarchic realms, unlike units interact. In an anarchic realm, the units are functionally similar and tend to remain so. Like units work to maintain a measure of independence and may even strive for autarchy. In a hierarchic realm, the units are differentiated, and they tend to increase the extent of their specialization. Differentiated units become closely interdependent, the more closely so as their specialization proceeds. Because of the difference of structure, interdependence within and interdependence among nations are two distinct concepts. So as to follow the logicians' admonition to keep a single meaning for a given term throughout one's discourse, I shall use "integration" to describe the condition within nations and "interdependence" to describe the condition among them.

Although states are like units functionally, they differ vastly in their capabilities. Out of such differences something of a division of labor develops. The division of labor across nations, however, is slight in comparison with the highly articulated division of labor within them. Integration draws the parts of a nation closely together. Interdependence among nations leaves them loosely connected. Although the integration of nations is often talked about, it seldom takes place. Nations could mutually enrich themselves by further dividing not just the labor that goes into the production of goods but also some of the other tasks they perform, such as political management and military defense. Why does their integration not take place? The structure of international politics limits the cooperation of states in two ways.

In a self-help system each of the units spends a portion of its effort, not in forwarding its own good, but in providing the means of protecting itself against others. Specialization in a system of divided labor works to everyone's advantage, though not equally so. Inequality in the expected distribution of the increased product works strongly against extension of the division of labor internationally. When faced with the possibility of cooperating for mutual gain, states that feel insecure must ask how the gain will be divided. They are compelled to ask not "Will both of us gain?" but "Who will gain more?" If an expected gain is to be divided, say, in the ratio of two to one, one state may use its disproportionate gain to implement a policy intended to damage or destroy the other. Even the prospect of large absolute gains for both parties does not elicit their cooperation so long as each fears how the other will use its increased capabilities. Notice that the impediments to collaboration may not lie in the character and the immediate intention of either party. Instead, the condition of insecurity—at the least, the uncertainty of each about the other's future intentions and actions—works against their cooperation. . . .

A state worries about a division of possible gains that may favor others more than itself. That is the first way in which the structure of international politics limits the cooperation of states. A state also worries lest it become dependent on others through cooperative endeavors and exchanges of goods and services. That is the second way in which the structure of international politics limits the cooperation of states. The more a state specializes, the more it relies on others to supply the materials and goods that it is not producing. The larger a state's imports and exports, the more it depends on others. The world's well-being would be increased if an ever more elaborate division of labor were developed, but states would thereby place themselves in situations of ever closer interdependence. Some states may not resist that. For small and ill-endowed states the costs of doing so are excessively high. But states that can resist becoming ever more enmeshed with others ordinarily do so in either or both of two ways. States that are heavily dependent, or closely interdependent, worry about securing that which they depend on. The high interdependence of states means that the states in question experience, or are subject to, the common vulnerability that high interdependence entails. Like other organizations, states seek to control what they depend on or to lessen the extent of their dependency. This simple thought explains quite a bit of the behavior of states: their imperial thrusts to widen the scope of their control and their autarchic strivings toward greater self-sufficiency.

Structures encourage certain behaviors and penalize those who do not respond to the encouragement. Nationally, many lament the extreme development of the division of labor, a development that results in the allocation of ever narrower tasks to individuals. And yet specialization proceeds, and its extent is a measure of the development of societies. In a formally organized realm a premium is put on each unit's being able to specialize in order to increase its value to others in a system of divided labor. The domestic imperative is "specialize"! Internationally, many lament the resources states spend unproductively for their own defense and the opportunities they miss to enhance the welfare of their people through cooperation with other states. And yet the ways of states change little. In an unorganized realm each unit's incentive is to put itself in a position to be able to take care of itself since no one else can be counted on to do so. The international imperative is "take care of yourself"! Some leaders of nations may understand that the well-being of all of them would increase through their participation in a fuller division of labor. But to act on the idea would be to act on a domestic imperative, an imperative that does not run internationally. What one might want to do in the absence of structural constraints is different from what one is encouraged to do in their presence. States do not willingly place themselves in situations of increased dependence. In a self-help system, considerations of security subordinate economic gain to political interest. . . .

6. Structures and Strategies

That motives and outcomes may well be disjoined should now be easily seen. Structures cause nations to have consequences they were not intended to have. Surely most of the actors will notice that, and at least some of them will be able to figure out why. They may develop a pretty good sense of just how structures work their effects. Will they not then be able to achieve their original ends by appropriately adjusting their strategies? Unfortunately, they often cannot. To show why this is so I shall give only a few examples; once the point is made, the reader will easily think of others.

If shortage of a commodity is expected, all are collectively better off if they buy less of it in order to moderate price increases and to distribute shortages equitably. But because some will be better off if they lay in extra supplies quickly, all have a strong incentive to do so. If one expects others to make a run on a bank, one's prudent course is to run faster then they do even while knowing that if few others run, the bank will remain solvent, and if many run, it will fail. In such cases, pursuit of individual interest produces collective results that nobody wants, yet individuals by behaving differently will hurt themselves without altering outcomes. These two much used examples establish the main point. Some courses of action I cannot sensibly follow unless we are pretty sure that many others will as well. . . .

We may well notice that our behavior produces unwanted outcomes, but we are also likely to see that such instances as these are examples of what Alfred E. Kahn describes as "large" changes that are brought about by the accumulation of "small" decisions. In such situations people are victims of the "tyranny of small decisions," a phrase suggesting that "if one hundred consumers choose option x, and this causes the market to make decision X (where X equals 100x), it is not necessarily true that those same consumers would have voted for that outcome if that large decision had ever been presented for their explicit consideration."[8] If the market does not present the large question for decision, then individuals are doomed to making decisions that are sensible within their narrow contexts even though they know all the while that in making such decisions they are bringing about a result that most of them do not want. Either that or they organize to overcome some of the effects of the market by changing its structure—for example, by bringing consumer units roughly up to the size of the units that are making producers' decisions. This nicely makes the point: So long as one leaves the structure unaffected it is not possible for changes in the intentions and the actions of particular actors to produce desirable outcomes or to avoid undesirable ones. . . . The only remedies for strong structural effects are structural changes.

Structural constraints cannot be wished away, although many fail to understand this. In every age and place, the units of self-help systems—nations, corporations, or whatever—are told that the greater good, along with their own, requires them to act for the sake of the system and not for their own narrowly defined advantage. In the 1950s, as fear of the world's destruction in nuclear war grew, some concluded that the alternative to world destruction was world disarmament. In the 1970s, with the rapid growth of population, poverty, and pollution, some concluded, as one political scientist put it, that "states must meet the needs of the political ecosystem in its global dimensions or court annihilation."[9] The international interest must be served; and if that means anything at all, it means that national interests are subordinate to it. The problems are found at the global level. Solutions to the problems continue to depend on national policies. What are the conditions that would make nations more or less willing to obey the injunctions that are so often laid on them? How can they resolve the tension between pursuing their own interests and acting for the sake of the system? No one has shown how that can be done, although many wring their hands and plead for rational behavior. The very problem, however, is that rational behavior, given structural constraints, does not lead to the wanted results. With each country constrained to take care of itself, no one can take care of the system.[10]

A strong sense of peril and doom may lead to a clear definition of ends that must be achieved. Their achievement is not thereby made possible. The possibility of effective action depends on the ability to provide necessary means. It depends even more so on the existence of conditions that permit nations and other organizations to follow appropriate policies and strategies. World-shaking problems cry for global solutions, but there is no global agency to provide them. Necessities do not create possibilities. Wishing that final causes were efficient ones does not make them so.

Great tasks can be accomplished only by agents of great capability. That is why states, and especially the major ones, are called on to do what is necessary for the world's survival. But states have to do whatever they think necessary for their own preservation, since no one can be relied on to do it for them. Why the advice to place the international interest above national interests is meaningless can be explained precisely in terms of the distinction between micro- and macrotheories. . . .

Some have hoped that changes in the awareness and purpose, in the organization and ideology of states would change the quality of international life. Over the centuries states have changed in many ways, but the quality of international life has remained much the same. States may seek reasonable and worthy ends, but they cannot figure out how to reach them. The problem is not in their stupidity or ill will, although one does not want to claim that those qualities are lacking. The depth of the difficulty is not understood until one realizes that intelligence and goodwill cannot discover and act on adequate programs. Early in this century Winston Churchill observed that the British-German naval race promised disaster *and* that Britain had no realistic choice other than to run it. States facing global problems are like individual consumers trapped by the "tyranny of small decisions." States, like consumers, can get out of the trap only by changing the structure of their field of activity. The message bears repeating: The only remedy for a strong structural effect is a structural change.

7. The Virtues of Anarchy

To achieve their objectives and maintain their security, units in a condition of anarchy—be they people, corporations, states, or whatever—must rely on the means they can generate and the arrangements they can make for themselves. Self-help is necessarily the principle of action in an anarchic order. A self-help situation is one of high risk—of bankruptcy in the economic realm and of war in a world of free states. It is also one in which organizational costs are low. Within an economy or within an international order, risks may be avoided or lessened by moving from a situation of coordinate action to one of super- and subordination, that is, by erecting agencies with effective authority and extending a system of rules. Government emerges where the functions of regulation and management themselves become distinct and specialized tasks. The costs of maintaining a hierarchic order are frequently ignored by those who deplore its absence. Organizations have at least two aims: to get something done and to maintain themselves as organizations. Many of their activities are directed toward the second purpose. The leaders of organizations, and political leaders preeminently, are not masters of the matters their organizations deal with. They have become leaders not by being experts on one thing or another but by excelling in the organizational arts—in maintaining control of a group's members, in eliciting predictable and satisfactory efforts from them, in holding a group together. In making political decisions, the first and most important concern is not to achieve the aims the members of an organization may have but to secure the continuity and health of the organization itself.[11]

Along with the advantages of hierarchic orders go the costs. In hierarchic orders, moreover, the means of control become an object of struggle. Substantive issues become entwined with efforts to influence or control the controllers. The hierarchic ordering of politics adds one to the already numerous objects of struggle, and the object added is at a new order of magnitude.

If the risks of war are unbearably high, can they be reduced by organizing to manage the affairs of nations? At a minimum, management requires controlling the military forces that are at the disposal of states. Within nations, organizations have to work to maintain themselves. As organizations, nations, in working to maintain themselves, sometimes have to use force against dissident elements and areas. As hierarchical systems, governments nationally or globally are disrupted by the defection of major parts. In a society of states with little coherence, attempts at world government would founder on the inability of an emerging central authority to mobilize the resources needed to create and maintain the unity of the system by regulating and managing its parts. The prospect of world government would be an invitation to prepare for world civil war. . . . States cannot entrust managerial powers to a central agency unless that agency is able to protect its client states. The more powerful the clients and the more the power of each of them appears as a threat to the others, the greater the power lodged in the center must be. The greater the power of the center, the stronger the incentive for states to engage in a struggle to control it.

States, like people, are insecure in proportion to the extent of their freedom. If freedom is wanted, insecurity must be accepted. Organizations that establish relations of authority and control may increase insecurity as they decrease freedom. If might does not make right, whether among people or states, then some institution or agency has intervened to lift them out of nature's realm. The more influential the agency, the stronger the desire to control it becomes. In contrast, units in an anarchic order act for their own sakes and not for the sake of preserving an organization and furthering their fortunes within it. Force is used for ones's own interest. In the absence of organization, people or states are free to leave one another alone. Even when they do not do so, they are better able, in the absence of the politics of the organization, to concentrate on the politics of the problem and to aim for a minimum agreement that will permit their separate existence rather than a maximum agreement for the sake of maintaining unity. If might decides, then bloody struggles over right can more easily be avoided.

Nationally, the force of a government is exercised in the name of right and justice. Internationally, the force of a state is employed for the sake of its own protection and advantage. Rebels challenge a government's claim to authority;

they question the rightfulness of its rule. Wars among states cannot settle questions of authority and right; they can only determine the allocation of gains and losses among contenders and settle for a time the question of who is the stronger. Nationally, relations of authority are established. Internationally, only relations of strength result. Nationally, private force used against a government threatens the political system. Force used by a state—a public body—is, from the international perspective, the private use of force; but there is no government to overthrow and no governmental apparatus to capture. Short of a drive toward world hegemony, the private use of force does not threaten the system of international politics, only some of its members. War pits some states against others in a struggle among similarly constituted entities. The power of the strong may deter the weak from asserting their claims, not because the weak recognize a kind of rightfulness of rule on the part of the strong, but simply because it is not sensible to tangle with them. Conversely, the weak may enjoy considerable freedom of action if they are so far removed in their capabilities from the strong that the latter are not much bothered by their actions or much concerned by marginal increases in their capabilities.

National politics is the realm of authority, of administration, and of law. International politics is the realm of power, of struggle, and of accommodation. The international realm is preeminently a political one. The national realm is variously described as being hierarchic, vertical, centralized, heterogeneous, directed, and contrived; the international realm, as being anarchic, horizontal, decentralized, homogeneous, undirected, and mutually adaptive. The more centralized the order, the nearer to the top the locus of decisions ascends. Internationally, decisions are made at the bottom level, there being scarcely any other. In the vertical horizontal dichotomy, international structures assume the prone position. Adjustments are made internationally, but they are made without a formal or authoritative adjuster. Adjustment and accommodation proceed by mutual adaptation.[12] Action and reaction, and reaction to the reaction, proceed by a piecemeal process. The parties feel each other out, so to speak, and define a situation simultaneously with its development. Among coordinate units, adjustment is achieved and accommodations arrived at by the exchange of "considerations," in a condition, as Chester Barnard put it, "in which the duty of command and the desire to obey are essentially absent."[13] Where the contest is over considerations, the parties seek to maintain or improve their positions by maneuvering, by bargaining, or by fighting. The manner and intensity of the competition is determined by the desires and the abilities of parties that are at once separate and interacting.

Whether or not by force, each state plots the course it thinks will best serve its interests. If force is used by one state or its use is expected, the recourse of other states is to use force or be prepared to use it singly or in combination. No appeal can be made to a higher entity clothed with the authority and equipped with the ability to act on its own initiative. Under such conditions the possibility that force will be used by one or another of the parties looms always as a threat in the background. In politics force is said to be the *ultima ratio*. In international politics force serves, not only as the *ultima ratio*, but indeed as the first and constant one. To limit force to being the *ultima ratio* of politics implies, in the words of Ortega y Gasset, "the previous submission of force to methods of reason."[14] The constant possibility that force will be used limits manipulations, moderates demands, and serves as an incentive for the settlement of disputes. One who knows that pressing too hard may lead to war has strong reason to consider whether possible gains are worth the risks entailed. The threat of force internationally is comparable to the role of the strike in labor and management bargaining. "The few strikes that take place are in a sense," as Livernash has said, "the cost of the strike option which produces settlements in the large mass of negotiations."[15] Even if workers seldom strike, their doing so is always a possibility. The possibility of industrial disputes leading to long and costly strikes encourages labor and management to face difficult issues, to try to understand each other's problems, and to work hard to find accommodations. The possibility that conflicts among nations may lead to long and costly wars has similarly sobering effects.

8. Anarchy and Hierarchy

I have described anarchies and hierarchies as though every political order were of one type or the other. Many, and I suppose most, political scientists who write of structures allow for a greater, and sometimes for a bewildering, variety of types. Anarchy is seen as one end of a continuum whose other end is marked by the presence of a legitimate and competent government. International politics is then described as being flecked with particles of government and alloyed with elements of community—supranational organizations whether universal or regional, alliances, multinational corporations, networks of trade, and whatnot. International-political systems are thought of as being more or less anarchic.

Those who view the world as a modified anarchy do so, it seems, for two reasons. First, anarchy is taken to mean not just the absence of government but also the presence of disorder and chaos. Since world politics, although not reliably peaceful, falls short of unrelieved chaos, students are inclined to see a lessening of anarchy in each outbreak of peace. Since world politics, although not formally organized, is not entirely without institutions and orderly procedures, students are inclined to see a lessening of anarchy when alliances form, when transactions across national borders increase, and when international agencies multiply. Such views confuse structure with process, and I have drawn attention to that error often enough.

Second, the two simple categories of anarchy and hierarchy do not seem to accommodate the infinite social variety our senses record. Why insist on reducing the types of structure to two instead of allowing for a greater variety? Anarchies are ordered by the juxtaposition of similar units, but those similar units are not identical. Some specialization by function develops among them. Hierarchies are ordered by the social division of labor among units specializing in different tasks, but the resemblance of units does not vanish. Much duplication of effort continues. All societies are organized segmentally or hierarchically in greater or lesser degree. Why not, then, define additional social types according to the mixture of organizing principles they embody? One might conceive of some societies approaching the purely anarchic, of others approaching the purely hierarchic, and of still others reflecting specified mixes of the two organizational types. In anarchies the exact likeness of units and the determination of relations by capability alone would describe a realm wholly of politics and power with none of the interaction of units guided by administration and conditioned by authority. In hierarchies the complete differentiation of parts and the full specification of their functions would produce a realm wholly of authority and administration with none of the interaction of parts affected by politics and power. Although such pure orders do not exist, to distinguish realms by their organizing principles is nevertheless proper and important.

Increasing the number of categories would bring the classification of societies closer to reality. But that would be to move away from a theory claiming explanatory power to a less theoretical system promising greater descriptive accuracy. One who wishes to explain rather than to describe should resist moving in that direction if resistance is reasonable. Is it? What does one gain by insisting on two types when admitting three or four would still be to simplify boldly? One gains clarity and economy of concepts. A new concept should be introduced only to cover matters that existing concepts do not reach. If some societies are neither anarchic or hierarchic, if their structures are defined by some third ordering principle, then we would have to define a third system.[16] All societies are mixed. Elements in them represent both of the ordering principles. That does not mean that some societies are ordered according to a third principle. Usually one can easily identify the principle by which a society is ordered. The appearance of anarchic sectors within hierarchies does not alter and should not obscure the ordering principle of the larger system, for those sectors are anarchic only within limits. The attributes and behavior of the units populating those sectors within the larger system differ, moreover, from what they should be and how they would behave outside of it. Firms in oligopolistic markets again are perfect examples of this. They struggle against one another, but because they need not prepare to defend themselves physically, they can afford to specialize and to participate more fully in the division of economic labor than states can. Nor do the states that populate an anarchic world find it impossible to work with one another, to make agreements limiting their arms, and to cooperate in establishing organizations. Hierarchic elements within international structures limit and restrain the exercise of sovereignty but only in ways strongly conditioned by the anarchy of the larger system. The anarchy of that order strongly affects the likelihood of cooperation, the extent of arms agreements, and the jurisdiction of international organizations. . . .

NOTES

1. S. F. Nadel, *The Theory of Social Structure* (Glencoe, Ill.: Free Press, 1957), pp. 8–11.
2. *Ibid.*, pp. 104–9.

3. William T. R. Fox, "The Uses of International Relations Theory," in William T. R. Fox, ed., *Theoretical Aspects of International Relations* (Notre Dame, Ind.: University of Notre Dame Press, 1959), p. 35.

4. Marriet Martineau, *The Positive Philosophy of Auguste Comte: Freely Translated and Condensed*, 3rd ed. (London: Kegan Paul, Trench, Trubner, 1983), vol. 2, pp. 51–53; George Katona, "Rational Behavior and Economic Behavior," *Psychological Review* 60 (September 1953).

5. Charles P. Kindleberger, *American Business Abroad* (New Haven, Ct.: Yale University Press, 1969), p. 207.

6. Smith should know better. Translated into terms that he has himself so effectively used, to say that states are sovereign is to say that they are segments of a plural society. See his "A Structural Approach to Comparative Politics" in David Easton, ed., *Varieties of Politics Theories* (Englewood Cliffs, N.J.: Prentice-Hall, 1966), p. 122; cf. his "On Segmentary Lineage Systems," *Journal of the Royal Anthropological Society of Great Britain and Ireland* 86 (July–December 1956).

7. Emile Durkheim, *The Division of Labor in Society*, trans. George Simpson (New York: Free Press, 1964), p. 212.

8. Alfred E. Kahn, "The Tyranny of Small Decision: Market Failure, Imperfections and Limits of Econometrics," in Bruce M. Russett, ed., *Economic Theories of International Relations* (Chicago, Ill.: Markham, 1966), p. 23.

9. Richard W. Sterling, *Macropolitics: International Relations in a Global Society* (New York: Knopf, 1974), p. 336.

10. Put differently, states face a "prisoners' dilemma." If each of two parties follows his own interest, both end up worse off than if each acted to achieve joint interests. For thorough examination of the logic of such situations, see Glenn H. Snyder and Paul Diesing, *Conflict among Nations* (Princeton, N.J.: Princeton University Press, 1977); for brief and suggestive international applications, see Robert Jervis, "Cooperation under the Security Dilemma," *World Politics* 30 (January 1978).

11. Cf. Paul Diesing, *Reason in Society* (Urbana, Ill.: University of Illinois Press, 1962), pp. 198–204; Anthony Downs, *Inside Bureaucracy* (Boston: Little, Brown, 1967), pp. 262–70.

12. Cf. Chester I. Bernard, "On Planning for World Government," in Chester I. Barnard, ed., *Organization and Management* (Cambridge, Mass.: Harvard University Press, 1948), pp. 148–152; Michael Polanyi, "The Growth of Thought in Society," *Economica* 8 (November 1941), pp. 428–456.

13. Barnard, "On Planning," pp. 150–51.

14. Quoted in Chalmers A. Johnson, *Revolutionary Change* (Boston: Little, Brown, 1966), p. 13.

15. E. R. Livernash, "The Relation of Power to the Structure and Process of Collective Bargaining," in Bruce M. Russett, ed., *Economic Theories of International Politics* (Chicago, Ill.: Markham, 1963), p. 430.

16. Emile Durkheim's depiction of solidary and mechanical societies still provides the best explication of the two ordering principles, and his logic in limiting the types of society to two continues to be compelling despite the efforts of his many critics to overthrow it (see esp. *The Division of Labor in Society*).

A Critique of Anarchy

Helen V. Milner

Anarchy *is one of the most vague and ambiguous words in language.*

George Cornewall Lewis, 1832.

In much current theorizing, anarchy has once again been declared to be the fundamental assumption about international politics. Over the last decade, numerous scholars, especially those in the Neorealist tradition, have posited anarchy as the single most important characteristic underlying international relations. This article explores implications of such an assumption. In doing so, it reopens older debates about the nature of international politics. First, I will examine various concepts of "anarchy" employed in the international relations literature. Second, I will probe the sharp dichotomy between domestic and international politics that is associated with this assumption. As others have, I question the validity and utility of such a dichotomy. Finally, this article suggests that a more fruitful way to understand the international system is one that combines anarchy and interdependence. . . .

The. . . focus on anarchy in international politics has led to the creation of a sharp distinction between domestic and international politics. Politics internationally is seen as characterized primarily by anarchy, while domestically centralized authority prevails. One of the most explicit statements of this position is in Waltz's *Theory of International Politics.* His powerful articulation of this dichotomy is interesting to examine closely since it is the clearest logical statement of the consequences of the anarchy assumption.

Waltz makes three separate claims about the distinction between the two areas. First, anarchy as a lack of central authority implies that international politics is a decentralized competition among sovereign equals. . . . A second distinction flows from the assumption of anarchy. As a lack of centralized control over force, anarchy implies that world politics is a self-help system reliant primarily on force. This also distinguishes international from national politics. . . . Finally, international politics is seen as the only true "politics". . . .

From "The Assumption of Anarchy in International Relations Theory" by Helen Milner from *The Review of International Studies* (1991). Reprinted by permission of Helen Milner and Cambridge University Press. Portions of the text and some footnotes have been omitted.

A very sharp distinction is drawn between the two political arenas on a number of different grounds, all of which flow from the assumption of anarchy. While some societies may possess elements of both ordering principles—anarchy and hierarchy—the conclusion of many is that such a rigid dichotomy is empirically feasible and theoretically useful. This section examines the utility of such a distinction. Is it empirically and heuristically helpful? To answer this question, it is important to examine Waltz's three distinctions because they represent the logical outcome of adopting the assumption of anarchy as the basis of international politics. While his views are the most explicit and perhaps extreme statement of this dichotomy, they do reflect the implicit understanding of Neorealist theory in general.

The first line of demarcation between domestic and international politics is the claim that centralization prevails in the former and decentralization in the latter. What is meant by centralization or its opposite? Centralization seems related to hierarchy. As Waltz notes, "The units—institutions and agencies—stand vis à vis each other in relations of super- and subordination."[1] Apparently, it refers to the number of, and relationship among, recognized centers of authority in a system. Domestic politics has fewer, more well-defined centers that are hierarchically ordered, while in international politics many centers exist and they are not so ordered. What counts as a center of authority, however? Waltz resorts to the legalistic notion of sovereignty to make his count internationally. He also assumes that domestically a well-defined hierarchy of authority exists. . . .

Such a view of domestic politics is hard to maintain. Who is the highest authority in the United States? The people, the states, the Constitution, the President, the Supreme Court, or even Congress? De jure, the Constitution is; but, de facto, it depends upon the issue. There is no single hierarchy of authority, as in some ideal military organization. Authority for deciding different issues rests with different groups in society. Authority is not highly concentrated; it is diffused. This was the intention of the writers of the Constitution, who wanted a system where power was not concentrated but rather dispersed. It was dispersed not only functionally through a structure of countervailing "checks and balances", but also geographically through federalism.[2]

Moreover, this decentralization is not unique to the United States. One of the main concerns in comparative politics has been to locate the centers of authority in various nations and plot their differing degrees of political centralization and decentralization along some continuum. Authority in some states may be fairly centralized, while in others it is highly decentralized, as demonstrated in the debate over "strong" and "weak" states.[3] But the central point is that states exhibit a very broad range of values along this continuum, and not all of them—or perhaps even the majority—may be more centralized than the international system.

A second issue is to what extent the international system is decentralized. The point made above that the concentration of authority in any system is best gauged along a continuum, and not a dichotomy, is relevant. Where along the continuum does the international system fit? The answer to this depends on two factors: What issue we are discussing (e.g., fishing rights, the use of nuclear weapons, or control of the seas) and what time period we have in mind. The first factor raises the issue of the fungibility of power. Curiously, Waltz assumes it is highly fungible: Force dominates and a hierarchy of power exists internationally, that is, "great powers" are identifiable. This view centralizes power much more than does the assumption that it is infungible. The issue of change over time is also important. The international system may evince different levels of centralization and decentralization, e.g., the nineteenth century Concert of Europe versus the post–World War II system.

To deal with these issues, Waltz has to relinquish his more legalistic notion of the international system as one of sovereign equals. At times, he indeed does this. In discussing anarchy, he posits that all states are equal and thus that authority internationally is highly decentralized. But, when talking of the distribution of capabilities, he recognizes that states are not equal and that only a few great powers count. In this latter discussion, he implies that capabilities are highly centralized in the international system. Waltz himself then does *not* find the assumption that all states are equal and thus that power is highly decentralized to be either empirically true or heuristically useful. As a "good" realist, he focuses upon the few strong powers in the system. . . .

The issue of the centralization of power internationally touches on another distinction between domestic and international politics. . . . The argument is that states are sovereign, implying that they are functionally equal and hence not interdependent. They are duplicates who do not need one another. Domestically, the units within states are differentiated, each filling some niche in the chain of command. For many domestic systems this is not accurate. For instance, in federal systems each state is functionally equal and no generally agreed-upon chain of command between the states and the national government exists. On some issues at some times, states have the final say; on others, the central government.

On the other hand, there is the question of whether all nation-states are functionally equivalent. If states are all "like units," why only examine the great powers? Waltz realizes this is a problem. He admits that "internationally, like units sometimes perform different tasks." Moreover, "the likelihood of their doing so, varies with their capabilities."[4] Thus he acknowledges that states with different capabilities perform different functions; hence, they are not all "like" units. Later he takes the point further:

> Although states are like units functionally, they differ vastly in their capabilities. Out of such differences something of a division of labor develops. . . . The division of labor across nations, however, is slight in comparison with the highly articulated division of labor within them.[5]

His position is that states do not perform the same tasks, that some international division of labor exists, but that this differentiation is *empirically* unimportant relative to that domestically. The dilemma is that two of Waltz's three central assumptions/ordering principles conflict. It is difficult to assume both that all states are equal (principles 1 and 2) *and* that all states are not equal as a result of the distribution of their capabilities (principle 3). Waltz might claim that they are equal in function but not in capabilities; however, as he himself states, one's capabilities shape one's functions. The point is, as others have noted before, the distribution of resources internationally creates a division of labor among states; differentiation and hierarchy exist and provide governing mechanisms for states, just as they do for individuals within states. Most importantly, the distinction among different international systems and within nation-states over the degree of centralization of authority as well as over the degree of differentiation among their units is variable and should be viewed along a continuum, rather than as a dichotomy.

A second means of separating domestic and international politics is to differentiate the role and importance of force in the two arenas. For Waltz, domestically force is less important as a means of control and is used to serve justice; internationally, force is widespread and serves no higher goal than to help the state using it. But is the importance of force so different in the two realms?. . . . For theorists like Waltz, Carr, and Weber, the threat of the use of force—in effect, deterrence—is ultimately the means of social control domestically. Threats of sanctions are the state's means of enforcement, as they are internationally. When norms and institutions fail to maintain social control, states internally and externally resort to threats of force. It may be that norms and institutions are more prevalent forms of control domestically than internationally. But this depends on the state in question. In some countries, belief in the legitimacy of government and institutions, being widespread and well-developed, might suffice to maintain control. However, the fact that more civil wars have been fought in this century than international ones and that since 1945 more have died in the former should make one pause when declaiming about the relative use of force in the two realms.[6]

Since at times the frequency of violence domestically is acknowledged, perhaps the point is that force is legitimate and serves justice domestically and not internationally.[7] Again, this depends upon the perceived legitimacy of the government and the particular instance of use. Have the majority of people in the Soviet Union, Poland, Ethiopia, South Africa, Iran, or the Philippines—to name just a few—felt that the state's use of force serves justice (all of the time? some of the time?)? Whether force serves justice domestically is an issue to be studied, not a given to be assumed. On the other hand, does force never serve justice internationally? Is it always, or most of the time, "for the sake of [the state's] own protection and advantage"? States have been known to intervene forcefully for larger purposes. The fight against Germany in World War II by the United States, for example, helped serve justice regardless of whether the United States' own protection was a factor. The distinction between international and domestic politics on this issue does not appear as clear as is claimed.

A third dichotomy between the two arenas asserts that power and politics operate internationally. Domestically, authority, administration, and law prevail; internationally, it is power, struggle, and accommodation. For some, the latter alone is politics. This distinction is the hardest to maintain. Disputes among political parties, local and national officials, the executive and the legislature, different geographic regions, different races, capital and labor, industry and finance, organized and unorganized groups, etc., over who gets how much and when occur constantly within the nation. Morgenthau recognizes this:

> The essence of international politics is identical with its domestic counterpart. Both domestic and international politics are a struggle for power, modified only by the different conditions under which this struggle takes place in the domestic and in the international spheres.
>
> The tendency to dominate, in particular, is an element of all human associations, from the family through fraternal and professional associations and local political organizations, to the state. . . . Finally, the whole political life of a nation, particularly of a democratic nation, from the local to the national level, is a continuous struggle for power.[8]

E. H. Carr, another realist, also disagrees with Waltz. Like Morgenthau, he sees the national and world arenas as being based on the same principles and processes: power politics. In talking of domestic politics, he echoes Thucydides' Melian dialogue: "The majority rules because it is stronger, the minority submits because it is weaker."[9] He maintains that the factors which supposedly distinguish domestic politics—for example, legitimacy, morality, ideology, and law—are just as political nationally as internationally.

Theories of social morality are always the product of a

> dominant group which identifies itself with the community as a whole, and which possesses facilities denied to subordinate groups or individuals for imposing its view of life on the community. Theories of international morality are, for the same reason and in virtue of the same process, the product of dominant nations or groups of nations.[10]

As an example of this, Carr notes that "laissez-faire, in international relations as in those between capital and labor, is the paradise of the economically strong."[11] He points out that even law, another factor that is supposed to make politics within the nation different, is merely a manifestation of power:

> Behind all law there is this necessary political background. The ultimate authority of law derives from politics.[12]

Others would reject Carr's insistence that law and morality spring from power, but would nonetheless agree that politics within nations and among them are similar. These authors see authority, law, and morality being as important to international relations as to domestic ones. For instance, Inis Claude holds that international order is maintained by a balance of power among opposing forces, just as it is domestically. In attacking the notion that governments maintain peace through some monopoly of force, Claude returns to Morgenthau to make his point:

> Morgenthau's espousal of the concept of the state's "monopoly of organized violence" is contradicted by his general conception of politics: "Domestic and interna-

tional politics are but two different manifestations of the same phenomenon: the struggle for power." In his terms, "The balance of power . . . is indeed a perennial element of all pluralistic societies."[13]

For him, as for Morgenthau, societies are pluralistic, and thus the role of government is "the delicate task of promoting and presiding over a constantly shifting equilibrium."[14] Politics domestically and internationally is about balancing power. To assume that a state has a monopoly of power and that this is "the key to the effectiveness of [it] as an order-keeping institution may lead to an exaggerated notion of the degree to which actual states can and do rely upon coercion."[15] Unlike Morgenthau and other realists, Claude sees factors other than coercion—such as, norms and institutions—as being more important both domestically and internationally to the maintenance of order, but like them he views the balance of power as fundamental to the two realms. Unlike Waltz, all of these authors find relations within nations and among them to be political and to be based on similar political processes. . . .

A second and related heuristic problem is the tendency implicit in this separation of the two fields to view all states as being the same. Waltz, for one, wants us to conceive of states as like units and to avoid looking within them at their internal arrangements. His is a systemic level theory. But the issue is whether it is possible and/or fruitful to abstract from all of domestic politics. All states are not the same, and their internal characteristics, including their goals and capabilities, affect international politics importantly, as Waltz is forced to admit. This is reflected in the tension between his ordering principles, the first two of which give primacy to structural pressures while the third makes certain agents key. Using systemic theory, he wants to "tell us about the forces the units are subject to," but he also notes that "in international politics, as in any self-help system, the units of greatest capability set the scene of action for others as well as for themselves.[16] The units do matter.

NOTES

1. Kenneth Waltz, *Theory of International Politics* (Reading, Mass.: Addison-Wesley, 1979), p. 81.
2. Waltz recognizes this: see *Theory of International Politics*, pp. 81. But it never influences his very sharp distinction between the ordering of domestic and international politics.
3. See, for example, Peter Katzenstein, ed., *Between Power and Plenty* (Ithaca: Cornell University Press, 1978).
4. Waltz, *Theory of International Politics*, p. 47.
5. Ibid, p. 105.
6. Melvin Small and J. David Singer, *Explaining War* (Beverly Hills: Sage, 1979), pp. 63, 65, 68–69.
7. Waltz, *Theory of International Politics*, p. 103.
8. Hans Morgenthau, *Politics Among Nations*, 6th ed. (New York: Knopf, 1985), pp. 39–40.
9. E. H. Carr, *The Twenty Years' Crisis* (New York: Harper and Row, 1964), p. 41.

10. Ibid. p. 79.
11. Ibid, p. 60.
12. Ibid, p. 180.
13. Inis Claude, *Power and International Relations* (New York: Random House, 1962), p. 231.
14. Ibid.
15. Ibid, p. 234.
16. Waltz, *Theory of International Politics*, p. 72.

The Conditions for Cooperation in World Politics

Kenneth A. Oye

I. INTRODUCTION

Nations dwell in perpetual anarchy, for no central authority imposes limits on the pursuit of sovereign interests. This common condition gives rise to diverse outcomes. Relations among states are marked by war and concert, arms races and arms control, trade wars and tariff truces, financial panics and rescues, competitive devaluation and monetary stabilization. At times, the absence of centralized international authority precludes attainment of common goals. Because, as states, they cannot cede ultimate control over their conduct to an supranational sovereign, they cannot guarantee that they will adhere to their promises. The possibility of a breach of promise can impede cooperation even when cooperation would leave all better off. Yet, at other times, states do realize common goals through cooperation under anarchy. Despite the absence of any ultimate international authority, governments often bind themselves to mutually advantageous courses of action. And, though no international sovereign stands ready to enforce the terms of agreement, states can realize common interests through tacit cooperation, formal bilateral and multilateral negotiation, and the creation of international regimes. The question is: if international relations can approximate both a Hobbesian state of nature and a Lockean evil society, why does cooperation emerge in some cases and not in others?

[Scholars] address both explanatory and prescriptive aspects of this perennial question. *First, what circumstances favor the emergence of cooperation under anarchy?* Given the lack of a central authority to guarantee adherence

"Explaining Cooperation under Anarchy: Hypothesis and Strategies" by Kenneth A. Oye from *World Politics*. Reprinted by permission of Johns Hopkins University Press. Portions of the text and some footnotes have been omitted.

to agreements, what features of situations encourage or permit states to bind themselves to mutually beneficial courses of action? What features of situations preclude cooperation? *Second, what strategies can states adopt to foster the emergence of cooperation by altering the circumstances they confront?* Governments need not necessarily accept circumstances as given. To what extent are situational impediments to cooperation subject to willful modification? Through what higher order strategies can states create the preconditions for cooperation?. . .

I submit that three circumstantial dimensions serve both as proximate explanations of cooperation and as targets of longer-term strategies to promote cooperation. Each of the three major sections of this piece defines a dimension, explains how that dimension accounts for the incidence of cooperation and conflict in the absence of centralized authority, and examines associated strategies for enhancing the prospects for cooperation.

In the section entitled "Payoff Structure: Mutual and Conflicting Preferences," I discuss how payoffs affect the prospects for cooperation and present strategies to improve the prospects for cooperation by altering payoffs. Orthodox game theorists identify optimal strategies *given* ordinally defined classes of games, and their familiar insights provide the starting point for the discussion. Recent works in security studies, institutional microeconomics, and international political economy suggest strategies to *alter* payoff structures and thereby improve the prospects for cooperation.[1]

In the next section, entitled "Shadow of the Future: Single-play and Iterated Games," I discuss how the prospect of continuing interaction affects the likelihood of cooperation; examine how strategies of reciprocity can provide direct paths to cooperative outcomes under iterated conditions; and suggest strategies to lengthen the shadow of the future.[2] In addition, this section shows that recognition and control capabilities—the ability to distinguish between cooperation and defection by others and to respond in kind—can affect the power of reciprocity, and suggests strategies to improve recognition capabilities.

In the third section, "Number of Players: Two-Person and N-Person Games," I explain why cooperation becomes more difficult as the number of actors increases; present strategies for promoting cooperation in N-actor situations; and offer strategies for promoting cooperation by reducing the number of actors necessary to the realization of common interests. Game theorists and oligopoly theorists have long noted that cooperation becomes more difficult as numbers increase, and their insights provide a starting point for discussion. Recent work in political economy focuses on two strategies for promoting cooperation in thorny N-person situations: functionalist analysts of regimes suggest strategies for increasing the likelihood and robustness of cooperation *given* large numbers of actors,[3] analysts of *ad hoc* bargaining in international political economy suggest strategies of bilateral and regional decomposition to *reduce* the number of actors necessary to the realization of some mutual interests, at the expense of the magnitude of gains from cooperation. . . .[4]

II. PLAYOFF STRUCTURE:
MUTUAL AND CONFLICTING PREFERENCES

The structure of payoffs in a given round of play—the benefits of mutual cooperation (CC) relative to mutual defection (DD) and the benefits of unilateral defection (DC) relative to unrequited cooperation (CD)—is fundamental to the analysis of cooperation. The argument proceeds in three stages. First, how does payoff
structure affect the significance of cooperation? More narrowly, when is cooperation, defined in terms of conscious policy coordination, necessary to the realization of mutual interests? Second, how does payoff structure affect the likelihood
and robustness of cooperation? Third, through what strategies can states increase
the long-term prospects for cooperation by altering payoff structures?

Before turning to these questions, consider briefly some tangible and intangible determinants of payoff structures. The security and political economy
literatures examine the effects of military force structure and doctrine, economic ideology, the size of currency reserves, macroeconomic circumstance,
and a host of other factors on national assessments of national interests. In
"Cooperation under the Security Dilemma," Robert Jervis has explained how
the diffusion of offensive military technology and strategies can increase rewards from defection and thereby reduce the prospects for cooperation. In
"International Regimes, Transactions, and Chance: Embedded Liberalism in
the Postwar Economic Order," John Ruggie has demonstrated how the diffusion
of liberal economic ideas increased the perceived benefits of mutual economic
openness over mutual closure (CC-DD), and diminished the perceived rewards
from asymmetric defection relative to asymmetric cooperation (DC-CD). In
"Firms and Tariff Regime Change," Timothy McKeown has shown how down-
turns in the business cycle alter national tastes for protection and thereby
decrease the perceived benefits of mutual openness relative to mutual closure
and increase the perceived rewards of asymmetric defection. . . .[5]

A. Payoff Structure and Cooperation

How does payoff structure determine the significance of cooperation? More
narrowly, when is *cooperation*, defined in terms of conscious policy coordination, *necessary* to the realization of *mutual benefits*? For a *mutual benefit* to
exist, actors must prefer mutual cooperation (CC) to mutual defection (DD).
For coordination to be *necessary* to the realization of the mutual benefit, actors
must prefer unilateral defection (DC) to unrequited cooperation (CD). These
preference orderings are consistent with the familiar games of Prisoners' Dilemma, Stag Hunt, and Chicken. Indeed, these games have attracted a disproportionate share of scholarly attention precisely because cooperation is desirable but not automatic. In these cases, the capacity of states to cooperate under
anarchy, to bind themselves to mutually beneficial courses of action without
resort to any ultimate central authority, is vital to the realization of a common
good. . . .

In the class of games—including Prisoners' Dilemma, Stag Hunt, and

Chicken—where cooperation is necessary to the realization of mutual benefits, how does payoff structure affect the likelihood and robustness of cooperation in these situations? Cooperation will be less likely in Prisoners' Dilemma than in Stag Hunt or Chicken. To understand why, consider each of these games in conjunction with the illustrative stories from which they derive their names.

Prisoners' Dilemma: Two prisoners are suspected of a major crime. The authorities possess evidence to secure conviction on only a minor charge. If neither prisoner squeals, both will draw a light sentence on the minor charge (CC). If one prisoner squeals and the other stonewalls, the rat will go free (DC) and the sucker will draw a very heavy sentence (CD). If both squeal, both will draw a moderate sentence (DD). Each prisoner's preference ordering is: DC > CC > DD > CD. If the prisoners expect to "play" only one time, each prisoner will be better off squealing than stonewalling, no matter what his partner chooses to do (DC > CC and DD > CD). The temptation of the rat payoff and fear of the sucker payoff will drive single-play Prisoners' Dilemmas toward mutual defection. Unfortunately, if both prisoners act on this reasoning, they will draw a moderate sentence on the major charge, while cooperation could have led to a light sentence on the minor charge (CC > DD). In single-play Prisoners' Dilemmas, individually rational actions produce a collectively suboptimal outcome.

Stag Hunt: A group of hunters surround a stag. If all cooperate to trap the stag, all will eat well (CC). If one person defects to chase a passing rabbit, the stag will escape. The defector will eat lightly (DC) and none of the others will eat at all (CD). If all chase rabbits, all will have some chance of catching a rabbit and eating lightly (DD). Each hunter's preference ordering is: CC > DC > DD > CD. The mutual interest in plentiful venison (CC) relative to all other outcomes militates strongly against defection. However, because a rabbit in the hand (DC) is better than a stag in the bush (CD), cooperation will be assured only if each hunter believes that all hunters will cooperate. In single-play Stag Hunt, the temptation to defect to protect against the defection of others is balanced by the strong universal preference for stag over rabbit.

Chicken: Two drivers race down the center of a road from opposite directions. If one swerves and the other does not, then the first will suffer the stigma of being known as a chicken (CD) while the second will enjoy being known as a hero (DC). If neither swerves, both will suffer grievously in the ensuing collision (DD). If both swerve, damage to the reputation of each will be limited (CC). Each driver's preference ordering is: DC > CC > CD > DD. If each believes that the other will swerve, then each will be tempted to defect by continuing down the center of the road. Better to be a live hero than a live chicken. If both succumb to this temptation, however, defection will result in collision. The fear that the other driver may not swerve decreases the appeal of continuing down the center of the road. In single-play Chicken, the temptations of unilateral defection are balanced by fear of mutual defection.

In games that are not repeated, only ordinally defined preferences matter. Under single-play conditions, interval-level payoffs in ordinally defined categories of games cannot (in theory) affect the likelihood of cooperation. In the illustrations above, discussions of dominant strategies do not hinge on the magnitude of differences among the payoffs. Yet the magnitude of differences between CC and DD and between DC and CD can be large or small, if not precisely measurable, and can increase or decrease. Changes in the magnitude of differences in the value placed on outcomes can influence the prospects for cooperation through two paths.

First, changes in the value attached to outcomes can transform situations from one ordinally defined class of game into another. For example, in "Cooperation under the Security Dilemma" Robert Jervis described how difficult Prisoners' Dilemmas may evolve into less challenging Stag Hunts if the gains from mutual cooperation (CC) increase relative to the gains from exploitation (DC). He related the structure of payoffs to traditional concepts of offensive and defensive dominance, and offensive and defensive dominance to technological and doctrinal shifts. Ernst Haas, Mary Pat Williams, and Don Babai have emphasized the importance of cognitive congruence as a determinant of technological cooperation. The diffusion of common conceptions of the nature and effects of technology enhanced perceived gains from cooperation and diminished perceived gains from defection, and may have transformed some Prisoners' Dilemmas into Harmony.[6]

Second, under iterated conditions, the magnitude of differences among payoffs *within* a given class of games can be an important determinant of co-operation. The more substantial the gains from mutual cooperation (CC-DD) and the less substantial the gains from unilateral defection (DC-CD), the greater the likelihood of cooperation. In iterated situations, the magnitude of the difference between CC and DD and between DC and CD in present and future rounds of play affects the likelihood of cooperation in the present. This point is developed at length in the section on the shadow of the future.

B. Strategies to Alter Payoff Structure

If payoff structure affects the likelihood of cooperation, to what extent can states alter situations by modifying payoff structures, and thereby increase the long-term likelihood of cooperation? Many of the tangible and intangible determinants of payoff structure, discussed at the outset of this section, are subject to willful modification through unilateral, bilateral, and multilateral strategies. In "Cooperation under the Security Dilemma," Robert Jervis has offered specific suggestions for altering payoff structures through unilateral strategies. Procurement policy can affect the prospects for cooperation. If one superpower favors procurement of defensive over offensive weapons, it can reduce its own gains from exploitation through surprise attack (DC) and reduce its adversary's fear of exploitation (CD). Members of alliances have often resorted to the device of deploying troops on troubled frontiers to increase the likelihood of cooperation. A state's use of troops as hostages is designed to diminish the payoff from its own defection—to reduce its gains from exploitation (DC)—and thereby render defensive defection by its partner less likely. Publicizing an agreement diminishes payoffs associated with defection from the agreement, and thereby lessens gains from exploitation. These observations in international relations are paralleled by recent developments in microeconomics. Oliver Williamson has identified unilateral and bilateral techniques used by firms to facilitate interfirm cooperation by diminishing gains from exploitation. He distinguishes between specific and nonspecific costs associated with adherence to agreements. Specific costs, such as specialized training, machine tools, and construction, cannot be recovered in the event of the breakdown of an agreement. When parties to an agreement incur high specific costs, repudiation of commitments will entail substantial losses. Firms can thus reduce their gains from exploitation through the technique of acquiring dedicated assets that serve as hostages to continuing cooperation. Nonspecific assets, such as general-purpose trucks and airplanes, are salvageable if agreements break down; firms can reduce their fear of being exploited by maximizing the use of nonspecific assets, but such assets cannot diminish gains from exploitation by serving as hostages.[7] Unilateral strategies can improve the prospects of cooperation by reducing both the costs of being exploited (CD) and the gains from exploitation (DC). The new literature on interfirm cooperation indirectly raises an old question on the costs of unilateral strategies to promote cooperation in international relations.

In many instances, unilateral actions that limit one's gains from exploitation may have the effect of increasing one's vulnerability to exploitation by others. For example, a state could limit gains from defection from liberal international economic norms by permitting the expansion of sectors of comparative advantage and by permitting liquidation of inefficient sectors. Because a specialized economy is a hostage to international economic cooperation, this strategy would unquestionably increase the credibility of the nation's commitment to liberalism. It also has the effect, however, of increasing the nation's vulnerability to protection by others. In the troops-as-hostage example, the government that stations troops may promote cooperation by diminishing an ally's fear of abandonment, but in so doing it raises its own fears of exploitation by the ally. . . .

Unilateral strategies do not exhaust the range of options that states may use to alter payoff structures. Bilateral strategies—most significantly strategies of issue linkage—can be used to alter payoff structures by combining dissimilar games. Because resort to issue linkage generally assumes iteration, analysis of how issue linkage can be used to alter payoffs is presented in the section on the shadow of the future. Furthermore, bilateral "instructional" strategies can aim at altering another country's understanding of cause-and-effect relationships, and result in altered perceptions of interest. For example, American negotiators in SALT I sought to instruct their Soviet counterparts on the logic of mutual assured destruction.[8]

Multilateral strategies, centering on the formation of international regimes, can be used to alter payoff structures in two ways. First, norms generated by regimes may be internalized by states, and thereby alter payoff structure. Second, information generated by regimes may alter states' understanding of their interests. As Ernst Haas argues, new regimes may gather and distribute information that can highlight cause-and-effect relationships not previously understood. Changing perceptions of means-ends hierarchies can, in turn, result in changing perceptions of interest.[9]

III. THE SHADOW OF THE FUTURE: SINGLE-PLAY AND ITERATED GAMES

The distinction between cases in which similar transactions among parties are unlikely to be repeated and cases in which the expectation of future interaction can influence decisions in the present is fundamental to the emergence of cooperation among egotists. As the previous section suggests, states confronting strategic situations that resemble single-play Prisoners' Dilemma and, to a lesser extent, single-play Stag Hunt and Chicken, are constantly tempted by immediate gains from unilateral defection, and fearful of immediate losses from unrequited cooperation. How does continuing interaction affect prospects for cooperation? The argument proceeds in four stages. First, why do iterated conditions improve the prospects for cooperation in Prisoners' Dilemma and Stag Hunt while diminishing the prospects for cooperation in Chicken? Second, how do strategies of reciprocity improve the prospects for cooperation under iterated conditions? Third, why does the effectiveness of reciprocity hinge on conditions of play—the ability of actors to distinguish reliably between cooperation and defection by others and to respond in kind? Fourth, through what strategies can states improve conditions of play and lengthen the shadow of the future?[10]

Before turning to these questions, consider the attributes of iterated situations. First, states must expect to continue dealing with each other. This condition is, in practice, not particularly restrictive. With the possible exception of global thermonuclear war, international politics is characterized by the expectation of future interaction. Second, payoff structures must not change substantially over time. In other words, each round of play should not alter the structure of the game in the future. This condition is, in practice, quite restrictive. For example, states considering surprise attack when offense is dominant are in a situation that has many of the characteristics of a single-play game: Attack alters options and payoffs in future rounds of interaction. Conversely, nations considering increases or decreases in their military budgets are in a situation that has many of the characteristics of an iterated game: Spending options and associated marginal increases or decreases in military strength are likely to remain fairly stable over future rounds of interaction. In international monetary affairs, governments considering or fearing devaluation under a gold-exchange standard are in a situation that has many of the characteristics of a single-play game: Devaluation may diminish the value of another state's foreign currency reserves on a one-time basis, while reductions in holdings of reserves would diminish possible losses on a one-time basis. Conversely, governments considering intervention under a floating system with minimal reserves are in a situation that has many of the characteristics of an iterated game: Depreciation or appreciation of a currency would not produce substantial one-time losses or gains. Third, the size of the discount rate applied to the future affects the iterativeness of games. If a government places little value on future payoffs, its situation has many of the characteristics of a single-play game. If it places a high value on future payoffs, its situation may have many of the characteristics of an interated game. For example, political leaders in their final term are likely to discount the future more substantially than political leaders running for, or certain of, reelection.

A. The Shadow of the Future and Cooperation

How does the shadow of the future affect the likelihood of cooperation? Under single-play conditions without a sovereign, adherence to agreements is often irrational. Consider the single-play Prisoners' Dilemma. Each prisoner is better off squealing, whether or not his partner decides to squeal. In the absence of continuing interaction, defection would emerge as the dominant strategy. Because the prisoners can neither turn to a central authority for enforcement of an agreement to cooperate nor rely on the anticipation of retaliation to deter present defection, cooperation will be unlikely under single-play conditions. If the prisoners expect to be placed in similar situations in the future, the prospects for cooperation improve. Experimental evidence suggests that under iterated Prisoners' Dilemma the incidence of cooperation rises substantially.[11] Even in the absence of centralized authority, tacit agreements to cooperate through mutual stonewalling are frequently reached and maintained. Under iterated Prisoners' Dilemma, a potential defector compares the immediate gain from squealing with the possible sacrifice of future gains that may result from squealing. In single-play Stag Hunt, each hunter is tempted to defect in order to defend himself against the possibility of defection by others. A reputation for reliability, for resisting temptation, reduces the likelihood of defection. If the hunters are a permanent group, and expect to hunt together again, the immediate gains from unilateral defection relative to unrequited cooperation must be balanced against the cost of diminished cooperation in the future. In both Prisoners' Dilemma and Stag Hunt, defection in the present *decreases* the likelihood of cooperation in the future. In both, therefore, iteration improves the prospects for cooperation. In Chicken, iteration may decrease the prospects for cooperation. Under single-play conditions, the temptation of unilateral defection is balanced by the fear of the collision that follows from mutual defection. How does iteration affect this balance? If the game is repeated indefinitely, then each driver may refrain from swerving in the present to coerce the other driver into swerving in the future. Each driver may seek to acquire a reputation for not swerving to cause the other driver to swerve. In iterated Chicken, one driver's defection in the present may decrease the likelihood of the other driver's defection in the future.

B. Strategies of Reciprocity and Conditions of Play

It is at this juncture that strategy enters the explanation. Although the expectation of continuing interaction has varying effects on the likelihood of cooperation in the illustrations above, an iterated environment permits resort to strategies of reciprocity that may improve the prospects of cooperation in Chicken as well as in Prisoners' Dilemma and Stag Hunt. Robert Axelrod argues that strategies of reciprocity have the effect of promoting cooperation by establishing a direct connection between an actor's present behavior and anticipated future benefits. Tit-for-tat, or conditional cooperation, can increase the likelihood of joint cooperation by shaping the future consequences of present cooperation or defection.

In iterated Prisoners' Dilemma and Stag Hunt, reciprocity underscores the future consequences of present cooperation and defection. The argument presented above—that iteration enhances the prospects for cooperation in these games—rests on the assumption that defection in the present will decrease the likelihood of cooperation in the future. Adoption of an implicit or explicit strategy of matching stonewalling with stonewalling, squealing with squealing, rabbit chasing with rabbit chasing, and cooperative hunting with cooperative hunting validates the assumption. In iterated Chicken, a strategy of reciprocity can offset the perverse effects of reputational considerations on the prospects for cooperation. Recall that in iterated Chicken, each driver may refrain from swerving in the present to coerce the other driver into swerving in the future. Adoption of an implicit or explicit strategy of tit-for-tat in iterated games of Chicken alters the future stream of benefits associated with present defection. If a strategy of reciprocity is credible, then the mutual losses associated with future collisions can encourage present swerving. In all three games, a promise to respond to present cooperation with future cooperation and a threat to respond to present defection with future defection can improve the prospects for cooperation.

The effectiveness of strategies of reciprocity hinges on conditions of play—the ability of actors to distinguish reliably between cooperation and defection by others and to respond in kind. In the illustrations provided above, the meaning of "defect" and "cooperate" is unambiguous. Dichotomous choices—between squeal and stonewall, chase the rabbit or capture the stag, continue down the road or swerve—limit the likelihood of misperception. Further, the actions of all are transparent. Given the definitions of the situations, prisoners, hunters, and drivers can reliably detect defection and cooperation by other actors. Finally, the definition of the actors eliminates the possibility of control problems. Unitary prisoners, hunters, and drivers do not suffer from factional, organizational, or bureaucratic dysfunctions that might hinder implementation of strategies of reciprocity.

In international relations, conditions of play can limit the effectiveness of reciprocity. The definition of cooperation and defection may be ambiguous. For example, the Soviet Union and the United States hold to markedly different definitions of "defection" from the terms of détente as presented in the Basic Principles Agreement;[12] the European Community and the United States differ over whether domestic sectoral policies comprise indirect export subsidies. Further, actions may not be transparent. For example, governments may not be able to detect one another's violations of arms control agreements or indirect export subsidies. If defection cannot be reliably detected, the effect of present cooperation on possible future reprisals will erode. Together, ambiguous definitions and a lack of transparency can limit the ability of states to recognize cooperation and defection by others.

Because reciprocity requires flexibility, control is as important as recognition. Internal factional, organizational, and bureaucratic dysfunctions may limit the ability of nations to implement tit-for-tat strategies. It may be easier to sell one unvarying line of policy than to sell a strategy of shifting between lines of policy in response to the actions of others. For example, arms suppliers and defense planners tend to resist the cancellation of weapons systems even if the cancellation is a response to the actions of a rival. Import-competing industries tend to resist the removal of barriers to imports, even if trade liberalization is in response to liberalization by another state. At times, national decision makers may be unable to implement strategies of reciprocity. On other occasions, they must invest heavily in selling reciprocity. For these reasons, national decision makers may display a bias against conditional strategies: The domestic costs of pursuing such strategies may partially offset the value of the discounted stream of future benefits that conditional policies are expected to yield. . . .

C. Strategies to Improve Recognition and Lengthen the Shadow of the Future

To what extent can governments promote cooperation by creating favorable conditions of play and by lengthening the shadow of the future? The literature on international regimes offers several techniques for creating favorable conditions of play. Explicit codification of norms can limit definitional ambiguity. The very act of clarifying standards of conduct, of defining cooperative and uncooperative behavior, can permit more effective resort to strategies of reciprocity. Further, provisions for surveillance—for example, mechanisms for verification in arms control agreements or for sharing information on the nature and effects of domestic sectoral policies—can increase transparency. In practice, the goal of enhancing recognition capabilities is often central to negotiations under anarchy.

The game-theoretic and institutional microeconomic literatures offer several approaches to increasing the iterative character of situations. Thomas Schelling and Robert Axelrod suggest tactics of decomposition over time to lengthen the shadow of the future.[13] For example, the temptation to defect in a deal promising thirty billion dollars for a billion barrels of oil may be reduced if the deal is sliced up into a series of payments and deliveries. Cooperation in arms reduction or in territorial disengagement may be difficult if the reduction or disengagement must be achieved in one jump. If a reduction or disengagement can be sliced up into increments, the problem of cooperation may be rendered more tractable. Finally, strategies of issue linkage can be used to alter payoff structures and to interject elements of iterativeness into single-play situations. Relations among states are rarely limited to one single-play issue of overriding importance. When nations confront a single-play game on one issue, present defection may be deterred by threats of retaliation on other iterated issues. In international monetary affairs, for instance, a government fearing one-time reserve losses if another state devalues its currency may link devaluation to an iterated trade game. By establishing a direct connection between present behavior in a single-play game and future benefits in an iterated game, tacit or explicit cross-issue linkage can lengthen the shadow of the future. . . .

IV. NUMBER OF PLAYERS: TWO-PERSON AND N-PERSON GAMES

Up to now, I have discussed the effects of payoff structure and the shadow of the future on the prospects of cooperation in terms of two-person situations. What happens to the prospects for cooperation as the number of significant actors rises? In this section, I explain why the prospects for cooperation diminish as the number of players increases; examine the function of international regimes as a response to the problems created by large numbers; and offer strategies to improve the prospects for cooperation by altering situations to diminish the number of significant players.

The numbers problem is central to many areas of the social sciences. Mancur Olson's theory of collective action focuses on N-person versions of Prisoners' Dilemma. The optimism of our earlier discussions of cooperation under iterated Prisoners' Dilemma gives way to the pessimism of analyses of cooperation in the provision of public goods. Applications of Olsonian theory to problems ranging from cartelization to the provision of public goods in alliances underscore the significance of "free-riding" as an impediment to cooperation.[14] In international relations, the numbers problem has been central to two debates. The longstanding controversy over the stability of bipolar versus multipolar systems reduces to a debate over the impact of the number of significant actors on international conflict.[15] A more recent controversy, between proponents of the theory of hegemonic stability and advocates of international regimes, reduces to a debate over the effects of large numbers on the robustness of cooperation.[16]

A. Number of Players and Cooperation

How do numbers affect the likelihood of cooperation? There are at least three important channels of influence.[17] First, cooperation requires recognition of opportunities for the advancement of mutual interests, as well as policy coordination once these opportunities have been identified. As the number of players increases, transactions and information costs rise. In simple terms, the complexity of N-person situations militates against identification and realization of common interests. Avoiding nuclear war during the Cuban missile crisis called for cooperation by the Soviet Union and the United States. The transaction and information costs in this particularly harrowing crisis, though substantial, did not preclude cooperation. By contrast, the problem of identifying significant actors, defining interests, and negotiating agreements that embodied mutual interests in the N-actor case of 1914 was far more difficult. These secondary costs associated with attaining cooperative outcomes in N-actor cases erode the difference between CC and DD. More significantly, the intrinsic difficulty of anticipating the behavior of other players and of weighing the value of the future goes up with the number of players. The complexity of solving N-person games, even in the purely deductive sense, has stunted the development of formal work on the problem. This complexity is even greater in real situations, and operates against multilateral cooperation.

Second, as the number of players increases, the likelihood of autonomous defection and of recognition and control problems increases. Cooperative behavior rests on calculations of expected utility—merging discount rates, payoff structures, and anticipated behavior of other players. Discount rates and approaches to calculation are likely to vary across actors, and the prospects for mutual cooperation may decline as the number of players and probable heterogeneity of actors increases. The chances of including a state that discounts the future heavily, that is too weak (domestically) to detect, react, or implement a strategy of reciprocity, that cannot distinguish reliably between cooperation and defection by other states, or that departs from even minimal standards of rationality increase with the number of states in a game. For example, many pessimistic analyses of the consequences of nuclear proliferation focus on how breakdowns of deterrence may become more likely as the number of countries with nuclear weapons increases.

Third, as the number of players increases, the feasibility of sanctioning defectors diminishes. Strategies of reciprocity become more difficult to implement without triggering a collapse of cooperation. In two-person games, tit-for-tat works well because the costs of defection are focused on only one other party. If defection imposes costs on all parties in an N-person game, however, the power of strategies of reciprocity is underminded. The infeasibility of sanctioning defectors creates the possibility of free-riding. What happens if we increase the number of actors in the iterated Prisoners' Dilemma from 2 to 20? Confession by any one of them could lead to the conviction of all on the major charge; therefore, the threat to retaliate against defection in the present with defection in the future will impose costs on all prisoners, and could lead to wholesale defection in subsequent rounds. For example, under the 1914 system of alliances, retaliation against one member of the alliance was the equivalent of retaliation against all. In N-person games, a strategy of conditional defection can have the effect of spreading, rather than containing, defection.

B. Strategies of Institutionalization and Decomposition

Given a large number of players, what strategies can states use to increase the likelihood of cooperation? Regime creation can increase the likelihood of cooperation in N-person games. First, conventions provide rules of thumb that can diminish transaction and information costs. Second, collective enforcement mechanisms both decrease the likelihood of autonomous defection and permit selective punishment of violators of norms. These two functions of international regimes directly address problems created by large numbers of players. For example, Japan and the members of NATO profess a mutual interest in limiting flows of militarily useful goods and technology to the Soviet Union. Obviously, all suppliers of militarily useful goods and technology must cooperate to deny the Soviet Union access to such items. Although governments differ in their assessment of the military value of some goods and technologies, there is consensus on a rather lengthy list of prohibited items. By facilitating agreement on the prohibited list, the Coordinating Committee on the Consultative Group of NATO (CoCom) provides a relatively clear definition of what exports would constitute defection. By defining the scope of defection, the CoCom list forestalls the necessity of retaliation against nations that ship technology or goods that do not fall within the consensual definition of defection. Generally, cooperation is a prerequisite of regime creation. The creation of rules of thumb and mechanisms of collective enforcement and the maintenance and administration of regimes can demand an extraordinary degree of cooperation. This problem may limit the range of situations susceptible to modification through regimist strategies.

What strategies can reduce the number of significant players in a game and thereby render cooperation more likely? When governments are unable to cooperate on a global scale, they often turn to discriminatory strategies to encourage bilateral or regional cooperation. Tactics of decomposition across actors can, at times, improve the prospects for cooperation. Both the possibilities and the limits of strategies to reduce the number of players are evident in the discussions that follow. First, reductions in the number of actors can usually be purchased at the expense of the magnitude of gains from cooperation. The benefits of regional openness are smaller than the gains from global openness. A bilateral clearing arrangement is less economically efficient than a multilateral clearing arrangement. Strategies to reduce the number of players in a game generally diminish the gains from cooperation while they increase the likelihood and robustness of cooperation. Second, strategies to reduce the number of players generally impose substantial costs on third parties. These externalities may motivate third parties to undermine the limited area of cooperation or may serve as an impetus for a third party to enlarge the zone of cooperation. In the 1930s, for example, wholesale resort to discriminatory trading policies facilitated creation of exclusive zones of commercial openness. When confronted by a shrinking market share, Great Britain adopted a less liberal and more discriminatory commercial policy in order to secure preferential access to its empire and to undermine preferential agreements between other countries. As the American market share diminished, the United States adopted a more liberal and more discriminatory commercial policy to increase its access to export markets. It is not possible, however, to reduce the number of players in all situations. For example, compare the example of limited commercial openness with the example of a limited strategic embargo. To reduce the number of actors in a trade war, market access can simply be offered to only one country and withheld from others. By contrast, defection by only one supplier can permit the target of a strategic embargo to obtain a critical technology. These problems may limit the range of situations susceptible to modification through strategies that reduce the number of players in games.

NOTES

1. For examples, see Robert Jervis, "Cooperation under the Security Dilemma," *World Politics* 30 (January 1978), pp. 167–214; Oliver E. Williamson, "Credible Commitments: Using Hostages to Support Exchange," *American Economic Review* (September 1983), pp. 519–40; John Gerard Ruggie, "International Regimes, Transactions, and Change: Embedded Liberalism in the Postwar Economic Order," in Stephen D. Krasner, ed., *International Regimes* (Ithaca, N.Y.: Cornell University Press, 1983).
2. For orthodox game-theoretic analyses of the importance of iteration, see R. Duncan Luce and Howard Raiffa, *Games and Decisions* (New York: Wiley, 1957), Appendix 8, and David M. Kreps, Paul Milgram, John Roberts, and Robert Wilson, "Rational Cooperation in Finitely-Repeated Prisoner's Dilemma," *Journal of Economic Theory* 27 (August 1982), pp. 245–52. For the results of laboratory experiments, see Robert Radlow, "An Experimental Study of Cooperation in the Prisoner's Dilemma Game," *Journal of Conflict Resolution* 9 (June 1965), pp. 221–27. On the importance of indefinite iteration to the emergence of cooperation in business transactions, see Robert Telsor, "A Theory of Self-Enforcing Agreements," *Journal of Business* 53 (January 1980), pp. 27–44.
3. See Robert O. Keohane, *After Hegemony: Cooperation and Discord in the World Political Economy* (Princeton, N.J.: Princeton University Press, 1984), and Krasner (fn. 5).
4. See John A. C. Conybeare, "International Organization and the Theory of Property Rights," *International Organization* 34 (Summer 1980), pp. 307–34, and Kenneth A. Oye, "Belief Systems, Bargaining, and Breakdown: International Political Economy 1929–1936," Ph.D. diss. (Harvard University, 1983), chap. 3.
5. See Jervis (fn. 1); Ruggie (fn. 1); Timothy J. McKeown, "Firms and Tariff Regime Change: Explaining the Demand for Protection," *World Politics* 36 (January 1984), pp. 215–33. On the effects of *ambiguity* of preferences on the prospects of cooperation, see the concluding sections of Jervis (fn. 1).
6. Haas, Williams, and Babai, *Scientists and World Order: The Uses of Technical Knowledge in International Organizations* (Berkeley: University of California Press, 1977).
7. Williamson (fn. 1).
8. See John Newhouse, *Cold Dawn: The Story of SALT I* (New York: Holt, Rinehart & Winston, 1973).
9. See Haas, "Words Can Hurt You; Or Who Said What to Whom About Regimes," in Krasner (fn. 5).
10. This section is derived largely from Axelrod (fn. 2) and Telsor (fn. 2).
11. See Anatol Rapoport and Albert Chammah, *Prisoner's Dilemma* (Ann Arbor: University of Michigan Press, 1965), and subsequent essays in *Journal of Conflict Resolution*.
12. See Alexander L. George, *Managing U.S.-Soviet Rivalry: Problems of Crisis Prevention* (Boulder, Colo.: Westview, 1983).
13. Schelling, *Strategy of Conflict* (Cambridge, Mass.: Harvard University Press, 1960), pp. 43–46, and Axelrod (fn. 2), pp. 126–132.

14. See Mancur Olson, Jr., *The Logic of Collective Action: Public Goods and the Theory of Groups* (Cambridge, Mass.: Harvard University Press, 1965), and Mancur Olson and Richard Zeckhauser, "An Economic Theory of Alliances," *Review of Economics and Statistics* 48 (August 1966), pp. 266–79. For a recent elegant summary and extension of the large literature on dilemmas of collective action, see Russell Hardin, *Collective Action* (Baltimore: Johns Hopkins University Press, 1982).

15. See Kenneth N. Waltz, "The Stability of a Bipolar World," *Daedalus* 93 (Summer 1964), and Richard N. Rosecrance, "Bipolarity, Multipolarity, and the Future," *Journal of Conflict Resolution* (September 1966), pp. 314–27.

16. On hegemony, see Robert Gilpin, *U.S. Power and the Multinational Corporation* (New York: Basic Books, 1975), pp. 258–59. On duopoly, see Timothy McKeown, "Hegemonic Stability Theory and 19th-Century Tariff Levels in Europe," *International Organization* 37 (Winter 1983), pp. 73–91.

17. See Keohane (fn. 3), chap. 6, for extensions of these points.

Anarchy and the Limits of Cooperation

Joseph M. Grieco

Realism has dominated international relations theory at least since World War II. For realists, international anarchy fosters competition and conflict among states and inhibits their willingness to cooperate even when they share common interests. Realist theory also argues that international institutions are unable to mitigate anarchy's constraining effects on interstate cooperation. Realism, then, presents a pessimistic analysis of the prospects for international cooperation and of the capabilities of international institutions.

The major challenger to realism has been what I shall call *liberal institutionalism*. . . . The new liberal institutionalists basically argue that even if the realists are correct in believing that anarchy constrains the willingness of states to cooperate, states nevertheless can work together and can do so especially with the assistance of international institutions.[1]

This point is crucial for students of international relations. If neoliberal institutionalists are correct, then they have dealt realism a major blow while providing the intellectual justification for treating their own approach, and the tradition from which it emerges, as the most effective for understanding world politics.

This essay's principal argument is that, in fact, neoliberal institutionalism misconstrues the realist analysis of international anarchy and therefore it misunderstands the realist analysis of the impact of anarchy on the preferences and actions of states. Indeed, the new liberal institutionalism fails to address a major constraint on the willingness of states to cooperate, which is generated by international anarchy and which is identified by realism. As a result, the new theory's optimism about international cooperation is likely to be proven wrong.

Neoliberalism's claims about cooperation are based on its belief that states are atomistic actors. It argues that states seek to maximize their individual *absolute* gains and are indifferent to the gains achieved by others. Cheating, the new theory suggests, is the greatest impediment to cooperation among rationally egoistic states, but international institutions, the new theory also suggests, can help states overcome this barrier to joint action. Realists understand that states seek absolute gains and worry about compliance. However, realists find that states are *positional*, not atomistic, in character, and therefore realists argue that, in addition to concerns about cheating, states in cooperative arrangements also worry that their partners might gain more from cooperation than they do. For realists, a state will focus both on its absolute and relative gains from cooperation, and a state that is satisfied with a partner's compliance in a joint arrangement might nevertheless exit from it because the partner is achieving relatively greater gains. Realism, then, finds that there are at least two major barriers to international cooperation: state concerns about cheating and state concerns about relative achievements of gains. Neoliberal institutionalism pays attention exclusively to the former, and is unable to identify, analyze, or account for the latter.

Realism's identification of the relative gains problem for cooperation is based on its insight that states in anarchy fear for their survival as independent actors. According to realists, states worry that today's friend may be tomorrow's enemy in war, and fear that achievements of joint gains that advantage a friend in the present might produce a more dangerous *potential* foe in the future. As a result, states must give serious attention to the gains of partners. Neoliberals fail to consider the threat of war arising from international anarchy, and this allows them to ignore the matter of relative gains and to assume that states only desire absolute gains. Yet, in doing so, they fail to identify a major source of state inhibitions about international cooperation. . . .

Neoliberals begin with assertions of acceptance of several key realist propositions; however, they end with a rejection of realism and with claims of affirmation of the central tenets of the liberal institutionalist tradition. To develop this argument, neoliberals first observe that states in anarchy often faced mixed interests and, in particular, situations that can be depicted by Prisoners' Dilemma. In the game, each state prefers mutual cooperation to mutual noncooperation (CC > DD), but also successful cheating to mutual cooperation (DC > CC) and mutual defection to victimization by another's cheating (DD > CD); overall, then, DC > CC > DD > CD. In these circumstances, and in the absence of a centralized authority or some other countervailing force to bind states to their promises, each defects regardless of what it expects the other to do.

However, neoliberals stress that countervailing forces often do exist— forces that cause states to keep their promises and thus to resolve the Prisoners' Dilemma. They argue that states may pursue a strategy of tit-for-tat and cooperate on a conditional basis—that is, each adheres to its promises so long as partners do so. They also suggest that conditional cooperation is more likely to occur in Prisoners' Dilemma if the game is highly iterated, since states that interact repeatedly in either a mutually beneficial or harmful manner are likely to find that mutual cooperation is their best long-term strategy. Finally, conditional cooperation is more attractive to states if the costs of verifying one an-

other's compliance, and of sanctioning cheaters, are low compared to the benefits of joint action. Thus, conditional cooperation among states may evolve in
the face of international anarchy and mixed interests through strategies of reciprocity, extended time horizons, and reduced verification and sanctioning costs.

Neoliberals find that one way states manage verification and sanctioning
problems is to restrict the number of partners in a cooperative arrangement.[2]
However, neoliberals place much greater emphasis on a second factor—
international institutions. In particular, neoliberals argue that institutions reduce
verification costs, create iterativeness, and make it easier to punish cheaters. As
Keohane suggests, "in general, regimes make it more sensible to cooperate by
lowering the likelihood of being double-crossed."[3] Similarly, Axelrod and
Keohane assert that "international regimes do not substitute for reciprocity;
rather, they reinforce and institutionalize it. Regimes incorporating the norm of
reciprocity delegitimize defection and thereby make it more costly."[4] In addition,
finding that "coordination conventions" are often an element of conditional cooperation in Prisoners' Dilemma, Charles Lipson suggests that "in international
relations, such conventions, which are typically grounded in ongoing reciprocal
exchange, range from international law to regime rules."[5] Finally, Arthur Stein
argues that, just as societies "create" states to resolve collective action problems
among individuals, so too "regimes in the international arena are also created to
deal with the collective suboptimality that can emerge from individual [state]
behavior."[6] Hegemonic power may be necessary to establish cooperation among
states, neoliberals argue, but it may endure after hegemony with the aid of
institutions. As Keohane concludes, "When we think about cooperation after
hegemony, we need to think about institutions."[7]

The new liberals assert that they can accept key realist views about states
and anarchy and still sustain classic liberal arguments about institutions and
international cooperation. Yet, in fact, realist and neoliberal perspectives on
states and anarchy differ profoundly, and the former provides a more complete
understanding of the problem of cooperation than the latter.

Neoliberals assume that states have only one goal in mixed-interest interactions: to achieve the greatest possible individual gain. For example, Axelrod
suggests that the key issue in selecting a "best strategy" in Prisoners' Dilemma—
offered by neoliberals as a powerful model of the problem of state cooperation in
the face of anarchy and mixed interests—is to determine "what strategy will yield
a player the highest possible score."[8] Similarly, Lipson observes that cheating is
attractive in a single play of Prisoners' Dilemma because each player believes
that defecting "can maximize his own reward," and, in turning to iterated plays,
Lipson retains the assumption that players seek to maximize individual payoffs
over the long run.[9] Indeed, reliance upon conventional Prisoners' Dilemma to
depict international relationships and upon iteration to solve the dilemma unambiguously requires neoliberalism to adhere to an individualistic payoff maximization assumption, for a player responds to an iterated conventional Prisoners'
Dilemma with conditional cooperation *solely out of a desire to maximize its
individual long-term total payoffs.* . . .

Given its understanding of anarchy, realism argues that individual well-being is not the key interest of states; instead, it finds that *survival* is their core interest. Raymond Aron, for example, suggested that "politics, insofar as it concerns relations among states, seems to signify—in both ideal and objective terms—simply the survival of states confronting the potential threat created by the existence of other states."[10] Similarly, Robert Gilpin observes that individuals and groups may seek truth, beauty, and justice, but he emphasizes that "all these more noble goals will be lost unless one makes provision for one's security in the power struggle among groups."[11]

Driven by an interest in survival, states are acutely sensitive to any erosion of their relative capabilities, which are the ultimate basis for their security and independence in an anarchical, self-help international context. Thus, realists find that the major goal of states in any relationship is not to attain the highest possible individual gain or payoff. Instead, *the fundamental goal of states in any relationship is to prevent others from achieving advances in their relative capabilities.* For example, E. H. Carr suggested that "the most serious wars are fought in order to make one's own country militarily stronger or, *more often*, to prevent another from becoming militarily stronger."[12] Along the same lines, Gilpin finds that the international system "stimulates, and may compel, a state to increase its power; at the least, it necessitates that the prudent state prevent relative increases in the power of competitor states."[13] Indeed, states may even forego increases in their absolute capabilities if doing so prevents others from achieving even greater gains. This is because, as Waltz suggests, "the first concern of states is not to maximize power but to maintain their position in the system."[14]

States seek to prevent increases in others' relative capabilities. As a result, states always assess their performance in any relationship in terms of the performance of others.[15] Thus, I suggest that states are positional, not atomistic, in character. Most significantly, *state positionality may constrain the willingness of states to cooperate.* States fear that their partners will achieve relatively greater gains; that, as a result, the partners will surge ahead of them in relative capabilities; and, finally, that their increasingly powerful partners in the present could become all the more formidable foes at some point in the future.

State positionality, then, engenders a "relative gains problem" for cooperation. That is, a state will decline to join, will leave, or will sharply limit its commitment to a cooperative arrangement if it believes that partners are achieving, or are likely to achieve, relatively greater gains. It will eschew cooperation even though participation in the arrangement was providing it, or would have provided it, with large absolute gains. Moreover, a state concerned about relative gains may decline to cooperate even if it is confident that partners will keep their commitments to a joint arrangement. Indeed, if a state believed that a proposed arrangement would provide all parties absolute gains, but would also generate gains favoring partners, then greater certainty that partners would adhere to the terms of the arrangement would only accentuate its relative-gains concerns. Thus, a state worried about relative gains might respond to greater certainty that partners would keep their promises with a lower, rather than a higher, willingness to cooperate.

NOTES

1. See Robert Axelrod, *The Evolution of Cooperation* (New York: Basic Books, 1984); Axelrod and Robert O. Keohane, "Achieving Cooperation under Anarchy: Strategies and Institutions," *World Politics* 38 (October 1985), pp. 226–54; Keohane, *After Hegemony: Cooperation and Discord in the World Political Economy* (Princeton, N.J.: Princeton University Press, 1984); Charles Lipson, "International Cooperation in Economic and Security Affairs," *World Politics* 37 (October 1984), pp. 1–23; and Arthur Stein, "Coordination and Collaboration: Regimes in an Anarchic World," in Stephen D. Krasner, ed., *International Regimes* (Ithaca, N.Y.: Cornell University Press, 1983), pp. 115–40.
2. See Keohane, *After Hegemony*, p. 77; Axelrod and Keohane, "Achieving Cooperation," pp. 234–38. For a demonstration, see Lipson, "Bankers' Dilemmas."
3. Keohane, *After Hegemony*, p. 97.
4. Axelrod and Keohane, "Achieving Cooperation," p. 250.
5. Lipson, "International Cooperation," p. 6.
6. Stein, "Coordination and Collaboration," p. 123.
7. Keohane, *After Hegemony*, p. 246.
8. Axelrod, *Evolution of Cooperation*, pp. 6, 14. Stein acknowledges that he employs an absolute-gains assumption and that the latter "is very much a liberal, not mercantilist, view of self-interest; it suggests that actors focus on their own returns and compare different outcomes with an eye to maximizing their own gains." See Stein, "Coordination and Collaboration," p. 134. It is difficult to see how Stein can employ a "liberal" assumption of state interest and assert that his theory of regimes, as noted earlier in note 34, is based on the "classic [realist?] characterization" of international politics.
9. Lipson, "International Cooperation," pp. 2, 5.
10. Raymond Aron, *International Relations: A Theory of Peace and War*, trans. Richard Howard and Annette Baker Fox (Garden City, N.J.: Doubleday, 1973), p. 7; also see pp. 64–65.
11. Robert Gilpin, "The Richness of the Tradition of Political Realism," in Robert O. Keohane, ed., *Neorealism and Its Critics* (New York: Columbia University Press, 1986), p. 305. Similarly, Waltz indicates that "in anarchy, security is the highest end. Only if survival is assured can states safely seek such other goals as tranquility, profit, and power." See Kenneth Waltz, *Theory of International Politics* (Reading, Mass: Addison-Wesley, 1979), p. 126. Also see pp. 91–92, and Waltz, "Reflections on Theory of International Politics: A Response to My Critics," in Keohane, ed., *Neorealism and Its Critics*, p. 334.
12. E. H. Carr, *Twenty Years Crisis, 1919–1939: An Introduction to the Study of International Relations* (London and New York: Harper Torchbooks, 1964), p. 111, emphasis added.
13. Robert Gilpin, *War and Change in World Politics* (Cambridge: Cambridge University Press, 1981), pp. 87–88.
14. Waltz, *Theory of International Politics*, p. 126; see also Waltz, "Reflections," p. 334.
15. On the tendency of states to compare performance levels, see Oran Young, "International Regimes: Toward a New Theory of Institutions," *World Politics* 39 (October 1986), p. 118.

Coping with Anarchy

Kant, Liberal Legacies, and Foreign Affairs

Michael W. Doyle

I

What difference do liberal principles and institutions make to the conduct of the foreign affairs of liberal states? A thicket of conflicting judgments suggests that the legacies of liberalism have not been clearly appreciated. For many citizens of liberal states, liberal principles and institutions have so fully absorbed domestic politics that their influence on foreign affairs tends to be either overlooked altogether or, when perceived, exaggerated. Liberalism becomes either unself-consciously patriotic or inherently "peace-loving." For many scholars and diplomats, the relations among independent states appear to differ so significantly from domestic politics that influences of liberal principles and domestic liberal institutions are denied or denigrated. They judge that international relations are governed by perceptions of national security and the balance of power; liberal principles and institutions, when they do intrude, confuse and disrupt the pursuit of balance-of-power politics.

Although liberalism is misinterpreted from both these points of view, a crucial aspect of the liberal legacy is captured by each. Liberalism is a distinct ideology and set of institutions that has shaped the perceptions of and capacities for foreign relations of political societies that range from social welfare or social democratic to laissez faire. It defines much of the content of the liberal patriot's nationalism. Liberalism does appear to disrupt the pursuit of balance-of-power politics. Thus its foreign relations cannot be adequately explained (or prescribed) by a sole reliance on the balance of power. But liberalism is not inherently "peace-loving"; nor is it consistently restrained or peaceful in intent. Furthermore, liberal practice may reduce the probability that states will successfully exercise the consistent restraint and peaceful intentions that a world peace may well require in the nuclear age. Yet the peaceful intent and restraint that liberalism does manifest in limited aspects of its foreign affairs announces the possibility of a world peace this side of the grave or of world conquest. It has strengthened the prospects for a world peace established by the steady expansion of a separate peace among liberal societies. . . .

II

Liberalism has been identified with an essential principle—the importance of the freedom of the individual. Above all, this is a belief in the importance of moral freedom, of the right to be treated and a duty to treat others as ethical subjects, and not as objects or means only. This principle has generated rights and institutions.

A commitment to a threefold set of rights forms the foundation of liberalism. Liberalism calls for freedom from arbitrary authority, often called "negative freedom," which includes freedom of conscience, a free press and free speech, equality under the law, and the right to hold, and therefore to exchange, property without fear of arbitrary seizure. Liberalism also calls for those rights necessary to protect and promote the capacity and opportunity for freedom, the "positive freedoms." Such social and economic rights as equality of opportunity in education and rights to health care and employment, necessary for effective self-expression and participation, are thus among liberal rights. A third liberal right, democratic participation or representation, is necessary to guarantee the other two. To ensure that morally autonomous individuals remain free in those areas of social action where public authority is needed, public legislation has to express the will of the citizens making laws for their own community.

These three sets of rights, taken together, seem to meet the challenge that Kant identified:

> To organize a group of rational beings who demand general laws for their survival, but of whom each inclines toward exempting himself, and to establish their constitution in such a way that, in spite of the fact their private attitudes are opposed, these private attitudes mutually impede each other in such a manner that [their] public behavior is the same as if they did not have such evil attitudes.[1]

But the dilemma within liberalism is how to reconcile the three sets of liberal rights. The right to private property, for example, can conflict with equality of opportunity and both rights can be violated by democratic legislation. During the 180 years since Kant wrote, the liberal tradition has evolved two high roads to individual freedom and social order; one is laissez-faire, or "conservative," liberalism and the other is social welfare, or social democratic, or "liberal," liberalism. Both reconcile these conflicting rights (though in differing ways) by successfully organizing free individuals into a political order.

The political order of laissez-faire and social welfare liberals is marked by a shared commitment to four essential institutions. First, citizens possess juridical equality and other fundamental civil rights such as freedom of religion and the press. Second, the effective sovereigns of the state are representative legislatures deriving their authority from the consent of the electorate and exercising their authority free from all restraint apart from the requirement that basic civic rights be preserved. Most pertinently for the impact of liberalism on foreign affairs, the state is subject to neither the external authority of other states nor to the internal authority of special prerogatives held, for example, by monarchs or military castes over foreign policy. Third, the economy rests on a recognition of the rights of private property, including the ownership of means of production. Property is justified by individual acquisition (for example, by labor) or by social agreement or social utility. This excludes state socialism or state capitalism, but it need not exclude market socialism or various forms of the mixed economy. Fourth, economic decisions are predominantly shaped by the forces of supply and demand, domestically and internationally, and are free from strict control by bureaucracies. . . .

III

In foreign affairs liberalism has shown, as it has in the domestic realm, serious weaknesses. But unlike liberalism's domestic realm, its foreign affairs have experienced startling but less than fully appreciated successes. Together they shape an unrecognized dilemma, for both these successes and weaknesses in large part spring from the same cause: the international implications of liberal principles and institutions.

The basic postulate of liberal international theory holds that states have the

Table 1   WARS INVOLVING LIBERAL REGIMES

Period	Liberal regimes and the pacific union (by date "liberal")[a]	Total number
18th century	Swiss Cantons[b] French Republic 1790–1795 the United States[b] 1776–	3
1800–1850	Swiss Confederation, the United States France 1830–1849 Belgium 1830– Great Britain 1832– Netherlands 1848– Piedmont 1848– Denmark 1849–	8
1850–1900	Switzerland, the United States, Belgium, Great Britain, Netherlands Piedmont 1861, Italy 1861– Denmark 1866 Sweden 1864– Greece 1864–	13

Table 1 (*Continued*)

Period	Liberal regimes and the pacific union (by date "liberal")[a]	Total number
1900–1945	Canada 1867– France 1871– Argentina 1880– Chile 1891– Switzerland, the United States, Great Britain, Sweden, Canada Greece 1911, 1928–1936 Italy 1922 Belgium 1940 Netherlands 1940 Argentina 1943 France 1940 Chile 1924, 1932 Australia 1901– Norway 1905–1940 New Zealand 1907– Colombia 1910–1949 Denmark 1914–1940 Poland 1917–1935 Latvia 1922–1934 Germany 1918–1932 Austria 1918–1934 Estonia 1919–1934 Finland 1919– Uruguay 1919– Costa Rica 1919– Czechoslovakia 1920–1939 Ireland 1920– Mexico 1928– Lebanon 1944–	29
1945[c]–	Switzerland, the United States, Great Britain, Sweden, Canada, Australia, New Zealand, Finland, Ireland, Mexico Uruguay 1973 Chile 1973 Lebanon 1975 Costa Rica 1948, 1953– Iceland 1944– France 1945– Denmark 1945– Norway 1945– Austria 1945– Brazil 1945–1954, 1955–1964 Belgium 1946– Luxemburg 1946– Netherlands 1946– Italy 1946–	49

Table 1 (*Continued*)

Period	Liberal regimes and the pacific union (by date "liberal")[a]	Total number
	Philippines 1946–1972	
	India 1947–1975, 1977–	
	Sri Lanka 1948–1961, 1963–1977, 1978–	
	Ecuador 1948–1963, 1979–	
	Israel 1949–	
	West Germany 1949–	
	Peru 1950–1962, 1963–1968, 1980–	
	El Salvador 1950–1961	
	Turkey 1950–1960, 1966–1971	
	Japan 1951–	
	Bolivia 1956–1969	
	Colombia 1958–	
	Venezuela 1959–	
	Nigeria 1961–1964, 1979–	
	Jamaica 1962–	
	Trinidad 1962–	
	Senegal 1963–	
	Malaysia 1963–	
	South Korea 1963–1972	
	Botswana 1966–	
	Singapore 1965–	
	Greece 1975–	
	Portugal 1976–	
	Spain 1978–	
	Dominican Republic 1978–	

[a]I have drawn up this approximate list of "Liberal Regimes" according to the four institutions described as essential: market and private property economies; polities that are externally sovereign; citizens who possess juridical rights; and "republican" (whether republican or monarchical), representative, government. This latter includes the requirement that the legislative branch have an effective role in public policy and be formally and competitively, either potentially or actually, elected. Furthermore, I have taken into account whether male suffrage is wide (that is, 30 percent) or open to "achievement" by inhabitants (for example, to poll-tax payers or householders) of the national or metropolitan territory. Female suffrage is granted within a generation of its being demanded; and representative government is internally sovereign (for example, including and especially over military and foreign affairs) as well as stable (in existence for at least three years).

Sources: Arthur Banks and W. Overstreet, eds., *The Political Handbook of the World, 1980* (New York: McGraw-Hill, 1980); Foreign and Commonwealth Office, *A Year Book of the Commonwealth 1980* (London: HMSO, 1980); *Europa Yearbook, 1981* (London: Europa, 1981); W. L. Langer, *An Encyclopedia of World History* (Boston: Houghton-Mifflin, 1968); Department of State, *Country Reports on Human Rights Practices* (Washington, D.C.: U.S. Government Printing Office, 1981); and *Freedom at Issue,* no. 54 (January–February 1980).

[b]There are domestic variations within these liberal regimes. For example, Switzerland was liberal only in certain cantons; the United States was liberal only north of the Mason-Dixon line until 1865, when it became liberal throughout. These lists also exclude ancient "republics," since none appear to fit Kant's criteria. See Stephen Holmes, "Aristippus in and out of Athens," *American Political Science Review* 73, no. 1 (March 1979).

[c]Selected list, excludes liberal regimes with populations less than one million.

right to be free from foreign intervention. Since morally autonomous citizens hold rights to liberty, the states that democratically represent them have the right to exercise political independence. Mutual respect for these rights then becomes the touchstone of international liberal theory. When states respect each other's rights, individuals are free to establish private international ties without state interference. Profitable exchanges between merchants and educational exchanges among scholars then create a web of mutual advantages and commitments that bolsters sentiments of public respect.

These conventions of mutual respect have formed a cooperative foundation for relations among liberal democracies of a remarkably effective kind. *Even though liberal states have become involved in numerous wars with nonliberal states, constitutionally secure liberal states have yet to engage in war with one another.*[2] No one should argue that such wars are impossible; but preliminary evidence does appear to indicate that there exists a significant predisposition against warfare between liberal states. Indeed, threats of war also have been regarded as illegitimate. A liberal zone of peace, a pacific union, has been maintained and has expanded despite numerous particular conflicts of economic and strategic interest. . . .

Statistically, war between any two states (in any single year or other short period of time) is a low probability event. War between any two adjacent states, considered over a long period of time, may be somewhat more probable. The apparent absence of war among the more clearly liberal states, whether adjacent or not, for almost two hundred years thus has some significance. Politically more significant, perhaps, is that, when states are forced to decide, by the pressure of an impinging world war, on which side of a world contest they will fight, liberal states wind up all on the same side, despite the real complexity of the historical, economic, and political factors that affect their foreign policies. And historically, we should recall that medieval and early modern Europe were the warring cockpits of states, wherein France and England and the Low Countries engaged in near constant strife. Then in the late eighteenth century there began to emerge liberal regimes. At first hesitant and confused, and later clear and confident as liberal regimes gained deeper domestic foundations and longer international experience, a pacific union of these liberal states became established.

The realist model of international relations, which provides a plausible explanation of the general insecurity of states, offers little guidance in explaining the pacification of the liberal world. Realism, in its classical formulation, holds that the state is and should be formally sovereign, effectively unbounded by individual rights nationally and thus capable of determining its own scope of authority. (This determination can be made democratically, oligarchically, or autocratically.) Internationally, the sovereign state exists in an anarchical society in which it is radically independent, neither bounded nor protected by international "law" or treaties or duties, and hence, insecure. Hobbes, one of the seventeenth-century founders of the realist approach drew the international implications of realism when he argued that the existence of international anarchy, the very independence of states, best accounts for the competition, the

Table 2 INTERNATIONAL WARS LISTED CHRONOLOGICALLY*

British-Maharattan (1817–1818)
Greek (1821–1828)
Franco-Spanish (1823)
First Anglo-Burmese (1823–1826)
Javanese (1825–1830)
Russo-Persian (1826–1828)
Russo-Turkish (1828–1829)
First Polish (1831)
First Syrian (1831–1832)
Texan (1835–1836)
First British-Afghan (1838–1842)
Second Syrian (1839–1840)
Franco-Algerian (1839–1847)
Peruvian-Bolivian (1841)
First British-Sikh (1845–1846)
Mexican-American (1846–1848)
Austro-Sardinian (1848–1849)
First Schleswig-Holstein (1848–1849)
Hungarian (1848–1849)
Second British-Sikh (1848–1849)
Roman Republic (1849)
La Plata (1851–1852)
First Turco-Montenegran (1852–1853)
Crimean (1853–1856)
Anglo-Persian (1856–1857)
Sepoy (1857–1859)
Second Turco-Montenegran (1858–1859)
Italian Unification (1859)
Spanish-Moroccan (1859–1860)
Italo-Roman (1860)
Italo-Sicilian (1860–1861)
Franco-Mexican (1862–1867)
Ecuadorian-Colombian (1863)
Second Polish (1863–1864)
Spanish-Santo Dominican (1863–1865)
Second Schleswig-Holstein (1864)
Lopez (1864–1870)
Spanish-Chilean (1865–1866)
Seven Weeks (1866)
Ten Years (1868–1878)
Franco-Prussian (1870–1871)
Dutch-Achinese (1873–1878)
Balkan (1875–1877)
Russo-Turkish (1877–1878)
Bosnian (1878)
Second British-Afghan (1878–1880)
Pacific (1879–1880)
British-Zulu (1879)

Franco-Indochinese (1882–1884)
Mahdist (1882–1885)
Sino-French (1884–1885)
Central American (1885)
Serbo-Bulgarian (1885)
Sino-Japanese (1894–1895)
Franco-Madagascan (1894–1895)
Cuban (1895–1898)
Italo-Ethiopian (1895–1896)
First Philippine (1896–1898)
Greco-Turkish (1897)
Spanish-American (1898)
Second Philippine (1899–1902)
Boer (1899–1902)
Boxer Rebellion (1900)
Ilinden (1903)
Russo-Japanese (1904–1905)
Central American (1906)
Central American (1907)
Spanish-Moroccan (1909–1910)
Italo-Turkish (1911–1912)
First Balkan (1912–1913)
Second Balkan (1913)
World War I (1914–1918)
Russian Nationalities (1917–1921)
Russo-Polish (1919–1920)
Hungarian-Allies (1919)
Greco-Turkish (1919–1922)
Riffian (1921–1926)
Druze (1925–1927)
Sino-Soviet (1929)
Manchurian (1931–1933)
Chaco (1932–1935)
Italo-Ethiopian (1935–1936)
Sino-Japanese (1937–1941)
Changkufeng (1938)
Nomohan (1939)
World War II (1939–1945)
Russo-Finnish (1939–1940)
Franco-Thai (1940–1941)
Indonesian (1945–1946)
Indochinese (1945–1954)
Madagascan (1947–1948)
First Kashmir (1947–1949)
Palestine (1948–1949)
Hyderabad (1948)
Korean (1950–1953)
Algerian (1954–1962)

Table 2   *(Continued)*

Russo-Hungarian (1956)	Yom Kippur (1973)
Sinai (1956)	Turco-Cypriot (1974)
Tibetan (1956–1959)	Ethiopian-Eritrean (1974–)
Sino-Indian (1962)	Vietnamese-Cambodian (1975–)
Vietnamese (1965–1975)	Timor (1975–)
Second Kashmir (1965)	Saharan (1975–)
Six Day (1967)	Ogaden (1976–)
Israeli-Egyptian (1969–1970)	Ugandan-Tanzanian (1978–1979)
Football (1969)	Sino-Vietnamese (1979)
Bangladesh (1971)	Russo-Afghan (1979–1989)
Philippine-MNLF (1972–)	Irani-Iraqi (1980–1988)

*The table is reprinted by permission from Melvin Small and J. David Singer from *Resort to Arms* (Beverly Hills, Calif.: Sage Publications, 1982), pp. 79–80. This is a partial list of international wars fought between 1816 and 1980. In Appendices A and B of *Resort to Arms,* Small and Singer identify a total of 575 wars in this period, but approximately 159 of them appear to be largely domestic or civil wars.

This definition of war excludes covert interventions, some of which have been directed by liberal regimes against other liberal regimes. One example is the United States' effort to destabilize the Chilean election and Allende's government. Nonetheless, it is significant (as will be apparent below) that such interventions are not pursued publicly as acknowledged policy. The covert destabilization campaign against Chile is recounted in U.S. Congress, Senate, Select Committee to Study Governmental Operations with Respect to Intelligence Activities, *Covert Action in Chile, 1963–73,* 94th Congress, 1st Session (Washington, D.C.: U.S. Government Printing Office, 1975).

fear, and the temptation toward preventive war that characterize international relations. Politics among nations is not a continuous combat, but it is in this view a "state of war . . . a tract of time, wherein the will to contend by battle is sufficiently known"[3]. . . .

Finding that all states, including liberal states, do engage in war, the realist concludes that the effects of differing domestic regimes (whether liberal or not) are overridden by the international anarchy under which all states live[4]. . . . But the ends that shape the international state of war are decreed for the realist by the anarchy of the international order and the fundamental quest for power that directs the policy of all states, irrespective of differences in their domestic regimes. As Rousseau argued, international peace therefore depends on the abolition of international relations either by the achievement of a world state or by a radical isolationism (Corsica). Realists judge neither to be possible.

Recent additions to game theory specify some of the circumstances under which prudence could lead to peace. Experience; geography; expectations of cooperation and belief patterns; and the differing payoffs to cooperation (peace) or conflict associated with various types of military technology all appear to influence the calculus.[5] But when it comes to acquiring the techniques of peaceable interaction, nations appear to be slow, or at least erratic, learners. The balance of power (more below) is regarded as a primary lesson in the realist primer, but centuries of experience did not prevent either France (Louis XIV, Napoleon I) or Germany (Wilhelm II, Hitler) from attempting to conquer Europe, twice each. Yet some, very new, black African states appear to have achieved a twenty-year-old system of impressively effective standards of mutual toleration. These standards are not completely effective (as in Tanzania's invasion of Uganda); but they have confounded expectations of a scramble to redivide Africa.[6] Geography—"insular security" and "continental insecurity"—may affect foreign policy attitudes; but it does not appear to determine behavior, as the bellicose records of England and Japan suggest. Beliefs, expectations, and attitudes of leaders and masses should influence strategic behavior. . . . Nevertheless, it would be difficult to determine if liberal leaders have had more peaceable attitudes than leaders who lead nonliberal states. But even if one did make that discovery, he also would have to account for why these peaceable attitudes only appear to be effective in relations with other liberals (since wars with nonliberals have not been uniformly defensive). . . .

Second, at the level of social determinants, some might argue that relations among any group of states with similar social structures or with compatible values would be peaceful. But again, the evidence for feudal societies, communist societies, fascist societies, or socialist societies does not support this conclusion. Feudal warfare was frequent and very much a sport of the monarchs and nobility. There have not been enough truly totalitarian, fascist powers (nor have they lasted long enough) to test fairly their pacific compatibility; but fascist powers in the wider sense of nationalist, capitalist, military dictatorships fought each other in the 1930s. Communist powers have engaged in wars more recently in East Asia. And we have not had enough socialist societies to consider the relevance of socialist pacification. The more abstract category of pluralism does not suffice. Certainly Germany was pluralist when it engaged in war with liberal states in 1914; Japan as well in 1941. But they were not liberal.

And third, at the level of interstate relations, neither specific regional attributes nor historic alliances or friendships can account for the wide reach of the liberal peace. The peace extends as far as, and no further than, the relations among liberal states, not including nonliberal states in an otherwise liberal region (such as the north Atlantic in the 1930s) nor excluding liberal states in a nonliberal region (such as Central America or Africa).

At this level, Raymond Aron has identified three types of interstate peace: empire, hegemony, and equilibrium.[7] An empire generally succeeds in creating an internal peace, but this is not an explanation of peace among independent liberal states. Hegemony can create peace by over-awing potential rivals. Although far from perfect and certainly precarious, United States hegemony, as Aron notes, might account for the interstate peace in South America in the postwar period during the height of the Cold War conflict. However, the liberal peace cannot be attributed merely to effective international policing by a predominant hegemon—Britain in the nineteenth century, the United States in the postwar period. Even though a hegemon might well have an interest in enforcing a peace for the sake of commerce or investments or as a means of enhancing its prestige or security; hegemons such as seventeenth-century France were not peace-enforcing police, and the liberal peace persisted in the interwar period when international society lacked a predominant hegemonic power. Moreover, this explanation overestimates hegemonic control in both periods. Neither England nor the United States was able to prevent direct challenges to its interests (colonial competition in the nineteenth century, Middle East diplomacy and conflicts over trading with the enemy in the postwar period). Where then was the capacity to prevent all armed conflicts between liberal regimes, many of which were remote and others strategically or economically insignificant? Liberal hegemony and leadership are important, but they are not sufficient to explain a liberal peace. . . .

Finally, some realists might suggest that the liberal peace simply reflects the absence of deep conflicts of interest among liberal states. Wars occur outside the liberal zone because conflicts of interest are deeper there. But this argument does nothing more than raise the question of why liberal states have fewer or less fundamental conflicts of interest with other liberal states than liberal states have with nonliberal, or nonliberal states have with other nonliberals. We must therefore examine the workings of liberalism among its own kind—a special pacification of the "state of war" resting on liberalism and nothing either more specific or more general.

IV

Most liberal theorists have offered inadequate guidance in understanding the exceptional nature of liberal pacification. Some have argued that democratic states would be inherently peaceful simply and solely because in these states citizens rule the polity and bear the costs of wars. Unlike monarchs, citizens are not able to indulge their aggressive passions and have the consequences suffered by someone else. Other liberals have argued that laissez-faire capitalism contains an inherent tendency toward rationalism, and that, since war is irrational, liberal capitalisms will be pacifistic. Others still, such as Montesquieu, claim that "commerce is the cure for the most destructive prejudices," and "Peace is the natural effect of trade."[8] While these developments can help account for the liberal peace, they do not explain the fact that liberal states are peaceful only in relations with other liberal states. France and England fought expansionist, colonial wars throughout the nineteenth century (in the 1830s and 1840s against Algeria and China); the United States fought a similar war with Mexico in 1848 and intervened again in 1914 under President Wilson. Liberal states are as aggressive and war prone as any other form of government or society in their relations with nonliberal states.

Immanuel Kant offers the best guidance. "Perpetual Peace," written in 1795, predicts the ever-widening pacification of the liberal pacific union, explains that pacification, and at the same time suggests why liberal states are not pacific in their relations with nonliberal states. . . .

Kant shows how republics, once established, lead to peaceful relations. he argues that once the aggressive interests of absolutist monarchies are tamed and once the habit of respect for individual rights is engrained by republican government, wars would appear as the disaster to the people's welfare that he and the other liberals thought them to be. The fundamental reason is this:

> If the consent of the citizens is required in order to decide that war should be declared (and in this constitution it cannot but be the case), nothing is more natural than that they would be very cautious in commencing such a poor game, decreeing for themselves all the calamities of war. Among the latter would be: having to fight, having to pay the costs of war from their own resources, having painfully to repair the devastation war leaves behind, and, to fill up the measure of evils, load themselves with a heavy national debt that would embitter peace itself and that can never be liquidated on account of constant wars in the future. But, on the other hand, in a constitution which is not republican, and under which the subjects are not citizens, a declaration of war is the easiest thing in the world to decide upon, because war does not require of the ruler, who is the proprietor and not a member of the state, the least sacrifice of the pleasure of his table, the chase, his country houses, his court functions, and the like. He may, therefore, resolve on war as on a pleasure party for the most trivial reasons, and with perfect indifference leave the justification which decency requires to the diplomatic corps who are ever ready to provide it.[9]

One could add to Kant's list another source of pacification specific to liberal constitutions. The regular rotation of office in liberal democratic polities is a nontrivial device that helps ensure that personal animosities among heads of government provide no lasting, escalating source of tension.

These domestic republican restraints do not end war. If they did, liberal states would not be warlike, which is far from the case. They do introduce Kant's "caution" in place of monarchical caprice. Liberal wars are only fought for popular, liberal purposes. To see how this removes the occasion of wars among liberal states and not wars between liberal and nonliberal states, we need to shift our attention from constitutional law to international law, Kant's second source.

Complementing the constitutional guarantee of caution, *international law* adds a second source—a guarantee of respect. The separation of nations that asocial sociability encourages is reinforced by the development of separate languages and religions. These further guarantee a world of separate states—an essential condition needed to avoid a "global, soul-less despotism." Yet, at the same time, they also morally integrate liberal states "as culture progresses and men gradually come closer together toward a greater agreement on principles for peace and understanding."[10] As republics emerge (the first source) and as culture progresses, an understanding of the legitimate rights of all citizens and of all republics comes into play; and this, now that caution characterizes policy, sets up the moral foundations for the liberal peace. Correspondingly, international law highlights the importance of Kantian publicity. Domestically, publicity helps ensure that the officials of republics act according to the principles they profess to hold just and according to the interests of the electors they claim to represent. Internationally, free speech and the effective communication of accurate conceptions of the political life of foreign peoples is essential to establish and preserve the understanding on which the guarantee of respect depends. In short, domestically just republics, which rest on consent, presume foreign republics to be also consensual, just, and therefore deserving of accommodation. The experience of cooperation helps engender further cooperative behavior when the consequences of state policy are unclear but (potentially) mutually beneficial.[11]

Lastly, *cosmopolitan law* adds material incentives to moral commitments. The cosmopolitan right to hospitality permits the "spirit of commerce" sooner or later to take hold of very nation, thus impelling states to promote peace and to try to avert war.

Liberal economic theory holds that these cosmopolitan ties derive from a cooperative international division of labor and free trade according to comparative advantage. Each economy is said to be better off than it would have been under autarky; each thus acquires an incentive to avoid policies that would lead the other to break these economic ties. Since keeping open markets rests upon the assumption that the next set of transactions will also be determined by prices rather than coercion, a sense of mutual security is vital to avoid security-motivated searches for economic autarky. Thus, avoiding a challenge to another liberal state's security or even enhancing each other's security by means of alliance naturally follows economic interdependence.

A further cosmopolitan source of liberal peace is that the international market removes difficult decisions of production and distribution from the direct sphere of state policy. A foreign state thus does not appear directly responsible for these outcomes; states can stand aside from, and to some degree above, these contentious market rivalries and be ready to step in to resolve crises. Furthermore, the interdependence of commerce and the connections of state officials help create crosscutting transnational ties that serve as lobbies for mutual accommodation. According to modern liberal scholars, international financiers and transnational, bureaucratic, and domestic organizations create interests in favor of accommodation and have ensured by their variety that no single conflict sours an entire relationship.[12]

No one of these constitutional, international or cosmopolitan sources is alone sufficient, but together (and only where together) they plausibly connect the characteristics of liberal polities and economies with sustained liberal peace. Liberal states have not escaped from the realists' "security dilemma," the insecurity caused by anarchy in the world political system considered as a whole. But the effects of international anarchy have been tamed in the relations among states of a similarly liberal character. Alliances of purely mutual strategic interest among liberal and nonliberal states have been broken, economic ties between liberal and nonliberal states have proven fragile, but the political bond of liberal rights and interests has proven a remarkably firm foundation for mutual nonaggression. A separate peace exists among liberal states.

NOTES

1. Immanuel Kant, "Perpetual Peace" (1795), in *The Philosophy of Kant*, ed. Carl J. Friedrich (New York: Modern Library, 1949), p. 453.

2. There appear to be some exceptions to the tendency for liberal states not to engage in a war with each other. Peru and Ecuador, for example, entered into conflict. But for each, the war came within one to three years after the establishment of a liberal regime, that is, before the pacifying effects of liberalism could become deeply ingrained. The Palestinians and the Israelis clashed frequently along the Lebanese border, which Lebanon could not hold secure from either belligerent. But at the beginning of the 1967 War, Lebanon seems to have sent a flight of its own jets into Israel. The jets were repulsed. Alone among Israel's Arab neighbors, Lebanon engaged in no further hostilities with Israel. Israel's recent attack on the territory of Lebanon was an attack on a country that had already been occupied by Syria (and the P.L.O.). Whether Israel actually will withdraw (if Syria withdraws) and restore an independent Lebanon is yet to be determined.

3. Thomas Hobbes, *Leviathan* (New York: Penguin, 1980), I, chap. 13, 62, p. 186.

4. Kenneth N. Waltz, *Man, the State, and War* (New York: Columbia University Press, 1954, 1959), pp. 120–23; and see his *Theory of International Politics* (Reading, Mass.: Addison-Wesley, 1979). The classic sources of this form of Realism are Hobbes and, more particularly, Rousseau's "Essay on St. Pierre's Peace Project" and his "State of War" in *A Lasting Peace* (London: Constable, 1917), E. H. Carr's *The Twenty Year's Crisis: 1919–1939* (London: Macmillan & Co., 1951), and the works of Hans Morgenthau.

5. Jervis, "Cooperation under the Security Dilemma," *World Politics* 30, no. 1 (January 1978), pp. 172–86.

6. Robert H. Jackson and Carl G. Rosberg, "Why West Africa's Weak States Persist," *World Politics* 35, no. 1 (October 1982).

7. Raymond Aron, *Peace and War* (New York: Praeger, 1968) pp. 151–54.

8. The incompatibility of democracy and war is forcefully asserted by Paine in *The Rights of Man*. The connection between liberal capitalism, democracy, and peace is argued by, among others, Joseph Schumpeter in *Imperialism and Social Classes* (New York: Meridian, 1955); and Montesquieu, *Spirit of the Laws* I, bk. 20, chap. 1. This literature is surveyed and analyzed by Albert Hirschman, "Rival Interpretations of Market Society: Civilizing, Destructive, or Feeble?" *Journal of Economic Literature* 20 (December 1982).

9. Immanuel Kant, "Perpetual Peace," in *The Enlightenment*, ed. Peter Gay (New York: Simon & Schuster, 1974), pp. 790–92.

10. Kant, *The Philosophy of Kant*, p. 454. These factors also have a bearing on Karl Deutsch's "compatibility of values" and "predictability of behavior" (see n. 20).

11. A highly stylized version of this effect can be found in the realist's "Prisoners' Dilemma" game. There, a failure of mutual trust and the incentives to enhance one's own position produce a noncooperative solution that makes both parties worse off. Contrarily, cooperation, a commitment to avoid exploiting the other party, produces joint gains. The significance of the game in this context is the character of its participants. The "prisoners" are presumed to be felonious, unrelated apart from their partnership in crime, and lacking in mutual trust—competitive nation-states in an anarchic world. A similar game between fraternal or sororal twins—Kant's republics—would be likely to lead to different results. See Robert Jervis, "Hypotheses on Misperception," *World Politics* 20, no. 3 (April 1968), for an exposition of the role of presumptions; and "Cooperation under the Security Dilemma," *World Politics* 30, no. 2 (January 1978), for the factors realists see as mitigating the security dilemma caused by anarchy.

Also, expectations (including theory and history) can influence behavior, making liberal states expect (and fulfill) pacific policies toward each other. These effects are explored at a theoretical level in R. Dacey, "Some Implications of 'Theory Absorption' for Economic Theory and the Economics of Information," in *Philosophical Dimensions of Economics*, ed. J Pitt (Dordrecht, Holland: D. Reidel, 1980).

12. Karl Polanyi, *The Great Transformation* (Boston: Beacon Press, 1944), chaps. 1–2 and Samuel Huntington and Z. Brzezinski, *Political Power: USA/USSR* (New York: Viking Press, 1963, 1964), chap. 9. And see Richard Neustadt, *Alliance Politics* (New York: Columbia University Press, 1970) for a detailed case study of interliberal politics.

Alliances: Balancing and Bandwagoning

Stephen M. Walt

When confronted by a significant external threat, states may either balance or bandwagon. *Balancing* is defined as allying with others against the prevailing threat; *bandwagoning* refers to alignment with the source of danger. Thus two distinct hypotheses about how states will select their alliance partners can be identified on the basis of whether the states ally against or with the principal external threat.[1]

These two hypotheses depict very different worlds. If balancing is more common than bandwagoning, then states are more secure, because aggressors will face combined opposition. But if bandwagoning is the dominant tendency, then security is scarce, because successful aggressors will attract additional allies, enhancing their power while reducing that of their opponents. . . .

BALANCING BEHAVIOR

The belief that states form alliances in order to prevent stronger powers from dominating them lies at the heart of traditional balance-of-power theory. According to this view, states join alliances to protect themselves from states or coalitions whose superior resources could pose a threat. States choose to balance for two main reasons.

First, they place their survival at risk if they fail to curb a potential hegemon before it becomes too strong. To ally with the dominant power means placing one's trust in its continued benevolence. The safer strategy is to join with those who cannot readily dominate their allies, in order to avoid being dominated by those who can. As Winston Churchill explained Britain's traditional alliance policy: "For four hundred years the foreign policy of England has been to oppose the strongest, most aggressive, most dominating power on the

Reprinted from Stephen M. Walt: *The Origins of Alliances*. Copyright © 1987 by Cornell University. Used by permission of the publisher, Cornell University Press. Portions of the text and some footnotes have been omitted.

Continent. . . . [I]t would have been easy . . . and tempting to join with the stronger and share the fruits of his conquest. However, we always took the harder course, joined with the less strong powers, . . . and thus defeated the Continental military tyrant whoever he was."[2] More recently, Henry Kissinger advocated a rapprochement with China, because he believed that in a triangular relationship it was better to align with the weaker side.

Second, joining the weaker side increases the new member's influence within the alliance, because the weaker side has greater need for assistance. Allying with the strong side, by contrast, gives the new member little influence (because it adds relatively less to the coalition) and leaves it vulnerable to the whims of its partners. Joining the weaker side should be the preferred choice.

BANDWAGONING BEHAVIOR

The belief that states will balance is unsurprising, given the many familiar examples of states joining together to resist a threatening state or coalition. Yet, despite the powerful evidence that history provides in support of the balancing hypothesis, the belief that the opposite response is more likely is widespread. According to one scholar: "In international politics, nothing succeeds like success. Momentum accrues to the gainer and accelerates his movement. The appearance of irreversibility in his gains enfeebles one side and stimulates the other all the more. The bandwagon collects those on the sidelines."[3]

The bandwagoning hypothesis is especially popular with statesmen seeking to justify overseas involvements or increased military budgets. For example, German admiral Alfred von Tirpitz's famous risk theory rested on this type of logic. By building a great battle fleet, Tirpitz argued, Germany could force England into neutrality or alliance with her by posing a threat to England's vital maritime supremacy.

Bandwagoning beliefs have also been a recurring theme throughout the Cold War. Soviet efforts to intimidate both Norway and Turkey into not joining NATO reveal the Soviet conviction that states will accommodate readily to threats, although these moves merely encouraged Norway and Turkey to align more closely with the West.[4] Soviet officials made a similar error in believing that the growth of Soviet military power in the 1960s and 1970s would lead to a permanent shift in the correlation of forces against the West. Instead, it contributed to a Sino-American rapprochement in the 1970s and the largest peacetime increase in U.S. military power in the 1980s.

American officials have been equally fond of bandwagoning notions. According to NSC-68, the classified study that helped justify a major U.S. military buildup in the 1950s: "In the absence of an affirmative decision [to increase U.S. military capabilities] . . . our friends will become more than a liability to us, they will become a positive increment to Soviet power."[5] President John F. Kennedy once claimed that "if the United States were to falter, the whole world . . . would inevitably begin to move toward the Communist bloc."[6] And though Henry Kissinger often argued that the United States should form balancing alliances to contain the Soviet Union, he apparently believed that U.S. allies were likely to bandwagon. As he put it, "If leaders around the world . . . assume that the U.S. lacked either the forces or the will . . . they will accommodate themselves to what they will regard as the dominant trend."[7] Ronald Reagan's claim, "If we cannot defend ourselves [in Central America] . . . then we cannot expect to prevail elsewhere. . . . [O]ur credibility will collapse and our alliances will crumble," reveals the same logic in a familiar role—that of justifying overseas intervention.[8]

Balancing and bandwagoning are usually framed solely in terms of capabilities. Balancing is alignment with the weaker side, bandwagoning with the stronger. This conception should be revised, however, to account for the other factors that statesmen consider when deciding with whom to ally. Although power is an important part of the equation, it is not the only one. It is more accurate to say that states tend to ally with or against the foreign power that poses the greatest threat. For example, states may balance by allying with other strong states if a weaker power is more dangerous for other reasons. Thus the coalitions that defeated Germany in World War I and World War II were vastly superior in total resources, but they came together when it became clear that the aggressive aims of the Wilhelmines and Nazis posed the greater danger. Because balancing and bandwagoning are more accurately viewed as a response to threats, it is important to consider other factors that will affect the level of threat that states may pose: aggregate power, geographic proximity, offensive power, and aggressive intentions. . . .

By defining the basic hypotheses in terms of threats rather than power alone, we gain a more complete picture of the factors that statesmen will consider when making alliance choices. One cannot determine a priori, however, which sources of threat will be most important in any given case; one can say only that all of them are likely to play a role. And the greater the threat, the greater the probability that the vulnerable state will seek an alliance.

THE IMPLICATIONS OF BALANCING AND BANDWAGONING

The two general hypotheses of balancing and bandwagoning paint starkly contrasting pictures of international politics. Resolving the question of which hypothesis is more accurate is especially important, because each implies very different policy prescriptions. What sort of world does each depict, and what policies are implied?

If balancing is the dominant tendency, then threatening states will provoke others to align against them. Because those who seek to dominate others will attract widespread opposition, status quo states can take a relatively sanguine view of threats. Credibility is less important in a balancing world, because one's allies will resist threatening states out of their own self-interest, not because they expect others to do it for them. Thus the fear of allies defecting will decline. Moreover, if balancing is the norm and if statesmen understand this tendency, aggression will be discouraged because those who contemplate it will anticipate resistance.

In a balancing world, policies that convey restraint and benevolence are best. Strong states may be valued as allies because they have much to offer their partners, but they must take particular care to avoid appearing aggressive. Foreign and defense policies that minimize the threat one poses to others make the most sense in such a world.

A bandwagoning world, by contrast, is much more competitive. If states tend to ally with those who seem most dangerous, then great powers will be rewarded if they appear both strong and potentially aggressive. International rivalries will be more intense, because a single defeat may signal the decline of one side and the ascendancy of the other. This situation is especially alarming in a bandwagoning world, because additional defections and a further decline in position are to be expected. Moreover, if statesmen believe that bandwagoning is widespread, they will be more inclined to use force. This tendency is true for both aggressors and status quo powers. The former will use force because they will assume that others will be unlikely to balance against them and because they can attract more allies through belligerence or brinkmanship. The latter will follow suit because they will fear the gains their opponents will make by appearing powerful and resolute.[9]

Finally, misperceiving the relative propensity to balance or bandwagon is dangerous, because the policies that are appropriate for one situation will backfire in the other. If statesmen follow the balancing prescription in a bandwagoning world, their moderate responses and relaxed view of threats will encourage their allies to defect, leaving them isolated against an overwhelming coalition. Conversely, following the bandwagoning prescription in a world of balancers (employing power and threats frequently) will lead others to oppose you more and more vigorously.[10]

These concerns are not merely theoretical. In the 1930s, France failed to recognize that her allies in the Little Entente were prone to bandwagon, a tendency that French military and diplomatic policies reinforced. As noted earlier, Soviet attempts to intimidate Turkey and Norway after World War II reveal the opposite error; they merely provoked a greater U.S. commitment to these regions and cemented their entry into NATO. Likewise, the self-encircling bellicosity of Wilhelmine Germany and Imperial Japan reflected the assumption, prevalent in both states, that bandwagoning was the dominant tendency in international affairs.

WHEN DO STATES BALANCE?
WHEN DO THEY BANDWAGON?

These examples highlight the importance of identifying whether states are more likely to balance or bandwagon and which sources of threat have the greatest impact on the decision. . . . In general, we should expect balancing behavior to *balancing occurs more often than bandwagoning rare so easier to specify characteristics*

be much more common than bandwagoning, and we should expect band-wagoning to occur only under certain identifiable conditions.

Although many statesmen fear that potential allies will align with the strongest side, this fear receives little support from most of international history. For example, every attempt to achieve hegemony in Europe since the Thirty Years War has been thwarted by a defensive coalition formed precisely for the purpose of defeating the potential hegemon. Other examples are equally telling. Although isolated cases of bandwagoning do occur, the great powers have shown a remarkable tendency to ignore other temptations and follow the balancing prescription when necessary.

This tendency should not surprise us. Balancing should be preferred for the simple reason that no statesman can be completely sure of what another will do. Bandwagoning is dangerous because it increases the resources available to a threatening power and requires placing trust in its continued forbearance. Because perceptions are unreliable and intentions can change, it is safer to balance against potential threats than to rely on the hope that a state will remain benevolently disposed.

But if balancing is to be expected, bandwagoning remains a possibility. Several factors may affect the relative propensity for states to select this course.

Strong versus Weak States   *weak states bwnd.*

In general, the weaker the state, the more likely it is to bandwagon rather than balance. This situation occurs because weak states add little to the strength of a defensive coalition but incur the wrath of the more threatening states nonetheless. Because weak states can do little to affect the outcome (and may suffer grievously in the process), they must choose the winning side. Only when their decision can affect the outcome is it rational for them to join the weaker alliance. By contrast, strong states can turn a losing coalition into a winning one. And because their decision may mean the difference between victory and defeat, they are likely to be amply rewarded for their contribution.

Weak states are also likely to be especially sensitive to proximate power. Where great powers have both global interests and global capabilities, weak states will be concerned primarily with events in their immediate vicinity. Moreover, weak states can be expeced to balance when threatened by states with roughly equal capabilities but they will be tempted to bandwagon when threatened by a great power. Obviously, when the great power is capable of rapid and effective action (i.e., when its offensive capabilities are especially strong), this temptation will be even greater.

The Availability of Allies   *allie availability*

States will also be tempted to bandwagon when allies are simply unavailable. This statement is not simply tautological, because states may balance by mobilizing their own resources instead of relying on allied support. They are more likely to do so, however, when they are confident that allied assistance will be available. Thus a further prerequisite for balancing behavior is an effective system of diplomatic communication. The ability to communicate enables potential allies to recognize their shared interests and coordinate their responses. If weak states see no possibility of outside assistance, however, they may be forced to accommodate the most imminent threat. Thus the first Shah of Iran saw the British withdrawal from Kandahar in 1881 as a signal to bandwagon with Russia. As he told the British representative, all he had received from Great Britain was "good advice and honeyed words—nothing else."[11] Finland's policy of partial alignment with the Soviet Union suggests the same lesson. When Finland joined forces with Nazi Germany during World War II, it alienated the potential allies (the United States and Great Britain) that might otherwise have helped protect it from Soviet pressure after the war.

Of course, excessive confidence in allied support will encourage weak states to free-ride, relying on the efforts of others to provide security. Free-riding is the optimal policy for a weak state, because its efforts will contribute little in any case. Among the great powers, the belief that allies are readily available encourages buck-passing; states that are threatened strive to pass to others the burdens of standing up to the aggressor. Neither response is a form of bandwagoning, but both suggest that effective balancing behavior is more likely to occur when members of an alliance are not convinced that their partners are unconditionally loyal.

Taken together, these factors help explain the formation of spheres of influence surrounding the great powers. Although strong neighbors of strong states are likely to balance, small and weak neighbors of the great powers may be more inclined to bandwagon. Because they will be the first victims of expansion, because they lack the capabilities to stand alone, and because a defensive alliance may operate too slowly to do them much good, accommodating a threatening great power may be tempting.

Peace and War

Finally, the context in which alliance choices are made will affect decisions to balance or bandwagon. States are more likely to balance in peacetime or in the early stages of a war, as they seek to deter or defeat the powers posing the greatest threat. But once the outcome appears certain, some will be tempted to defect from the losing side at an opportune moment. Thus both Rumania and Bulgaria allied with Nazi Germany initially and then abandoned Germany for the Allies, as the tides of war ebbed and flowed across Europe in World War II.

The restoration of peace, however, restores the incentive to balance. As many observers have noted, victorious coalitions are likely to disintegrate with the conclusion of peace. Prominent examples include Austria and Prussia after their war with Denmark in 1864, Britain and France after World War I, the Soviet Union and the United States after World War II, and China and Vietnam after the U.S. withdrawal from Vietnam. This recurring pattern provides further support for the proposition that balancing is the dominant tendency in international politics and that bandwagoning is the opportunistic exception.

SUMMARY OF HYPOTHESES ON BALANCING AND BANDWAGONING

Hypotheses on Balancing

1. *General form:* States facing an external threat will align with others to oppose the states posing the threat.
2. The greater the threatening state's aggregate power, the greater the tendency for others to align against it.
3. The nearer a powerful state, the greater the tendency for those nearby to align against it. Therefore, neighboring states are less likely to be allies than are states separated by at least one other power.
4. The greater a state's offensive capabilities, the greater the tendency for others to align against it. Therefore, states with offensively oriented military capabilities are likely to provoke other states to form defensive coalitions.
5. The more aggressive a state's perceived intentions, the more likely others are to align against that state.
6. Alliances formed during wartime will disintegrate when the enemy is defeated.

Hypotheses on Bandwagoning

The hypotheses on bandwagoning are the opposite of those on balancing.

1. *General form:* States facing an external threat will ally with the most threatening power.
2. The greater a state's aggregate capabilities, the greater the tendency for others to align with it.
3. The nearer a powerful state, the greater the tendency for those nearby to align with it.
4. The greater a state's offensive capabilities, the greater the tendency for others to align with it.
5. The more aggressive a state's perceived intentions, the less likely other states are to align against it.
6. Alliances formed to oppose a threat will disintegrate when the threat becomes serious.

Hypotheses on the Conditions Favoring Balancing or Bandwagoning

1. Balancing is more common than bandwagoning.
2. The stronger the state, the greater its tendency to balance. Weak states will balance against other weak states but may bandwagon when threatened by great powers.
3. The greater the probability of allied support, the greater the tendency

to balance. When adequate allied support is certain, however, the tendency for free-riding or buck-passing increases.

4. The more unalterably aggressive a state is perceived to be, the greater the tendency for others to balance against it.

5. In wartime, the closer one side is to victory, the greater the tendency for others to bandwagon with it.

NOTES

1. My use of the terms *balancing* and *bandwagoning* follows that of Kenneth Waltz (who credits it to Stephen Van Evera) in his *Theory of International Politics* (Reading, Mass., 1979). Arnold Wolfers uses a similar terminology in his essay "The Balance of Power in Theory and Practice," in *Discord and Collaboration: Essays on International Politics* (Baltimore, Md., 1962), pp. 122–24.

2. Winston S. Churchill, *The Second World War*, vol. 1: *The Gathering Storm* (Boston, 1948), pp. 207–8.

3. W. Scott Thompson, "The Communist International System," *Orbis* 20, no. 4 (1977).

4. For the effects of the Soviet pressure on Turkey, see George Lenczowski, *The Middle East in World Affairs*, 4th ed. (Ithaca, 1980), pp. 134–38; and Bruce R. Kuniholm, *The Origins of the Cold War in the Near East* (Princeton, N.J., 1980), pp. 355–78. For the Norwegian response to Soviet pressure, see Herbert Feis, *From Trust to Terror: The Onset of the Cold War, 1945–50* (New York, 1970), p. 381; and Geir Lundestad, *America, Scandinavia, and the Cold War: 1945–1949* (New York, 1980), pp. 308–9.

5. NSC-68 ("United States Objectives and Programs for National Security"), reprinted in Gaddis and Etzold, *Containment*, p. 404. Similar passages can be found on pp. 389, 414, and 434.

6. Quoted in Seyom Brown, *The Faces of Power: Constancy and Change in United States Foreign Policy from Truman to Johnson* (New York, 1968), p. 217.

7. Quoted in U.S. House Committee on Foreign Affairs, *The Soviet Union and the Third World: Watershed in Great Power Policy?* 97th Cong., 1st sess., 1977, pp. 157–58.

8. *New York Times*, April 28, 1983, p. A12. In the same speech, Reagan also said: "If Central America were to fall, what would the consequences be for our position in Asia and Europe and for alliances such as NATO? . . . Which ally, which friend would trust us then?"

9. It is worth noting that Napoleon and Hitler underestimated the costs of aggression by assuming that their potential enemies would bandwagon. After Munich, for example, Hitler dismissed the possibility of opposition by claiming that British and French statesmen were "little worms." Napoleon apparently believed that England could not "reasonably make war on us unaided" and assumed that the Peace of Amiens guaranteed that England had abandoned its opposition to France. On these points, see Fest, *Hitler*, pp. 594–95; Liska, *Nations in Alliance*, p. 45; and Geoffrey Bruun, *Europe and the French Imperium: 1799–1814* (New York, 1938), p. 118. Because Hitler and Napoleon believed in a bandwagoning world, they were excessively eager to go to war.

10. This situation is analogous to Robert Jervis's distinction between the deterrence model and the spiral model. The former calls for opposition to a suspected aggressor, the latter for appeasement. Balancing and bandwagoning are the alliance equivalents of deterring and appeasing. See Robert Jervis, *Perception and Misperception in International Politics* (Princeton, N.J., 1976), chap. 3.

11. Quoted in C. J. Lowe, *The Reluctant Imperialists* (New York, 1967), p. 85.

The Future of Diplomacy

Hans J. Morgenthau

FOUR TASKS OF DIPLOMACY

. . . Diplomacy [is] an element of national power. The importance of diplomacy for the preservation of international peace is but a particular aspect of that general function. For a diplomacy that ends in war has failed in its primary objective: the promotion of the national interest by peaceful means. This has always been so and is particularly so in view of the destructive potentialities of total war.

Taken in its widest meaning, comprising the whole range of foreign policy, the task of diplomacy is fourfold: (1) Diplomacy must determine its objectives in the light of the power actually and potentially available for the pursuit of these objectives. (2) Diplomacy must assess the objectives of other nations and the power actually and potentially available for the pursuit of these objectives. (3) Diplomacy must determine to what extent these different objectives are compatible with each other. (4) Diplomacy must employ the means suited to the pursuit of its objectives. Failure in any one of these tasks may jeopardize the success of foreign policy and with it the peace of the world.

A nation that sets itself goals which it has not the power to attain may have to face the risk of war on two counts. Such a nation is likely to dissipate its strength and not to be strong enough at all points of friction to deter a hostile nation from challenging it beyond endurance. The failure of its foreign policy may force the nation to retrace its steps and to redefine its objectives in view of its actual strength. Yet it is more likely that, under the pressure of an inflamed public opinion, such a nation will go forward on the road toward an unattainable goal, strain all its resources to achieve it, and finally, confounding the national interest with that goal, seek in war the solution to a problem that cannot be solved by peaceful means.

A nation will also invite war if its diplomacy wrongly assesses the objectives of other nations and the power at their disposal. . . . A nation that mistakes a policy of imperialism for a policy of the status quo will be unprepared to meet the threat to its own existence which the other nation's policy entails. Its weakness will invite attack and may make war inevitable. A nation that mistakes a policy of the status quo for a policy of imperialism will evoke through its disproportionate reaction the very danger of war which it is trying to avoid. For as A mistakes B's policy for imperialism, so B might mistake A's defensive reaction for imperialism. Thus both nations, each intent upon forestalling imaginary aggression from the other side, will rush to arms. Similarly, the confusion of one type of imperialism with another may call for disproportionate reaction and thus evoke the risk of war.

As for the assessment of the power of other nations, either to overrate or to underrate it may be equally fatal to the cause of peace. By overrating the power of B, A may prefer to yield to B's demands until, finally, A is forced to fight for its very existence under the most unfavorable conditions. By underrating the power of B, A may become overconfident in its assumed superiority. A may advance demands and impose conditions upon B which the latter is supposedly too weak to resist. Unsuspecting B's actual power of resistance, A may be faced with the alternative of either retreating and conceding defeat or of advancing and risking war.

A nation that seeks to pursue an intelligent and peaceful foreign policy cannot cease comparing its own objectives and the objectives of other nations in the light of their compatibility. If they are compatible, no problem arises. If they are not compatible, nation A must determine whether its objectives are so vital to itself that they must be pursued despite that incompatibility with the objectives of B. If it is found that A's vital interests can be safeguarded without the attainment of these objectives, they ought to be abandoned. On the other hand, if A finds that these objectives are essential for its vital interests, A must then ask itself whether B's objectives, incompatible with its own, are essential for B's vital interests. If the answer seems to be in the negative, A must try to induce B to abandon its objectives, offering B equivalents not vital to A. In other words, through diplomatic bargaining, the give and take of compromise, a way must be sought by which the interests of A and B can be reconciled.

Finally, if the incompatible objectives of A and B should prove to be vital to either side, a way might still be sought in which the vital interests of A and B might be redefined, reconciled, and their objectives thus made compatible with each other. Here, however—even provided that both sides pursue intelligent and peaceful policies—A and B are moving dangerously close to the brink of war.

It is the final task of an intelligent diplomacy, intent upon preserving peace, to choose the appropriate means for pursuing its objectives. The means at the disposal of diplomacy are three: persuasion, compromise, and threat of force. No diplomacy relying only upon the threat of force can claim to be both intelligent and peaceful. No diplomacy that would stake everything on persuasion and compromise deserves to be called intelligent. Rarely, if ever, in the conduct of the foreign policy of a great power is there justification for using only one method to the exclusion of the others. Generally, the diplomatic representative of a great power, in order to be able to serve both the interests of his country and the interests of peace, must at the same time use persuasion, hold out the advantages of a compromise, and impress the other side with the military strength of his country.

The art of diplomacy consists in putting the right emphasis at any particular moment on each of these three means at its disposal. A diplomacy that has been successfully discharged in its other functions may well fail in advancing the national interest and preserving peace if it stresses persuasion when the give and take of compromise is primarily required by the circumstances of the case. A diplomacy that puts most of its eggs in the basket of compromise when the military might of the nation should be predominantly displayed, or stresses military might when the political situation calls for persuasion and compromise, will likewise fail. . . .

The Promise of Diplomacy: Its Nine Rules[1]

Diplomacy could revive if it would part with [the] vices, which in recent years have well-nigh destroyed its usefulness, and if it would restore the techniques which have controlled the mutual relations of nations since time immemorial. By doing so, however, diplomacy would realize only one of the preconditions for the preservation of peace. The contribution of a revived diplomacy to the cause of peace would depend upon the methods and purposes of its use. . . .

We have already formulated the four main tasks with which a foreign policy must cope successfully in order to be able to promote the national interest and preserve peace. It remains for us now to reformulate those tasks in the light of the special problems with which contemporary world politics confront diplomacy. . . .

The main reason for [the] threatening aspect of contemporary world politics [lies] in the character of modern war, which has changed profoundly under the impact of nationalistic universalism* and modern technology. The effects of modern technology cannot be undone. The only variable that remains subject to deliberate manipulation is the new moral force of nationalistic universalism. The attempt to reverse the trend toward war through the techniques of a revived diplomacy must start with this phenomenon. That means, in negative terms, that a revived diplomacy will have a chance to preserve peace only when it is not used as the instrument of a political religion aiming at universal dominion.

Four Fundamental Rules

Diplomacy Must Be Divested of the Crusading Spirit   This is the first of the rules that diplomacy can neglect only at the risk of war. In the words of William Graham Sumner:

---

*[Editors' Note: By this term Professor Morgenthau refers to the injection of ideology into international politics and to each nation's claim that its own ethical code would serve as the basis of international conduct for all nations.]

If you want war, nourish a doctrine. Doctrines are the most frightful tyrants to which men ever are subject, because doctrines get inside of a man's own reason and betray him against himself. Civilised men have done their fiercest fighting for doctrines. The reconquest of the Holy Sepulcher, "the balance of power," "no universal dominion," "trade follows the flag," "he who holds the land will hold the sea," "the throne and the altar," the revolution, the faith—these are the things for which men have given their lives. . . . Now when any doctrine arrives at that degree of authority, the name of it is a club which any demagogue may swing over you at any time and apropos of anything. In order to describe a doctrine, we must have recourse to theological language. A doctrine is an article of faith. It is something which you are bound to believe, not because you have some rational grounds for believing it is true, but because you belong to such and such a church or denomination. . . . A policy in a state we can understand; for instance, it was the policy of the United States at the end of the eighteenth century to get the free navigation of the Mississippi to its mouth, even at the expense of war with Spain. That policy had reason and justice in it; it was founded in our interests; it had positive form and definite scope. A doctrine is an abstract principle; it is necessarily absolute in its scope and abstruse in its terms; it is metaphysical assertion. It is never true, because it is absolute, and the affairs of men are all conditioned and relative. . . . Now to turn back to politics, just think what an abomination in statecraft an abstract doctrine must be. Any politician or editor can, at any moment, put a new extension on it. The people acquiesce in the doctrine and applaud it because they hear the politicians and editors repeat it, and the politicians and editors repeat it because they think it is popular. So it grows. . . . It may mean anything or nothing, at any moment, and no one knows how it will be. You accede to it now, within the vague limits of what you suppose it to be; therefore, you will have to accede to it tomorrow when the same name is made to cover something which you never have heard or thought of. If you allow a political catchword to go on and grow, you will awaken some day to find it standing over you, the arbiter of your destiny, against which you are powerless, as men are powerless against delusions. . . . What can be more contrary to sound statesmanship and common sense than to put forth an abstract assertion which has no definite relation to any interest of ours now at stake, but which has in it any number of possibilities of producing complications which we cannot foresee, but which are sure to be embarrassing when they arise![2]

The Wars of Religion have shown that the attempt to impose one's own religion as the only true one upon the rest of the world is as futile as it is costly. A century of almost unprecedented bloodshed, devastation, and barbarization was needed to convince the contestants that the two religions could live together in mutual toleration. The two political religions of our time have taken the place of the two great Christian denominations of the sixteenth and seventeenth centuries. Will the political religions of our time need the lesson of the Thirty Years' War, or will they rid themselves in time of the universalistic aspirations that inevitably issue in inconclusive war?

Upon the answer to that question depends the cause of peace. For only if it is answered in the affirmative can a moral consensus, emerging from shared convictions and common values, develop—a moral consensus within which a peace-preserving diplomacy will have a chance to grow. Only then will diplomacy have a chance to face the concrete political problems that require peaceful solution. If the objectives of foreign policy are not to be defined in terms of a

world-embracing political religion, how are they to be defined? This is a fundamental problem to be solved once the crusading aspirations of nationalistic
universalism have been discarded.

*The Objectives of Foreign Policy Must Be Defined in Terms of the National
Interest and Must Be Supported with Adequate Power*   This is the second rule
of a peace-preserving diplomacy. The national interest of a peace-loving nation
can only be defined in terms of national security, and national security must be
defined as integrity of the national territory and of its institutions. National
security, then, is the irreducible minimum that diplomacy must defend with
adequate power without compromise. But diplomacy must ever be alive to the
radical transformation that national security has undergone under the impact of
the nuclear age. Until the advent of that age, a nation could use its diplomacy to
purchase its security at the expense of another nation. Today, short of a radical
change in the atomic balance of power in favor of a particular nation, diplomacy,
in order to make one nation secure from nuclear destruction, must make them
all secure. With the national interest defined in such restrictive and transcen-
dent terms, diplomacy must observe the third of its rules.

*Diplomacy Must Look at the Political Scene from the Point of View of Other
Nations*   "Nothing is so fatal to a nation as an extreme of self-partiality, and the
total want of consideration of what others will naturally hope or fear."[3] What are
the national interests of other nations in terms of national security and are they
compatible with one's own? The definition of the national interest in terms of
national security is easier, and the interests of the two opposing nations are
more likely to be compatible in a bipolar system than in any other system of the
balance of power. The bipolar system, as we have seen, is more unsafe from the
point of view of peace than any other, when both blocs are in competitive
contact throughout the world and the ambition of both is fired by the crusading
zeal of a universal mission. ". . . Vicinity, or nearness of situation, constitutes
nations natural enemies."[4]

Yet once they have defined their national interests in terms of national
security, they can draw back from their outlying positions, located close to, or
within, the sphere of national security of the other side, and retreat into their
respective spheres, each self-contained within its orbit. Those outlying positions add nothing to national security; they are but liabilities, positions that
cannot be held in case of war. Each bloc will be the more secure the wider it
makes the distance that separates both spheres of national security. Each side
can draw a line far distant from each other, making it understood that to touch
or even to approach it means war. What then about the interjacent spaces,
stretching between the two lines of demarcation? Here the fourth rule of diplomacy applies.

*Nations Must Be Willing to Compromise on All Issues that Are Not Vital to
Them*

All government, indeed every human benefit and enjoyment, every virtue and
every prudent act, is founded on compromise and barter. We balance inconve-

niences; we give and take; we remit some rights, that we may enjoy others; and we choose rather to be happy citizens than subtle disputants. As we must give away some natural liberties, for the advantages to be derived from the communion and fellowship of a great empire. But, in all fair dealings, the thing bought must bear some proportion to the purchase paid. None will barter away the immediate jewel of his soul.[5]

Here diplomacy meets its most difficult task. For minds not beclouded by the crusading zeal of a political religion and capable of viewing the national interests of both sides with objectivity, the delimitation of these vital interests should not prove too difficult. Compromise on secondary issues is a different matter. Here the task is not to separate and define interests that by their very nature already tend toward separation and definition, but to keep in balance interests that touch each other at many points and may be intertwined beyond the possibility of separation. It is an immense task to allow the other side a certain influence in those interjacent spaces without allowing them to be absorbed into the orbit of the other side. It is hardly a less immense task to keep the other side's influence as small as possible in the regions close to one's own security zone without absorbing those regions into one's own orbit. For the performance of these tasks, no formula stands ready for automatic application. It is only through a continuous process of adaptation, supported both by firmness and self-restraint, that compromise on secondary issues can be made to work. It is, however, possible to indicate a priori what approaches will facilitate or hamper the success of policies of compromise.

First of all, it is worth noting to what extent the success of compromise— that is, compliance with the fourth rule—depends upon compliance with the other three rules, which in turn are similarly interdependent. As the compliance with the second rule depends upon the realization of the first, so the third rule must await its realization from compliance with the second. A nation can only take a rational view of its national interests after it has parted company with the crusading spirit of a political creed. A nation is able to consider the national interests of the other side with objectivity only after it has become secure in what it considers its own national interests. Compromise on any issue, however minor, is impossible so long as both sides are not secure in their national interests. Thus nations cannot hope to comply with the fourth rule if they are not willing to comply with the other three. Both morality and expediency require compliance with these four fundamental rules.

Compliance makes compromise possible, but it does not assure its success. To give compromise, made possible through compliance with the first three rules, a chance to succeed, five other rules must be observed.

Five Prerequisites of Compromise

Give up the Shadow of Worthless Rights for the Substance of Real Advantage   A diplomacy that thinks in legalistic and propagandistic terms is particularly tempted to insist upon the letter of the law, as it interprets the law, and to lose sight of the consequences such insistence may have for its own nation and for humanity. Since there are rights to be defended, this kind of diplomacy thinks that the issue cannot be compromised. Yet the choice that confronts the diplomat is not between legality and illegality, but between political wisdom and political folly. "The question with me," said Edmund Burke, "is not whether you have a right to render your people miserable, but whether it is not your interest to make them happy. It is not what a lawyer tells me I *may* do, but what humanity, reason and justice tell me I ought to do."[6]

Never Put Youself in a Position from which you Cannot Retreat Without Losing Face and from which You Cannot Advance without Grave Risks   The violation of this rule often results from disregard for the preceding one. A diplomacy that confounds the shadow of legal right with the actuality of political advantage is likely to find itself in a position where it may have a legal right, but no political business, to be. In other words, a nation may identify itself with a position, which it may or may not have a right to hold, regardless of the political consequences. And again compromise becomes a difficult matter. A nation cannot retreat from that position without incurring a serious loss of prestige. It cannot advance from that position without exposing itself to political risks, perhaps even the risk of war. That heedless rush into untenable positions and, more particularly, the stubborn refusal to extricate oneself from them in time is the earmark of incompetent diplomacy. Its classic examples are the policy of Napoleon III on the eve of the Franco-Prussian War of 1870 and the policies of Austria and Germany on the eve of the First World War. These examples also show how closely the risk of war is allied with the violation of this rule.

Never Allow a Weak Ally to Make Decisions for You   Strong nations that are oblivious to the preceding rules are particularly susceptible to violating this one. They lose their freedom of action by identifying their own national interests completely with those of the weak ally. Secure in the support of its powerful friend, the weak ally can choose the objectives and methods of its foreign policy to suit itself. The powerful nation then finds that it must support interests not its own and that it is unable to compromise on issues that are vital not to itself, but only to its ally.

The classic example of the violation of this rule is to be found in the way in which Turkey forced the hand of Great Britain and France on the eve of the Crimean War in 1853. The Concert of Europe had virtually agreed upon a compromise settling the conflict between Russia and Turkey, when Turkey, knowing that the Western powers would support it in a war with Russia, did its best to provoke that war and thus involved Great Britain and France in it against their will. Thus Turkey went far in deciding the issue of war and peace for Great Britain and France according to its own national interests. Great Britian and France had to accept that decision even though their national interests did not require war with Russia and they had almost succeeded in preventing its outbreak. They had surrendered their freedom of action to a weak ally, which used its control over their policies for its own purposes.

The Armed Forces Are the Instrument of Foreign Policy, not Its Master   No successful and no peaceful foreign policy is possible without observance of this rule. No nation can pursue a policy of compromise with the military determining the ends and means of foreign policy. The armed forces are instruments of war; foreign policy is an instrument of peace. It is true that the ultimate objectives of the conduct of war and of the conduct of foreign policy are identical: Both serve the national interest. Both, however, differ fundamentally in their immediate objective, in the means they employ, and in the modes of thought they bring to bear upon their respective tasks.

The objective of war is simple and unconditional: to break the will of the enemy. Its methods are equally simple and unconditional: to bring the greatest amount of violence to bear upon the most vulnerable spot in the enemy's armor. Consequently, the military leader must think in absolute terms. He lives in the present and in the immediate future. The sole question before him is how to win victories as cheaply and quickly as possible and how to avoid defeat.

The objective of foreign policy is relative and conditional: to bend, not to break, the will of the other side as far as necessary in order to safeguard one's own vital interests without hurting those of the other side. The methods of foreign policy are relative and conditional: not to advance by destroying the obstacles in one's way, but to retreat before them, to circumvent them, to maneuver around them, to soften and dissolve them slowly by means of persuasion, negotiation, and pressure. In consequence, the mind of the diplomat is complicated and subtle. It sees the issue in hand as a moment in history, and beyond the victory of tomorrow it anticipates the incalculable possibilities of the future. In the words of Bolingbroke:

> Here let me only say, that the glory of taking towns, and winning battles, is to be measured by the utility that results from those victories. Victories that bring honour to the arms, may bring shame to the councils, of a nation. To win a battle, to take a town, is the glory of a general, and of an army. . . . But the glory of a nation is to proportion the ends she proposes, to her interest and her strength; the means she employs to the ends she proposes, and the vigour she exerts to both.[7]

To surrender the conduct of foreign affairs to the military, then, is to destroy the possibility of compromise and thus surrender the cause of peace. The military mind knows how to operate between the absolutes of victory and defeat. It knows nothing of that patient intricate and subtle maneuvering of diplomacy, whose main purpose is to avoid the absolutes of victory and defeat and meet the other side on the middle ground of negotiated compromise. A foreign policy conducted by military men according to the rules of the military art can only end in war, for "what we prepare for is what we shall get."[8]

For nations conscious of the potentialities of modern war, peace must be the goal of their foreign policies. Foreign policy must be conducted in such a way as to make the preservation of peace possible and not make the outbreak of war inevitable. In a society of sovereign nations, military force is a necessary instrument of foreign policy. Yet the instrument of foreign policy should not become the master of foreign policy. As war is fought in order to make peace possible, foreign policy should be conducted in order to make peace permanent. For the performance of both tasks, the subordination of the military under the civilian authorities which are constitutionally responsible for the conduct of foreign affairs is an indispensable prerequisite.

The Government Is the Leader of Public Opinion, not Its Slave   Those responsible for the conduct of foreign policy will not be able to comply with the foregoing principles of diplomacy if they do not keep this principle constantly in mind. As has been pointed out above in greater detail, the rational requirements of good foreign policy cannot from the outset count upon the support of a public opinion whose preferences are emotional rather than rational. This is bound to be particularly true of a foreign policy whose goal is compromise, and which, therefore, must concede some of the objectives of the other side and give up some of its own. Especially when foreign policy is conducted under conditions of democratic control and is inspired by the crusading zeal of a political religion, statesmen are always tempted to sacrifice the requirements of good foreign policy to the applause of the masses. On the other hand, the statesmen who would defend the integrity of these requirements against even the slightest contamination with popular passion would seal his own doom as a political leader and, with it, the doom of his foreign policy, for he would lose the popular support which put and keeps him in power.

The statesman, then, is allowed neither to surrender to popular passions nor disregard them. He must strike a prudent balance between adapting himself to them and marshaling them to the support of his policies. In one word, he must lead. He must perform that highest feat of statesmanship: trimming his sails to the winds of popular passion while using them to carry the ship to the port of good foreign policy, on however roundabout and zigzag a course.

CONCLUSION

The road to international peace which we have outlined cannot compete in inspirational qualities with the simple and fascinating formulae that for a century and a half have fired the imagination of a war-weary world. There is something spectacular in the radical simplicity of a formula that with one sweep seems to dispose of the problem of war once and for all. This has been the promise of such solutions as free trade, arbitration, disarmament, collective security, universal socialism, international government, and the world state. There is nothing spectacular, fascinating, or inspiring, at least for the people at large, in the business of diplomacy.

We have made the point, however, that these solutions, insofar as they deal with the real problem and not merely with some of its symptoms, presuppose the existence of an integrated international society, which actually does not exist. To bring into existence such an international society and keep it in being, the accommodating techniques of diplomacy are required. As the integration of domestic society and its peace develop from the unspectacular and almost unnoticed day-by-day operations of the techniques of accommodation and change, so the ultimate ideal of international life—that is, to transcend itself in a supranational society—must await its realization from the techniques of persuasion, negotiation, and pressure, which are the traditional instruments of diplomacy.

The reader who has followed us to this point may well ask: But has not diplomacy failed in preventing war in the past? To that legitimate question two answers can be given.

Diplomacy has failed many times, and it has succeeded many times, in its peace-preserving task. It has failed sometimes because nobody wanted it to succeed. We have seen how different in their objectives and methods the limited wars of the past have been from the total war of our time. When war was the normal activity of kings, the task of diplomacy was not to prevent it, but to bring it about at the most propitious moment.

On the other hand, when nations have used diplomacy for the purpose of preventing war, they have often succeeded. The outstanding example of a successful war-preventing diplomacy in modern times is the Congress of Berlin of 1878. By the peaceful means of an accommodating diplomacy, that Congress settled, or at least made susceptible of settlement, the issues that had separated Great Britain and Russia since the end of the Napoleonic Wars. During the better part of the nineteenth century, the conflict between Great Britain and Russia over the Balkans, the Dardanelles, and the Eastern Mediterranean hung like a suspended sword over the peace of the world. Yet, during the fifty years following the Crimean War, though hostilities between Great Britain and Russia threatened to break out time and again, they never actually did break out. The main credit for the preservation of peace must go to the techniques of an accommodating diplomacy which culminated in the Congress of Berlin. When British Prime Minister Disraeli returned from that Congress to London, he declared with pride that he was bringing home "peace . . . with honor." In fact, he had brought peace for later generations, too; for a century there has been no war between Great Britain and Russia.

We have, however, recognized the precariousness of peace in a society of sovereign nations. The continuing success of diplomacy in preserving peace depends, as we have seen, upon extraordinary moral and intellectual qualities that all the leading participants must possess. A mistake in the evaluation of one of the elements of national power, made by one or the other of the leading statesmen, may spell the difference between peace and war. So may an accident spoiling a plan or a power calculation.

Diplomacy is the best means of preserving peace which a society of sovereign nations has to offer, but, especially under the conditions of contemporary world politics and of contemporary war, it is not good enough. It is only when nations have surrendered to a higher authority the means of destruction which modern technology has put in their hands—when they have given up their sovereignty— that international peace can be made as secure as domestic peace. Diplomacy can make peace more secure than it is today, and the world state can make peace more secure than it would be if nations were to abide by the rules of diplomacy.

Yet, as there can be no permanent peace without a world state, there can be no world state without the peace-preserving and community-building processes of diplomacy. For the world state to be more than a dim vision, the accommodating processes of diplomacy, mitigating and minimizing conflicts, must be revived. Whatever one's conception of the ultimate state of international affairs may be, in the recognition of that need and in the demand that it be met all men of good will can join.

NOTES

1. We by no means intend to give here an exhaustive account of rules of diplomacy. We propose to discuss only those which seem to have a special bearing upon the contemporary situation.
2. "War." *Essays of William Graham Sumner* (New Haven: Yale University Press, 1934), vol. I, pp. 169 ff.
3. Edmund Burke, "Remarks on the Policy of the Allies with Respect to France" (1793), *Works*, vol. IV (Boston: Little, Brown and Company, 1889), p. 447.
4. *The Federalist*, no. 6.
5. Edmund Burke, "Speech on the Conciliation with America," *loc. cit.*, vol. II, p. 169.
6. "Speech on Conciliation with the Colonies" (1775), *The Works of Edmund Burke*, vol. II (Boston: Little, Brown and Company, 1865), p. 140.
7. *Bolingbroke's Defense of the Treaty of Utrecht* (Cambridge, Cambridge University Press, 1932), p. 95.
8. William Graham Sumner, *op. cit.*, p. 173.

The Uses and Limits of International Law

Stanley Hoffmann

The student of international law who examines its functions in the present international system and in the foreign policy of states will, unless he takes refuge in the comforting seclusion from reality that the pure theory of law once provided, be reduced to one of three attitudes. He will become a cynic, if he chooses to stress, like Giraudoux in *Tiger at the Gates*, the way in which legal claims are shaped to support any position a state deems useful or necessary on nonlegal grounds, or if he gets fascinated by the combination of cacophony and silence that characterizes international law as a system of world public order. He will become a hypocrite, if he chooses to rationalize either the conflicting interpretations and uses of law by states as a somehow converging effort destined to lead to some such system endowed with sufficient stability and solidity, or else if he endorses one particular construction (that of his own statesmen) as a privileged and enlightened contribution to the achievement of such a system. He will be overcome by consternation, if he reflects upon the gap between, on the one hand, the ideal of a world in which traditional self-help will be at least moderated by procedures and rules made even more indispensable by the proliferation both of states and of lethal weapons, and, on the other hand, the realities of inexpiable conflicts, sacred egoisms, and mutual recriminations. . . .

1. Some of the functions of international law constitute *assets both for the policy maker and from the viewpoint of world order*, i.e., of providing the international milieu with a framework of predictability and with procedures for the transaction of interstate business.

    (a) International law is an instrument of *communication*. To present one's claims in legal terms means, 1, to signal to one's partner or opponent which "basic conduct norms" (to use Professor Scheinman's expression) one considers relevant or essential, and 2, to indicate which procedures one intends to follow and would like the other side to follow. At a time when both the size of a highly heterogeneous international milieu and the imperatives of prudence in the resort to force make communication essential and often turn international relations into a psychological contest, international law provides a kind of common language that does not amount to a common code of legitimacy yet can serve as a joint frame of reference. (One must however remember, one, that communication is no guarantee against misperception and, two, that what is being communicated may well determine the other side's response to the message: If "we" communicate to "them" an understanding of the situation that threatens their basic values or goals—like our interpretation of the war in South Vietnam as a case of aggression—there will be no joint frame of reference at all, and in fact the competition may become fiercer.)

   (b) International law affords means of *channeling conflict*—of diverting inevitable tensions and clashes from the resort to force. Whenever there have been strong independent reasons for avoiding armed conflict—in an international system in which the superpowers in particular have excellent reasons for "managing" their confrontations, either by keeping them nonviolent, or by using proxies—international law has provided statesmen both with alibis for shunning force and with alternatives to violence. . . . In Berlin, both the Soviets and the West shaped their moves in such a way as to leave to the other side full responsibility for a first use of force, and to avoid the kind of frontal collision with the other side's legal claim that could have obliged the opponent to resort to force in order not to lose power or face. Thus, today as in earlier periods, law can indeed . . . serve as an alternative to confrontation whenever states are eager or forced to look for an alternative.

2. International law also plays various useful roles in the policy process, which however do not ipso facto contribute to world order. Here, we are concerned with *law as a tool of policy* in the competition of state visions, objectives, and tactics.

   (a) The establishment of a network of rights and obligations, or the resort to legal arguments can be useful for the *protection or enhancement of a position:* if one wants to give oneself a full range of means with which to buttress a threatened status quo (cf. the present position of the West in Berlin; this is also what treaties of alliance frequently are for); if one wants to enhance one's power in a way that is demonstrably authorized by principles in international law (cf. Nasser's claim when he nationalized the Suez Canal, and Sukarno's invocation of the principle of self-determination against Malaysia); if one wants to restore a political position badly battered by an adversary's move, so that the resort to legal arguments becomes part of a strategy of restoring the status quo ante (Western position during the Berlin blockade; Kennedy's strategy during the Cuban missile crisis; Western powers' attempts during the first phase of the Suez crisis; Soviet tactics in the U.N. General Assembly debates on the financing of peace-keeping operations).

(b) In all those instances, policy makers use law as a way of putting pressure on an opponent by *mobilizing international support* behind the legal rules invoked: law serves as a focal point, as the tool for "internationalizing" a national interest and as the cement of a political coalition. States that may have political misgivings about pledging direct support to a certain power whose interests only partly coincide with theirs, or because they do not want to antagonize another power thereby, may find it both easier and useful to rally to the defense of a legal principle in whose maintenance or promotion they may have a stake.

(c) . . . A policy maker who ignores international law leaves the field of political-competition-through-legal-manipulation open to his opponents or rivals. International law provides one of the numerous *chessboards* on which state contests occur.

3. Obviously, this indicates not only that to the statesmen international law provides an instrument rather than a guide for action, but also that this tool is often *not used*, when resort to it would hamper the state's interest as defined by the policy maker.

(a) One of the reasons why international law often serves as a technique of political mobilization is the appeal of reciprocity: "You must support my invocation of the rule against him, because if you let the rule be violated at my expense, someday it may be breached at yours; and we both have an interest in its preservation." But *reciprocity cuts both ways:* My using a certain legal argument to buttress my case against him may encourage him, now or later, to resort to the same argument against me; I may therefore be unwise to play on a chessboard in which, given the solemn and abstract nature of legal rights and obligations, I may not be able to make the kind of distinction between my (good) case and your (bad) one that can best be made by resort to ad hoc, political and circumstantial evidence that is irrelevant or ruled out in legal argumentation. Thus . . . during the Cuban crisis, when the United States tried to distinguish between Soviet missiles in Cuba and American ones in Turkey in order to build its case and get support, America's use of the OAS [Organization of American States] Charter as the legal basis for its "quarantine" established a dangerous precedent which the Soviets could use some day, against the U.S. or its allies, on behalf of the Warsaw Pact. And in the tragicomedy of the battle over Article 19 of the U.N. Charter, one reason why the U.S. finally climbed down from its high legal horse and gave up the attempt to deprive the Soviets of their right to vote, unless they paid their share, was the growing awareness of the peril which the principle of the exercise of the U.N. taxing power by the General Assembly could constitute some day for the United States if it lost control of the Assembly.

(b) One of the things that international law "communicates" is the solemnity of a commitment: a treaty, or a provision of the Charter, serves as a kind of tripwire or burglar alarm. When it fails to deter, the victim and third parties have a fateful choice between upholding the legal principle by all means, at the cost of a possible escalation in violence, and choosing to settle the dispute more peacefully, at the cost of *fuzzing the legal issue.* For excellent political reasons, the latter course is frequently adopted . . . in the form of dropping any reference to the legal principle at stake. . . .

(c) The very *ambiguity* of international law, which in many essential areas displays either gaping holes or conflicting principles, allows policy makers in an emergency to act as if international law were irrelevant— as if it were neither a restraint nor a guide. . . .

However, precisely because there is a legal chessboard for state competition, the fact that international law does not, in a crisis, really restrict one's freedom of action, does not mean that one will forgo legal rationalizations of the moves selected. Here we come to the last set of considerations about the role of law:

4. The resort to legal arguments by policy makers may be *detrimental to world order and thereby counterproductive for the state* that used such arguments.

(a) In the legal vacuum or confusion which prevails in areas as vital to states as internal war or the use of force, each state tries to justify its conduct with legal rationalizations. The result is a kind of *escalation of claims and counterclaims,* whose consequence, in turn, is both a further devaluation of international law and a "credibility gap" at the expense of those states who have debased the currency. America's rather indiscriminate resort to highly debatable legal arguments to support its Vietnam policy is a case in point. The unsubtle reduction of international law to a mere storehouse of convenient *ex post* justifications (as in the case of British intervention at Suez, or American interventions in Santo Domingo and Vietnam) undermines the very pretense of contributing to world order with which these states have tried to justify their unilateral acts.

(b) Much of contemporary international law authorizes states to *increase their power.* In this connection, Nasser's nationalization of the Suez Canal Company was probably quite legal, and those who accept the rather tortured argument put forth by the State Department's legal advisers to justify the Cuban "quarantine" have concluded that this partial blockade was authorized by the OAS Charter and not in contradiction with the U.N. Charter. Yet it is obvious that a full exploitation by all states of all permissions granted by international law would be a perfect recipe for chaos.

(c) *Attempts to enforce or to strengthen international law,* far from consolidating a system of desirable restraints on state (mis)behavior, may actually *backfire* if the political conditions are not ripe. This is the central lesson of the long story of the financing of U.N. peace-keeping operations. American self-intoxication with the importance of the rule of law, fed by misleading analogies between the U.N. Charter and the U.S. Constitution, resulted ultimately in a weakening of the influence of the World Court (which largely followed America's line of reasoning), and in an overplaying of America's hand during the "non-session" of the General Assembly in the fall of 1964 and winter of 1965.

These are sobering considerations. But what they tell us is not, as so many political scientists seem to believe, that international law is, at best, a farce, and, at worst, even a potential danger; what they tell us is that *the nature of the international system condemns international law to all the weaknesses and perversions that it is so easy to deride.* International law is merely a magnifying mirror that reflects faithfully and cruelly the essence and the logic of international politics. In a fragmented world, there is no "global perspective" from which anyone can authoritatively assess, endorse, or reject the separate national efforts at making international law serve national interests above all. Like the somber universe of Albert Camus' Caligula, this is a judgeless world where no one is innocent. . . .

The permanent plight of international law is that, now as before, it shows on its body of rules all the scars inflicted by the international state of war. The tragedy of contemporary international law is that of a double divorce: first, between the old liberal dream of a world rule of law, and the realities of an international system of multiple minidramas that always threaten to become major catastrophes; second, between the old dream and the new requirements of moderation which in the circumstances of the present system suggest a *down-playing* of formal law in the realm of peace-and-war issues, and an *upgrading* of more flexible techniques, until the system has become less fierce. The interest of international law for the political scientist is that there is no better way of grasping the continuing differences between order within a national society and the fragile order of international affairs than to study how and when states use legal language, symbols, and documents, and with what results. . . .

Nbo ideal + real.

A Functional Theory of Regimes

Robert O. Keohane

COOPERATION IN THEORY

. . . Since governments put a high value on the maintenance of their own autonomy, it is usually impossible to establish international institutions that exercise authority over states. This fact is widely recognized by officials of international organizations and their advocates in national governments as well as by scholars. It would therefore be mistaken to regard international regimes, or the organizations that constitute elements of them, as characteristically unsuccessful attempts to institutionalize centralized authority in world politics. They cannot establish patterns of legal liability that are as solid as those developed within well-ordered societies, and their architects are well aware of this limitation.

Of course, the lack of a hierarchical structure of world politics does not prevent regimes from developing bits and pieces of law. But the principal significance of international regimes does not lie in their formal legal status, since any patterns of legal liability and property rights established in world politics are subject to being overturned by the actions of sovereign states. . . . These arrangements . . . are designed not to implement centralized enforcement of agreements, but rather to establish stable mutual expectations about others' patterns of behavior and to develop working relationships that will allow the parties to adapt their practices to new situations. Contracts, conventions, and quasi-agreements provide information and generate patterns of transaction costs: Costs of reneging on commitments are increased, and the costs of operating within these frameworks are reduced.

Both these arrangements and international regimes are often weak and fragile. Like contracts and quasi-agreements, international regimes are frequently altered: Their rules are changed, bent, or broken to meet the exigencies of the

From "A Functional Theory of Regimes," pp. 31–46, 88–103, from *After Hegemony: Cooperation and Discord in the World Political Economy* by Robert O. Keohane. Copyright © 1984 by Princeton University Press. Reprinted by permission of Princeton University Press.

moment. They are rarely enforced automatically, and they are not self-executing. Indeed, they are often matters for negotiation and renegotiation. . . .

Transaction Costs

Like oligopolistic quasi-agreements, international regimes alter the relative costs of transactions. Certain agreements are forbidden. Under the provisions of the General Agreement on Tariffs and Trade (GATT), for instance, it is not permitted to make discriminatory trade arrangements except under specific conditions. Since there is no centralized government, states can nevertheless implement such actions, but their lack of legitimacy means that such measures are likely to be costly. Under GATT rules, for instance, retaliation against such behavior is justified. By elevating injunctions to the level of principles and rules, furthermore, regimes construct linkages between issues. No longer does a specific discriminatory agreement constitute merely a particular act without general significance; on the contrary, it becomes a "violation of GATT" with serious implications for a large number of other issues. In the terms of Prisoners' Dilemma, the situation has been transformed from a single-play to an iterated game. In market-failure terms, the transaction costs of certain possible bargains have been increased, while the costs of others have been reduced. In either case, the result is the same: Incentives to violate regime principles are reduced. International regimes reduce transaction costs of legitimate bargains and increase them for illegitimate ones.

International regimes also affect transaction costs in the more mundane sense of making it cheaper for governments to get together to negotiate agreements. It is more convenient to make agreements within a regime than outside of one. International economic regimes usually incorporate international organizations that provide forums for meetings and secretariats that can act as catalysts for agreement. Insofar as their principles and rules can be applied to a wide variety of particular issues, they are efficient: Establishing the rules and principles at the outset makes it unnecessary to renegotiate them each time a specific question arises.

International regimes thus allow governments to take advantage of potential economies of scale. Once a regime has been established, the marginal cost of dealing with each additional issue will be lower than it would be without a regime. If a policy area is sufficiently dense, establishing a regime will be worthwhile. Up to a point there may even be what economists call "increasing returns to scale." In such a situation, each additional issue could be included under the regime at lower cost than the previous one. . . . In world politics, we should expect increasing returns to scale to lead to more extensive international regimes.

In view of the benefits of economies of scale, it is not surprising that specific agreements tend to be "nested" within regimes. For instance, an agreement by the United States, Japan, and the European Community in the Multilateral Trade Negotiations to reduce a particular tariff will be affected by the rules and principles of GATT—that is, by the trade regime. The trade regime, in turn, is

nested within a set of other arrangements, including those for monetary relations, energy, foreign investment, aid to developing countries, and other issues,
which together constitute a complex and interlinked pattern of relations among
the advance market-economy countries. These, in turn, are related to military-
security relations among the major states.[1]

The nesting patterns of international regimes affect transaction costs by
making it easier or more difficult to link particular issues and to arrange side-
payments, giving someone something on one issue in return for her help on
another. Clustering of issues under a regime facilitates side-payments among
these issues: more potential *quids* are available for the *quo*. Without international regimes linking clusters of issues to one another, side-payments and
linkages would be difficult to arrange in world politics; in the absence of a price
system for the exchange of favors, institutional barriers would hinder the construction of mutually beneficial bargains.

Suppose, for instance, that each issue were handled separately from all
others, by a different governmental bureau in each country. Since a side-
payment or linkage always means that a government must give up something on
one dimension to get something on another, there would always be a bureaucratic loser within each government. Bureaus that would lose from proposed
side-payments, on issues that matter to them, would be unlikely to bear the
costs of these linkages willingly on the basis of other agencies' claims that the
national interest required it.

Of course, each issue is not considered separately by a different governmental department or bureau. On the contrary, issues are grouped together, in
functionally organized departments such as Treasury, Commerce, and Energy
(in the United States). Furthermore, how governments organize themselves to
deal with foreign policy is affected by how issues are organized internationally;
issues considered by different regimes are often dealt with by different bureaucracies at home. Linkages and side-payments among issues grouped in the same
regime thus become easier, since the necessary internal tradeoffs will tend to
take place within rather than across bureaus; but linkages among issues falling
into different regimes will remain difficult, or even become more so (since the
natural linkages on those issues will be with issues within the same regime).

Insofar as issues are dealt with separately from one another on the international level, it is often hard, in simply bureaucratic terms, to arrange for them to
be considered together. There are bound to be difficulties in coordinating
policies of different international organizations—GATT, the IMF, and the IEA
all have different memberships and different operating styles—in addition to
the resistance that will appear to such a move within member governments.
Within regimes, by contrast, side-payments are facilitated by the fact that
regimes bring together negotiators to consider sets of issues that may well lie
within the negotiators' bureaucratic bailiwicks at home. GATT negotiations, as
well as deliberations on the international monetary system, have been characterized by extensive bargaining over side-payments and the politics of issue-
linkage. The well-known literature on "spillover" in bargaining, relating to the
European Community and other integration schemes, can also be interpreted

as concerned with side-payments. According to these writings, expectations that an integration arrangement can be expanded to new issue-areas permit the broadening of potential side-payments, thus facilitating agreement.

We conclude that international regimes affect the costs of transactions. The value of a potential agreement to its prospective participants will depend, in part, on how consistent it is with principles of legitimacy embodied in international regimes. Transactions that violate these principles will be costly. Regimes also affect bureaucratic costs of transactions: successful regimes organize issue-areas so that productive linkages (those that facilitate agreements consistent with the principles of the regime) are facilitated, while destructive linkages and bargains that are inconsistent with regime principles are discouraged.

Uncertainty and Information

From the perspective of market-failure theories, the informational functions of regimes are the most important of all. . . . Even in games of pure coordination with stable equilibria, this may be a problem. Conventions—commuters meeting under the clock at Grand Central Station, suburban families on a shopping trip "meeting at the car"—become important. But in simple games of coordination, severe information problems are not embedded in the structure of relationships, since actors have incentives to reveal information and their own preferences fully to one another. In these games the problem is to reach some point of agreement; but it may not matter much which of several possible points is chosen. Conventions are important and ingenuity may be required, but serious systemic impediments to the acquisition and exchange of information are lacking.

Yet as we have seen in our discussions of collective action and Prisoners' Dilemma, many situations—both in game theory and in world politics—are characterized by conflicts of interest as well as common interests. In such situations, actors have to worry about being deceived and double-crossed, just as the buyer of a used car has to guard against purchasing a "lemon." The literature on market failure elaborates on its most fundamental contention— that, in the absence of appropriate institutions, some mutually advantageous bargains will not be made because of uncertainty—by pointing to three particularly important sources of difficulty: *asymmetrical information; moral hazard;* and *irresponsibility.*

Asymmetrical Information   Some actors may know more about a situation than others. Expecting that the resulting bargains would be unfair, "outsiders" will be reluctant to make agreements with "insiders." This is essentially the problem of "quality uncertainty" as discussed by Akerlof.[2] This is a problem not merely of insufficient information, but rather of *systematically biased* patterns of information, which are recognized in advance of any agreement both by the holder of more information (the seller of the used car) and by its less well-informed prospective partner (the potential buyer of the "lemon" or "cream-puff," as the case may be). Awareness that others have greater knowledge than oneself, and are therefore capable of manipulating a relationship or even engaging successful deception and double-cross, is a barrier to making agreements. When this suspicion is unfounded—that is, the agreement would be mutually benefical—it is an obstacle to improving welfare through cooperation.

This problem of asymmetrical information only appears when dishonest behavior is possible. In a society of saints, communication would be open and no one would take advantage of superior information. In our imperfect world, however, asymmetries of information are not rectified simply by communication. Not all communication reduces uncertainty, since communication may lead to asymmetrical or unfair bargaining outcomes as a result of deception. Effective communication is not measured well by the amount of talking that used-car salespersons do to customers or that governmental officials do to one another in negotiating international regimes! The information that is required in entering into an international regime is not merely information about other governments' resources and formal negotiating positions, but also accurate knowledge of their future positions. In part, this is a matter of estimating whether they will keep their commitments. As the "market for lemons" example suggests, . . . a government's reputation therefore becomes an important asset in persuading others to enter into agreements with it. International regimes help governments to assess others' reputations by providing standards of behavior against which performance can be measured, by linking these standards to specific issues, and by providing forums, often through international organizations, in which these evaluations can be made. Regimes may also include international organizations whose secretariats act not only as mediators but as providers of unbiased information that is made available, more or less equally to all members. By reducing asymmetries of information through a process of upgrading the general level of available information, international regimes reduce uncertainty. Agreements based on misapprehension and deception may be avoided; mutually beneficial agreements are more likely to be made. . . .

The significance of asymmetrical information and quality uncertainty in theories of market failure therefore calls attention to the importance not only of international regimes but also of variations in the degree of closure of different states' decision-making processes. Some governments maintain secrecy much more zealously than others. American officials, for example, often lament that the U.S. government leaks information "like a sieve" and claim that this openness puts the United States at a disadvantage vis à vis its rivals.

Surely there are disadvantages in openness. The real or apparent incoherence in policy that often accompanies it may lead the open government's partners to view it as unreliable because its top leaders, whatever their intentions, are incapable of carrying out their agreements. A cacophony of messages may render all of them uninterpretable. But some reflection on the problem of making agreements in world politics suggests that there are advantages for the open government that cannot be duplicated by countries with more tightly closed bureaucracies. Governments that cannot provide detailed and reliable information about their intentions—for instance, because their decision-making processes are closed to the outside world and their officials are prevented from developing frank informal relationships with their foreign counterparts—may be unable convincingly to persuade their potential partners of their commitment to the contemplated arrangements. Observers from other countries will be uncertain about the genuineness of officials' enthusiasm or the depth of their support for the cooperative scheme under consideration. These potential partners will therefore insist on discounting the value of prospective agreements to take account of their uncertainty. As in the "market for lemons," some potential agreements, which would be beneficial to all parties, will not be made because of "quality uncertainty"—about the quality of the closed government's commitment to the accord.

Moral Hazard   Agreements may alter incentives in such a way as to encourage less cooperative behavior. Insurance companies face this problem of "moral hazard." Property insurance, for instance, may make people less careful with their property and therefore increase the risk of loss. The problem of moral hazard arises quite sharply in international banking. The solvency of a major country's largest banks may be essential to its financial system, or even to the stability of the entire international banking network. As a result, the country's central bank may have to intervene if one of these banks is threatened. The U.S. Federal Reserve, for instance, could hardly stand idly by while the Bank of America or Citibank became unable to meet its liabilities. Yet this responsibility creates a problem of moral hazard, since the largest banks, in effect, have automatic insurance against diastrous consequences of risky but (in the short run at least) profitable loans. They have incentives to follow risk-seeking rather than risk-averse behavior at the expense of the central bank.

Irresponsibility   Some actors may be irresponsible, making commitments that they may not be able to carry out. Governments or firms may enter into agreements that they intend to keep, assuming that the environment will continue to be benign; if adversity sets in, they may be unable to keep their commitments. Banks regularly face this problem, leading them to devise standards of creditworthiness. Large governments trying to gain adherents to international agreements may face similar difficulties: countries that are enthusiastic about cooperation are likely to be those that expect to gain more, proportionately, than they contribute. This is a problem of self-selection, as discussed in the market-failure literature. For instance, if rates are not properly adjusted, people with high risks of heart attack will seek life insurance more avidly that those with longer life expectancies; people who purchased "lemons" will tend to sell them earlier on the used-car market than people with "creampuffs." In international politics, self-selection means that for certain types of activities—such as sharing research and development information—weak states (with much to gain but little to give) may have more incentive to participate than strong ones, but less incentive actually to spend funds on research and development. Without the strong states, the enterprise as a whole will fail. . . .

Concl: asymmetry will decrease

Regimes and Market Failure

International regimes help states to deal with all of these problems. As the principles and rules of a regime reduce the range of expected behavior, uncertainty declines, and as information becomes more widely available, the asymmetry of its distribution is likely to lessen. ② Arrangements within regimes to monitor actors' behavior—discussed more fully below under the heading of "compliance"—mitigate problems of moral hazard. ③ Linkages among particular issues within the context of regimes raise the costs of deception and irresponsibility, since the consequences of such behavior are likely to extend beyond the issue on which they are manifested ④ Close ties among officials involved in managing international regimes increase the ability of governments to make mutually beneficial agreements, because intergovernmental relationships characterized by ongoing communication among working-level officials, informal as well as formal, are inherently more conducive to exchange of information than are traditional relationships between closed bureaucracies. ⑤ In general, regimes make it more sensible to cooperate by lowering the likelihood of being double-crossed. . . .

regimes work ie

Thus international regimes are useful to governments. Far from being threats to governments (in which case it would be hard to understand why they exist at all), they permit governments to attain objectives that would otherwise be unattainable. They do so in part by facilitating intergovernmental agreements. Regimes facilitate agreements by raising the anticipated costs of violating others' property rights, by altering transaction costs through the clustering of issues, and by providing reliable information to members. Regimes are relatively efficient institutions, compared with the alternative of having a myriad of unrelated agreements, since their principles, rules, and institutions create linkages among issues that give actors incentives to reach mutually beneficial agreements. They thrive in situations where states have common as well as conflicting interests on multiple, overlapping issues and where externalities are difficult but not impossible to deal with through bargaining. Where these conditions exist, international regimes can be of value to states.

regimes pro

NOTES

1. For the idea of "nesting," I am indebted to Vinod Aggarwal, *Liberal Protectionism: The International Politics of Organized Textile Trade* (Berkeley: University of California Press, 1985).
2. Oliver Williamson, *Markets and Hierarchies: Analysis and Anti-Trust Implications* (New York: Free Press, 1975), pp. 31–33; George Akerlof "The Market for 'Lemons'" *Quarterly Journal of Economics*, vol. 84 (August 1970), pp. 488–500.

The U.N. in a
New World Order

Bruce Russett
James S. Sutterlin

The new world order envisioned by Presidents Bush and Gorbachev would be founded on the rule of law and on the principle of collective security. That principle necessarily entails the possibility of military enforcement measures by the United Nations. Twice in its history the Security Council has authorized such action. The first instance was in the Korean War in 1950; the second was in the Persian Gulf in 1990. More occasions are likely to follow.

The U.N. Charter gives the Security Council the authority "to maintain or restore international peace and security," and to enforce the will of the council on a state that has broken the peace. Use of military force by the council for these purposes was foreseen by the founders of the United Nations. Indeed it was seen almost half a century ago as an essential element in the world order that the United Nations was intended to establish. Should the need arise, countries would be protected from aggression by forces provided to the Security Council by member states, serving as a U.N. army at the council's will. Military forces, however, have not been available to the council on this basis and improvisation has therefore been required. The action taken by the Security Council in response to the Iraqi invasion of Kuwait amounted to just that— an improvisation to permit enforcement of the council's will without the specific means provided in the charter for that purpose.

Military force has much more frequently been used by the United Nations for the purpose of peacekeeping, something not foreseen in the charter at all. This improvisation was first devised in haste to facilitate an end to the 1956 hostilities in the Middle East. Since that beginning, which amply demonstrated the value of the technique, U.N. use of military and civilian pesonnel provided by member states for peacekeeping has become a well-established practice now supported by all the major powers.

The use of military force by the United Nations for both of these purposes— enforcement and peacekeeping—is surely essential to a world order in which international security is heavily dependent on the Security Council. The experience of the Gulf War and of the more distant past offers important lessons and raises trenchant questions as to how this can most effectively be done in the gulf (as action moves from military victory to the maintenance of peace in the region) and wherever else peace may be endangered.

Since the Suez crisis of 1956, the United Nations has developed a notable elasticity in using peacekeeping forces, to the point that it is now difficult to formulate a precise definition—or the limits—of what peacekeeping functions may be. The original role of standing between hostile forces has been expanded to encompass, among other functions, the maintenance of security or stability within a given area (as in southern Lebanon), the monitoring of elections (Namibia, Haiti), the provision of humanitarian assistance (Cyprus), and the disarmament of insurgents (Nicaragua). This flexibility greatly increases the value of peacekeeping forces as an instrument available to the Security Council in dealing with potential or existing conflicts. For example, the permanent members of the Security Council have recently developed a plan to bring peace to Cambodia that would use peacekeeping forces—both military and civilian—for broad purposes of pacification, stabilization, and administration.

Three limitations on the use of peacekeeping have been consistently honored: (1) peacekeeping has been interpreted, as originally articulated by U.N. Secretary General Dag Hammarskjöld, as a provisional measure under the U.N. Charter, that is, as a measure undertaken without prejudice to the rights, claims, or positions of the parties concerned; (2) peacekeeping operations have been undertaken only with the consent of all the parties concerned; (3) peacekeeping forces may use arms only in self-defense. Again, in accordance with the original decision by Hammarskjöld, U.S. and Soviet troops have never been included in peacekeeping forces.

In domestic conflicts the consent of all the parties is likely to remain a compelling requirement. It was clearly shown in non–U.N. peacekeeping undertakings, in Lebanon in 1983–84 and more recently in Liberia, that without the consent of the parties grave risks are involved and the results can be disastrous. This may not, however, be the case in interstate conflicts. When peacekeeping forces are deployed between hostile forces after a truce or ceasefire has been achieved, an essential purpose is to deter a renewal of hostilities. In this sense deterrence is already an accepted function of peacekeeping. Yet in interstate conflicts a situation could well rise in which peacekeeping forces are needed for deterrence purposes but the consent of one of the parties is not obtainable. This should not, a priori, preclude a Security Council decision to deploy them if the other characteristic limitations are maintained. . . .

It is worth emphasizing that nothing in the charter prohibits the Security Council from deploying peacekeeping forces without the consent of all the parties, or from including troop contingents from the permanent members of the council in such forces where the need for deterrence arises. (U.S. and Soviet military personnel already serve in U.N. military observer missions.) Such action would still fall under the definition of a provisional measure to be taken by the council "to prevent an aggravation of the situation" before deciding on enforcement action as foreseen in Articles 41 and 42 of the U.N. Charter. The provision of troops by member states for such deterrence operations would remain voluntary, as in other peacekeeping missions, with financing determined on an ad hoc basis by the council, either through assessment of all members or through payment of the cost by the countries requesting the deployment, as could be the case in a situation like the gulf where wealthy states are involved as parties. . . .

A good number of countries might well oppose in principle the idea of deploying peacekeeping forces without the consent of all the parties concerned, fearing that it would open the way to action contrary to their own national interests. Unlike the United States and the other four permanent members of the Security Council, they would not enjoy the protection of the veto. When a similar idea was put forward some years ago, in the course of confidential consultations in the Security Council on how its effectiveness might be enhanced, there was little response. The Gulf War has served, however, to heighten interest in effective deterrence using multilateral means not under the domination of one or several U.N. members. There is certainly now a broad recognition that adequate means of deterrence will be essential to a peaceful world order.

The second broad purpose for the Security Council's use of military force falls largely under the heading of compellence, or coercion, rather than simply deterrence. In the context of the Security Council such action is best understood as enforcement action. Use of "air, sea or land forces" for enforcement is specifically foreseen in Chapter VII, Articles 39–46 of the U.N. Charter, in which all members undertake to make available to the Security Council "on its call and in accordance with a special agreement or agreements, armed forces, assistance and facilities, including rights of passage, necessary for the purpose of maintaining international peace and security."

Since no such special agreements have been concluded, no standing multilateral force has been available to the Security Council. Therefore the Security Council authorized the use of ad hoc forces to restore international peace in Korea and the Persian Gulf. When the North Korean attacks on South Korea were formally brought to the Security Council's attention, the council's resolution of July 7, 1950—adopted in the temporary absence of the Soviet Union—called on member states to assist South Korea in resisting the North Korean aggression. It recommended "that all members providing military forces and other assistance pursuant to the aforesaid Security Council resolutions make such forces and other assistance available to a unified command under the United States." It requested further that the United States designate the commander of such forces. The same resolution authorized use of the U.N. flag.

Thus in the case of Korea the Security Council requested one member state to lead a combined effort on behalf of the United Nations to resist aggression.

Notwithstanding his designation as commander of U.N. forces in Korea, General Douglas MacArthur, the commander named by the United States, never reported directly to the Security Council. (Routine, unclassified status reports were provided by the United States.) Neither the Military Staff Committee—a body composed of military representatives of the five permanent members intended to advise the council on military matters—nor the council itself had any role in directing military operations of the unified command. The General Assembly did, however, establish a three-nation ceasefire committee that sought a formula to end the war, and the secretary general suggested the procedure of direct talks between the military commanders that was ultimately followed and through which an armistice was achieved.

The advantages offered by this procedure were:

—Expeditous action to resist aggression. Only the United States had troops deployed in South Korea capable of taking quick military action.

—The unambiguous command structure needed for large-scale field operations.

—A practical way to meet the responsibilities of the United Nations under the charter in the absence of a multilateral force under the Security Council for which the necessary agreements with member states had not been reached.

—Validation of the concept of collective security, since states acted jointly in response to Security Council (and subsequently General Assembly) decisions.

The disadvantages of this procedure (which became more evident in the course of time) were:

—The United Nations lacked control or influence over the course of military action or the precise purposes for which it was exercised (e.g., to repel and punish aggression, to reunify the country).

—The military operation became identified with the policy of the nation leading the effort rather than with the United Nations.

—Divisive forces within the United Nations were encouraged by the dominant role of one member state pursuing goals not universally shared.

—Opportunities were afforded the aggressor to identify the struggle with one country, the United States, rather than with the international community as a whole.

All of these disadvantages were intensified in the Korean case by the bitter disagreements that prevailed at the time between the Soviet Union and the United States. Under conditions of harmony among the permanent members of the Security Council, these various disadvantages could have considered less force.

In the Persian Gulf crisis the Security Council authorized, albeit in oblique language, the use of force for enforcement in another interstate conflict. After imposing a comprehensive embargo in order to bring about Iraqi withdrawal from Kuwait and the restoration of its legitimate government, the council called upon "those member states cooperating with the government of Kuwait which are deploying maritime forces to the area to use such measures commensurate to the specific circumstances as may be necessary under the authority of the Security Council . . . to ensure strict implementation" of the provisions laid down in the resolution relating to economic sanctions. Then, in Resolution 678 of November 29, 1990, the Security Council authorized "member states cooperating with the government of Kuwait . . . to use all necessary means to uphold and implement Security Council Resolution 660 and all subsequent relevant resolutions and to restore international peace and security in the area." All states were requested to provide appropriate support for "the actions undertaken."

This action, with specific reference to Chapter VII of the charter, constituted a new approach to implementation of the collective security concept. As in the earlier enforcement action in Korea, when there was no reference to Chapter VII, a basis for the council to mobilize a U.N. force for military enforcement action did not exist. Therefore the council again turned to member states to act in its behalf through such measures as might be necessary. But this time no unified command was established, and the use of the U.N. flag was not authorized.

The gulf action became possible because the permanent members of the Security Council cooperated on a matter of peace and security in the way originally foreseen when the United Nations was founded. Representatives of the United States and the Soviet Union have repeatedly suggested that such action is an important element in a new world order; that is, a world in which nations will be secure because of the capacity of the United Nations to guarantee their security through collective measures. This fundamental goal of the United Nations is unquestionably brought closer through the sustained cooperation and a notably increased commonality of interests among the major powers, evident not only in the Gulf War but also in other conflicts such as Cambodia and Angola. Two questions nonetheless warrant careful examination: Is the approach that was taken to enforce the council's decisions with regard to the Iraq-Kuwait crisis necessarily a viable model for implementing collective security in the future? Is there a realistic alternative that would offer greater advantages?

With regard to the first question, it is clear that the Security Council, in deciding on action to counter the Iraqi aggression, prescribed action for all member states. While it authorized individual states to take "the necessary action," it requested "all states to provide appropriate support for the actions undertaken." Thus all states were called on to assist in defending one state, Kuwait, from aggression. Actions to be taken for this purpose would seem clearly to constitute "effective collective measures for the prevention and removal of threats to the peace, and for the suppression of acts of aggression" as foreseen in Article 1 of the charter.

But the procedure adopted is not without its difficulties. The Security Council has no means of controlling when, how, or in what degree the collective measures are applied. In the gulf case, the states concerned were only requested "to keep the council regularly informed"; some measures taken might not have had majority support in the Security Council or the General Assembly. The state that is in command may have from the outset an interpretation of U.N. goals different from that of other Security Council members, or its aims may become more expansive in the course of the operation. The latter happened in Korea with the U.S. decision to cross the 38th parallel and try to reunify the country by force. It would have been the case in the gulf had the United States pursued military action beyond the Kuwaiti theater of operations.

If the measures taken cease to have the endorsement of the majority of the Security Council, can they still be considered collective measures taken in the council's behalf? This problem is inherent in a procedure in which action is taken on behalf of the council but without any council control over the nature, timing, or extent of the action. The major danger is that the entire undertaking will be identified with the country or countries actually involved in military action rather than with the United Nations. In any case, many U.N. members will not view the military action as an appropriate application of collective security if the action appears to conflict with the Security Council's goals.

The gulf operation and the terms for ending military action against Iraq offer a case in point. None of the 12 Security Council resolutions called for eliminating Iraq's war-making capability or deposing Saddam Hussein. But the former clearly became a goal of some coalition members, and the latter was widely suspected. President Bush and the coalition partners felt free to give their own interpretation to the Security Council resolutions. Those members, including the Soviet Union, that interpreted the resolutions more narrowly may be reluctant next time to give such unconstrained authority to member states acting on the council's behalf. In any operation, if the Security Council has asserted no control over the military action authorized, will it be possible for it to assert control over the terms of peace?

Such questions indicate the problems that can arise when a procedure such as that developed for the Gulf War is followed. Moreover, the approach adopted in the gulf case is not likely to be viable unless vital interests of one or more major military powers are at risk. For example, the United States might not be interested in deploying substantial forces, even if authorized to do so by the Security Council, to deter or repel an Egyptian attack on Libya.

There are alternative procedures that might in the future be followed by the Security Council, ones that would offer the prospect of effective enforcement action without the disadvantages and problems associated with according responsibility to individual member states.

One would be a variant of the procedure followed in Korea. National forces could be brought together in ad hoc fashion under a unified U.N. command, with the commander designated by whichever happened to be the major troop-contributing country. The problems that arose in the Korean case could conceivably be alleviated if the unified commander were required to consult with the Security Council, or with some form of military authority appointed by the council, on the mission of the military operation and the basic strategy to be followed in achieving it. The country supplying the major troop contingent can be expected to resist such a procedure as inhibiting unacceptably the freedom of action of the commander and subjecting its forces to perilous uncertainties. But if favorable relations among the permanent members of the Security Council persist, such a consultative, though not command, procedure might be feasible. It would have the distinct advantage of maintaining a close U.N. identification with all action taken and of giving the Security Council some influence, if not control, over any military action.

The other alternative is the procedure defined in Articles 42 and 43 of the U.N. Charter, according to which all members of the United Nations undertake "to make available to the Security Council on its call in accordance with a special agreement or agreements, armed forces, facilities and assistance." In the Korean War, the "uniting for peace" resolution of 1950 recommended that each member maintain within its armed forces earmarked units so trained that they could promptly be made available for service "as a United Nations unit or units."

The hostile relations between the United States and the Soviet Union were long perceived as the major obstacle to implementing such provisions. If after the Gulf War the two countries remain in accord on using the United Nations, that obstacle may be lifted. The willingness of member states to commit themselves in advance to provide troops and facilities at the request of the Security Council for enforcement purposes has never been tested. It can be argued that such commitment is inherent in U.N. membership, a condition for which is acceptance of the obligations contained in the charter and ability and willingness to carry out those obligations. For such a commitment to be reliable, however, it must be embodied in agreements between the Security Council and those member states prepared to assume the obligations. Such commitments will not be undertaken lightly.

The subject was discussed in detail in 1945 in the U.S. Senate when the U.N. Charter was under consideration. John Foster Dulles, a member of the U.S. delegation to the San Francisco conference at which the charter was signed, told the Senate Foreign Relations Committee that an agreement with the United Nations on the provision of troops should be regarded as a treaty requiring approval of a two-thirds majority of the Senate. The recorded comments of the senators indicate wide agreement with that interpretation. It was also discussed whether the president would need to obtain the consent of Congress to provide troops, when called upon by the United Nations after completion of an agreement. No consensus emerged on the question, but one senator suggested at the time that the size of the force requested could be decisive. Two or three thousand troops for "police action" would not need congressional approval, whereas a battle force would.

Soviet representatives have recently expressed a positive view of a U.N. agreement on the provision of troops for enforcement purposes, but they have emphasized that in no case could the troops be provided without the specific approval of the Soviet parliament.

Once agreements on the provision of troops were completed with a fair portion of member states, the Security Council would have the capacity to call into being a multilateral force (land, sea, and air) under a U.N. commander "to maintain or restore international peace and security." In military operations the commander would presumably have full tactical authority but would operate under the guidance of the Security Council or a body established by the council to serve this purpose. Subsequent understandings would be required on command, intelligence, logistics, and other more or less centralized functions. The Military Staff Committee could, as foreseen 46 years ago, "advise and assist the Security Council on all questions relating to military requirements." It could do this without acquiring any command authority, which would be advisable since it functions on the basis of consensus.

In some ways a U.N. force of this type would be quite similar to a peacekeeping force, since it would be made up of troops provided by member states and would have a U.N. commander. It would differ markedly, however, in mission, armament, composition, and command.

A U.N. force of this nature would not entail the problems and disadvantages that the other identified approaches could present. Identification with the United Nations from initiation to end of any operation would be assured, and control could be clearly in the hands of the Security Council. The likelihood of sustained support among U.N. members for the action undertaken would be strong. Yet in this approach, too, likely problems can be identified.

First of all, it is not clear how many states will be willing to conclude the agreements foreseen in the U.N. Charter—or how long this will take. It can only be said that international circumstances, especially in the wake of the Gulf War, appear more favorable than at any time since 1945. It is also questionable whether a force as large and elaborately equipped as one needed to maintain peace in the gulf, for example, could have been organized quickly on this basis. Any very large operation is bound to depend heavily on a major contingent from one or more of the principal military powers; the larger and more sophisticated the contingent provided, the less likely the contributing country will be willing to place it under non-national command.

Organization and deployment of a multilateral force by the Security Council would likely require more time than if action were delegated to one or more member states, especialy if a large-scale operation were foreseen. To shorten the lead time, the secretary general might be given authority, not subject to the veto, to send an unarmed observer corps to any international border at any time. According to Article 99 of the U.N. Charter, the secretary general "may bring to the attention of the Security Council any matter which in his opinion may threaten the maintenance of international peace and security." To do so he needs to be informed. An authorization to send observers without specific consent of the parties raises difficulties, but it would allow the Security Council to be forewarned and to make quick preparations if an enforcement action were required. The very presence of observers can have a deterrent effect, possibly avoiding the need for subsequent enforcement.

Then, too, there is a very basic question as to whether a military action can be successfully carried out under multilateral strategic command, or as successfully as under national command. Administrative aspects of managing the use of force by the Security Council have received little attention. . . .

One question inherent in any big multilateral action concerns the level at which integration of command of multinational forces would occur. The distinction in U.S. military terminology between command and operational control (OPCON) is useful in this respect. Command applies to such matters as discipline, pay, morale, and logistics; most of these (perhaps not logistics) would be carried out at the level of the national military contingents. OPCON is likely to be different. If U.S. troops were involved there would probably have to be, under an overall U.N. commander from some country, a U.S. "component commander" operating with substantial independence. OPCON can be decentralized by confining each member's forces to a specific sector, physically dividing up the ground, as has been done in most U.N. peacekeeping operations.

Some other functions may be even harder to divide than OPCON. Intelligence gathering, for example, will be dominated by states with vast technological capacities for overhead electronic surveillance. In the gulf operation other coalition members presumably accepted U.S. control of intelligence, but if there were substantial Soviet participation the Soviets would likely not accept it. Secure communications would be required among participating forces in the field, either through sharing encryption (politically very sensitive) or cumbersome procedures for transmission and delivery. It is likely that some states will be unable or unwilling to provide adequate logistical support for their troops, and that those with the motivation and ability to do so will have to provide for others. Some U.N. "headquarters" personnel and facilities will be required for these functions, probably drawing on the experience and capabilities of the secretary general's staff.

The problem of financing such military actions demands careful attention. The history of financing past peacekeeping efforts by voluntary contribution is, to say the least, not encouraging. The gulf operation was heavily dependent on the willingness and ability of the most deeply involved states—the United States, Saudi Arabia, and Kuwait—to pay most of the immediate costs, and in turn their willingness depended upon their ability to control the means and ends of military operations. A future operation that less directly engaged the interests of such states would have to rely on broader support, probably through an assessment of all member governments. Reasonably complete and prompt payment of those assessments would have to be assured.

Such problems may be equally severe for the peacetime maintenance of standing earmarked forces. Unless any additional costs incurred can be covered by the United Nations, Third World states may be unable to participate. Certain central (non-state-specific) services, such as administration, intelligence, command, and control, perhaps logistics and transport, must be prepared and institutionalized in advance. Provision in the regular budget of the United Nations might cover such ongoing costs of multilateral readiness, with special assessments made to cover the cost of any enforcement actions undertaken.

The credibility of U.N. action to repel aggression and restore international peace and security, as foreseen in the U.N. Charter, has been profoundly affected by the response to the Iraqi invasion of Kuwait. The Security Council showed itself capable of taking decisive action. Its ability to impose comprehensive sanctions and see them enforced was clearly demonstrated, even though the ultimate effectiveness of the sanctions was not adequately tested. By authorizing the use of military force the council gained compliance with all of its relevant resolutions. The Security Council has shown that it has the capacity to initiate collective measures essential for the maintenance of peace in a new world order.

This development can enhance the United Nations' ability not just to restore the status quo as it existed prior to a breach of the peace, but also to change the parameters of the global order to something more favorable than existed under the prior status quo. In this it may even go beyond the vision of the U.N. founders. Furthermore, knowledge that the United Nations has such a capability will also enhance its ability to deter breaches of the peace, and so make actual enforcement or later peacekeeping less necessary. Collective security may suppress incipient acts of aggression as well as defeat or punish those that do emerge.

Nevertheless, it should not be assumed that any U.N. role in enforcement during the 1990s will be automatic. It will require a deliberate political judgment that can only be made by members of the Security Council acting collectively, and will depend on some continuing commonality of interests among the five permanent members of the council—the United States and the Soviet Union in particular. The effectiveness of the United Nations in dealing with international security problems, whether by enforcement measures, peacekeeping or mediation, will always be sensitive to the nature of relations between these two superpowers. A United Nations whose credibility in dealing with aggression and threats to peace has been restored, however, can serve to moderate any revival of tension between them by lessening the need for, or likelihood of, unilateral intervention in regional crises.

The manner in which the gulf military action was executed by the United States and its coalition partners will likely limit the willingness of council members to follow a similar procedure in the future—a procedure that leaves council members little control over the course of military operations and over the conclusion of hostilities. Neither the United States nor any other country will be ready to act under all circumstances to preserve or restore peace. Nor will other states always be ready to endorse unilateral actions. Some states may not wish to contribute to an operation, and the council may not always wish to depend disproportionately on a particular state's contribution.

Some U.N. capacity to carry out these functions on a permanent basis will therefore be desirable. For this reason, as well as others previously mentioned, the Security Council should be able to mobilize a force to serve under U.N. command for enforcement purposes. That capacity may be virtually indispensable in an emergent world order. The chance to achieve it should not be missed.

PART
Two

The Uses of Force

As states formed, individuals lost the right and the need to use force. Nations, by contrast, retain the right and must be prepared to fight in order to protect what they have. Because one state can use violence to achieve its aims, all states must be prepared to do so. Threats and use of armed force are therefore integral parts of a state's foreign policy. A state that fails to calculate the military prerequisites and implications of its foreign policies or, conversely, that allows military planning to proceed without reference to its foreign-policy assumptions, is courting disaster. Military "requirements" cannot be drawn up without analysis of a state's interests, of the objectives that seem worth a war, and of possible alliances. But neither can a nation formulate and implement foreign-policy goals without considering how strong its forces are relative to those of its opponents, how quickly they can be brought to bear, and how much they can be augmented. The use of force is not always necessary, but it must always be available.

THE NATURE AND FUNCTIONS OF MILITARY POWER

The use of force almost always represents the partial failure of a policy. The exception, of course, is the case in which fighting is valued for its own sake—when it is believed that war brings out manly values and purifies individuals and cultures, or when fighting is seen as entertainment. Changes in states' values and the increased destructiveness of war, however, have led statesmen to view armed conflicts as the last resort. Threats are a second choice to diplomatic maneuvers; actual use of force follows only if the threats fail.

Because of the high costs of violence, its use is tempered by restraints and bargaining. As bloody as most wars are, they could always be bloodier. Brutalities are limited in part by the combatants' shared interests, if not by their scruples. Because two states differ enough to go to war, it does not follow that they have no common interests. Only when everything that is good for one side is bad for the other (a "zero-sum" situation), do the opponents gain nothing by bargaining. In most cases, however, some outcomes are clearly bad for both sides; and therefore, even though they are at war, each side shares an interest in avoiding them.

The shared nature of the interest, as Thomas Schelling points out, stems from the fact that it is easier to destroy than to create. Force can be used to take—or to bargain. If you can take what you want, you do not need your adversary's cooperation and do not have to bargain with him. A country may use force to seize disputed territory just as a robber may kill you to get your wallet. Most of the things people and nations want, however, cannot be taken in this way. A nation not only wants to take territory, it wants to govern and exploit it. A nation may want others to stop menacing it; it may even want others to adopt its values. Brute force alone cannot achieve these goals. A nation that wants to stop others from menacing it may not want to fight them in order to remove the threat. A nation that wants others to adopt its values cannot impose them solely through conquest. Where the cooperation of an adversary is needed, bargaining will ensue. The robber does not need the cooperation of his victim if he kills him to get his wallet. The thief, however, who must obtain the combination of a safe from the hostage, who carries it only in his head, does need such cooperation. The thief may use force to demonstrate that the hostage can lose his life if he does not surrender the combination. But the thief no more wishes to kill the hostage and lose the combination than the hostage wishes to die. The hostage may trade the combination for his life. The bargain may be unequal or unfair, but it is still a bargain.

The mutual avoidance of certain outcomes explains why past wars have not been as bloody as they could have been; but an analysis of why wars were not more destructive should not blind us to the factors that made them as destructive as they were. By 1914, for example, all the statesmen of Europe believed a war inevitable, and all were ready to exploit it. None, however, imagined the staggering losses that their respective nations would inflict and bear in the field, or the extent to which noncombatants would be attacked. Yet by the second year of the war, the same men were accepting the deaths of hundreds or thousands for a few yards' gain in the front lines; and by the end of the war, they were planning large-scale aerial gas attacks on each other's major cities. The German bombing of Guernica in 1937 and Rotterdam in 1940 shocked statesmen and citizens alike, but by the middle of the war both were accepting as routine the total destruction of German and Japanese cities.

Three factors largely account for the increasing destructiveness of the wars of the last two centuries. First was the steady technological improvement in weaponry. Weapons such as machine guns, submarines, poison gas, and aircraft made it feasible to maim or kill large numbers of people quickly. The rapidity of destruction that is possible with nuclear weapons is only the most recent, albeit biggest, advance. Second was the growth in the capacity, and thus the need, of states to field ever larger numbers of forces. As states became more industrialized and centralized, they acquired the wealth and developed the administrative apparatus to move men on a grand scale. Concomitant with the increase in military potential was the necessity to realize the potential. As soon as one state expanded the forces at its disposal, all other states had to follow suit. Thus when Prussia instituted universal conscription and the general-staff system and then demonstrated their advantages by her swift victories over Austria and France, the rest of the continent quickly adopted her methods. Because of the security dilemma, an increase in the potential power of states led to an increase in their standing power.

Third was the gradual "democratization" of war: the expansion of the battlefield and hence the indiscriminate mass killing of noncombatants. Everyone, citizens and soldiers alike, began fighting and dying. World War II, with its extensive use of airpower, marked not the debut but the zenith of this mass killing. Once war became the burden of the masses, not the province of the princes, the distinction between combatants and noncombatants increasingly blurred. Most of the wars of the eighteenth century did impinge upon the citizenry, but mainly financially; few civilians died in them. With the widespread use of conscription in the nineteenth and twentieth centuries, however, more citizens became soldiers. With the advent of industrialization and with the increasing division of labor, the citizens who did not fight remained behind to produce weapons. Now a nation not only had to conquer its enemy's armies, but also to destroy the industrial plant that supplied their weapons. Gradually the total energy of a country was diverted into waging wars. And, of course, as the costs of wars increased, so did the justifications given for them and the benefits claimed to derive from them. The greater the sacrifices asked, the larger the victory spoils demanded. Because wars became literally wars of, by, and for the people, governments depended increasingly upon the support of their citizens. As wars became democratized, so too did they become popularized and propagandized.

The readings in the first section explore how force has been and can be used in a changing world. Thomas Schelling examines the differences between the uses of conventional and nuclear weapons and the links between force and foreign policy goals. Robert Art notes that the threat and use of force has four distinct functions and shows how their relative importance varies from one situation to another. Robert Jervis argues that the extent to which states can make themselves more secure without menacing others depends in large part on whether offensive postures can be distinguished from defensive ones and whether the offense is believed to be more efficacious than the defense.

THE UTILITY OF FORCE IN THE CONTEMPORARY WORLD

The fundamental change in the use of military force among the great powers since 1945 is the premium put on deterrence. Before 1945, military planners concentrated, not on preventing the next general war, but on winning it. In the contingency planning prior to World War I, for example, the military staffs of Europe became obsessed with the swift strike that would knock the opponent out of the war. These men concentrated on victory partly because they believed that the first strike, if properly executed, could be militarily decisive and that the side that conquered the other's military forces could in the process protect its own population. The possibility of nuclear retaliation makes this no longer feasible; in a nuclear war neither side could save itself. Nuclear weapons have brought, not overkill, but *mutual* kill. Because each side can destroy the other no matter which attacks first, each has an interest in avoiding all-out war. But this raises the question of what exactly is the utility of force in the contemporary world.

Even if nuclear weapons are a force for peace, they are not the only such force. Robert Keohane and Joseph Nye contrast the models or "ideal types" of Realism and complex interdependence. The former, which is well known and represented in many of the readings in Part I, stresses the importance of power, especially military power. Complex interdependence, by contrast, is designed to capture relations, not among military adversaries, but among those states with close economic and political ties in which force plays a smaller role. In these cases international organizations, economic issues and resources, and relations among nongovernmental groups within the countries are of increased importance. Although America's relations with her major allies do not completely fit the ideal type, nevertheless there are major elements of complex interdependence in them.

The standard argument about nuclear weapons is that, by vastly increasing the costs of war, they played a major role in seeing that the Cold War never turned into a general war. John Mueller, however, argues that nuclear weapons were not all that important for the sustained peace between the superpowers. Conventional war would have been so enormously destructive that this prospect would have been sufficient to have produced peace. Furthermore, because both the U.S. and the USSR were satisfied with the status quo, they had little reason to fight. Robert Jervis finds this argument not sufficient to explain superpower peace and points to those special characteristics of nuclear weapons that enhance deterrence. But even if nuclear weapons have played a significant role in ensuring that neither the United States nor the USSR would attack the other, have they helped these states reach other goals? Have they been useful bargaining instruments and tools of statecraft? McGeorge Bundy's analysis of the historical record indicates that they have not. With the passing of the Cold War, we will gain increasing evidence about these questions, but continuing debates rather than definitive answers are likely. It is conventional rather than nuclear force the remains central in the Third World and, as Yezid Sayigh shows, the 1990s are not likely to provide a benign security environment for these countries.

The Nature and Functions of Force

The Diplomacy of Violence
Thomas C. Schelling

The usual distinction between diplomacy and force is not merely in the instruments, words or bullets, but in the relation between adversaries—in the interplay of motives and the role of communication, understandings, compromise, and restraint. Diplomacy is bargaining; it seeks outcomes that, though not ideal for either party, are better for both than some of the alternatives. In diplomacy each party somewhat controls what the other wants, and can get more by compromise, exchange, or collaboration than by taking things in his own hands and ignoring the other's wishes. The bargaining can be polite or rude, entail threats as well as offers, assume a status quo or ignore all rights and privileges, and assume mistrust rather than trust. But whether polite or impolite, constructive or aggressive, respectful or vicious, whether it occurs among friends or antagonists and whether or not there is a basis for trust and goodwill, there must be some common interest, if only in the avoidance of mutual damage, and an awareness of the need to make the other party prefer an outcome acceptable to oneself.

With enough military force a country may not need to bargain. Some things a country wants it can take, and some things it has it can keep, by sheer strength, skill, and ingenuity. It can do this *forcibly*, accommodating only to opposing strength, skill, and ingenuity and without trying to appeal to an enemy's wishes. Forcibly a country can repel and expel, penetrate and occupy, seize, exterminate, disarm and disable, confine, deny access, and directly frustrate intrusion or attack. It can, that is, if it has enough strength. "Enough" depends on how much an opponent has.

There is something else, though, the force can do. It is less military, less heroic, less impersonal, and less unilateral; it is uglier, and has received less attention in Western military strategy. In addition to seizing and holding, disarming and confining, penetrating and obstructing, and all that, military force can be used to *hurt*. In addition to taking and protecting things of value it can destroy value. In addition to weakening an enemy militarily it can cause an enemy plain suffering. . . .

THE CONTRAST OF BRUTE FORCE WITH COERCION

There is a difference between taking what you want and making someone give it to you, between fending off assault and making someone afraid to assault you, between holding what people are trying to take and making them afraid to take it, between losing what someone can forcibly take and giving it up to avoid risk or damage. It is the difference between defense and deterrence, between brute force and intimidation, between conquest and blackmail, between action and threats. It is the difference between the unilateral, "undiplomatic" recourse to strength, and coercive diplomacy based on the power to hurt.

The contrasts are several. The purely "military" or "undiplomatic" recourse to forcible action is concerned with enemy strength, not enemy interests; the coercive use of the power to hurt, though, is the very exploitation of enemy wants and fears. And brute strength is usually measured relative to enemy strength, the one directly opposing the other, while the power to hurt is typically not reduced by the enemy's power to hurt in return. Opposing strengths may cancel each other, pain and grief do not. The willingness to hurt, the credibility of a threat, and the ability to exploit the power to hurt will indeed depend on how much the adversary can hurt in return but there is little or nothing about an adversary's pain or grief that directly reduces one's own. Two sides cannot both overcome each other with superior strength; they may both be able to hurt each other. With strength they can dispute objects of value; with sheer violence they can destroy them.

And brute force succeeds when it is used, whereas the power to hurt is most successful when held in reserve. It is the *threat* of damage, or of more damage to come, that can make someone yield or comply. It is *latent* violence that can influence someone's choice—violence that can still be withheld or inflicted or that a victim believes can be withheld or inflicted. The threat of pain tries to structure someone's motives, while brute forces tries to overcome his strength. Unhappily, the power to hurt is often communicated by some performance of it. Whether it is sheer terroristic violence to induce an irrational response, or cool premeditated violence to persuade somebody that you mean it and may do it again, it is not the pain and damage itself but its influence on somebody's behavior that matters. It is the expectation of *more* violence that gets the wanted behavior, if the power to hurt can get it at all.

To exploit a capacity for hurting and inflicting damage one needs to know what an adversary treasures and what scares him and one needs the adversary to understand what behavior of his will cause the violence to be inflicted and what will cause it to be withheld. The victim has to know what is wanted, and he may have to be assureed of what is not wanted. The pain and suffering have to appear *contingent* on his behavior; it is not alone the threat that is effective—

the threat of pain or loss if he fails to comply—but the corresponding assurance, possibly an implicit one, that he can avoid the pain or loss if he does comply. The prospect of certain death may stun him, but it gives him no choice.

Coercion by threat of damage also requires that our interests and our opponent's not be absolutely opposed. If his pain were our greatest delight and our satisfaction his great woe, we would just proceed to hurt and to frustrate each other. It is when his pain gives us little or no satisfaction compared with what he can do for us, and the action or inaction that satisfies us costs him less than the pain we can cause, that there is room for coercion. Coercion requires finding a bargain, arranging for him to be better off doing what we want—worse off not . . . doing what we want—when he takes the threatened penalty into account. . . .

This difference between coercion and brute force is as often in the intent as in the instrument. To hunt down Comanches and to exterminate them was brute force; to raid their villages to make them behave was coercive diplomacy, based on the power to hurt. The pain and loss to the Indians might have looked much the same one way as the other; the difference was one of purpose and effect. If Indians were killed because they were in the way, or somebody wanted their land, or the authorities despaired of making them behave and could not confine them and decided to exterminate them, that was pure unilateral force. If *some* Indians were killed to make *other* Indians behave, that was coercive violence—or intended to be, whether or not it was effective. The Germans at Verdun perceived themselves to be chewing up hundreds of thousands of French soldiers in a gruesome "meatgrinder." If the purpose was to eliminate a military obstacle—the French infantryman, viewed as a military "asset" rather than as a warm human being—the offensive at Verdun was a unilateral exercise of military force. If instead the object was to make the loss of young men—not of impersonal "effectives," but of sons, husbands, fathers and the pride of French manhood—so anguishing as to be unendurable, to make surrender a welcome relief and to spoil the foretaste of an Allied victory, then it was an exercise in coercion, in applied violence, intended to offer relief upon accommodation. And of course, since any use of force tends to be brutal, thoughtless, vengeful, or plain obstinate, the motives themselves can be mixed and confused. The fact that heroism and brutality can be either coercive diplomacy or a contest in pure strength does not promise that the distinction will be made, and the strategies enlightened by the distinction, every time some vicious enterprise gets launched. . . .

. . . . War appears to be, or threatens to be, not so much a contest of strength as one of endurance, nerve, obstinacy, and pain. It appears to be, and threatens to be, not so much a contest of military strength as a bargaining process—dirty, extortionate, and often quite reluctant bargaining on one side or both—nevertheless a bargaining process.

The differecen cannot quite be expressed as one between the *use* of force and the *threat* of force. The actions involved in forcible accomplishment, on the one hand, and in fulfilling a threat, on the other, can be quite different. Sometimes the most effective direct action inflicts enough cost or pain on the enemy to serve as a threat, sometimes not. The United States threatens the Soviet Union with virtual destruction of its society in the event of a surprise attack on the United States; a hundred million deaths are awesome as pure damage, but they are useless in stopping the Soviet attack—especially if the threat is to do it all afterward anyway. So it is worthwhile to keep the concepts distinct—to distinguish forcible action from the threat of pain—recognizing that some actions serve as both a means of forcible accomplishment and a means of inflicting pure damage; some do not. Hostages tend to entail almost pure pain and damage, as do all forms of reprisal after the fact. Some modes of self-defense may exact so little in blood or treasure as to entail negligible violence; and some forcible actions entail so much violence that their threat can be effective by itself.

The power to hurt, though it can usually accomplish nothing directly, is potentially more versatile than a straightforward capacity for forcible accomplishment. By force alone we cannot even lead a horse to water—we have to drag him—much less make him drink. Any affirmative action, any collaboration, almost anything but physical exclusion, expulsion, or extermination, requires that an opponent or a victim do something, even if only to stop or get out. The threat of pain and damage may make him want to do it, and anything he can do is potentially susceptible to inducement. Brute force can only accomplish what requires no collaboration. The principle is illustrated by a technique of unarmed combat: One can disable a man by various stunning, fracturing, or killing blows, but to take him to jail one has to exploit the man's own efforts. "Come-along" holds are those that threaten pain or disablement, giving relief as long as the victim complies, giving him the option of using his own legs to get to jail. . . .

The fact that violence—pure pain and damage—can be used or threatened to coerce and to deter, to intimidate and to blackmail, to demoralize and to paralyze, in a conscious process of dirty bargaining, does not by any means imply that violence is not often wanton and meaningless or, even when purposive, in danger of getting out of hand. Ancient wars were often quite "total" for the loser, the men being put to death, the women sold as slaves, the boys castrated, the cattle slaughtered, and the buildings leveled, for the sake of revenge, justice, personal gain, or merely custom. If an enemy bombs a city, by design or by carelessness, we usually bomb his if we can. In the excitement and fatigue of warfare, revenge is one of the few satisfactions that can be savored. . . . Pure violence, like fire, can be harnessed to a purpose; that does not mean that behind every holocaust is a shrewd intention successfully fulfilled.

But if the occurrence of violence does not always bespeak a shrewd purpose, the absence of pain and destruction is no sign that violence was idle. Violence is most purposive and most successful when it is threatened and not used. Successful threats are those that do not have to be carried out. . . .

THE STRATEGIC ROLE OF PAIN AND DAMAGE

Pure violence, nonmilitary violence, appears most conspicuously in relations between unequal countries, where there is no substantial military challenge and the outcome of military engagement is not in question: Hitler could make his threats contemptuously and brutally against Austria; he could make them, if he wished, in a more refined way against Denmark. It is noteworthy that it was Hitler, not his generals, who used this kind of language; proud military establishments do not like to think of themselves as extortionists. Their favorite job is to deliver victory, to dispose of opposing military force and to leave most of the civilian violence to politics and diplomacy. But if there is no room for doubt how a contest in strength will come out, it may be possible to bypass the military stage altogether and to proceed at once to the coervice bargaining.

A typical confrontation of unequal forces occurs at the *end* of a war, between victor and vanquished. Where Austria was vulnerable before a shot was fired, France was vulnerable after its military shield had collapsed in 1940. Surrender negotiations are the place where the threat of civil violence can come to the fore. Surrender negotiations are often so one-sided, or the potential violence so unmistakable, that bargaining succeeds and the violence remains in reserve. But the fact that most of the actual damage was done during the military stage of the war, prior to victory and defeat, does not mean that violence was idle in the aftermath, only that it was latent and the threat of it successful. . . .

. . . The Russians crushed Budapest in 1956 and cowed Poland and other neighboring countries. There was a lag of ten years between military victory and this show of violence, but the principle was the one [just] explained. . . . Military victory is often the prelude to violence, not the end of it, and the fact that successful violence is usually held in reserve should not deceive us about the role it plays.

What about pure violence during war itself, the infliction of pain and suffering as a military technique? Is the threat of pain involved only in the political use of victory, or is it a decisive technique of war itself?

Evidently between unequal powers it has been part of warfare. Colonial conquest has often been a matter of "punitive expeditions" rather than genuine military engagements. If the tribesmen escape into the brush you can burn their villages without them until they assent to receive what, in strikingly modern language, used to be known as the Queen's "protection." . . .

Pure hurting, as a military tactic, appeared in some of the military actions against the plains Indians. In 1868, during the war with the Cheyennes, General Sheridan decided that his best hope was to attack the Indians in their winter camps. His reasoning was that the Indians could maraud as they pleased during the seasons when their ponies could subsist on grass, and in the winter hide away in remote places. "To disabuse their minds from the idea that they were secure from punishment, and to strike at a period when they were helpless to move their stock and villages, a winter campaign was projected against the large bands hiding away in the Indian territory."[1]

These were not military engagements; they were punitive attacks on people. They were an effort to subdue by the use of violence, without a futile attempt to draw the enemy's military forces into decisive battle. They were "massive retaliation" on a diminutive scale, with local effects not unlike those of Hiroshima. The Indians themselves totally lacked organization and discipline, and typically could not afford enough ammunition for target practice and were no military match for the calvary; their own rudimentary strategy was at best one of harassment and reprisal. Half a century of Indian fighting in the West left us a legacy of cavalry tactics; but it is hard to find a serious treatise on American strategy against the Indians or Indian strategy against the whites. The twentieth is not the first century in which "retaliation" has been part of our strategy, but it is the first in which we have systematically recognized it. . . .

Making it "terrible beyond endurance" is what we associate with Algeria and Palestine, the crushing of Budapest, and the tribal warfare in Central Africa. But in the great wars of the last hundred years it was usually military victory, not the hurting of the people, that was decisive; General Sherman's attempt to make war hell for the Southern people did not come to epitomize military strategy for the century to follow. To seek out and destroy the enemy's military force, to achieve a crushing victory over enemy armies, was still the avowed purpose and the central aim of American strategy in both world wars. Military action was seen as an *alternative* to bargaining, not a *process* of bargaining.

The reason is not that civilized countries are so averse to hurting people that they prefer "purely military" wars. (Nor were all of the participants in these wars entirely civilized.) The reason is apparently that the technology and geography of warfare, at least for a war between anything like equal powers during the century ending in World War II, kept coercive violence from being decisive before military victory was achieved. Blockade indeed was aimed at the whole enemy nation, not concentrated on its military forces; the German civilians who died of influenza in the First World War were victims directed at the whole country. It has never been quite clear whether blockade—of the South in the Civil War or of the Central Powers in both world wars, or submarine warfare against Britain—was expected to make war unendurable for the people or just to weaken the enemy forces by denying economic support. Both arguments were made, but there was no need to be clear about the purpose as long as either purpose was regarded as legitimate and either might be served. "Strategic bombing" of enemy homelands was also occasionally rationalized in terms of the pain and privation it could inflict on people and the civil damage it could do to the nation, as an effort to display either to the population or to the enemy leadership that surrender was better than persistence in view of the damage that could be done. It was also rationalized in more "military" terms, as a way of selectively denying war material to the troops or as a way of generally weakening the economy on which the military effort rested.

But terrorism—as violence intended to coerce the enemy rather than to weaken him militarily—blockade and strategic bombing by themselves were not quite up to the job in either world war in Europe. (They might have been sufficient in the war with Japan after straightforward military action had brought American aircraft into range.) Airplanes could not quite make punitive, coercive violence decisive in Europe, at least on a tolerable time schedule, and preclude the need to defeat or to destroy enemy forces as long as they had nothing but conventional explosives and incendiaries to carry. Hitler's V-1 buzz bomb and his V-2 rocket are fairly pure cases of weapons whose purpose was to intimidate, to hurt Britain itself rather than Allied military forces. What the V-2 needed was a punitive payload worth carrying, and the Germans did not have it. Some of the expectations in the 1920s and the 1930s that another major war would be one of pure civilian violence, of shock and terror from the skies, were not borne out by the available technology. The threat of punitive violence kept occupied countries quiescent; but the wars were won in Europe on the basis of brute strength and skill and not by intimidation, not by the threat of civilian violence but by the application of military force. Military victory was still the price of admission. Latent violence against people was reserved for the politics of surrender and occupation.

The great exception was the two atomic bombs on Japanese cities. These were weapons of terror and shock. They hurt, and promised more hurt, and that was their purpose. The few "small" weapons we had were undoubtedly of some direct military value but their enormous advantage was in pure violence. In a military sense the United States could gain a little by destruction of two Japanese industrial cities; in a civilian sense, the Japanese could lose much. The bomb that hit Hiroshima was a threat aimed at all of Japan. The political target of the bomb was not the dead of Hiroshima or the factories they worked in, but the survivors of Tokyo. The two bombs were in the tradition of Sheridan against the Comanches and Sherman in Georgia. Whether in the end those two bombs saved lives or wasted them, Japanese lives or American lives; whether punitive coercive violence is uglier than straightforward military force or more civilized; whether terror is more or less humane than military destruction; we can at least perceive that the bombs on Hiroshima and Nagasaki represented violence against the country itself and not mainly an attack on Japan's material strength. The effect of the bombs, and their purpose, was not mainly the military destruction they accomplished but the pain and the shock and the promise of more.

THE NUCLEAR CONTRIBUTION TO TERROR AND VIOLENCE

Man has, it is said, for the first time in history enough military power to eliminate his species from the earth, weapons against which there is no conceivable defense. War has become, it is said, so destructive and terrible that it ceases to be an instrument of national power. "For the first time in human history," says Max Lerner in a book whose title, *The Age of Overkill*, conveys the point, "men have bottled up a power . . . which they have thus far not dared to use." And Soviet military authorities, whose party dislikes having to accommodate an entire theory of history to a single technological event, have had to re-examine a set of principles that had been given the embarrassing name of "permanently operating factors" in warfare. Indeed, our era is epitomized by words like "the first time in human history," and by the abdication of what was "permanent."

For dramatic impact these statements are splendid. Some of them display a tendency, not at all necessary, to belittle the catastrophe of earlier wars. They may exaggerate the historical novelty of deterrence and the balance of terror.[2] More important, they do not help to identify just what is new about war when so much destructive energy can be packed in warheads at a price that permits advanced countries to have them in large numbers. Nuclear warheads are incomparably more devastating than anything packaged before. What does that imply about war?

It is not true that for the first time in history man has the capability to destroy a large fraction, even the major part, of the human race. Japan was defenseless by August 1945. With a combination of bombing and blockade, eventually invasion, and if necessary the deliberate spread of disease, the United States could probably have exterminated the population of the Japanese islands without nuclear weapons. . . .

It is a grisly thing to talk about. We did not do it and it is not imaginable that we would have done it. We had no reason; if we had had a reason, we would not have the persistence of purpose once the fury of war had been dissipated in victory and we had taken on the task of the executioner. If we and our enemies might do such a thing to each other now, and to others as well, it is not because nuclear weapons have for the first time made it feasible.

Nuclear weapons can do it quickly. . . . To compress a catastrophic war within the span of time that a man can stay awake drastically changes the politics of war, the process of decision, the possibility of central control and restraint, the motivations of people in charge, and the capacity to think and reflect while war is in progress. It *is* imaginable that we might destroy 200,000,000 Russians in a war of the present, though not 80,000,000 Japanese in a war of the past. It is not only imaginable, it is imagined. It is imaginable because it could be done "in a moment, in the twinkling of an eye, at the last trumpet."

This may be why there is so little discussion of how an all-out war might be brought to a close. People do not expect it to be "brought" to a close, but just to come to an end when everything has been spent. It is also why the idea of "limited war" has become so explicit in recent years. Earlier wars, like the World Wars I and II or the Franco-Prussian War, were limited by *termination,* by an ending that occurred before the period of greatest potential violence, by negotiation that brought the *threat* of pain and privation to bear but often precluded the massive *exercise* of civilian violence. With nuclear weapons available, the restraint of violence cannot await the outcome of a contest of military strength; restraint, to occur at all, must occur during war itself.

This is a difference between nuclear weapons and bayonets. It is not in the number of people they can eventually kill but in the speed with which it can be done, in the centralization of decision, in the divorce of the war from political process, and in computerized programs that threaten to take the war out of human hands once it begins.

That nuclear weapons make it *possible* to compress the fury of global war into a few hours does not mean that they make it *inevitable.* We have still to ask whether that is the way a major nuclear war would be fought, or ought to be fought. Nevertheless, that the whole war might go off like one big string of firecrackers makes a critical difference between our conception of nuclear war and the world wars we have experienced. . . .

There is another difference. In the past it has usually been the victors who could do what they pleased to the enemy. War has often been "total war" for the loser. With deadly monotony the Persians, Greeks and Romans "put to death all men of military age, and sold the women and children into slavery," leaving the defeated territory nothing but its name until new settlers arrived sometime later. But the defeated could not do the same to their victors. The boys could be castrated and sold only after the war had been won, and only on the side that lost it. The power to hurt could be brought to bear only after military strength had achieved victory. The same sequence characterized the great wars of this century; for reasons of technology and geography, military force has usually had to penetrate, to exhaust, or to collapse opposing military force—to achieve military victory—before it could be brought to bear on the enemy nation itself. The Allies in World War I could not inflict coercive pain and suffering directly on the Germans in a decisive way until they could defeat the German army; and the Germans could not coerce the French people with bayonets unless they first beat the Allied troops that stood in their way. With two-dimensional warfare, there is a tendency for troops to confront each other, shielding their own lands while attempting to press into each other's. Small penetrations could not do major damage to the people; large penetrations were so destructive of military organization that they usually ended the military phase of the war.

Nuclear weapons make it possible to do monstrous violence to the enemy without first achieving victory. With nuclear weapons and today's means of delivery, one expects to penetrate an enemy homeland without first collapsing his military force. What nuclear weapons have done, or appear to do, is to promote this kind of warfare to first place. Nuclear weapons threaten to make war less military, and are responsible for the lowered status of "military victory" at the present time. *Victory is no longer a prerequisite for hurting the enemy.* And it is no assurance against being terribly hurt. One need not wait until he has won the war before inflicting "unendurable" damages on his enemy. One need not wait until he has lost the war. There was a time when the assurance of victory—false or genuine assurance—could make national leaders not just willing but sometimes enthusiastic about war. Not now.

Not only *can* nuclear weapons hurt the enemy before the war has been won, and perhaps hurt decisively enough to make the military engagement academic, but it is widely assumed that in a major war that is *all* they can do. Major war is often discussed as though it would be only a contest in national destruction. If this is indeed the case—if the destruction of cities and their populations has become, with nuclear weapons, the primary object in an all-out war—the sequence of war has been reversed. Instead of destroying enemy forces as a prelude to imposing one's will on the enemy nation, one would have to destroy the nation as a means or a prelude to destroying the enemy forces. If one cannot disable enemy forces without virtually destroying the country, the victor does not even have the option of sparing the conquered nation. He has already destroyed it. Even with blockade and strategic bombing it could be supposed that a country would be defeated before it was destroyed, or would elect surrender before annihilation had gone far. In the Civil War it could be hoped that the South would become too weak to fight before it became too weak to survive. For "all-out" war, nuclear weapons threaten to reverse this sequence.

So nuclear weapons do make a differnce, marking an epoch in warfare. The difference is not just in the amount of destruction that can be accomplished but in the role of destruction and in the decision process. Nuclear weapons can change the speed of events, the control of events, the sequence of events, the relation of victor to vanquished, and the relation of homeland to fighting front. Deterrence rests today on the threat of pain and extinction, not just on the threat of military defeat. We may argue about the wisdom of announcing "unconditional surrender" as an aim in the last major war, but seem to expect "unconditional destruction" as a matter of course in another one.

Something like the same destruction always *could* be done. With nuclear weapons there is an expectation that it would be done. . . . What is new is . . . the idea that major war might be just a contest in the killing of countries, or not even a contest but just two parallel exercises in devastation.

That is the difference nuclear weapons make. At least they *may* make the difference. They also may not. If the weapons themselves are vulnerable to attack, or the machines that carry them, a successful surprise might eliminate the opponent's means of retribution. That an enormous explosion can be packaged in a single bomb does not by itself guarantee that the victor will receive deadly punishment. Two gunfighters facing each other in a Western town had an unquestioned capacity to kill one another; that did not guarantee that both would die in a gunfight—only the slower of the two. Less deadly weapons, permitting an injured one to shoot back before he died, might have been more conducive to a restraining balance of terror, or of caution. The very efficiency of nuclear weapons could make them ideal for starting war, if they can suddenly eliminate the enemy's capability to shoot back.

And there is a contrary possibility: that nuclear weapons are not vulnerable to attack and prove not to be terribly effective against each other, posing no need to shoot them quickly for fear they will be destroyed before they are launched, and with no task available but the systematic destruction of the enemy country and no necessary reason to do it fast rather than slowly. Imagine that nuclear destruction had to go slowly—that the bombs could be dropped only one per day. The prospect would look very different, something like the most terroristic guerilla warfare on a massive scale. It happens that nuclear war does not have to go slowly; but it may also not have to go speedily. The mere existence of nuclear weapons does not itself determine that everything must go off in a blinding flash, any more than that it must go slowly. Nuclear weapons do not simplify things quite that much. . . .

In World Wars I and II one went to work on enemy military forces, not his people, because until the enemy's military forces had been taken care of there was typically not anything decisive that one could do to the enemy nation itself. The Germans did not, in World War I, refrain from bayoneting French citizens by the millions in the hopes that the Allies would abstain from shooting up the

German population. They could not get at the French citizens until they had breached the Allied lines. Hitler tried to terrorize London and did not make it. The Allied air forces took the war straight to Hitler's territory, with at least some thought of doing in Germany what Sherman recognized he was doing in Georgia; but with the bombing technology of World War II one could not afford to bypass the troops and go exclusively for enemy populations—not, anyway, in Germany. With nuclear weapons one has that alternative.

To concentrate on the enemy's military installations while deliberately holding in reserve a massive capacity for destroying his cities, for exterminating his people and eliminating his society, on condition that the enemy observe similar restraint with respect to one's own society is not the "conventional approach." In World Wars I and II the first order of business was to destroy enemy armed forces because that was the only promising way to make him surrender. To fight a purely military engagement "all-out" while holding in reserve a decisive capacity for violence, on condition the enemy do likewise, is not the way military operations have traditionally been approached.

. . . In the present era noncombatants appear to be not only deliberate targets but primary targets. . . . In fact, noncombatants appeared to be primary targets at both ends of the scale of warfare; thermonuclear war threatened to be a contest in the destruction of cities and populations; and, at the other end of the scale, insurgency is almost entirely terroristic. We live in an era of dirty war.

Why is this so? Is war properly a military affair among combatants, and is it a depravity peculiar to the twentieth century that we cannot keep it within decent bounds? Or is war inherently dirty?

To answer this question it is useful to distinguish three stages in the involvement of noncombatants—of plain people and their possessions—in the fury of war. These stages are worth distinguishing; but their sequence is merely descriptive of Western Europe during the past three hundred years, not a historical generalization. The first stage is that in which the people may get hurt by inconsiderate combatants. This is the status that people had during the period of "civilized warfare" that the International Committee had in mind.

From about 1648 to the Napoleonic era, war in much of Western Europe was something superimposed on society. It was a contest engaged in by monarchies for stakes that were measured in territories, and, occasionally, money or dynastic claims. The troops were mostly mercenaries and the motivation for war was confined to the aristocratic elite. Monarchs fought for bits of territory, but the residents of disputed terrain were more concerned with protecting their crops and their daughters from marauding troops than with whom they owed allegiance to. They were, as Quincy Wright remarked in his classic *Study of War*, little concerned that the territory in which they lived had a new sovereign.[3] Furthermore, as far as the King of Prussia and the Emperor of Austria were concerned, the loyalty and enthusiasm of the Bohemian farmer were not decisive considerations. It is an exaggeration to refer to European war during this period as a sport of kings, but not a gross exaggeration. And the military logistics of those days confined military operations to a scale that did not require the enthusiasm of a multitude.

Hurting people was not a decisive instrument in warfare. Hurting people or destroying property only reduced the value of things that were being fought over, to the disadvantage of both sides. Furthermore, the monarchs who conducted wars often did not want to discredit the social institutions they shared with their enemies. Bypassing an enemy monarch and taking the war straight to his people would have had revolutionary implications. Destroying the opposing monarchy was often not in the interest of either side; opposing sovereigns had much more in common with each other than with their own subjects, and to discredit the claims of a monarchy might have produced a disastrous backlash. It is not surprising—or, if it is surprising, not altogether astonishing—that on the European continent in that particular era war was fairly well confined to military activity.

One could still, in those days and in that part of the world, be concerned for the rights of noncombatants and hope to devise rules that both sides in the war might observe. The rules might well be observed because both sides had something to gain from preserving social order and not destroying the enemy. Rules might be a nuisance, but if they restricted both sides the disadvantages might cancel out.

This was changed during the Napoleonic wars. In Napoleon's France, people cared about the outcome. The nation was mobilized. The war was a national effort, not just an activity of the elite. It was both political and military genius on the part of Napoleon and his ministers that an entire nation could be mobilized for war. Propaganda became a tool of warfare, and war became vulgarized.

Many writers deplored this popularization of war, this involvement of the democratic masses. In fact, the horrors we attribute to thermonuclear war were already foreseen by many commentators, some before the First World War and more after it, but the new "weapon" to which these terrors were ascribed was people, millions of people, passionately engaged in national wars, spending themselves in a quest for total victory and desperate to avoid total defeat. Today we are impressed that a small number of highly trained pilots can carry enough energy to blast and burn tens of millions of people and the buildings they live in; two or three generations ago there was concern that tens of millions of people using bayonets and barbed wire, machine guns and shrapnel, could create the same kind of destruction and disorder.

That was the second stage in the relation of people to war, the second in Europe since the middle of the seventeenth century. In the first stage people had been neutral but their welfare might be disregarded; in the second stage people were involved because it was *their* war. Some fought, some produced materials of war, some produced food, and some took care of children; but they were all part of a war-making nation. When Hitler attacked Poland in 1939, the Poles had reason to care about the outcome. When Churchill said the British would fight on the beaches, he spoke for the British and not for a mercenary army. The war was about something that mattered. If people would rather fight a dirty war than lose a clean one, the war will be between nations and not just between governments. If people have an influence on whether the war is continued or on the terms of a truce, making the war hurt people serves a purpose. It is a dirty purpose, but war itself is often about something dirty. The Poles and the Norwegians, the Russians and the British, had reason to believe that if they lost the war the consequences would be dirty. This is so evident in modern civil wars—civil wars that involve popular feelings—that we expect them to be bloody and violent. To hope that they would be fought cleanly with no violence to people would be a little like hoping for a clean race riot.

There is another way to put it that helps to bring out the sequence of events. If a modern war were a clean one, the violence would not be ruled out but merely saved for the postwar period. Once the army has been defeated in the clean war, the victorious enemy can be as brutally coercive as he wishes. A clean war would determine which side gets to use its power to hurt coercively after victory, and it is likely to be worth some violence to avoid being the loser.

"Surrender" is the process following military hostilities in which the power to hurt is brought to bear. If surrender negotiations are successful and not followed by overt violence, it is because the capacity to inflict pain and damage was successfully used in the bargaining process. On the losing side, prospective pain and damage were averted by concessions; on the winning side, the capacity for inflicting further harm was traded for concessions. The same is true in a successful kidnapping. It only reminds us that the purpose of pure pain and damage is extortion; it is *latent* violence that can be used to advantage. A well-behaved occupied country is not one in which violence plays no part; it may be one in which latent violence is used so skillfully that it need not be spent in punishment.

This brings us to the third stage in the relation of civilian violence to warfare. If the pain and damage can be inflicted during war itself, they need not wait for the surrender negotiation that succeeds a military decision. If one can coerce people and their governments while war is going on, one does not need to wait until he has achieved victory or risk losing that coercive power by spending it all in a losing war. General Sherman's march through Georgia might have made as much sense, possibly more, had the North been losing the war, just as the German buzz bombs and V-2 rockets can be thought of as coercive instruments to get the war stopped before suffering military defeat.

In the present era, since at least the major East-West powers are capable of massive civilian violence during war itself beyond anything available during the Second World War, the occasion for restraint does not await the achievement of military victory or truce. The principal restraint during the Second World War was a temporal boundary, the date of surrender. In the present era we find the violence dramatically restrained during war itself. The Korean War was furiously "all-out" in the fighting, not only on the peninsular battlefield but in the resources used by both sides. It was "all-out," though, only within some dramatic restraints; no nuclear weapons, no Russians, no Chinese territory, no Japanese territory, no bombing of ships at sea or even airfields on the United Nations side of the line. It was a contest in military strength circumscribed by the threat of unprecedented civilian violence. Korea may or may not be a good model for speculation on limited war in the age of nuclear violence, but it was dramatic evidence that the capacity for violence can be consciously restrained even under the provocation of war that measures its military dead in tens of thousands and that fully preoccupies two of the largest countries in the world.

A consequence of this third stage is that "victory" inadequately expresses what a nation wants from its military forces. Mostly it wants, in these times, the influence that resides in latent force. It wants the bargaining power that comes from its capacity to hurt, not just the direct consequence of successful military action. Even total victory over an enemy provides at best an opportunity for unopposed violence against the enemy population. How to use that opportunity in the national interest, or in some wider interest, can be just as important as the achievement of victory itself; but traditional military science does not tell us how to use that capacity for inflicting pain. And if a nation, victor or potential loser, is going to use its capacity for pure violence to influence the enemy, there may be no need to await the achievement of total victory.

Actually, this third stage can be analyzed into two quite different variants. In one, sheer pain and damage are primary instruments of coercive warfare and may actually be applied, to intimidate or to deter. In the other, pain and destruction *in* war are expected to serve little or no purpose but *prior threats* of sheer violence, even of automatic and uncontrolled violence, are coupled to military force. The difference is in the all-or-none character of deterrence and intimidation. Two acute dilemmas arise. One is the choice of making prospective violence as frightening as possible or hedging with some capacity for reciprocated restraint. The other is the choice of making retaliation as automatic as possible or keeping deliberate control over the fateful decisions. The choices are determined partly by governments, partly by technology. Both variants are characterized by the coercive role of pain and destruction—of threatened (not inflicted) pain and destruction. But in one the threat either succeeds or fails altogether, and any ensuing violence is gratuitous; in the other, progressive pain and damage may actually be used to threaten more. The present era, for countries possessing nuclear weapons, is a complex and uncertain blend of the two. . . .

The power to hurt is nothing new in warfare, but for the United States modern technology has drastically enhanced the strategic importance of pure, unconstructive, unacquisitive pain and damage, whether used against us or in our own defense. This in turn enhances the importance of war and threats of war as techniques of influence, not of destruction; of coercion and deterrence, not of conquest and defense; of bargaining and intimidation. . . .

War no longer looks like just a contest of strength. War and the brink of war are more a contest of nerve and risk-taking, of pain and endurance. Small wars embody the threat of a larger war; they are not just military engagements but "crisis diplomacy." The threat of war has always been somewhere underneath international diplomacy, but for Americans it is now much nearer the surface. Like the threat of a strike in industrial relations, the threat of divorce in a family dispute, or the threat of bolting the party at a political convention, the threat of violence continuously circumscribes international politics. Neither strength nor goodwill procures immunity.

Military strategy can no longer be thought of, as it could for some countries in some eras, as the science of military victory. It is now equally, if not more, the art of coercion, of intimidation and deterrence. The instruments of war are more punitive than acquisitive. Military strategy, whether we like it or not, has become the diplomacy of violence.

NOTES

1. Paul I. Wellman, *Death on the Prairie* (New York: Macmillan, 1934), 82.
2. Winston Churchill is often credited with the term, "balance of terror," and the following quotation succinctly expresses the familiar notion of nuclear mutual deterrence. This, though, is from a speech in Commons in November 1934. "The fact remains that when all is said and done as regards defensive methods, pending some new discovery the only direct measure of defense upon a great scale is the certainty of being able to inflict simultaneously upon the enemy as great damage as he can inflict upon ourselves. Do not let us undervalue the efficiency of this procedure. It may well prove in practice—I admit I cannot prove it in theory—capable of giving complete immunity. If two Powers show themselves equally capable of inflicting damage upon each other by some particular process of war, so that neither gains an advantage from its adoption and both suffer the most hideous reciprocal injuries, it is not only possible but it seems probable that neither will employ that means. . . ."
3. (Chicago: University of Chicago Press), 1942, 296.

The Four Functions of Force

Robert J. Art

In view of what is likely to be before us, it is vital to think carefully and precisely about the uses and limits of military power. That is the purpose of this essay. It is intended as a backdrop for policy debates, not a prescription of specific policies. It consciously eschews elaborate detail on the requisite military forces for scenarios *a . . . n* and focuses instead on what military power has and has not done, can and cannot do. Every model of how the world works has policy implications. But not every policy is based on a clear view of how the world works. What, then, are the uses to which military power can be put? How have nuclear weapons affected these uses? And what is the future of force in a world of nuclear parity and increasing economic interdependence?

WHAT ARE THE USES OF FORCE?

The goals that states pursue range widely and vary considerably from case to case. Military power is more useful for realizing some goals than others, though it is generally considered of some use by most states for all of the goals that they hold. If we attempt, however, to be descriptively accurate, to enumerate all of the purposes for which states use force, we shall simply end up with a bewildering list. Descriptive accuracy is not a virtue *per se* for analysis. In fact, descriptive accuracy is generally bought at the cost of analytical utility. (A concept that is descriptively accurate is usually analytically useless.) Therefore, rather than compile an exhaustive list of such purposes, I have selected four categories that themselves analytically exhaust the functions that force can serve: defense, deterrence, compellence, and "swaggering".[1]

Not all four functions are necessarily well or equally served by a given military posture. In fact, usually only the great powers have the wherewithall to develop military forces that can serve more than two functions at once. Even

From "To What Ends Military Power" by Robert J. Art, in *International Security*, vol. 4 (Spring 1980), pp. 4–35. Portions of the text and some footnotes have been omitted.

then, this is achieved only vis à vis smaller powers, not vis à vis the other great ones. The measure of the capabilities of a state's military forces must be made relative to those of another state, not with reference to some absolute scale. A state that can compel another state can also defend against it and usually deter it. A state that can defend against another state cannot thereby automatically deter or compel it. A state can deter another state without having the ability to either defend against or compel it. A state that can swagger vis à vis another may or may not be able to perform any of the other three functions relative to it. Where feasible, defense is the goal that all states aim for first. If defense is not possible, deterrence is generally the next priority. Swaggering is the function most difficult to pin down analytically; deterrence, the one whose achievement is the most difficult to demonstrate; compellence, the easiest to demonstrate but among the hardest to achieve. The following discussion develops these points more fully.

The *defensive* use of force is the deployment of military power so as to be able to do two things—to ward off an attack and to minimize damage to oneself if attacked. For defensive purposes, a state will direct its forces against those of a potential or actual attacker, but not against his unarmed population. For defensive purposes, a state can deploy its forces in place prior to an attack, use them after an attack has occurred to repel it, or strike first if it believes that an attack upon it is imminent or inevitable. The defensive use of force can thus involve both peaceful and physical employment and both repellent (second) strikes and offensive (first) strikes.[2] If a state strikes first when it believes an attack upon it is imminent, it is launching a preemptive blow. If it strikes first when it believes an attack is inevitable but not momentary, it is launching a preventive blow. Preemptive and preventive blows are undertaken when a state calculates, first, that others plan to attack it and, second, that to delay in striking offensively is against its interests. A state preempts in order to wrest the advantage of the first strike from an opponent. A state launches a preventive attack because it believes that others will attack it when the balance of forces turns in their favor and therefore attacks while the balance of forces is in its favor. In both cases it is better to strike first than to be struck first. The major distinction between preemption and prevention is the calculation about when an opponent's attack will occur. For preemption, it is a matter of hours, days, or even a few weeks at the most; for prevention, months or even a few years. In the case of preemption, the state has almost no control over the timing of its attack; in the case of prevention, the state can in a more leisurely way contemplate the timing of its attack. For both cases, it is the belief in the certainty of war that governs the offensive, defensive attack. For both cases, the maxim, "the best defense is a good offense," makes good sense.

The *deterrent* use of force is the deployment of military power so as to be able to prevent an adversary from doing something that one does not want him to do and that he might otherwise be tempted to do by threatening him with unacceptable punishment if he does it. Deterrence is thus the threat of retaliation. Its purpose is to prevent something undesirable from happening. The threat of punishment is directed at the adversary's population and/or industrial infrastructure. The effectiveness of the threat depends upon a state's ability to convince a potential adversary that it has both the will and power to punish him severely if he undertakes the undesirable action in question. Deterrence therefore employs force peacefully. It is the threat to resort to force in order to punish that is the essence of deterrence. If the threat has to be carried out, deterrence by definition has failed. A deterrent threat is made precisely with the intent that it will not have to be carried out. Threats are made to prevent actions from being undertaken. If the threat has to be implemented, the action has already been undertaken. Hence deterrence can be judged successful only if the retaliatory threats have not been implemented.

Deterrence and defense are alike in that both are intended to protect the state or its closest allies from physical attacks. The purpose of both is dissuasion—persuading others *not* to undertake actions harmful to oneself. The defensive use of force dissuades by convincing an adversary that he cannot conquer one's military forces. The deterrent use of force dissuades by convincing the adversary that his population and territory will suffer terrible damage if he initiates the undesirable action. Defense dissuades by presenting an unvanquishable military force. Deterrence dissuades by presenting the certainty of retaliatory devastation.

Defense is possible without deterrence, and deterrence is possible without defense. A state can have the military wherewithall to repel an invasion without also being able to threaten devastation to the invader's population or territory. Similarly, a state can have the wherewithall credibly to threaten an adversary with such devastation and yet be unable to repel his invading force. Defense, therefore, does not necessarily buy deterrence, nor deterrence defense. A state that can defend itself from attack, moreover, will have little need to develop the wherewithall to deter. If physical attacks can be repelled or if the damage from them drastically minimized, the incentive to develop a retaliatory capability is low. A state that cannot defend itself, however, will try to develop an effective deterrent if that be possible. No state will leave its population and territory open to attack if it has the means to redress the situation. Whether a given state can defend or deter or do both vis à vis another depends upon two factors: (1) the quantitative balance of forces between it and its adversary; and (2) the qualitative balance of forces, that is, whether the extant military technology favors the offense or the defense. These two factors are situation-specific and therefore require careful analysis of the case at hand.

The *compellent* use of force is the deployment of military power so as to be able either to stop an adversary from doing something that he has already undertaken or to get him to do something that he has not yet undertaken. Compellence, in Schelling's words, "involves initiating an action . . . that can cease, or become harmless, only if the opponent responds."[3] Compellence can employ force either physically or peacefully. A state can start actually harming another with physical destruction until the latter abides by the former's wishes. Or, a state can take actions against another that do not cause physical harm but that require the latter to pay some type of significant price until it changes its behavior. America's bombing of North Vietnam in early 1965 was an example of physical compellence; Tirpitz's building of a German fleet aimed against England's in the two decades before World War I, an example of peaceful compellence. In the first case, the United States started bombing North Vietnam in order to compel it to stop assisting the Vietcong forces in South Vietnam. In the latter case, Germany built a battlefleet that in an engagement threatened to cripple England's in order to compel her to make a general political settlement advantageous to Germany. In both cases, one state initiated some type of action against another precisely so as to be able to stop it, to bargain it away for the appropriate response from the "put upon" state.

The distinction between compellence and deterrence is one between the active and passive use of force. The success of a deterrent threat is measured by its not having to be used. The success of a compellent action is measured by how closely and quickly the adversary conforms to one's stipulated wishes. In the case of successful deterrence, one is trying to demonstrate a negative, to show why something did not happen. It can never be clear whether one's actions were crucial to, or irrelevant to, why another state chose *not* to do something. In the case of successful compellence, the clear sequence of actions and reactions lends a compelling plausibility to the centrality of one's actions. Figure 1 illustrates the distinction. In successful compellence, state B can claim that its pressure deflected state A from its course of action. In successful deterrence, state B has no change in state A's behavior to point to, but instead must resort to claiming that its threats were responsible for the continuity in A's behavior. State A may have changed its behavior for reasons other than state B's compellent action. State A may have continued with its same behavior for

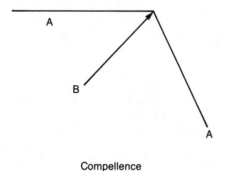

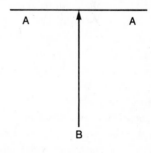

Compellence	Deterrence
(1) A is doing something that B cannot tolerate	(1) A is presently not doing anything that B finds intolerable
(2) B initiates action against A in order to get him to stop his intolerable actions	(2) B tells A that if A changes his behavior and does something intolerable, B will punish him
(3) A stops his tolerable actions and B stops his (or both cease simultaneously)	(3) A continues not to do anything B finds intolerable

Figure 1

reasons other than state B's deterrent threat. "Proving" the importance of B's influence on A for either case is not easy, but it is more plausible to claim that B influenced A when there is a change in A's behavior than when there is not. Explaining why something did not happen is more difficult than explaining why something did.

Compellence may be easier to demonstrate than deterrence, but it is harder to achieve. Schelling argues that compellent actions tend to be vaguer in their objectives than deterrent threats and for that reason more difficult to attain.[4] If an adversary has a hard time understanding what it is that one wished him to do, his compliance with one's wishes is made more difficult. There is, however, no inherent reason why a compellent action must be vaguer than a deterrent threat with regard to how clearly the adversary understands what is wanted from him. "Do not attack me" is not any clearer in its ultimate meaning that "stop attacking my friend." A state can be as confused or as clear about what it wishes to prevent as it can be about what it wishes to stop. The clarity, or lack of it, of the objectives of compellent actions and deterrent threats does not vary according to whether the given action is compellent or deterrent in nature, but rather according to a welter of particularities associated with the given action. Some objectives, for example, are inherently clearer and hence easier to perceive than others. Some statesmen communicate more clearly than others. Some states have more power to bring to bear for a given objective than others. It is the specifics of a given situation, not any intrinsic difference between compellence and deterrence, that determines the clarity with which an objective is perceived.

We must, therefore, look elsewhere for the reason as to why compellence is comparatively harder to achieve than deterrence. It lies, not in what one asks another to do, but in *how* one asks. With deterrence, state B asks something of state A in this fashion: "Do not take action X; for if you do, I will bash you over the head with this club." With compellence, state B asks something of state A in this fashion: "I am now going to bash you over the head with this club and will continue to do so until you do that I want." In the former case, state A can easily deny with great plausibility any intention of having planned to take action X. In the latter case, state A cannot deny either that it is engaged in a given course of action or that it is being subjected to pressure by state B. If they are to be successful, compellent actions require a state to alter its behavior in a manner quite visible to all in response to an equally visible forceful initiative taken by another state. In contrast to compellent actions, deterrent threats are both easier to appear to have ignored or easier to acquiesce to without great loss of face. In contrast to deterrent threats, compellent actions more directly engage the prestige and the passions of the put-upon state. Less prestige is lost in not doing something than in clearly altering behavior due to pressure from another. In the case of compellence, a state has publicly committed its prestige and resources to a given line of conduct that it is now asked to give up. This is not so for deterrence. Thus, compellence is intrinsically harder to attain than deterrence, not because its objectives are vaguer, but because it demands more humiliation from the compelled state.

The fourth purpose to which military power can be put is the most difficult to be precise about. *Swaggering* is in part a residual category, the deployment of military power for purposes other than defense, deterrence, or compellence. Force is not aimed directly at dissuading another state from attacking, at repelling attacks, nor at compelling it to do something specific. The objectives for swaggering are more diffuse, ill-defined, and problematic than that. Swaggering almost always involves only the peaceful use of force and is expressed usually in one of two ways: displaying one's military might at military exercises and national demonstrations and buying or building the era's most prestigious weapons. The swagger use of force is the most egoistic: It aims to enhance the national pride of a people or to satisfy the personal ambitions of its ruler. A state or statesman swaggers in order to look and feel more powerful and important, to be taken seriously by others in the councils of international decision making, to enhance the nation's image in the eyes of others. If its image is enhanced, the nation's defense, deterrent, and compellent capabilities may also be enhanced; but swaggering is not undertaken solely or even primarily for these specific purposes. Swaggering is pursued because it offers to bring prestige "on the cheap." Swaggering is pursued because of the fundamental yearning of states and statesmen for respect and prestige. Swaggering is more something to be enjoyed for itself than to be employed for a specific, consciously thought-out end.

And yet, the instrumental role of swaggering cannot be totally discounted because of the fundamental relation between force and foreign policy that obtains in an anarchic environment. Because there is a connection between the military might that a nation is thought to possess and the success that it achieves in attaining its objectives, the enhancement of a state's stature in the eyes of others can always be justified on *realpolitik* lines. If swaggering causes other states to take one's interests more seriously into account, then the general interests of the state will benefit. Even in its instrumental role, however, swaggering is undertaken less for any given end than for all ends. The swaggering function of military power is thus at one and the same time the most comprehensive and the most diffuse, the most versatile in its efects and the least focused in its immediate aims, the most instrumental in the long run and the least instrumental in the short run, easy to justify on hardheaded grounds and often undertaken on emotional grounds. Swaggering mixes the rational and irrational more than the other three functions of military power and, for that reason, remains both pervasive in international relations and elusive to describe.

Defense, deterrence, compellence, and swaggering—these are the four general purposes for which force can be employed. Discriminating among them analytically, however, is easier than applying them in practice. This is due to two factors. First, we need to know the motives behind an act in order to judge its purpose; but the problem is that motives cannot be readily inferred from actions because several motives can be served by the same action. But neither can one readily infer the motives of a state from what it publicly or officially proclaims them to be. Such statements should not necessarily be taken at face value because of the role that bluff and dissimulation play in statecraft. Such statements are also often concocted with domestic political, not foreign audiences in mind, or else are deliberate exercises in studied ambiguity. Motives are important in order to interpret actions, but neither actions nor words always clearly delineate motives.

It is, moreover, especially difficult to distinguish defensive from compellent actions and deterrent from swaggering ones unless we know the reasons for which they were undertaken. Peaceful defensive preparations often look largely the same as peaceful compellent ones. Defensive attacks are nearly indistinguishable from compellent ones. Is he who attacks first the defender or the compeller? Deterrence and swaggering both involve the acquisition and display of an era's prestigious weapons. Are such weapons acquired to enhance prestige or to dissuade an attack?

Second, to make matters worse, consider the following example. Germany launched an attack upon France and Russia at the end of July 1914 and thereby began World War I. There are two schools of thought as to why Germany did this. One holds that its motives were aggressive—territorial aggrandizement, economic gain, and elevation to the status of a world empire. Another holds that her motives were preventive and hence defensive. She struck first because she feared encirclement, slow strangulation, and then inevitable attack by her two powerful neighbors, foes whom she felt were daily increasing their military might faster than she was. She struck while she had the chance to win.

It is not simple to decide which school is the more nearly correct because both can marshall evidence to build a powerful case. Assume for the moment, though, that the second is closer to the truth. There are then two possibilities to consider: (1) Germany launched an attack because it *was* the case that her foes were planning to attack her ultimately, and Germany had the evidence to prove it; or (2) Germany felt she had reasonable evidence of her foes' *intent* to attack her eventually, but in fact her evidence was wrong because she misperceived their intent from their actions. If the first was the case, then we must ask this question: How responsible was Germany's diplomacy in the fifteen years before 1914, aggressive and blundering as it was, in breeding hostility in her neighbors? Germany attacked in the knowledge that they would eventually have struck her, but if her fifteen-year diplomatic record was a significant factor in causing them to lay these plans, must we conclude that Germany in 1914 was merely acting defensively? Must we confine our judgment about the defensive or aggressive nature of the act to the month or even the year in which it occurred? If not, how many years back in history do we go in order to make a judgment? If the second was the case, then we must ask this question: If Germany attacked in the belief, mistakenly as it turns out, that she would be attacked, must we conclude that Germany was acting defensively? Must we confine our judgment about the defensive or aggressive nature of the act simply to Germany's beliefs about others' intent, without reference to their actual intent?

It is not easy to answer these questions. Fortunately, we do not have to. Asking them is enough because it illustrates that an assessment of the *legitimacy* of a state's motives in using force is integral to the task of determining what its motives are. One cannot, that is, specify motives without at the same time making judgments about their legitimacy. The root cause of this need lies in the nature of state action. In anarchy every state is a valid judge of the legitimacy of its goals because there is no supranational authority to enforce agreed upon rules. Because of the lack of universal standards, we are forced to examine each case within its given context and to make individual judgments about the meaning of the particulars. When individual judgment is exercised, individuals may well differ. Definitive answers are more likely to be the exception rather than the rule.

Where does all of this leave us? Our four categories tell us what are the four possible purposes for which states can employ military power. The attributes of each alert us to the types of evidence for which to search. But because the context of an action is crucial in order to judge its ultimate purpose, these four categories cannot be applied mindlessly and ahistorically. Each state's purpose in using force in a given instance must fall into one of these four categories. We know *a priori* what the possibilities are. Which one it is, is an exercise in judgment, an exercise that depends as much upon the particulars of the given case as it does upon the general features of the given category. . . . (See Table 1).

WHAT IS THE FUTURE OF FORCE?

If the past be any guide to the future, then military power will remain central to the course of international relations. Those states that do not have the wherewithal to field large forces (for example, Denmark) or those that choose to field forces far smaller than their economies can bear (for example, Japan) will pay the price. Both will find themselves with less control over their own fate than would otherwise be the case. Those states that field powerful military forces will find themselves in greater control, but also that their great military power can produce unintended effects and that such power is not a solution to all their problems. For both the strong and the weak, however, as long as anarchy obtains, force will remain the final arbiter to resolve the disputes that arise among them. As has always been the case, most disputes will be settled short of the physical use of force. But as long as the physical use of force remains a viable option, military power will vitally affect the manner in which all states in peacetime deal with one another.

This is a conclusion not universally nor even widely held today. Three schools of thought challenge it. First are those who argue that nuclear weapons make war, nuclear or conventional, between American and Russia or between the NATO Alliance and the Warsaw Pact unthinkable. Hopefully, that is the case. But, as we have argued, one does not measure the utility of force simply by the frequency with which it is used physically. To argue that force is on the wane because war in Europe has not occurred is to confuse effect with cause. The probability of war between America and Russia or between NATO and the Warsaw Pact is practically nil precisely because the military planning and deployments of each, together with the fears of escalation to general nuclear war,

Table 1 THE PURPOSES OF FORCE

Type	Purpose	Mode	Targets	Characteristics
Defensive	Fend off attacks and/or reduce damage of an attack	Peaceful and physical	Primarily military Secondarily industrial	Defensive preparations can have dissuasion value; Defensive preparations can look aggressive; First strikes can be taken for defense.
Deterrent	Prevent adversary from initiating an action	Peaceful	Primarily civilian Secondarily industrial Tertiarily military	Threats of retaliation made so as not to have to be carried out; Second strike preparations can be viewed as first strike preparations.
Compellent	Get adversary to stop doing something or start doing something	Peaceful and physical	All three with no clear ranking	Easy to recognize but hard to achieve; Compellent actions can be justified on defensive grounds.
Swaggering	Enhance prestige	Peaceful	None	Difficult to describe because of instrumental and irrational nature; Swaggering can be threatening.

keep it that way. The absence of war in the European theater does not thereby signify the irrelevance of military power to East-West relations but rather the opposite. The estimates of relative strength between these two sets of forces, moreover, intimately affect the political and economic relations between Eastern and Western Europe. A stable balance of forces creates a political climate conducive to trade. An unstable balance of forces heightens political tensions that are disruptive to trade. The chances for general war are quite small, but the fact that it nevertheless remains possible vitally shapes the peacetime relations of the European powers to one another and to their superpower protectors.

Second are those who argue that the common problems of mankind, such as pollution, energy and other raw material scarcities, have made war and military power passé. In fact, their argument is stronger: The common problems that all nations now confront make it *imperative* that they cooperate in order to solve them. This argument, however, is less a statement of fact about the present than a fervent hope for the future. Unfortunately, proof of how the future will look is not available in the present. Cooperation among nations today, such as it is, should not make us sanguine about their ability to surmount their conflicts for the good of all. It takes a strong imagination, moreover, to assume that what some nations term common problems are viewed as such by all. One man's overpopulation, for example, is another man's source of strength. China and India are rightly concerned about the deleterious effects of their population growth on their standard of living. But Nigeria, whose source of power and influence within Africa rests partly on a population that is huge by African standards, is not. The elemental rule of international relations is that the circumstances of states differ. Hence so too do their interests and perspectives. Not only do they have different solutions to the same problem, they do not always or often agree on what are the problems. As long as anarchy obtains, therefore, there will be no agency above states powerful enough to create and enforce a consensus. As long as anarchy obtains, therefore, military power deployed by individual states will play a vital role both in defining what are the problems and in hastening or delaying their solutions. Only when world government arrives will the ability of every nation to resort to force cease to be an option. But even then, the importance of force will endure. For every government has need of an army.

Finally, there are those who proclaim that the nations of the world have become so economically intertwined that military power is no longer of use because its use is no longer credible. A nation whose economic interests are deeply entangled with another's cannot use force against it because to do so would be to harm itself in the process. Interests intertwined render force unusable—so believe the "interdependencia theorists." . . . This view of the world is odd. . . . American military power has created and sustained the political preconditions necessary for the evolutionary intertwining of the American, Canadian, Japanese, and Western European economies. . . . Military preeminence has never ensured political and economic preeminence. But it does put one nation in a stronger bargaining position that, if skillfully exploited, can be fashioned for non-military goals. Force cannot be irrelevant as a tool of policy for

America's economic relations with her great power allies: America's military preeminence politically pervades these relations. It is the cement of economic interdependence.

A simple example will clarify the point. In 1945, convinced that competitive devaluations of currencies made the depression of the 1930s deeper and longer than need be, America pushed for fixed exchange rates. Her view prevailed, and the Bretton Woods structure of fixed exchange rates, with small permissible variations monitored by the International Monetary Fund, was set up and lasted until 1971. In that year, because of the huge outflow of dollars over a twenty-five year period, the United States found it to its best interests to close the gold window—that is, to suspend the commitment to pay out gold for dollars that any nation turned in. Under Bretton Woods the relations of the free world's currencies to one another were fixed in the relation of each to the dollar, which in turn was fixed in value by its relation to the standard "one ounce of gold equals thirty-five dollars." By closing the gold window, the United States shattered that standard, caused the price of an ounce of gold in dollars to soar, destroyed the fixed benchmark according to which all currencies were measured, and ushered in the era of floating exchange rates. In sum, America both made and unmade the Bretton Woods system. In 1945 she persuaded her allies. In 1971 she acted unilaterally and against their wishes.

Under both fixed and floating exchange rates, moreover, the United States has confronted her great power allies with an unpleasant choice. Either they could accept and hold onto the dollars flowing out of the United States and thereby add to their inflation at home by increasing their money supplies; or they could refuse the dollars, watch the value of their currencies in relation to the dollar rise, make their exports more expensive (exports upon which all these nations heavily rely), and threaten a decline in exports with the concomitant risk of a recession. America's economic and military strength has enabled her for over twenty years to confront her great power allies with the choice of inflation or recession for their economies. America did not have to use her military power directly to structure the choice this way, nor to make and break the system. Her economic strength, still greater than that of most of her great power allies combined, gave her considerable bargaining power. But without her military preeminence and their military dependence, she could never have acted as she did. America used her military power politically to cope with her dollar valuation problem.

In a similar vein, others argue that the United States can no longer use its military power against key Third World nations to achieve its aims because of its dependence on their raw materials or because of its needs to sell them manufactured goods. In order to assess the validity of this argument, four factors must be kept in mind. First, the efficacy of military power should not be confused with the will to use it. In the mid- and late 1970s, as a consequence of the experience with Vietnam, America's foreign policy elite was reluctant to commit American conventional forces to combat. Its calculation has been that the American public would not tolerate such actions, except for the most compelling and extreme of circumstances. The non-use of American military power in

Asia, Africa, and Latin American in the late 1970s stems as much from American domestic political restraints as from anything else.

Second, it is important to recall a point made earlier about the inherent limits of military power to achieve economic objectives. A superior military position can give one state a bargaining edge over another in the conduct of their bilateral economic relations, but bargains must still be struck. And that requires compromise by both parties. Only by conquest, occupation, and rule, or by a credible threat to that effect, can one state guarantee that another will conduct its economic relations on terms most favorable to the (would-be) conqueror. Short of that, the economic relations between two states are settled on the basis of each state's perception of its own economic interests, on differences in the strength, size, and diversity of their economies, on differences in the degree to which each state coordinates the activities of its interest groups and hence centrally manages its economy, and on the differential in their military capabilites. Because military power is only one of the ingredients that determine the economic relations between two states, its role is not always, nor usually, overriding. By itself superiority in arms does not guarantee, nor has it ever guaranteed, superiority in economic leverage. In this sense, although there may be clear limits on what the United States through its military power can achieve in its economic relations with the Third World, much of the constraint stems from the limits that inhere in translating military power into economic ends.

Third, America's economic power relative to others has waned in the 1970s. The 1950s were characterized by a United States whose economic and military power far surpassed that of any other nation. With the emergence of the Soviet Union as a global military power in the 1970s, America's freedom to intervene militarily around the world, unimpeded by concerns about the counteractions of another global power, has drastically declined. But America's economic freedom worldwide has also waned. Whether measured by the diminished role of the dollar as the world's reserve currency, by the persistent lack of a favorable trade balance, by a smaller percentage of the world's trade accounted for by American imports and exports, by a decline in the productivity of its labor force, or by a greater dependence on imported raw materials, the United States economy is not as self-sufficient and immune from economic events beyond its borders as it once was. Analysts disagree over the extent to which, and the reasons why, the health of the American economy has become more dependent on the actions of other nations; but they do not disagree on the fact of greater dependence. If the hallmark of the fifties and sixties was America's military and economic preeminence, the hallmark of the seventies has been America's passing the zenith of her power and the consequent waning of this dual preeminence.

A diminishment in the economic power of a state is not easily compensated for by an edge in military capability. When that military edge also wanes, such compensation becomes even more difficult. Although the United States remains the world's strongest economic *and* military power, the gap between her strength in each dimension and that of other nations has narrowed in the seventies from that which was the case in the fifties and sixties. It is therefore wrongheaded to assert that America's diminished ability to get what it wants economically from allies and neutrals is due solely to the devaluation of military power. It is wrongheaded to assert that military power is devalued because it cannot solve economic problems when economic problems have never been readily or totally solved by military measures. It is wrongheaded to blame on military power that which has military and economic causes. The utility of force to a state for compellent purposes does diminish as the relative military power of a state declines. But the utility of force for compellent economic purposes declines even more when a state's economic bargaining power concomitantly wanes.

Fourth, force cannot be efficiently used to achieve goals when ambivalence exists over the goal to be attained. . . . It would be absurd to deny the fact that the potency of the Third World's virulent nationalism has restrained the great powers in their military adventures against those nations. It would be absurd to deny that the 1970s are not different from the 1870s and 1880s, when the European great powers, restrained only by their fears of each other's counteractions, intervened militarily at will in Asia and Africa against poorly armed and politically fragmented "nations." Clearly the political and military conditions for great power military intervention in such areas have drastically changed since then. . . .

The efficacy of force endures. It must. For in anarchy, force and politics are connected. By itself, military power guarantees neither survival nor prosperity. But it is almost always the essential ingredient for both. Because resort to force is the ultimate card of all states, the seriousness of a state's intentions is conveyed fundamentally by its having a credible military posture. Without it, a state's diplomacy generally lacks effectiveness. Force need not be physically used to be politically useful. Threats need not be overtly made to be communicated. The mere presence of a credible military option is often sufficient to make the point. It is the capability to resort to military force if all else fails that serves as the most effective brake against having to do so. Lurking behind the scenes, unstated but explicit, lies the military muscle that gives meaning to the posturings of the diplomats. Diplomacy is the striking of compromises by parties with differing perspectives and clashing interests. The ultimate ability of each to resort to force disciplines the diplomats. Precisely because each knows that all can come to blows if they do not strike compromises do the diplomats engage in the hard work necessary to construct them. There is truth to the old adage: "The best way to keep the peace is first to prepare for war."

NOTES

1. The term "compellence" was coined by Thomas C. Schelling in his *Arms and Influence* (New Haven: Yale University Press, 1966). Part of my discussion of compellence and deterrence draws upon his as it appears in Chapter 2 (69–86), but, as will be made clear below, I disagree with some of his conclusions.
2. Military power can be used in one of two modes—"physically" and "peacefully." The

physical use of force refers to its actual employment against an adversary, usually but not always in a mutual exchange of blows. The peaceful use of force refers either to an explicit threat to resort to force, or to the implicit threat to use it that is communicated simply by a state's having it available for use. The physical use of force means that one nation is literally engaged in harming, destroying, or crippling those possessions which another nation holds dear, including its military forces. The peaceful use of force is referred to as such because, while force is "used" in the sense that it is employed explicitly or implicitly for the assistance it is thought to render in achieving a given goal, it does not result in any physical destruction to another nation's valued possessions. There is obviously a gray area between these two modes of use—the one in which a nation prepares (that is, gears up or mobilizes or moves about) its military forces for use against another nation but has not yet committed them such that they are inflicting damage.

3. Schelling, *Arms and Influence*, 72.
4. Ibid., 72–73.

Offense, Defense, and the Security Dilemma

Robert Jervis

Another approach starts with the central point of the security dilemma—that an increase in one state's security decreases the security of others—and examines the conditions under which this proposition holds. Two crucial variables are involved: whether defensive weapons and policies can be distinguished from offensive ones, and whether the defense or the offense has the advantage. The definitions are not always clear, and many cases are difficult to judge, but these two variables shed a great deal of light on the question of whether status-quo powers will adopt compatible security policies. All the variables discussed so far leave the heart of the problem untouched. But when defensive weapons differ from offensive ones, it is possible for a state to make itself more secure without making others less secure. And when the defense has the advantage over the offense, a large increase in one state's security only slightly decreases the security of the others, and status-quo powers can all enjoy a high level of security and largely escape from the state of nature.

OFFENSE-DEFENSE BALANCE

When we say that the offense has the advantage, we simply mean that it is easier to destroy the other's army and take its territory than it is to defends one's own. When the defense has the advantage, it is easier to protect and to hold than it is to move forward, destroy, and take. If effective defenses can be erected quickly, an attacker may be able to keep territory he has taken in an initial victory. Thus, the dominance of the defense made it very hard for Britain and France to push Germany out of France in World War I. But when superior defenses are difficult for an aggressor to improvise on the battlefield and must be constructed during peacetime, they provide no direct assistance to him.

From "Cooperation Under the Security Dilemma" from *World Politics*, vol. 30, no. 2 (Jan. 1978), pp. 186–214 by Robert Jervis. Reprinted with permission of Johns Hopkins University Press. Portions of the text and some footnotes have been omitted.

The security dilemma is at its most vicious when commitments, strategy, or technology dictate that the only route to security lies through expansion. Status-quo powers must then act like aggressors; the fact that they would gladly agree to forego the opportunity for expansion in return for guarantees for their security has no implications for their behavior. Even if expansion is not sought as a goal in itself, there will be quick and drastic changes in the distribution of territory and influence. Conversely, when the defense has the advantage, status-quo states can make themselves more secure without gravely endangering others.[1] Indeed, if the defense has enough of an advantage and if the states are of roughly equal size, not only will the security dilemma cease to inhibit status-quo states from cooperating, but aggression will be next to impossible, thus rendering international anarchy relatively unimportant. If states cannot conquer each other, then the lack of sovereignty, although it presents problems of collective goods in a number of areas, no longer forces states to devote their primary attention to self-preservation. Although, if force were not usable, there would be fewer restraints on the use of nonmilitary instruments, these are rarely powerful enough to threaten the vital interests of a major state.

Two questions of the offense-defense balance can be separated. First, does the state have to spend more or less than one dollar on defensive forces to offset each dollar spent by the other side on forces that could be used to attack? If the state has one dollar to spend on increasing its security, should it put it into offensive or defensive forces? Second, with a given inventory of forces, is it better to attack or to defend? Is there an incentive to strike first or to absorb the other's blow? These two aspects are often linked: If each dollar spent on offense can overcome each dollar spent on defense, and if both sides have the same defense budgets, then both are likely to build offensive forces and find it attractive to attack rather than to wait for the adversary to strike.

These aspects affect the security dilemma in different ways. The first has its greatest impact on arms races. If the defense has the advantage, and if the status-quo powers have reasonable subjective security requirements, they can probably avoid an arms race. Although an increase in one side's arms and security will still decrease the other's security, the former's increase will be larger than the latter's decrease. So if one side increases its arms, the other can bring its security back up to its previous level by adding a smaller amount to its forces. And if the first side reacts to this change, its increase will also be smaller than the stimulus that produced it. Thus a stable equilibrium will be reached. Shifting from dynamics to statics, each side can be quite secure with forces roughly equal to those of the other. Indeed, if the defense is much more potent than the offense, each side can be willing to have forces much smaller than the other's, and can be indifferent to a wide range of the other's defense policies.

The second aspect—whether it is better to attack or to defend—influences short-run stability. When the offense has the advantage, a state's reaction to international tension will increase the chances of war. The incentives for preemption and the "reciprocal fear of surprise attack" in this situation have been made clear by analyses of the dangers that exist when two countries have first-strike capabilities.[2] There is no way for the state to increase its security without menacing, or even attacking, the other. Even Bismarck, who once called preventive war "committing suicide from fear of death," said that "no government, if it regards war as inevitable even if it does not want it, would be so foolish as to leave to the enemy the choice of time and occasion and to wait for the moment which is most convenient for the enemy."[3] In another arena, the same dilemma applies to the policeman in a dark alley confronting a suspected criminal who appears to be holding a weapon. Though racism may indeed be present, the security dilemma can account for many of the tragic shootings of innocent people in the ghettos.

Beliefs about the course of a war in which the offense has the advantage further deepen the security dilemma. When there are incentives to strike first, a successful attack will usually so weaken the other side that victory will be relatively quick, bloodless, and decisive. It is in these periods when conquest is possible and attractive that states consolidate power internally—for instance, by destroying the feudal barons—and expand externally. There are several consequences that decrease the chance of cooperation among status-quo states. First, war will be profitable for the winner. The costs will be low and the benefits high. Of course, losers will suffer; the fear of losing could induce states to try to form stable cooperative arrangements, but the temptation of victory will make this particularly difficult. Second, because wars are expected to be both frequent and short, there will be incentives for high levels of arms, and quick and strong reaction to the other's increases in arms. The state cannot afford to wait until there is unambiguous evidence that the other is building new weapons. Even large states that have faith in their economic strength cannot wait, because the war will be over before their products can reach the army. Third, when wars are quick, states will have to recruit allies in advance.[4] Without the opportunity for bargaining and realignments during the opening stages of hostilities, peacetime diplomacy loses a degree of the fluidity that facilitates balance-of-power policies. Because alliances must be secured during peacetime, the international system is more likely to become bipolar. It is hard to say whether war therefore becomes more or less likely, but this bipolarity increases tension between the two camps and makes it harder for status-quo states to gain the benefits of cooperation. Fourth, if wars are frequent, statesmen's perceptual thresholds will be adjusted accordingly and they will be quick to perceive ambiguous evidence as indicating that others are aggressive. Thus, there will be more cases of status-quo powers arming against each other in the incorrect belief that the other is hostile.

When the defense has the advantage, all the foregoing is reversed. The state that fears attack does not preempt—since that would be a wasteful use of its military resources—but rather prepares to receive an attack. Doing so does not decrease the security of others, and several states can do it simultaneously; the situation will therefore be stable, and status-quo powers will be able to cooperate. When Herman Kahn argues that ultimatums "are vastly too dangerous to give because . . . they are quite likely to touch off a pre-emptive strike,"[5] he incorrectly assumes that it is always advantageous to strike first.

More is involved than short-run dynamics. When the defense is dominant, wars are likely to become stalemates and can be won only at enormous cost. Relatively small and weak states can hold off larger and stronger ones, or can deter attack by raising the costs of conquest to an unacceptable level. States then approach equality in what they can do to each other. Like the .45-caliber pistol in the American West, fortifications were the "great equalizer" in some periods. Changes in the status quo are less frequent and cooperation is more common wherever the security dilemma is thereby reduced.

Many of these arguments can be illustrated by the major powers' policies in the periods preceding the two world wars. Bismarck's wars surprised statesmen by showing that the offense had the advantage, and by being quick, relatively cheap, and quite decisive. Falling into a common error, observers projected this pattern into the future.[6] The resulting expectations had several effects. First, states sought semi-permanent allies. In the early stages of the Franco-Prussian War, Napoleon III had thought that there would be plenty of time to recruit Austria to his side. Now, others were not going to repeat this mistake. Second, defense budgets were high and reacted quite sharply to increases on the other side. It is not surprising that Richardson's theory of arms races fits this period well. Third, most decision makers thought that the next European war would not cost much blood and treasure.[7] That is one reason why war was generally seen as inevitable and why mass opinion was so bellicose. Fourth, once war seemed likely, there were strong pressures to preempt. Both sides believed that whoever moved first could penetrate the other deep enough to disrupt mobilization and thus gain an insurmountable advantage. (There was no such belief about the use of naval forces. Although Churchill made an ill-advised speech saying that if German ships "do not come out and fight in time of war they will be dug out like rats in a hole,"[8] everyone knew that submarines, mines, and coastal fortifications made this impossible. So at the start of the war each navy prepared to defend itself rather than attack, and the short-run destabilizing forces that launched the armies toward teach other did not operate.)[9] Furthermore, each side knew that the other saw the situation the same way, thus increasing the perceived danger that the other would attack, and giving each added reasons to precipitate a war if conditions seemed favorable. In the long and the short run, there were thus both offensive and defensive incentives to strike. This situation casts light on the common question about German motives in 1914: "Did Germany unleash the war deliberately to become a world power or did she support Austria merely to defend a weakening ally," thereby protecting her own position?[10] To some extent, this question is misleading. Because of the perceived advantage of the offense, war was seen as the best route both to gaining expansion and to avoiding drastic loss of influence. There seemed to be no way for Germany merely to retain and safeguard her existing position.

Of course the war showed these beliefs to have been wrong on all points. Trenches and machine guns gave the defense an overwhelming advantage. The fighting became deadlocked and produced horrendous casualties. It made no sense for the combatants to bleed themselves to death. If they had known the power of the defense beforehand, they would have rushed for their own trenches rather than for the enemy's territory. Each side could have done this without increasing the other's incentives to strike. War might have broken out anyway; but at least the pressures of time and the fear of allowing the other to get the first blow would not have contributed to this end. And, had both sides known the costs of the war, they would have negotiated much more seriously. The obvious question is why the states did not seek a negotiated settlement as soon as the shape of the war became clear. Schlieffen had said that if his plan failed, peace should be sought.[11] The answer is complex, uncertain, and largely outside of the scope of our concerns. But part of the reason was the hope and sometimes the expectation that breakthroughs could be made and the dominance of the offensive restored. Without that hope, the political and psychological pressures to fight to a decisive victory might have been overcome.

The politics of the interwar period were shaped by the memories of the previous conflict and the belief that any future war would resemble it. Political and military lessons reinforced each other in ameliorating the security dilemma. Because it was believed that the First World War had been a mistake that could have been avoided by skillful conciliation, both Britain and, to a lesser extent, France were highly sensitive to the possibility that interwar Germany was not a real threat to peace, and alert to the danger that reacting quickly and strongly to her arms could create unnecessary conflict. And because Britain and France expected the defense to continue to dominate, they concluded that it was safe to adopt a more relaxed and nonthreatening military posture.[12] Britain also felt less need to maintain tight alliance bonds. The Allies' military posture then constituted only a slight danger to Germany; had the latter been content with the status quo, it would have been easy for both sides to have felt secure behind their lines of forticiations. Of course the Germans were not content, so it is not surprising that they devoted their money and attention to finding ways out of a defense-dominated stalemate. *Blitzkrieg* tactics were necessary if they were to use force to change the status quo.

The initial stages of the war on the Western Front also contrasted with the First World War. Only with the new air arm were there any incentives to strike first, and these forces were too weak to carry out the grandiose plans that had been both dreamed and feared. The armies, still the main instrument, rushed to defensive positions. Perhaps the allies could have successfully attacked while the Germans were occupied in Poland.[13] But belief in the defense was so great that this was never seriously contemplated. Three months after the start of the war, the French Prime Minister summed up the view held by almost everyone but Hitler: on the Western Front there is "deadlock. Two Forces of equal strength and the one that attacks seeing such enormous casualties that it cannot move without endangering the continuation of the war or of the aftermath."[14] The Allies were caught in a dilemma they never fully recognized, let alone solved. On the one hand, they had very high war aims; although unconditional surrender had not yet been adopted, the British had decided from the start that the removal of Hitler was a necessary condition for peace.[15] On the other hand, there were no realistic plans or instruments for allowing the Allies to impose their will on the other side. The British Chief of the Imperial General Staff noted, "The French have no intention of carrying out an offensive for years, if at all"; the British were only slightly bolder.[16] So the Allies looked to a long war that would wear the Germans down, cause civilian suffering through shortages, and eventually undermine Hitler. There was little analysis to support this view—and indeed it probably was not supportable—but as long as the defense was dominant and the numbers on each side relatively equal, what else could the Allies do?

To summarize, the security dilemma was much less powerful after World War I than it had been before. In the later period, the expected power of the defense allowed status-quo states to pursue compatible security policies and avoid arms races. Furthermore, high tension and fear of war did not set off short-run dynamics by which each state, trying to increase its security, inadvertently acted to make war more likely. The expected high costs of war, however, led the Allies to believe that no sane German leader would run the risks entailed in an attempt to dominate the Continent, and discouraged them from risking war themselves.

Technology and Geography

Technology and geography are the two main factors that determine whether the offense or the defense has the advantage. As Brodie notes, "On the tactical level, as a rule, few physical factors favor the attacker but many favor the defender. The defender usually has the advantage of cover. He characteristically fires from behind some form of shelter while his opponent crosses open ground."[17] Anything that increases the amount of ground the attacked has to cross, or impedes his progress across it, or makes him more vulnerable while crossing, increases the advantage accruing to the defense. When states are separated by barriers that produce these effects, the security dilemma is eased, since both can have forces adequate for defense without being able to attack. Impenetrable barriers would actually prevent war; in reality, decision makers have to settle for a good deal less. Buffer zones slow the attacker's progress; they thereby give the defender time to prepare, increase problems of logistics, and reduce the number of soldiers available for the final assault. At the end of the nineteenth century, Arthur Balfour noted Afghanistan's "non-conducting" qualities. "So long as it possesses few roads, and no railroads, it will be impossible for Russia to make effective use of her great numerical superiority at any point immediately vital to the Empire." The Russians valued buffers for the same reasons; it is not surprising that when Persia was being divided into Russian and British spheres of influence some years later, the Russians sought assurances that the British would refrain from building potentially menacing railroads in their sphere. Indeed, since railroad construction radically altered the abilities of countries to defend themselves and to attack others, many diplomatic notes and much intelligence activity in the late nineteenth century centered on this subject.[18]

Oceans, large rivers, and mountain ranges serve the same function as buffer zones. Being hard to cross, they allow defense against superior numbers. The defender has merely to stay on his side of the barrier and so can utilize all the men he can bring up to it. The attacker's men, however, can cross only a few at a time, and they are very vulnerable when doing so. If all states were self-sufficient islands, anarchy would be much less of a problem. A small investment in shore defenses and a small army would be sufficient to repel invasion. Only very weak states would be vulnerable, and only very large ones could menace others. As noted above, the United States, and to a lesser extent Great Britain, have partly been able to escape from the state of nature because their geographical positions approximated this ideal.

Although geography cannot be changed to conform to borders, borders can and do change to conform to geography. Borders across which an attack is easy tend to be unstable. States living within them are likely to expand or be absorbed. Frequent wars are almost inevitable since attacking will often seem the best way to protect what one has. This process will stop, or at least slow down, when the state's borders reach—by expansion or contraction—a line of natural obstacles. Security without attack will then be possible. Furthermore, these lines constitute salient solutions to bargaining problems and, to the extent that they are barriers to migration, are likely to divide ethnic groups, thereby raising the costs and lowering the incentives for conquest.

Attachment to one's state and its land reinforce one quasi-geographical aid to the defense. Conquest usually becomes more difficult the deeper the attacker pushes into the other's territory. Nationalism spurs the defenders to fight harder; advancing not only lengthens the attacker's supply lines, but takes him through unfamiliar and often devastated lands that require troops for garrison duty. These stabilizing dynamics will not operate, however, if the defender's war matériel is situated near its borders, or if the people do not care about their state, but only about being on the winning side. In such cases, positive feedback will be at work and initial defeats will be insurmountable.[19]

Imitating geography, men have tried to create barriers. Treaties may provide for demilitarized zones on both sides of the border, although such zones will rarely be deep enough to provide more than warning. Even this was not possible in Europe, but the Russians adopted a gauge for their railroads that was broader than that of the neighboring states, thereby complicating the logistics problems of any attacker—including Russia.

Perhaps the most ambitious and at least temporarily successful attempts to construct a system that would aid the defenses of both sides were the interwar naval treaties, as they affected Japanese-American relations. As mentioned earlier, the problem was that the United States could not defend the Philippines without denying Japan the ability to protect her home islands.[20] (In 1941 this dilemma became insoluble when Japan sought to extend her control to Malaya and the Dutch East Indies. If the Philippines had been invulnerable, they could have provided a secure base from which the United States could interdict Japanese shipping between the homeland and the areas she was trying to conquer.) In the 1920s and early 1930s each side would have been willing to grant the other security for its possessions in return for a reciprocal grant, and the

Washington Naval Conference agreements we designed to approach this goal. As a Japanese diplomat later put it, their country's "fundamental principle" was to have "a strength insufficient for attack and adequate for defense."[21] Thus Japan agreed in 1922 to accept a navy only three-fifths as large as that of the United States, and the United States agreed not to fortify its Pacific islands.[22] (Japan had earlier been forced to agree not to fortify the islands she had taken from Germany in World War I.) Japan's navy would not be large enough to defeat America's anywhere other than close to the home islands. Although the Japanese could still take the Philippines, not only would they be unable to move farther, but they might be weakened enough by their efforts to be vulnerable to counterattack. Japan, however, gained security. An American attack was rendered more difficult because the American bases were unprotected and because, until 1930, Japan was allowed unlimited numbers of cruisers, destroyers, and submarines that could weaken the American fleet as it made its way across the ocean.[23]

The other major determinant of the offense-defense balance is technology. When weapons are highly vulnerable, they must be employed before they are attacked. Others can remain quite invulnerable in their bases. The former characteristics are embodied in unprotected missiles and many kinds of bombers. (It should be noted that it is not vulnerability *per se* that is crucial, but the location of the vulnerability. Bombers and missiles that are easy to destroy only after having been launched toward their targets do not create destabilizing dynamics.) Incentives to strike first are usually absent for naval forces that are threatened by a naval attack. Like missiles in hardened silos, they are usually well protected when in their bases. Both sides can then simultaneously be prepared to defend themselves successfully.

In ground warfare under some conditions, forts, trenches, and small groups of men in prepared positions can hold off large numbers of attackers. Less frequently, a few attackers can storm the defenses. By and large, it is a contest between fortifications and supporting light weapons on the one hand, and mobility and heavier weapons that clear the way for the attack on the other. As the erroneous views held before the two world wars show, there is no simple way to determine which is dominant. "[T]hese oscillations are not smooth and predictable like those of a swinging pendulum. They are uneven in both extent and time. Some occur in the course of a single battle or campaign, others in the course of a war, still others during a series of wars." Longer-term oscillations can also be detected:

> The early Gothic age, from the twelfth to the late thirteenth century, with its wonderful cathedrals and fortified places, was a period during which the attackers in Europe generally met serious and increasing difficulties, because the improvement in the strength of fortresses outran the advance in the power of destruction. Later, with the spread of firearms at the end of the fifteenth century, old fortresses lost their power to resist. An age ensued during which the offense possessed, apart from short-term setbacks, new advantages. Then, during the seventeenth century, especially after about 1660, and until at least the outbreak of the War of the Austrian Succession in 1740, the defense regained much of the ground it had lost since the

great medieval fortresses had proved unable to meet the bombardment of the new and more numerous artillery.[24]

Another scholar has continued the argument: "The offensive gained an advantage with new forms of heavy mobile artillery in the nineteenth century, but the stalemate of World War I created the impression that the defense again had an advantage; the German invasion in World War II, however, indicated the offensive superiority of highly mechanized armies in the field."[25]

The situation today with respect to conventional weapons is unclear. Until recently it was believed that tanks and tactical air power gave the attacker an advantage. The initial analyses of the 1973 Arab-Israeli war indicated that new anti-tank and anti-aircraft weapons have restored the primacy of the defense. These weapons are cheap, easy to use, and can destroy a high proportion of the attacking vehicles and planes that are sighted. It then would make sense for a status-quo power to buy lots of $20,000 missiles rather than buy a few half-million dollar fighter-bombers. Defense would be possible even against a large and well-equipped force; states that care primarily about self-protection would not need to engage in arms races. But further examinations of the new technologies and the history of the October War cast doubt on these optimistic conclusions and leave us unable to render any firm judgment.[26]

Concerning nuclear weapons, it is generally agreed that defense is impossible—a triumph not of the offense, but of deterrence. Attack makes no sense, not because it can be beaten off, but because the attacker will be destroyed in turn. In terms of the questions under consideration here, the result is the equivalent of the primacy of the defense. First, security is relatively cheap. Less than one percent of the G.N.P. is devoted to deterring a direct attack on the United States; most of it is spent on acquiring redundant systems to provide a lot of insurance against the worst conceivable contingencies. Second, both sides can simultaneously gain security in the form of second-strike capability. Third, and related to the foregoing, second-strike capability can be maintained in the face of wide variations in the other side's military posture. There is no purely military reason why each side has to react quickly and strongly to the other's increases in arms. Any spending that the other devotes to trying to achieve first-strike capability can be neutralized by the state's spending much smaller sums on protecting its second-strike capability. Fourth, there are no incentives to strike first in a crisis.

Important problems remain, of course. Both sides have interests that go well beyond defense of the homeland. The protection of these interests creates conflicts even if neither side desires expansion. Furthermore, the shift from defense to deterrence has greatly increased the importance and perceptions of resolve. Security now rests on each side's belief that the other would prefer to run high risks of total destruction rather than sacrifice its vital interests. Aspects of the security dilemma thus appear in a new form. Are weapons procurements used as an index of resolve? Must they be so used? If one side fails to respond to the other's buildup, will it appear weak and thereby invite predation? Can both sides simultaneously have images of high resolve or is there a zero-sum element involved? Although these problems are real, they are not as severe as those in the prenuclear era: There are many indices of resolve, and states do not so much judge images of resolve in the abstract as ask how likely it is that the other will stand firm in a particular dispute. Since states are most likely to stand firm on matters which concern them most, it is quite possible for both to demonstrate their resolve to protect their own security simultaneously.

OFFENSE-DEFENSE DIFFERENTIATION

The other major variable that affects how strongly the security dilemma operates is whether weapons and policies that protect the state also provide the capability for attack. If they do not, the basic postulate of the security dilemma no longer applies. A state can increase its own security without decreasing that of others. The advantage of the defense can only ameliorate the security dilemma. A differentiation between offensive and defensive stances comes close to abolishing it. Such differentiation does not mean, however, that all security problems will be abolished. If the offense has the advantage, conquest and aggression will still be possible. And if the offense's advantage is great enough, status-quo powers may find it too expensive to protect themselves by defensive forces and decide to procure offensive weapons even though this will menace others. Furthermore, states will still have to worry that even if the other's military posture shows that it is peaceful now, it may develop aggressive intentions in the future.

Assuming that the defense is at least as potent as the offense, the differentiation between them allows status-quo states to behave in ways that are clearly different from those of aggressors. Three beneficial consequences follow. First, status-quo powers can identify each other, thus laying the foundations for cooperation. Conflicts growing out of the mistaken belief that the other side is expansionist will be less frequent. Second, status-quo states will obtain advance warning when others plan aggression. Before a state can attack, it has to develop and deploy offensive weapons. If procurement of these weapons cannot be disguised and takes a fair amount of time, as it almost always does, a status-quo state will have the time to take countermeasures. It need not maintain a high level of defensive arms as long as its potential adversaries are adopting a peaceful posture. (Although being so armed should not, with the one important exception noted below, alarm other status-quo powers.) States do, in fact, pay special attention to actions that they believe would not be taken by a status-quo state because they feel that states exhibiting such behavior are aggressive. Thus the seizure or development of transportation facilities will alarm others more if these facilities have no commercial value, and therefore can only be wanted for military reasons. In 1906, the British rejected a Russian protest about their activities in a district of Persia by claiming that this area was "only of [strategic] importance [to the Russians] if they wished to attack the Indian frontier, or to put pressure upon us by making us think that they intend to attack it."[27]

The same inferences are drawn when a state acquires more weapons than observers feel are needed for defense. Thus, the Japanese spokesman at the 1930 London naval conference said that his country was alarmed by the American refusal to give Japan a 70 percent ratio (in place of a 60 percent ratio) in heavy cruisers: "As long as America held that ten percent advantage, it was possible for her to attack. So when America insisted on sixty percent instead of seventy percent, the idea would exist that they were trying to keep that possibility, and the Japanese people could not accept that."[28] Similarly, when Mussolini told Chamberlain in January 1939 that Hitler's arms program was motivated by defensive considerations, the Prime Minister replied that "German military forces were now so strong as to make it impossible for any Power or combination of Powers to attack her successfully. She could not want any further armaments for defensive purposes; what then did she want them for?"[29]

Of course these inferences can be wrong—as they are especially likely to be because states underestimate the degree to which they menace others.[30] And when they are wrong, the security dilemma is deepened. Because the state thinks it has received notice that the other is aggressive, its own arms building will be less restrained and the chances of cooperation will be decreased. But the dangers of incorrect inferences should not obscure the main point: When offensive and defensive postures are different, much of the uncertainty about the other's intentions that contributes to the security dilemma is removed.

The third beneficial consequence of a difference between offensive and defensive weapons is that if all states support the status quo, an obvious arms control agreement is a ban on weapons that are useful for attacking. As President Roosevelt put it in his message to the Geneva Disarmament Conference in 1933: "If all nations will agree wholly to eliminate from possession and use the weapons which make possible a successful attack, defenses automatically will become impregnable, and the frontiers and independence of every nation will become secure."[31] The fact that such treaties have been rare—the Washington naval agreements discussed above and the anti-ABM treaty can be cited as examples—shows either that states are not always willing to guarantee the security of others, or that it is hard to distinguish offensive from defensive weapons. .

Is such a distinction possible? Salvador de Madariaga, the Spanish statesman active in the disarmament negotiations of the interwar years, thought not: "A weapon is either offensive or defensive according to which end of it you are looking at." The French Foreign Minister agreed (although French policy did not always follow this view): "Every arm can be employed offensively or defensively in turn. . . . The only way to discover whether arms are intended for purely defensive purposes or are held in a spirit of aggression is in all cases to enquire into the intentions of the country concerned." Some evidence for the validity of this argument is provided by the fact that much time in these unsuccessful negotiations was devoted to separating offensive from defensive weapons. Indeed, no simple and unambiguous definition is possible and in many cases no judgment can be reached. Before the American entry into World War I, Woodrow Wilson wanted to arm merchantmen only with guns in the back of the ship so they could not initiate a fight, but this expedient cannot be applied to more common forms of armaments.[32]

There are several problems. Even when a differentiation is possible, a status-quo power will want offensive arms under any of three conditions: (1) If the offense has a great advantage over the defense, protection through defensive forces will be too expensive. (2) Status-quo states may need offensive weapons to regain territory lost in the opening stages of war. It might be possible, however, for a state to wait to procure these weapons until war seems likely, and they might be needed only in relatively small numbers, unless the aggressor was able to construct strong defenses quickly in the occupied areas. (3) The state may feel that it must be prepared to take the offensive either because the other side will make peace only if it loses territory or because the state has commitments to attack if the other makes war on a third party. As noted above, status-quo states with extensive commitments are often forced to behave like aggressors. Even when they lack such commitments, status-quo states must worry about the possibility that if they are able to hold off an attack, they will still not be able to end the war unless they move into the other's territory to damage its military forces and inflict pain. Many American naval officers after the Civil War, for example, believed that "only by destroying the commerce of the opponent could the United States bring him to terms."[33]

A further complication is introduced by the fact that aggressors as well as status-quo powers require defensive forces as a prelude to acquiring offensive ones, to protect one frontier while attacking another, or for insurance in case the war goes badly. Criminals as well as policemen can use bulletproof vests. Hitler as well as Maginot built a line of forts. Indeed, Churchill reports that in 1936 the German Foreign Minister said: "As soon as our fortifications are constructed [on our western borders] and the countries in Central Europe realize that France cannot enter German territory, all these countries will begin to feel very differently about their foreign policies, and a new constellation will develop."[34] So a state may not necessarily be reassured if its neighbor constructs strong defenses.

More central difficulties are created by the fact that whether a weapon is offensive or defensive often depends on the particular situation—for instance, the geographical setting and the way in which the weapon is used. "Tanks . . . spearheaded the fateful German thrust through the Ardennes in 1940, but if the French had disposed of a properly concentrated armored reserve, it would have provided the best means for their cutting off the penetration and turning into a disaster for the Germans what became instead an overwhelming victory."[35] Anti-aircraft weapons seem obviously defensive—to be used, they must wait for the other side to come to them. But the Egyptian attack on Israel in 1973 would have been impossible without effective air defenses that covered the battlefield. Nevertheless, some distinctions are possible. Sir John Simon, then the British Foreign Secretary, in response to the views cited earlier, stated that just because a fine line could not be drawn, "that was no reason for saying that there were not stretches of territory on either side which all practical men and women knew to be well on this or that side of the line." Although there are almost no weapons and strategies that are useful only for attacking, there are some that are almost exclusively defensive. Aggressors could want them for protection, but a state that relied mostly on them could not menace others. More frequently, we cannot "determine the absolute character of a weapon, but [we can] make a comparison . . . [and] discover whether or not the offensive potentialities predominate, whether a weapon is more useful in attack or in defense."[36]

The essence of defense is keeping the other side out of your territory. A purely defensive weapon is one that can do this wihout being able to penetrate the enemy's land. Thus a committee of military experts in an interwar disarmament conference declared that armaments "incapable of mobility by means of self-contained power," or movable only after long delay, were "only capable of being used for the defense of a State's territory."[37] The most obvious examples are fortifications. They can shelter attacking forces, especially when they are built right along the frontier,[38] but they cannot occupy enemy territory. A state with only a strong line of forts, fixed guns, and a small army to man them would not be much of a menace. Anything else that can serve only as a barrier against attacking troops is similarly defensive. In this category are systems that provide warning of an attack, the Russian's adoption of a different railroad gauge, and nuclear land mines that can seal off invasion routes.

If total immobility clearly defines a system that is defensive only, limited mobility is unfortunately ambiguous. As noted above, short-range fighter aircraft and anti-aircraft missiles can be used to cover an attack. And, unlike forts, they can advance with the troops. Still, their inability to reach deep into enemy territory does make them more useful for the defense than for the offense. Thus, the United States and Israel would have been more alarmed in the early 1970s had the Russians provided the Egyptians with long-range instead of short-range aircraft. Naval forces are particularly difficult to classify in these terms, but those that are very short-legged can be used only for coastal defense.

Any forces that for various reasons fight well only when on their own soil in effect lack mobility and therefore are defensive. The most extreme example would be passive resistance. Noncooperation can thwart an aggressor, but it is very hard for large numbers of people to cross the border and stage a sit-in on another's territory. Morocco's recent march on the Spanish Sahara approached this tactic, but its success depended on special circumstances. Similarly, guerrilla warfare is defensive to the extent to which it requires civilian support that is likely to be forthcoming only in opposition to a foreign invasion. Indeed, if guerrilla warfare were easily exportable and if it took ten defenders to destroy each guerrilla, then this weapon would not only be one which could be used as easily to attack the other's territory as to defend one's own, but one in which the offense had the advantage: so the security dilemma would operate especially strongly.

If guerrillas are unable to fight on foreign soil, other kinds of armies may be unwilling to do so. An army imbued with the idea that only defensive wars were just would fight less effectively, if at all, if the goal were conquest. Citizen militias may lack both the ability and the will for aggression. The weapons employed, the short term of service, the time required for mobilization, and the spirit of repelling attacks on the homeland, all lend themselves much more to defense than to attacks on foreign territory.[39]

Less idealistic motives can produce the same result. A leading student of medieval warfare has described the armies of that period as follows: "Assembled with difficulty, insubordinate, unable to maneuver, ready to melt away from its standard the moment that its short period of service was over, a feudal force presented an assemblage of unsoldierlike qualities such as have seldom been known to coexist. Primarily intended to defend its own borders from the Magyar, the Northman, or the Saracen . . . , the institution was utterly un-adapted to take the offensive."[40] Some political groupings can be similarly described. International coalitions are more readily held together by fear than by hope of gain. Thus Castlereagh was not being entirely self-serving when in 1816 he argued that the Quadruple Alliance "could only have owed its origin to a sense of common danger; in its very nature it must be conservative; it cannot threaten either the security or the liberties of other States."[41] It is no accident that most of the major campaigns of expansion have been waged by one domi-nant nation (for example, Napoleon's France and Hitler's Germany), and that coalitions among relative equals are usually found defending the status quo. Most gains from conquest are too uncertain and raise too many questions of future squabbles among the victors to hold an alliance together for long. Al-though defensive coalitions are by no means easy to maintain—conflicting na-tional objectives and the free-rider problem partly explain why three of them dissolved before Napoleon was defeated—the common interest of seeing that no state dominates provides a strong incentive for solidarity.

Weapons that are particularly effective in reducing fortifications and barri-ers are of great value to the offense. This is not to deny that a defensive power will want some of those weapons if the other side has them: Brodie is certainly correct to argue that while their tanks allowed the Germans to conquer France, properly used French tanks could have halted the attack. But France would not have needed these weapons if Germany had not acquired them, whereas even if France had no tanks, Germany could not have foregone them since they pro-vided the only chance of breaking through the French lines. Mobile heavy artillery is, similarly, especially useful in destroying fortifications. The defender, while needing artillery to fight off attacking troops or to counterattack, can usually use lighter guns since they do not need to penetrate such massive obstacles. So it is not surprising that one of the few things that most nations at the interwar disarmament conferences were able to agree on was that heavy tanks and mobile heavy guns were particularly valuable to a state planning an attack.[42]

Weapons and strategies that depend for their effectiveness on surprise are almost always offensive. That fact was recognized by some of the delegates to the interwar disarmament conferences and is the principle behind the common national ban on concealed weapons. An earlier representative of this widespread view was the mid-nineteenth-century Philadelphia newspaper that argued: "As a measure of defense, knives, dirks, and sword canes are entirely useless. They are fit only for attack, and all such attacks are of murderous character. Whoever carries such a weapon has prepared himself for homicide."[43]

It is, of course, not always possible to distinguish between forces that are most effective for holding territory and forces optimally designed for taking it. Such a distinction could not have been made for the strategies and weapons in Europe during most of the period between the Franco-Prussian War and World War I. Neither naval forces nor tactical air forces can be readily classified in these terms. But the point here is that when such a distinction is possible, the central characteristic of the security dilemma no longer holds, and one of the most troublesome consequences of anarchy is removed.

Offense-Defense Differentiation and Strategic Nuclear Weapons

In the interwar period, most statesmen held the reasonable position that weapons that threatened civilians were offensive.[44] But when neither side can protect its civilians, a counter-city posture is defensive because the state can credibly threaten to retaliate only in response to an attack on itself or its closest allies. The costs of this strike are so high that the state could not threaten to use it for the less-than-vital interest of compelling the other to abandon an established position.

In the context of deterrence, offensive weapons are those that provide defense. In the now familiar reversal of common sense, the state that could take its population out of hostage, either by active or passive defense or by destroying the other's strategic weapons on the ground, would be able to alter the status quo. The desire to prevent such a situation was one of the rationales for the anti-ABM agreements; it explains why some arms controllers opposed building ABMs to protect cities, but favored sites that covered ICBM fields. Similarly, many analysts want to limit warhead accuracy and favor multiple re-entry vehicles (MRVs), but oppose multiple independently targetable re-entry vehicles (MIRVs). The former are more useful than single warheads for penetrating city defenses, and ensure that the state has a second-strike capability. MIRVs enhance counterforce capabilities. Some arms controllers argue that this is also true of cruise missiles, and therefore do not want them to be deployed either. There is some evidence that the Russians are not satisfied with deterrence and are seeking to regain the capability for defense. Such an effort, even if not inspired by aggressive designs, would create a severe security dilemma.

What is most important for the argument here is that land-based ICBMs are both offensive and defensive, but when both sides rely on Polaris-type systems (SLBMs), offense and defense use different weapons. ICBMs can be used either to destroy the other's cities in retaliation or to initiate hostilities by attacking the other's strategic missiles. Some measures—for instance, hardening of missile sites and warning systems—are purely defensive, since they do not make a first strike easier. Others are predominantly offensive—for instance, passive or active city defenses, and highly accurate warheads. But ICBMs themselves are useful for both purposes. And because states seek a high level of insurance, the desire for protection as well as the contemplation of a counterforce strike can explain the acquisition of extremely large numbers of missiles. So it is very difficult to infer the other's intentions from its military posture. Each side's efforts to increase its own security by procuring more missiles decreases, to an extent determined by the relative efficacy of the offense and the defense, the other side's security. That is not the case when both sides use SLBMs. The point is not that sea-based systems are less vulnerable than land-based ones (this bears on the offense-defense ratio) but that SLBMs are defensive, retaliatory weapons. First, they are probably not accurate enough to destroy many military targets.[45] Second, and more important, SLBMs are not the main instrument of attack against other SLBMs. The hardest problem confronting a state that wants to take its cities out of hostage is to locate the other's SLBMs, a job that requires not SLBMs but anti-submarine weapons. A state might use SLBMs to attack the other's submarines (although other weapons would probably be more efficient), but without anti-submarine warfare (ASW) capability the task cannot be performed. A status-quo state that wanted to forego offensive capability could simply forego ASW research and procurement.

There are two difficulties with this argument, however. First, since the state's SLBMs are potentially threatened by the other's ASW capabilities, the state may want to pursue ASW research in order to know what the other might be able to do and to design defenses. Unless it does this, it cannot be confident that its submarines are safe. Second, because some submarines are designed to attack surface ships, not launch missiles, ASW forces have missions other than taking cities out of hostage. Some U.S. officials plan for a long war in Europe, which would require keeping the sea lanes open against Russian submarines. Designing an ASW force and strategy that would meet this threat without endangering Soviet SLBMs would be difficult but not impossible, since the two missions are somewhat different.[46] Furthermore, the Russians do not need ASW forces to combat submarines carrying out conventional missions; it might be in America's interest to sacrifice the ability to meet a threat that is not likely to materialize in order to reassure the Russians that we are not menacing their retaliatory capability.

When both sides rely on ICBMs, one side's missiles can attack the other's, and so the state cannot be indifferent to the other's building program. But because one side's SLBMs do not menace the other's, each side can build as many as it wants and the other need not respond. Each side's decision on the size of its force depends on technical questions, its judgment about how much destruction is enough to deter, and the amount of insurance it is willing to pay for—and these considerations are independent of the size of the other's strategic force. Thus the crucial nexus in the arms race is severed.

Here two objections not only can be raised but have been, by those who feel that even if American second-strike capability is in no danger, the United States must respond to a Soviet buildup. First, the relative numbers of missiles and warheads may be used as an index of each side's power and will. Even if there is no military need to increase American arms as the Russians increase theirs, a failure to respond may lead third parties to think that the United States has abandoned the competition with the USSR and is no longer willing to pay the price of world leadership. Furthermore, if either side believes that nuclear "superiority" matters, then, through the bargaining logic, it will matter. The side with "superiority" will be more likely to stand firm in a confrontation if it thinks its "stronger" military position helps it, or if it thinks that the other thinks its own "weaker" military position is a handicap. To allow the other side to have more SLBMs—even if one's own second-strike capability is unimpaired—will give the other an advantage that can be translated into political gains.

The second objection is that superiority *does* matter, and not only because of mistaken beliefs. If nuclear weapons are used in an all-or-none fashion, then all that is needed is second-strike capability. But limited, gradual, and controlled strikes are possible. If the other side has superiority, it can reduce the state's forces by a slow-motion war of attrition. For the state to strike at the other's cities would invite retaliation; for it to reply with a limited counterforce attack would further deplete its supply of missiles. Alternatively, the other could employ demonstration attacks—such as taking out an isolated military base or exploding a warhead high over a city—in order to demonstrate its resolve. In either of these scenarios, the state will suffer unless it matches the other's arms posture.[47]

These two objections, if valid, mean that even with SLBMs one cannot distinguish offensive from defensive strategic nuclear weapons. Compellence may be more difficult than deterrence.[48] But if decision makers believe that numbers of missiles or of warheads influence outcomes, or if these weapons can be used in limited manner, then the posture and policy that woud be needed for self-protection is similar to that useful for aggression. If the second objection has merit, security would require the ability to hit selected targets on the other side, enough ammunition to wage a controlled counterforce war, and the willingness to absorb limited countervalue strikes. Secretary Schlesinger was correct in arguing that this capability would not constitute a first-strike capability. But because the "Schlesinger Doctrine" could be used not only to cope with a parallel Russian policy, but also to support an American attempt to change the status quo, the new American stance would decrease Russian security. Even if the USSR were reassured that the present U.S. government lacked the desire or courage to do this, there could be no guarantee that future governments would not use the new instruments for expansion. Once we move away from the simple idea that nuclear weapons can only be used for all-out strikes, half the advantage of having both sides rely on a sea-based force would disappear because of the lack of an offensive-defensive differentiation. To the extent that military policy affects political relations, it would be harder for the United States and the Soviet Union to cooperate even if both supported the status quo.

Although a full exploration of these questions is beyond the scope of this paper, it should be noted that the objections rest on decision makers' beliefs—beliefs, furthermore, that can be strongly influenced by American policy and American statements. The perceptions of third nations of whether the details of the nuclear balance affect political conflicts—and, to a lesser extent, Russian beliefs about whether superiority is meaningful—are largely derived from the

American strategic debate. If most American spokesmen were to take the position that a secure second-strike capability was sufficient and the increments over that (short of a first-strike capability) would only be a waste of money, it is doubtful whether America's allies or the neutrals would judge the superpowers' useful military might or political will by the size of their stockpiles. Although the Russians stress war-fighting ability, they have not contended that marginal increases in strategic forces bring political gains; any attempt to do so could be rendered less effective by an American assertion that this is nonsense. The bargaining advantages of possessing nuclear "superiority" work best when both sides acknowledge them. If the "weaker" side convinces the other that it does not believe there is any meaningful difference in strength, then the "stronger" side cannot safely stand firm because there is no increased chance that the other will back down.

This kind of argument applies at least as strongly to the second objection. Neither side can employ limited nuclear options unless it is quite confident that the other accepts the rules of the game. For if the other believes that nuclear war cannot be controlled, it will either refrain from responding—which would be fine—or launch all-out retaliation. Although a state might be ready to engage in limited nuclear war without acknowledging this possibility—and indeed, that would be a reasonable policy for the United States—it is not likely that the other would have sufficient faith in that prospect to initiate limited strikes unless the state had openly avowed its willingness to fight this kind of war. So the United States, by patiently and consistently explaining that it considers such ideas to be mad and that any nuclear wars will inevitably get out of control, could gain a large measure of protection against the danger that the Soviet Union might seek to employ a "Schlesinger Doctrine" against an America that lacked the military ability or political will to respond in kind. Such a position is made more convincing by the inherent implausibility of the arguments for the possibility of a limited nuclear war.

In summary, as long as states believe that all that is needed is second-strike capability, then the differentiation between offensive and defensive forces that is provided by reliance on SLBMs allows each side to increase its security without menacing the other, permits some inferences about intentions to be drawn from military posture, and removes the main incentive for status-quo powers to engage in arms races.

FOUR WORLDS

The two variables we have been discussing—whether the offense or the defense has the advantage, and whether offensive postures can be distinguished from defensive ones—can be combined to yield four possible worlds.

The first world is the worst for status-quo states. These is no way to get security without menacing others, and security through defense is terribly difficult to obtain. Because offensive and defensive postures are the same,

Table 1

	Offense has the advantage	Defense has the advantage
Offensive posture not distinguishable from defensive one	1 Doubly dangerous.	2 Security dilemma, but security requirements may be compatible.
Offensive posture distinguishable from defensive one	3 No security dilemma, but aggression possible. Status-quo states can follow different policy than aggressors. Warning given.	4 Doubly stable.

status-quo states acquire the same kind of arms that are sought by aggressors. And because the offense has the advantage over the defense, attacking is the best route to protecting what you have; status-quo states will therefore behave like aggressors. The situation will be unstable. Arms races are likely. Incentives to strike first will turn crises into wars. Decisive victories and conquests will be common. States will grow and shrink rapidly, and it will be hard for any state to maintain its size and influence without trying to increase them. Cooperation among status-quo powers will be extremely hard to achieve.

There are no cases that totally fit this picture, but it bears more than a passing resemblance to Europe before World War I. Britain and Germany, although in many respects natural allies, ended up as enemies. Of course much of the explanation lies in Germany's ill-chosen policy. And from the perspective of our theory, the powers' ability to avoid war in a series of earlier crises cannot be easily explained. Nevertheless, much of the behavior in this period was the product of technology and beliefs that magnified the security dilemma. Decision makers thought that the offense had a big advantage and saw little difference between offensive and defensive military postures. The era was characterized by arms races. And once war seemed likely, mobilization races created powerful incentives to strike first.

In the nuclear era, the first world would be one in which each side relied on vulnerable weapons that were aimed at similar forces and each side understood the situation. In this case, the incentives to strike first would be very high—so high that status-quo powers as well as aggressors would be sorely tempted to preempt. And since the forces could be used to change the status quo as well as to preserve it, there would be no way for both sides to increase their security simultaneously. Now the familiar logic of deterrence leads both sides to see the dangers in this world. Indeed, the new understanding of this situation was one reason why vulnerable bombers and missiles were replaced. Ironically, the 1950s would have been more hazardous if the decision makers had been aware of the dangers of their posture and had therefore felt greater pressure to strike first. This situation could be recreated if both sides were to rely on MIRVed ICBMs.

In the second world, the security dilemma operates because offensive and defensive postures cannot be distinguished; but it does not operate as strongly as in the first world because the defense has the advantage, and so an increment in one side's strength increases its security more than it decreases the other's. So, if both sides have reasonable subjective security requirements, are of roughly equal power, and the variables discussed earlier are favorable, it is quite likely that status-quo states can adopt compatible security policies. Although a state will not be able to judge the other's intentions from the kinds of weapons it procures, the level of arms spending will give important evidence. Of course a state that seeks a high level of arms might be not an aggressor but merely an insecure state, which if conciliated will reduce its arms, and if confronted will reply in kind. To assume that the apparently excessive level of arms indicates aggressiveness could therefore lead to a response that would deepen the dilemma and create needless conflict. But empathy and skillful statesmanship can reduce this danger. Furthermore, the advantageous position of the defense means that a status-quo state can often maintain a high degree of security with a level of arms lower than that of its expected adversary. Such a state demonstrates that it lacks the ability or desire to alter the status quo, at least at the present time. The strength of the defense also allows states to react slowly and with restraint when they fear that others are menacing them. So, although status-quo powers will to some extent be threatening to others, that extent will be limited.

This world is the one that comes closest to matching most periods in history. Attacking is usually harder than defending because of the strength of fortifications and obstacles. But purely defensive postures are rarely possible because fortifications are usually supplemented by armies and mobile guns which can support an attack. In the nuclear era, this world would be one in which both sides relied on relatively invulnerable ICBMs and believed that limited nuclear war was impossible. Assuming no MIRVs, it would take more than one attacking missile to destroy one of the adversary's. Preemption is therefore unattractive. If both sides have large inventories, they can ignore all but drastic increases on the other side. A world of either ICBMs or SLBMs in which both sides adopted the "Schlesinger Doctrine" would probably fit in this category too. The means of preserving the status quo would also be the means of changing it, as we discussed earlier. And the defense usually would have the advantage, because compellence is more difficult than deterrence. Although a state might succeed in changing the status quo on issues that matter much more to it than to others, status-quo powers could deter major provocations under most circumstances.

In the third world there may be no security dilemma, but there are security problems. Because states can procure defensive systems that do not threaten others, the dilemma need not operate. But because the offense has the advantage, aggression is possible, and perhaps easy. If the offense has less of an advantage, stability and cooperation are likely because the status-quo states will procure defensive forces. They need not react to others who are similarly armed, but can wait for the warning they would receive if others started to deploy offensive weapons. But each state will have to watch the others carefully, and there is room for false suspicions. The costliness of the defense and the allure of the offense can lead to unnecessary mistrust, hostility, and war, unless some of the variables discussed earlier are operating to restrain defection.

A hypothetical nuclear world that would fit this description would be one in which both sides relied on SLBMs, but in which ASW techniques were very effective. Offense and defense would be different, but the former would have the advantage. This situation is not likely to occur; but if it did, a status-quo state could show its lack of desire to exploit the other by refraining from threatening its submarines. The desire to have more protecting you than merely the other side's fear of retaliation is a strong one, however, and a state that knows that it would not expand even if its cities were safe is likely to believe that the other would not feel threatened by its ASW program. It is easy to see how such a world could become unstable, and how spirals of tensions and conflict could develop.

The fourth world is doubly safe. The differentiation between offensive and defensive systems permits a way out of the security dilemma; the advantage of the defense disposes of the problems discussed in the previous paragraphs. There is no reason for a status-quo power to be tempted to procure offensive forces, and aggressors give notice of their intentions by the posture they adopt. Indeed, if the advantage of the defense is great enough, there are no security problems. The loss of the ultimate form of the power to alter the status quo would allow greater scope for the exercise of nonmilitary means and probably would tend to freeze the distribution of values.

This world would have existed in the first decade of the twentieth century if the decision makers had understood the available technology. In that case, the European powers would have followed different policies both in the long run and in the summer of 1914. Even Germany, facing powerful enemies on both sides, could have made herself secure by developing strong defenses. France could also have made her frontier almost impregnable. Furthermore, when crises arose, no one would have had incentives to strike first. There would have been no competitive mobilization races reducing the time available for negotiations.

In the nuclear era, this world would be one in which the superpowers relied on SLBMs, ASW technology was not up to its task, and limited nuclear options were not taken seriously. We have discussed this situation earlier; here we need only add that, even if our analysis is correct and even if the policies and postures of both sides were to move in this direction, the problem of violence below the nuclear threshold would remain. On issues other than defense of the homeland, there would still be security dilemmas and security problems. But the world would nevertheless be safer than it has usually been.

NOTES

1. Thus, when Wolfers argues that a status-quo state that settles for rough equality of power with its adversary, rather than seeking preponderance, may be able to convince the other to reciprocate by showing that it wants only to protect itself, not menace the other, he assumes that the defense has an advantage. See Arnold Wolfers, *Discord and Collaboration* (Balitmore: Johns Hopkins Press, 1962), 126.
2. Thomas Schelling, *The Strategy of Conflict* (New York: Oxford University Press, 1963), chap. 9.
3. Quoted in Fritz Fischer, *War of Illusions* (New York: Norton, 1975), 377, 461.
4. George Quester, *Offense and Defense in the International System* (New York: John Wiley, 1977), 105.
5. Herman Kahn, *On Thermonuclear War* (Princeton: Princeton University Press, 1960), 211 (also see 144).
6. For a general discussion of such mistaken learning from the past, see Jervis, *Perception and Misperception in International Relations* (Princeton: Princeton University Press, 1976), chap. 6. The important and still not completely understood question of why this belief formed and was maintained throughout the war is examined in Bernard Brodie, *War and Politics* (New York: Macmillan, 1973), 262–70; Brodie: "Technological Change, Strategic Doctrine, and Political Outcomes," in Klaus Knorr, ed., *Historical Dimensions of National Security Problems* (Lawrence: University Press of Kansas, 1976), 290–92; and Douglas Porch, "The French Army and the Spirit of the Offensive, 1900–14," in Brian Bond and Ian Roy, eds., *War and Society* (New York: Holmes & Meier, 1975), 117–43.
7. Some were not so optimistic. Grey's remark is well-known: "The lamps are going out all over Europe; we shall not see them lit again in our life-time." The German Prime Minister, Bethmann Hollweg, also feared the consequences of the war. But the controlling view was that it would certainly pay for the winner.
8. Quoted in Martin Gilbert, *Winston S. Churchill*, III, *The Challenge of War*, 1914–1916 (Boston: Houghton Mifflin, 1971), 84.
9. Quester (fn. 4), 98–99. Robert Art, *The Influence of Foreign Policy on Seapower*, II (Beverly Hills: Sage Professional Papers in International Studies Series, 1973), 14–18, 26–28.
10. Konrad Jarausch, "The Illusion of Limited War: Chancellor Bethmann Hollweg's Calculated Risk, July 1914," *Central European History*, II (March 1969): 50.
11. Brodie, *War and Politics* (New York: Macmillan, 1973), 58.
12. President Roosevelt and the American delegates to the League of Nations Disarmament Conference maintained that the tank and the mobile heavy artillery had reestablished the dominance of the offensive, thus making disarmament more urgent (Marion Boggs, *Attempts to Define and Limit "Aggressive" Armament in Diplomacy and Strategy* [Columbia: University of Missouri Studies, XVI, no. 1, 1941]: 31, 108), but this was a minority position and may not even have been believed by the Americans. The reduced prestige and influence of the military, and the high pressures to cut government spending throughout this period also contributed to the lowering of defense budgets.
13. Jon Kimche, *The Unfought Battle* (New York: Stein, 1968); Nicholas William Bethell, *The War Hitler Won: The Fall of Poland, September 1939* (New York: Holt, 1972); Alan Alexandroff and Richard Rosecrance, "Deterrence in 1939," *World Politics*, XXIX (April 1977): 404–24.

14. Roderick Macleod and Denis Kelly, eds., *Time Unguarded: The Ironside Diaries, 1937–1940* (New York; McKay, 1962), 173.

15. For a short time, as France was falling, the British Cabinet did discuss reaching a negotiated peace with Hitler. The official history downplays this, but it is covered in P.M.H. Bell, *A Certain Eventuality* (Farnborough, England: Saxon House, 1974), 40–48.

16. Macleod and Kelly (fn. 14), 174. In flat contradiction to common sense and almost everything they believed about modern warfare, the Allies planned an expedition to Scandinavia to cut the supply of iron ore to Germany and to aid Finland against the Russians. But the dominant mood was the one described above.

17. Brodie (fn. 11), 179.

18. Arthur Balfour, "Memorandum," Committee on Imperial Defence, April 30, 1903, 2–3; see the telegrams by Sir Arthur Nicolson, in G.P. Gooch and Harold Temperley, eds., *British Documents on the Origins of the War*, vol. 4 (London: H.M.S.O., 1929): 429, 524. These barriers do not prevent the passage of long-range aircraft; but even in the air, distance usually aids the defender.

19. See, for example, the discussion of warfare among Chinese warlords in Hsi-Sheng Chi, "The Chinese Warlord System as an International System," in Morton Kaplan, ed., *New Approaches to International Relations* (New York: St. Martin's, 1968), 405–25.

20. Some American decision makers, including military officers, thought that the best way out of the dilemma was to abandon the Philippines.

21. Quoted in Elting Morrison, *Turmoil and Tradition: A Study of the Life and Times of Henry L. Stimson* (Boston: Houghton Mifflin, 1960), 326.

22. The U.S. "refused to consider limitations on Hawaiian defenses, since these works posed no threat to Japan." William Braisted, *The United States Navy in the Pacific, 1909–1922* (Austin: University of Texas Press, 1971), 612.

23. That is part of the reason why the Japanese admirals strongly objected when the civilian leaders decided to accept a seven-to-ten ratio in lighter craft in 1930. Stephen Pelz, *Race to Pearl Harbor* (Cambridge: Harvard University Press, 1974), 3.

24. John Nef, *War and Human Progress* (New York: Norton, 1963), 185. Also see ibid., 237, 242–43, and 323; C. W. Oman, *The Art of War in the Middle Ages* (Ithaca, N.Y.: Cornell University Press, 1953), 70–72; John Beeler, *Warfare in Feudal Europe, 730–1200* (Ithaca, N.Y.: Cornell University Press, 1971), 212–14; Michael Howard, *War in European History* (London: Oxford University Press 1976), 33–37.

25. Quincy Wright, *A Study of War* (abridged ed.; Chicago: University of Chicago Press, 1964), 142. Also see 63–70, 74–75. There are important exceptions to these generalizations—the American Civil War, for instance, falls in the middle of the period Wright says is dominated by the offense.

26. Geoffrey Kemp, Robert Pfaltzgraff, and Uri Ra'anan, eds., *The Other Arms Race* (Lexington, Mass.: D.C. Heath, 1975); James Foster, "The Future of Conventional Arms Control," *Policy Sciences*, no. 8 (Spring 1977): 1–19.

27. Richard Challener, *Admirals, Generals, and American Foreign Policy, 1898–1914* (Princeton: Princeton University Press, 1973); Grey to Nicolson, in Gooch and Temperley (fn. 18), 414.

28. Quoted in James Crowley, *Japan's Quest for Autonomy* (Princeton: Princeton University Press, 1966), 49. American naval officers agree with the Japanese that a ten-to-six ratio would endanger Japan's supremacy in her home waters.

29. E.L. Woodward and R. Butler, ed., *Documents on British Foreign Policy, 1919–1939*. 3d ser. III (London: H.M.S.O., 1950): 526.

30. Jervin (fn. 6), 69–72, 352–55.
31. Quoted in Merze Tate, *The United States and Armaments* (Cambridge: Harvard University Press, 1948), 108.
32. Boggs (fn. 12), 15, 40.
33. Kenneth Hagan, *American Gunboat Diplomacy and the Old Navy, 1877–1899* (Westport, Conn.: Greenwood Press, 1973), 20.
34. Winston Churchill, *The Gathering Storm* (Boston: Houghton, 1948), 206.
35. Brodie, *War and Politics* (fn. 6), 325.
36. Boggs (fn. 12), 42, 83. For a good argument about the possible differentiation between offensive and defensive weapons in the 1930s, see Basil Liddell Hart, "Aggression and the Problem of Weapons," *English Review*, 55 (July 1932): 71–78.
37. Quoted in Boggs (fn. 12), 39.
38. On these grounds, the Germans claimed in 1932 that the French forts were offensive (ibid., 49). Similarly, fortified forward naval bases can be necessary for launching an attack; see Braisted (fn. 22), 643.
39. The French made this argument in the interwar period; see Richard Challener, *The French Theory of the Nation in Arms* (New York: Columbia University Press, 1955), 181–82. The Germans disagreed; see Boggs (fn. 12), 44–45.
40. Oman (fn. 24), 57–58.
41. Quoted in Charles Webster, *The Foreign Policy of Castlereagh, II, 1815–1822* (London: G. Bell and Sons, 1963), 510.
42. Boggs (fn. 12), 14–15, 47–48, 60.
43. Quoted in Philip Jordan, *Frontier Law and Order* (Lincoln: University of Nebraska Press, 1970), 7; also see 16–17.
44. Boggs (fn. 12), 20, 28.
45. See, however, Desmond Ball, "The Counterforce Potential of American SLBM Systems," *Journal of Peace Research*, XIV (No. I, 1977): 23–40.
46. Richard Garwin, "Anti-Submarine Warfare and National Security," *Scientific American*, 227 (July 1972): 14–25.
47. The latter scenario, however, does not require that the state closely match the number of missiles the other deploys.
48. Thomas Schelling, *Arms and Influence* (New Haven: Yale University Press, 1966), 69–78. Schelling's arguments are not entirely convincing, however. For further discussion, see Jervis, "Deterrence Theory Re-Visited," Working Paper No. 14, UCLA Program in Arms Control and International Security.

The Utility of Force in the Modern World

Complex Interdependence and the Role of Force

Robert O. Keohane and Joseph S. Nye

Interdependence.

We live in an era of interdependence. This vague phrase expressed a poorly understood but widespread feeling that the very nature of world politics is changing. The power of nations—that age-old touchstone of analysts and statesmen—has become more elusive: "calculations of power are even more delicate and deceptive than in previous ages."[1] Henry Kissinger, though deeply rooted in the classical tradition, has stated that "the traditional agenda of international affairs—the balance among major powers, the security of nations—no longer defines our perils or our possibilities. . . . Now we are entering a new era. Old international patterns are crumbling; old slogans are uninstructive; old solutions are unavailing. The world has become interdependent in economics, in communications, in human aspirations."[2]

How profound are the changes? A modernist school sees telecommunications and jet travel as creating a "global village" and believes that burgeoning social and economic transactions are creating a "world without borders."[3] To greater or lesser extent, a number of scholars see our era as one in which the territorial state, which has been dominant in world politics for the four centuries since feudal times ended, is being eclipsed by nonterritorial actors such as multinational corporations, transnational social movements, and international organizations. As one economist put it, "the state is about through as an economic unit."[4]

Traditionalists call these assertions unfounded "globaloney." They point to the continuity in world politics. Military interdependence has always existed, and military power is still important in world politics—witness nuclear deterrence; the Vietnam, Middle East, and Indian-Pakistan wars; and Soviet influence in Eastern Europe or American influence in the Caribbean. Moreover, as

---

the Soviet Union has shown, authoritarian states can, to a considerable extent, control telecommunications and social transactions that they consider disruptive. Even poor and weak countries have been able to nationalize multinational corporations, and the prevalence of nationalism casts doubt on the proposition that the nation-state is fading away.

Neither the modernists nor the traditionalists have an adequate framework for understanding the politics of global interdependence.[5] Modernists point correctly to the fundamental changes now taking place, but they often assume without sufficient analysis that advances in technology and increases in social and economic transactions will lead to a new world in which states, and their control of force, will no longer be important.[6] Traditionalists are adept at showing flaws in the modernist vision by pointing out how military interdependence continues, but find it very difficult accurately to interpret today's multidimensional economic, social, and ecological interdependence.

Our task . . . is not to argue either the modernist or traditionalist position. Because our era is marked by both continuity and change, this would be fruitless. Rather, our task is to provide a means of distilling and blending the wisdom in both positions by developing a coherent theoretical framework for the political analysis of interdependence. We shall develop several different but potentially complementary models, or intellectual tools, for grasping the reality of interdependence in contemporary world politics. Equally important, we shall attempt to explore the *conditions* under which each model will be most likely to produce accurate predictions and satisfactory explanations. Contemporary world politics is not a seamless web; it is a tapestry of diverse relationships. In such a world, one model cannot explain all situations. The secret of understanding lies in knowing which approach or combination of approaches to use in analyzing a situation. There will never be a substitute for careful analysis of actual situations. . . .

THE NEW RHETORIC OF INTERDEPENDENCE

During the Cold War, "national security" was a slogan American political leaders used to generate support for their policies. The rhetoric of national security justified strategies designed, at considerable cost, to bolster the economic, military, and political structure of the "free world." It also provided a rationale for international cooperation and support for the United Nations, as well as justification for alliances, foreign aid, and extensive military involvements.

National security became the favorite symbol of the internationalists who favored increased American involvement in world affairs. The key foreign policy coordinating unit in the White House was named the National Security Council. The Truman administration used the alleged Soviet threat to American security to push the loan to Britain and then the Marshall Plan through Congress. The Kennedy administration employed the security argument to promote the 1962 Trade Expansion Act. Presidents invoked national security to control certain sectoral economic interests in Congress, particularly those favoring protectionist trade policies. Congressmen who protested adverse economic effects on their districts or increased taxes were assured—and in turn explained to constituents—that the "national security interests" required their sacrifice. At the same time, special interests frequently manipulated the symbolism of national security for their own purposes, as in the case of petroleum import quotas, promoted particularly by domestic oil producers and their political allies.[7]

National security symbolism was largely a product of the Cold War and the severe threat Americans then felt. Its persuasiveness was increased by realist analysis, which insisted that national security is the primary national goal and that in international politics security threats are permanent. National security symbolism, and the realist mode of analysis that supported it, not only epitomized a certain way of reacting to events, but helped to codify a perspective in which some changes, particularly those toward radical regimes in Third World countries, seemed inimical to national security, while fundamental changes in the economic relations among advanced industrialized countries seemed insignificant.

As the Cold War sense of security threat slackened, foreign economic competition and domestic distributional conflict increased. The intellectual ambiguity of "national security" became more pronounced as varied and often contradictory forms of involvement took shelter under a single rhetorical umbrella.[8] In his imagery of a world balance of power among five major centers (the United States, the Soviet Union, China, Europe, Japan), President Nixon tried unsuccessfully to extend traditional realist concepts to apply to the economic challenge posed by America's postwar allies, as well as the political and military actions of the Soviet Union and China.

As the descriptive accuracy of a view of national security dominated by military concerns declined, so did the term's symbolic power. This decline reflected not only the increased ambiguity of the concept, but also American reaction to the Vietnam imbroglio, to the less hostile relationship with Russia and China summed up by the word *detente,* and to misuse of national security rhetoric by President Nixon in the Watergate affair. National security had to share its position as the prime symbol in the internationalists' lexicon with *interdependence.*

Political leaders often use interdependence rhetoric to portray interdependence as a natural necessity, as a fact to which policy (and domestic interest groups) must adjust, rather than as a situation partially created by policy itself. They usually argue that conflicts of interest are reduced by interdependence, and that cooperation alone holds the answer to world problems.

"We are all engaged in a common enterprise. No nation or group of nations can gain by pushing beyond the limits that sustain world economic growth. No one benefits from basing progress on tests of strength."[9] These words clearly belong to a statesman intending to limit demands from the Third World and influence public attitudes at home, rather than to analyze contemporary reality. For those who wish the United States to retain world leadership, interdependence has become part of the new rhetoric, to be used against both economic nationalism at home and assertive challenges abroad. Although the connotations of interdependence rhetoric may seem quite different from those of national security symbolism, each has often been used to legitimize American presidential leadership in world affairs. . . .

Yet interdependence rhetoric and national security symbolism coexist only uneasily. In its extreme formulation, the former suggests that conflicts of interest are passé, whereas the latter argues that they are, and will remain, fundamental, and potentially violent. The confusion in knowing what analytical models to apply to world politics (as we noted earlier) is thus paralleled by confusion about the policies that should be employed by the United States. Neither interdependence rhetoric nor national security symbolism provides reliable guidelines for problems of extensive interdependence.

Rhetoriticians of interdependence often claim that since the survival of the human race is threatened by environmental as well as military dangers, conflicts of interest among states and people no longer exist. This conclusion would only follow if three conditions were met: an international economic system on which everyone depended or our basic life-supporting ecological system were in danger; all countries were significantly vulnerable to such a catastrophe; and there were only one solution to the problem (leaving no room for conflict about how to solve it and who should bear the costs). Obviously these conditions are rarely all present.

Yet balance of power theories and national security imagery are also poorly adapted to analyzing problems of economic or ecological interdependence. Security, in traditional terms, is not likely to be the principal issue facing governments. Insofar as military force is ineffective on certain issues, the conventional notion of power lacks precision. In particular, different power resources may be needed to deal with different issues. Finally, in the politics of interdependence, domestic and transnational as well as governmental interests are involved. Domestic and foreign policy become closely linked. The notion of national interest—the traditionalists' lodestar—becomes increasingly difficult to use effectively. Traditional maxims of international politics—that states will act in their national interests or that they will attempt to maximize their power—become ambiguous.

We are not suggesting that international conflict disappears when interdependence prevails. On the contrary, conflict will take new forms, and may even increase. But the traditional approaches to understanding conflict in world politics will not explain interdependence conflict particularly well. Applying the wrong image and the wrong rhetoric to problems will lead to erroneous analysis and bad policy. . . .

Manipulating economic or sociopolitical vulnerabilities, however, also bears risks. Strategies of manipulating interdependence are likely to lead to counterstrategies. It must always be kept in mind, furthermore, that military power dominates economic power in the sense that economic means alone are likely to be ineffective against the serious use of military force. Thus, even effective manipulation of asymmetrical interdependence within a nonmilitary area can create risks of military counteraction. When the United States exploited Japanese vulnerability to economic embargo in 1940–41, Japan countered by attacking Pearl Harbor and the Philippines. Yet military actions are usually very costly; and for many types of actions, these costs have risen steeply during the last thirty years.

Table 1 shows the three types of asymmetrical interdependence that we have been discussing. The dominance ranking column indicates that the power resources provided by military interdependence dominate those provided by nonmilitary vulnerability, which in turn dominate those provided by asymmetries in sensitivity. Yet exercising more dominant forms of power brings higher costs. Thus, *relative to cost*, there is no guarantee that military means will be more effective than economic ones to achieve a given purpose. We can expect, however, that as the interests at stake become more important, actors will tend to use power resources that rank higher in both dominance and cost. . . .

One's assumptions about world politics profoundly affect what one sees and how one constructs theories to explain events. We believe that the assumptions of political realists, whose theories dominated the postwar period, are often an inadequate basis for analyzing the politics of interdependence. The realist assumptions about world politics can be seen as defining an extreme set of conditions or *ideal type*. One could also imagine very different conditions. In this chapter, we shall construct another ideal type, the opposite of realism. We call it *complex interdependence*. After establishing the differences between realism and complex interdependence, we shall argue that complex interdependence sometimes comes closer to reality than does realism. When it does, traditional explanations of change in international regimes become questionable and the search for new explanatory models becomes more urgent.

For political realists, international politics, like all other politics, is a strug-

Table 1   ASYMMETRICAL INTERDEPENDENCE AND ITS USES

Source of interdependence	Dominance ranking	Cost ranking	Contemporary use
Military (costs of using military force)	1	1	Used in extreme situations or against weak foes when costs may be slight.
Nonmilitary vulnerability (costs of pursuing alternative policies)	2	2	Used when normative constraints are low, and international rules are not considered binding (including nonmilitary relations between adversaries, and situations of extremely high conflict between close partners and allies).
Nonmilitary sensitivity (costs of change under existing policies)	3	3	A power resource in the short run or when normative constraints are high and international rules are binding. Limited, since if high costs are imposed, disadvantaged actors may formulate new policies.

gle for power but, unlike domestic politics, a struggle dominated by organized violence. In the words of the most influential postwar textbook, "All history shows that nations active in international politics are continuously preparing for, actively involved in, or recovering from organized violence in the form of war."[10] Three assumptions are integral to the realist vision. First, states as coherent units are the dominant actors in world politics. This is a double assumption: States are predominant; and they act as coherent units. Second, realists assume that force is a usable and effective instrument of policy. Other instruments may also be employed, but using or threatening force is the most effective means of wielding power. Third, partly because of their second assumption, realists assume a hierarchy of issues in world politics, headed by questions of military security: the "high politics" of military security dominates the "low politics" of economic and social affairs.

These realist assumptions define an ideal type of world politics. They allow us to imagine a world in which politics is continually characterized by active or potential conflict among states, with the use of force possible at any time. Each state attempts to defend its territory and interests from real or perceived threats. Political integration among states is slight and lasts only as long as it serves the national interests of the most powerful states. Transitional actors either do not exist or are politically unimportant. Only the adept exercise of force or the threat of force permits states to survive, and only while statesmen succeed in adjusting their interests, as in a well-functioning balance of power, is the system stable.

Each of the realist assumptions can be challenged. If we challenge them all simultaneously, we can imagine a world in which actors other than states participate directly in world politics, in which a clear hierarchy of issues does not exist, and in which force is an ineffective instrument of policy. Under these conditions—which we call the characteristics of complex interdependence—one would expect world politics to be very different than under realist conditions. . . .

We do not argue, however, that complex interdependence faithfully reflects world political reality. Quite the contrary: Both it and the realist portrait are ideal types. Most situations will fall somewhere between these two extremes. Sometimes, realist assumptions will be accurate, or largely accurate, but frequently complex interdependence will provide a better portrayal of reality. Before one decides what explanatory model to apply to a situation or problem, one will need to understand the degree to which realist or complex interdependence assumptions correspond to the situation.

THE CHARACTERISTICS OF COMPLEX INTERDEPENDENCE

Complex interdependence has three main characteristics:

1. *Multiple channels* connect societies, including: informal ties between governmental elites as well as formal foreign office arrangements; infor-

mal ties among nongovernmental elites (face-to-face and through tele-communications); and transnational organizations (such as multinational banks or corporations). These channels can be summarized as interstate, transgovernmental, and transnational relations. *Interstate* relations are the normal channels assumed by realists. *Transgovernmental* applies when we relax the realist assumption that states act coherently as units; *transnational* applies when we relax the assumption that states are the only units.

2. The agenda of interstate relationships consists of multiple issues that are not arranged in a clear or consistent hierarchy. This *absence of hierarchy among issues* means, among other things, that military security does not consistently dominate the agenda. Many issues arise from what used to be considered domestic policy, and the distinction between domestic and foreign issues becomes blurred. These issues are considered in several government departments (not just foreign offices), and at several levels. Inadequate policy coordination on these issues involves significant costs. Different issues generate different coalitions, both within governments and across them, and involve different degress of conflict. Politics does not stop at the waters' edge.

3. Military force is not used by governments toward other governments within the region, or on the issues, when complex interdependence prevails. It may, however, be important in these governments' relations with governments outside that region, or on other issues. Military force could, for instance, be irrelevant to resolving disagreements on economic issues among members of an alliance, yet at the same time be very important for the alliance's political and military relations with a rival bloc. For the former relationships this condition of complex interdependence would be met; for the latter, it would not.

Traditional theories of international politics implicitly or explicitly deny the accuracy of these three assumptions. Traditionalists are therefore tempted also to deny the relevance of criticisms based on the complex interdependence ideal type. We believe, however, that our three conditions are fairly well approximated on some global issues of economic and ecological interdependence and that they come close to characterizing the entire relationship between some countries. One of our purposes here is to prove that contention. . . .

Multiple Channels

A visit to any major airport is a dramatic way to confirm the existence of multiple channels of contact among advanced industrial countries; there is a voluminous literature to prove it.[11] Bureaucrats from different countries deal directly with one another at meetings and on the telephone as well as in writing. Similarly, nongovernmental elites frequently get together in the normal course of business, in organizations such as the Trilateral Commission, and in conferences sponsored by private foundations.

In addition, multinational firms and banks affect both domestic and inter-state relations. The limits on private firms, or the closeness of ties between government and business, vary considerably from one society to another; but the participation of large and dynamic organizations, not controlled entirely by governments, has become a normal part of foreign as well as domestic relations.

interdep

These actors are important not only because of their activities in pursuit of their own interests, but also because they act as transmission belts, making government policies in various countries more sensitive to one another. As the scope of governments' domestic activities has broadened, and as corporations, banks, and (to a lesser extent) trade unions have made decisions that transcend national boundaries, the domestic policies of different countries impinge on one another more and more. Transnational communications reinforce these effects. Thus, foreign economic policies touch more domestic economic activity than in the past, blurring the lines between domestic and foreign policy and increasing the number of issues relevant to foreign policy. Parallel developments in issues of environmental regulation and control over technology reinforce this trend.

Absence of Hierarchy Among Issues

Foreign affairs agendas—that is, sets of issues relevant to foreign policy with which governments are concerned—have become larger and more diverse. No longer can all issues be subordinated to military security. As Secretary of State Kissinger described the situation in 1975:

> progress in dealing with the traditional agenda is no longer enough. A new and unprecedented kind of issue has emerged. The problems of energy, resources, environment, population, the uses of space and the seas now rank with questions of military security, ideology and territorial rivalry which have traditionally made up the diplomatic agenda.[12]

Kissinger's list, which could be expanded, illustrates how governments' policies, even those previously considered merely domestic, impinge on one another. The extensive consultative arrangements developed by the OECD, as well as the GATT, IMF, and the European Community, indicate how character-istic the overlap of domestic and foreign policy is among developed pluralist countries. The organization within nine major departments of the United States government (Agriculture, Commerce, Defense, Health, Education and Welfare, Interior, Justice, Labor, State, and Treasury) and many other agencies reflects their extensive international commitments. The multiple, overlapping issues that result make a nightmare of governmental organization.[13]

When there are multiple issues on the agenda, many of which threaten the interests of domestic groups but do not clearly threaten the nation as a whole, the problems of formulating a coherent and consistent foreign policy increase. In 1975 energy was a foreign policy problem, but specific remedies, such as a tax on gasoline and automobiles, involved domestic legislation opposed by auto workers and companies alike. As one commentator observed, "virtually every time Congress has set a national policy that changed the way people live . . .

the action came after a consensus had developed, bit by bit, over the years, that a problem existed and that there was one best way to solve it."[14] Opportunities for delay, for special protection, for inconsistency and incoherence abound when international politics requires aligning the domestic policies of pluralist democratic countries.

Minor Role of Military Force

Political scientists have traditionally emphasized the role of military force in international politics. . . . [F]orce dominates other means of power: *if* there are no constraints on one's choice of instruments (a hypothetical situation that has only been approximated in the two world wars), the state with superior military force will prevail. If the security dilemma for all states were extremely acute, military force, supported by economic and other resources, would clearly be the dominant source of power. Survival is the primary goal of all states, and in the worst situations, force is ultimately necessary to guarantee survival. Thus military force is always a central component of national power.

Yet particularly among industrialized, pluralist countries, the perceived margin of safety has widened: Fears of attack in general have declined, and fears of attacks *by one another* are virtually nonexistent. France has abandoned the *tous azimuts* (defense in all directons) strategy that President de Gaulle advocated (it was not taken entirely seriously even at the time). Canada's last war plans for fighting the United States were abandoned half a century ago. Britain and Germany no longer feel threatened by each other. Intense relationships of mutual influence exist between these countries, but in most of them force is irrelevant or unimportant as an instrument of policy.

Moreover, force is often not an appropriate way of achieving other goals (such as economic and ecological welfare) that are becoming more important. It is not impossible to imagine dramatic conflict or revolutionary change in which the use or threat of military force over an economic issue or among advanced industrial countries might become plausible. Then realist assumptions would again be a reliable guide to events. But in most situations, the effects of military force are both costly and uncertain.[15]

Even when the direct use of force is barred among a group of countries, however, military power can still be used politically. Each superpower continues to use the threat of force to deter attacks by other superpowers on itself or its allies; its deterrence ability thus serves an indirect, protective role, which it can use in bargaining on other issues with its allies. This bargaining tool is particularly important for the United States, whose allies are concerned about potential Soviet threats and which has fewer other means of influence over its allies than does the Soviet Union over its Eastern European partners. The United States has, accordingly, taken advantage of the Europeans' (particularly the Germans') desire for its protection and linked the issue of troop levels in Europe to trade and monetary negotiations. Thus, although the first-order effect of deterrent force is essentially negative—to deny effective offensive power to a superpower opponent—a state can use the force positively—to gain political influence.

Thus, even for countries whose relations approximate complex interdependence, two serious qualifications remain: (1) drastic social and political change could cause force again to become an important direct instrument of policy; and (2) even when elites' interests are complementary, a country that uses military force to protect another may have significant political influence over the other country.

In North-South relations, or relations among Third World countries, as well as in East-West relations, force is often important. Military power helps the Soviet Union to dominate Eastern Europe economically as well as politically. The threat of open or covert American military intervention has helped to limit revolutionary changes in the Caribbean, especially in Guatemala in 1954 and in the Dominican Republic in 1965. Secretary of State Kissinger, in January 1975, issued a veiled warning to members of the Organization of Petroleum Exporting Countries (OPEC) that the United States might use force against them "where there is some actual strangulation of the industrialized world."[16]

Even in these rather conflictual situations, however, the recourse to force seems less likely now than at most times during the century before 1945. The destructiveness of nuclear weapons makes any attack against a nuclear power dangerous. Nuclear weapons are mostly used as a deterrent. Threats of nuclear action against much weaker countries may occasionally be efficacious, but they are equally or more likely to solidify relations between one's adversaries. The limited usefulness of conventional force to control socially mobilized populations has been shown by the United States failure in Vietnam as well as by the rapid decline of colonialism in Africa. Furthermore, employing force on one issue against an independent state with which one has a variety of relationships is likely to rupture mutually profitable relations on other issues. In other words, the use of force often has costly effects on nonsecurity goals. And finally, in Western democracies, popular opposition to prolonged military conflicts is very high.[17]

It is clear that these constraints bear unequally on various countries, or on the same countries in different situations. Risks of nuclear escalation affect everyone, but domestic opinion is far less constraining for communist states, or for authoritarian regional powers, than for the United States, Europe, or Japan. Even authoritarian countries may be reluctant to use force to obtain economic objectives when such use might be ineffective and disrupt other relationships. Both the difficulty of controlling socially mobilized populations with foreign troops and the changing technology of weaponry may actually enhance the ability of certain countries, or nonstate groups, to use terrorism as a political weapon without effective fear of reprisal.

The fact that the changing role of force has uneven effects does not make the change less important, but it does make matters more complex. This complexity is compounded by differences in the usability of force among issue areas. When an issue arouses little interest or passion, force may be unthinkable. In such instances, complex interdependence may be a valuable concept for analyzing the political process. But if that issue becomes a matter of life and death—as some people thought oil might become—the use or threat of force could become decisive again. Realist assumptions would then be more relevant.

It is thus important to determine the applicability of realism or of complex interdependence to each situation. Without this determination, further analysis is likely to be confused. Our purpose in developing an alternative to the realist description of world politics is to encourage a differentiated approach that distinguishes among dimensions and areas of world politics—not (as some modernist observers do) to replace one oversimplification with another.

THE POLITICAL PROCESS OF COMPLEX INTERDEPENDENCE

The three main characteristics of complex interdependence give rise to distinctive political processes, which translate power resources into power as control of outcomes. As we argued earlier, something is usually lost or added in the translation. Under conditions of complex interdependence the translation will be different than under realist conditions, and our predictions about outcomes will need to be adjusted accordingly.

In the realist world, military security will be the dominant goal of states. It will even affect issues that are not directly involved with military power or territorial defense. Nonmilitary problems will not only be subordinated to military ones; they will be studied for their politico-military implications. Balance of payments issues, for instance, will be considered at least as much in the light of their implications for world power generally as for their purely financial ramifications. McGeorge Bundy conformed to realist expectations when he argued in 1964 that devaluation of the dollar should be seriously considered if necessary to fight the war in Vietnam.[18] To some extent, so did former Treasury Secretary Henry Fowler when he contended in 1971 that the United States needed a trade surplus of $4 billion to $6 billion in order to lead in Western defense.[19]

In a world of complex interdependence, however, one expects some officials, particularly at lower levels, to emphasize the *variety* of state goals that must be pursued. In the absence of a clear hierarchy of issues, goals will vary by issue, and may not be closely related. Each bureaucracy will pursue its own concerns; and although several agencies may reach compromises on issues that affect them all, they will find that a consistent pattern of policy is difficult to maintain. Moreover, transnational actors will introduce different goals into various groups of issues.

Linkage Strategies

Goals will therefore vary by issue area under complex interdependence, but so will the distribution of power and the typical political processes. Traditional analysis focuses on *the* international system, and leads us to anticipate similar political processes on a variety of issues. Militarily and economically strong states will dominate a variety of organizations and a variety of issues, by linking their own policies on some issues to other states' policies on other issues. By using their overall dominance to prevail on their weak issues, the strongest states will, in the traditional model, ensure a congruence between the overall structure of military and economic power and the pattern of outcomes on any one issue area. Thus world politics can be treated as a seamless web.

Under complex interdependence, such congruence is less likely to occur. As military force is devalued, militarily strong states will find it more difficult to use their overall dominance to control outcomes on issues in which they are weak. And since the distribution of power resources in trade, shipping, or oil, for example, may be quite different, patterns of outcomes and distinctive political processes are likely to vary from one set of issues to another. If force were readily applicable, and military security were the highest foreign policy goal, these variations in the issue structures of power would not matter very much. The linkages drawn from them to military issues would ensure consistent dominance by the overall strongest states. But when military force is largely immobilized, strong states will find that linkage is less effective. They may still attempt such links, but in the absence of hierarchy of issues, their success will be problematic.

Dominant states may try to secure much the same result by using overall economic power to affect results on other issues. If only economic objectives are at stake, they may succeed: Money, after all, is fungible. But economic objectives have political implications, and economic linkage by the strong is limited by domestic, transnational, and transgovernmental actors who resist having their interests traded off. Furthermore, the international actors may be different on different issues, and the international organizations in which negotiations take place are often quite separate. Thus it is difficult, for example, to imagine a military or economically strong state linking concessions on monetary policy to reciprocal concessions in oceans policy. On the other hand, poor weak states are not similarly inhibited from linking unrelated issues, partly because their domestic interests are less complex. Linkage of unrelated issues is often a means of extracting concessions or side payments from rich and powerful states. And unlike powerful states whose instrument for linkage (military force) is often too costly to use, the linkage instrument used by poor, weak states—international organization—is available and inexpensive.

Thus as the utility of force declines, and as issues become more equal in importance, the distribution of power within each issue will become more important. If linkages become less effective on the whole, outcomes of political bargaining will increasingly vary by issue area.

The differentiation among issue areas in complex interdependence means that linkages among issues will become more problematic and will tend to reduce rather than reinforce international hierarchy. Linkage strategies, and defense against them, will pose critical strategic choices for states. Should issues be considered separately or as a package? If linkages are to be drawn, which issues should be linked, and on which of the linked issues should concessions be made? How far can one push a linkage before it becomes counterproductive? For instance, should one seek formal agreements or informal, but less politically sensitive, understandings? The fact that world politics under complex interdependence is not a seamless web leads us to expect that efforts to stitch seams together advantageously, as reflected in linkage strategies, will, very often, determine the shape of the fabric.

The negligible role of force leads us to expect states to rely more on other instruments in order to wield power. For the reasons we have already discussed, less vulnerable states will try to use asymmetrical interdependence in particular groups of issues as a source of power; they will also try to use international organizations and transnational actors and flows. States will approach economic interdependence in terms of power as well as its effects on citizens' welfare, although welfare considerations will limit their attempts to maximize power. Most economic and ecological interdependence involves the possibility of joint gains or joint losses. Mutual awareness of potential gains and losses and the danger of worsening each actor's position through overly rigorous struggles over the distribution of the gains can limits the use of asymmetrical interdependence.

Agenda Setting

Our second assumption of complex interdependence, the lack of clear hierarchy among multiple issues, leads us to expect that the politics of agenda formation and control will become more important. Traditional analyses lead statesmen to focus on politico-military issues and to pay little attention to the broader politics of agenda formation. Statesmen assume that the agenda will be set by shifts in the balance of power, actual or anticipated, and by perceived threats to the security of states. Other issues will only be very important when they seem to affect security and military power. In these cases, agendas will be influenced strongly by considerations of the overall balance of power.

Yet, today, some nonmilitary issues are emphasized in interstate relations at one time, whereas others of seemingly equal importance are neglected or quietly handled at a technical level. International monetary politics, problems of commodity terms of trade, oil, food, and multinational corporations have all been important during the last decade; but not all have been high on interstate agendas throughout that period.

Traditional analysts of international politics have paid little attention to agenda formation: to how issues come to receive sustained attention by high officials. The traditional orientation toward military and security affairs implies that the crucial problems of foreign policy are imposed on states by the actions or threats of other states. These are high politics as opposed to the low politics of economic affairs. Yet, as the complexity of actors and issues in world politics increases, the utility of force declines and the line between domestic policy and foreign policy becomes blurred: As the conditions of complex interdependence are more closely approximated, the politics of agenda formation becomes more subtle and differentiated.

Under complex interdependence we can expect the agenda to be affected by the international and domestic problems created by economic growth and increasing sensitivity interdependence. . . . Discontented domestic groups will politicize issues and force more issues once considered domestic onto the inter-state agenda. Shifts in the distribution of power resources within sets of issues will also affect agendas. During the early 1970s the increased power of oil-producing governments over the transnational corporation and the consumer countries dramatically altered the policy agenda. Moreover, agendas for one group of issues may change as a result of linkages from other groups in which power resources are changing; for example, the broader agenda of North-South trade issues changed after the OPEC price rises and the oil embargo of 1973–74. Even if capabilities among states do not change, agendas may be affected by shifts in the importance of transnational actors. The publicity surrounding multi-national corporations in the early 1970s, cooupled with their rapid growth over the past twenty years, put the regulation of such corporations higher on both the Union Nations agenda and national agendas.

Politicization—agitation and controversy over an issue that tend to raise it to the top of the agenda—can have many sources, as we have seen. Govern-ments whose strength is increasing may politicize issues by linking them to other issues. An international regime that is becoming ineffective or is not serving important issues may cause increasing politicization, as dissatisfied gov-ernments press for change. Politicization, however, can also come from below. Domestic groups may become upset enough to raise a dormant issue, or to interfere with interstate bargaining at high levels. In 1974 the American secre-tary of state's tacit linkage of a Soviet-American trade pact with progress in detente was upset by the success of domestic American groups working through Congress to link a trade agreement with Soviet policies on emigration.

The technical characteristics and institutional setting in which issues are raised will strongly affect politicization patterns. In the United States, congres-sional attention is an effective instrument of politicization. Generally, we expect transnational economic organizations and transgovernmental networks of bu-reaucrats to seek to avoid politicization. Domestically based groups (such as trade unions) and domestically oriented bureaucracies will tend to use politiciza-tion (particularly congressional attention) against their transnationally mobile competitors. At the international level, we expect states and actors to "shop among forums" and struggle to get issues raised in international organizations that will maximize their advantage by broadening or narrowing the agenda.

Transnational and Transgovernmental Relations

Our third condition of complex interdependence, multiple channels of contact among societies, further blurs the distinction between domestic and interna-tional politics. The availability of partners in political coalitions is not necessar-ily limited by national boundaries as traditional analysis assumes. The nearer a situation is to complex interdependence, the more we expect the outcomes of political bargaining to be affected by transnational relations. Multinational cor-porations may be significant both as independent actors and as instruments manipulated by governments. The attitudes and policy stands of domestic groups are likely to be affected by communications, organized or not, between them and their counterparts abroad.

Thus the existence of multiple channels of contact leads us to expect limits, beyond those normally found in domestic politics, on the ability of statesmen to calculate the manipulation of interdependence or follow a consistent strategy of linkage. Statesmen must consider differential as well as aggregate effects of interdependence strategies and their likely implications for politicization and agenda control. Transactions among societies—economic and social transactions more than security ones—affect groups differently. Opportunities and costs from increased transnational ties may be greater for certain groups—for instance, American workers in the textile or shoe industries—than for others. Some organizations or groups may interact directly with actors in other societies or with other governments to increase their benefits from a network of interaction. Some actors may therefore be less vulnerable as well as less sensitive to changes elsewhere in the network than are others, and this will affect patterns of political action.

The multiple channels of contact found in complex interdependence are not limited to nongovernmental actors. Contacts between governmental bureaucracies charged with similar tasks may not only alter their perspectives but lead to transgovernmental coalitions on particular policy questions. To improve their chances of success, government agencies attempt to bring actors from other governments into their own decision-making processes as allies. Agencies of powerful states such as the United States have used such coalitions to penetrate weaker governments in such countries as Turkey and Chile. They have also been used to help agencies of other governments penetrate the United States bureaucracy.[20] . . . [T]ransgovernmental politics frequently characterizes Canadian-American relations, often to the advantage of Canadian interests.

The existence of transgovernmental policy networks leads to a different interpretation of one of the standard propositions about international politics—that states act in their own interest. Under complex interdependence, this conventional wisdom begs two important questions: Which self and which interest? A government agency may pursue its own interests under the guise of the national interest; and recurrent interactions can change official perceptions of their interests. As a careful study of the politics of United States trade policy has documented, concentrating only on pressures of various interests for decisions leads to an overly mechanistic view of a continuous process and neglects the important role of communications in slowly changing perceptions of self-interest.[21]

The ambiguity of the national interest raises serious problems for the top political leaders of governments. As bureaucracies contact each other directly across national borders (without going through foreign offices), centralized control becomes more difficult. There is less assurance that the state will be united when dealing with foreign governments or that its components will interpret national interests similarly when negotiating with foreigners. The state may prove to be multifaceted, even schizophrenic. National interest will be defined differently on different issues, at different times, and by different governmental units. States that are better placed to maintain their coherence (because of a centralized political tradition such as France's) will be better also be manipulate uneven interdependence than fragmented states that at first glance seem to have more resources in an issue area.

NOTES

1. Stanley Hoffman, "Notes on the Elusiveness of Modern Power," *International Journal* 30 (Spring 1975): 184.
2. "A New National Partnership," speech by Secretary of State Henry A. Kissinger at Los Angeles, January 24, 1975. News release, Department of State, Bureau of Public Affairs, Office of Media Services, 1.
3. See, for example, Lester R. Brown, *World Without Borders: The Interdependence of Nations* (New York: Foreign Policy Association, Headline Series, 1972).
4. Charles Kindleberger, *American Business Abroad* (New Haven: Yale University Press, 1969), 207.
5. The terms are derived from Stanley Hoffmann, "Choices," *Foreign Policy* 12 (Fall 1973): 6.
6. For instance, see Robert Angell, *Peace on the March: Transnational Participation* (New York: Van Nostrand, 1969).
7. See Robert Engler, *The Politics of Oil: Private Power and Democratic Directions* (Chicago: University of Chicago Press, 1962).
8. Arnold Wolfers' "National Security as an Ambiguous Symbol" remains the classic analysis. See his collection of essays, *Discord and Collaboration* (Baltimore: Johns Hopkins University Press, 1962). Daniel Yergin's study of the emergence of the doctrine of national security (in place of the traditional concept of defense) portrays it as a "commanding idea" of the Cold War era. See Daniel Yergin, *The Shattered Peace: The Rise of the National Security State* (Boston: Houghton Mifflin, 1976).
9. Secretary of State Henry A. Kissinger, Address before the Sixth Special Session of the United Nations General Assembly, April 15, 1974. News release, Department of State, Office of Media Services, 2. Reprinted in *International Organization* 28, no. 3 (Summer 1974): 573–83.
10. Hans J. Morgenthau, *Politics Among Nations: The Struggle for Power and Peace*, 4th ed. (New York: Knopf, 1967), 36.
11. See Edward L. Morse, "Transnational Economic Processes," in Robert O. Keohane and Joseph S. Nye, Jr., eds., *Transnational Relations and World Politics* (Cambridge, Mass.: Harvard University Press, 1972).
12. Henry A. Kissinger, "A New National Partnership," *Department of State Bulletin*, February 17, 1975, 199.
13. See the report of the Commission on the Organization of the Government for the Conduct of Foreign Policy (Murphy Commission) (Washington, D.C.: U.S. Government Printing Office, 1975), and the studies prepared for that report. See also Raymond Hopkins, "The International Role of 'Domestic' Bureaucracy," *International Organization* 30, no. 3 (Summer 1976).
14. *The New York Times*, May 22, 1975.
15. For a valuable discussion, see Klaus Knorr, *The Power of Nations: The Political Economy of International Relations* (New York: Basic Books, 1975).

16. *Business Week*, January 13, 1975.
17. Stanley Hoffmann, "The Acceptability of Military Force," and Laurence Martin, "The Utility of Military Force," in *Force in Modern Societies: Its Place in International Politics* (Adelphi Paper, International Institute for Strategic Studies, 1973). See also Korr, *The Power of Nations*.
18. Henry Brandon, *The Retreat of American Power* (New York: Doubleday, 1974), 218.
19. *International Implications of the New Economic Policy*, U.S. Congress, House of Representatives, Committee on Foreign Affairs, Subcommittee on Foreign Economic Policy, Hearings, September 16, 1971.
20. For a more detailed discussion, see Robert O. Keohane and Joseph S. Nye, Jr., "Transgovernmental Relations and International Organizations," *World Politics* 27, no. 1 (October 1974): 39–62.
21. Raymond Bauer, Ithiel de Sola Pool, and Lewis Dexter, *American Business and Foreign Policy* (New York: Atherton, 1963), chap. 35, esp. 472–75.

The Obsolescence of War in the Modern Industrialized World

John Mueller

It is widely assumed that, for better or worse, the existence of nuclear weapons has profoundly shaped our lives and destinies. Some find the weapons supremely beneficial. Defense analyst Edward Luttwak says, "we have lived since 1945 without another world war precisely because rational minds . . . extracted a durable peace from the very terror of nuclear weapons."[1] And Robert Art and Kenneth Waltz conclude, "the probability of war between America and Russia or between NATO and the Warsaw Pact is practically nil precisely because the military planning and deployments of each, together with the fear of escalation to general nuclear war, keep it that way."[2] Others argue that, while we may have been lucky so far, the continued existence of the weapons promises eventual calamity: The doomsday clock on the cover of the *Bulletin of the Atomic Scientists* has been pointedly hovering near midnight for over 40 years now, and in his influential bestseller, *The Fate of the Earth*, Jonathan Schell dramatically concludes that if we do not "rise up and cleanse the earth of nuclear weapons," we will "sink into the final coma and end it all."[3]

This article takes issue with both of these points of view and concludes that nuclear weapons neither crucially define a fundamental stability nor threaten severely to disturb it.

The paper is in two parts. In the first it is argued that, while nuclear weapons may have substantially influenced political rhetoric, public discourse, and defense budgets and planning, it is not at all clear that they have had a significant impact on the history of world affairs since World War II. They do not seem to have been necessary to deter World War III, to determine alliance patterns, or to cause the United States and the Soviet Union to behave cautiously.

In the second part, these notions are broadened to a discussion of stability

International Security, Fall 1988 (Vol. 13, No. 2). © 1988 by the President and Fellows of Harvard College and of the Massachusetts Institute of Technology. Portions of the text and some footnotes have been omitted.

in the postwar world. It is concluded that there may be a long-term trend away from war among developed countries and that the long peace since World War II is less a peculiarity of the nuclear age than the logical conclusion of a substantial historical process. Seen broadly, deterrence seems to be remarkably firm; major war—a war among developed countries, like World War II or worse—is so improbable as to be obsolescent; imbalances in weapons systems are unlikely to have much impact on anything except budgets; and the nuclear arms competition may eventually come under control not so much out of conscious design as out of atrophy born of boredom.

THE IMPACT OF NUCLEAR WEAPONS

The postwar world might well have turned out much the same even in the absence of nuclear weapons. Without them, world war would have been discouraged by the memory of World War II, by superpower contentment with the postwar status quo, by the nature of Soviet ideology, and by the fear of escalation. Nor do the weapons seem to have been the crucial determinants of Cold War developments, of alliance patterns, or of the way the major powers have behaved in crises.

Deterrence of World War

It is true that there has been no world war since 1945 and it is also true that nuclear weapons have been developed and deployed in part to deter such a conflict. It does not follow, however, that it is the weapons that have prevented the war—that peace has been, in Winston Churchill's memorable construction, "the sturdy child of [nuclear] terror." To assert that the ominous presence of nuclear weapons has prevented a war between the two power blocs, one must assume that there would have been a war had these weapons not existed. This assumption ignores several other important war-discouraging factors in the postwar world.

The Memory of World War II   A nuclear war would certainly be vastly destructive, but for the most part nuclear weapons simply compound and dramatize a military reality that by 1945 had already become appalling. Few with the experience of World War II behind them would contemplate its repetition with anything other than horror. Even before the bomb had been perfected, world war had become spectacularly costly and destructive, killing some 50 million worldwide. . . .

Postwar Contentment   For many of the combatants, World War I was as destructive as World War II, but its memory did not prevent another world war. Of course, as will be discussed more fully in the second half of this article, most nations *did* conclude from the horrors of World War I that such an event must never be repeated. If the only nations capable of starting World War II had been Britain, France, the Soviet Union, and the United States, the war would probably never have occurred. Unfortunately other major nations sought direct territorial expansion, and conflicts over these desires finally led to war.

Unlike the situation after World War I, however, the only powers capable of creating another world war since 1945 have been the big victors, the United States and the Soviet Union, each of which has emerged comfortably dominant in its respective sphere. As Waltz has observed, "the United States, and the Soviet Union as well, have more reason to be satisfied with the status quo than most earlier great powers had."[4] (Indeed, except for the dismemberment of Germany, even Hitler might have been content with the empire his arch-enemy Stalin controlled at the end of the war.) While there have been many disputes since the war, neither power has had a grievance so essential as to make a world war—whether nuclear or not—an attractive means for removing the grievance.

Soviet Ideology   Although the Soviet Union and international communism have visions of changing the world in a direction they prefer, their ideology stresses revolutionary procedures over major war. The Soviet Union may have hegemonic desires as many have argued but, with a few exceptions (especially the Korean War) to be discussed below, its tactics, inspired by the cautiously pragmatic Lenin, have stressed subversion, revolution, diplomatic and economic pressure, seduction, guerrilla warfare, local uprising, and civil war—levels at which nuclear weapons have little relevance. The communist powers have never—before or after the invention of nuclear weapons—subscribed to a Hitler-style theory of direct, Armageddon-risking conquest, and they have been extremely wary of provoking Western powers into large-scale war. Moreover, if the memory of World War II deters anyone, it probably does so to an extreme degree for the Soviets. Officially and unofficially they seem obsessed by the memory of the destruction they suffered. . . .

based on subvert

Soviet Union no large threat

The Belief in Escalation   Those who started World Wars I and II did so not because they felt that costly wars of attrition were desirable, but because they felt that escalation to wars of attrition could be avoided. In World War I the offensive was believed to be dominant, and it was widely assumed that conflict would be short and decisive.[5] In World War II, both Germany and Japan experienced repeated success with bluster, short wars in peripheral areas, and blitzkrieg, aided by the counterproductive effects of their opponents' appeasement and inaction.

World war in the post–1945 era has been prevented not so much by visions of nuclear horror as by the generally accepted belief that conflict can easily escalate to a level, nuclear or not, that the essentially satisfied major powers would find intolerably costly.

many countries fear major escalation

To deal with the crucial issue of escalation, it is useful to assess two important phenomena of the early postwar years: the Soviet preponderance in conventional arms and the Korean War.

First, it has been argued that the Soviets would have been tempted to take advantage of their conventional strength after World War II to snap up a prize like Western Europe if its chief defender, the United States, had not possessed nuclear weapons. As Winston Churchill put it in 1950, "nothing preserves Europe from an overwhelming military attack except the devastating resources of the United States in this awful weapon."[6]

This argument requires at least three questionable assumptions: (1) that the Soviets really think of Western Europe as a prize worth taking risks for; (2) that, even without the atomic bomb to rely on, the United States would have disarmed after 1945 as substantially as it did; and (3) that the Soviets have actually ever had the strength to be quickly and overwhelmingly successful in a conventional attack in Western Europe.[7]

However, even if one accepts these assumptions, the Soviet Union would in all probability still have been deterred from attacking Western Europe by the enormous potential of the American war machine. Even if the USSR had the ability to blitz Western Europe, it could not have stopped the United States from repeating what it did after 1941: mobilizing with deliberate speed, putting its economy onto a wartime footing, and wearing the enemy down in a protracted conventional major war of attrition massively supplied from its unapproachable rear base.

The economic achievement of the United States during the war was astounding. While holding off one major enemy, it concentrated with its allies on defeating another, then turned back to the first. Meanwhile, it supplied everybody. With 8 million of its ablest men out of the labor market, it increased industrial production 15 percent per year and agricultural production 30 percent overall. Before the end of the 1943 it was producing so much that some munitions plants were closed down, and even so it ended the war with a substantial surplus of wheat and over $90 billion in surplus war goods. (National governmental expenditures in the first peacetime year, 1946, were only about $60 billion.) As Denis Brogan observed at the time, "to the Americans war is a business, not an art."[8]

If anyone was in a position to appreciate this, it was the Soviets. By various circuitous routes the United States supplied the Soviet Union with, among other things, 409,526 trucks; 12,161 combat vehicles (more than the Germans had in 1939); 32,200 motorcycles; 1,966 locomotives; 16,000,000 pairs of boots (in two sizes); and over one-half pound of food for every Soviet soldier for every day of the war (much of it Spam)[9] It is the kind of feat that concentrates the mind, and it is extremely difficult to imagine the Soviets willingly taking on this somewhat lethargic, but ultimately hugely effective juggernaut. That Stalin was fully aware of the American achievement—and deeply impressed by it—is clear. Adam Ulam has observed that Stalin had "great respect for the United States' vast economic and hence military potential, quite apart from the bomb," and that his "whole career as dictator had been a testimony to his belief that production figures were a direct indicator of a given country's power."[10] As a member of the Joint Chiefs of Staff put it in 1949, "if there is any single factor today which would deter a nation seeking world domination, it would be the great industrial capacity of this country rather than its armed strength."[11] Or, as

Hugh Thomas has concluded, "if the atomic bomb had not existed, Stalin would still have feared the success of the U.S. wartime economy."[12]

After a successful attack on Western Europe the Soviets would have been in a position similar to that of Japan after Pearl Harbor: They might have gains aplenty, but they would have no way to stop the United States (and its major unapproachable allies, Canada and Japan) from eventually gearing up for, and then lauching, a war of attrition. All they could hope for, like the Japanese in 1941, would be that their victories would cause the Americans to lose their fighting spirit. But if Japan's Asian and Pacific gains in 1941 propelled the United States into war, it is to be expected that the United States would find a Soviet military takeover of an area of far greater importance to it—Western Europe—to be alarming in the extreme. Not only would the United States be outraged at the American casualties in such an attack and at the loss of an important geographic area, but it would very likely conclude (as many Americans did conclude in the late 1940s even without a Soviet attack) that an eventual attack on the United States itself was inevitable. . . .

Second, there is the important issue of the Korean War. Despite the vast American superiority in atomic weapons in 1950, Stalin was willing to order, approve, or at least acquiesce in an outright attack by a communist state on a noncommunist one, and it must be assumed that he would have done so at least as readily had nuclear weapons not existed. The American response was essentially the result of the lessons learned from the experiences of the 1930s: Comparing this to similar incursions in Manchuria, Ethiopia, and Czechoslovakia (and partly also to previous Soviet incursions into neighboring states in East Europe and the Baltic area), Western leaders resolved that such provocations must be nipped in the bud. If they were allowed to succeed, they would only encourage more aggression in more important locales later. Consequently it seems likely that the Korean War would have occurred in much the same way had nuclear weapons not existed.

For the Soviets the lessons of the Korean War must have enhanced those of World War II: Once again the United States was caught surprised and underarmed, once again it rushed hastily into action, once again it soon applied itself in a forceful way to combat—in this case for an area that it had previously declared to be of only peripheral concern. If the Korean War was a limited probe of Western resolve, it seems the Soviets drew the lessons the Truman administration intended. . . .

The Korean experience may have posed a somewhat similar lesson for the United States. In 1950, amid talk of "rolling back" communism and sometimes even of liberating China, American-led forces invaded North Korea. This venture led to a costly and demoralizing, if limited, war with China, and resulted in a considerable reduction in American enthusiasm for such maneuvers. Had the United States been successful in taking over North Korea, there might well have been noisy calls for similar ventures elsewhere—though, of course, these calls might well have gone unheeded by the leadership.

It is not at all clear that the United States and the Soviet Union needed the Korean War to become viscerally convinced that escalation was dangerously easy. But the war probably reinforced that belief for both of them and, to the degree that it did, Korea was an important stabilizing event.

Cold War and Crisis

If nuclear weapons have been unnecessary to prevent world war, they also do not seem to have crucially affected other important developments, including development of the Cold War and patterns of alliance, as well as behavior of the superpowers in crisis.

The Cold War and Alliance Patterns   The Cold War was an outgrowth of various disagreements between the United States and the USSR over ideology and over the destinies of Eastern, Central, and Southern Europe. The American reaction to the perceived Soviet threat in this period mainly reflects prenuclear thinking, especially the lessons of Munich.

For example, the formation of the North Atlantic Treaty Organization and the division of the world into alliances centered on Washington and Moscow suggests that the participants were chiefly influenced by the experience of World War II. If the major determinant of these alliance patterns had been nuclear strategy, one might expect the United States and, to a lesser extent, the Soviet Union, to be only lukewarm members, for in general the alliances include nations that contribute little to nuclear defense but possess the capability unilaterally of getting the core powers into trouble. And one would expect the small countries in each alliance to tie themselves as tightly as possible to the core nuclear power in order to have maximum protection from its nuclear weapons. However, the weakening of the alliance which has taken place over the last three decades has not come from the major partners.

The structure of the alliances therefore better reflects political and ideological bipolarity than sound nuclear strategy. As military economist (and later Defense Secretary) James Schlesinger has noted, the Western alliance "was based on some rather obsolescent notions regarding the strength and importance of the European nations and the direct contribution that they could make to the security of the United States. There was a striking failure to recognize the revolutionary impact that nuclear forces would make with respect to the earlier beliefs regarding European defense."[13] Or, as Warner Schilling has observed, American policies in Europe were "essentially pre-nuclear in their rationale. The advent of nuclear weapons had not influenced the American determination to restore the European balance of power. It was, in fact, an objective which the United States would have had an even greater incentive to undertake if the fission bomb had not been developed."[14]

Crisis Behavior   Because of the harrowing image of nuclear war, it is sometimes argued, the United States and the Soviet Union have been notably more restrained than they might otherwise have been, and thus crises that might have escalated to dangerous levels have been resolved safely at low levels.[15]

There is, of course, no definitive way to refute this notion since we are unable to run the events of the last forty years over, this time without nuclear weapons. And it is certainly the case that decision makers are well aware of the horrors of nuclear war and cannot be expected to ignore the possibility that a crisis could lead to such devastation.

However, this idea—that it is the fear of nuclear war that has kept behavior restrained—looks far less convincing when its underlying assumption is directly confronted: that the major powers would have allowed their various crises to escalate if all they had to fear at the end of the escalatory ladder was something like a repetition of World War II. Whatever the rhetoric in these crises, it is difficult to see why the unaugmented horror of repeating World War II, combined with considerable comfort with the status quo, wouldn't have been enough to inspire restraint.

Once again, escalation is the key: What deters is the belief that escalation to something intolerable will occur, not so much what the details of the ultimate unbearable punishment are believed to be. Where the belief that the conflict will escalate is absent, nuclear countries *have* been militarily challenged with war—as in Korea, Vietnam, Afghanistan, Algeria, and the Falklands.

To be clear: None of this is meant to deny that the sheer horror of nuclear war is impressive and mind-concentratingly dramatic, particularly in the speed with which it could bring about massive destruction. Nor it is meant to deny that decision makers, both in times of crisis and otherwise, are fully conscious of how horribly destructive a nuclear war could be. It is simply to stress that the sheer horror of repeating World War II is not all that much *less* impressive or dramatic, and that powers essentially satisfied with the status quo will strive to avoid anything that they feel could lead to *either* calamity. World War II did not cause total destruction in the world, but it did utterly annihilate the three national regimes that brought it about. It is probably quite a bit more terrifying to think about a jump from the 50th floor than about a jump from the 5th floor, but anyone who finds life even minimally satisfying is extremely unlikely to do either.

Did the existence of nuclear weapons keep the Korean conflict restrained? As noted, the communist venture there seems to have been a limited probe—though somewhat more adventurous than usual and one that got out of hand with the massive American and Chinese involvement. As such, there was no particular reason—or meaningful military opportunity—for the Soviets to escalate the war further. In justifying *their* restraint, the Americans continually stressed the danger of escalating to a war with the Soviet Union—something of major concern whether or not the Soviets possessed nuclear weapons. . . .

Much the same could be said about other instances in which there was a real or implied threat that nuclear weapons might be brought into play: the Taiwan Straits crises of 1954–55 and 1958, the Berlin blockade of 1948–49, the Soviet-Chinese confrontation of 1969, the Six-Day War in 1967, the Yom Kippur War of 1973, Cold War disagreements over Lebanaon in 1958, Berlin in 1958 and 1961, offensive weapons in Cuba in 1962. All were resolved, or allowed to dissipate, at rather low rungs on the escalatory ladder. While the horror of a possible nuclear war was doubtless clear to the participants, it is certainly not apparent that they would have been much more casual about escalation if the worst they had to visualize was a repetition of World War II.

Of course nuclear weapons add new elements to international politics: new pieces for the players to move around the board (missiles in and out of Cuba, for example), new terrors to contemplate. But in counter to the remark attributed to Albert Einstein that nuclear weapons have changed everything except our way of thinking, it might be suggested that nuclear weapons have changed little except our way of talking, gesturing, and spending money.

STABILITY

The argument thus far leads to the conclusion that stability is overdetermined—that the postwar situation contains redundant sources of stability. The United States and the Soviet Union have been essentially satisfied with their lot and, fearing escalation to another costly war, have been quite willing to keep their conflicts limited. Nuclear weapons may well have enhanced this stability—they are certainly dramatic reminders of how horrible a big war could be. But it seems highly unlikely that, in their absence, the leaders of the major powers would be so unimaginative as to need such reminding. Wars are not begun out of casual caprice or idle fancy, but because one country or another decides that it can profit from (not simply win) the war—the combination of risk, gain, and cost appears preferable to peace. Even allowing considerably for stupidity, ineptness, miscalculation, and self-deception in these considerations, it does not appear that a large war, nuclear or otherwise, has been remotely in the interest of the essentially contented, risk-averse, escalation-anticipating powers that have dominated world affairs since 1945.

It is *conceivable* of course that the leadership of a major power could be seized by a lucky, clever, risk-acceptant, aggressive fanatic like Hitler; or that an unprecedentedly monumental crisis could break out in an area, like Central Europe, that is of vital importance to both sides; or that a major power could be compelled toward war because it is consumed by desperate fears that it is on the verge of catastrophically losing the arms race. It is not obvious that any of these circumstances would necessarily escalate to a major war, but the existence of nuclear weapons probably does make such an escalation less likely; thus there are imaginable circumstances under which it might be useful to have nuclear weapons around. In the world we've actually lived in, however, those extreme conditions haven't come about, and they haven't every really even been in the cards. This enhancement of stability is, therefore, purely theoretical—extra insurance against unlikely calamity.

Crisis Stability, General Stability, and Deterrence

In further assessing these issues, it seems useful to distinguish crisis stability from a more general form of stability. Much of the literature on defense policy has concentrated on crisis stability, the notion that it is desirable for both sides

[handwritten margin note: postwar inherently stable.]

[handwritten margin note: wars caused rationally]

in a crisis to be so secure that each is able to wait out a surprise attack fully confident that it would be able to respond with a punishing counterattack. In an ideal world, because of its fear of punishing retaliation, neither side would have an incentive to start a war no matter how large or desperate the disagreement, no matter now intense the crisis. Many have argued that crisis stability is "delicate": easily upset by technological or economic shifts.[16]

There is a more general form of stability, on the other hand, that is concerned with balance derived from broader needs, desires, and concerns. It prevails when two powers, taking all potential benefits, costs, and risks into account, greatly prefer peace to war—in the extreme, even to victorious war—whether crisis stability exists or not. For example, it can be said that general stability prevails in the relationship between the United States and Canada. The United States enjoys a massive military advantage over its northern neighbor since it could attack at any time with little concern about punishing military retaliation or about the possibility of losing the war (that is, it has a full "first strike capability"), yet the danger that the United States will attack Canada is nil. General stability prevails.

Although the deterrence literature is preoccupied with military considerations, the deterrence concept may be more useful if it is broadened to include nonmilitary incentives and disincentives. For example, it seems meaningful to suggest that the United States is "deterred" from attacking Canada, but not, obviously, by the Canadians' military might. If anyone in Washington currently were even to contemplate a war against Canada (a country, it might be noted, with which the United States has been at war in the past and where, not too long ago, many Americans felt their "manifest destiny" lay), the planner would doubtless be dissuaded by nonmilitary factors. For example, the war would disrupt a beneficial economic relationship; the United States would have the task of occupying a vast new area with sullen and uncooperative inhabitants; the venture would produce political turmoil in the United States. Similar cases can be found in the Soviet sphere. Despite an overwhelming military superiority, the USSR has been far from anxious to attack such troublesome neighboring states as Poland and Romania. It seems likely that the vast majority of wars that never take place are caused by factors that have little to do with military considerations. . . .

If a kind of overwhelming general stability really prevails, it may well be that the concerns about arms and the arms race are substantially overdone. That is, the often-exquisite numerology of the nuclear arms race has probably had little to do with the important dynamics of the Cold War era, most of which have taken place at militarily subtle levels such as subversion, guerrilla war, local uprising, civil war, and diplomatic posturing. As Benjamin Lambeth has observed, "it is perhaps one of the notable ironies of the nuclear age that while both Washington and Moscow have often lauded superiority as a military force-posture goal, neither has ever behaved as though it really believed superiority significantly mattered in the resolution of international conflicts.[17] In their extensive study of the use of the threat and force since World War II, Blechman and Kaplan conclude that, "especially noteworthy is the fact that our data do not support a hypothesis that the strategic weapons balance between the United States and the USSR influences outcomes."[18]

A special danger of weapons imbalance is often cited: A dominant country might be emboldened to use its superiority for purposes of pressure and intimidation. But unless its satisfaction with the status quo falls enormously and unless its opponent's ability to respond becomes very low as well, the superior power is unlikely to push its advantage very far, and certainly not anywhere near the point of major war. Even if the war could be kept nonnuclear and even if that power had a high probability of winning, the gains are likely to be far too low, the costs far too high.

Stability: Trends

Curiously, in the last twenty-five years crisis stability between the United States and the USSR has probably gotten worse while general stability has probably improved.

With the development of highly accurate multiple warhead missiles, there is a danger that one side might be able to obtain a first-strike counterforce capability, at least against the other side's land-based missiles and bombers, or that it might become able to cripple the other's command and control operations. At the same time, however, it almost seems—to put it very baldly—that the two major powers have forgotten how to get into a war. Although on occasion they still remember how to say nasty things about each other, there hasn't been a true, bone-crunching confrontational crisis for over a quarter-century. Furthermore, as Bernard Brodie notes, even the last crisis, over missiles in Cuba, was "remarkably different . . . from any previous one in history" in its "unprecedented candor, direct personal contact, and at the same time mutual respect between the chief actors."[19] Events since then that seem to have had some warlike potential, such as the military alert that attended the Yom Kippur War of 1973, fizzled while still at extremely low levels. . . .

It seems reasonable, though perhaps risky, to extrapolate from this trend and to suggest that, whatever happens with crisis stability in the future, general stability is here to stay for quite some time. That is, major war—war among developed countries—seems so unlikely that it may well be appropriate to consider it obsolescent. Perhaps World War II was indeed the war to end war—at least war of that scale and type.

The Hollandization Phenomenon   There are, of course, other possibilities. Contentment with the status-quo could diminish in time and, whatever the traumas of World War II, its lessons could eventually wear off, especially as postwar generations come to power. Somehow the fear of escalation could diminish, and small, cheap wars among major countries could again seem viable and attractive. We could get so used to living with the bomb that its use becomes almost casual. Some sort of conventional war could reemerge as a viable possibility under nuclear stalemate. But, as noted, the trends seem to be substantially in the opposite direction: Discontent does not seem to be on the rise, and visceral hostility seems to be on the decline.

Moreover, it might be instructive to look at some broad historical patterns. For centuries now, various countries, once warlike and militaristic, have been quietly dropping out of the war system to pursue neutrality and, insofar as they are allowed to do so, perpetual peace. Their existence tends to go unremarked because chroniclers have preferred to concentrate on the antics of the "Great Powers." "The story of international politics," observes Waltz, "is written in terms of the great powers of an era."[20] But it may be instructive for the story to include Holland, a country which chose in 1713, centuries before the invention of nuclear weapons, to abandon the fabled "struggle for power," or Sweden, which followed Holland's lead in 1721. Spain and Denmark dropped out too, as did Switzerland, a country which fought its last battle in 1798 and has shown a "curious indifference" to "political or territorial aggrandizement," as one historian has put it.[21]

While Holland's bandwagon was quietly gathering riders, an organized movement in opposition to war was arising. The first significant peace organizations in Western history emerged in the wake of the Napoleonic Wars in 1815, and during the next century they sought to promote the idea that war was immoral, repugnant, inefficient, uncivilized, and futile. They also proposed remedies like disarmament, arbitration, and international law and organization, and began to give out prizes for prominent peaceable behavior. They had become a noticeable force by 1914 but, as one of their number, Norman Angell, has recalled, they tended to be dismissed as "cranks and faddists . . . who go about in sandals and long beards, live on nuts."[22] Their problem was that most people living within the great power system were inclined to disagree with their central premise: that war was bad. As Michael Howard has observed, "before 1914 war was almost universally considered an acceptable, perhaps an inevitable and for many people a desirable way of settling international differences."[23] One could easily find many prominent thinkers declaring that war was progressive, beneficial, and necessary; or that war was a thrilling test of manhood and a means of moral purification and spiritual enlargement, a promoter of such virtues as orderliness, cleanliness, and personal valor.

It should be remembered that a most powerful effect of World War I on the countries that fought it was to replace that sort of thinking with a revulsion against wars and with an overwhelming, and so far permanent, if not wholly successful, desire to prevent similar wars from taking place. Suddenly, after World War I, peace advocates were a decided majority. As A.A. Milne put it in 1935, "in 1913, with a few exceptions we all thought war was a natural and fine thing to happen, so long as we were well prepared for it and had no doubt about coming out the victor. Now, with a few exceptions, we have lost our illusions; we are agreed that war is neither natural nor fine, and that the victor suffers from it equally with the vanquished."[24]

For the few who didn't get the point, the lesson was substantially reinforced by World War II. In fact, it almost seems that after World War I the only person left in Europe who was willing to risk another total war was Adolf Hitler. He had a vision of expansion and carried it out with ruthless and single-minded determination. Many Germans found his vision appealing, but unlike the situation in 1914 where enthusiasm for war was common, Hitler found enormous reluctance at all levels within Germany to use war to quest after the vision. As Gerhard Weinberg has concluded, "whether any other German leader would indeed have taken the plunge is surely doubtful, and the very warnings Hitler received from some of his generals can only have reinforced his belief in his personal role as the one man able, willing, and even eager to lead Germany and drag the world into war."[25] Hitler himself told his generals in 1939 "in all modesty" that he alone possessed the nerve required to lead Germany to fulfill what he took to be its mission. In Italy, Benito Mussolini also sought war, but only a small one, and he had to deceive his own generals to get that.[26] Only in Japan, barely touched by World War I, was the willingness to risk major war fairly widespread.

Since 1945 the major nuclear powers have stayed out of war with each other, but equally interesting is the fact that warfare of *all* sorts seems to have lost its appeal within the developed world. With only minor and fleeting exceptions (the Falklands War of 1982, the Soviet invasions of Hungary and Czechoslovakia), there have been no wars among the 48 wealthiest countries in all that time. Never before have so many well-armed countries spent so much time not using their arms against each other. This phenomenon surely goes well beyond the issue of nuclear weapons; they have probably been no more crucial to the non-war between, say, Spain and Italy than they have been to the near-war between Greece and Turkey or to the small war between Britain and Argentina.

Consider the remarkable cases of France and Germany, important countries which spent decades and centuries either fighting each other or planning to do so. For this age-old antagonism, World War II was indeed the war to end war. Like Greece and Turkey, they certainly retained the creativity to discover a motivation for war if they had really wanted to, even under an over-arching superpower balance; yet they have now lived side-by-side for nearly half a century, perhaps with some bitterness and recrimination, but without even a glimmer of war fever. They have become Hollandized with respect to one another. The case of Japan is also instructive: Another formerly aggressive major power seems now to have embraced fully the virtues and profits of peace.

The existence of nuclear weapons also does not help very much to explain the complete absence since 1945 of civil war in the developed world (with the possible exception of the 1944–49 Greek civil war, which could be viewed instead as an unsettled carryover of World War II). The sporadic violence in Northern Ireland or the Basque region of Spain has not really been sustained enough to be considered civil war, nor have the spurts of terrorism carried out by tiny bands of self-styled revolutionaries elsewhere in Western Europe. Except for the case of Hungary in 1956, Europeans under Soviet domination have not (so far) resorted to major violence, no matter how desperate their disaffection. . . .

As a form of activity, war in the developed world may be following once-fashionable dueling into obsolescence: The perceived wisdom, value, and efficacy of war may have moved gradually toward terminal disrepute. Where war was often casually seen as beneficial, virtuous, progressive, and glorious, or at least as necessary or inevitable, the conviction has now become widespread that war in the developed world would be intolerably costly, unwise, futile, and debased.

World war would be catastrophic, of course, and so it is sensible to be concerned about it even if its probability is microscopic. Yet general stability seems so firm and the trends so comforting that the concerns of Schell and others about our eventual "final coma" seem substantially overwrought. By themselves, weapons do not start wars, and if nuclear weapons haven't had much difference, reducing their numbers probably won't either. They may be menacing, but a major war seems so spectacularly unlikely that for those who seek to save lives it may make sense to spend less time worrying about something so improbable as major war and more time dealing with limited conventional wars outside the developed world, where war still can seem cheap and tempting, where romantic notions about holy war and purifying revolution still persist and sometimes prevail, and where developed countries sometimes still fight carefully delimited surrogate wars. Wars of that sort are still far from obsolete and have killed millions since 1945.

Over a quarter century ago, strategist Herman Kahn declared that "it is most unlikely that the world can live with an uncontrolled arms race lasting for several decades." He expressed his "firm belief" that "we are not going to reach the year 2000—and maybe not even the year 1965—without a cataclysm" unless we have "much better mechanisms than we have had for forward thinking."[27] Reflecting again on the cases of the United States and Canada, of Sweden and Denmark, of Holland, of Spain and Switzerland, of France and Germany, and of Japan, it might be suggested that there is a long-term solution to the arms competition between the United States and the Soviet Union, and that it doesn't have much to do with "mechanisms." Should political tensions decline, as to a considerable degree they have since the classic Cold War era of 1945–63, it may be that the arms race will gradually dissipate. And it seems possible that this condition might be brought about not principally by ingenious agreements over arms control, but by atrophy stemming from a dawning realization that, since preparations for major war are essentially irrelevant, they are profoundly foolish.

NOTES

1. Edward N. Luttwak, "Of Bombs and Men," *Commentary*, August 1983, 82.
2. Robert J. Art and Kenneth N. Waltz, "Technology, Strategy, and the Uses of Force," in Robert J. Art and Kenneth N. Waltz, eds., *The Use of Force* (Lanham, Md.: University Press of America, 1983), 28. See also Klaus Knorr, "Controlling Nuclear War," *International Security*, 9, no. 4 (Spring 1985): 79; John J. Mearsheimer, "Nuclear Weapons and Deterrence in Europe," *International Security*, 9, no. 3 (Winter 1984/85): 25–26; Robert Gilpin, *War and Change in World Politics* (Cambridge: Cambridge University Press, 1981), 213–19.

3. Jonathan Schell, *The Fate of the Earth* (New York: Knopf, 1982), 231.

4. Kenneth N. Waltz, *Theory of International Politics* (Reading, Mass.: Addison-Wesley, 1979), 190. See also Joseph S. Nye, Jr., "Nuclear Learning and U.S.-Soviet Security Regimes," *International Organization*, 41, no. 3 (Summer 1987): 377.

5. Jack Snyder, *The Ideology of the Offensive* (Ithaca: Cornell University Press, 1984); Stephen Van Evera, "Why Cooperation Failed in 1914," *World Politics*, 38, no. 1 (October 1985): 80–117. See also the essays on "The Great War and the Nuclear Age" in *International Security*, 9, no. 1 (Summer 1984): 7–186.

6. Matthew A. Evangelista, "Stalin's Postwar Army Reappraised," *International Security*, 7, no. 3 (Winter 1982/83), 110.

7. This assumption is strongly questioned in ibid., 110–38.

8. Despite shortages, rationing, and tax surcharges, American consumer spending increased by 12 percent between 1939 and 1944. Richard R. Lingeman, *Don't You Know There's a War On?* (New York: Putnam, 1970), 133, 357, and ch. 4; Alan S. Milward, *War, Economy and Society 1939–1945* (Berkeley and Los Angeles: University of California Press, 1977), 63–74, 271–75; Mercedes Rosebery, *This Day's Madness* (New York: Macmillan, 1944), xii.

9. John R. Deane, *The Strange Alliance* (New York: Viking, 1947), 92–95; Robert Huhn Jones, *The Roads to Russia* (Norman: University of Oklahoma Press, 1969), Appendix A. Additional information from Harvey DeWeerd.

10. Adam Ulam, *The Rivals: America and Russia Since World War II* (New York: Penguin, 1971), 95 and 5. In essence, Stalin seems to have understood that in Great Power wars, as Paul Kennedy put it, "victory has always gone to the side with the greatest material resources." Paul Kennedy, *The Rise and Fall of the Great Powers* (New York: Random House, 1987), 439.

11. Samuel P. Huntington, *The Common Defense* (New York: Columbia University Press, 1961), 46. See also Walter Mills, ed., *The Forrestal Diaries* (New York: Viking, 1951), 350–51.

12. Thomas, *Armed Truce*, 548.

13. James Schlesinger, *On Reading Non-technical Elements to Systems Studies*, P-3545 (Santa Monica, Cal.: RAND, February 1967), 6.

14. Warner R, Schilling, "The H-Bomb Decision," *Political Science Quarterly*, 76, no. 1 (March 1961): 26. See also Waltz: "Nuclear weapons did not cause the condition of bipolarity. . . . Had the atom never been split, [the US and the USSR] would far surpass others in military strength, and each would remain the greatest threat and source of potential damage to the other." Waltz, *Theory of International Politics*, 180–81.

15. John Lewis Gaddis, *The Long Peace* (New York: Oxford University Press, 1987), 229–232; Gilpin, *War and Change in World Politics*, 218; Coit D. Blacker, *Reluctant Warriors* (New York: Freeman, 1987), 46.

16. The classic statement of this position is, of course, Albert Wohlstetter, "The Delicate Balance of Terror," *Foreign Affairs*, 27, no. 2 (January 1959): 211–34. See also Glenn H. Snyder, *Deterrence and Defense* (Princeton: Princeton University Press, 1961), 97–109.

17. Benjamin S. Lambeth, "Deterrence in the MIRV Era," *World Politics*, 24, no. 2 (January 1972): 234n.

18. Barry M. Blechman and Stephen S. Kaplan, *Force Without War* (Washington, D.C.: Brookings, 1978), 132. See also Jacek Kugler, "Terror Without Deterrence: Reassessing the Role of Nuclear Weapons," *Journal of Conflict Resolution*, 28, no. 3 (September 1984): 470–506.

19. Bernard Brodie, *War and Politics* (New York: Macmillan, 1973), 426.

20. Waltz, *Theory of International Politics*, 72.

21. Lynn Montross, quoted in Jack S. Levy, *War in the Modern Great Power System* (Lexington: University Press of Kentucky), 45. On this issue, see also Brodie, *War and Politics*, 314.

22. Norman Angell, *After All* (New York: Farrar, Straus, and Young, 1951), 147. See also A.C.F. Beales, *The History of Peace* (New York: Dial, 1931); Roger Chickering, *Imperial Germany and a World Without War* (Princeton: Princeton University Press, 1975).

23. Howard, "The Causes of Wars," 92.

24. A.A. Milne, *Peace With Honour* (New York: Dutton, 1935), 9–10. See also Paul Fussell, *The Great War and Modern Memory* (New York: Oxford University Press, 1975); I.F. Clarke, *Voices Prophesying War 1763–1984* (London: Oxford University Press, 1966), chap. 5.

25. Gerhard Weinberg, *The Foreign Policy of Hitler's Germany* (Chicago: University of Chicago Press, 1982), 664.

26. MacGregor Knox, *Mussolini Unleashed 1939–1941* (Cambridge: Cambridge University Press, 1982), chap. 3.

27. Herman Kahn, *On Thermonuclear War* (Princeton: Princeton University Press, 1961), 574, x, 576.

The Utility of Nuclear Deterrence

Robert Jervis

Perhaps the most striking characteristic of the postwar world is just that—it can be called "postwar" because the major powers have not fought each other since 1945. Such a lengthy period of peace among the most powerful states is unprecedented.[1] Almost as unusual is the caution with which each superpower has treated the other. Although we often model superpower relations as a game of chicken, in fact the United States and USSR have not behaved like reckless teenagers. Indeed, superpower crises are becoming at least as rare as wars were in the past. Unless one strains and counts 1973, we have gone over a quarter of a century without a severe crisis. Furthermore, in those that have occurred, each side has been willing to make concessions to avoid venturing too near the brink of war. Thus the more we see of the Cuban missile crisis, the more it appears as a compromise rather than an American victory. Kennedy was not willing to withhold all inducements and push the Russians as hard as he could if this required using force or even continuing the volatile confrontation.[2]

It has been common to attribute these effects to the existence of nuclear weapons. Because neither side could successfully protect itself in an all-out war, no one could win—or, to use John Mueller's phrase, profit from it.[3] Of course this does not mean that wars will not occur. It is rational to start a war one does not expect to win (to be more technical, whose expected utility is negative), if it is believed that the likely consequences of not fighting are even worse.[4] War could also come through inadvertence, loss of control, or irrationality. But if decision makers are "sensible,"[5] peace is the most likely outcome. Furthermore, nuclear weapons can explain superpower caution: When the cost of seeking excessive gains is an increased probability of total destruction, moderation makes sense.

Some analysts have argued that these effects either have not occurred or are not likely to be sustained in the future. Thus Fred Iklé is not alone in asking

International Security, Fall 1988 (Vol. 13, No. 2) © 1988 by the President and Fellows of Harvard College and of the Massachusetts Institute of Technology. Portions of the text and some footnotes have beem omitted.

whether nuclear deterrence can last out the century.[6] It is often claimed that the threat of all-out retaliation is credible only as a response to the other side's all-out attack: Thus Robert McNamara agrees with more conservative analysts whose views he usually does not share that the "sole purpose" of strategic nuclear force "is to deter the other side's first use of its strategic forces."[7] At best, then, nuclear weapons will keep the nuclear peace; they will not prevent—and, indeed, may even facilitate—the use of lower levels of violence.[8] It is then not surprising that some observers attribute Soviet adventurism, particularly in Africa, to the Russians' ability to use the nuclear stalemate as a shield behind which they can deploy pressure, military aid, surrogate troops, and even their own forces in areas they had not previously controlled. The moderation mentioned earlier seems, to some, to be only one-sided. Indeed, American defense policy in the past decade has been driven by the felt need to create limited nuclear options to deter Soviet incursions that, while deeply menacing to our values, fall short of threatening immediate destruction of the United States.

Furthermore, while nuclear weapons may have helped keep the peace between the United States and USSR, ominous possibilities for the future are hinted at by other states' experiences. Allies of nuclear-armed states have been attacked: Vietnam conquered Cambodia and China attacked Vietnam. Two nuclear powers have fought each other, albeit on a very small scale: Russia and China skirmished on their common border. A nonnuclear power has even threatened the heartland of a nuclear power: Syria nearly pushed Israel off the Golan Heights in 1973 and there was no reason for Israel to be confident that Syria was not trying to move into Israel proper. Some of those who do not expect the United States to face such a menace have predicted that continued reliance on the threat of mutual destruction "would lead eventually to the demoralization of the West. It is not possible indefinitely to tell democratic republics that their security depends on the mass extermination of civilians . . . without sooner or later producing pacifism and unilateral disarmament."[9]

John Mueller has posed a different kind of challenge to claims for a "nuclear revolution." He disputes, not the existence of a pattern of peace and stability, but the attributed cause. Nuclear weapons are "essentially irrelevant" to this effect; modernity and highly destructive nonnuclear weapons would have brought us pretty much to the same situation had it not been possible to split the atom.[10] Such intelligent revisionism makes us think about questions whose answers had seemed self-evident. But I think that, on closer inspection, the conventional wisdom turns out to be correct. Nevertheless, there is much force in Mueller's arguments, particularly in the importance of what he calls "general stability" and the reminder that the fact that nuclear war would be so disastrous does not mean that conventional wars would be cheap.

Mueller is certainly right that the atom does not have magical properties. There is nothing crucial about the fact that people, weapons, industry, and agriculture may be destroyed as a result of a particular kind of explosion, although fission and fusion do produce special byproducts like fallout and electromagnetic pulse. What is important are the political effects that nuclear weapons produce, not the physics and chemistry of the explosion. We need to determine what these effect are, how they are produced, and whether modern conventional weapons would replicate them.

POLITICAL EFFECTS OF NUCLEAR WEAPONS

The existence of large nuclear stockpiles influences superpower politics from three directions. Two perspectives are familiar: First, the devastation of an all-out war would be unimaginably enormous. Second, neither side—nor, indeed, third parties—would be spared this devastation. As Bernard Brodie, Thomas Schelling, and many others have noted, what is significant about nuclear weapons is not "overkill" but "mutual kill."[11] That is, no country could win an all-out nuclear war, not only in the sense of coming out of the war better than it went in, but in the sense of being better off fighting than making the concessions needed to avoid the conflict. It should be noted that although many past wars, such as World War II for all the Allies except the United States (and, perhaps, the USSR), would not pass the first test, they would pass the second. For example: Although Britain and France did not improve their positions by fighting, they were better off than they would have been had the Nazis succeeded. Thus it made sense for them to fight even though, as they feared at the outset, they would not profit from the conflict. Furthermore, had the Allies lost the war, the Germans—or at least the Nazis—would have won in a very meaningful sense, even if the cost had been extremely high. But "a nuclear war," as Reagan and Gorbachev affirmed in their joint statement after the November 1985 summit, "cannot be won and must never be fought."[12]

A third effect of nuclear weapons on superpower politics springs from the fact that the devastation could occur extremely quickly, within a matter of days or even hours. This is not to argue that a severe crisis or the limited use of force—even nuclear force—would inevitably trigger total destruction, but only that this is a possibility that cannot be dismissed. At any point, even in calm times, one side or the other could decide to launch an unprovoked all-out strike. More likely, a crisis could lead to limited uses of force which in turn, through a variety of mechanisms, could produce an all-out war. Even if neither side initially wanted this result, there is a significant, although impossible to quantify, possibility of quick and deadly escalation.

Mueller overstates the extent to which conventional explosives could substitute for nuclear ones in these characteristics of destructiveness, evenhandedness, and speed. One does not have to underestimate the horrors of previous wars to stress that the level of destruction we are now contemplating is much greater. Here, as in other areas, there comes a point at which a quantitative difference becomes a qualitative one. Charles De Gaulle put it eloquently: After a nuclear war, the "two sides would have neither powers, nor laws, nor cities, nor cultures, nor cradles, nor tombs."[13] While a total "nuclear winter" and the extermination of human life would not follow a nuclear war, the world-wide effects would be an order of magnitude greater than those of any previous war.[14] Mueller understates the differences in the scale of potential destruction: "World War II did not cause total destruction in the world, but it did utterly annihilate the three national regimes that brought it about. It is probably quite a bit more terrifying to think about a jump from the 50th floor than about a jump from the 5th floor, but anyone who finds life even minimally satisfying is extremely unlikely to do either."[15] The war did indeed destroy these national regimes, but it did not utterly destroy the country itself or even all the values the previous regimes supported. Most people in the Axis countries survived World War II; many went on to prosper. Their children, by and large, have done well. There is an enormous gulf between this outcome—even for the states that lost the war—and a nuclear holocaust. It is far from clear whether societies could ever be reconstituted after a nuclear war or whether economies would ever recover.[16] Furthermore, we should not neglect the impact of the prospect of destruction of culture, art, and national heritage: even a decision maker who was willing to risk the lives of half his population might hesitate at the thought of destroying what has been treasured throughout history.

Mueller's argument just quoted is misleading on a second count as well: The countries that started World War II were destroyed, but the Allies were not. It was more than an accident but less than predetermined that the countries that were destroyed were those that sought to overturn the status quo; what is crucial in this context is that with conventional weapons at least one side can hope, if not expect, to profit from the war. Mueller is quite correct to argue that near-absolute levels of punishment are rarely required for deterrence, even when the conflict of interest between the two sides is great—i.e., when states believe that the gross gains (as contrasted with the net gains) from war would be quite high. The United States, after all, could have defeated North Vietnam. Similarly, as Mueller notes, the United States was deterred from trying to liberate East Europe even in the era of American nuclear monopoly.

But, again, one should not lose sight of the change in scale that nuclear explosives produce. In a nuclear war the "winner" might end up distinguishably less worse off than the "loser," but we should not make too much of this difference. Some have. As Harold Brown put it when he was Secretary of the Air Force, "if the Soviets thought they may be able to recover in some period of time while the U.S. would take three or four times as long, or would never recover, then the Soviets might not be deterred."[17] Similarly, one of the criteria that Secretary of Defense Melvin Laird held necessary for the essential equivalence of Soviet and American forces was: "preventing the Soviet Union from gaining the ability to cause considerably greater urban/industrial destruction than the United States would in a nuclear war."[18] A secret White House memorandum in 1972 used a similar formulation when it defined "strategic sufficiency" as the forces necessary "to ensure that the United States would emerge from a nuclear war in discernably better shape than the Soviet Union."[19]

But this view is a remarkably apolitical one. It does not relate the costs of the war to the objectives and ask whether the destruction would be so great that the "winner," as well as the loser, would regret having fought it. Mueller avoids this trap, but does not sufficiently consider the possibility that, absent nuclear explosives, the kinds of analyses quoted above would in fact be appropriate. Even very high levels of destruction can rationally be compatible with a focus on who will come out ahead in an armed conflict. A state strongly motivated to change the status quo could believe that the advantages of domination were sufficiently great to justify enormous blood-letting. For example, the Russians may feel that World War II was worth the cost not only when compared with being conquered by Hitler, but also when compared with the enormous increase in Soviet prestige, influence, and relative power.

Furthermore, without nuclear weapons, states almost surely would devote great energies to seeking ways of reducing the costs of victory. The two world wars were enormously destructive because they lasted so long. Modern technology, especially when combined with nationalism and with alliances that can bring others to the rescue of a defeated state, makes it likely that wars will last long: Defense is generally more efficacious than offense. But this is not automatically true; conventional wars are not necessarily wars of attrition, as the successes of Germany in 1939–40 and Israel in 1967 remind us. Blitzkrieg can work under special circumstances, and when these are believed to apply, conventional deterrence will no longer be strong.[20] Over an extended period of time, one side or the other could on occasion come to believe that a quick victory was possible. Indeed, for many years most American officials have believed not only that the Soviets could win a conventional war in Europe or the Persian Gulf, but that they could do so at low cost. Were the United States to be pushed off the continent, the considerations Mueller gives might well lead it to make peace rather than pay the price of refighting World War II. Thus, extended deterrence could be more difficult without nuclear weapons. Of course, in their absence, NATO might build up a larger army and better defenses, but each side would continually explore new weapons and tactics that might permit a successful attack. At worst, such efforts would succeed. At best, they would heighten arms competition, national anxiety, and international tension. If both sides were certain that any new conventional war would last for years, the chances of war would be slight. But we should not be too quick to assume that conventional war with modern societies and weapons is synonymous with wars of attrition.

The length of the war is important in a related way as well. The fact that a war of attrition is slow makes a difference. It is true, as George Quester notes, that for some purposes all that matters is the amount of costs and pain the state has to bear, not the length of time over which it is spread.[21] But a conventional war would have to last a long time to do an enormous amount of damage; and it would not *necessarily* last a long time. Either side can open negotiations or make concessions during the war if the expected costs of continued fighting seem intolerable. Obviously, a timely termination is not guaranteed—the fitful attempts at negotiation during World War II and the stronger attempts during World War I were not fruitful. But the possibility of ending the war before the costs become excessive is never foreclosed. Of course, states can believe that a nuclear war would be prolonged, with relatively little damage being done each day, thus permitting intra-war bargaining. But no one can overlook the possibility that at any point the war could escalate to all-out destruction. Unlike the past, neither side could be certain that there would be a prolonged period for negotiation and intimidation. This blocks another path which statesmen in nonnuclear eras could see as a route to meaningful victory.

Furthermore, the possibility that escalation could occur even though neither side desires this outcome—what Schelling calls "the threat that leaves something to chance"[22]—induces caution in crises as well. The fact that sharp confrontations can get out of control, leading to the eventual destruction of both sides, means that states will trigger them only when the incentives to do so are extremely high. Of course, crises in the conventional era also could escalate, but the possibility of quick and total destruction means that the risk, while struggling near the brink, of falling into the abyss is greater and harder to control than it was in the past. Fears of this type dominated the bargaining during the Cuban missile crisis: Kennedy's worry was "based on fear, not of Khrushchev's intention, but of human error, of something going terribly wrong down the line." Thus when Kennedy was told that a U-2 had made a navigational error and was flying over Russia, he commented: "There is always some so-and-so who doesn't get the word."[23] The knowledge of these dangers—which does not seem lacking on the Soviet side as well[24]—is a powerful force for caution.

Empirical findings on deterrence failure in the nuclear era confirm this argument. George and Smoke show that: "The initiator's belief that the risks of his action are calculable and that the unacceptable risks of it can be controlled and avoided is, with very few exceptions, a necessary (though not sufficient) condition for a decision to challenge deterrence."[25] The possibility of rapid escalation obviously does not make such beliefs impossible, but it does discourage them. The chance of escalation means that local military advantage cannot be confidently and safely employed to drive the defender out of areas in which its interests are deeply involved. Were status quo states able to threaten only a war of attrition, extended deterrence would be more difficult.

GENERAL STABILITY

But is very much deterrence needed? Is either superpower strongly driven to try to change the status quo? On these points I agree with much of Mueller's argument—the likely gains from war are now relatively low, thus producing what he calls general stability.[26] The set of transformations that go under the heading of "modernization" have not only increased the costs of war, but have created alternative paths to established goals, and, more profoundly, have altered values in ways that make peace more likely. Our focus on deterrence and, even more narrowly, on matters military has led to a distorted view of international behavior. In a parallel manner, it has adversely affected policy prescriptions. We have not paid sufficient attention to the incentives states feel to change the status quo, or to the need to use inducements and reassurance, as well as threats and deterrence.[27]

States that are strongly motivated to challenge the status quo may try to do so even if the military prospects are bleak and the chances of destruction considerable. Not only can rational calculation lead such states to challenge the status quo, but people who believe that a situation is intolerable feel strong psychological pressures to conclude that it can be changed.[28] Thus nuclear weapons by themselves—and even mutual second-strike capability—might not be sufficient to produce peace. Contrary to Waltz's argument, proliferation among strongly dissatisfied countries would not necessarily recapitulate the Soviet-American pattern of stability.[29]

The crucial questions in this context are the strength of the Soviet motivation to change the status quo and the effect of American policy on Soviet drives and calculations. Indeed, differences of opinion on these matters explain much of the debate over the application of deterrence strategies toward the USSR.[30] Most of this dispute is beyond our scope here. Two points, however, are not. I think Mueller is correct to stress that not only Nazi Germany, but Hitler himself, was exceptional in the willingness to chance an enormously destructive war in order to try to dominate the world. While of course such a leader could recur, we should not let either our theories or our policies be dominated by this possibility.

A second point is one of disagreement: Even if Mueller is correct to believe that the Soviet Union is basically a satisfied power—and I share his conclusion—war is still possible. Wars have broken out in the past between countries whose primary goal was to preserve the status quo. States' conceptions of what is necessary for their security often clash with one another. Because one state may be able to increase its security only by making others less secure, the premise that both sides are basically satisfied with the status quo does not lead to the conclusion that the relations between them will be peaceful and stable. But here too nuclear weapons may help. As long as all-out war means mutual devastation, it cannot be seen as a path to security. The general question of how nuclear weapons make mutual security more feasible than it often was in the past is too large a topic to engage here. But I can at least suggest that they permit the superpowers to adopt military doctrines and bargaining tactics that make it possible for them to take advantage of their shared interest in preserving the status quo. Winston Churchill was right: "Safety [may] be the sturdy child of terror."

NOTES

1. Paul Schroeder, "Does Murphy's Law Apply to History?" *Wilson Quarterly*, 9, no. 1 (New Year's 1985): 88; Joseph S. Nye, Jr., "The Long-Term Future of Nuclear Deterrence," in Roman Kolkowicz, *The Logic of Nuclear Terror* (Boston: Allen & Unwin, 1987), 234.
2. See the recent information in McGeorge Bundy, transcriber, and James G. Blight, ed., "October 27, 1962: Transcripts of the Meetings of the ExComm," *International Security*, 12, no. 3 (Winter 1987/88): 30–92; and James G. Blight, Joseph S. Nye, Jr., and David A. Welch, "The Cuban Missile Crisis Revisited," *Foreign Affairs*, 66

(Fall 1987): 178–79. Long before this evidence became available, Alexander George stressed Kennedy's moderation; see Alexander L. George, David K. Hall, and William E. Simons, *The Limits of Coercive Diplomacy: Laos, Cuba, Vietnam* (Boston: Little Brown, 1971), 86–143.

3. "The Essential Irrelevance of Nuclear Weapons: Stability in the Postwar World." But as we will discuss below, it can be rational for states to fight even when profit is not expected.

4. Alternatively, to be even more technical, a decision maker could expect to lose a war and at the same time could see its expected utility as positive if the slight chance of victory was justified by the size of the gains that victory would bring. But the analysis here requires only the simpler formulation.

5. See the discussion in Patrick M. Morgan, *Deterrence: A Conceptual Analysis* (Beverly Hills, Calif.: Sage, 1977), 101–24.

6. Fred Iklé, "Can Nuclear Deterrence Last Out the Century?" *Foreign Affairs*, 51, no. 2 (January 1973): 267–85.

7. Robert McNamara, "The Military Role of Nuclear Weapons," *Foreign Affairs*, 62, no. 4 (Fall 1983): 68. For his comments on how he came to this view, see his interview in Michael Charlton, *From Deterrence to Defense* (Cambridge: Harvard University Press, 1987), 18.

8. See Glenn Snyder's discussion of the "stability-instability paradox," in "The Balance of Power and the Balance of Terror," in Paul Seabury, ed., *The Balance of Power* (San Francisco: Chandler, 1965), 184–201.

9. Henry Kissinger, "After Reykjavik: Current East-West Negotiations," *The San Francisco Meeting of the Tri-Lateral Commission, March 1987* (New York: The Trilateral Commission, 1987), 4; see also ibid., 7, and his interview in Charlton, *From Deterrence to Defense*, 34.

10. Mueller, "The Essential Irrelevance." Waltz offers yet a third explanation for peace and stability—the bipolar nature of the international system, which, he argues, is not merely a product of nuclear weapons. See Kenneth Waltz, *Theory of International Politics* (Reading, Mass.: Addison-Wesley, 1979). But in a later publication he places more weight on the stabilizing effect of nuclear weapons: *The Spread of Nuclear Weapons: More May be Better*, Adelphi, Paper No. 171 (London: International Institute for Strategic Studies, 1981).

11. Bernard Brodie, ed., *The Absolute Weapon: Atomic Power and World Order* (New York: Harcourt Brace, 1946); Thomas Schelling, *Arms and Influence* (New Haven: Yale University Press, 1966).

12. *New York Times*, November 22, 1985, A12.

13. Speech of May 31, 1960, in Charles De Gaulle, *Discours Et Messages*, 3 (Paris: Plon, 1970): 218. I am grateful to McGeorge Bundy for the reference and translation.

14. Starley Thompson and Stephen Schneider, "Nuclear Winter Reappraised," *Foreign Affairs*, 64, no. 5 (Summer 1986): 981–1005.

15. "The Essential Irrelevance," 66–67.

16. For a discussion of economic recovery models, see Michael Kennedy and Kevin Lewis, "On Keeping Them Down: Or, Why Do Recovery Models Recover So Fast?" in Desmond Ball and Jeffrey Richelson, *Strategic Nuclear Targeting* (Ithaca, N.Y.: Cornell University Press, 1986), 194–208.

17. U.S. Senate, Preparedness Investigating Subcommittee of the Committee on Armed Services, *Hearings on Status of U.S. Strategic Power*, 90th Cong., 2d sess., April 30, 1968 (Washington, D.C.: U.S. Government Printing Office, 1968), 186.

18. U.S. House of Representatives, Subcommittee on Department of Defense, *Appro-*

priations for the FY 1973 Defense Budget and FY 1973–1977 Program, 92nd Cong., 2d sess., February 22, 1972, 65.

19. Quoted in Gregg Herken, *Counsels of War* (New York: Knopf, 1985), 266.

20. John J. Mearsheimer, *Conventional Deterrence* (Ithaca, N.Y.: Cornell University Press, 1983). It should be noted, however, that even a quick and militarily decisive war might not bring the fruits of victory. Modern societies may be even harder to conquer than are modern governments. A high degree of civilian cooperation is required if the victor is to reach many goals. We should not assume it will be forthcoming. See Gene Sharp, *Making Europe Unconquerable* (Cambridge, Mass.: Ballinger, 1985).

21. George Quester, "Crisis and the Unexpected," *Journal of Interdisciplinary History*, 18, no. 3 (Spring 1988): 701–3.

22. Thomas Schelling, *The Strategy of Conflict* (Cambridge: Harvard University Press, 1960), 187–203; Schelling, *Arms and Influence*, 92–125. Also see Jervis, *The Illogic of American Nuclear Strategy* (Ithaca, N.Y.: Cornell University Press, 1984), ch. 5; Jervis, " 'MAD is a Fact, not a Policy': Getting the Arguments Straight," in Jervis, *Meaning of the Nuclear Revolution* (Ithaca, N.Y.: Cornell University Press, 1989); and Robert Powell, "The Theoretical Foundations of Strategic Nuclear Deterrence," *Political Science Quarterly*, 100, no. 1 (Spring 1985): 75–96.

23. Arthur M. Schlesinger, Jr., *Robert Kennedy and His Times* (Boston: Houghton Mifflin, 1978), 529; quoted in Roger Hilsman, *To Move A Nation* (Garden City, N.Y.: Doubleday, 1964), 221.

24. See Benjamin Lambeth, "Uncertainties for the Soviet War Planner," *International Security*, 7, no. 3 (Winter 1982/83): 139–66.

25. Alexander L. George and Richard Smoke, *Deterrence in American Foreign Policy* (New York: Columbia University Press, 1974), 529.

26. Mueller, "Essential Irrelevance," 69–70; also see Waltz, *Theory of International Politics*, 190.

27. For discussions of this topic, see George, Hall, and Simons, *Limits of Coercive Diplomacy*; George and Smoke, *Deterrence in American Foreign Policy*; Richard Ned Lebow, *Between Peace and War* (Baltimore: Johns Hopkins University Press, 1981); Robert Jervis, "Deterrence Theory Revisited," *World Politics*, 31, no. 2 (January 1979): 289–324; Jervis, Lebow, and Janice Gross Stein, *Psychology and Deterrence* (Baltimore: Johns Hopkins University Press, 1985); David Baldwin, "The Power of Positive Sanctions," *World Politics*, 24, no. 1 (October 1971): 19–38; and Janice Gross Stein, "Deterrence and Reassurance," in Philip E. Tetlock, et al., eds., *Behavior, Society and Nuclear War*, vol. 2 (New York: Oxford University Press, 1991).

28. George and Smoke, *Deterrence in American Foreign Policy*; Lebow, *Between Peace and War*; Jervis, Lebow, and Stein, *Psychology and Deterrence*.

29. Waltz, *Spread of Nuclear Weapons*.

30. See Robert Jervis, *Perception and Misperception in International Politics* (Princeton: Princeton University Press, 1976), chap. 3.

The Unimpressive Record of Atomic Diplomacy

McGeorge Bundy

In addressing the question of the role of nuclear weapons in diplomacy, it is well to begin with an expression of one's own general position on the nuclear problem. My view of these weapons is that for my own country they are a necessary evil. I do not think it acceptable for the United States to renounce the possession of nuclear capabilities while they are maintained in the Soviet Union. In that most basic sense I accept the need for nuclear deterrence and am unimpressed by arguments that neglect this requirement. . . .

I also believe that not all the consequences of the nuclear arsenals are bad. The very existence of nuclear stockpiles has created and enforced a considerable caution in the relations among nuclear-weapon states, so that where the interests of those states are clear and their political and military engagement manifest, as with the Soviet Union and the United States in Eastern and Western Europe respectively, there is an intrinsic inhibition on adventure which is none the less real for being essentially independent of doctrines—and even of nuclear deployments—on either side. I have elsewhere called this phenomenon "existential deterrence,"[1] and I think it has more to do with the persisting peace—and division—of Europe than all the particular nuclear doctrines and deployments that have so often bedeviled the European scene. . . .

Indeed the acceptance of nuclear deterrence, for me as for the American Catholic bishops, is "strictly conditioned," not only on a constant readiness to move to agreed arms reductions as drastic as the most skillful and dedicated negotiations permit, but also on a reluctance to depend on nuclear weapons for purposes beyond that of preventing nuclear war. On the historical record since Nagasaki, I think that these weapons have not been of great use to any government for such wider purposes, and I also think a misreading of that record has led to grossly mistaken judgments and to unnecessary, costly, and sometimes dangerous nuclear deployments by both superpowers, and perhaps by others.

"The Unimpressive Record of Atomic Diplomacy" by McGeorge Bundy from *The Choice: Nuclear Weapons vs. Security*, edited by Gwyn Prins. Reprinted by permission of Chatto & Windus, one of the publishers in The Random Century Group Ltd. Portions of the text and some footnotes have been omitted.

Let us begin by considering what good these weapons have done the United States, which was their first and for a short four years their only possessor. I am willing to concede, though it cannot be proven, that in the years of American monopoly, and perhaps for a short time thereafter (in my view, not beyond 1955, at the latest) American nuclear superiority had some military and political value in Europe. We must recognize that fear of what the Russians would otherwise do with what was then an enormous advantage in conventional strength was not limited to Winston Churchill. Niels Bohr too believed that the American atomic bomb was a necessary balancing force, and so did many other highly peaceable men. But the time has long since passed when either side could hope to enjoy either monopoly or overwhelming superiority, so from the standpoint of the present and the future it is not necessary to challenge this particular bit of conventional wisdom. We do not really know that the American monopoly saved Europe in the early postwar years, but we do not know it did not, and we need not decide.

What is more interesting is to examine these years of evident American nuclear advantage from another angle, to try to see what usefulness that advantage may have had in supporting American diplomacy or in restraining specific adventures of others outside Western Europe. Aside from this debatable European case, there is very little evidence that American atomic supremacy was helpful in American diplomacy. Broadly speaking, the years from 1945 to 1949 were a time in which Soviet power and the power of such major Soviet allies as the Chinese communists was expanding and consolidating itself at a rate not remotely equaled since then, and there is no evidence whatever that fear of the American bomb had any restraining effect on this enormous process. It is true that for a short time in the autumn of 1945 Secretary of States James Byrnes believed that the silent presence of the bomb might constructively affect Soviet behavior at the negotiating table, but in fact it had no such impact, and before the end of the year Byrnes himself had changed his tactics. The importance of this brief and foolish flirtation with atomic diplomacy has been grossly exaggerated by students misreading a marginal and passing state of mind into a calculated effort in which Hiroshima itself is read largely as an effort to impress the Russians.[2] But this misreading is less important than the deeper point that to whatever degree atomic diplomacy may have tempted this or that American leader at this or that moment in those years, it did not work.

The point becomes still more evident when we look at moments which American presidents themselves, in later years, came to see as evidence of the power of the atomic possibility. The two most notable cases are the Soviet withdrawal from Iran in 1946 and the armistice agreement that ended the Korean War in 1953.

In April 1952 President Harry Truman told an astonished press conference that not long after the end of World War II he had given Joseph Stalin "an ultimatum"—to get his troops out of Iran—and "they got out." Truman was referring to events in March 1946, when the Soviet union kept troops in northern Iran after the expiration of an agreed date for British and Russian withdrawal that had been honored by the British. The Soviet stance stirred a vigorous international reaction, and after three weeks of increasing tension there came a Soviet announcement of a decision to withdraw that was executed over the following weeks. Truman never doubted that his messages had been decisive. Out of office, in 1957, he described his action still more vividly: "The Soviet Union persisted in its occupation until I personally saw to it that Stalin was informed that I had given orders to our military chiefs to prepare for the movement of our ground, sea and air forces. Stalin then did what I knew he would do. He moved his troops out." If this statement were accurate, it would be an extraordinary confirmation of the effectiveness of American threats in the age of atomic monopoly, because a troop movement of this sort, in 1946, into an area so near the Soviet Union and so far from the United States could only have been ventured, or feared, because of the nuclear monopoly.[3]

The only trouble with this picture is that no such message ever went to Stalin and no such orders to American officers. What actually happened is wholly different. Stalin did indeed attempt to gain a special position in Iran by keeping his troops beyond the deadline, but what made his effort a failure was not an ultimatum from Truman but primarily the resourceful resistance of the Iranian government, supported indeed by American diplomacy (especially at the United Nations) and still more by a wide and general international reaction. Stalin's was a low-stake venture in an area of persistent Soviet hope. He pulled back when he found the Iranian government firm but not belligerent, his Iranian supporters weak, and the rest of the watching world critical. One of the critics was Harry Truman, and we need not doubt the strength of his feelings. But the messages he actually sent (all now published) were careful and genuinely diplomatic. The United States Government "cannot remain indifferent," and "expresses the earnest hope" of immediate Soviet withdrawal, all "in the spirit of friendly association." There is no deadline and no threat. What we have here is no more than an understandable bit of retrospective braggadocio. As George Kennan later remarked—he had been *chargé d'affaires* in Moscow at the time and was the man who would have had to deliver any ultimatum—Truman "had an unfortunate tendency to exaggerate, in later years, certain aspects of the role that he played" in relations with Stalin.[4]

Regrettably, Truman's retrospective version of events was not harmless. Among stouthearted and uncomplicated anticommunists it became a part of the folklore showing that Harry Truman knew how to stop aggression by toughness, when in fact what he and his colleagues knew, in this case, was something much more important: that their task was to help keep up Iranian courage, but precisely *not* to confront Stalin directly. American diplomacy was adroit but not menacing, and Kennan is right again in describing the result: "It was enough for Stalin to learn that a further effort by the Soviet Union to retain its forces in Persia would create serious international complications. He had enough problems at the moment without that." Truman's messages had certainly helped in this learning process, and not least because they had expressly avoided the kind of threat he later came to believe he made. So his faulty memory led others to learn the wrong lesson.

Dwight Eisenhower contributed even more than Harry Truman to the folklore of atomic diplomacy. He believed that it was the threat of atomic war that brought an armistice in Korea in 1953. In his memoirs he cited a number of warnings and signals to make his case, and his Secretary of State, John Foster Dulles, told allied statesmen in private a lurid tale of nuclear deployments made know to the Chinese. But here again the historical record raises questions. The decisive shift in the position of the communists, a shift away from insistence on the forced repatriation of prisoners, occurred before any of these signals was given, shortly after the death of Stalin in March. While Eisenhower certainly intended the whiff of nuclear danger to reach Peking, the records now available make it clear that he in fact held back from any audible threat because of his recognition that it would be as divisive in 1953 as it had been in 1950, when Harry Truman, by a casual press conference response to a question on the possibility of using nuclear weapons, had brought Prime Minister Attlee across the Atlantic to receive assurance that no such step was in prospect. Quite aside from any nuclear threat, there were other and excellent reasons in 1953 for the communist side to want to end the war: their own heavy losses, the absence of any prospect for further gains, and the continuing high cost of unsuccessful probes of United Nations forces on the ground. At the most the springtime signals of a nuclear possibility were a reinforcement to Chinese preferences already established before those signals were conveyed.

Yet Eisenhower clearly did believe that the Korean case showed the value of nuclear threats, and indeed he and Dulles made the threat permanent in the language of a public declaration after the armistice that those who had supported South Korea would respond to any renewed aggression in ways that might not be limited. In two later crises, over the offshore islands of Quemoy and Matsu in 1955 and 1958, Eisenhower used both open references to nuclear weapons and visible deployments of nuclear-armed forces to underline the risks Mao was running. What actually held off the attacking Chinese forces, in both crises, was not these threats but the effective use of local air and naval superiority, but it cannot be denied that the nuclear possibility may have contributed to Chinese unwillingness to raise the stakes. It is also possible that the readiness of the United States to help defend these small and unimportant islands was increased by the fact that against China the United States then held a nuclear monopoly.

In this case too the threat was almost as alarming to friends as to opponents. Fully aware of the fiercely divisive consequences of any actual use of a nuclear weapon, Eisenhower devoted himself in these crises to the energetic and skillful support of the conventional forces and tactics which fended off the Chinese attacks. He was very careful indeed not to lose his control over the nuclear choice, either by any unconditional public threat or by an delegation of authority. The nuclear reply remained a possibility, not a policy. As he told Nixon in 1958, "You should never let the enemy know what you will not do." In the offshore islands affair as in Korea, Eisenhower kept the use of nuclear weapons as something the enemy could not know he would not do, and believed he gained from this stance.[5]

But the President was teaching his Vice President a lesson that was going out of date even as he explained it. The offshore islands crisis of 1958, so far from being a model for the future, turns out to be the last case we have of a crisis between the United States and a nation not the Soviet Union in which nuclear weapons or threats of their use play any role whatever. Consider the war in Vietnam. Here the president whose inaction proves the point conclusively is the same Richard Nixon who had been Eisenhower's eager student. Nixon came to the White House in 1969 determined to apply to Hanoi the same techniques of credible threat that he thought he had seen used successfully in Korea. If he had continued to believe a nuclear threat would be credible, he would surely have conveyed it. But once he considered the matter carefully he was forced to recognize that there was in reality no way of making a credible nuclear threat because the men in Hanoi knew as well as he did that no American president, by 1969, could in fact have used nuclear weapons in Indochina. To do so would plainly outrage allies and split his own country in half. What you cannot conceivably execute, you cannot plausibly threaten.[6]

The evolution from what Eisenhower believed in 1958 to what Nixon was forced to recognize in 1969 is extraordinarily important, and not all the reasons for it are clear. One of them certainly is the spreading awareness of the danger inherent in the thermonuclear age. The end of the 1950s saw the first large-scale popular reactions to nuclear danger, and the searing experience of the Cuban Missile Crisis gave the threat of nuclear warfare new meaning. More broadly, if less consciously, men had come to believe more and more strongly in the value and importance of respecting the "firebreak" between conventional and nuclear weapons. In September 1964, President Lyndon Johnson had stated the case with characteristic passion and force during his campaign against Barry Goldwater:

> Make no mistake. There is no such thing as a conventional nuclear weapon. For nineteen peril-filled years no nation has loosed the atom against another. To do so now is a political decision of the highest order. And it would lead us down an uncertain path of blows and counterblows whose outcome none may know.[7]

To all these general considerations one must add that by 1969 the morality of the Vietnam War was a profoundly divisive question in the United States. To resort to nuclear weapons in such a war would be to outrage still further the angry opponents of the war and probably to multiply their numbers.

So what Richard Nixon thought he had learned turned out only ten years later not to be so, and by his own wise refusal to present a nuclear threat to Hanoi he reinforced the very tradition whose strength he had not at first understood. If the United States could not threaten the use of nuclear weapons even in such a long and painful contest as Vietnam, in what case was such a threat possible? The answer, today, on all the evidence, is that the only places where a nuclear threat remains remotely plausible are those where it has been present for decades—in Western Europe and in Korea, because of the special historical connections noted above, and much more diffusely and existentially in the general reality that any prospect of direct confrontation between the United States and the Soviet Union presents nuclear risks which enforce caution.

A stronger proposition may be asserted. International support for the maintenance of the nuclear firebreak now operates not only to make nuclear threats largely ineffective, but also to penalize any government that resorts to them. This rule applies as much to the Soviet Union as to the United States. The Soviet government, in the heyday of Nikita Khrushchev, set international records for nuclear bluster. The favorite target was the United Kingdom, not only in the Suez crisis but more generally. Khrushchev clearly believed that his rockets gave him a politically usable superiority and talked accordingly. Yet in fact Soviet threats were not decisive at Suez; they were not even issued until what really was decisive—American opposition to the adventure—had been clear for several days. By 1957 Soviet reminders of British vulnerability, so logical from the point of view of believers in the political value of atomic superiority, were serving only to strengthen the Macmillan government in its determination to maintain and improve its own deterrent. The Soviet triumph in launching Sputnik did indeed help Soviet prestige, but attempts to capitalize on it by crude threats were unproductive.

Still more striking is the failure of Soviet atomic diplomacy in relation to China. Having first made the enormous mistake of helping the Chinese toward nuclear weapons, the Soviets reversed their field at the end of the 1950s and addressed themselves assiduously, but with no success whatever, to an effort to persuade the Chinese that they would be happier without any nuclear weapons of their own. Neither cajolery nor the withdrawal of assistance was effective. Probably nothing could have changed the Chinese purpose, but Soviet unreliability only intensified it, and at no time before the first Chinese explosion in 1964 was the Kremlin prepared to make the matter one of war or peace. By the time that possibility was actively considered, in 1969, the Chinese bomb was a reality requiring caution: In a limited but crucial way the Chinese themselves now had an existential deterrent.

But of course Khrushchev's greatest adventure in atomic diplomacy was also his worst fiasco: the deployment of missiles to Cuba in 1962. It is not clear yet how he hoped to gain from the adventure, but he must have believed that placing these weapons in Cuba would produce advantages of some sort. Whether they were there to be bargained against concessions in Europe, or to demonstrate Soviet will and American impotence, or to establish a less uneven strategic balance, we cannot know. That they were there merely to be traded for a pledge against a US invasion of Cuba we must doubt. Nor need we linger on the fact of the failure.

What deserves attention is rather that in this most important crisis of all we can see clearly three persistent realities: First, it was not what the weapons could actually do but the political impact of the deployment that counted most to both sides; second, both leaders understood that any nuclear exchange would be a personal, political, and national catastrophe; third, as a consequence the determinant of the crisis must be in the level of will and ability to act by less than nuclear means. While this set of propositions does not of itself justify President Kennedy's course, it does make clear the folly of Khrushchev's: He left himself open to the use of conventional superiority by an opponent for whom the choice of inaction was politically impossible. I recognize that many students have asserted the commanding importance of U.S. nuclear superiority in the Cuban Missile Crisis, but I am deeply convinced that they are wrong. Along with five other senior members of the Kennedy Administration, including Dean Rusk and Robert McNamara, I am convinced that the missile crisis illustrates "not the significance but the insignificance of nuclear superiority in the face of survivable thermonuclear retaliatory forces."[8]

The missile crisis had powerful and lasting consequences for the notion of atomic diplomacy. It showed the world that both great governments had a profound lack of enthusiasm for nuclear war, and in so doing it reduced the plausibility of nuclear threats of any kind. It also increased the political costs of such posturing. Even before 1962 Khrushchev had learned to try to couch his threats in relatively civil terms—of course I don't want to crush you, but it's only sensible to note that I can.[9] In October 1962, it was precisely nuclear war that both sides plainly chose to stay clear of, and the world took note. Since that time there has been no open nuclear threat by any government. I think it is not too much to say that this particular type of atomic diplomacy has been permanently discredited.

Even the very occasional use of nuclear signals in a crisis has had low importance in recent decades. The most notable case available is the short alert called in President Nixon's name on October 24, 1973, at the height of Yom Kippur war for the purpose of deterring unilateral Soviet action. This alert, by Henry Kissinger's authoritative account, was intended as a general show of resolution and in no way as a specifically thermonuclear threat. More significantly still, Kissinger's account makes it clear that the alert was unnecessary. The possibility of a unilateral Soviet troop movement to Egypt was effectively blocked by Sadat's overnight decision, before he ever heard of the U.S. alert, to back away from the Soviet proposals.

In recent years there has been one remarkable revival of the notion of atomic diplomacy, together with an equally remarkable demonstration of its lack of content. The revival occurred among frightened American hawks eager to demonstrate that the Soviet nuclear build-up of the 1970s was conferring on Moscow a level of superiority that would inescapably translate into usable political leverage. In its most dramatic form the argument was that the Russians were getting a superiority in large, accurate ICBMs that would soon allow them to knock out our own ICBMs and defy us to reply for fear of annihilation. This was the famous "window of vulnerability," and the argument was that this kind of strategic superiority, because both sides would be aware of it, would make the Soviet Union's political pressures irresistible around the world. It was all supposed to happen before now—in the early 1980s. The argument was riddled with analytical errors, ranging from the over-simplification of the problems of such an attack through the much too facile assumption that no credible reply could be offered, and on to the quite untested notion that a threat of this kind would have useful results for the threat-maker. It is not at all surprising that history has shown the notion empty. There has been no Soviet action anywhere that can be plausibly attributed to the so-called window of vulnerability, and indeed after riding this wave of fear—and others—into the White House, the

Reagan Administration eventually managed to discover that the window did not exist. First, in the spring of 1983, the Scowcroft Commission concluded that the existing capabilities of American forces, taken as a whole, made such a scenario implausible, and in early 1984 Ronald Reagan himself concluded that we are all safer now because "America is back—standing tall," though out there in the real world the strategic balance remains almost exactly the one which led to the foolish fears in the first place. The notion of a new vulnerability to nuclear diplomacy was unreal; perhaps we were dealing instead with a little atomic politics. . . .

My general moral is a simple one. The more we learn about living with nuclear arsenals, the less we are able to find any good use for them but one— the deterrence of nuclear aggression by others—and the more we are led to the conclusion that this one valid and necessary role is not nearly as demanding as the theorists of countervailing strategy assert. No sane government wants nuclear war, and the men in the Kremlin, brutal and cynical tyrants to be sure, are eminently sane. There are two places still—Western Europe and South Korea—where we Americans do have outstanding undertakings to go first with nuclear weapons if necessary. I believe those commitments are increasingly implausible and ripe for revision. They may also create pressure for, though they do not in fact require, special and politically neuralgic deployments.

Such deployments are a subset of the competition in weapons systems that is now itself becoming the largest single threat to peace. The systems now coming in sight, especially those that might seem to offer effective prospects for defense, do indeed raise the specter of a world in which at some moment of great tension in the future one side or the other might feel that its only hope was to "preempt"—to go first—to aim at a simultaneous offensive and defensive knockout. That would be another and much nastier world than the one we now have, and it is worth great efforts to see to it that it does not come into being.

Meanwhile what remains remarkable about the enormous arsenals of the superpowers is how little political advantage they have conferred. It is a question for another essay whether other nuclear powers have gained more.

NOTES

1. McGeorge Bundy, "The bishops and the bomb," *New York Review of Books*, June 16, 1983.
2. The case for the prosecution was presented by Gar Alperowitz in *Atomic Diplomacy: Hiroshima and Potsdam* (New York, 1956). His thesis has not fared well under analysis by more careful historians, many themselves revisionists—see, e.g., Barton J. Bernstein, ed., *The Atomic Bomb: The Critical Issues* (Boston, 1976), 69–71.
3. Truman's press conference is in the *Public Papers of the Presidents* (1952), at pages 290–96. His 1957 remarks appeared in the *New York Times*, August 25, 1957, and are quoted in Stephen S. Kaplan, *Diplomacy of Power* (Washington, D.C., 1981), 70–71.
4. Truman's message of March 6 is printed in part in his own *Memoirs, II, Years of Trial and Hope* (Garden City, New York, 1956), 94–95, and is available also now in

Foreign Relations of the United States (1946), 7: 340–43. The whole episode is covered with great clarity in Bruce R. Kuniholm, *The Origins of the Cold War in the Near East: Great Power Conflict and Diplomacy in Iran, Turkey and Greece* (Princeton, N.J., 1980), 304–37. Kennan's later remark and the one quoted below are in a letter to Kuniholm printed at 321.

5. Eisenhower to Nixon is in Richard Nixon, *The Real War* (New York, 1980), 255.
6. Nixon's recognition that he could not use nuclear weapons in Vietnam is described in his *Memoirs* at 347.
7. *Public Papers of the Presidents, 1963–4*, 2: 1051.
8. See "The lessons of the Cuban Missile Crisis," *Time*, September 27, 1982, 85.
9. For a good example of this sort of thing, see Adam Ulam, *Expansion and Coexistence*, 2nd ed. (New York, 1974), 612.

Security in the Developing Countries

Yezid Sayigh

One of the remarkable features of the evolution of the Third World since 1945 has been its gradual militarization: violent conflict, interstate arms transfers, massive military development. In a broad sense much of this was the result of decolonization. The colonial era had affected the direction and pace of indigenous social, economic, and political evolution of most developing countries. Independence created a new context in which certain old issues, suppressed by the fact of colonial rule, resurfaced. These were mixed with the challenge inherent in the achievement of independence, namely the struggle to define the new nation-states and determine the distribution of power within them. That struggle frequently took a violent form. Even when physical conflict was not involved, expansion of the armed forces and their role in society has, for many emerging states, been viewed alternately as a modernizing agent, pillar of national security, and guarantor of security and stability for socioeconomic development. Compounding the internal dynamic, the bipolarity and superpower rivalry that characterized the world order after 1945 provided a massive stimulus to militarization in the Third World.

At the beginning of the 1990s, many developing countries still face major internal and external challenges. Communal conflict, competition for resources, disputes over territory, and ambitions of regional power continue to provoke insecurity and suspicion. Most are midway in the process of consolidating their nation-states and constructing durable political systems. The perception of threat remains strong, instilling a pervasive sense of vulnerability in the minds of ruling elites. Attempts to achieve security and consolidate state-building in the developing countries spur further military development. . . .

A consequence of this process has been to militarize Third World societies and impose severe financial and structural pressures on the economies. Lack of political stability and social cohesion has also encouraged the military to main-

From "Confronting the 1990's—Security in the Developing Countries" by Yezid Sayigh from *Adelphi Paper* No. 251 (Summer 1990). Reprinted by permission of the International Institute of Strategic Studies. Portions of the text and some footnotes have been omitted.

tain a high profile in many countries and even to assume power. A second consequence has been to encourage a network of military relationships between the developing and industrialized countries, involving the transfer of arms, services, and forces, and the provision of training for indigenous forces. Both processes have gone hand in hand with regional military buildups, and allowed for the introduction of superpower confrontation into local conflicts. Furthermore, some developing countries have embarked on additional programs of military development besides the buildup of conventional arms, in response partly to perceived security needs and partly to developments in the regional and international balances of power. The establishment of local arms industries and the proliferation of nuclear and other mass destruction capabilities are major examples. . . .

PATTERNS OF CONFLICT

Since 1945, most armed conflicts in the developing countries have taken one form or another of "internal war," with only a small number being interstate wars. The frequency of the latter has remained constant in that period, but the incidence of internal conflict—especially tribal and ethnic—has risen markedly. This underlines the significance of social heterogeneity in the developing countries, and the crisis of their state structures. Another pattern has been the increase in military intervention by Third World states in local conflicts, partially replacing the role of the advanced industrialized powers. While reflecting a growth in self-confidence and physical capabilities in some cases, this trend results too from the relative lack of definition of nation-states in the Developing World. The increase in local interventions also highlights the transitional nature of regional power balances and the gradual emergence of would-be regional hegemons.

Up until the very recent past, however, the Advanced Industrialized Countries (AICs) have played an important role in Third World wars, whether through encouraging superpower confrontation "by proxy" or by expanding local conflicts into "internationalized" civil wars. In the first instance, the Iran-Iraq War would have soon reduced to a low-level war of attrition had it not been for massive arms shipments, principally from the USSR, France, and China. Afghanistan, Angola, Nicaragua, and Cambodia are examples of conflicts where the flow of external support to the warring parties altered the balance of forces in the field, and so made decisive resolution even more difficult. Furthermore, the major AICs remain prepared for direct intervention in crisis areas in the Third World, as the US invasion of Grenada and Panama, and French deployment to Chad show. Arms transfers from Europe, especially those East European states eager for hard currency, will continue to affect the combat capacity of Third World states, even if the political interest such conflict inspires in AICs is much diminished. . . .

A further implication is that the shift in superpower behavior in the 1990s with its new emphasis on deescalation and nonviolent resolution of regional conflicts (reflected in the increased interest in UN peacekeeping operations)—will highlight the impact on local security of factors indigenous to the developing countries. It is difficult to tell whether U.S. and Soviet self-restraint will relax the constraints on Third World conflict and so lead to an upsurge in violence, or if the reduction in external largesse will combine with growing economic crises to limit military expenditure (and activity) in the developing countries. The continuation of U.S. and Soviet arms shipments to the opposing sides in Afghanistan, Angola, and Cambodia—despite interim settlements or talks—suggests an attenuation rather than cancellation of previous patterns.

It remains the case that certain important local powers will have regional security interests and objectives which will call into place military force. Countries such as India, Syria, Israel, Iraq, China, Vietnam, and others (such as Israel and South Africa, which although not part of the Developing World, are situated physically within it) will continue to seek the preservation and establishment of a regional security order attractive to them. Calculations of a regional balance of power (which *may* be little affected by superpower interests or deployments) will move them to acquire arms and intervene in local crises to ensure that their own regional positions are maintained. The new international *détente* could thus lead to more complicated regional balances and struggles; it might also set ceilings, because of the decline of external support, on the capacity of certain states (like Syria and Vietnam) to project force confident of outside financial and military assistance. . . .

REGIONAL MILITARY BUILDUPS

Despite the past importance and continued significance of the role of foreign military power within the Third World, this has been paralleled, even overshadowed, by the impact on local security of regional arms races. The developing countries have witnessed a continuous upward spiral in military spending since 1945, much of which has gone into importing modern weapon systems. . . . Three main factors appear to fuel arms races.

First is the pervasive sense of insecurity (both internal and external) felt by the developing countries. . . . The second and third factors are what Thomas Ohlson terms "externally generated stimuli": the cycle of modernization in conventional weapons that occurs every 15–20 years and prompts Third World "middle powers" to seek early acquisition in order to extend equipment currency and delay obsolescence; and arms transfers to selected countries in regions of tensions by an AIC in pursuit of certain policy aims.[1] There is also the factor of the AIC "sales push" not only commercially inspired but also seeking, by securing long production runs, to achieve economies of scale and reduce costs of procurement for their own armed forces. . . .

Ultimately, the local factor—domestic or regional threats—is the determinant one, as without it there is no lasting demand for arms purchases. This is strongly borne out in South Asia and the Middle East, where the Indo-Pakistani, Arab-Israeli, and Gulf conflicts are highly volatile. Southeast Asia offers another example: although ASEAN has achieved a degree of security within its area, its members continue to register heavy military growth in reflection of a general sense of insecurity towards their regional environment. In Latin America, however, the arms race has been kept under control, largely due to the stability of national boundaries and to the relative marginalization of interstate and superpower conflicts within the continent. Border disputes abound, but there is no basic external threat to the continued existence of nation-states. Internal threats pose a different type of challenge that can be met without important state-of-the-art weapon systems, a fact reflected in the armament of most Latin American countries.

The example of South America also highlights the importance of the external factor: in this case the absence of active U.S.–Soviet rivalry in the continent has greatly weakened the drive for a regional arms race. The role of the major AICs—motivated by strategic concerns and material self-interest—is often decisive (though by no means a solitary factor), as without it needed arms supplies may not be forthcoming and certain levels of conflict then become impracticable. Until recently, the superimposition of East–West rivalry onto the pattern of Third World conflict made resolution more intractable, and also strengthened the mutual incentive for each superpower (and other AICs) to pour more arms into the area and indeed to help create conditions making such transfers necessary and justifiable. Ironically, the defusing of Soviet–U.S. rivalry in the late 1980s seems unlikely to curtail arms-marketing efforts by the AICs. Evidently the continuing insecurity of developing countries creates a market, but so does the desire of the AICs to maintain a lucrative market worth some $35bn annually. In 1988 the USSR stepped up efforts to export its modern MiG-29 aircraft, while the U.S. planned to increase its foreign arms sales by 28% in 1989.[2] The arms-exporting AICs are set to face a growing contradiction between their need for markets and the logic of their professed interest in seeing a decline in regional conflict.

A cutoff of external arms supplies will not eliminate conflict within the Third World; indeed, it will hardly even slow local conflict down, as the move towards local weapons production and South–South trade compensates partially for embargoes. Iran's ability to pursue the Gulf War is the best recent example of this. But Iran also provides a good example of the opposite too: however determined a developing country may be to wage war, its success remains dependent on finding major outside sources of weaponry. No developing country is yet free of this constraint, and even the exceptional cases of arms-producing Israel and South Africa (both of which fall outside the LDC category) display the same problem. The Iran–Iraq War moreover showed the marginality of East–West rivalry to the regional arms race, which was dominated by the security objectives of local parties.

What emerges from this debate is that the factors driving regional arms buildups in the Third World are lasting ones. The incentives for AICs to continue supplying arms to developing countries are sufficiently strong and varied as to survive changes in any one of them. Moreover, any unwillingness to export arms by one supplier will almost always be exploited by another, especially with the emergence of China, some additional AICs, and other Third World countries as new arms producers and exporters. However, the fundamental driving force remains the sense of insecurity within the developing countries, most of which view a certain level of arms imports as necessary for their minimum defense requirements and to promote a stable security environment, itself essential for social and economic development. Only progress by these countries in consolidating their nation-states and developing viable political systems will reduce their incentive to arm extensively, by reducing their vulnerability.

ARMS PRODUCTION

Another domestic manifestation of the drive for military development in the developing countries since 1945 is the growth of indigenous defense industries. However, possibly contrary to expectation, this has not been linked necessarily to the incidence of military government. Indeed, a review of Third World arms producers shows powerful evidence for the opposite. Developing countries have various incentives to expand their military industries. Local production is seen as a vehicle for technology transfer, with added potential for interaction between the civilian and military industrial sectors. Development of human skills and basic technical infrastructure can play an important role in providing local repair and maintenance services, reducing overall costs and saving hard currency. The desire for regional prestige is often an additional motivating factor. Nonetheless, the principal incentive to embark on military industrialization for decision makers in most developing countries, military or civilian, is the desire to strengthen national security by guaranteeing supplies of necessary combat material. Of interest here, though, is not the causes for establishing Third World defense industries, but their impact on regional security.

The last decade has seen the emergence of Third World arms producers as a growing force in international relations. According to one study, they were responsible for 22 percent (nearly 17 percent even without China) of all military assistance to Third World combatants during hostilities up to 1984, worth $3.6bn ($2.7bn without China).[3] Statistics of the arms trade are imprecise, it is true, but the broad trend suggested here and demonstrated during the Gulf War shows the impact Third World military production can have on regional security, with major implications for international security too. Elsewhere, imports of Taiwanese equipment have followed Israeli and South African products into Central America, allowing local governments to compensate for the suspension of American arms shipments due to their human rights abuses.[4] What Third World suppliers cannot always do, however, is provide all the necessary backup and most notably the training assistance and support necesary to optimize the introduction of new weapons. . . .

All this suggests that an important distinction between the policies of Third World arms producers and those of the AICs is the way exports fall within a broader strategic context. For the major AICs, sales usually form part of a political relationship with the recipient, and are therefore used to reinforce it. One aspect of this reinforcement is negative: the actual or threatened withholding of equipment as a means of political pressure. Third World arms producers cannot exert such leverage and do not employ military exports to gain it; so they have less incentive to withhold supplies and face fewer constraints than the AICs in exporting to areas of active conflict.

By the same token, Third World producers are less constrained in exporting hardware and technology related to special categories of weapons that may have strategic impact. Sales of Chinese *Silkworm* anti-ship missiles to Iran in 1987 were seen as threatening the regional balance by invoking the possibility of escalating the "tanker war" and extending it to other countries and navies besides Iraq. (This possibility existed with or without *Silkworm*—by means of air and surface ship attack, and sea mines.) Owing to the rise in local tensions and the threat to international shipping, the issue became a point of immediate contention in Sino-American ties. Similarly, external assistance was instrumental in extending the range of Iraqi *Scud* missiles, while both Brazil and Argentina have cooperated with Egypt and Iraq to develop indigenous ballistic missiles. . . .

The scale of Third World arms sales needs to be set in proper proportion. Military exports from the LDCs have been estimated to be worth $1.718m, or only about 2.6 percent of world trade (excluding China, Israel, and South Africa) in 1981–85, a peak period. Once re-exports of imported weapons are deducted, the Third World share of production (whether indigenous or licensed) drops to 1.1 percent, or $749m. Furthermore, Third World military products tend to be at the low end of the technological scale, with the high end still dominated by the AICs. In regions such as the Middle East, significant changes in the actual or perceived balance of power can often only be made by increases in high-tech weaponry whose principal source is still likely to be the AICs. However, in other areas, such as some parts of Africa, low- or medium-tech armaments can substantially affect combat capacities and thus transfers made by Third World states may affect outcomes significantly. Of particular regional and international concern is the proliferation or the local production of NBC weapons and sophisticated delivery systems, especially those with an over-the-horizon capacity.

NBC WEAPONS AND DELIVERY SYSTEMS

The growing proliferation of weapons of mass destruction in the Third World is one illustration of regional arms races and indicates the potential impact of indigenous military industrialization in developing countries. This proliferation emerged in the 1960s and 1970s, accelerated throughout the 1980s, and now poses a major arms-control problem for the 1990s. An increasing number of developing countries have developed nuclear infrastructures with actual or potential military capabilities since the Non-Proliferation Treaty regime went into force in 1970. Several of them may have reached the weapons production stage, with serious implications for future arms control and crisis management.

The spread of delivery means, including medium-range ballistic missiles, increases the threat, as does the appearance of chemical weapons in a number of conflict zones.

The overall picture seems alarming. The AICs generally, and the West specifically, have responded by seeking to limit the proliferation both of weapons of mass destruction, and of the technology necessary to produce them. This concern extends to delivery systems, such as ballistic missiles with an over-the-horizon capacity. In April 1987 the United States, Japan, and five West European states set up a Missile Technology Control Regime (MTCR), and in spring 1988 formed a special committee, designed to prevent the spread of missile technology and materials. Later in 1988, the U.S. administration also started talks with Egypt and Israel on ways of limiting the proliferation of ballistic missiles and of avoiding accidental war in the Middle East. In parallel, a series of international conferences have also been convened to discuss ways of prohibiting the use or development of chemical weapons. In July 1989 the Bush administration gave an example of the control it hoped to exert by banning the sale to India of a combined acceleration vibration climatic test system that could be used to test nuclear-capable reentry vehicles. U.S. pressure was also instrumental in bringing the Egyptian-Iraqi-Argentinian *Condor/Badr 2000* ballistic missile program close to collapse in 1989, and in causing the withdrawal of Italian and West German firms from the transfer to Brazil, proposed by France, of the *Viking* rocket engine used as a first-stage booster for the *Ariane* rocket.[5]

However, these efforts tend to overlook the reasons for proliferation and to exaggerate the effectiveness of nonnuclear (biological or chemical) weapons or ballistic missiles. The basic motivation for the acquisition of such capabilities is a pervasive sense of insecurity. This is most evident in the Middle East and South Asia, where Israeli and Indian possession of nuclear capability has deepened the anxiety of the Arab states and Pakistan. In each case, the neighboring country has sought either to develop its own nuclear capability or to acquire an alternative deterrent: ballistic missiles or the "poor man's bomb"—chemical weapons or both.

Although the appearance of chemical weapons and ballistic missiles in Third World areas of actual or potential conflict gives cause for serious concern, nuclear military capability remains for many the preeminent threat to international security. This is borne out by the reaction to reports that both Iraq and Iran were trying to restart their nuclear programs in late 1987. Had either been successful the consequences could have been calamitous. In South Asia Rajiv Gandhi and Benazir Bhutto agreed to a "no strike" policy against each other's nuclear facilities during their meeting on 30 December 1988. A positive development as such, it nonetheless reflected the degree to which the nuclear issue has become part of the regional balance there. Nuclear technology is no longer the exclusive domain of the AICs, moreover, and several developing countries are entering the world market as traders, thus raising the question of how to achieve broader adherence to safeguard regimes. Brazil, India, and Argentina have emerged as major exporters, offering technology, research reactors, and enriched uranium—occasionally to countries in conflict. Brazil and India are also both developing nuclear reactors for use on submarines, which could become another export item in the future. . . .

In the Third World, nuclear proliferation may tend to undermine hegemony by a single regional power, as Barry Buzan and Gowher Rizvi suggest, though this is not yet evident in the case of India and Pakistan.[6] Conversely, superiority may be reinforced if the leading military power in the region is also the sole local nuclear-capable state, as is the case with both Israel and South Africa (non-LDCs that nonetheless abut on developing countries). One can speculate on whether stability may be achieved through a natural evolution towards a regional balance or by formal arrangements for nuclear weapons-free zones (NWFZs). It may, of course, not be achieved through either means. It is notable, however, that proliferation does not occur or is controlled in areas such as Southeast Asia and Latin America where NWFZs have been suggested or in effect implemented owing to the relatively low intensity of regional rivalries. The Middle East and South Asia are not likely candidates, therefore, for NWFZs or other CBMS, since fundamental interstate conflicts remain active and several imbalances in conventional and nuclear power persist. . . .

PROSPECTS FOR REGIONAL ORGANIZATION

In the past a variety of incentives have prompted developing countries to seek institutional frameworks for collective action. One is awareness of the relatively disadvantageous position that LDCs occupy as a group within the world system, measured in military, economic, and political power. A second is the desire to improve their material conditions, principally by coordinating economic and trade policies. A third is fear of specific threats, whether external or internal. A wide range of regional and international agencies has emerged within the Third World since 1945 in response to these challenges; the scope and nature of each varies according to the specific objective it was established to achieve.

The existence of common problems is not a guarantee of regional cooperation, however. The attitude of each developing country towards collective security arrangements is based on its own perception of the national interest. Not surprisingly, any state will place its own policy preferences first, and will promote regional agencies to the extent that they accommodate or even enhance its individual security. This may appear a universal truism, but it is particularly relevant for the Developing World, where nation-states remain unstable and intraregional ties are relatively loose. More specifically, given the general crisis of state structures in the developing countries, achievement of individual national security is a *sine qua non* for adhering to regional security arrangements. The experience of the Gulf Cooperation Council (GCC) demonstrates this: Faced with the destabilizing effect of the Gulf War, each member effectively took a separate stand on critical issues—Kuwait reflagged its tankers and invited a U.S. naval presence without consulting Saudi Arabia or the GCC, and at Arab summit meetings Oman refused to condemn Iran, with which several emirates maintained strikingly good political and financial ties.

That the formation of regional agencies specifically aimed at security co-operation is a problematic issue in the developing world is indicated by the fact that the founding objectives most frequently cited are economic or general political cooperation. Among the causes for reticence about the security dimension are the wish of individual member states to avoid external interference in their internal affairs, the attitude of the local population or opposition groups, and the reaction of rival powers. Such considerations stand in the way particularly of setting up joint military forces; given the problems of legitimacy that governments and their security apparatuses face in many LDCs, recourse to foreign forces during internal crises would be especially hazardous. In some cases, it is precisely because security is not a stated objective that regional agencies are successful. ASEAN has emerged as a relatively effective security agency (in terms of approving certain measures within its zone and managing collective policy towards the external environment), though founded as a body for economic cooperation.

The fact that the security function of regional agencies in the Third World has been either nonexistent or else important but undeclared raises a question about the nature and substance of intraregional ties. Is there any incentive, besides national security traditionally defined, and any "currency" of exchange and influence between states besides military power, that may come to underlie regional cooperation in the Third World? Put differently, regional organizations have not generally addressed the complete security problem. Special issues such as indebtedness, the drug problem, and environmental challenges may yet alter this lack of formal connections between individual and collective state fortunes—though the momentum to date has been inadequate—but there are few signs of effective joint efforts to deal with the problems of technology transfer, or economic development, through formal regional structures. Regional agencies have not attempted to deal with water management concerns, or other issues that clearly affect regional stability, in the same manner as they have examined politico-military relations between them. . . .

Looking to regional security organization in the 1990s, in conclusion, there appears to be little prospect of change in basic incentives. True, powerful reasons for cooperation exist in the form of issues such as indebtedness, but this is unlikely to generate moves to construct regional security frameworks as a second step. Nor are the undeniably crucial problems of food shortages, the greenhouse effect, or distribution of water resources necessarily conducive to regional organization based solely on local states. Indeed, the fact that the majority of the commercial, economic, and military relations of virtually any developing country are maintained with the AICs acts as a major disincentive to effective and autonomous regional security cooperation.

NOTES

1. Thomas Ohlson, *Arms Transfer Limitations and Third World Security* (Oxford: Oxford University Press, 1988), 37.

2. Robert Pear, "White House Seeks 28% Increase in Weapons Sales," *International Herald Tribune*, May 3, 1988.

3. Stephanie Neuman, "Third World Military Industries," in Stephanie Neuman and Robert Harkavy, eds., *The Lessons of Recent Wars in the Third World: Comparative Dimensions*, 2 (Lexington: Lexington Books, 1987): 159.

4. Jane Hunter, *Israeli Foreign Policy: South Africa and Central America*, (London: Spokesman, 1987); Joel Millman, "Taiwan's Central American Links," *Jane's Defence Weekly*, vol. 10, no. 21, November 26, 1988.

5. "U.S. Bans Sale of Missile Device to India," *International Herald Tribune*, July 17, 1989.

6. Barry Buzan and Gowher Rizvi, "The Future of the South Asian Security Complex," in Buzan and Rizvi et al., *South Asian Insecurity and Great Powers*, (London: Macmillan, 1986), 243.

PART
Three

THE INTERNATIONAL POLITICAL ECONOMY

*I*n Part One, we examined the meaning of anarchy and saw the consequences for state behavior that flowed from it. In Part Two, we analyzed in more detail one of the primary instruments that states can and must use, namely, military power. In Part Three, we are concerned with the other primary instrument of state action, economic power.

Disparities in power, as we saw earlier, have important effects on state behavior. Such disparities occur, not simply because of the differences in the military power that states wield, but also because of the differences in economic resources that they generate. In the first instance, the force that a nation can field is dependent in part on the economic wealth that it can muster to support and sustain its military forces. Wealth is therefore a component of state power. But the generation of wealth, unlike the generation of military power, is also an end of state action. Except in the rarest of circumstances, military power is never sought as an end in itself, but rather is acquired as a means to attain security or the other ends that a state pursues. By contrast, wealth is both a component of state power and a good that can be consumed by its citizenry. Force is mustered primarily for the external arena. Wealth is sought for both the external and the domestic arena. Moreover, wealth and power differ in the degree that states can pursue each without detriment to the positions and interests of other nations. No situation in international politics is ever totally cooperative or conflictual, but the potential for cooperative behavior is greater in the realm of wealth than in the realm of power.

It is the duality of economic power (as a component and end of state action) and its greater potential for common gains that makes the analysis of the role it plays in state behavior and international interactions complex and elusive. The study of international political economy, as it has been tradition-ally understood, encompasses both these aspects of economic power.

THE RELATION OF POLITICS AND ECONOMICS

"The science of economics presupposes a given political order, and cannot be profitably studied in isolation from politics." So wrote E. H. Carr in his seminal work, *The Twenty Year's Crisis,* in 1939. Fifty years earlier, in an essay entitled "Socialism: Utopian or Scientific" Friedrich Engels asserted: "The materialist conception of history starts from the proposition that the production of the means to support human life . . . is the basis of all social structure. . . ." These two views—that economic processes are not autono-mous but require political structures to support them and that economic factors determine the social and political structures of states—represent the polar extremes on the relationship of politics and economics.

Which view is correct? To this question there is no simple or single answer. Any reply is as much philosophical as it is empirical. The economic interests of individuals in a state and of states within the international arena do powerfully affect the goals that are sought and the degree of success with which they are attained. But the political structure of international action is also a constraint. Anarchy makes cooperative actions more difficult to attain than would otherwise be the case and requires that statesmen consider both relative and absolute positions when framing actions in the international eco-nomic realm. And often in international politics the imperatives of security and survival override the dictates of economic interests. War, after all, al-most never pays in a strict balance-sheet sense, particularly when waged between states of roughly equal power. The economic wealth lost in fighting is usually not recouped in the peace that follows.

The best answers to the question, what is the relation between politics and economics in international affairs, have been given by the classical theo-rists of international politics. Robert Gilpin examines three schools of thought—the liberals, the marxists, and the mercantilists. Unlike the other two, liberal political economists have stressed the cooperative, not the con-flictual, nature of international economic relations. They have extended Adam Smith's arguments about the domestic economy to the international economy. Smith argued that the specialization of function by individuals within a state, together with their unfettered pursuit of their own self-interests, would increase the wealth of a nation and thereby benefit all. Col-lective harmony and national wealth could thus be the product of self-interested behavior, if only the government would provide as little restraint on individual action as was necessary. The eighteenth-century Philosophes and the nineteenth- and twentieth-century free traders argued that what was good for the individuals within a state would also be good for states in the international arena. By trading freely with one another, states could specialize according to their respective comparative advantages and the wealth of all nations would, as a consequence, increase. "Make trade not war" has been the slogan of the liberal free traders.

By contrast, both mercantilists and marxists have seen state relations as inherently conflictual. For marxists, this is so because capitalists within and among states compete fiercely with one another to maximize their profits. Driven by their greed, they are incapable of cooperating with one another. Because a state's policy is determined by the capitalist ruling class, states will wage wars for profit and, under Lenin's dictum, will wage wars to redivide the world's wealth. Imperialism as the highest stage of capitalism is a classic zero-sum situation. Mercantilists also argue that economic factors make relations among states conflictual. But their analysis rests, not on the externalization of class conflict, but on the nature of political and economic power. For eighteenth-century mercantilists, the world's wealth was fixed and could only be redivided. For nineteenth- and twentieth-century mercantilists, wealth could be increased for all, but because wealth contributes to national power and power is relative, not absolute, conflict would continue.

All three schools of thought are motivated by their views on the relation of politics to economics. Mercantilists stress the primacy of politics and the consequent pursuit of national power and relative position in the international arena. Both liberals and marxists stress the primacy of economics. For the former, the potential for economic harmony can override the forces of nationalism if only free trade is pursued. For the latter, economic interests determine political behavior and, since the first is conflictual, the second must be also. Both liberals and marxists want to banish politics from international relations, the former through free trade, the latter through the universal spread of communism. Mercantilists, like realists, view these prescriptions as naive and believe that the national interests of every state are only partly determined by their economic interests.

Contemporary writers continue to wrestle with the relation between politics and economics in international affairs. Robert O. Keohane analyzes what types of international political structures are conducive to economic cooperation among nations. He finds the theory of hegemonic stability—that a dominant power is necessary to create and sustain a stable international economic order—a suggestive but not definitive way to understand the last one hundred years. A hegemonic power can foster economic cooperation among states, as the United States did after World War II, but cooperation can occur in the absence of such a power. A hegemonic power is neither a necessary nor a sufficient condition for interstate cooperation.

Stephen D. Krasner looks at the political-economic relations between the United States and the Third World. He argues that Third World states want both wealth and power and have used international organizations and international regimes to advance their interests in ways that are not beneficial to the United States and the other nations of the industrialized world. Due to a peculiar set of conditions in the 1970s and 1980s, the Third World nations were able to advance their interests, with varying degrees of success, in international fora under the rubric of the New International Economic Order (NIEO).

Finally, Robert Gilpin sets forth three models of the future—the sovereignty-at-bay model, the dependencia model, and the mercantilist model—that lay out in clear terms the directions that the international economy can take. The sovereignty-at-bay model represents the traditional liberal vision of an international economy organized along the dictates of economic efficiency and comparative advantage, with little interference by states. The dependencia model stresses that the workings of the international economy only make the strong states stronger and the weak states weaker, because of the exploitative nature of trade between the rich and poor nations. Finally, the mercantilist model resurrects the importance of the nation-state to the international economy and maintains that the political interests of a state dictates the nature of its foreign economic activity as much as does the international marketplace. No one model captures the whole truth, but, taken together, they represent a comprehensive picture of the contemporary international political economy.

THE DEBATE ABOUT INTERDEPENDENCE

At the end of the twentieth century, which way will the international political economy go? Can the nations of the world muster the political will necessary to preserve a relatively open international system that has benefitted them all, even if they have benefitted unequally? Or, have the political costs of severe economic dislocations, which the open system of the last two decades has produced, been too great? Will states lapse into protectionism? Does free trade still make sense when factor endowments (land, labor, capital, and technology) are no longer fixed and when, therefore, comparative advantages are no longer static but can be created behind protectionist barriers, as Japan, to take an example, has so successfully shown?

These are difficult questions to answer. How they are answered depends heavily on how economically interdependent one sees the nations of the world today. "Interdependence" is one of those terms that has developed a myriad of meanings. The most fruitful way to use the term, when considering the relationship between this concept and peaceful cooperation among states, is as follows: Interdependence is the size of the stake that a state believes it has in seeing other states' economies prosper, so as to help its own economy prosper too. Interdependence can be high or low. The higher perceived interdependence is, the larger a state's stake in the economic well-being of the countries with which it heavily interacts; the lower interdependence, the smaller is its stake. High levels of interdependence should facilitate cooperation among states for their mutual gain.

After World War II, the United States used its considerable economic and military power to create an open international economic order by working to lower the barriers among nations to the flow of manufactured goods, raw materials other than agriculture, and capital. The result of this international economic openness was a rise in the level of interdependence, particularly among the industrialized nations of the world, but also, to a considerable degree, among the industrializing nations in the Far East and Latin America as well. But interdependence has its costs as well as its benefits. High levels of participation in the international economy can bring the benefits of efficiency that flow from specialization, but also the destruction of national industries that can no longer compete internationally. States today must reconcile the imperatives of what Robert Gilpin has called "Keynes at home" with "Smith abroad": the maintenance of full employment domestically and the competitive participation in the international economy. Through exports and capital inflows, interdependence can help a state increase its wealth; but it also brings vulnerabilities that derive from the need to rely partially on others for one's own prosperity. Balancing the two imperatives is a difficult political act.

How interdependent the world actually is today, how different this era's interdependence is compared to what obtained before 1914, how important ownership of manufacturing assets is compared to where they are located, whether the world is moving towards economic closure, and how significant trade remains in light of the vast daily flows of capital among nations today—all these issues bear upon the nature and resiliency of today's interdependence. None are settled matters among the experts.

Janice Thomson and Stephen Krasner argue that by whatever indices one uses, today's interdependence is little different from what obtained before 1914. Exports as a percentage of gross domestic product are no higher today among the industrialized nations that they were in the four decades before 1914. Neither is the growth of world trade, nor the international movement of capital. Moreover, as Robert Gilpin argues, in the mid-1980s, the world began moving away from openness towards a more closed order characterized by mercantilistic competition, economic regionalism, and sectoral protectionism. This may not bring a return to the economic warfare of the 1930s, but it presages a return to the mercantilism of old, even if a more benign variety.

Richard Rosecrance disagrees with this picture of the contemporary international economic order. He sees this era's interdependence more deeply rooted than the one before 1914 because the nature of cross-national capital investments among the rich nations has changed. There is a greater level of direct, as opposed to indirect (portfolio), investment amongst these nations. As a consequence of the higher levels of direct cross-national investment, a state's interest in seeing other national economies prosper has grown. The reason is that it is easier to dispose of shares in an industry on the stock exchange than it is to sell complete factories and other pieces of real estate. Moreover, as Peter Drucker shows, the daily movement of capital among nations overwhelms the exchange of goods among them. This has changed the world economy in fundamental ways, in part by making all nations more dependent upon the international capital market and, thereby, more interdependent on one another's national capital markets. Finally, as Robert Reich stresses, the central question for a nation competing in the international economy is not who owns the factories within its borders, but how efficient those factories are. Prospering in today's global economy requires an educated, skilled work force and sufficient capital investment. If capital and other types of investment enhance the efficiency of a nation's workforce, it makes no difference which investor—foreign or national—provided the capital, only that it was provided.

Which vision of interdependence today's statesmen hold will largely determine the future of the global economy.

The Relation of Politics and Economics

The Nature of Political Economy

Robert Gilpin

> The international corporations have evidently declared ideological war on the "anti-quated" nation state. . . . The charge that materialism, modernization and internationalism is the new liberal creed of corporate capitalism is a valid one. The implication is clear: The nation state as a political unit of democratic decision-making must, in the interest of "progress," yield control to the new mercantile mini-powers.[1]

> While the structure of the multinational corporation is a modern concept, designed to meet the requirements of a modern age, the nation state is a very old-fashioned idea and badly adapted to serve the needs of our present complex world.[2]

These two statements—the first by Kari Levitt, a Canadian nationalist, the second by George Ball, a former United States undersecretary of state—express a dominant theme of contemporary writings on international relations. International society, we are told, is increasingly rent between its economic and its political organization. On the one hand, powerful economic and technological forces are creating a highly interdependent world economy, thus diminishing the traditional significance of national boundaries. On the other hand, the nation-state continues to command men's loyalties and to be the basic unit of political decision making. As one writer has put the issue, "The conflict of our era is between ethnocentric nationalism and geocentric technology."[3]

Ball and Levitt represent two contending positions with respect to this conflict. Whereas Ball advocates the diminution of the power of the nation-state in order to give full rein to the productive potentialities of the multinational corporation. Levitt argues for a powerful nationalism which could counterbalance American corporate domination. What appears to one as the logical and desirable consequence of economic rationality seems to the other to be an effort

---

on the part of American imperialism to eliminate all contending centers of power.

Although the advent of the multinational corporation has put the question of the relationship between economics and politics in a new guise, it is an old issue. In the nineteenth century, for example, it was this issue that divided classical liberals like John Stuart Mill from economic nationalists, represented by Georg Friedrich List. Whereas the former gave primacy in the organization of society to economics and the production of wealth, the latter emphasized the political determination of economic relations. As this issue is central both to the contemporary debate on the multinational corporation and to the argument of this study, this chapter analyzes the three major treatments of the relationship between economics and politics—that is, the three major ideologies of political economy.

THE MEANING OF POLITICAL ECONOMY

The argument of this study is that the relationship between economics and politics, at least in the modern world, is a reciprocal one. On the one hand, politics largely determines the framework of economic activity and channels it in directions intended to serve the interests of dominant groups; the exercise of power in all its forms is a major determinant of the nature of an economic system. On the other hand, the economic process itself tends to redistribute power and wealth; it transforms the power relationships among groups. This in turn leads to a transformation of the political system, thereby giving rise to a new structure of economic relationships. Thus, the dynamics of international relations in the modern world is largely a function of the reciprocal interaction between economics and politics.

First of all, what do I mean by "politics" or "economics"? Charles Kindleberger speaks of economics and politics as two different methods of allocating scarce resources: the first through a market mechanism, the latter through a budget.[4] Robert Keohane and Joseph Nye, in an excellent analysis of international political economy, define economics and politics in terms of two levels of analysis: those of structure and of process.[5] Politics is the domain "having to do with the establishment of an order of relations, a structure. . . ."[6] Economics deals with "short-term allocative behavior (i.e., holding institutions, fundamental assumptions, and expectations constant). . . ."[7] Like Kindleberger's definition, however, this definition tends to isolate economic and politcal phenomena except under certain conditions, which Keohane and Nye define as the "politicization" of the economic system. Neither formulation comes to terms adequately with the dynamic and intimate nature of the relationship between the two.

In this study, the issue of the relationship between economics and politics translates into that between wealth and power. According to this statement of the problem, economics takes as its province the creation and distribution of wealth; politics is the realm of power. I shall examine their relationship from several ideological perspectives, including my own. But what is wealth? What is power?

In response to the question, What is wealth?, an economist-colleague responded, "What do you want, my thirty-second or thirty-volume answer?" Basic concepts are elusive in economics, as in any field of inquiry. No unchallengeable definitions are possible. Ask a physicist for his definition of the nature of space, time, and matter, and you wil not get a very satisfying response. What you will get is an *operational* definition, one which is usable: It permits the physicist to build an intellectual edifice whose foundations would crumble under the scrutiny of the philosopher.

Similarly, the concept of wealth, upon which the science of economics ultimately rests, cannot be clarified in a definitive way. Paul Samuelson, in his textbook, doesn't even try, though he provides a clue in his definition of economics as "the study of how men and society *choose* . . . to employ *scarce* productive resources . . . to produce various commodities . . . and distribute them for consumption."[8] Following this lead, we can say that wealth is anything (capital, land, or labor) that can generate future income; it is composed of physical assets and human capital (including embodied knowledge).

The basic concept of political science is power. Most political scientists would not stop here; they would include in the definition of political science the purpose for which power is used, whether this be the advancement of the public welfare or the domination of one group over another. In any case, few would dissent from the following statement of Harold Lasswell and Abraham Kaplan:

> The concept of power is perhaps the most fundamental in the whole of political science: The political process is the shaping, distribution, and exercise of power (in a wider sense, of all the deference values, or of influence in general.)[9]

Power as such is not the sole or even the principal goal of state behavior. Other goals or values constitute the objectives pursued by nation-states: welfare, security, prestige. But power in its several forms (military, economic, psychological) is ultimately the necessary means to achieve these goals. For this reason, nation-states are intensely jealous of and sensitive to their relative power position. The distribution of power is important because it profoundly affects the ability of states to achieve what they perceive to be their interests.

The nature of power, however, is even more elusive than that of wealth. The number and variety of definitions should be an embarrassment to political scientists. Unfortunately, this study cannot bring the intradisciplinary squabble to an end. Rather, it adopts the definition used by Hans Morgenthau in his influential *Politics Among Nations:* "man's control over the minds and actions of other men."[10] Thus, power, like wealth, is the capacity to produce certain results.

Unlike wealth, however, power cannot be quantified; indeed, it cannot be over-emphasized that power has an imporant psychological dimension. Perceptions of power relations are of critical importance; as a consequence, a fundamental task of statesmen is to manipulate the perceptions of other statesmen regarding the distribution of power. Moreover, power is relative to a specific situation or set of circumstances; there is no single hierarchy of power in international relations. Power may take many forms—military, economic, or psychological—though, in the final analysis, force is the ultimate form of power. Finally, the inability to predict the behavior of others or the outcome of events is of great significance. Uncertainty regarding the distribution of power and the ability of the statesmen to control events plays an important role in international relations. Ultimately, the determination of the distribution of power can be made only in retrospect as a consequence of war. It is precisely for this reason that war has had, unfortunately, such a central place in the history of international relations. In short, power is an elusive concept indeed upon which to erect a science of politics.

Such mutually exclusive definitions of economics and politics as these run counter to much contemporary scholarship by both economists and political scientists, for both disciplines are invading the formerly exclusive jurisdictions of the other. Economists, in particular, have become intellectual imperialists; they are applying their analytical techniques to traditional issues of political science with great success. These developments, however, really reinforce the basic premise of this study, namely, the inseparability of economics and politics.

The distinction drawn above between economics as the science of wealth and politics as the science of power is essentially an analytical one. In the real world, wealth and power are ultimately joined. This, in fact, is the basic rationale for a political economy of international relations. But in order to develop the argument of this study, wealth and power will be treated, at least for the moment, as analytically distinct.

To provide a perspective on the nature of political economy, the next section will discuss the three prevailing conceptions of political economy: liberalism, Marxism, and mercantilism. Liberalism regards politics and economics as relatively separable and autonomous spheres of activities; I associate most professional economists as well as many other academics, businessmen, and American officials with this outlook. Marxism refers to the radical critique of capitalism identified with Karl Marx and his contmeporary disciples; according to this conception, economics determines politics and political structure. Mercantilism is a more questionable term because of its historical association with the desire of nation-states for a trade surplus and for treasure (money). One must distinguish, however, between the specific form mercantilism took in the seventeenth and eighteenth centuries and the general outlook of mercantilistic thought. The essence of the mercantilistic perspective, whether it is labeled economic nationalism, protectionism, or the doctrine of the German Historical School, is the subservience of economy to the state and its interests—interests that range from matters of domestic welfare to those of international security. It is this more general meaning of mercantilism that is implied by the use of the term in this study.

Following the discussion of these three schools of thought, I shall elaborate my own, more eclectic, view of political economy and demonstrate its relevance for understanding the phenomenon of the multinational corporation.

THREE CONCEPTIONS OF POLITICAL ECONOMY

The three prevailing conceptions of political economy differ on many points. Several critical differences will be examined in this brief comparison. (See Table 1.)

The Nature of Economic Relations

The basic assumption of liberalism is that the nature of international economic relations is essentially harmonious. Herein lay the great intellectual innovation of Adam Smith. Disputing his mercantilist predecessors, Smith argued that international economic relations could be made a positive-sum game; that is to say, everyone could gain, and no one need lose, from a proper ordering of economic relations, albeit the distribution of these gains may not be equal. Following Smith, liberalism assumes that there is a basic harmony between true national interest and cosmopolitan economic interest. Thus, a prominent member of this school of thought has written, in response to a radical critique, that the economic effeciency of the sterling standard in the nineteenth century and that of the dollar standard in the twentieth century serve "the cosmopolitan interest in a national form."[11] Although Great Britain and the United States gained the most from the international role of their respective currencies, everyone else gained as well.

Liberals argue that, given this underlying identity of national and cosmopolitan interests in a free market, the state should not interfere with economic transactions across national boundaries. Through free exchange of commodities, removal of restrictions on the flow of investment, and an international division of labor, everyone will benefit in the long run as a result of a more efficient utilization of the world's scarce resources. The national interest is therefore best served, liberals maintain, by a generous and cooperative attitude regarding economic relations with other countries. In essence, the pursuit of self-interest

Table 1   COMPARISON OF THE THREE CONCEPTIONS OF POLITICAL ECONOMY

	Liberalism	Marxism	Mercantilism
Nature of economic relations	Harmonious	Conflictual	Conflictual
Nature of the actors	Households and firms	Economic classes	Nation-states
Goal of economic activity	Maximization of global welfare	Maximization of class interests	Maximization of national interest
Relationship between economics and politics	Economics *should* determine politics	Economics *does* determine politics	Politics determines economics
Theory of change	Dynamic equilibrium	Tendency toward disequilibrium	Shifts in the distribution of power

in a free, competitive economy achieves the greatest good for the greatest number in international no less than in the national society.

Both mercantilists and Marxists, on the other hand, begin with the premise that the essence of economic relations is conflictual. There is no underlying harmony; indeed, one group's gain is another's loss. Thus, in the language of game theory, whereas liberals regard economic relations as a non-zero-sum game, Marxists and mercantilists view economic relations as essentially a zero-sum game.

The Goal of Economic Activity

For the liberal, the goal of economic activity is the optimum or efficient use of the world's scarce resources and the maximization of world welfare. While most liberals refuse to make value judgments regarding income distribution, Marxists and mercantilists stress the distributive effects of economic relations. For the Marxist the distribution of wealth among social classes is central; for the mercantilist it is the distribution of employment, industry, and military power among nation-states that is most significant. Thus, the goal of economic (and political) activity for both Marxists and mercantilists is the redistribution of wealth and power.

The State and Public Policy

These three perspectives differ decisively in their view regarding the nature of the economic actors. In Marxist analysis, the basic actors in both domestic and international relations are economic classes; the interests of the dominant class determine the foreign policy of the state. For mercantilists, the real actors in international economic relations are nation-states; national interest determines foreign policy. National interest may at times be influenced by the peculiar economic interests of classes, elites, or other subgroups of the society; but factors of geography, external configurations of power, and the exigencies of national survival are primary in determining foreign policy. Thus, whereas liberals speak of world welfare and Marxists of class interests, mercantilists recognize only the interests of particular nation-states.

Although liberal economists such as David Ricardo and Joseph Schumpeter recognized the importance of class conflict and neoclassical liberals analyze economic growth and policy in terms of national economies, the liberal emphasis is on the individual consumer, firm, or entrepreneur. The liberal ideal is summarized in the view of Harry Johnson that the nation-state has no meaning as an economic entity.[12]

Underlying these contrasting views are differing conceptions of the nature of the state and public policy. For liberals, the state represents an aggregation of private interests: public policy is but the outcome of a pluralistic struggle among interest groups. Marxists, on the other hand, regard the state as simply the "executive committee of the ruling class," and public policy reflects its interests. Mercantilists, however, regard the state as an organic unit in its own right: the whole is greater than the sum of its parts. Public policy, therefore, embodies the national interest or Rousseau's "general will" as conceived by the political elite.

The Relationship Between Economics and Politics: Theories of Change

Liberalism, Marxism, and mercantilism also have differing views on the relationship between economics and politics. And their differences on this issue are directly relevant to their contrasting theories of international political change.

Although the liberal ideal is the separation of economics from politics in the interest of maximizing world welfare, the fulfillment of this ideal would have important political implications. The classical statement of these implications was that of Adam Smith in *The Wealth of Nations*.[13] Economic growth, Smith argued, is primarily a function of the extent of the division of labor, which in turn is dependent upon the scale of the market. Thus he attacked the barriers erected by feudal principalities and mercantilistic states against the exchange of goods and the enlargement of markets. If men were to multiply their wealth, Smith argued, the contradiction between political organization and economic rationality had to be resolved in favor of the latter. That is, the pursuit of wealth should determine the nature of the political order.

Subsequently, from nineteenth-century economic liberals to twentieth-century writers on economic integration, there has existed "the dream . . . of a great republic of world commerce, in which national boundaries would cease to have any great economic importance and the web of trade would bind all the people of the world in the prosperity of peace."[14] For liberals the long-term trend is toward world integration, wherein functions, authority, and loyalties will be transferred from "smaller units to larger ones; from states to federalism; from federalism to supranational unions and from these to superstates."[15] The logic of economic and technological development, it is argued, has set mankind on an inexorable course toward global political unification and world peace.

In Marxism, the concept of the contradiction between economic and political relations was enacted into historical law. Whereas classical liberals— although Smith less than others—held that the requirements of economic rationality *ought* to determine political relations, the Marxist position was that the mode of production does in fact determine the superstructure of political relations. Therefore, it is argued, history can be understood as the product of the dialectical process—the contradiction between the evolving techniques of production and the resistant sociopolitical system.

Although Marx and Engels wrote remarkably little on international economics, Engels, in his famous polemic, *Anti-Duhring*, explicitly considers whether economics or politics is primary in determining the structure of international relations.[16] E. K. Duhring, a minor figure in the German Historical School, had argued, in contradiction to Marxism, that property and market relations resulted less from the economic logic of capitalism than from extraeconomic political factors: "The basis of the exploitation of many by man was an historical act of force which created an exploitative economic system for the benefit of the stronger man or class."[17] Since Engels, in his attack on Duhring, used the example of the unification of Germany through the Zollverein or customs union of 1833, his analysis is directly relevant to this discussion of the relationship between economics and political organization.

Engels argued that when contradictions arise between economic and political structures, political power adapts itself to the changes in the balance of economic forces; politics yields to the dictates of economic development. Thus, in the case of nineteenth-century Germany, the requirements of industrial production had become incompatible with its feudal, politically fragmented structure. "Though political reaction was victorious in 1815 and again in 1848," he argued, "it was unable to prevent the growth of large-scale industry in Germany and the growing participation of German commerce in the world market."[18] In summary, Engels wrote, "German unity had become an economic necessity."[19]

In the view of both Smith and Engels, the nation-state represented a progressive stage in human development, because it enlarged the political realm of economic activity. In each successive economic epoch, advances in technology and an increasing scale of production necessitate an enlargement of political organization. Because the city-state and feudalism restricted the scale of production and the division of labor made possible by the Industrial Revolution, they prevented the efficient utilization of resources and were, therefore, superseded by larger political units. Smith considered this to be a desirable objective; for Engels it was an historical necessity. Thus, in the opinion of liberals, the establishment of the Zollverein was a movement toward maximizing world economic welfare;[20] for Marxists it was the unavoidable triumph of the German industrialists over the feudal aristocracy.

Mercantilist writers from Alexander Hamilton to Frederich List to Charles de Gaulle, on the other hand, have emphasized the primacy of politics; politics, in this view, determines economic organization. Whereas Marxists and liberals have pointed to the production of wealth as the basic determinant of social and political organization, the mercantilists of the German Historical School, for example, stressed the primacy of national security, industrial development, and national sentiment in international political and economic dynamics.

In response to Engels's interpretation of the unification of Germany, mercantilists would no doubt agree with Jacob Viner that "Prussia engineered the customs union primarily for political reasons, in order to gain hegemony or at least influence over the lesser German states. It was largely in order to make certain that the hegemony should be Prussian and not Austrian that Prussia continually opposed Austrian entry into the Union, either openly or by pressing for a customs union tariff lower than highly protectionist Austria could stomach."[21] In pursuit of this strategic interest, it was "Prussian might, rather than a common zeal for political unification arising out of economic partnership, [that] . . . played the major role."[22]

In contrast to Marxism, neither liberalism nor mercantilism has a developed theory of dynamics. The basic assumption of orthodox economic analysis (liberalism) is the tendency toward equilibrium; liberalism takes for granted the existing social order and given istitutions. Change is assumed to be gradual and adaptive—a continuous process of dynamic equilibrium. There is no necessary connection between such political phenomena as war and revolution and the evolution of the economic system, although they would not deny that misguided statesmen can blunder into war over economic issues or that revolutions are conflicts over the distribution of wealth; but neither is inevitably linked to the evolution of the productive system. As for mercantilism, it sees change as taking place owing to shifts in the balance of power; yet, mercantilist writers such as members of the German Historical School and contemporary political realists have not developed a systematic theory of how this shift occurs.

On the other hand, dynamics is central to Marxism; indeed Marxism is essentially a theory of social *change*. It emphasizes the tendency toward *dis*equilibrium owing to changes in the means of production and the consequent effects on the everpresent class conflict. When these tendencies can no longer be contained, the sociopolitical system breaks down through violent upheaval. Thus war and revolution are seen as an integral part of the economic process. Politics and economics are intimately joined.

Why an International Economy?

From these differences among the three ideologies, one can get a sense of their respective explanations for the existence and functioning of the international economy.

An interdependent world economy constitutes the normal state of affairs for most liberal economists. Responding to technological advances in transportation and communications, the scope of the market mechanism, according to this analysis, continuously expands. Thus, despite temporary setbacks, the long-term trend is toward global economic integration. The functioning of the international economy is determined primarily by considerations of efficiency. The role of the dollar as the basis of the international monetary system, for example, is explained by the preference for it among traders and nations as the vehicle of international commerce.[23] The system is maintained by the mutuality of the benefits provided by trade, monetary arrangements, and investment.

A second view—one shared by Marxists and mercantilists alike—is that every interdependent international economy is essentially an imperial or hierarchical system. The imperial or hegemonic power organizes trade, monetary, and investment relations in order to advance its own economic and political interests. In the absence of the economic and especially the political influence of the hegemonic power, the system would fragment into autarkic economies or regional blocs. Whereas for liberalism maintenance of harmonious international market relations is the norm, for Marxism and mercantilism conflicts of class or national interests are the norm.

PERSPECTIVE OF THE AUTHOR

My own perspective on political economy rests on what I regard as a fundamental difference in emphasis between economics and politics; namely, the distinction between absolute and relative gains. The emphasis of economic science—or, at least, of liberal economics—is on *absolute* gains; the ultimate defense of liberalism is that over the long run everyone gains, albeit in varying degrees, from a liberal economic regime. Economics, according to this formulation, need not be a zero-sum game. Everyone can gain in wealth through a more efficient division of labor; moreover, everyone can lose, in absolute terms, from economic inefficiency. Herein lies the strength of liberalism.

This economic emphasis on absolute gains is in fact embodied in what one can characterize as the ultimate ideal of liberal economics: the achievement of a "Pareto optimum" world. Such a properly ordered world would be one wherein "by improving the position of one individual (by adding to his possessions) no one else's position is deteriorated." As Oskar Morgenstern has observed, "[e]conomic literature is replete with the use of the Pareto optimum thus formulated or in equivalent language."[24] It is a world freed from "interpersonal comparisons of utility," and thus a world freed from what is central to politics, i.e., ethical judgment and conflict regarding the just and relative distribution of utility. That the notion of a Pareto optimum is rife with conceptual problems and is utopian does not detract from its centrality as the implicit objective of liberal economics. And this emphasis of economics on absolute gains for all differs fundamentally from the nature of political phenomena as studied by political scientists: viz., struggles for power as a goal itself or as a means to the achievement of other goals.

The essential fact of politics is that power is always relative; one state's gain in power is by necessity another's loss. Thus, even though two states may be gaining absolutely in wealth, in political terms it is the effect of these gains on relative power positions which is of primary importance. From this *political* perspective, therefore, the mercantilists are correct in emphasizing that in power terms, international relations is a zero-sum game.

In a brilliant analysis of international politics, the relativity of power and its profound implications were set forth by Jean-Jacques Rousseau:

> the state, being an artifical body is not limited in any way. . . . It can always increase; it always feels itself weak if there is another that is stronger. Its security and preservation demand that it make itself more powerful than its neighbors. It can increase, nourish and exercise its power only at their expense . . . while the inequality of man has natural limits that between societies can grow without cease, until one absorbs all the others. . . . Because the grandeur of the state is purely relative it is forced to compare itself with that of the others. . . . It is in vain that it wishes to keep itself to itself; it becomes small or great, weak or strong, according to whether its neighbor expands or contracts, becomes stronger or declines. . . .
>
> The chief thing I notice is a patent contradiction in the condition of the human race. . . . Between man and man we live in the condition of the civil state, subjected to laws; between people and people we enjoy natural liberty, which makes

the situation worse. Living at the same time in the social order and in the state of nature, we suffer from the inconveniences of both without finding . . . security in either. . . . We see men united by artifical bonds, but united to destroy each other; and all the horrors of war take birth from the precautions they have taken in order to prevent them. . . . War is born of peace, or at least of the precautions which men have taken for the purpose of achieving durable peace.[25]

Because of the relativity of power, therefore, nation-states are engaged in a never-ending struggle to improve or preserve their relative power positions.

This rather stark formulation obviously draws too sharp a distinction between economics and politics. Certainly, for example, liberal economists may be interested in questions of distribution; the distributive issue was, in fact, of central concern to Ricardo and other classical writers. However, when economists stop taking the system for granted and start asking questions about distribution, they have really ventured into what I regard as the essence of politics, for distribution is really a political issue. In a world in which power rests on wealth, changes in the relative distribution of wealth imply changes in the distrubtion of power and in the political system itself. This, in fact, is what is meant by saying that politics is about relative gains. Politics concerns the effects of groups to redistribute gains to their own advantage.

Similarly, to argue that politics is about relative gains is not to argue that it is a constant-sum game. On the contrary, man's power over nature and his fellow man has grown immensely in absolute terms over the past several centuries. It is certainly the case that eveyone's absolute capabilities can increase due to the development of new weaponry, the expansion of productive capabilities, or changes in the political system itself. Obviously such absolute increases in power are important politically. Who can deny, for example, that the advent of nuclear weapons has profoundly altered international politics? Obviously, too, states can negotiate disarmament and other levels of military capability.

Yet recognition of these facts does not alter the prime consideration that changes in the relative distribution of power are of fundamental significance politically. Though all may be gaining or declining in absolute capability, what will concern states principally are the effects of these absolute gains or losses on relative positions. How, for example, do changes in productive capacity or military weaponry affect the ability of one state to impose its will an another? It may very well be that in a particular situation absolute gains will not affect relative positions. But the efforts of groups to cause or prevent such shifts in the relative distribution of power constitute the critical issue of politics.

This formulation of the nature of politics obviously does not deny that nations may cooperate in order to advance their mutual interest. But even cooperative actions may have important consequences for the distribution of power in the system. For example, the Strategic Arms Limitation Talks (SALT) between the United States and the Soviet Union are obviously motivated by a common interest in preventing thermonuclear war. Other states will also benefit if the risk of war between the superpowers is reduced. Yet, SALT may also be seen as an attempt to stabilize the international distribution of power to the disadvantage of China and other third powers. In short, in terms of the system as a whole, political cooperation can have a profound effect on the relative distribution of power among nation-states.

The point may perhaps be clarified by distinguishing between two aspects of power. When one speaks of absolute gains in power, such as advances in economic capabilities or weapons development, one is referring principally to increases in physical or material capabilities. But while such capabilities are an important component of power, power, as we have seen, is more than physical capability. Power is also a psychological relationship: Who can influence whom to do what? From this perspective, what may be of most importance is how changes in capability affect this psychological relationship. Insofar as they do, they alter the relative distribution of power in the system.

In a world in which power rests increasingly on economic and industrial capabilities, one cannot really distinguish between wealth (resources, treasure, and industry) and power as national goals. In the short run there may be conflicts between the pursuit of power and the pursuit of wealth; in the long run the two pursuits are identical. Therefore, the position taken in this study is similar to Viner's interpretation of classical mercantilism:

> What then is the correct interpretation of mercantilist doctrine and practice with respect to the roles of power and plenty as ends of national policy? I believe that practically all mercantilists, whatever the period, country, or status of the particular individual, would have subscribed to all of the following propositions: (1) wealth is an absolutely essential means to power, whether for security or for aggression; (2) power is essential or valuable as a means to the acquisition or retention of wealth; (3) wealth and power are each proper ultimate ends of national policy; (4) there is long-run harmony between these ends, although in particular circumstances it may be necessary for a time to make economic sacrifices in the interest of military security and therefore also of long-run prosperity.[26]

This interpretation of the role of the economic motive in international relations is substantially different from that of Marxism. In the Marxist framework of analysis, the economic factor is reduced to the profit motive, as it affects the behavior of individuals or firms. Accordingly, the foreign policies of capitalist states are determined by the desire of capitalists for profits. This is, in our view, far too narrow a conception of the economic aspect of international relations. Instead, in this study we label "economic" those sources of wealth upon which national power and domestic welfare are dependent.

Understood in these broader terms, the economic motive and economic activities are fundamental to the struggle for power among nation-states. The objects of contention in the struggles of the balance of power include the centers of economic power. As R. G. Hawtrey has expressed it, "the political motives at work can only be expressed in terms of the economic. Every conflict is one of power and power depends on resources."[27] In pursuit of wealth *and* power, therefore, nations (capitalist, socialist, or fascist) contend over the territorial division and exploitation of the globe.

Even at the level of peaceful economic intercourse, one cannot separate out the political element. Contrary to the attitude of liberalism, international economic relations are in reality political relations. The interdependence of national economies creates economic power, defined as the capacity of one state to damage another through the interruption of commercial and financial relations.[28] The attempts to create and to escape from such dependency relationships constitute an important aspect of international relations in the modern era.

The primary actors in the international system are nation-states in pursuit of what they define as their national interest. This is not to argue, however, that nation-states are the only actors, nor do I believe that the "national interest" is something akin to Rousseau's "general will"—the expression of an organic entity separable from its component parts. Except in the abstract models of political scientists, it has never been the case that the international system was composed solely of nation-states. In an exaggerated acknowledgment of the importance of nonstate or transnational actors at an earlier time, John A. Hobson asked rhetorically whether "a great war could be undertaken by any European state, or a great state loan subscribed, if the House of Rothschild and its connexions set their face against it."[29] What has to be explained, however, are the economic and political circumstances that enable such transnational actors to play their semi-independent role in international affairs. The argument of this study is that the primary determinants of the role played by these non-state actors are the larger configurations of power among nation-states. What is determinant is the interplay of national interests.

As for the concept of "national interest," the national interest of a given nation-state is, of course, what its political and economic elite determines it to be. In part, as Marxists argue, this elite will define it in terms of its own group or class interests. But the national interest comprehends more than this. More general influences, such as cultural values and considerations relevant to the security of the state itself—geographical position, the evolution of military technology, and the international distribution of power—are of greater importance. There is a sense, then, in which the factors that determine the national interest are objective. A ruling elite that fails to take these factors into account does so at its peril. In short, then, there is a basis for considering the nation-state itself as an actor pursuing its own set of security, welfare, and status concerns in competition or cooperation with other nation-states.

Lastly, in a world of conflicting nation-states, how does one explain the existence of an interdependent international economy? Why does a liberal international economy—that is, an economy characterized by relatively free trade, currency convertibility, and freedom of capital movement—remain intact rather than fragment into autarkic national economies and regional or imperial groupings? In part, the answer is provided by liberalism: economic cooperation, interdependence, and an international division of labor enhance efficiency and the maximization of aggregate wealth. Nation-states are induced to enter the international system because of the promise of more rapid growth; greater benefits can be had than could be obtained by autarky or a fragmentation of the world economy. The historical record suggests, however, that the existence of mutual economic benefits is not always enough to induce nations to pay the costs of a market system or to forgo opportunities of advancing their own interests at the expense of others. There is always the danger that a nation may pursue certain short-range policies, such as the imposition of an optimum tariff, in order to maximize its own gains at the expense of the system as a whole.

For this reason, a liberal international economy requires a power to manage and stabilize the system. As Charles Kindleberger has convincingly shown, this governance role was performed by Great Britain throughout the nineteenth century and up to 1931, and by the United States after 1945.[30] The inability of Great Britain in 1929 to continue running the system and the unwillingness of the United States to assume this responsibility led to the collapse of the system in the "Great Depression." The result was the fragmentation of the world economy into rival economic blocs. Both dominant economic powers had failed to overcome the divisive forces of nationalism and regionalism.

The argument of this study is that the modern world economy has evolved through the emergence of great national economies that have successively become dominant. In the words of the distinguished French economist François Perroux, "the economic evolution of the world has resulted from a succession of dominant economies, each in turn taking the lead in international activity and influence. . . . Throughout the nineteenth century the British economy was the dominant economy in the world. From the [eighteen] seventies on, Germany was dominant in respect to certain other Continental countries and in certain specified fields. In the twentieth century, the United States economy has clearly been and still is the internationally dominant economy."[31]

An economic system, then, does not arise spontaneously owing to the operation of an invisible hand and in the absence of the exercise of power. Rather, every economic system rests on a particular political order; its nature cannot be understood aside from politics. This basic point was made some years ago by E. H. Carr when he wrote that "the science of economics presupposes a given political order, and cannot be profitably studied in isolation from politics."[32] Carr sought to convince his fellow Englishmen that an international economy based on free trade was not a natural and inevitable state of affairs but rather one that reflected the economic and political interests of Great Britain. The system based on free trade had come into existence through, and was maintained by, the exercise of British economic and military power. With the rise after 1880 of new industrial and military powers with contrasting economic interests—namely, Germany, Japan, and the United States—an international economy based on free trade and British power became less and less viable. Eventually this shift in the locus of industrial and military power led to the collapse of the system in World War I. Following the interwar period, a liberal international economy was revived through the exercise of power by the world's newly emergent dominant economy—the United States.

Accordingly, the regime of free investment and the preeminence of the multinational corporation in the contemporary world have reflected the economic and political interests of the United States. The multinational corporation has prospered because it has been dependent on the power of, and consistent with the political interests of, the United States. This is not to deny the analyses of economists who argue that the multinational corporation is a response to contemporary technological and economic developments. The argument is rather that these economic and technological factors have been able to exercise their profound effects because the United States—sometimes with the cooperation of other states and sometimes over their opposition—has created the necessary political framework. As former Secretary of the Treasury Henry Fowler stated several years ago, "it is . . . impossible to overestimate the extent to which the efforts and opportunities for American firms abroad depend upon the vast presence and influence and prestige that America holds in the world."[33]

By the mid-1970s, however, the international distribution of power and the world economy resting on it were far different from what they had been when Fowler's words were spoken. The rise of foreign economic competitors, America's growing dependence upon foreign sources of energy and other resources, and the expansion of Soviet military capabilities have greatly diminished America's presence and influence in the world. One must ask if, as a consequence, the reign of the American multinationals over international economic affairs will continue into the future.

In summary, although nation-states, as mercantilists suggest, do seek to control economic and technological forces and channel them to their own advantage, this is impossible over the long run. The spread of economic growth and industrialization cannot be prevented. In time the diffusion of industry and technology undermines the position of the dominant power. As both liberals and Marxists have emphasized, the evolution of economic relations profoundly influences the nature of the international political system. The relationship between economics and politics is a reciprocal one.

Although economic and accompanying political change may well be inevitable, it is not inevitable that the process of economic development and technological advance will produce an increasingly integrated world society. In the 1930s, Eugene Staley posed the issue.

> A conflict rages between technology and politics. Economics, so closely linked to both, has become the major battlefield. Stability and peace will reign in the world economy only when, somehow, the forces on the side of technology and the forces on the side of politics have once more become accommodated to each other.[34]

Staley believed, as do many present-day writers, that politics and technology must ultimately adjust to one another. But he differed with contemporary writers with regard to the inevitability with which politics would adjust to technology. Reflecting the intense economic nationalism of the period in which he wrote, Staley pointed out that the adjustment may very well be the other way around. As he reminds us, in his own time and in earlier periods economics has had to adjust to political realities: "In the 'Dark Ages' following the collapse of the Roman Empire, technology adjusted itself to politics. The magnificent Roman roads fell into disrepair, the baths and aqueducts and amphitheatres and villas into ruins. Society lapsed back to localism in production and distribution, forgot much of the learning and the technology and the governmental systems of earlier days."[35]

CONCLUSION

The purpose of this chapter has been to set forth the analytical framework that will be employed in this study. This framework is a statement of what I mean by "political economy." In its eclecticism it has drawn upon, while differing from, the three prevailing perspectives of political economy. It has incorporated their respective strengths and has attempted to overcome their weaknesses. In brief, political economy in this study means the reciprocal and dynamic interaction in international relations of the pursuit of wealth and the pursuit of power. In the short run, the distribution of power and the nature of the political system are major determinants of the framework within which wealth is produced and distributed. In the long run, however, shifts in economic efficiency and in the location of economic activity tend to undermine and transform the existing political system. This political transformation in turn gives rise to changes in economic relations that reflect the interests of the politically ascendant state in the system.

NOTES

1. Kari Levitt, "The Hinterland Economy," *Canadian Forum 50* (July-August 1970): 163.
2. George W. Ball, "The Promise of the Multinational Corporation," *Fortune*, June 1, 1967, p. 80.
3. Sidney Rolfe, "Updating Adam Smith," *Interplay* (November 1968): 15.
4. Charles Kindleberger, *Power and Money: The Economics of International Politics and the Politics of International Economics* (New York: Basic Books, 1970), p. 5.
5. Robert Keohane and Joseph Nye, "World Politics and the International Economic System," in C. Fred Bergsten, ed., *The Future of the International Economic Order: An Agenda for Research (Lexington, Mass: D. C. Heath, 1973), p. 116.
6. Ibid.
7. Ibid., p. 117.
8. Paul Samuelson, *Economics: An Introductory Analysis* (New York: McGraw-Hill, 1967), p. 5.
9. Harold Lasswell and Abraham Kaplan, *Power and Society: A Framework for Political Inquiry* (New Haven: Yale University Press, 1950), p. 75.
10. Hans Morgenthau, *Politics Among Nations* (New York: Alfred A. Knopl), p. 26. For a more complex but essentially identical view, see Robert Dahl, *Modern Political Analysis* (Englewood Cliffs, N.J.: Prentice-Hall, 1963).
11. Kindleberger, *Power and Money*, p. 227.
12. For Johnson's critique of economic nationalism, see Harry Johnson, ed., *Economic Nationalism in Old and New States* (Chicago: University of Chicago Press, 1967).
13. Adam Smith, *The Wealth of Nations* (New York: Modern Library, 1937).

14. J. B. Condliffe, *The Commerce of Nations* (New York: W. W. Norton, 1950), p. 136.
15. Amitai Etzioni, "The Dialectics of Supernational Unification" in *International Political Communities* (New York: Doubleday, 1966), p. 147.
16. The relevant sections appear in Ernst Wangerman, ed., *The Role of Force in History: A Study of Bismarck's Policy of Blood and Iron*, trans. Jack Cohen (New York: International Publishers, 1968).
17. Ibid., p. 12.
18. Ibid., p. 13.
19. Ibid., p. 14.
20. Gustav Stopler, *The German Economy* (New York: Harcourt, Brace and World, 1967), p. 11.
21. Jacob Viner, *The Customs Union Issue*, Studies in the Administration of International Law and Organization, no. 10 (New York: Carnegie Endowment for International Peace, 1950), pp. 98–99.
22. Ibid., p. 101.
23. Richard Cooper, "Eurodollars, Reserve Dollars, and Asymmetrics in the International Monetary System," *Journal of International Economics 2* (September 1972): 325–44.
24. Oskar Morgenstern, "Thirteen Critical Points in Contemporary Economic Theory: An Interpretation," *Journal of Economic Literature* 10 (December 1972): 1169.
25. Quoted in F. H. Hinsley, *Power and the Pursuit of Peace* (Cambridge: Cambridge University Press, 1963), pp. 50–51.
26. Jacob Viner, "Power versus Plenty as Objectives of Foreign Policy in the Seventeenth and Eighteenth Centuries," in *The Long View and the Short: Studies in Economic Theory and Practice* (Glencoe, Ill.: The Free Press, 1958), p. 286.
27. R. G. Hawtrey, *Economic Aspects of Sovereignty* (London: Longmans, Green, 1952), p. 120
28. Albert Hirshman, *National Power and the Structure of Foreign Trade* (Berkeley: University of California Press, 1969), p. 16.
29. John A. Hobson, *Imperialism: A Study* (1902; 3rd ed., rev., London: G. Allen and Unwin, 1938), p. 57.
30. Charles Kindleberger, *The World in Depression 1929–1939* (Berkeley: University of California Press, 1973), p. 293.
31. François Perroux, "The Domination Effect and Modern Economic Theory," in *Power in Economics*, ed. K. W. Rothschild (London: Penguin, 1971), p. 67.
32. E. H. Carr, *The Twenty Years' Crisis, 1919–1939* (New York: Macmillan, 1951), p. 117.
33. Quoted in Kari Levitt, *Silent Surrender: The American Economic Empire in Canada* (New York: Liveright Press, 1970). p. 100.
34. Eugene Staley, *World Economy in Transition: Technology vs. Politics, Laissez Faire vs. Planning, Power vs. Welfare* (New York: Council on Foreign Felations [under the auspices of the American Coordinating Committee for International Studies], 1939), pp. 51–52.
35. Ibid., p. 52.

Hegemony in the World Political Economy

Robert O. Keohane

It is common today for troubled supporters of liberal capitalism to look back with nostalgia on British preponderance in the nineteenth century and American dominance after World War II. Those eras are imagined to be simpler ones in which a single power, possessing superiority of economic and military resources, implemented a plan for international order based on its interests and its vision of the world. As Robert Gilpin has expressed it, "the *Pax Britannica* and *Pax Americana*, like the *Pax Romana*, ensured an international system of relative peace and security. Great Britain and the United States created and enforced the rules of a liberal international economic order."

Underlying this statement is one of the two central propositions of the theory of hegemonic stability[1]: that order in world politics is typically created by a single dominant power. Since regimes constitute elements of an international order, this implies that the formation of international regimes normally depends on hegemony. The other major tenet of the theory of hegemonic stability is that the maintenance of order requires continued hegemony. As Charles P. Kindleberger has said, "for the world economy to be stabilized, there has to be a stabilizer, one stabilizer".[2] This implies that cooperation, . . . [the] mutual adjustment of state policies to one another, also depends on the perpetuation of hegemony.

I discuss hegemony before elaborating my definitions of cooperation and regimes because my emphasis on how international institutions such as regimes facilitate cooperation only makes sense if cooperation and discord are not determined simply by interests and power. In this chapter I argue that a deterministic version of the theory of hegemonic stability, relying only on the realist concepts of interests and power, is indeed incorrect. There is some validity in a modest version of the first proposition of the theory of hegemonic stability—that hegemony can facilitate a certain type of cooperation—but there is little reason to believe that hegemony is either a necessary or a sufficient condition for the emergence of cooperative relationships. Furthermore, and even more important for the argument presented here, the second major proposition of the theory is erroneous: Cooperation does not necessarily require the existence of a hegemonic leader after international regimes have been established. Post-hegemonic cooperation is also possible. . . .

The task of the present chapter is to explore in a preliminary way the value and limitations of the concept of hegemony for the study of cooperation. The first section analyzes the claims of the theory of hegemonic stability; the second section briefly addresses the relationship between military power and hegemony in the world political economy; and the final section seeks to enrich our understanding of the concept by considering Marxian insights. Many Marxian interpretations of hegemony turn out to bear an uncanny resemblance to Realist ideas, using different language to make similar points. Antonio Gramsci's conception of ideological hegemony, however, does provide an insightful supplement to purely materialist arguments, whether Realist or Marxist.

EVALUATING THE THEORY OF HEGEMONIC STABILITY

The theory of hegemonic stability, as applied to the world political economy, defines hegemony as preponderance of material resources. Four sets of resources are especially important. Hegemonic powers must have control over raw materials, control over sources of capital, control over markets, and competitive advantages in the production of highly valued goods.

The importance of controlling sources of raw materials has provided a traditional justification for territorial expansion and imperialism, as well as for the extension of informal influence. . . . [S]hifts in the locus of control over oil affected the power of states and the evolution of international regimes. Guaranteed access to capital, though less obvious as a source of power, may be equally important. Countries with well-functioning capital markets can borrow cheaply and may be able to provide credit to friends or even deny it to adversaries. Holland derived political and economic power from the quality of its capital markets in the seventeenth century; Britain did so in the eighteenth and nineteenth centuries; and the United States has similarly benefited during the last fifty years.

Potential power may also be derived from the size of one's market for imports. The threat to cut off a particular state's access to one's own market, while allowing other countries continued access, is a "potent and historically relevant weapon of economic 'power'."[3] Conversely, the offer to open up one's own huge market to other exporters, in return for concessions or deference, can be an effective means of influence. The bigger one's own market, and the greater the government's discretion in opening it up or closing it off, the greater one's potential economic power.

The final demension of economic preponderance is competitive superiority in the production of goods. Immanuel Wallerstein has defined hegemony in economic terms as "a situation wherein the products of a given core state are produced so efficiently that they are by and large competitive even in other core states, and therefore the given core state will be the primary beneficiary of a maximally free world market."[4] As a definition of economic preponderance this is interesting but poorly worked out, since under conditions of overall balance of payments equilibrium each unit—even the poorest and least developed—will have some comparative advantage. The fact that in 1960 the United States had a trade deficit in textiles and apparel and in basic manufactured goods (established products not, on the whole, involving the use of complex or new technology) did not indicate that it had lost predominant economic status.[5] Indeed, one should expect the economically preponderant state to import products that are labor-intensive or that are produced with well-known production techniques. Competitive advantage does not mean that the leading economy exports *everything*, but that it produces and exports the most profitable products and those that will provide the basis for producing even more advanced goods and services in the future. In general, this ability will be based on the technological superiority of the leading country, although it may also rest on its political control over valuable resources yielding significant rents.

To be considered hegemonic in the world political economy, therefore, a country must have access to crucial raw materials, control major sources of capital, maintain a large market for imports, and hold comparative advantages in goods with high value added, yielding relatively high wages and profits. It must also be stronger, on these dimensions taken as a whole, than any other country. The theory of hegemonic stability predicts that the more one such power dominates the world political economy, the more cooperative will interstate relations be. This is a parsimonious theory that relies on . . . a "basic force model," in which outcomes reflect the tangible capabilities of actors.

Yet, like many such basic force models, this crude theory of hegemonic stability makes imperfect predictions. In the twentieth century it correctly anticipates the relative cooperativeness of the twenty years after World War II. It is at least partially mistaken, however, about trends of cooperation when hegemony erodes. Between 1900 and 1913 a decline in British power coincided with a decrease rather than an increase in conflict over commercial issues. . . . [R]ecent changes in international regimes can only partially be attributed to a decline in American power. How to interpret the prevalence of discord in the interwar years is difficult, since it is not clear whether any country was hegemonic in material terms during those two decades. The United States, though considerably ahead in productivity, did not replace Britain as the most important financial center and lagged behind in volume of trade. Although American domestic oil production was more than sufficient for domestic needs during these years, Britain still controlled the bulk of major Middle Eastern oil fields. Nevertheless, what prevented American leadership of a cooperative world political economy in these years was less lack of economic resources than an absence of political willingness to make and enforce rules for the system. Britain, despite its efforts, was too weak to do so effectively. The crucial factor in producing discord lay in American politics, not in the material factors to which the theory points.

Unlike the crude basic force model, a refined version of hegemonic stability theory does not assert an automatic link between power and leadership. Hegemony is defined as a situation in which "one state is powerful enough to maintain the essential rules governing interstate relations, and willing to do so."[6] This interpretive framework retains an emphasis on power but looks more seriously than the crude power theory at the internal characteristics of the strong state. It does not assume that strength automatically creates incentives to project one's power abroad. Domestic attitudes, political structures, and decision making processes are also important.

This argument's reliance on state decisions as well as power capabilities puts it into the category of what March calls "force activation models." Decisions to exercise leadership are necessary to "activate" the posited relationship between power capabilities and outcomes. Force activation models are essentially *post hoc* rather than *a priori*, since one can always "save" such a theory after the fact by thinking of reasons why an actor would not have wanted to use all of its available potential power. In effect, this modification of the theory declares that states with preponderant resources will be hegemonic except when they decide not to commit the necessary effort to the tasks of leadership, yet it does not tell us what will determine the latter decision. As a causal theory this is not very helpful, since whether a given configuration of power will lead the potential hegemon to maintain a set of rules remains indeterminate unless we know a great deal about its domestic politics.

Only the cruder theory generates predictions. When I refer without qualification to the theory of hegemonic stability, therefore, I will be referring to this basic force model. We have seen that the most striking contention of this theory—that hegemony is both a necessary and a sufficient condition for cooperation—is not strongly supported by the experience of this century. Taking a longer period of about 150 years, the record remains ambiguous. International economic relations were relatively cooperative both in the era of British hegemony during the mid-to-late nineteenth century and in the two decades of American dominance after World War II. But only in the second of these periods was there a trend toward the predicted disruption of established rules and increased discord. And a closer examination of the British experience casts doubt on the causal role of British hegemony in producing cooperation in the nineteenth century.

Both Britain in the nineteenth century and the United States in the twentieth met the material prerequisites for hegemony better than any other states since the Industrial Revolution. In 1880 Britain was the financial center of the world, and it controlled extensive raw materials, both in its formal empire and through investments in areas not part of the Imperial domain. It had the highest per capita income in the world and approximately double the share of world trade and investment of its nearest competitor, France. Only in the aggregate size of its economy had it already fallen behind the United States.[7] Britain's share of world trade gradually declined during the next sixty years, but in 1938 it was still the world's largest trader, with 14 percent of the world total. In the nineteenth century Britain's relative labor productivity was the highest in the world, although it declined rather precipitously thereafter. As Table 1 shows, Britain in the late nineteenth century and the United States after World War II were roughly comparable in their proportions of world trade, although until 1970 or so the United States had maintained much higher levels of relative productivity than Britain had done three-quarters of a century earlier.

Yet, despite Britain's material strength, it did not always enforce its preferred rules. Britain certainly did maintain freedom of the seas. But it did not induce major continental powers, after the 1870s, to retain liberal trade policies. A recent investigation of the subject has concluded that British efforts to make and enforce rules were less extensive and less successful than hegemonic stability theory would lead us to believe they were.[8]

Attempts by the United States after World War II to make and enforce rules for the world political economy were much more effective than Britain's had ever been. America after 1945 did not merely replicate earlier British experience; on the contrary, the differences between Britain's "hegemony" in the nineteenth century and America's after World War II were profound. As we have seen, Britain had never been as superior in productivity to the rest of the world as the United States was after 1945. Nor was the United States ever as dependent on foreign trade and investment as Britain. Equally important, America's economic partners—over whom its hegemony was exercised, since America's ability to make the rules hardly extended to the socialist camp—were also its military allies; but Britain's chief trading partners had been its major military and political rivals. In addition, one reason for Britain's relative ineffectiveness in maintaining a free trade regime is that it had never made extensive

Table 1 MATERIAL RESOURCES OF BRITAIN AND THE UNITED STATES AS HEGEMONS: PROPORTIONS OF WORLD TRADE AND RELATIVE LABOR PRODUCTIVITY

	Proportion of world trade	Relative labor productivity*
Britain, 1870	24.0	1.63
Britain, 1890	18.5	1.45
Britain, 1913	14.1	1.15
Britain, 1938	14.0	.92
United States, 1950	18.4	2.77
United States, 1960	15.3	2.28
United States, 1970	14.4	1.72
United States, 1977	13.4	1.45

*As compared with the average rate of productivity in the other members of the world economy
Source: David A. Lake, "International Economic Structures and American Foreign Economic Policy, 1887–1934," *World Politics*, vol. 35, no. 4 (July 1983), table 1 (p. 525) and table 3 (p. 541).

use of the principle of reciprocity in trade.[9] It thus had sacrificed potential leverage over other countries that preferred to retain their own restrictions while Britain practiced free trade. The policies of these states might well have been altered had they been confronted with a choice between a closed British market for their exports on the one hand and mutual lowering of barriers on the other. Finally, Britain had an empire to which it could retreat, by selling less advanced goods to its colonies rather than competing in more open markets. American hegemony, rather than being one more instance of a general phenomenon, was essentially unique in the scope and efficacy of the instruments at the disposal of a hegemonic state and in the degree of success attained.

That the theory of hegemonic stability is supported by only one or at most two cases casts doubt on its general validity. Even major proponents of the theory refrain from making such claims. In an article published in 1981, Kindleberger seemed to entertain the possibility that two or more countries might "take on the task of providing leadership together, thus adding to legitimacy, sharing the burdens, and reducing the danger that leadership is regarded cynically as a cloak for domination and exploitation."[10] In *War and Change in World Politics*, Gilpin promulgated what appeared to be a highly deterministic conception of hegemonic cycles: "the conclusion of one hegemonic war is the beginning of another cycle of growth, expansion, and eventual decline."[11] Yet he denied that his view was deterministic, and he asserted that "states can learn to be more enlightened in their definitions of their interests and can learn to be more cooperative in their behavior."[12] Despite the erosion of hegemony, "there are reasons for believing that the present disequilibrium in the international system can be resolved without resort to hegemonic war."[13]

The empirical evidence for the general validity of hegemonic stability theory is weak, and even its chief adherents have doubts about it. In addition, the logical underpinnings of the theory are suspect. Kindleberger's strong claim for the necessity of a single leader rested on the theory of collective goods. He argued that "the danger we face is not too much power in the international economy, but too little, not an excess of domination, but a superfluity of would-be free riders, unwilling to mind the store, and waiting for a storekeeper to appear."[14] . . . some of the "goods" produced by hegemonic leadership are not genuinely collective in character, although the implications of this fact are not necessarily as damaging to the theory as might be imagined at first. More critical is the fact that in international economic systems a few actors typically control a preponderance of resources. This point is especially telling, since the theory of collective goods does not properly imply that cooperation among a few countries should be impossible. Indeed, one of the original purposes of Olson's use of the theory was to show that in systems with only a few participants these actors "can provide themselves with collective goods without relying on any positive inducements apart from the good itself."[15] Logically, hegemony should not be a necessary condition for the emergence of cooperation in an oligopolistic system.

The theory of hegemonic stability is thus suggestive but by no means definitive. Concentrated power alone is not sufficient to create a stable international economic order in which cooperation flourishes, and the argument that hegemony is necessary for cooperation is both theoretically and empirically weak. If hegemony is redefined as the ability and willingness of a single state to make and enforce rules, furthermore, the claim that hegemony is sufficient for cooperation becomes virtually tautological.

The crude theory of hegemonic stability establishes a useful, if somewhat simplistic, starting-point for an analysis of changes in international cooperation and discord. Its refined version raises a looser but suggestive set of interpretive questions for the analysis of some eras in the history of the international political economy. Such an interpretive framework does not constitute an explanatory systemic theory, but it can help us think of hegemony in another way—less as a concept that helps to explain outcomes in terms of power than as a way of describing an international system in which leadership is exercised by a single state. Rather than being a component of a scientific generalization—that power is a necessary or sufficient condition for cooperation—the concept of hegemony, defined in terms of willingness as well as ability to lead, helps us think about the incentives facing the potential hegemon. Under what conditions, domestic and international, will such a country decide to invest in the construction of rules and institutions?

Concern for the incentives facing the hegemon should also alert us to the frequently neglected incentives facing other countries in the system. What calculus do they confront in considering whether to challenge or defer to a would-be leader? Thinking about the calculations of secondary powers raises the question of deference. Theories of hegemony should seek not only to analyze dominant powers' decisions to engage in rule-making and rule-enforcement, but also to explore why secondary states defer to the leadership of the hegemon. That is, they need to account for the legitimacy of hegemonic regimes and for the coexistence of cooperation, as defined in the next chapter, with hegemony. We will see later that Gramsci's notion of "ideological hegemony" provides some valuable clues helping us understand how cooperation and hegemony fit together.

MILITARY POWER AND HEGEMONY IN THE WORLD POLITICAL ECONOMY

Before taking up these themes, we need to clarify the relationship between this analysis of hegemony in the world political economy and the question of military power. A hegemonic state must possess enough military power to be able to protect the international political economy that it dominates from incursions by hostile adversaries. This is essential because economic issues, if they are crucial enough to basic national values, may become military-security issues as well. For instance, Japan attacked the United States in 1941 partly in response to the freezing of Japanese assets in the United States, which denied Japan "access to all the vitally needed supplies outside her own control, in particular her most crucial need, oil".[16] During and after World War II the United States used its military power to assure itself access to the petroleum of the Middle

East; and at the end of 1974 Secretary of State Henry A. Kissinger warned that the United States might resort to military action if oil-exporting countries threatened "some actual strangulation of the industrialized world."[17]

Yet the hegemonic power need not be militarily dominant worldwide. Neither British nor American power ever extended so far. Britain was challenged militarily during the nineteenth century by France, Germany, and especially Russia; even at the height of its power after World War II the United States confronted a recalcitrant Soviet adversary and fought a war against China. The military conditions for economic hegemony are met if the economically preponderant country has sufficient military capabilities to prevent incursions by others that would deny it access to major areas of its economic activity.

The sources of hegemony therefore include sufficient military power to deter or rebuff attempts to capture and close off important areas of the world political economy. But in the contemporary world, at any rate, it is difficult for a hegemon to use military power directly to attain its economic policy objectives with its military partners and allies. Allies cannot be threatened with force without beginning to question the alliance; nor are threats to cease defending them unless they conform to the hegemon's economic rules very credible except in extraordinary circumstances. Many of the relationships within the hegemonic international political economy dominated by the United States after World War II approximated more closely the ideal type of "complex interdependence"—with multiple issues, multiple channels of contact among societies, and inefficacy of military force for most policy objectives—than the converse ideal type of realist theory.[18]

This does not mean that military-force has become useless. It has certainly played an indirect role even in U.S. relations with its closest allies, since Germany and Japan could hardly ignore the fact that American military power shielded them from Soviet pressure. It has played a more overt role in the Middle East, where American military power has occasionally been directly employed and has always cast a shadow and where U.S. military aid has been conspicuous. Yet changes in relations of military power have not been the major factors affecting patterns of cooperation and discord among the advanced industrialized countries since the end of World War II. Only in the case of Middle Eastern oil have they been highly significant as forces contributing to changes in international economic regimes, and even in that case . . . shifts in economic interdependence, and therefore in economic power, were more important. Throughout the period between 1945 and 1983 the United States remained a far stronger military power than any of its allies and the only country capable of defending them from the Soviet Union or of intervening effectively against serious opposition in areas such as the Middle East. . . .

Some readers may wish to criticize this account by arguing that military power has been more important than claimed here. By considering military power only as a background condition for postwar American hegemony rather than as a variable, I invite such a debate. Any such critique, however, should keep in mind what I am trying to explain [here] . . . not the sources of hegemony (in domestic institutions, basic resources, and technological advances any more than in military power), but rather the effects of changes in hegemony on cooperation among the advanced industrialized countries. I seek to account for the impact of American dominance on the creation of international economic regimes and the effects of an erosion of that preponderant position on those regimes. Only if *these* problems—not other questions that might be interesting—could be understood better by exploring more deeply the impact of changes in relations of military power would this hypothetical critique be damaging to my argument.

MARXIAN NOTIONS OF HEGEMONY

For Marxists, the fundamental forces affecting the world political economy are those of class struggle and uneven development. International history is dynamic and dialectical rather than cyclical. The maneuvers of states reflect the stages of capitalist development and the contradictions of that development. For a Marxist, it is futile to discuss hegemony, or the operation of international institutions, without understanding that they operate, in the contemporary world system, within a capitalist context shaped by the evolutionary patterns and functional requirements of capitalism. Determinists may call these requirements laws. Historicists may see the patterns as providing some clues into a rather open-ended process that is nevertheless affected profoundly by what has gone before: people making their own history, but not just as they please.

Any genuinely Marxian theory of world politics begins with an analysis of capitalism. According to Marxist doctrine, no smooth and progressive development of productive forces within the confines of capitalist relations of production can persist for long. Contradictions are bound to appear. It is likely that they will take the form of tendencies toward stagnation and decline in the rate of profit, but they may also be reflected in crises of legitimacy for the capitalist state, even in the absence of economic crises.[19] Any "crisis of hegemony" will necessarily be at the same time—and more fundamentally—a crisis of capitalism.

For Marxists, theories of hegemony are necessarily partial, since they do not explain changes in the contradictions facing capitalism. Nevertheless, Marxists have often used the concept of hegemony, implicitly defined simply as dominance, as a way of analyzing the surface manifestations of world politics under capitalism. for Marxists as well as mercantilists, wealth and power are complementary: each depends on the other . . . the analyses of the Marxist Fred Block and the Realist Robert Gilpin are quite similar: both emphasize the role of U.S. hegemony in creating order after the Second World War and the disturbing effects of the erosion of American power.

Immanuel Wallerstein's work also illustrates this point. He is at pains to stress that modern world history should be seen as the history of capitalism as a world system. Apart from "relatively minor accidents" resulting from geography, peculiarities of history, or luck, "it is the operations of the world-market forces which accentuate the differences, institutionalize them, and make them impossible to surmount over the long run."[20] Nevertheless, when considering particular epochs, Wallerstein emphasizes hegemony and the role of military force. Dutch economic hegemony in the seventeenth century was destroyed not by the operation of the world-market system or contradictions of capitalism, but by the force of British and French arms.[21]

The Marxian adoption of mercantilist categories raises analytical ambiguities having to do with the relationship between capitalism and the state. Marxists who adopt this approach have difficulty maintaining a class focus, since their unit of analysis shifts to the country, rather than the class, for purposes of explaining international events. This is a problem for both Block and Wallerstein, as it often appears that their embrace of state-centered analysis has relagated the concept of class to the shadowy background of political economy. The puzzle of the relationship between the state and capitalism is also reflected in the old debate between Lenin and Kautsky about "ultra-imperialism."[22] Lenin claimed that contradictions among the capitalist powers were fundamental and could not be resolved, against Kautsky's view that capitalism could go through a phase in which capitalist states could maintain unity for a considerable period of time.

The successful operation of American hegemony for over a quarter-century after the end of World War II supports Kautsky's forecast that ultra-imperialism could be stable and contradicts Lenin's thesis that capitalism made inter-imperialist war inevitable. It does not, however, resolve the issue of whether ultra-imperialism could be maintained in the absence of hegemony. An analysis of the contemporary situation in marxian terminology would hold that one form of ultra-imperialism—American hegemony—is now breaking down, leading to increased disorder, and that the issue at present is "whether all this will ultimately result in a new capitalist world order, in a revolutionary reconstitution of world society, or in the common ruin of the contending classes and nations."[23] The issue from a Marxian standpoint is whether ultra-imperialism could be revived by new efforts at inter-capitalist collaboration or, on the contrary, whether fundamental contradictions in capitalism or in the coexistence of capitalism with the state system prevent any such recovery.

The key question of this book—how international cooperation can be maintained among the advanced capitalist states in the absence of American hegemony—poses essentially the same problem. The view taken here is similar to that of Kautsky and his followers, although the terminology is different. My contention is that the common interests of the leading capitalist states, bolstered by the effects of existing international regimes (mostly created during a period of American hegemony), are strong enough to make sustained cooperation possible, though not inevitable. One need not go so far as . . . the "internationalization of capital" to understand the strong interests that capitalists have in maintaining some cooperation in the midst of rivalry. Uneven development in the context of a state system maintains rivalry and ensures that cooperation will be incomplete and fragile . . . but it does not imply that the struggle must become violent or that compromises that benefit all sides are impossible.

Despite the similarities between my concerns and those of many Marxists, I do not adopt their categories in this study. Marxian explications of the "laws of capitalism" are not sufficiently well established that they can be relied upon for inferences about relations among states in the world political economy or for the analysis of future international cooperation. Insofar as there are fundamental contradictions in capitalism, they will surely have great impact on future international cooperation; but the existence and nature of these contradictions seem too murky to justify incorporating them into my analytical framework.

As this discussion indicates, Marxian insights into international hegemony derive in part from combining Realist conceptions of hegemony as dominance with arguments about the contradictions of capitalism. But this is not the only Marxian contribution to the debate. In the thought of Antonio Gramsci and his followers, hegemony is distinguished from sheer dominance. As Robert W. Cox has expressed it:

> Antonio Gramsci used the concept of hegemony to express a unity between objective material forces and ethico-political ideas—in Marxian terms, a unity of structure and superstructure—in which power based on dominance over production is rationalized through an ideology incorporating compromise or consensus between dominant and subordinate groups. A hegemonial structure of world order is one in which power takes a primarily consensual form, as distinguished from a nonhegemonic order in which there are manifestly rival powers and no power has been able to establish the legitimacy of its dominance.[24]

The value of this conception of hegemony is that it helps us understand the willingness of the partners of a hegemon to defer to hegemonial leadership. Hegemons require deference to enable them to construct a structure of world capitalist order. It is too expensive, and perhaps self-defeating, to achieve this by force; after all, the key distinction between hegemony and imperialism is that a hegemon, unlike an empire, does not dominate societies through a cumbersome political superstructure, but rather supervises the relationships between politically independent societies through a combination of hierarchies of control and the operation of markets.[25] Hegemony rests on the subjective awareness by elites in secondary states that they are benefiting, as well as on the willingness of the hegemon itself to sacrifice tangible short-term benefits for intangible long-term gains.

Valuable as the conception of ideological hegemony is in helping us understand deference, it should be used with some caution. First, we should not assume that leaders of secondary states are necessarily the victims of "false consciousness" when they accept the hegemonic ideology, or that they constitute a small, parasitical elite that betrays the interests of the nation to its own selfish ends. It is useful to remind ourselves, as Robert Gilpin has, that during both the *Pax Britannica* and the *Pax Americana* countries other than the hegemon prospered, and that indeed many of them grew faster than the hegemon itself.[26] Under some conditions—not necessarily all—it may be not only in the self-interest of peripheral elites, but conducive to the economic growth of their countries, for them to defer to the hegemon.[27]

We may also be permitted to doubt that ideological hegemony is as enduring internationally as it is domestically. The powerful ideology of nationalism is not available for the hegemon, outside of its own country, but rather for its enemies. Opponents of hegemony can often make nationalism the weapon of the weak and may also seek to invent cosmopolitan ideologies that delegitimize hegemony, such as the current ideology of a New International Economic Order, instead of going along with legitimating ones. Thus the potential for challenges to hegemonic ideology always exists.

CONCLUSIONS

Claims for the general validity of the theory of hegemonic stability are often exaggerated. The dominance of a single great power may contribute to order in world politics, in particular circumstances, but it is not a sufficient condition and there is little reason to believe that it is necessary. But Realist and Marxian arguments about hegemony both generate some important insights.

Hegemony is related in complex ways to cooperation and to institutions such as international regimes. Successful hegemonic leadership itself depends on a certain form of asymmetrical cooperation. The hegemon plays a distinctive role, providing its partners with leadership in return for deference; but, unlike an imperial power, it cannot make and enforce rules without a certain degree of consent from other sovereign states. As the interwar experience illustrates, material predominance alone does not guarantee either stability or effective leadership. Indeed, the hegemon may have to invest resources in institutions in order to ensure that its preferred rules will guide the behavior of other countries.

Cooperation may be fostered by hegemony, and hegemons require cooperation to make and enforce rules. Hegemony and cooperation are not alternatives; on the contrary, they are often found in symbiotic relationships with one another. To analyze the relationships between hegemony and cooperation, we need a conception of cooperation that is somewhat tart rather than syrupy-sweet. It must take into account the facts that coercion is always possible in world politics and that conflicts of interest never vanish even when there are important shared interests. . . . [C]ooperation should be defined not as the absence of conflict—which is always at least a potentially important element of international relations—but as a process that involves the use of discord to stimulate mutual adjustment.

NOTES

1. Robert O. Keohane, "The Theory of Hegemonic Stability and Changes in International Economic Regimes, 1967–1977," in Ole Holsti et al., *Change in the International System* (Boulder: Westview Press, 1980), pp. 131–162.
2. Charles P. Kindleberger, *The World in Depression. 1929–1939* (Berkeley: University of California Press, 1973), p. 305.
3. Timothy J. NcKeown, "Hegemonic Stability Theory and Nineteenth Century Tariff Levels in Europe," *International Organization*, vol. 37, no. 1 (Winter 1980), p. 78.
4. Immanuel Wallerstein, *The Modern World-System II: Mercantilism and the Consolidation of the European World-Economy. 1600–1750* (New York: Academic Press, 1980), p. 38.

5. Stephen D. Krasner, "United States Commercial and Monetary Policy: Unravelling the Paradox of External Strength and Internal Weakness," in Peter J. Katzenstein, ed., *Between Power and Plenty: Foreign Economic Policies of Advanced Industrial States* (Madison: University of Wisconsin Press, 1978), pp. 68–69.

6. Robert O. Keohane and Joseph S. Nye, *Power and Interdependence: World Politics in Transition* (Boston: Little, Brown), p. 44.

7. Stephen D. Krasner, "State Power and the Structure of International Trade," *World Politics*, vol. 28, no. 3 (April 1976), p. 333.

8. McKeown, p. 88.

9. Ibid.

10. Charles P. Kindleberger, "Dominance and Leadership in the International Economy," *International Studies Quarterly*, vol. 25, no. 3 (June 1981), p. 252.

11. Robert Gilpin, *War and Change in World Politics* (Cambridge: Cambridge University Press, 1981), p. 210.

12. Ibid., p. 227.

13. Ibid., p. 234.

14. Ibid., p. 253.

15. Mancur Olson, quoted in McKeown, p. 79.

16. Paul Schroeder, *The Axis Alliance and Japanese-American Relations* (Ithaca: Cornell University Press, 1958), p. 53;

17. Seyom Brown, *The Faces of Power: Constancy and Change in United States Foreign Policy from Truman to Reagan* (New York: Columbia University Press, 1983), p. 428.

18. Keohane and Nye, chapter 2.

19. Jurgen Haberman, *Legitimation Crisis* (London: Heinemann, 1976).

20. Immanuel Wallerstein, *The Capitalist World Economy* (Cambridge: Cambridge University Press, 1979), p. 21.

21. Wallerstein, *The Modern World-System II*, pp. 38–39.

22. V. I. Lenin, *Imperialism: The Highest Stage of Capitalism* (New York: International Publishers, 1939), pp. 93–94.

23. Giovanni Arrighi, "A Crisis of Hegemony," in Samir Amin, Giovanni Arrighi, Andre Gunder Frank, and Immanuel Wallerstein, *Dynamics of Global Crisis* (New York: Monthly Review Press, 1982), p. 108.

24. Robert W. Cox, "Social Forces, States, and World Orders: Beyond International Relations Theory," *Journal of Internation Studies, Millennium*, vol. 10, no. 2 (Summer 1981), p. 153., note 27.

25. Immanuel Wallerstein, *The Modern World System: Capitalist Agriculture and the Origins of the European World-Economy in the Sixteenth Century* (New York: Academic Press, 1974), pp. 15–17.

26. Robert Gilpin, pp. 175–185.

27. This is not to say that hegemony in general benefits small or weak countries. There certainly is no assurance that this will be the case. Hegemons may prevent middle-sized states from exploiting small ones and may construct a structure of order conducive to world economic growth; but they may also exploit smaller states economically or distort their patterns of autonomous development through economic, political, or military intervention. The issue of whether hegemony helps poor countries cannot be answered unconditionally, because too many other factors intervene. Until a more complex and sophisticated theory of the relationships among hegemony, other factors, and welfare is developed, it remains an empirically open question.

Power vs Wealth in North-South Economic Relations

Stephen D. Krasner

What do Third World countries want? More wealth. How can they get it? By adopting more economically rational policies. What should the North do? Facilitate these policies. How should the North approach global negotiations? With cautious optimism. What is the long-term prognosis for North-South relations? Hopeful, at least if economic development occurs. This is the common wisdom about relations between industrialized and developing areas in the United States and in much of the rest of the North. Within this fold there are intense debates among adherents of conventional liberal, basic human needs, and interdependence viewpoints. But the emphasis on economics at the expense of politics, on material well-being as opposed to power and control, pervades all of these orientations.

[Here], I set forth an alternative perspective. I assume that Third World states, like all states in the international system, are concerned about vulnerability and threat; and I note that national political regimes in almost all Third World countries are profoundly weak both internationally and domestically. This . . . offers a very different set of answers to the questions posed in the preceding paragraph. Third World states want power and control as much as wealth. One strategy for achieving this objective is to change the rules of the game in various international issue areas. In general, these efforts will be incompatible with long-term Northern interests. Relations between industrialized and developing areas are bound to be conflictual because most Southern countries cannot hope to cope with their international vulnerability except by challenging principles, norms, and rules preferred by industrialized countries.

Political weakness and vulnerability are fundamental sources of Third

World behavior. This weakness is a product of both external and internal factors. Externally, the national power capabilities of most Third World states are extremely limited. The national economic and military resources at the disposal of their leaders are unlikely to alter the behavior of Northern actors or the nature of international regimes. Southern states are subject to external pressures that they cannot influence through unilateral action. The international weakness of almost all less developed countries (LDCs) is compounded by the internal underdevelopment of their political and social systems. The social structures of most LDCs are rigid, and their central political institutions lack the power to make societal adjustments that could cushion external shocks. They are exposed to vacillations of an international system from which they cannot extricate themselves but over which they have only limited control.[1] The gap between Northern and Southern capabilities is already so great that even if the countries of the South grew very quickly and those of the North stagnated (an unlikely pair of assumptions in any event), only a handful of developing countries would significantly close the power gap within the next one hundred years. The physical conditions of individuals in developing areas may improve dramatically without altering the political vulnerabilities that confront their political leaders.

Third World states have adopted a range of strategies to cope with their poverty and vulnerability. Strategies directed primarily toward alleviating vulnerability are most frequently played out in international forums concerned with the establishment on maintenance of international regimes. Regimes are principles, norms, rules, and decision-making procedures around which actor expectations converge. Principles are a coherent set of theoretical statements about how the world works. Norms specify general standards of behavior. Rules and decision-making procedures refer to specific prescriptions for behavior in clearly defined areas. For instance, a liberal international regime for trade is based on a set of neoclassical economic principles that demonstrate that global utility is maximized by the free flow of goods. The basic norm of a liberal trading regime is that tariff and nontariff barriers should be reduced and ultimately eliminated. Specific rules and decision-making procedures are spelled out in the General Agreement on Tariffs and Trade. Principles and norms define the basic character of any regime. Although rules and decision-making procedures can be changed without altering the fundamental nature of a regime, principles and norms cannot. Regimes define basic property rights. They establish acceptable patterns of behavior. They coordinate decision making. They can enhance global well-being by allowing actors to escape from situations in which individual decision making leads to Pareto-suboptimal outcomes. Changes in regimes can alter the control and allocation of resources among actors in the international system. Every state wants more control over international regimes in order to make its own basic values and interests more secure.[2]

The Third World has supported international regimes that would ameliorate its weakness. As a group, the developing countries have consistently endorsed principles and norms that would legitimate more authoritative as opposed to more market-oriented modes of allocation. Authoritative allocation involves either the direct allocation of resources by political authorities, or indirect allocation by limiting the property rights of nonstate actors, including private corporations. A market-oriented regime is one in which the allocation of resources is determined by the endowments and preferences of individual actors who have the right to alienate their property according to their own estimations of their own best interests.

For developing countries, authoritative international regimes are attractive because they can provide more stable and predictable transaction flows. External shocks and pressures are threatening to developing countries because their slack resources and adjustment capabilities are so limited. Shocks are particularly troubling for political leaders because they are the likely targets of unrest generated by sudden declines in material well-being. Authoritative regimes may also provide a level of resource transfer that developing countries could not secure through market-oriented exchange. Given equal levels of resource transfer, developing states prefer authoritative to market-oriented regimes. Even when market-oriented regimes are accompanied by substantial increases in wealth, as has been the case in the post-World War II period, developing states have still sought authoritative regimes that would provide more security. I do not claim in this study that developing countries prefer control to wealth; rather I argue that authoritative regimes can provide them with both, whereas market-oriented ones cannot. I do not claim the LDCs are uninterested in wealth for its own sake. Purely wealth-oriented activities can be pursued within existing international regimes at the same time that developing states seek basic changes in principles and norms. But I do claim that the South has fundamentally challenged the extant liberal order, most visibly in the call for a New International Economic Order.

The general goal of moving toward more authoritative international regimes has been pursued using two, more specific, strategies. First, the Third World has sought to alter existing international institutions, or create new ones that would be more congruent with its preferred principles and norms. Second, developing countries have pressed for regimes that would legitimate the unilateral assertion of sovereign authority by individual states. With regard to international institutions, Third World states have demanded greater participation in global forums. They have supported universal organizations with one-nation, one-vote decision-making procedures. They have pressed for the creation of new bureaucracies that would be more sympathetic to regimes based on authoritative allocation. For instance, in the area of trade, UNCTAD (the United Nations Conference on Trade and Development) was created to offer a counterweight to the General Agreement on Tariffs and Trade (GATT), which was perceived by developing countries as an institution dedicated to a market-oriented approach. International organizations based on authoritative rather than market-oriented principles can limit the discretionary behavior of Northern actors by redefining property rights including, in the most extreme case, compelling additional resource transfers from the North to the South. For instance, the Law of the Sea Convention provides for the compulsory transfer of technology from multinational corporations to an international entity called the

Enterprise, the operating instrument of the International Sea-Bed Authority. The UNCTAD Liner Code states that liners from developing countries (ocean freighters plying regular routes on regular schedules) ought to have 40 percent of the cargo originating in their own home ports.

The second strategy pursued by the Third World has been to support international regimes that legitimate the right of individual states to exercise sovereign control over a wider range of activities than previously. The Third World has sought to enhance the scope of activities that are universally accepted as subject to the unilateral control of the state. For instance, Latin American countries led the fight for extended economic zones in the ocean. By securing international acceptance of this right at the United Nations Conference on the Law of the Sea, developing coastal countries were able to secure both greater economic returns and more control than would have been the case if narrower limits had been recognized. By accepting property-right claims that were being unilaterally asserted by developing countries, the international community greatly reduced the costs of enforcement. Similarly, in dealing with multinational corporations, the Third World has sought international legitimation of national controls. Such legitimation limits competition among developing countries and makes it more difficult for multinational corporations and their home governments to challenge host-country policies either legally or diplomatically. The South has also resisted Northern efforts to create new international regimes that would delimit existing sovereign powers. For instance, the Third World has rejected Northern efforts to legitimate new international norms regarding population control and individual human rights. The regime objectives pursued by the Third World are designed to limit the market power of the North by enhancing the sovereign prerogatives of the South, either through universal international organizations in which each nation has a single vote, or by widening the scope of activities exclusively subject to the unilateral sovereign will of individual developing states.

The demands associated with proposals for the New International Economic Order (NIEO), which assumed their greatest saliency in the mid-1970s, are the clearest manifestation of Third World efforts to restructure market-oriented international regimes. The NIEO and related proposals covered a wide range of issue areas, including trade, primary commodities, aid, debt, space, multinational corporations, journalism, and shipping. The NIEO was the culmination of Third World efforts that had begun in the 1940s.

The degree to which developing countries have succeeded in altering international regimes has been a function of three variables: the nature of existing institutional structures; the ability to formulate a coherent system of ideas, which set the agenda for international negotiations and cemented Third World unity; and the attitude and power of the North, especially the United States, toward both the demands of the South and the forums in which they have been made.

The nature of existing regime structures, including existing international organizations, has influenced the ability of Third World states to secure an environment governed by authoritative, as opposed to market, allocation. The most important general institutional advantage enjoyed by the Third World has been the acceptance of the principle of the sovereign equality of states. There have always been weak states in the international system, although in recent years disparities in per capita income have magnified distinctions in size and population. Before the twentieth century, however, the great powers were accepted as the dominant actors in the system, possessing rights of unilateral action that were denied to smaller states: the principle of great-power primacy dominated that of sovereign equality. At best, small states could maintain a precarious neutrality, relying on the balance of power to provide them with some freedom of action. In the present system the principle of sovereign equality dominates that of great-power primacy, and states with the most exiguous national power capabilities deny that others have special prerogatives.

The most important organizational manifestation of the principle of sovereign equality has been the United Nations. The UN system provided the major forums at which developing countries could present their demands. Developing states have had automatic access to United Nations agencies. With the exception of international financial institutions and the Security Council, states have had equal voting power. New agencies such as UNCTAD and UNIDO (UN Industrial Development Organization) have been created. The standard operating procedures of agencies have been changed. In areas where existing institutions limited access, such as with the Antarcitc, developing states have had little success. If the United Nations had not existed, it would have been impossible for the Third World to articulate a general program for altering international regimes.

Aside from nonspecialized universal institutions, the principles, norms, rules, and decision-making procedures confronting Third World countries in a number of specific issue areas conditioned their ability to secure their objectives. For developing states the most attractive situations have been ones in which existing international regimes, supported by the North, already embodied norms of authoritative, rather than market, allocation. If developing countries could secure access to these regimes, they could make claims on resources that would have been barred to them in a market-oriented world. For instance, the regime governing civil aviation has, since its inception after World War I, been governed by principles emphasizing state security, and norms that call for an equal allocation of traffic between foreign and domestic carriers in any given national market. Furthermore, fares have been influenced by agreements among airline companies, which are subject to state approval. This regime gave any Third World country that wanted to begin its own national airline a presumptive right to passengers, a reciprocal right to landing privileges, and some guarantee against competitive rate-cutting. Many Third World states took advantage of this situation. In contrast, critical aspects of ocean shipping have been governed by norms and rules (some of whose antecedents stretch back to the late Middle Ages) which are predominantly based on commercial principles emphasizing market allocation. Some rate structures have been negotiated by cartels, to which developing country shipping lines have limited access. The legitimation of flags of convenience has offset some of the competitive advantage that developing countries might have had from cheap labor. Developing countries have been less successful in establishing their own shipping lines than in establishing their own commercial airlines, in part because of the nature of existing international regimes.

The second variable affecting the ability of developing countries to secure their preferred international regimes has been the coherence of the ideological arguments used to rationalize and justify their demands. The degree of coherence has increased over time. Developing states were never entranced with the liberal market-oriented regimes established at the conclusion of the Second World War. But their initial forays were limited to sniping at bits and pieces of this order and calling attention to areas where developed states had violated their own liberal principles. However, beginning with the work of Raul Prebisch at the Economic Commission for Latin America in the late 1940s, spokesmen for Third World countries developed a set of arguments that placed the major reponsibility for underdevelopment on the workings of the international system rather than on the specific characteristics of developing countries and the policies adopted by their leaders. This line of argument was developed and propagated over time, drawing on Marxist as well as conventional economic analyses. The ability of the Third World to present a coherent world view—one which depicted the exploitation of the Third World as an inherent feature of the global economy—provided a rationale for making demands on the North, helped the Group of 77 (formed at the first UNCTAD meeting by seventy-seven LDCs) to coordinate its programs across several issue areas, and reduced negotiating costs among developing countries by suggesting specific policy proposals. By the early 1970s the industrialized world was on the defensive in major international forums. The agenda was being set by the Third World. The Gramscian hegemony enjoyed by liberal doctrines in the immediate post-war period had been totally undermined. It was rejected by almost all Third World leaders and questioned by many specific groups, including some policymakers, in the North.

The final variable influencing the degree of success realized by the Third World in securing international regimes based upon authoritative allocation has been the power of the North, especially that of the United States. This too changed over time. The United States emerged from the Second World War in an extrordinarily dominant position. Its physical plant had not been damaged by the fighting. Its gross national product was three times as large as that of its main rival, the Soviet Union. It had a monopoly on nuclear weapons. It enjoyed a technological advantage over its major competitors in most industrial sectors. Over time this domination has eroded. The Europeans and the Japanese recovered. The Soviet Union and several other countries secured nuclear weapons. The Japanese challenged the United States even in the most technologically advanced industries. Dependence on imported energy supplies increased dramatically. Vietnam undermined the domestic consensus that had supported U.S. foreign policy.[3]

The early 1970s proved to be the most propitious moment for the developing world to launch a major attack on the liberal international order that had been so assiduously cultivated by U.S. policymakers. The United States had been the moving force behind the international organizations created at the conclusion of the Second World War. For a hegemonic power, the purpose of such organizations is to legitimate its preferences, and values. Legitimation requires that the organizations be given autonomy. If they are seen merely as handmaidens of the hegemon, they will be ineffective. Despite formal autonomy, the United States had great influence over specific decisions and general policies in all major international organizations through the 1950s.

Decolonization eroded American influence. In the United Nations, and in other international organizations, voting majorities changed. Third World states questioned both the underlying values and specific policy preferences of the United States. This did not immediately lead to an American renunciation of existing institutions, however, or even to a decline in American commitments. In the absence of alternatives, such a radical shift was unattractive because Third World behavior could be interpreted as a temporary aberration, and the reaction of other countries to a dramatic change could not be easily gauged. At least some American policymakers were committed to the strategy, deeply rooted in basic American attitudes toward international affairs, of resolving conflicts through negotiations and international agreements. Thus, despite a growing inability to influence decisions in the United Nations and other international forums, the United States did not simply walk out. Had it done so the developing world would have been reduced to vacuous rhetoric in chambers devoid of influence, if not of individuals.

The early 1970s offered a unique window of opportunity for the Third World because it was a period characterized by Third World control of major international forums but continued Northern commitment. Through the 1960s the South had not wielded itself into a disciplined voting block or presented a coherent program across many issue areas. By the late 1970s, Northern commitments had begun to erode, especially those of the United States. Financial contributions declined. The United States temporarily withdrew from the International Labor Organization in the late 1970s, and in January 1985 formally withdrew from UNESCO. Other industrialized market-economy states, notably Great Britain, also indicated their deep dissatisfaction with UNESCO. In 1982, several Northern states, including the United States, rejected the United Nations Law of the Sea Convention. Without American participation the Convention is of limited utility. In January 1985 the United States, for the first time, refused to take part in a World Court case, an action in defiance of the Court's rules.

In sum, the desire to secure international regimes embodying authoritative rather than market allocation of resources has been an enduring aspect of Third World policy in the postwar period. It reflects the profound national weakness of most developing countries. This weakness stems from the inability to influence unilaterally or to adjust internally to the pressures of global markets. Larger industrialized states are able to influence the international environment and can adjust internally. Smaller industrialized states have little influence over the global pattern of transactions, but their domestic political economies allow them to adjust. Small size and inflexible domestic structures make Third World states vulnerable: severe domestic political and economic dislocation can occur as a result of shocks and fluctuations emanating from the international system. Such dislocation can be especially painful for political leaders who become the targets of a counter-elite or of popular discontent. By changing the nature of international regimes, Third World leaders hope not only to increase the flow of material resources but also to create a more predictable and stable environment. The success of developing countries in pursuing their regime objectives has depended on the nature of extant institutional arrangements, their ability to articulate a coherent viewpoint, and the willingness of the North, particularly the United States, to tolerate international forums that produced undesired results. These last two factors explain why the North-South conflict reached such intensity during the mid-1970s. At that moment, the South had developed an effective ideological position, the international forums were available, and the United States was still committed to global negotiations. Ironically, it was the last years of the American hegemonic apogee that provided weak states with their greatest opportunity to attack the prevailing order.

This interpretation of Southern behavior draws upon a structural, or third-image, approach to international politics which maintains that the behavior of states is determined by their relative power capabilities.[4] The countries of the South are not purveyors of some new and superior morality, nor are their policies any less reasonable than those of the industrialized world. They are behaving the way states have always behaved; they are trying to maximize their power—their ability to control their own destinies. The claims of the Group of 77 have been based on the equality of sovereign states and have been made for the state and the state alone, not for individual citizens.[5] For developing countries, restructuring regimes was an attractive strategy, particularly in the early 1970s, because of their lack of national power capabilities, their ability to break the ideological hegemony of the North, and the access provided by international organizations.

The implications of this analysis for maintaining universal principles and norms are not sanguine. Effective international regime construction, as opposed to regime maintenance, is difficult. Historically, new regimes are most easily created by hegemonic states possessing overwhelming military, economic, and ideological power. Once regimes are created, narrow calculations of interests, uncertainty about alternatives, and habit may provide support even if the power of the hegemonic state fades and its policy preferences change. The countries of the developing world are, however, interested in altering liberal international regimes, not in maintaining them. They want new principles, norms, rules, and decision-making procedures. They can bring to bear powerful ideological arguments to legitimate their preferences, but they lack national economic and military capabilities.

Existing international regimes are likely to continue to weaken, not only because of attacks from the South but also because of disaffection in the North. Especially for the United States, declining power will make policymakers less willing to tolerate free riders or to bear a disproportionate share of the costs of maintaining international regimes. Although the South will not abandon calls for a New International Economic Order, it will give less emphasis to this program because the prospects for success are dim. The behavior of both the North and the South will be increasingly motivated by short-term calculations of interest rather than by long-term goals that require efficacious regimes. When mutual interests are high, such calculations can lead to cooperative relations. Where specific interests are not present, interaction will decline. For both developing and industrialized states this is not such a daunting prospect. Given fundamental conflicts stemming from outlandish disparities in power, there would be more security in a world with lower levels of transnational interactions. Self-reliance and collective self-reliance rather than interdependence may serve the interests of the North as well as those of the South.

THE VARIETY OF THIRD WORLD GOALS

By emphasizing weakness, vulnerability, and the quest for control in this study, I do not mean to imply that LDCs are uninterested in purely economic objectives. Third World states have pursued a wide variety of goals. These include economic growth, international political equality, influence in international decision-making arenas, autonomy and independence, the preservation of territorial integrity from external invasion or internal fragmentation, the dissemination of new world views at the global level, and the maintenance of domestic regime stability. They have used a wide variety of tactics to promote these objectives, including international commodity organizations such as OPEC and CIPEC (*Conseil Intergouvernment des Pays Exportateurs Cuivre*), regional organizations such as the Organization of African Unity (OAU) and the Association of Southeast Asian Nations (ASEAN), universal coalitions such as the Group of 77 (G-77) at UNCTAD and the United Nations, alliances with major powers, local wars to manipulate major powers, irregular violence such as national liberation movements, bilateral economic arrangements, national regulation of multinational corporations, nationalization of foreign holdings, foreign exchange manipulation, and international loans. . . .

The boundaries of this work can be more clearly delineated by distinguishing between two categories of political behavior. Relational power behavior refers to efforts to maximize values within a given set of institutional structures; meta-power behavior refers to efforts to change the institutions themselves. Relational power refers to the ability to change outcomes or affect the behavior of others within a given regime. Metapower refers to the ability to change the rules of the game.[6]

Outcomes can be changed both by altering the resources available to individual actors and by changing the regimes that condition action. Changing the outcome of struggles fought with relational power requires changing actor capability. But such changes do not necessarily imply an alteration in meta-power. An individual may win more money by learning to become a better poker player without being able to change the rules of poker. A political party may win more offices by attracting more voters without altering the laws governing elections. A state may prevail more frequently in disputes with other international actors by enhancing its national power capabilities without altering the principles, norms, and rules that condition such disputes.

Outcomes can also be changed by changing regimes. Meta-power behavior is designed to do this. When successfully implemented, it usually means a change in relational power as well. Individuals who win at poker may lose at bridge; political parties that secure seats under a proportional representation system might be excluded by single-seat districts; states that secure greater revenue from cartelized exports would be poorer if the price of their product were dictated by those with the greatest military capability. An actor capable of changing the game from poker to bridge, from proportional representation to single-seat, from economic to military capability, possesses meta-power. Actors may seek to enhance their relational power by enhancing their own national capabilities, or they may attempt to secure more favorable outcomes by pursuing a meta-power strategy designed to change regimes. . . .

The exercise of relational power involves only questions of formal rationality. Relational power behavior accepts existing goals and institutional structures. The challenge is to achieve these goals most efficiently. Meta-power rejects existing goals and institutional structures. It employs formal, rational calculations to promote new goals and institutions. Behavior that is formally rational given one set of substantive objectives may be formally irrational given another.

Third World states are interested in employing both relational power and meta-power. Proposals for international regime change, voiced by the less developed countries, are an effort to exercise meta-power. The objective of these proposals, of which the program associated with the New International Economic Order is the most salient, is to alter the principles, norms, rules, and decision-making procedures that condition international transactions. Such transformation is attractive because in a market-oriented regime the ability of Third World states to achieve their objectives solely through the exercise of relational power is limited by the exiguousness of their national capabilities. These capabilities alone could not resolve the vulnerability problems of poorer states. For the Third World, altering international regimes is a relatively attractive way to secure some control over the environment.

Third World efforts to change regimes have been most clearly manifest in international organizations. Debates within these organizations have concerned principles, norms, rules, and decision-making procedures, not just the transfer of resources. LDCs have also used national legislation to try to alter international rules of the game. However, the NIEO and other proposals for regime change have been but one of many kinds of interactions between the North and the South. With regard to actual resource movements, the most important settings have been national and bilateral. In such settings, developing states have used relational power to enhance specific economic interests. When, for instance, a developing country borrows on the Eurodollar market, it attempts to get the best possible terms; it does not, however, challenge the right of private financial institutions to base their decisions on maximizing private economic returns. When a developing country accepts foreign assistance, it tries to alter both the amounts and the terms on which it is dispensed; it does not, however, usually challenge the prerogative of donor countries to base aid allocations on self-determined principles or interests. When a state negotiates a standby agreement with the International Monetary Fund (IMF) it attempts to use relational power to adjust the terms and conditions of the arrangement; it does not, however, challenge the authority of the IMF to sign such an agreement. The modal form of interaction between industrialized and developing areas has involved the transfer of resources and the exercise of relational power, and has taken place in bilateral arenas.

Some examples of relational power and meta-power policies in national and bilateral, as opposed to multilateral, settings are shown in Table 1. Multilateral settings are further broken down into North-South and South-South arrangements.

Behavior that falls within one of the cells in not incompatible with behavior that falls in another. It is not inconsistent for developing countries to pursue different goals in various arenas at the same time. During the 1970s the Group of 77 pressed for generalized debt relief for the least developed states at universal international forums such as UNCTAD and the United Nations General Assembly, while downplaying this issue at multilateral financial institutions such as the World Bank and the IMF.[7] In the area of raw materials, the less developed countries sought both compensatory finance, which would enhance their economic well-being without altering basic regime characteristics, as well as the formation of the Integrated Program for Commodities, which would fundamentally change the principles and norms governing the international movement of primary products. Under the *sexenio* Luis Echeverría, Mexico played a prominent role in the Third World movement. At the same time, the Mexican finance and development ministries were engaged in extensive pragmatic discussions with multinational corporations about conditions for their entry into Mexico. Similarly, Algeria pursued purely economic policies with respect to liquefied natural gas exports while Boumedienne acted as the leader of the Non-Aligned Movement. The pursuit of different goals in various forums is not inconsistent or incoherent.[8] It does not reflect disagreement between politically oriented foreign affairs officials, who do not understand economics, and finance ministry officials, who recognize the "realities" of global interdependence. Rather, the variety of Third World strategies is a manifestation of a variety of objectives. . . .

ALTERNATIVE APPROACHES TO NORTH-SOUTH RELATIONS

The interpretation presented in this study both complements and challenges a number of prominent alternatives: basic human needs, conventional liberalism, and global interdependence. Analysts concerned with basic human needs em-

Table 1

Negotiating forum	Behavior type	
	Relational power behavior (formal rationality)	Meta-power behavior (substantive rationality)
National and bilateral	Eurodollar loans Taxtreaties Bilateral aid	Some regulation of MNCs (1960s) Control of oil production (1970s) Expansive national claims to ocean resources (1945–1970) Unilateral alteration of loan terms (early 1980s)
Multilateral South-South	Existing trade arrangements among LDCs	OPEC Andean Pact Collective self-reliance
Multilateral Universal, including North-South	Civil aviation Nuclear nonproliferation	New International Information Order (NIIO) NIEO Generalized systems of preferences Commodity agreements Aspects of Lome Convention Integrated Program for Commodities UNCLOS

278

phasize the material well-being of individuals rather than the political concerns of states. Advocates of free enterprise and liberal economics focus on problems of economic growth. Those who see interdependence as the defining characteristic of the present international system emphasize the ties that bind the North to the fate of the South. Both those of interdependence orientation and those embracing some variants of the liberal approach are sensitive to the political demands made by developing countries. However, basic human needs, conventional liberal, and interdependence arguments all include the implication that accelerated economic growth accompanied by equitable distribution would eliminate the basic source of North-South conflict. Demands for the restructuring of international regimes are understood as instrumental tactics whose ultimate purpose is to enhance economic well-being. Economic well-being for either individuals or the collectivity, rather than state concerns with vulnerability and control, is (tacitly or explicitly) seen as the fundamental motivation for Southern behavior.

As president of the World Bank, Robert McNamara was a prominent exponent of the basic human needs orientation. Under his leadership the bank emphasized the alleviation of absolute poverty. The bank's allocation of funds shifted away from infrastructure and industry toward projects that had a direct effect on the poor, especially small-scale agriculture. In his 1979 address to the board of governors of the bank, McNamara . . . maintained that income gaps between rich and poor are "largely irrelevant for determining the long-term objectives of the developing countries themselves."[9] In a 1977 talk he argued that it would quickly become apparent that "it is relatively unimportant whether the assistance is to take the form of commodity agreements, debt relief, trade concessions, bilateral or multilateral financing—or any particular combination of these—provided the overall total is adequate.[10]

The alleviation of absolute poverty has also been a major theme of American foreign aid doctrines. It has been embodied in legislation and instructions to American executive directors at international financial institutions. Secretary of State Vance maintained in a 1979 speech that "Programs such as those I have mentioned today are not a cure-all. But they come to grips with the most pressing problems of the developing countries, and they will make a difference where it counts most—in the daily lives of people. They will insure that more people in the developing countries will have enough food to eat, that fewer children will die in infancy, that there is sufficient energy to power more irrigation pumps and to bring more heat and light to distant villages."[11]

The emphasis on basic needs exemplifies a wider trend explicated by Robert W. Tucker. Tucker argues that some Western elites are advocates of what he terms the "politics of sensibility." These elites have come to assume that the Third World is primarily concerned with improving the well-being of individuals. They maintain that justice cannot tolerate existing inequalities. They argue that men should no longer distinguish between fellow citizens and the rest of mankind in the provision of basic needs. The countries of the South are seen by such elites, Tucker argues, as expositors of a new international morality that extends across national boundaries.[12]

General economic performance in the South has been a second focus of attention for Northern policymakers and analysts. Discussion of Third World growth has been deeply influenced by the precepts of liberal neoclassical economics. Within this general approach orthodox liberals have emphasized domestic factors in the Third World, while reformist liberals have also taken global systemic factors into account.

For orthodox liberals the problems of developing countries must be resolved internally. Low per capita incomes are the result of inadequate factor endowments. The rate of capital formation is low; infrastructures are underdeveloped; soil conditions are poor; education is limited. To some extent these conditions, and the consequent unsatisfactory economic performance of many developing countries, are blamed on inappropriate economic policies. Underdeveloped countries have authored their own failures. Orthodox liberals are especially perturbed by the Third World's rejection of market mechanisms. Trade barriers promote inefficient domestic industries. Investment regulations discourage multinational corporations. Low payments to farmers reduce food production. Artificial exchange rates distort production and consumption. Taxes on primary exports encourage smuggling. Enforced collectivization destroys individual incentives. . . .

The policy implications for the North of orthodox liberal views are readily apparent. The New International Economic Order (NIEO) program should be rejected in its entirety. There is no need to change the international economic system. Third World policies are responsible for Third World poverty. Indeed, such change would be counterproductive because it would substitute state activity for the market. The NIEO is seen as a cockeyed set of proposals inspired by erroneous dependency arguments at best, and economic stupidity at worst.

Orthodox liberals have not paid much attention to Northern policies that impede the functioning of the market. Such policies are unfortunate, even reprehensible. But the fate of the South will not be determined by anything that the North does; while the present system may be flawed in modest ways, it still offers enormous opportunities to those developing countries, such as Taiwan, South Korea, Hong Kong, and Singapore, which are prepared to seize them.

Reformist liberals start with the same basic presuppositions as orthodox liberals, but place more emphasis on the need for more forthcoming Northern policies. Such policies, they say, should recognize the peculiar circumstances of LDCs as well as making markets work more effectively. Reformist liberals strongly condemn import restrictions imposed by developed countries, which not only discourage adjustment in the North but impede exports from the South. They support criticisms of the system which point to imperfections in existing markets. For instance, the transfer of technology is carried out largely by multinational corporations that often have oligopoly if not monopoly power. International agreements concerning technology-transfer and restrictive business practices are needed because, like American antitrust legislation, they facilitate the functioning of the market.

Reformist liberals are also more tolerant than their orthodox colleagues of domestic policies in developing countries which do not strictly accord with market principles. They more readily accept the infant-industry argument. Given market imperfections, developing countries' domestic subsidies may be the second-best solution. When basic human needs are at stake, the state may have to allocate. But reformist liberals are as unhappy about inefficient domestic policies in developing countries as their orthodox brethren.

This analysis leads reformist liberals to a more sympathetic view of the New International Economic Order. The demands of the Third World are seen as reformist, not revolutionary. The Third World is understood to believe that the world economy can provide benefits for all. Rhetoric that condemns the system as a whole is just rhetoric. Compromise is possible at the international level. Moreover, the North needs to reform its own policies. Northern restrictions on imports from the South can seriously impede economic development. Present structures do not necessarily provide the price signals needed to maximize global efficiency. A more efficient system would provide benefits for both industrialized and developing areas. . . .

The special situation confronting developing countries must be appreciated. Industrialized nations should lower trade barriers and accept some temporary LDC export subsidization. Compensatory finance schemes should be encouraged for primary commodity exporters. Financial flows should be increased by providing more resources for international financial institutions and by creating international tax funds for the poorest countries. There should be more disclosure of information regarding technology to lessen the imperfections resulting from oligopolistic control. . . .

Liberal orientations of one cast or another have dominated American attitudes toward the Third World during the postwar period. Democratic administrations have tended to accept reformist liberal arguments. Such arguments were particularly prevalent under Jimmy Carter. Republicans have been more sympathetic to orthodox liberal perspectives, a viewpoint strongly reflected in the positions taken by the Reagan administration. Undergirding both these approaches is a set of beliefs about the relationship between economic well-being and political behavior which incorporates a reductionist, or second-image, understanding of international politics. Louis Hartz has argued that American views of foreign affairs are dominated by the prevailing liberal approach to politics within the United States. Because America's historical experience isolated it from the mainstream of both conservative and socialist developments in Europe, Lockean liberalism with its emphasis on individualism, free enterprise, and political democracy has set the boundaries of political discourse.[13] The leitmotif of American foreign policy has been to reconstruct the American experience in other parts of the world. The external behavior of states has been understood as a manifestation of their domestic sociopolitical characteristics rather than their international power capabilities.

In a study written before the demands for a New International Economic Order came to dominate North-South relations, Robert Packenham used Hartz's insights to analyze American foreign aid doctrines. He argued that the liberal roots of American attitudes led to four basic precepts. First, change and development are easy. Second, all good things go together. Third, radicalism and revolution are bad. Forth, distributing power is more important than accumulating power. American leaders saw the poorer countries of the world moving along the same path that had been followed by the United States. Economic development would promote political development. Political development meant democracy. Democratic regimes would follow international policies that coincided with the interests of the United States. . . .[14]

The world view of American policymakers has not changed much in the postwar period, and the American response to the New International Economic Order was not very different from the response to earlier Third World demands. Economic development within the countries of the Third World has been seen as the key to their domestic evolution, and domestic political evolution as the key to their international behavior.

For reformist liberals the analogies used to clarify Third World behavior are drawn from domestic politics rather than from international relations. John Sewell of the Overseas Development Council writes that the demands of LDCs bear "some similarity to the emergence of organized labor in this country in the late 1920s and 1930s."[15]

Few Northern commentators have perceived the NIEO as a challenge to the basic nature of the liberal regime. Rather, the Third World has been understood to be calling for adjustments within an existing set of principles and norms. Radical transformation was not necessary because a reformed version of the extant liberal order could meet many Third World economic needs. And it was these needs, not the desire to compensate for vulnerability by regime control, which were understood to be the gravamen of LDC dissatisfaction.

While the focus of various liberal and basic human needs perspectives is on the well-being of the South, the emphasis in interdependence approaches is on the links between the North and the South. The fate of all countries is intertwined. The basic assumptions of the realist approach, which underlies this study, are rejected. Viewing states as the only constitutive element of the international system obscures the inability of ostensibly sovereign political institutions to control many transnational flows. The formal imprimatur of sovereignty may remain, but revolutionary changes in the technology of communication and transportation have transformed the global system into a web of interdependence from which states can extricate themselves only at extremely high cost, if at all. Various private and subnational actors have developed their own transnational relations. Multinational corporations orchestrate subsidiaries in various parts of the world. Billions of dollars can be transferred electronically from one financial center to another in a matter of seconds. Domestic economic policies can be undermined or reinforced by choices made by other countries for purely domestic reasons. Partisans of an interdependence perspective maintain that this is a world that cannot be adequately understood by focusing on states and power. Economic failure for the South would have dire consequences for the North.[16]

The first report of the Independent Commission for International Economic Cooperation offers elegant testimony for this approach.[17] The commission was chaired by Willy Brandt, and included notables from the industrialized and developing worlds. The report includes the statement that "the world is now a fragile and interlocking system, whether for its people, its ecology or its resources" (p. 33). Brandt avers that "this Report deals with peace. War is often thought of in terms of military conflict, or even annihilation. But there is a growing awareness that an equal danger might be chaos—as a result of mass hunger, economic disaster, environmental catastrophes, and terrorism" (p. 13). The report contains a number of specific arguments about the way in which developments in the South affect the North. For instance, a surging demand for grain in the South, a result of local crop failures, would contribute to inflation in the North. Rapid population growth could have a deleterious impact on the earth's ecosystem. Developing countries are increasingly important trading partners for the North. Economic collapse in the South could spawn international terrorism and even nuclear blackmail.

The commission's analysis led it to policy conclusions that were more sympathetic to the Third World than those arrived at by analysts with liberal or basic human needs perspectives. While recognizing that the developing countries themselves must carry "the major share of the burden" for effectively attacking poverty, substantial changes in the global economic system were called for in the report (p. 29). Economic forces cannot be left entirely to themselves because they "tend to produce growing inequality" (p. 33). Aid levels should be increased, and the international provision of capital should be more automatic. Levies on armaments and luxury goods trade, taxes on the use of the global commons, or the sale of more gold by the IMF could provide the resources for such transfers. Commodity prices, it is argued in the report, should be stabilized through international agreement. Northern barriers to exports from the South should be eliminated.

The approach taken by the Brandt Commission, and by other analysts who see interdependence as the basic characteristic of the current world system, are closer in some ways to the perspective I have taken in this study than to other interpretations of the North-South situation. Like this study, interdependence arguments have a strong systemic orientation. They address not only the domestic poverty of the South but also the consequences of conditions in the South for the North. While those with basic human needs and liberal orientations focus on the relational power behavior of developing countries, those using interdependence arguments do address meta-power concerns as well. However, while economic growth and prosperity as the center of Third World concerns is stressed in interdependence arguments, I seek to demonstrate in this study that questions of vulnerability and control are more important, at least for some aspects of Third World behavior. Enhancing economic utility will not resolve conflicts between the North and the South. Vulnerability, not simply poverty, is the motivating force for the Third World's meta-power program for transforming international regimes. Those following basic human needs, liberal, and interdependence approaches have failed to comprehend the fundamentally political character of many Third World demands. . . .

CONCLUSION

The meta-political goals of Third World states, and many of their relational goals as well, can be understood in reference to the minimalist objective of preserving political integrity. Most developing countries have very weak domestic political institutions. Nonconstitutional regime changes occur frequently. Domestic violence is common. Slack resources are limited. The material resources controlled by Third World states are typically heavily dependent on international economic transactions, which can be taxed relatively easily compared with domestic transactions. Declines in the value of trade can deprive state officials of revenues that are critical for maintaining domestic political control. Hence, the positions of Third World political leaders are very vulnerable to changes in the international economic environment. Making that environment more predictable and stable would contribute to domestic political stability. Regimes legitimating authoritative, rather than market, allocation can provide more stability as well as greater transfers of wealth.

In this study, however, unlike those presenting conventional structural arguments, I have taken seriously not only international power but also international regimes. Those using conventional structural arguments view international politics as a zero-sum conflict among states. Regimes have little autonomy. They are regarded as being only one small step removed from the underlying power configurations that support them. When national power capabilities change, regimes will change as well. For conventional realists, regimes are purely epiphenomenal. The direct clash of interests among states is the basic characteristic of international life.

Because I have adopted the modified structural, or modified realist, orientation in this study I accept the critical importance of political power for regime creation. It is impossible to establish *de novo* durable principles, norms, rules, and decision-making procedures unless they are supported by the more powerful states in the system. Once regimes are actually in place, however, the relationship between power and regimes can become more attenuated. Established regimes generate inertia if only because of sunk costs and the absence of alternatives.[18] Bureaucrats in international organizations actively cultivate supportive clientele. The distribution of influence within organizations may not reflect underlying national power capabilities, one-nation, one-vote procedures being the most obvious example. Regimes with norms and rules giving open access can be altered by new members. Agendas within established regimes can be influenced not only be voting power but also by the persuasiveness and coherence of intellectual arguments. Hence, regimes do not move in lockstep with changes in underlying national power capabilities. Third World states cannot establish new regimes from scratch, but they have been able to change existing regimes, sometimes in very significant ways.

From a modified structuralist perspective, the normative implications of regime autonomy depend on the degree of disparity between underlying national power capabilities and regime characteristics. Some moderate degree of disparity is acceptable, even desirable. It makes it possible for regimes to have enough longevity and stability to produce mutually beneficial outcomes. The greater the disparity, however, the greater the probability of a sudden rupture. Powerful states can destroy regimes that are antithetical to their interests. By disrupting existing patterns of behavior and introducing high levels of uncertainty, such ruptures can be particularly damaging to global well-being and can exacerbate international tensions.

From a modified structural perspective, therefore, the Third World's quest for regimes based more on authoritative allocation is not quixotic, but it is normatively suspect. Developing states do not have the power to create completely new international regimes that involve the North. A minimum condition for Southern initiatives has been access to existing international organizations. Given access, the Third World has consistently attempted to move regimes away from market-oriented principles, norms, and rules. Ideological coherence and declining Northern capabilities have made possible some genuine success despite the lack of national power resources in the South. However, Third World accomplishments only rarely contribute to a stable international environment. The greater the success of the Third World in changing regimes against Northern preferences, the more likely the North is to rupture existing practices by withdrawing support.

The tensions between the South and the North, between weak and vulnerable states on the one hand and strong and resilient ones on the other, cannot be resolved through either economic growth or regime change. Even if very optimistic projections of economic performance for the South were realized, national vulnerabilities would not be significantly reduced even with substantial improvements in individual well-being. In only a limited number of cases will the South's support for regimes based on authoritative allocation coincide with the desires of the North. For industrialized states, market-oriented regimes in which resource allocation is determined by present endowments and preferences are more economically attractive and, given developed domestic political and economic structures, disruptions and dislocations can be managed so that political integrity is not put in jeopardy. The international system would be more stable and less conflictual if the North and the South had less to do with each other. From a Northern as well as a Southern perspective collective self-reliance is preferable to greater interdependence.

NOTES

1. The two major exceptions to this generalization are the small number of developing countries that are so large that they can limit external interactions, notably China and India, and a few smaller developing states that have flexible and effective sociopolitical and economic structures that allow them to adjust to international conditions, such as the newly industrializing countries (NICs) in Southeast Asia— South Korea, Taiwan, Singapore, and Hong Kong.
2. Robert Gilpin, *War and change in World Politics* (New York: Cambridge University Press, 1981), p. 50.

3. Ole Holsti and James N. Rosenau, "Vietnam, Consensus, and the Belief Systems of American Leaders," *World Politics,* vol. 32 (October, 1979).

4. Kenneth N. Waltz, *Man, the State, and War,* (New York: Columbia University Press, 1959); and Waltz, *Theory of International Politcs* (Reading: Addison-Wesley, 1979).

5. Robert W. Tucker, *The Inequality of Nations* (New York: Basic Books, 1977).

6. The terms are from Tom Baumgartner et al., "Unequal Exchange and Uneven Development," *working paper* no. 45, Institute of Sociology, University of Oslo, 1976.

7. *Wall Street Journal,* October 4, 1976, 8:3; Rothstein, *Global Bargaining,* p. 161.

8. For a similar conclusion, see Branislov Gosovic and John G. Ruggie, "On the Creation of a New International Economic Order," *International Organization,* vol. 30 (Spring 1976), p, 32.

9. Robert S. McNamara, *Address to the Board of Governors,* International Bank for Reconstruction and Development, October 2, 1979, Washington, DC, p. 6.

10. *The New York Times.* January 15, 1977, 33:6

11. U.S. State Department *Bulletin,* May 1979, p. 37.

12. Tucker, *Inequality of Nations,* esp. pp. 138 ff. Tucker thoroughly rejects the "politics of sensibility."

13. Hartz, *The Liberal Tradition in America* (New York: Harcourt, Brace and World, 1955).

14. Packenham, *Liberal America and the Third World* (Princeton: Princeton University Press, 1973), esp. ch. 3.

15. John Sewell, *The United States and World Development: Agenda 1977* (New York: Prager, 1977) p. 8.

16. See Robert O. Keohane and Joseph Nye, *Power and Interdependence* (Boston: Little, Brown, 1977), for a discussion of complex interdependence.

17. Independent Commission on International Development Issues (Brandt Commission), *North South: A Program for Survival* (Cambridge: MIT Press, 1980).

18. Robert O. Keohane, "The Demand for International Regimes," *International Organization,* vol. 36 (Spring 1982).

Three Models of the Future

Robert Gilpin

Edward Hallet Carr observed that "the science of economics presupposes a given political order, and cannot be profitably studied in isolation from politics.[1] Throughout history, the larger configurations of world politics and state interests have in large measure determined the framework of the international economy. Succeeding imperial and hegemonic powers have sought to organize and maintain the international economy in terms of their economic and security interests.

From this perspective, the contemporary international economy was the creation of the world's dominant economic and military power, the United States. At the end of the Second World War, there were efforts to create a universal and liberal system of trade and monetary relations. After 1947, however, the world economy began to revive on the foundations of the triangular relationship of the three major centers of noncommunist industrial power: the United States, Western Europe, and Japan. Under the umbrella of American nuclear protection and connected with the United States through military alliances, Japan and Western Europe were encouraged to grow and prosper. In order to rebuild these industrial economies adjacent to the Sino-Soviet bloc, the United States encouraged Japanese growth, led by exports, into the American market and, through the European Economic Community's (EEC) common external tariff and agricultural policy, also encouraged discrimination against American exports.[2]

Today, the triangular relationship of the noncommunist industrial powers upon which the world economy has rested is in disarray. . . .

In this brief article . . . my purpose is to present and evaluate three models of the future drawn from current writings on international relations. These models are really representative of the three prevailing schools of thought on political economy: liberalism, Marxism, and economic nationalism. Each model

Reprinted from *International Organization*, Winter 1975, pp. 37–60, by permission of The MIT Press, Cambridge, Massachussets and the author. © 1975 by the World Peace Foundation and the Massachusetts Institute of Technology. Portions of the text and some footnotes have been omitted.

is an amalgam of the ideas of several writers who, in my judgment (or by their own statements), fall into one or another of these three perspectives on the relationship of economic and political affairs.

Each model constitutes an ideal type. Perhaps no one individual would subscribe to each argument made by any one position. Yet the tendencies and assumptions associated with each perception of the future are real enough; they have a profound influence on popular, academic, and official thinking on trade, monetary, and investment problems. One, in fact, cannot really escape being influenced by one position or another.

Following the presentation of the three models, I present a critique that sets forth the strengths and weaknesses of each. On the basis of this critique, I draw some general conclusions with respect to the future of international economic organization and the nature of future international relations in general.

THE SOVEREIGNTY-AT-BAY MODEL

Nation state as anachronism.

I label the first model *sovereignty at bay,* after the title of Raymond Vernon's influential book on the multinational corporation.[3] According to this view, increasing economic interdependence and technological advances in communication and transportation are making the nation state an anachronism. These economic and technological developments are said to have undermined the traditional economic rationale of the nation state. In the interest of world efficiency and domestic economic welfare, the national state's control over economic affairs will continually give way to the multinational corporation, to the Eurodollar market, and to other international institutions better suited to the economic needs of mankind.

Perhaps the most forceful statement of the sovereignty-at-bay thesis is that of Harry Johnson—the paragon of economic liberalism. Analyzing the international economic problems of the 1970s, Johnson makes the following prediction:

> In an important sense, the fundamental problem of the future is the conflict between the political forces of nationalism and the economic forces pressing for world intergration. This conflict currently appears as one between the national government and the international corporation, in which the balance of power at least superficially appears to lie on the side of the national government. But in the longer run economic forces are likely to predominate over political, and may indeed come to do so before the end of this decade. Ultimately, a world federal government will appear as the only rational method for coping with the world's economic problems[4]

Though not all adherents of the sovereignty-at-bay thesis would go as far as Johnson, and an interdependent world economy is quite conceivable without unbridled scope for the activities of multinational corporation, most do regard the multinational corporation as the embodiment par excellence of the liberal ideal of an interdependent world economy. It has taken the intergration of national economies beyond trade and money to the internationalization of production. For the first time in history, production, marketing, and investment are being organized on a global scale rather than in terms of isolated national economies. The multinational corporations are increasingly indifferent to national boundaries in making decisions with respect to markets, production, and sources of supply.

The sovereignty-at-bay thesis argues that national economies have become enmeshed in a web of economic interdependence from which they cannot easily escape, and from which they derive great economic benefits. Through trade, monetary relations, and foreign investment, the destinies and well-being of societies have become too inexorably interwoven for these bonds to be severed. The costs of the ensuing inefficiencies in order to assert national autonomy or some other nationalistic goal would be too high. The citizenry, so this thesis contends, would not tolerate the sacrifices of domestic economic well-being that would be entailed if individual nation states sought to hamper unduly the successful operation of the international economy.

Underlying this development, the liberal position argues, is a revolution in economic needs and expectations. Domestic economic goals have been elevated to a predominant position in the hierarchy of national goals. Full employment, regional development, and other economic welfare goals have become the primary concerns of political leadership. More importantly, these goals can only be achieved, this position argues, through participation in the world economy. No government, for example, would dare shut out the multinational corporations and thereby forego employment, regional development, or other benefits these corporations bring into countries. In short, the rise of the welfare state and the increasing sensitivity of national goverments to the rising economic expectations of their societies have made them dependent upon the benefits provided by a liberal world-economic system.

In essence, this argument runs, one must distinguish between the creation of the interdependent world economy and the consequences of its subsequent dynamics.[5] Though the postwar world economy was primarily a creation of the United States, the system has since become essentially irreversible. The intermeshing of interests across national boundaries and the recognized benefits of interdependence now cement the system together for the future. Therefore, even though the power of the United States and security concerns may be in relative decline, this does not portend a major transformation of the international economy and policial system.

The multinational corporation, for example, is now believed to be sufficiently strong to stand and survive on its own. The flexibility, mobility, and vast resources of the corporations give them an advantage in confrontations with nation states. A corporation always has the option of moving its production facilities elsewhere. If it does, the nation state is the loser in terms of employment, corporate resources, and access to world markets. Thus the multinationals are escaping the control of nation states, including that of their home (source) governments. They are emerging as sufficient powers in their own right to survive the changing context of international political relations.

On the other hand, it is argued that the nation state has been placed in a dilemma it cannot hope to resolve.[6] It is losing control over economic affairs to transnational actors like the multinational corporation.[7] It cannot retain its traditional independence and sovereignty and simultaneously meet the expanding economic needs and desires of its populace. The efforts of nation states to enhance their security and power *relative* to others are held to be incompatible with an interdependent world economy that generates *absolute* gains for everyone. In response to the growing economic demands of its citizens, the national state must adjust to the forces of economic rationality and efficiency.

In the contemporary world, the costs of disrupting economic interdependence, of territorial conquest, and of risking nuclear warfare are believed to be far greater than any conceivable benefits. The calculus of benefits and risks has changed, and "the rational relationship between violence as a means of foreign policy and the ends of foreign policy has been destroyed by the possibility of all-out nuclear war."[8] In contrast to the nineteenth century, the cost of acquiring territory is viewed as having simply become too great. In the contemporary world, there is more to be gained through economic cooperation and international division of labor than through strife and conflict. . . .

Just as the nuclear revolution in warfare now inhibits the exercise of military power, the revolution in economic relations now inhibits the national exercise of economic power by increasing the cost. Advances in transportation and communications have integrated national economies to the point where many believe it is too costly to threaten the severance of economic relations in order to achieve particular political and economic goals. Economically as well as militarily in the contemporary world, nations are said to be mutually deterred from actions that would disrupt the interdependent economy. This mutual vulnerability of necessity limits and moderates the economic and political struggle among nation states. It provides the necessary minimum political order where the multinational corporations of all the major industrial powers can flourish and bring benefits to the whole of mankind.

The sovereignty-at-bay view also envisages a major transformation of the relationships among developed and underdeveloped countries. The multinational corporations of the developed, industrial economies must not only produce in each other's markets, but the locus of manufacturing industry will increasingly shift to underdeveloped countries.[9] As the economies of developed countries become more service oriented, as their terms of trade for raw materials continue to deteriorate, and as their labor costs continue to rise, manufacturing will migrate to lesser-developed countries. United States firms already engage in extensive offshore production in Asia and Latin America. Western Europe has reached the limits of importing Mediterranean labor, which is the functional equivalent of foreign direct investment. Japan's favorable wage structure and undervalued currency have eroded. With the end of the era of cheap energy and of favorable terms of trade for raw materials, the logic of industrial location favors the underdeveloped periphery. Increasingly, the multinational corporations of all industrial powers will follow the logic of this manufacturing revolution. Manufacturing, particularly of components and semiprocessed goods, will migrate to lesser-developed countries.

This vision of the future has been portrayed most dramatically by Norman

Macrae, in an issue of *The Economist,* who foresees a world of spreading affluence energized perhaps by "small transnational companies run in West Africa
by London telecommuters who live in Honolulu?[10] New computer-based training methods and information systems will facilitate the rapid diffusion of skills,
technologies, and industries to lesser-developed countries. The whole system
will be connected by modern telecommunications and computers; the rich will
concentrate on the knowledge-creating and knowledge-processing industries.
More and more of the old manufacturing industries will move to the underdeveloped world. The entire West and Japan will be a service-oriented island in a
labor-intensive global archipelago. Thus, whereas the telephone and jet aircraft
facilitated the internationalization of production in the Northern Hemisphere,
the contemporary revolution in communications and transportation will encompass the whole globe.

"The logical and eventual development of this possibility," according to
management consultant John Diebold, "would be the end of nationality and
national governments as we know them."[11] This sovereignty-at-bay world, then,
is one of voluntary and cooperative relations among interdependent economies,
the goal of which is to accelerate the economic growth and welfare of everyone.
In this model, development of the poor is achieved through the transfer of
capital, technology, and managerial know-how from the continually advancing
developed lands to the lesser-developed nations; it is a world in which the tide
of economic growth lifts all boats. In this liberal vision of the future, the multinational corporation, freed from the nation state, is the critical transmission belt of
capital, ideas, and growth.

THE DEPENDENCIA MODEL

In contrast to the sovereignty-at-bay vision of the future is what may be characterized as the *dependencia* model.[12] Although the analysis underlying the two approaches has much in common, the dependencia model challenges the partners-
in-development motif of the sovereignty-at-bay model. Its Marxist conception is
one of a hierarchical and exploitative world order. The sovereignty-at-bay model
envisages a relatively benevolent system in which growth and wealth spread from
the developed core to the lesser-developed periphery. In the dependencia
model, on the other hand, the flow of wealth and benefits is seen as moving—via
the same mechanisms—from the global, underdeveloped periphery to the centers of industrial financial power and decision. It is an exploitative system that
produces affluent development for some and dependent underdevelopment for
the majority of mankind. In effect, what is termed transnationalism by the
sovereignty-at-bay advocates is considered imperialism by the Marxist proponents of the dependencia model.

In the interdependent world economy of the dependencia model, the multinational corporation also reigns supreme. But the world created by these corporations is held to be far different from that envisaged by the sovereignty-at-bay
school of thought. In the dependencia model the political and economic conse-

quences of the multinational corporation are due to what Stephen Hymer has called the two laws of development: the law of increasing firm size, and the law of uneven development. The law of increasing firm size, Hymer argues, is the tendency since the Industrial Revolution for firms to increase in size "from the *workshop* to the *factory* to the *national* corporation to the *multidivisional corporation* and now to the multinational corporation."[13] The law of uneven development, he continues, is the tendency of the international economy to produce poverty as well as wealth, underdevelopment as well as development. Together, these two economic laws are producing the following consequence:

> . . . a regime of North Atlantic Multinational Corporations would tend to produce a hierarchical division of labor within the firm. It would tend to centralize high-level decision-making occupations in a few key cities in the advanced countries, surrounded by a number of regional sub-capitals, and confine the rest of the world to lower levels of activity and income, i.e., to the status of towns and villages in a new Imperial system. Income, status, authority, and consumption patterns would radiate out from these centers along a declining curve, and the existing pattern of inquality and dependency would be perpetrated. The pattern would be complex, just as the structure of the corporation is complex, but the basic relationship between different countries would be one of superior and subordinate, head office and branch office.[14]

In this hierarchical and exploitative world system, power and decision would be lodged in the urban financial and industrial cores of New York, London, Tokyo, etc. Here would be located the computers and data banks of the closely integrated global systems of production and distribution; the main computer in the core would control subsidiary computers in the periphery. The higher functions of management, research and development, entrepreneurship, and finance would be located in these Northern metropolitan centers. "Lower" functions and labor-intensive manufacturing would be continuously diffused to the lesser-developed countries where are found cheap pliable labor, abundant raw materials, and an indifference to industrial pollution. This global division of labor between higher and lower economic functions would perpetuate the chasm between the affluent northern one-fifth of the globe and the destitute southern four-fifths of the globe.

The argument of the dependencia thesis is that the economic dependence of the underdeveloped periphery upon the developed core is responsible for the impoverishment of the former. Development and underdevelopment are simultaneous processes; the developed countries have progressed and have grown rich through exploiting the poor and making them poorer. Lacking true autonomy and being economically dependent upon the developed countries, the underdeveloped countries have suffered because the developed have a veto over their development. . . .

Much of the dependence literature is addressed to the issue of foreign direct investments. In content, most of this literature is of a piece with traditional Marxist and radical theories of imperialism. Whether because of the falling rate of profit in capitalist economies or the attraction of superprofits abroad, multinational corporations are believed to exploit the underdeveloped countries. Thus, Paul Baran and Paul Sweezy see the multinationals necessarily impelled to invest in lesser-developed countries.[15] Constantine Vaitsos has sought to document the superprofits available to American corporations in Latin America.[16] The message conveyed by this literature is that the imperialism of free investment has replaced the imperialism of free trade in the contemporary world.

THE MERCANTILIST MODEL

A key element missing in both the sovereignty-at-bay and the dependencia models is the nation state. Both envisage a world organized and managed by powerful North American, European, and Japanese corporations. In the beneficial corporate order of the first model and the imperialist corporate order of the second, there is little room for national states, save as servants of corporate power and ambition. In opposition to both these models, therefore, the third model of the future—the mercantilist model—views the nation state and the interplay of national interests (as distinct from corporate interests) as the primary determinants of the future role of the world economy.[17]

According to this mercantilist view, the interdependent world economy, which has provided such a favorable environment for the multinational corporation, is coming to an end. In the wake of the relative decline of American power and of growing conflicts among the capitalist economies, a new international political order less favorable to the multinational corporation is coming into existence. Whether it is former President Nixon's five-power world (US, USSR, China, the EEC, and Japan), a triangular world (US, USSR, and China), or some form of American-Soviet condominium, the emergent world order will be characterized by intense international economic competition for markets, investment outlets, and sources of raw materials.

By *mercantilism* I mean the attempt of governments to manipulate economic arrangements in order to maximize their own interests, whether or not this is at the expense of others. These interests may be related to domestic concerns (full employment, price stability, etc.) or to foreign policy (security, independence, etc).

This use of the term *mercantilism* is far broader than its eighteenth-century association with a trade and balance-of-payments surplus. The essence of mercantilism, as the concept is used in this article, is the priority of *national* economic and political objectives over considerations of *global* economic efficiency. The mercantilist impulse can take many forms in the contemporary world: the desire for a balance-of-payments surplus; the export of unemployment, inflation, or both; the imposition of import and/or export controls; the expansion of world market shares; and the stimulation of advanced technology. In short, each nation will pursue economic policies that reflect domestic economic needs and external political ambitions without much concern for the effects of these policies on other countries or on the international economic system as a whole.

The mercantilist position in effect reverses the argument of the liberals with respect to the nature and success of the interdependent world economy. In contrast to the liberal view that trade liberalization has fostered economic growth, the mercantilist thesis is that several decades of uninterrupted economic growth permitted interdependence. Growth, based in part on relatively cheap energy and other resources as well as on the diffusion of American technology abroad, facilitated the reintroduction of Japan into the world economy and the development of a closely linked Atlantic economy. Now both cheap energy and a technological gap, which were sources of rapid economic growth and global interdependence, have ceased to exist.

International competition has intensified and has become disruptive precisely because the United States has lost much of its technological lead in products and industrial processes. As happened in Britain in the latter part of the nineteenth century, the United States no longer holds the monopoly position in advanced technologies. Its exports must now compete increasingly on the basis of price and a devalued dollar. As was also the case with Great Britain, the United States has lost the technological rents associated with its previous industrial superiority. This loss of industrial supremacy on the part of the dominant industrial power threatens to give rise to economic conflict between the rising and declining centers of industrial power.[18]

From the mercantilist perspective, the fundamental problem of modern international society has been how to organize an industrial world economy. This issue arose with the spread of industrialism from Great Britain and the emergence of several competing capitalist economies in the latter part of the nineteenth century.[19] In the decades prior to the First World War, the issue of how to organize a world economy composed of several competing industrial economies was at the heart of international politics. The resulting commercial and imperial struggle was a major factor in the subsequent outbreak of the First World War.

The issue was never resolved during the interwar period. During the Second World War, the organization of the world economy was regarded, at least in the United States, as a central question for the postwar era. Would it be a universal liberal system or a fragmented system of regional blocs and preference arrangements? With the outbreak of the cold war and the undisputed hegemony of the United States over other capitalist economies, however, the issue faded into the background. Former President Nixon's 15 August 1971 speech signaled to mercantilist writers that with the easing of the cold war the issue has once again moved to the fore.

These mercantilist writers tend to fall into the two camps of malevolent and benign mercantilism. Both tend to believe the world economy is fragmenting into regional blocs. In the wake of the relative decline of American power, nation-states will form regional economic alliances or blocs in order to advance their interests in opposition to other nation-states. International trade, monetary arrangements, and investment will be increasingly interregional. This regionalization of economic relations will replace the present American emphasis on multilateral free trade, the international role of the dollar, and the reign of the American multinational corporation.

Malevolent mercantilism believes regionalization will intensify international economic conflict.[20] Each bloc centered on the large industrial powers— the United States, Western Europe, Japan, and the Soviet Union—will clash over markets, currency, and investment outlets. This would be a return to the lawlessness and beggar-thy-neighbor policies of the 1930s.

Benign mercantilism, on the other hand, believes regional blocs would stabilize world economic relations.[21] It believes that throughout modern history universalism and regionalism have been at odds. The rationale of regional blocs is that one can have simultaneously the benefits of greater scale and interdependence and minimal accompanying costs of economic and political interdependence. Though the material gains from a global division of labor and free trade could be greater, regionalism is held to provide security and protection against external economic and political forces over which the nation state, acting alone, has little influence or control. In short, the organization of the world economy into regional blocs could provide the basis for a secure and peaceful economic order.[22]

Benign mercantilism derives from the view of John Maynard Keynes and other Englishmen who were highly critical of an increasingly interdependent world economy. The loss of national self-sufficiency, this more benign view of mercantilism holds, is a source of economic-political insecurity and conflict.[23] Liberalism, moreover, is detrimental to national cultural and political development. Therefore, this benign mercantilist position advocates a regionalization of the world economy as the appropriate middle road between a declining American-centered world economy and a global conflict between the capitalist economies. An inevitable clash between industrial economies can be prevented through the carving out of regional spheres of influence and the exercise of mutual self-restraint among them.

In the opinion of benign mercantilism, the thrust of much domestic and international economic policy, especially since the end of the First World War, has in fact been away from interdependence. Nations have placed a higher priority on domestic stability and policies of full employment than on the maintenance of international links; they have sought to exert national control over their monetary and other economic policies. This is what the Keynesian revolution and its emphasis on management of the domestic economy is said to be all about. The same desire for greater latitude in domestic policy underlies the increasing popularity today of flexible over fixed exchange rates and the movement toward regional blocs. Mercantilists point out that in many industrialized economies there is, in fact, a renewed questioning of whether the further benefits of trade liberalization and interdependence are worth the costs. Interdependence accentuates domestic economic adjustment problems as economic instabilities in one economy spill over into others. It causes labor dislocations, may accentuate inqualities of income distribution, and makes national planning more difficult. In short, according to these mercantilists, the world has reached the limits of interdependence and loss of national self-sufficiency.

A CRITIQUE OF THE THREE MODELS

In this section of the article, I evaluate the three models and draw from each what I consider to be important insights into the nature of contemporary international economic relations. This critique is not meant to cover all the points of each model but only those most directly relevant to this essay.

Sovereignty at Bay

Fundamentally, the sovereignty-at-bay thesis reduces to a question of interests and power: Who has the power to make the world economy serve its interests? This point may be best illustrated by considering the relationship of the multinational corporation and the nation state. In the writings I identified with the sovereignty-at-bay thesis, this contest is held to be most critical.

On one side of this contest is the host nation state. Its primary source of power is its control over access to its territory, that is, access to its internal market, investment opportunities, and source of raw material. On the other side is the corporation with its capital, technology, and access to world markets.[24] Each has something the other wants. Each seeks to maximize its benefits and minimize its costs. The bargain they strike is dependent upon how much one wants what the other has to offer and how skillfully one or the other can exploit its respective advantages. In most cases, the issue is how the benefits and costs of foreign investment are to be divided between the foreign corporation and the host economy.

The sovereignty-at-bay thesis assumes that the bargaining advantages are and always will be on the side of the corporation. In contrast to the corporation's vast resources and flexibility, the nation state has little with which to bargain. Most nation states lack the economies of scale, indigenous technological capabilities, or native entrepreneurship to free themselves from dependence upon American (or other) multinational corporations. According to this argument, the extent to which nation states reassert their sovereignty is dependent upon the economic price they are willing to pay, and it assumes that when confronted with this cost, they will retreat from nationalistic policies.

In an age of rising economic expectations, the sovereignty-at-bay thesis rests on an important truth: A government is reluctant to assert its sovereignty and drive out the multinational corporations if this means a dramatic lowering of the standard of living, increasing unemployment, and the like. But in an age when the petroleum-producing states, through cooperation, have successfully turned the tables on the multinational corporations, it becomes obvious that the sovereignty-at-bay thesis also neglects the fact that the success of the multinational corporation has been dependent upon a favorable political order. As this order changes, so will the fortunes of the multinationals.

This political order has been characterized by an absence of unity on the part of the economies that have been host to American and other corporations. The divisions between and within the host countries themselves, and the influence of the American government, left the host countries with little power to bargain effectively or to increase their relative benefits from foreign investments in their countries. Thus, in the case of Canada, the competition between the provinces and particularly between English Canada and Quebec greatly weakened Canada's position vis à vis American investors. Similarly, nationalistic competition for investment has weakened attempts, such as the Andean Pact, that have tried to develop common policy toward foreign corporations. But the importance of political factors in the overseas expansion of American corporations may be best illustrated by the case of Western Europe and Japan.

American corporations coveted both the Japanese and Western European markets; they have been able to establish hundreds of subsidiaries in the latter but only a few in the former. The reason for this difference is largely political. Whereas the former has one central government controlling access to Japan's internal market of 100 million population, six (now nine) political centers have controlled access to the European Common Market. By interposing itself between powerful American corporations and intensely competitive Japanese firms that desired American capital and technology, the Japanese government has been able to prevent the latter from making agreements not desired by the government. As a consequence, the Japanese home market has been protected as the almost exclusive domain of Japanese industry. American firms have had, therefore, a strong incentive to license their technology to the Japanese or to form corporate arrangements in which the American firms were no more than a minor partner.

What the Japanese succeeded in doing was to break up the package of capital, technology, and entrepreneurship that foreign direct investment entails. The Japanese did not need the capital; they got the technology without managerial control by American corporations; entrepreneurship remained in the hands of Japanese. This Japanese example of untying the package and obtaining the technology, and in many cases the capital, required for development without loss of control has become an inspiration for economic nationalists in Latin America, Canada, and elsewhere.

In Western Europe, on the other hand, an American firm denied the right to establish a subsidiary in one Common Market country has had the option of trying another country and thereby still gaining access to the whole Market. Moreover, the strong desire of individual European countries for American investment has enabled American corporations to invest on very favorable terms. In certain cases, the firms have followed a divide-and-conquer strategy. Denied permission by President de Gaulle to invest in France, General Motors established in Belgium one of the largest automobile assembly plants in the Common Market. Through this route, the corporation gained access to the French market as well as to other European markets.

In response to this situation, de Gaulle sought to obtain West German cooperation against American investment in EEC countries. Together these two most powerful of the Six could dictate a policy the others would be forced to accept. Through the instrumentality of the Franco-German Friendship Treaty of 1963, therefore, de Gaulle sought to form a Bonn-Paris axis directed against American hegemony in Western Europe.

Although there was sentiment in West Germany favorable to taking measures to limit the rapidly growing role of American subsidiaries in EEC countries, the West German government refused to take any action that might weaken the American commitment to defend Western Europe. The United States government not only reminded the West Germans that a continued American military presence was dependent upon West German support of measures to lessen the American balance-of-payments deficit, but it also pressured West Germany to increase its military purchases from the United States and to avoid competitive arrangements with France. Largely as a result of these American pressures, the Friendship Treaty was, in effect, aborted. The first serious counteroffensive of the nation state against the multinational corporation collapsed. It is clear, however, that the outcome of this tale would have been altogether different if West Germany had desired greater military and economic independence from the United States. In short, the American corporate penetration of the European Common Market has been dependent upon the special security relationship of the United States and West Germany.

One could extend this type of analysis for the whole of American overseas investment. American investment in the Middle East, Africa, Latin America, Canada, and elsewhere has benefited from America's dominant position in the world. This position is now seriously challenged not only by the Soviet Union but by Japan, Western Europe, China, the Arabs, and Brazil in Latin America. Throughout these areas, economic nationalism is on the rise, threatening American investments and the income they bring to the United States. The thrust of this attack has been to break up the package of capital, technology, and management in order to acquire the first two without the third; the goal is greater local control through joint ventures, nationalization, and other policies. While the host countries are unlikely to "kill off" the American multinational corporations, they will increasingly make them serve local interests. This in turn will undoubtedly make direct investment abroad less attractive to American corporations.

A reversal of fortunes has already been seen in the case of the oil multinationals. The significance of the offensive by the oil-producing states against the large international oil companies is not merely that the price of oil to the United States and to the rest of the world has risen but also that the United States may lose one of its most lucrative sources of investment income. The oil crisis and Arab oil boycott which followed the 1973 Arab-Israeli war was a profound learning experience for Europe, Japan, and even the United States. The oil boycott and the behavior of the oil multinationals set into motion a series of events that cannot help but transform national attitudes and policies toward the oil multinationals. The sudden appreciation of how vulnerable governments were to the policies of the oil multinationals and how far their "sovereignty" had been compromised awakened them to the inherent dangers of overdependence on the corporations and their policies.

The French and, to a lesser extent, the Japanese responses to this experience have received the most attention. But perhaps more noteworthy was the reaction of the West German government—after the United States the nation most committed to a liberal world economy. It was the West German representative at the February 1973 Washington conference of oil-consuming nations who demanded that the United States and Western Europe undertake "a joint analysis of the price policies, profits, and taxes of oil-multinationals." While the proposal, which became part of the Washington Declaration, does not mean demise of the oil multinationals, it does suggest that the policies of nation states will increasingly impinge on the freedom of action of these particular multinational corporations.

This change in attitude toward the oil multinationals can be witnessed in the United States itself. The role of the companies as instruments of the Arab boycott has had a significant impact on American perceptions. Prior to that time, few probing questions about the oil multinationals had been raised in the press or in Congress. Other than a few "radicals," few had challenged the fact that Exxon, Gulf, and other oil multinationals paid virtually no taxes to the United States government and that they acted as sovereign entities in their dealings with the oil-producing countries. When the tables were turned, however, and the oil companies became the instruments of the Arab boycott against the United States, then even their staunchest defenders began to raise questions about tax avoidance. More importantly, the United States government took into its own hands some of the task of negotiating with the oil-producing states. Thus, when the multinationals were perceived as no longer supportive of the national interests of the United States, there was a reassertion of national sovereignty.

The case of oil and the oil multinationals is perhaps unique. Yet is does suggest that nation states have not lost their power or their will to act when they believe the multinational corporations are threatening their perceived national interests and sovereignty. The experience of the oil boycott and the role of the multinationals in carrying it out reveal the extent to which the operators and the success of these corporations have been dependent upon American power. With the relative decline of American power and the rise of governments hostile to American interests and policies, this case history at least raises the question of how the weakening of the *Pax Americana* will effect the status of other American multinational corporations throughout the world.

DEPENDENCIA

The weakness of the dependencia, or ultraimperialism, model is that it makes at least three unwarranted assumptions. In the first place, it assumes much greater common interest among the noncommunist industrial powers—the United States, Western Europe, and Japan—than is actually the case. Secondly, it treats the peripheral states of Asia, Africa, Latin America, Canada, and the Middle East solely as objects of international economic and political relations. Neither assumption is true. As the first assumption is considered in more detail in the next section, let us consider the second for a moment.

After nearly two centuries, the passivity of the periphery is now past. The Soviet challenge to the West and the divisions among the capitalist powers themselves have given the emerging elites in the periphery room for maneuver. These nationalist elites are no longer ignorant and pliable colonials. Within the periphery, there are coalescing centers of power that will weigh increasingly in the future world balance of power: China, Indonesia, India, Iran, Nigeria, Brazil, and some form of Arab oil power. Moreover, if properly organized and led, such centers of power in control over a vital resouce, as the experience of the Organization of Petroleum Exporting Countries (OPEC) demostrates, may reverse the tables and make the core dependent upon the periphery. For the moment at least, a perceptible shift appears to be taking place in the global balance of economic power from the owners of capital to the owners of natural resources.[25]

The third unwarranted assumption it that a quasi-Marxist theory of capital-ist imperialism is applicable to the relationship of developed and lesser-developed economies today. Again, I illustrate my argument by considering the role of the multinational corporation in the lesser-developed countries, since its allegedly exploitative function is stressed by almost all dependencia theorists.

The dependencia theory undoubtedly has a good case with respect to for-eign direct investment in petroleum and other extractive industries. The oil, copper, and other multinationals have provided the noncommunist industrial world with a plentiful and relatively cheap supply of minerals and energy. The dramatic reversal of this situation by the oil-producing countries in 1973–74 and the steady rise of prices of other commodities support the contention that the producing countries were not getting the highest possible price and possibly not a just price for their nonrenewable resources. But what constitutes the just price for a natural endowment that was worthless until the multinationals found it is not an easy issue to resolve.

With respect to foreign direct investment in manufacturing, the case is far more ambiguous. Even if technological rents are collected, does the foreign corporation bring more into the economy in terms of technology, capital, and access to world markets than it takes out in the form of earnings? The research of Canadian, Australian, and other economists, for example, suggest that it does. They find no differences in the corporate behavior of domestic and foreign firms; on the contrary, foreign firms are given higher marks in terms of export performance, industrial research and development, and other economic indica-tors.[26] Nonetheless, it would be naive to suggest that no exploitation or severe distortions of host economies have taken place.

On the other hand, it may not be unwarranted to suggest that a strong presumption exists for arguing that in terms of economic growth and industrial development, foreign direct investment in *manufacturing* is to the advantage of the host economy. A major cause of foreign direct investment is the sector-specific nature of knowledge and capital in the home economy.[27] In order to prevent a fall in their rate of profits through overinvesting at home or diversify-ing into unknown areas, American corporations frequently go abroad to guard against a lower rate of profit at home rather than because the superprofits abroad are attractive. Insofar as this is true, and there is sufficient evidence to warrant its plausibility, foreign direct investment benefits both the corporations and the host economy at a cost to other factors of production in the home economy. Thus, though the Marxists may be right in saying that there is an imperative for capitalism to go abroad, the effect is not to exploit but to benefit the recipient economy—a conclusion, by the way, the Marx himself would have accepted.[28]

While it is true that, in general, lesser-developed countries are economically dependent upon developed countries, the conclusions to be drawn from this fact are not self-evident. Are the countries underdeveloped because they are dependent, as dependencia theorists assume, or are they dependent because they are underdeveloped? China is underdeveloped, but it is not dependent upon any external power (though one could argue a historical case). As Benjamin Cohen has pointed out, the critical question is whether the poor are worse off economically because of this dependence.[27] Does dependence upon the developed countries entail a new loss, or foreclose opportunities of greater benefit to the economy of the undeveloped country? While the opportunity to exploit may be there, is it exercised? These are empirical questions to which no general answers can be given. Whether foreign direct investment is exploitative or beneficial depends on the type of investment, its terms, and the policies of the recipient economy itself.

The dependencia argument that foreign direct investment by multinational corporations preempts the emergence of an indigenous entrepreneurial middle class and creates a situation of technological dependence provides a clue to what is the central concern of dependence theory. Though most frequently couched solely in economic terms, the concepts of underdevelopment and dependence are more political than economic in nature. They involve an assessment of the political costs of foreign investment. They refer both to the internal political development of the recipient country and its external relations. As one of the better dependence theorists has put it, the problem "is not so much growth, i.e., expansion of a given socio-economic system, as it is 'development,' i.e., rapid and fundamental politico-socio-economic transformation."[30] In other words, foreign direct investment fosters an international division of labor that perpetuates underdevelopment and politico-economic dependencia.

This distinction between *growth* and *development* is crucial.[31] Economic growth is defined by most development economists simply as an increase in output or income per capita; it is essentially a positive and quantitative concept. The concepts of development and underdevelopment as used by dependence theorists are primarily normative and qualitative; they refer to structural changes internal to the lesser-developed economy and in external relations with the developed world. Dependencia theory really calls for a change in the current international division of labor between the core and the periphery of the international economy, in which the periphery is a supplier of raw materials and whose industries are branch plants of the core's multinational corporations.

Whatever its economic merits, the dependencia model will continue to generate opposition against the structure of the contemporary world economy and the multinational corporation throughout the underdeveloped periphery of the world economy. As these peripheral societies grow in power, one can anticipate that they will undertake initiatives that attempt to lessen their dependence upon developed countries.

MERCANTILISM

It seems to me that mercantilists either ignore or ascribe too little significance to certain primary facts. Although the relative power of the United States has declined, the United States remains the dominant world economy. The scale, diversity, and dynamics of the American economy will continue to place the United States at the center of the international economic system. The universal desire for access to the huge American market, the inherent technological dynamism of the American economy, and America's additional strength in both agriculture and resources—which Europe and Japan do not have—provide a cement sufficient to hold the world economy together and to keep the United States at its center.[32]

Furthermore, the United States can compensate for its loss of strength in one issue area by its continued strength in another. For example, the American economic position has indeed declined relative to Europe and Japan. Yet the continued dependence of Europe and Japan on the United States for their security provides the United States with a strong lever over the economic policies of each.

Thus, the fundamental weakness of the mercantilist model is the absence of a convincing alternative to an American-centered world economy. Western Europe, the primary economic challenger to the United States, remains internally divided; it is as yet unable to develop common policies in such areas as industry and energy or with respect to economic and monetary union. It is merely a customs union with a comon agricultural policy. Moreover, like Japan, it continues to be totally dependent upon the United States for its security. As long as both Europe and Japan lack an alternative to their military and economic dependence on the United States, the mercantilist world of regional blocs lacks credibility.

The so-called energy crisis has affirmed this assessment. In the first place, the Arab oil boycott revealed the fragility of European unity. Threatened with the loss of vital supplies of Middle Eastern oil, every nation fended for itself. But subsequently, despite their reluctance, both Europe and Japan participated in the American-sponsored Washington energy conference. The American purpose in calling the conference was in part to reinforce its Middle Eastern diplomacy. But the purpose was also to reassert America's influence over its allies and to forestall policies such as competitive currency depreciation, creation of new trade barriers, and bilateral deals the would tend to fragment the world economy. No doubt, too, as the French and others charge, the United States hoped to find a solution to the energy crisis that did not threaten the position of the American oil multinationals.

Calling for cooperation from its European and Japanese allies, the United States reminded them that their security still rested on American goodwill. Moreover, in the event of a conflict over oil, America's economic weapons were far superior. Thus chastened and reminded where power continued to rest, all but the French fell into line. For the time being at least, the United States demonstrated that it retained sufficient power to maintain intact an American-centered world economy.

Yet sufficient tensions and conflicts of interests remain within this world economy to prevent one from dismissing so quickly the mercantilist thesis. Undoubtedly, the interstate conflict that will be the most vexing is the growing demand and competition for raw materials, particularly petroleum.[33] The loss of energy self-sufficiency by the United States and the growth in demand for petroleum and other raw materials have already shifted the terms of trade against developed economies, and commodity prices have become major factors in world inflation. In the longer term, these changes have put the industrial powers in competition for these limited resources. They are also competing for export markets in order to finance these vital imports and for the capital the oil-producing states now have to invest. Thus, whereas in the past America's virtual control over the noncommunist world's supply of petroleum was a source of unity, today the United States is struggling with other industrial powers to insure its own position in a highly competitive environment.

In fact, one witnesses in the contemporary world the reemergence of the neo-Malthusian and Social Darwinist fears that swept industrial society and were so disruptive in the latter part of the nineteenth century. A common factor in the several imperialisms that burst forth after 1880 and fragmented the world economy was the growing fear of the potential consequences of exclusion from resources and markets. With expanding populations and productive industries believed to be dependent on foreign sources of food and raw materials, the insecurity of European states was magnified by the loss of their former relative self-sufficiency. The paradox of an interdependent world economy is that it creates sources of insecurity and competition. The very dependence of one state on another and the necessity for access to external markets and sources of raw materials cause anxieties and suspicions that exacerbate international relations.

The other reason for believing that there may be some validity in the mercantilist vision of the future is the weakening of political bonds between the United States, Western Europe, and Japan. During the height of the cold war, the foreign economic policies of these three countries were complementary. Potential conflicts over economic matters were subordinated to the necessity for political unity against the Soviet Union and China. The United States encouraged export-led growth and accepted anti-American trade discrimination in order to enable Japan and Europe to rebuild their shattered economies. Reciprocally, Japan and Europe supported the international position of the dollar. Through foreign direct investment, American corporations were able to maintain their relative share of world markets. Neither the Europeans nor the Japanese challenged America's dominant position with respect to the industrial world's access to vital raw materials, particularly Middle Eastern petroleum.

Until the early 1970s, the political benefits of this arrangement were regarded as outweighing the economic costs to each partner. With the movement toward détente and with the revival of the European and Japanese economies, however, the political benefits have receded in importance and the concern over costs has increased. As a consequence, the United States and its industrial partners now desire reforms of the world's trading and monetary systems that would enable each to pursue its own particular set of interests and to limit that of the others. For example, the United States has proposed reforms of the trade and monetary systems that would limit the ability of the Europeans and the Japanese to run up huge trade surpluses. Europe and Japan, for their part, desire to preserve this scope and to limit the privileges of the United States as world banker.

Regardless of the outcome of the negotiations over the future of the international monetary system, one thing is certain: Whatever privilege is retained by the dollar will not be sufficient to enable the United States to behave as it has in the past. Gone are the days when the United States could run an immense balance-of-payments deficit in order to support foreign commitments, to buy up foreign assets, and at the same time pursue a full employment policy at home. It will no longer be able to expand overseas at a relatively low cost to the American standard of living. Having already lost its technological superiority and technological rents, the United States will have to finance its economic and military position abroad through currency devaluation and a current account surplus. Thus the cost of any effort to maintain US political and economic hegemony will bear upon the American people themselves. The weight and popular appreciation of this cost will profoundly alter American attitudes toward America's world role and toward its European and Japanese allies. These changes in political interests and perceptions cannot but help to push the world in a mercantilistic direction.

IMPLICATIONS FOR INTERNATIONAL ORGANIZATION

What then do these three models and their relative merits tell us about the future of international economic organizations? As a consequence of the relative decline of American power and of other developments treated in this article, there is little reason to believe that many new international institutions will be created, but it is likely that the nature and functioning of existing institutions will be profoundly altered.

In a world of national states, international organizations tend to reflect the power and interests of the dominant states in the international system. From this perspective, the international organizations founded at the end of the Second World War reflected the then predominant states in the system. As the structure of the United Nations reflected the distribution of power between the United States and the Soviet Union, so the so-called Bretton Woods system and the institutions associated with it—the International Monetary Fund (IMF), the World Bank, and subsequently the General Agreement on Trade and Tariffs (GATT)—reflected the power and interests of the dominant world economy, the United States.

In both cases, the relative decline of American power over the past several decades has led to profound modifications of these political and economic institutions. Thus, with the growth of Soviet power in the United Nations Security Council and of the so-called nonaligned bloc in the General Assembly, the United Nation's role in American foreign policy and as an institution have been altered significantly. In terms of the major political issues of the world, the United Nations has moved from center stage to the sidelines. A similar transformation can be seen in the area of international economic institutions. This can be witnessed, for example, in the case of the IMF and the negotiations for the reform of the international monetary system which have taken place outside its aegis.

The transformation of the IMF began in the late 1950s with the gradual weakening of the dollar as an international currency. After 1958 the American balance-of-payments deficit began to assume major proportions. The moderate deficits of the previous decade became severe. A drain began on the large gold hoard the United States had accumulated before and during the Second World War. Between 1957 and 1963, U.S. gold holdings fell from $22.8 billion to $15.5 billion, and foreign dollar holdings (official and private) rose from $15.1 to $28.8 billion. By 1968, American gold holdings fell to $10.9 billion, and foreign dollar holdings rose to $31.5 billion.

As Europeans and others began to turn dollars into gold, it became obvious that the United States could not continue to meet all gold claims. The immediate American response was to initiate numerous makeshift expedients—the gold pool, currency swap arrangements, the General Arrangements to Borrow, etc.—to reinforce the position of the dollar. Additionally, the United States undertook unilateral measures such as the Interest Equalization Tax (1963), "voluntary" controls on the export of capital (1965), and, eventually, mandatory controls on foreign direct investment (1968) to stem the outflow of dollars.

Despite these and other measures, monetary crises continued to mount throughout the 1960s. In response to these crises, demands mounted for a fundamental reform of the international monetary system. In the ensuing monetary negotiations, as in trade negotiations, the Western powers divided into three positions. On one side were ranged the United States and Great Britain. On the other stood France. In the middle was West Germany, which attempted to reconcile the Common Market and the Atlantic powers.

Whereas the United States wanted a reform that would ensure the continued privileged position of the dollar, France under de Gaulle wanted a reform that would dethrone the dollar and thus would redistribute economic power in the West. This would allegedly be achieved if the world returned to what de Gaulle believed was the true measure of wealth and guarantor of political independence, namely, gold. A return to the gold standard would not only enhance the power of France, which had replenished its gold reserves, but the United States would have to expend real wealth in order to maintain and/or expand its hegemony. If other nations refused to accept any more dollars and demanded gold, the United States would be forced to bring its payments into balance and to liquidate its global economic and military position. In short, a shift from the dollar to gold as the world's reserve currency would mean a retrenchment of American power in Europe, Asia, and around the globe.

At the same time that the United States desired to maintain the privileged position of the dollar, the basic instability of the system was appreciated by all. An international monetary system and an expanding trade system that depended upon the deficits of the United States were prone to crisis. From the perspective of most countries, a return to gold was both politically and economically undesirable, however. In the late sixties, therefore, extensive IMF negotiations produced an "international money" called special drawing rights (SDRs).

The United States had desired the SDRs to relieve the pressure on the dollar while preserving its ultimate reserve role. France wanted nothing less than the reimposition of monetary restraints on the United States. Between the two of them stood West Germany and its desire to hold together the European and Atlantic powers. Due largely to German initiatives, a compromise solution was finally reached, which gave the Americans their SDRs in exchange for greater European voting power in the International Monetary Fund. Thus, while the IMF would have the power to "issue" SDRs as an international reserve on a limited scale, Europe (if it were united) could exercise a veto over American policy in the IMF.

In short, the internal structure and functioning of the IMF was reconstituted to reflect the redistribution of world economic and monetary power. The United States no longer ran the organization. Control over it was now shared by the European powers. Similarly, one can anticipate that the immense growth of Arab monetary balances will lead to a further internal transformation of the IMF. By one method or other, this redistribution of monetary power will be given an institutional form.

In the areas of trade and investment, the continuing redistribution of power among nation states will find a response in the nature and functioning of international economic organizations. In trade this has already begun to happen, as the United States and other industrial nations ponder the future of the GATT. Perhaps the German initiative at the Washington energy conference in calling for an international investigation of the oil multinationals presages what many have long advocated—a GATT for investment. If so, it too will reflect the changes that have taken place in the world's distribution of economic and industrial power.

CONCLUSION

In conclusion, what does this redistribution of world power imply for the future of the interdependent world economy? Today, the liberal world economy is challenged by powerful groups (especially organized labor) within the dominant economy; the dominant economy itself is in relative decline. With the decline of the dominant economic power, the world economy may be following the pattern of the latter part of the nineteenth century and of the 1930s and may be fragmenting into regional trading and monetary blocs. This would be prevented, of course, if the United States, as it is presently trying to do, were to reassert its waning hegemony over Western Europe, Japan, and the rest of the noncommunist world economy.

In the wake of the decline of American power and the erosion of the political base upon which the world economy has rested, the question arises whether the wisest policy for the United States is to attempt to reassert its dominance. May not this effort in the areas of trade, money, investment, and energy exacerbate the conflicts between the United States, Western Europe, and Japan? If so, a future that could be characterized increasingly by benign mercantilism could well be transformed into its more malevolent relative. If this were to happen, the United States and its allies would be the losers.

This admonition suggests that the United States should accept a greater regionalization of the world economy than it has been wont to accept in the past. It implies greater representation and voice for other nations and regional blocs in international economic organizations. While such a policy of retrenchment would no doubt harm the interests of American corporations and other sectors of the American economy, the attempt to hold on to rather than adjust to the shifting balance of world power could be even more costly for the United States in the long run.

In a world economy composed of regional blocs and centers of power, economic bargaining and competition would predominate. Through the exercise of economic power and various trade-offs, each center of the world economy would seek to shift the costs and benefits of economic interdependence to its own advantage. Trade, monetary, and investment relations would be the consequence of negotiations as nation states and regional blocs sought to increase the benefits of interdependence and to decrease the costs. This in fact has been the direction of the evolution of the international economy, from a liberal to a negotiated system, since the rise of large and rival economic entities in the latter part of the nineteenth century.

Therefore, debate and policy planning today should not focus on economic independence or dependence but on the nature and consequences of economic interdependence. Economic interdependence may take many forms; it may affect the welfare of nations in very different ways. Some will emphasize security; others, efficiency, low rates of inflation, or full employment. The question of how these benefits and costs will be distributed is at the heart of the increasingly mercantilistic policies of nation states in the contemporary world.

NOTES

1. Edward Hallet Carr, *The Twenty Year's Crisis 1919–1939* (London: Macmillan and Co., 1951), p. 117.
2. This theme is developed in Robert Gilpin, "The Politics of Transnational Economic Relations," *International Organization* 25 (Summer 1971): 398–419. This article was part of a special issue of the journal, entitled "Transnational Relations and World Politics," which was edited by Robert O. Keohane and Joseph S. Nye, Jr., and was

subsequently published under the same title as a book by Harvard University Press in 1972.

3. Raymond Vernon, *Sovereignty at Bay* (New York: Basic Books, 1971).

4. Harry G. Johnson, *International Economic Questions Facing Britain, the United States, and Canada in the 70's,* British-North American Research Association, June 1970, p. 24.

5. Samuel Huntington, "Transnational Organizations in World Politics," *World Politics* 25 (April 1973): 361.

6. Edward Morse, "Crisis Diplomacy, Interdependence, and the Politics of International Economic Relations," *World Politics* 24, supplement (Spring 1972): 123–50.

7. Keohane and Nye.

8. Hans Morgenthau, "Western Values and Total War," *Commentary*, October 1961, p. 280.

9. John Diebold, "Multinational Corporations—Why be Scared of Them?," *Foreign Policy*, no. 12 (Fall 1973): 79–95.

10. "The Future of International Business," *The Economist*, 22 January 1972.

11. Diebold, p. 87.

12. The literature on dependencia, or underdevelopment, has now become legend. One of the better statements of this thesis is Osvaldo Sunkel, "Big Business and 'Dependencia': A Latin American View," *Foreign Affairs* 50 (April 1972): 517–31. For an excellent and critical view of the dependencia thesis, see Benjamin J. Cohen, *The Question of Imperialism—The Political Economy of Dominance and Dependence* (New York: Basic Books, 1973), chapter 6.

13. "The Multinational Corporation and the Law of Uneven Development," in *Economics and World Order—From the 1970's to the 1990's*, ed. Jagdish Bhagwati (New York: The Macmillan Co., 1972). p. 113 and passim.

14. Ibid., p. 114.

15. *Monopoly Capital—An Essay on the American Economic and Social Order* (New York: Monthly Review Press, 1966).

16. Constantine Vaitsos, "Transfer of Resources and Preservation of Monopoly Rents," Economic Development Report No. 168, Development Advisory Service, Harvard University. 1970. (Mimeographed.)

17. See, for example, David Calleo and Benjamin Rowland, *American and the World Political Economy* (Bloomington, Ind.: Indiana University Press, 1973). Mercantilism is also the real theme of Ernest Mandel's *Europe vs. America—Contradictions of Imperialism* (New York: Monthly Review Press, 1970).

18. Vietnam-generated inflation was also a factor in the decline of American competitiveness in the late 1960s. But mercantilists and others (such as Richard Nelson and Michael Boretsky) respond that it is precisely because the US has lost much of its technological lead in products and industrial processes that pure competition has become so important. For an analysis of this debate, see Philip Boffey. "Technology and World Trade: Is There Cause for Alarm?," *Science*, 2 April 1971.

19. I have benefited very much from the as yet unpublished writings of Kendall Myers on this subject. Myers's manuscript entitled "Appeasement and Nazi Germany—Regional Blocs or Universalism" was the basis of a seminar held at the Lehrman Institute in New York. See also the reflections of Simon Kuznets, *Modern Economy Growth* (New Haven, Conn.: Yale University Press, 1966. The issue, of course, is fundamental to the radical and Marxist critique of capitalism.

20. Ernest Mandel, in his *Europe vs. America*, is more malevolent mercantilist than Marxist in his argument.

21. Calleo and Rowland.

22. For a recent analysis of this issue, see Ernest Preeg, *Economic Blocs and U.S. Foreign Policy* (Washington, D. C.: National Planning Association, 1974).

23. This paradox is analyzed by Eugene Staley, *World Economy in Transition* (New York: Council on Foreign Relations, 1939), chapter 6, especially p. 15.

24. For an excellent examination of this relationship, see Huntington.

25. See C. Fred Bergsten, "The Threat From The Third World," *Foreign Policy*, no. 11 (Summer 1973): 102–24.

26. See, for example, A. E. Safarian, *Foreign Ownership of Canadian Industry* (Toronto: University of Toronto Press, 1973).

27. This point is developed in US Congress, Senate Committee on Labor and Public Welfare, *The Multinational Corporation and the National Interest* (report prepared for the Committee), 93rd Cong., 1st sess., 1973, Committee print.

28. Karl Marx, "The Future Results of British Rule in India," in *Karl Marx on Colonialism and Modernization*, ed. Shlomo Avineri (Garden City, N.Y.: Doubleday, 1968), pp. 125–31.

29. Cohen, chapter 6.

30. This distinction is developed by Keith Griffin, *Underdevelopment in Spanish America* (Cambridge, Mass.: the M.I.T. Press, 1969), p. 117.

31. For a more detailed analysis of the distinction, see J. D. Gould, *Economic Growth in History* (London: Methuen and Co., 1972), chapter 1.

32. A forceful statement of this position is Raymond Vernon's "Rogue Elephant in the Forest: An Appraisal of Transatlantic Relations," *Foreign Affairs* 51 (April 1973): 573–87.

33. See Helmut Schmidt, "The Struggle for the Global Product," *Foreign Affairs* 52 (April 1974): 437–51.

The Debate about Interdependence

Global Transactions and the Consolidation of Sovereignty

Janice E. Thomson
Stephen D. Krasner

Challenges to state-centric paradigms are nothing new in the study of international affairs. Before World War I some analysts maintained that the level of economic interdependence in Europe was so high that war was basically unthinkable. After World War II functionalists argued that specific functions could be assumed by political entities that would eventually supersede individual states. Advocates of the concept of transnational relations saw a world not only of interaction among national-states but also a transnational world involving interactions among nonstate actors or between nonstate actors and states (Keohane and Nye 1972). Some analysts saw multinational corporations escaping from the jurisdiction of any one state or any set of states. Hence the concern with the relationship between micro-macro interactions expressed in James Rosenau's micro formulation (Rosenau 1988), and especially the impact of greater individual competence on macroprocesses, has a lengthy intellectual pedigree.

One thread that runs through most of these arguments is that technological innovation is the most important factor explaining changes in the international system. Technological change is itself an exogenous variable; it is left unexplained, at least in relation to the political system. Technological change has reduced transactions costs. Transportation and communication are much cheaper than they have been in the past. The importance of geographic propinquity, of the territoriality that is at the core of the modern state system, has declined. Japan could become the world's most efficient steel producer even though both its coal and iron are thousands of miles away, a feat that would have been impossible in the nineteenth and early twentieth centuries before the development of bulk shipping. Billions of dollars can be transferred from one end of the world to the other in a matter of seconds—a far cry from the Rothschilds' use of carrier pigeons to secure information on the outcome of the Battle of Waterloo so that they could decide whether to buy or sell British sovereigns. Technological change may increase the competence of specific actors, whether individuals or organizations, by providing them with a vastly improved knowledge base.

The argument that interdependence has undermined the effective sovereignty of the state (the ability of the state to control activities that are nominally or juridicially subject to authoritative decisions) has been most fully elaborated for economic transactions. International flows have made it more difficult for national governments to independently manage their own economies. Policies could be nullified by new international transactions over which national decision makers had no control. For instance, the effort by a small state to dampen domestic economic activity by raising interest rates could be frustrated by international capital inflows attracted by these same higher interest rates, which would increase the state's money supply and lead to lower interest rates (Cooper 1968). Formal sovereignty remains but actual control diminishes or even disappears. The basic causal sequence is as follows: Technological change leads to increased economic flows, which erodes state control.

Realists have been extremely skeptical of all variants of the interdependence position. Realism has attempted to incorporate, to swallow up, the kinds of empirical evidence pointed to by interdependence formulations and to endogenize their theoretical variables. Realists argued first that growing interdependence has been a function of political power and political choice, not of exogenous technological change. The international rules of the game that are necessary for an open international economic system (the precondition for growing interdependence) precede, rather than follow, technological change. These rules had to be created by political choice and political power. In the postwar world only the United States could play an effective leadership role and even then only for those political entities that were not part of the Soviet bloc. The United States' desire for global liberalism has been explained in a variety of ways, including domestic preferences: a desire to internationalize the market-oriented economy that characterized the domestic U.S. economy; lessons drawn from the past: the conclusion accepted by U.S. leaders that the protectionism of the 1930s, especially the Smoot-Hawley Tariff Act, had contributed to economic breakdown, economic breakdown to authoritarian regimes, and authoritarian regimes to war; and finally to the realpolitik and national interest preferences that would be natural for any dominant state (Goldstein 1986; Krasner 1976; Maier 1977; Gilpin 1975). All of these arguments presuppose a hegemonic position for the United States, a level of dominance that would allow it to propagate its domestic preferences, act on the lessons its leaders drew from the past, and attain its realpolitik goals. The fact that technology has not led to an integration of the communist and noncommunist worlds strongly suggests that technology alone is not an adequate explanation for the pattern of international economic transactions.

Some realists, notably Kenneth Waltz, took a somewhat different tack.

They argued that interdependence and global power were being confused. Transactions in and of themselves did not have any political significance. What counted was the ability of a state to adjust to change or to use its economic position for political leverage. A state that is heavily involved in the international economy, but could easily shift to relative autarky, is not vulnerable. Such a state may even be in a strong position to exercise political leverage over its economic partners because the relative opportunity costs of change weigh heavily in its favor (Waltz 1970; Hirschman 1945).

This chapter points to three other problems with arguments that see the macro structure of the international system (national-states) being undermined by micro processes driven by changes in individual competencies. First, such arguments lack historical perspective, often tacitly assuming that states have, in some golden age in the past, been able to effortlessly control transborder movements, or taking recent changes as indicative of long-term trends. In comparison with the past, contemporary changes in the level of international transactions do not appear particularly spectacular. The kinds of technological changes that have reduced international transaction costs have also reduced domestic transaction costs. Although some ratios of international to domestic transactions have increased, others have gone down. To the extent that historical data can be obtained they do not suggest any powerful long-term trends.

Second, interdependence arguments have ignored different trajectories of state consolidation that have occurred in different issue areas. They have focused on economic transactions and ignored military and security concerns. Indeed, the analysis of international security issues has, with a few exceptions such as discussions of terrorism, hardly dealt with any of the concerns raised by the interdependence literature. In the past, however, the ability of states to control the international use of force was not at all clear. Mercenaries were an important component of European militaries into the nineteenth, and in some cases even the twentieth, centuries. States would charter private, that is, nonstate actors to conduct military as well as commercial activities. Mercantile companies acted like quasi-states, maintaining their own courts and armed forces. Privateers were authorized to attack foreign shipping. Private citizens did engage in military intervention. (The fact that the activities of private citizens associated with Irangate are considered illegitimate is an indication of how much attitudes and legal stipulations have changed since the early nineteenth century.) One of the achievements of the state over the last two centuries has been to curtail the number, activities, and kinds of nonstate actors in the security issue area. Thus, though some aspects of international economic relations might suggest that micro processes have become more important, others, such as the private use of coercion, indicate that they have declined.

Third, and most important, interdependence arguments ignore the relationship between the growing level of some transactions, both domestic and international, and the consolidation of sovereignty; that is, of the control of a defined territory by a stable government that exercises final authority. High levels of exchange and market-rational outcomes (outcomes that reach the Pareto-optimal frontier given existing preferences and distributions of income) require stable property rights which, in a capitalist economic system, internalize costs and benefits. The only actors currently able to provide such rights are national-states. National-states may not always establish such property rights: socialist states will not routinely vest the right to freely alienate property in private entities; many states have arbitrarily altered the distribution of property rights. Nevertheless, in the modern world consolidated national states are the necessary if not sufficient condition for stable property rights that internalize costs and benefits. Other things being equal, the more stable the pattern of property rights the higher the level of economic transactions. Hence the commonplace notion that there is an inherent conflict between sovereignty and economic transactions is fundamentally misplaced. The consolidation of sovereignty— that is, the establishment of a set of institutions exercising final authority over a defined territory—was a necessary condition for more international economic transactions.

CHALLENGES TO STATE CONTROL

At least some of the literature on economic interdependence regards recent challenges to state control as qualitatively different from challenges that have arisen in the past. There has not, however, been any golden age of state control. States, conceived of as central administrative apparatuses, have never been able to free themselves from concerns about external and internal challenges. The Peace of Westphalia went some way toward domesticating and routinizing the international and civil conflicts generated by religious differences. The eighteenth century saw persistent conflict between the major European powers, culminating in Napoleon's attempt to establish complete dominance over the continent of Europe, an effort that was also a threat to the existing domestic orders of the major European states. High levels of war placed persistent strains on the financial resources of states, compelling them to alter their relationships with their own civil societies.[1]

Compared to earlier periods the nineteenth century was relatively peaceful. The number of international challenges to state boundaries, or even the existence of states, declined. In the center of Europe, however, internal challenges increased. The enervation of the Ottoman and Hapsburg empires precipitated a series of nationalist challenges that led to the creation of new states in the Balkans. In Germany and Italy fragmented political entities were consolidated into nation-states. There has been no past golden age in which Machiavelli's Prince could take a nap secure in the knowledge that external and internal challenges had disappeared.

The kinds of international economic flows that have attracted the attention of analysts who see micro phenomena altering macro structures in the international system are not unprecedented. Technological change has reduced transaction costs domestically as well as internationally. The direction of the long-term trend in the relative importance of international as opposed to domestic flows has not always been clear.

State control over the movement of capital and goods in the international system is the primary focus of interdependence arguments. Huge increases in the absolute volume of world trade, international capital movements, and multinational manufacturing are taken as indicators of declining state control. If these observations are put in the context of domestic activities, it is not clear that international flows are relatively more important today than they were a century or more ago.

Table 1 presents a measure of the volume of international flows of goods, corrected for changes in world GNP. With some exceptions (1900 and 1910), world trade progressively increased, and grew more rapidly than GNP, until World War I. From 1830 to 1913 the volume of world trade increased more than twice as fast as world GNP. In the post-World War II period, trade has also outstripped the growth in world GNP. However, the ratio of trade to GNP did not reach its pre–World War I high of 11 percent until the early 1970s. During the thirty years immediately following World War II, the trade-to-GNP ratio was at a level comparable to that of the 1850–70 period. One interpretation of these data is that between 1950 and 1975, world trade was simply recovering from the disruptions caused by two world wars.

It is true that world trade increased much more rapidly than GNP in the

Table 1   WORLD TRADE

Year	World exports/world GNP
1830	0.046
1840	0.057
1850	0.068
1860	0.093
1870	0.098
1880	0.114
1890	0.111
1900	0.104
1910	0.104
1913	0.114
1950	0.081
1960	0.092
1965	0.090
1970	0.100
1975	0.139
1980	0.169

Sources: Paul Bairoch, Commerce Extérieur et Développement Économique de l'Europe au XIXe Siècle (Paris: École des Hautes Études en Sciences Sociales, 1976): 78; UN Statistical Yearbook, various years; UNCTAD, 1983 Handbook of International Trade and Development Statistics; and B.R. Mitchell, International Historical Statistics: The Americas and Australasia (Detroit: Gale Research): 886–89.

Note: Data for 1830–1913 only include the United States and Europe (including European and Asian Russia, but not Turkey). The gap in the data (1913–1950) is due to the paucity of reliable figures in the war and interwar years.

Table 2   INDICES OF WORLD OUTPUT AND TRADE OF COMMODITIES[a]

Year	Agricultural products		Minerals[b]		Manufactures	
	Output	Exports	Output	Exports	Output	Exports
1950	58	42	38	23	26	16
1955	66	50	49	35	38	25
1960	78	68	59	50	49	37
1965	88	82	79	64	72	58
1970	100	100	100	100	100	100
1975	114	106	109	103	122	143
1980	124	141	131	118	152	199
1985	141	150	115	98	177	252

Source: GATT, International Trade 1985–86. Geneva, 1986, 139.

[a]Based on volume.

[b]Includes fuels and nonferrous metals

1970s, but the differential slowed markedly during the recession of the early 1980s. Whether the increased level of trade to GNP will persist remains to be seen.

Disaggregated figures for world output and exports in agricultural products, minerals, and manufactures are presented in Table 2. Between 1950 and 1970, exports increased more rapidly than production in all three categories. Agricultural production grew by 70 percent as exports more than doubled. Although the output of minerals nearly tripled during the twenty-year period, exports in 1970 were four times their 1950 level. In manufacturing, output quadrupled, while exports grew by a factor of six.

After 1970, however, the picture is decidedly mixed. Though the export of manufactures more than doubled between 1970 and 1985, and production increased by nearly 80 percent, increases in the other commodity categories were more modest. No real trend is evident in agricultural commodities, though it appears that exports and output have increased at about the same rate. As of 1985, production was up about 41 percent over the 1970 level; exports were up 50 percent. More striking are the post-1970 trends in the minerals category. Here exports have consistently grown less rapidly than output. In 1985, mineral production was only 15 percent greater than in 1970; the volume of exports was actually less than the 1970 level.

Both output and trade in manufactures have increased dramatically over the past thirty-five years, but this does not necessarily imply an increase in interdependence—if growing interdependence is meant to imply increasing vulnerability to external forces. Rather, the agricultural and mineral commodities production and export statistics suggest that dependence on items that are basic to the reproduction of labor and the production of manufactures has stabilized or even declined. This implies that vulnerability to disruptions in the flow of basic raw materials, and therefore at least one measure of interdependence, has diminished. Moreover, one of the striking characteristics of trade in manufactures is the growth of intrasectoral trade. This is especially true for the United States and Western Europe. Trade has increased most in commodities where countries are most able to adjust to external changes.

In the area of trade, institutional structures (as opposed to actual patterns of behavior) have deteriorated. There are more departures from the General Agreement on Tariffs and Trade (GATT) principles of nondiscrimination and reductions in trade barriers. Efforts to expand the GATT regime to nontariff barriers (NTBs) have met with mixed results. Only relatively few countries have signed the NTB codes negotiated during the Tokyo Round, and the provisions of these codes are limited to the signatories. The Department of Commerce has estimated that barter trade rose from 2 to 3 percent of world trade in 1976 to 25 to 30 percent in 1983. The percentage of automobile trade among advanced industrialized countries affected by NTBs increased from 1 percent in 1973 to 50 percent in 1983 (Gilpin 1987, 195, 207).

Another indicator of the volume of international economic transactions is capital flows, including direct foreign investment, loans, and bonds. Table 3 presents the ratio of foreign investments to GNP for Western industrialized countries. Here again, the pre-World War I period was one in which foreign investment increased much faster than GNP. Unlike world trade, however, foreign investment has yet to reattain the level it reached in 1913. Foreign investment in the 1950s and 1960s stabilized at 12 percent of GNP, well below the 19 percent it reached in 1840.

The Western industrialized countries have been investing relatively decreasing amounts of capital abroad since 1965. From 0.25 percent of GNP in 1965, to 0.22 percent in 1970, the amount of new foreign investment declined to 0.17 percent in 1981 (United Nations Conference on Trade and Development, 1983, 446; Organisation for Economic Co-operation and Development 1981, 39, 52).

Bank loans and bonds emanating from Eurocurrency markets are other

Table 3   TOTAL FOREIGN INVESTMENT

Year	Foreign investment/GNP
1840	0.19
1870	0.57
1900	1.02
1913	1.08
1929	0.24
1938	0.27
1960	0.12
1970	0.12

Source: Bairoch (1976), 99.

Note: Data for 1840–1913 include only Germany, Belgium, France, Sweden, Switzerland, the United Kingdom, and Holland. All Western developed countries are included for 1929 and later.

forms of international capital movements that have attracted a great deal of attention. This involves lending in currencies other than that of the country in which the venture is taking place, such as dollar transactions in London, or yen transactions in Frankfurt. Eurocurrency markets first developed in the 1950s when the Soviet Union and China deposited dollars in European banks because they were afraid that holdings in the United States might be seized. U.S. corporations began making Eurodollar deposits in the 1960s to secure higher interest rates, and they greatly increased their borrowing in Eurodollar markets when capital controls were imposed in the United States in the mid-1960s. The influx of petrodollars during the 1970s further enlarged Euromarkets, although activity decelerated sharply with the onset of the Third World debt crisis in the 1980s. In aggregate Eurocurrency markets in the European reporting area grew from $12 billion in 1964 to $920 billion in 1984. This was a rate of growth far higher than for any other major international economic activity (Frieden 1987, 81–84; Cohen 1986, 21–25).

The increase in size of international capital markets has been accompanied by what appears to be a dramatic change in institutional structures. National capital markets have become integrated. Staggering sums of money can be transferred across international boundaries almost instantaneously by modern communication links. Bankers can respond instantaneously to developments in any part of the globe (Frieden 1987, 80). There is always a major financial market open in some part of the world.

Both the size and institutional character of Eurocurrency markets have led many observers to regard them as a quintessential example of the impact of micro developments on macro structures. Eurocurrency markets have not been subject to much supervision by national regulatory authorities. The size of the international currency pool has made it extremely difficult for central banks to intervene effectively to manage exchange rates. Walter Wriston, president of Citibank during the 1970s, has argued that there is a new world information standard that "is exerting discipline on the countries of the world, which they all hate. For the first time in history, the politicians can't stop it. It's beyond the political control of the world, and that's good news" (quoted in Frieden 1987, 115).

As in the area of trade, however, this viewpoint is woefully lacking in historical perspective. International banking has been important since the Renaissance. Lending rose dramatically during the nineteenth century, with Britain at the core of the system. Almost half of all British savings were lent overseas. The United States replaced Britain as the world's leading creditor after World War I, and lending grew considerably during the 1920s. The amount owed to U.S. banks by foreign borrowers was, as a percentage of GNP, about the same in 1929 as in the mid 1980s—in both cases around 12 percent (Frieden 1987, 89; Cohen 1986, 84–90). The Depression and the aftermath of World War II were the aberrant periods. In the 1970s, as in the case of trade, international lending approximated levels that had been reached in the nineteenth century and the 1920s.

Nor is it obvious that new institutional structures and the ability to rapidly deploy capital around the world indicate that state control is more tenuous than it has been in the past. At least some Renaissance sovereigns were more dependent on international capital markets than contemporary rulers. International capital movements were seen as a threat to domestic financial stability by the end of the nineteenth century. When a major British banking house, Baring Brothers, was threatened with bankruptcy in the early 1890s by Argentine defaults, an international rescue operation was put together by the Bank of England which included not only the Bank but also the British Treasury, the Bank of France, other London banks, and J.P. Morgan (Cohen 1986, 94–95; Frieden 1987, 117–18).

In general national governments, especially Britain, took a more laissez-faire attitude toward international lending in the nineteenth century than is presently the case. Most lending was in the form of bonds rather than bank loans, making it easier for states to argue that responsibility lay with private bondholders, rather than with the national regulatory authorities that were, in any event, much less well developed. Despite the increase in international banking operations in New York during the 1920s, the U.S. government was extremely reluctant to become involved, an attitude that contributed to the onset of the Great Depression (Cohen 1986, 110–11). There were private bondholder committees in the nineteenth century that tried to deal with default, and as gunboat diplomacy (which was often prompted by defaults) indicates, governments did become involved. But the institutional structure for state or at least official involvement in international lending is much more elaborated now, including Paris Clubs and the IMFs as well as private arrangements.

Jeffrey Frieden, who is in many ways quite sympathetic to the autonomy of international capital markets, sums up the present situation in the following terms:

> Nevertheless, the Euromarkets are not stateless; they rest on the implicit, and sometimes explicit support of major western governments. The offshore markets arose, after all, in response to actions by national governments, and they grew because national governments tolerated or encouraged them. At any point in the last thirty years, the U.S. government could have put a stop to much Euromarket activity by prohibiting American banks from participating and by blocking the use of the U.S. dollar offshore [1987, 116].

We do not mean to imply that states cannot be affected by international capital markets that they cannot directly control, but it is critical to recognize that this is not a new development and that these markets have only been able to develop within a broader institutional structure delineated by the power and policies of states.

International travel is another area in which microprocesses have been seen as challenging or altering macrostructures. Technological developments in transportation have facilitated world travel, making it economically feasible for millions of people. Yet the increase in the international flows of people is not so striking if we look at the ratio of foreign to domestic travel. Table 4 presents data on air travel for the world and for the United States. Since 1950, the number of foreign travelers has fluctuated between 20 and 30 percent of the number of domestic travelers. The data for U.S. air travel shows similar fluctuations, but between 7 and 11 percent of the domestic volume. Although the number of international travelers leaving the United States in 1980 was almost six hundred times what it was in 1930, the number of domestic air travelers has increased even more rapidly. In fact, the postwar high for the United States, 11 percent in 1970, was still less—albeit marginally—than it was in 1930. Neither U.S. nor world air traffic demonstrates any trend in the ratio of international to domestic travel.

James Rosenau and others have placed considerable emphasis on the communications revolution as a source of micro changes that may alter macro structures. Telecommunications and computer technology make possible dramatic increases in the flow of information across state borders. They make, so the argument goes, state control of information problematic. Though it is premature to gauge the impact these developments will have on state control of international communications, it is instructive to examine what happened with an earlier communication technology. Table 5 presents data on the ratio of international to domestic mail flows for the world, Europe, and the United States. Europe and the world as a

Table 4   AIR TRAVEL

Year	International/domestic (world)	International/domestic (U.S.)
1930		0.114
1940		0.075
1950	0.29	0.097
1955	0.21	
1960	0.27	0.105
1965	0.29	
1970	0.31	0.110
1980		0.088

Sources: ICAO, *Digest of Statistics: Traffic 1961–71;* Air Transport Association of America, *Air Transport Facts and Figures,* various years; and FAA, *Airport Activity Statistics,* various years

Table 5   MAIL FLOWS

| Year | Foreign mail sent/total domestic mail | | |
	World	United States	Europe
1928–29	0.072	0.018	0.067
1936–38	0.058	0.014	0.051
1948–49	0.058	0.009	0.054
1958–59	0.069	0.009	0.065
1967–68	0.068	0.008	0.071
1975–77	0.093	0.010	0.083

Source: *U.N. Statistical Yearbook,* various years.

whole reattained their pre–World War II highs only in the late 1960s and 1970s; the United States has yet to reach the level it saw in 1928–29. By the late 1970s, the ratio of foreign to domestic mail had reached new highs both worldwide and in Europe, though not in the United States.

The ratio of international to domestic telephone calls for selected countries is presented in Table 6. Data on telephone traffic are more difficult to obtain and—at best—available for only the last twenty years.[2] However, the figures in Table 6 do suggest a general trend toward the internationalization of this mode of communication. With only four exceptions, the number of international calls has increased more rapidly than that of domestic calls. The four exceptions (Mozambique, Rwanda, Pakistan, and Burma) are all LDCs whose flat or declining ratios are due not so much to a reduction in their international telephone calls as to rapid growth in the amount of domestic traffic. Though these data must be interpreted with a great deal of caution, they do suggest that in the realm of telephone communications, international flows are growing more rapidly than domestic ones.

These data on the flow of goods, money, people, and information do not definitively answer the question of whether state control has eroded. All of the data presented here are in the form of ratios between international and domes-

Table 6   TELEPHONE TRAFFIC

Country	International/domestic traffic (%)				
	1966	1970	1975	1980	1984
Bahamas	0.48	0.91	0.78	1.78	—
Burma	0.008	0.006	0.005	0.008[a]	—
Canada	0.15	0.18	0.25	0.35	0.38[b]
Chile	0.014	0.028	0.024	0.042[a]	—
Costa Rica	—	0.26	0.24	0.30	0.33
Czechoslovakia	0.04	0.05	0.05	0.12	0.13
Gambia	0.29	0.51	0.63	1.36[a]	—
Mexico	—	0.14[d]	0.17	0.23	0.26
Mozambique	0.62	1.05	0.56	0.33[a]	0.36[b]
Pakistan	1.06	1.05	0.36	0.98	0.90[b]
Philippines	—	11.2	12.5	18.8	25.0
Poland	0.18	0.16	0.24	0.07	0.25
Rwanda	0.43	0.58	0.57	0.39	0.27[c]
United Kingdom	0.12	0.16	0.23	0.54	0.81[b]
West Germany	0.43	0.60	0.85	1.18	1.42

Source: International Telecommunication Union, *Yearbook of Common Carrier Telecommunication Statistics.* Geneva: various years.

[a]Data are for 1979.

[b]Data are for 1983.

[c]Data are for 1981.

[d]Data are for 1971.

tic flows. The worldwide flow of goods has reached new highs since the 1970s, but it took ninety years to attain the previous historic high achieved in the 1880s. Capital flows, in the form of foreign investment, increased dramatically until World War I, but consistently declined after 1938. Lending in the 1970s was at a level comparable to that of the nineteenth century. International air travel in comparison with domestic has been relatively stable for the past thirty years. Mail flows in the late 1960s were about the same as they were in the 1920s, though they increased slightly in the 1970s. Among the indicators we have considered here, it is only the pattern of telephone communications that is consistent with growing interdependence.

International flows of all kinds have increased dramatically during the last century. But domestic transactions have increased as well. The relative importance of domestic and international flows has not followed any clear trend. Perhaps states have lost control over all kinds of economic and noneconomic activities in domestic society, and interdependence analyses of the loss of control at the international level could be married with similar arguments about domestic activities. But given the growing scope of state activities, and the steady increase in the ability of states to extract resources from their own societies, arguments about the domestic loss of state control are problematic at best. At the very least the effectiveness of state control domestically, coupled with the absence of any clear increase in the relative importance of international transactions, suggest that there is no prima facie case for the assertion that international flows are more of a challenge to state control now than they have been in the past.

THE CONSOLIDATION OF SOVEREIGNTY

A second problem with interdependence arguments is that they ignore the consolidation of final authority within a defined territory. Historically, the overarching problem for statesmen has been the survival of their state. Although Kant was right to argue that the state of nature of the international system was less malignant than the state of nature for individuals, the existence of states, or at least their geographic boundaries, has often been threatened (Kant 1963). The minimalist goals of preserving territorial and political integrity could not be taken for granted in the past.

Annihilation Rates

The contemporary international system is not nirvana, but the situation for individual states has become more secure. The number of official actors in the international system declined until the Napoleonic Wars; it began to increase in the nineteenth century. After World War II the number of states in the international system exploded. At the same time the number of states that have disappeared has continued at a low level. Figures for the last two centuries are shown in Table 7.

Table 7   CREATION AND DISAPPEARANCE OF STATES

Decade	Number created	Number destroyed	Total
			34
1816–25	7	0	41
1826–35	5	0	46
1836–45	6	0	52
1846–55	1	0	53
1856–65	2	6[a]	49
1866–75	3	9[b]	43
1876–85	3	0	46
1886–95	1	0	47
1896–1905	5	1[c]	51
1906–15	3	0	54
1916–25	14	3[d]	65
1926–35	1	0	66
1936–45	1	4[e]	63
1946–55	21	0	84
1956–65	43	1[f]	126
1966–73	17	0	143

Source: Arthur S. Banks, Cross-National Time Series Data Archive User's Manual. Bingham: SUNY, 1975.

[a]These were Modena, the Papal States, Parma, Sardinia, Tuscany, and Two Sicilies in 1862.

[b]The nine were Hanover, Hesse (Electorate), Hesse (Grand Duchy), Mecklenburg, Prussia, and Saxony in 1867, and Württemburg, Baden, and Bavaria in 1870.

[c]In 1905 Russia recognized Japan's "paramount interest" in Korea, though Japan did not formally annex Korea until 1910.

[d]These were Austria-Hungary (1918), Montenegro (1919) and Serbia (1919).

[e]These were Estonia, Latvia, and Lithuania (1940) and Germany (1945).

[f]This was Zanzibar, which joined Tanganyika in 1964 to form Tanzania.

The low annihilation rate of states since World War II can be explained in several ways. Nuclear weapons have made force less usable. The weapons themselves are most credible when they are associated with maintaining the central balance between the Soviet Union and the United States, although even here their utility has been challenged.[3] Nuclear weapons may also, however, play some role in deterring conventional conflicts because of the fear of escalation.[4]

The survival rate of states may also be enhanced by the growing significance of juridical sovereignty. Jackson and Rosberg (1982) have pointed out that many of the states created since the conclusion of World War II do not have the attributes that have been traditionally associated with the recognition of sovereignty. Some have not been able to effectively control activities within their own territory. Most lack the material resources that would be needed to resist an external attack by more powerful states in the system. Despite this they have survived. Jackson and Rosberg argue that the most efficacious resource that these states have is juridical sovereignty: the fact that they are recognized as sovereign by other states in the international system. This gives them access to international resources and discourages depredations by other states.

Finally, the high survival rate of states since World War II may reflect the bipolar balance of power. The interests of the two superpowers in Europe are well defined. Any change, particularly a change as dramatic as the elimination of a state, would be very threatening to either the Soviet Union or the United States, a development that neither would welcome. In the Third World the superpowers have cautiously tracked each other's initiatives. There is no playing field where the superpowers are indifferent to outcomes. The most recent disappearance of an arguably sovereign entity, South Vietnam, occurred only after an extended and bloody conflict in which one of the superpowers committed its own forces. Hence, the bipolar distribution of power, which engenders balancing by the poles, may also contribute to the security of states in the postwar world.

Regardless of whether the consolidation of the state system (as indicated by the low annihilation rate for states in the postwar period) is attributable to nuclear weapons, juridical sovereignty, or bipolarity, the pattern of development here does not suggest that basic macro structures are being undermined by micro processes or anything else.

The Control of Military Activity

State control over the use of violence in the international system today is substantially greater than it was as recently as the mid-nineteenth century. In the eighteenth century, most European armies depended on large contingents of foreign mercenaries. Privateers played an important role in sea warfare. The great mercantile companies of Britain, France, and the Netherlands fought wars with each other, governments, and pirates. Piracy was rampant everywhere. Filibustering—"private" military expeditions into neighboring states launched by adventurers, politicians, and renegade military officers, often in collusion with local government officials—flourished in the Americas until the 1860s.

These activities suggest that as recently as the mid-nineteenth century, state control over the exercise of coercion beyond its borders was far from complete. Control was incomplete because state authority claims on coercion were minimal, conflictual, or unsettled. States did not claim the exclusive authority to raise an army within their own borders. They did not claim the exclusive right to employ the military services of individuals residing in their jurisdiction. Individuals were quite free to exercise violence in the international system for their own ends.

The story of how the state gained a monopoly over the coercive forces domestically is well known (Tilly 1975). Less familiar is the process through which the state achieved the exclusive right to deploy violence beyond its borders. This process involved the assertion of new authority claims and the development of appropriate enforcement capabilities. It began in the fourteenth and fifteenth centuries when the Hundred Years' War (1337–1453) marked the demise of the feudal methods of warfare (Preston and Wise 1970, 85) and culminated in the late eighteenth and early nineteenth centuries.

One way to view the process is in terms of the allocation of military capabilities. Valued goods, including coercive forces, can be allocated by the market or an authoritative body.[5] The feudal levy was an authoritative allocation of military capabilities. Nobles and knights had a duty to provide military force in behalf of the king in exchange for the privilege of landholding. Men served, not for pay, but because they were obligated to serve. By the time of the Hundred Years' War, however, the market had already begun to erode this system, with many knights fighting for pay. In Europe, the fifteenth and sixteenth centuries were the age of the mercenaries (Mockler 1969, 25–27). Market forces were even more evident in sea warfare where "until the end of the fifteenth century maritime warfare was largely in the hands of privateers" (Jessup and Deak 1935, 12). Mercenaries, mercantile companies, privateers, pirates, and filibusters appeared as authoritative allocations gave way to more market-oriented allocations.

Yet by the end of the nineteenth century, all of these nonstate actors had virtually disappeared. Market forces had been supplanted by state authority. State claims to a monopoly on the use of violence in the international system had replaced market allocation of military forces. State control, which for centuries had been problematic, was virtually uncontested in 1990. . . .

PROPERTY RIGHTS AND THE CONSOLIDATION OF SOVEREIGNTY

Let us accept for the moment the proposition that the relative importance of international economic transactions has increased and that effective state control has been eroded. This is a position that supports the contention that major changes may be afoot in the international system. At the same time, however, state control has been consolidated in other areas, especially core areas related to survival and the use of force; this is a development that supports the contention that the existing macro structure (that is, a world of national states) will persist. In fact, these apparently contradictory trends may be causally related.

Optimal market resource allocation, and the high levels of economic exchange with which such allocation is likely to be associated, requires secure property rights. Property rights can be thought of as a set of economic and social relations among individuals that defines "the position of each individual with respect to the utilization of scarce resources" (Furubotn and Pejovich 1972, 1139). Without secure property rights market activities would be constrained because of uncertainty about the possessor's right to sell the commodity and the threat to achieve transfers through force and coercion rather than voluntary exchange.[6] Individuals would place a high discount rate on the future. Capital allocation would be aimed at maximizing short-term gain—getting out before the rules of the game were changed. International trade would concentrate on luxury goods that offered the possibility of very high payoffs if a transaction were successfully completed.

In the present environment the state is the only actor capable of establishing stable property rights. The transaction costs of allocating such rights privately could be prohibitive, especially in cases involving externalities and collective goods (Calabresi and Melamed 1972). The state also has the most developed legal apparatus for enforcing property rights including contractual arrangements.

Stability alone, however, is not a guarantee of an optimal market allocation of economic resources. To achieve this end, property rights must also internalize costs and benefits. States are more than capable of establishing stable property rights that encourage suboptimal economic behavior. Douglass North (1981) has argued that states are torn between securing revenue by seizing a larger slice of the existing pie (which discourages market rational economic behavior), and limiting revenues to encourage a more productive allocation of resources. Robert Bates (1981) has elegantly delineated how the policies pursued by many African states have discouraged agricultural production. Hence the extent to which a particular pattern of exchange approaches market rationality is a function of both the stability of property rights and their specific substance. These two dimensions are depicted in Figure 1.

The highest level of exchange activity will occur in the upper right quadrant, where property rights are both stable and market rational. (We assume here that all other things being equal, optimal allocation will be associated with higher levels of exchange at least up to the point where transaction costs outweigh further market activity.) Industrialized market economy states fall somewhere in this quadrant. Market activity will be least in the lower left quadrant. Perhaps Afghanistan is now an example. Centrally planned economies fall in the upper left quadrant. Neoclassical economists have also generally argued that many Third World states also belong in this quadrant by having established stable property rights that encourage misallocation. To some extent economists have tended to view entitlements through property rules as a natural state of affairs and restrictions on such entitlements as a product of misinformed or pernicious government policies.[7] The economist's prescription calls for moving from the upper-left-hand quadrant to the upper-right-hand quadrant of Figure 1.

The history of property rights is, however, much richer than this economist's prescription suggests. Property rights, as Hobbes, Locke, and Smith

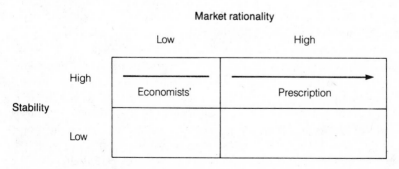

Figure 1 Property rights.

recognized, were not endowed by nature. Rights are not always stable. Political authority can disappear. New revolutionary regimes may, or may not, honor the international commitments of their predecessors. Private actors caught in the midst of boundary changes may have their property rights radically altered.[8] The movement from feudalism to capitalism was not always functionally optimal; that is, it did not always represent a shift from the upper-left quadrant to the upper-right quadrant of Figure 1. Japan did, in fact, make such a move after the Meiji Restoration. In Europe, however, some areas moved from the upper-left to the lower-right quadrant only later shifting to the upper-right quadrant. Depending on how colonial property rights are assessed some might argue that recently independent states have moved from the upper-right to the upper-left quadrant or even from the upper-right to the lower-left.

The increase in international economic transactions (absolute if not relative) to which the adherents of interdependence arguments so frequently point has occurred primarily in countries that fall in the upper-right-hand quadrant. But almost all areas of the world have, to some extent, participated in the absolute growth of international transactions. At least in part this must be attributed to the consolidation of sovereignty at the global level. Property rights are, in the contemporary world, only rarely threatened by external invasion or boundary changes. Disorder has emanated primarily from internal sources.[9] The consolidation of the state system has facilitated, indeed made possible, increased levels of exchange, both domestic and international.

At the international level, as suggested earlier in this chapter, the hegemonic distribution of power in the noncommunist world did facilitate the creation of a set of international property rights that encouraged international exchange. The trading regime embodied in GATT gave some assurance that the international flow of goods would not be arbitrarily changed by states.[10] Bilateral treaties helped to secure stable treatment for direct foreign investment. The Bretton Woods agreements, which reflected U.S. initiatives, power, and values, contributed to stability in international capital markets. National laws were, however, the base on which these international arrangements were erected. Without stable property rights enforced by national governments, international regimes would have been meaningless. In a world of national states, transactions take place within national jurisdictions.

CONCLUSION

Arguments that contend that changes in micro processes driven by exogenous technological innovations are fundamentally altering macro structures are vulnerable to several objections. First, they have exaggerated the growth in international transactions relative to domestic ones and have ignored the difficulties that states have always encountered in trying to control at least some transborder movements. Second, such conceptualizations have not taken sufficient account of the importance of hegemonic powers in at least initially creating stable international regimes. Third, they have not confronted the fact that in some issues areas, especially those related to security and the international use of coercion, states have become more consolidated: they have successfully eliminated almost all nonstate actors; and their existence and borders have become more secure. Finally, interdependence arguments have paid little attention to the way in which the consolidation of sovereignty has facilitated the creation of stable property rights that are a necessary if not sufficient condition for a market-rational allocation of resources.

If macro structures crumbled micro processes would almost certainly collapse as well. The transition from the present macro structure to some alternative will not be accomplished by the burrowing from below of micro processes, a fact that students of functionalism and neofunctionalism recognized more than a decade ago (Haas 1975). If such a transition is accomplished at all, more subtle and symbiotic changes will have to take place, and the new institutional forms that emerge will be different from any that exist now, and different than those the more mundane among us could even imagine.

NOTES

1. Skocpol (1979) argues that in one case, France, the financial pressures were so great that the king was compelled to enter into negotiations with civil society (through the Estates General) which ultimately precipitated the French Revolution. For a discussion of the relationship between war and taxation see Tilly (1975) and Ardant (1975). For a discussion of the benefits of an efficient domestic tax system for international military power see Rasler and Thompson (1983).
2. Problems with the ITU series are numerous. Many countries did not provide any statistics before the 1970s; others use different means for measuring international and domestic telephone traffic (for example, pulses versus number of calls), or change the method of measurement in the middle of the series. Of the countries for which twenty years of consistently reported data exist, we have selected countries from as many geographical regions, levels of development, and political systems as possible.
3. Jonathan Schell (1982), for instance, has argued that once a first strike has been launched, the original rationale for retaliation (which was to prevent that strike) has disappeared. But if the rationale is undermined by a preemptive strike then the logic of deterrence unravels. The standard response to this line of argument is the threat that leaves something to chance.
4. For a discussion of the declining utility of force see Keohane and Nye (1977) and Rosecrance (1986). For the ability of nuclear weapons to deter nonnuclear conflict see Robert Jervis (1984).
5. McNeill (1982) argues that the history of modern European warfare reflects the transition from the feudal command (that is, authoritative) allocation of military capabilities to a market-based system, and back to a command system.
6. Calabresi and Melamèd (1972, 1092) have argued that an entitlement may be protected by property rules, liability rules, or it may be inalienable. If an entitlement is protected by property rules then its ownership or use can only be changed through the voluntary agreement of the current owner by, for instance, sale in a market. An entitlement protected by liability rules may be destroyed by another party so long as

that party is willing to pay an objectively determined value. A right is inalienable if it cannot be transferred, even if there are willing buyers and willing sellers.

7. For example, see Furubotn and Pejovich (1972, 1140).

8. The movie *The Mission* gives a graphic example of such a change when the shift from Spanish to Portuguese rule transformed some South American Indians from recognized Christian individuals into slaves.

9. As U.S. assistance to the Nicaraguan contras illustrates, however, external intervention has hardly come to an end.

10. It is not clear whether the recent U.S. imposition of tariffs on $300 million worth of Japanese goods, given a bilateral trade deficit of tens of billions of dollars, should be taken as an indication of the strength of existing rules or of their malleability.

REFERENCES

Ardant, Gabriel (1975). "Financial Policy and Economic Infrastructure of Modern States and Nations." In C. Tilly, ed., *The Formation of National States in Western Europe.* Princeton: Princeton University Press.

Bairoch, Paul (1976). *Commerce extérieur et développement économique de l'Europe au XIXe siécle.* Paris: École des Hautes Études en Sciences Sociales.

Bates, Robert (1981). *Markets and States in Tropical Africa: The Political Basis of Agricultural Policies.* Berkeley: University of California Press.

Baumgart, Winfried (1981). *The Peace of Paris 1856.* Santa Barbara, Calif.: ABC-Clio.

Bayley, C. C. (1977). *Mercenaries for the Crimea.* London: McGill-Queen's University Press.

Brown, Charles H. (1980). *Agents of Manifest Destiny.* Chapel Hill: University of North Carolina Press.

Burchett, Wilfred, and Derek Roebuck (1977). *The Whores of War.* New York: Penguin Books.

Calabresi, Guido, and A. Douglas Melamed (1972). "Property Rules, Liability Rules, and Inalienability: One View of the Cathedral." *Harvard Law Review* 85 (April).

Cohen, Benjamin J. (1986). *In Whose Interest? International Banking and American Foreign Policy.* New Haven: Yale University Press.

Cooper, Richard (1968). *The Economics of Interdependence.* New York: McGraw-Hill.

Frieden, Jeffrey (1987). *Banking on the World: The Politics of American International Finance.* New York: Random House.

Furubotn, Eirik G., and Svetozar Pejovich (1972). "Property Rights and Economic Theory: A Survey of Recent Literature." *Journal of Economic Literature* 10 (December).

Gilpin, Robert (1975). *U.S. Power and the Multinational Corporation.* New York: Basic Books.

—— (1987). *The Political Economy of International Relations.* Princeton: Princeton University Press.

Goldstein, Judith (1986). "The Political Economy of Trade: Institutions of Protection." *American Political Science Review* 80, no. 1 (March).

Gooch, John (1980). *Armies in Europe*. London: Routledge & Kegan Paul.

Haas, Ernst (1975). *The Obsolescence of Regional Integration Theory*. Berkeley, Calif.: Institute for International Studies.

Hall, William E. (1924). *A Treatise on International Law*. Oxford: Clarendon Press.

Hirschman, Albert (1945). *National Power and the Structure of Foreign Trade*. Berkeley: University of California Press.

Jackson, Robert H., and Carl G. Rosberg (1982). "Why Africa's Weak States Persist: The Empirical and Juridical in Statehood." *World Politics* 35 (October).

Jervis, Robert (1984). *The Illogic of American Nuclear Strategy*. Ithaca: Cornell University Press.

Jessup, Philip, and Francis Deak (1935). *Neutrality: Its History, Economics, and Law*. Vol. 1. New York: Columbia University Press.

Kant, Immanuel (1963). *On History*. New York: Bobbs-Merrill.

Keohane, Robert, and Joseph Nye (1972). *Transnational Relations and World Politics*. Cambridge: Harvard University Press.

— (1977). *Power and Interdependence*. Boston: Little, Brown.

Krasner, Stephen (1976). "State Power and the Structure of International Trade." *World Politics* 28 (April).

McNeill, William H. (1982). *The Pursuit of Power*. Chicago: University of Chicago Press.

Maier, Charles (1977). "The Politics of Productivity." In Peter J. Katzenstein, ed., *Between Power and Plenty*. Madison: University of Wisconsin Press.

Malloy, William M. (1910). *Treaties, Conventions, International Acts, Protocols, and Agreements between the United States of America and Other Powers, 1776–1909*. Washington, D.C.: G.P.O.

Mitchell, B.R. (1983). *International Historical Statistics: The Americas and Australasia*. Detroit: Gale Research.

Mockler, Anthony (1969). *The Mercenaries*. New York: Macmillan.

Mukherjee, Ramkrishna (1974). *The Rise and Fall of the East India Company*. New York: Monthly Review Press.

Murdoch, Richard K. (1951). *The Georgia-Florida Frontier 1793–96: Spanish Reaction to French Intrigue and American Designs*. University of California Publications in History, J.W. Caughey, D.K. Bjork, and R.H. Fisher, eds., Vol. 40. Berkeley: University of California Press.

North, Douglass (1981). *Structure and Change in Economic History*. New York: Norton.

Organisation for Economic Co-operation and Development (OECD) (1981). *International Investment and Multinational Enterprises*. Paris: OECD.

Phillips, W.A., and Arthur H. Reede (1936). *Neutrality: Its History, Economics, and Law*. New York: Columbia University Press.

Preston, Richard A., and Sydney F. Wise (1970). *Men in Arms*. New York: Praeger.

Rasler, Karen, and William Thompson (1983). "Global Wars, Public Debts, and the Long Cycle." *World Politics* 35.

Ritchie, Robert C. (1986). *Captain Kidd and the War against the Pirates*. Cambridge: Harvard University Press.

Roche, James J. (1891). *The Story of the Filibusters*. New York: Macmillan.

Rosecrance, Richard (1986). *The Rise of the Trading State*. New York: Basic Books.

Rosenau, James N. (1988). "Post-International Politics: The Micro Dimension." Paper presented at the fourteenth World Congress of the International Political Science Association. Washington, D.C., 28 August–1 September.

Schell, Jonathan (1982). *The Fate of the Earth*. New York: Knopf.

Sherry, Frank (1986). *Raiders and Rebels*. New York: Hearst Marine Books.

Skocpol, Theda (1979). *States and Social Revolutions*. New York: Cambridge University Press.

Stout, Joseph A. (1973). *The Liberators*. Los Angeles: Westernlore Press.

Tilly, Charles (1975). *The Formation of National States in Western Europe*. Princeton: Princeton University Press.

United Nations Conference on Trade and Development (UNCTAD) (1983). *1983 Handbook of International Trade and Development Statistics*. Geneva: UNCTAD.

United Nations (various years). *U.N. Statistical Yearbook*. New York: United Nations.

Wallace, Edward S. (1957). *Destiny and Glory*. New York: Coward-McCann.

Waltz, Kenneth (1970). "The Myth of National Interdependence." In Charles P. Kindleberger, ed., *The International Corporation*. Cambridge: MIT Press.

—(1979). *Theory of International Relations*. Reading, Mass.: Addison-Wesley.

Emergent International Economic Order

Robert Gilpin

INTERNATIONAL NORMS VERSUS DOMESTIC AUTONOMY

After decades of unprecedented success, the postwar "compromise of embedded liberalism" deteriorated and the clash between domestic autonomy and international norms reasserted itself in the major economies of the international system. The increasing interdependence of national economies in trade, finance, and macroeconomic policy conflicted more and more with domestic economic and social priorities. As this occurred, the fundamental question initially posed by late nineteenth-century Marxists and subsequently by Keynes regarding the ultimate compatibility of domestic welfare capitalism with a liberal international economic order once again came to the fore. In the 1930s Keynes, believing that they were *not* compatible, chose domestic autonomy. The Keynes who helped put together the Bretton Woods system was more optimistic, and for a while he seemed to have been justified. By the 1980s, however, the Keynes of the 1930s, who believed that "goods [should] be homespun," might have felt vindicated.

The growth in global interdependence increased the relevance of domestic social structures and economic policies to the successful operation of the international economy. In a world where tax policies, social preferences, and government regulations significantly affect trading patterns and other international economic relations, the clash between domestic autonomy and international norms has become of central importance. As "embedded liberalism" seems less relevant, other possible solutions are: increased policy coordination and international cooperation, harmonization of domestic structures, and, in the event the first two options fail, a move toward greater autonomy and the delinking of national economies.

Although the resolution of this issue will be known only with the passage of time, the shifting attitudes and policies of the major centers of economic power—the United States, Western Europe, and Japan—toward international regimes suggests that domestic priorities are triumphing over international norms. In Western Europe and the United States, new constellations of interests and concerns have been leading to a greater stress on domestic economic interests and a deemphasis on international norms and policy coordination. Meanwhile, the new demands placed on Japan by its economic partners have begun to raise new anxieties in the Japanese people. Because of Japan's emerging key role in the world economy, "the Japan problem" and the challenge that it poses for international regimes are particularly important.

In response to complaints from its trading partners and its own economic success, Japan by the mid-1980s, had begun to change its highly protectionist policies and, in fact, had become the foremost advocate of free trade. As their strength increased the Japanese were beginning to open their traditionally closed markets and relaxing the control of the state bureaucracy over the economy. By the mid-1980s the Japanese had become, at least in their *formal* trade barriers with respect to manufacturers, the least protectionist of the advanced capitalist countries.

Even so, the liberalization measures that had been carried out by the Japanese were clearly not enough for their partners. The United States, Western Europe, and even Asian countries intensified their pressures on Japan for still more liberalization, the exercise of greater economic leadership, and the harmonization of Japanese institutions and practices with those of its major trading partners. These external pressures for liberalization raised particularly acute problems for Japanese society and its leaders.

Different interpretations of the meaning of the term "liberalization" are central to the debate between Japan and its critics. "Liberalization" has traditionally meant implementation of the basic principles and objectives of the GATT, that is, simply the removal of formal, external trade restrictions and, under certain circumstances, giving foreign firms "National Treatment"—treating them as if they were national firms and hence in a nondiscriminatory manner. For other countries, however, this interpretation is not sufficient in the case of Japan, due to the nature of the Japanese economy, and foreign demands for liberalization have challenged inherent and crucial features of Japanese culture, social relations, and political structure.

The Japanese economy is highly regulated, compartmentalized, and segmented in myriad ways. The existence of long-established informal relationships and institutional structures effectively restricts entry into many industrial and service sectors not only by foreign firms but also by Japanese firms. For example, as noted above, although it began to change in the 1970s and 1980s, the financial sector has been highly fragmented, with Japanese financial institutions confined to relatively narrow segments of the market; they have operated under tight government control by the Ministry of Finance, which tenaciously resists entry by either foreign or other Japanese firms. As has frequently been observed, the Japanese pattern in many economic sectors has been to discriminate against any "outside" firm, whether it is a foreign or even a Japanese business.

Moreover, in almost all economic sectors the reluctance of Japanese to "buy foreign," the interlocking networks of Japanese firms, and the crucial importance of personal relationships as well as the existence of numerous other informal barriers have constituted formidable obstacles to foreign penetration of the Japanese economy. (Some of Japan's more severe critics appear to believe that the Japanese language itself constitutes a nontariff barrier.) The distribution system is among the most important restrictions on entry to the market. Many believe that if the Japanese would only behave like Americans or Europeans, the economic conflicts would go away.

Westerners and Japanese also appear to have quite different conceptions of free trade. Whereas the West thinks in terms of "fairness" and full participation in the Japanese economy, Japan thinks in terms of "openness," preserving traditional structures, and not becoming overly dependant on imports. The Japanese firmly believe that they are playing by the rules; their foreign critics believe just as firmly to the contrary. Because of these cultural barriers, Americans and others regard the GATT principle of National Treatment to be an insufficient guarantor of greater access to Japanese markets. Instead, critics argue that a major overhaul of Japanese business practices and economic institutions is necessary. What is required, they argue, is a greater harmonization of Japanese institutions and behavior with those of other countries. In effect Japan must not only remove its formal and external barriers to trade, but it must become a liberal society in the Western sense of free markets open to all. The demands of the United States on the Japanese for greater reciprocity have reflected this attitude.

Although these pressures undoubtedly have contained a large element of resentment over Japan's economic success, they also arise from genuine concerns about whether or not the Japanese have indeed been "playing fair." As Gary Saxonhouse has commented, "a good share of the expanded agenda of international economic diplomacy, and, in particular, a good share of the interest in the harmonization of domestic economic practices in the name of transparency has been motivated by a desire to ensure that the very successful, but traditionally illiberal Japanese economy is competing fairly with its trading partners".[1] In international economic matters as in other spheres, justice must not only *be* done but be *seen* to be done. With increasing economic interdependence, questions of the legitimacy of national structures and practices have gained in importance. Microeconomic policy coordination as well as macroeconomic policy coordination appear to be necessary.

Western liberal societies find Japanese economic success particularly threatening because it is the first non-Western and nonliberal society to outcompete them. Whereas Western economies are based on belief in the superior efficiency of the free market and individualism, the market and the individual in Japan are not relatively autonomous but are deeply embedded in a powerful nonliberal culture and social system. . . .

Critics have argued that Japan must assume responsibility in trade, finance, and other areas commensurate with its new economic power; Japan cannot continue to respond merely by adjusting its policies to outside pressures. Although this sentiment has been vociferously expressed in the United States and, to a lesser extent, in Western Europe, it has appeared in Asian countries as well. As was noted earlier, the Japanese response to the demands of ASEAN countries and Asian NICs for greater access to the Japanese economy has been that these countries should copy its own early industrialization and should export labor-intensive goods to the United States rather than export to Japan. For those Asian neighbors with huge trade deficits with Japan, this refusal to open the Japanese market and to exercise greater leadership has been a source of great resentment.

These outside pressures for harmonization, reciprocity, and leadership have raised the stakes in economic struggles between Japan and its trading partners. The clash with the United States became especially acute by the mid-1980s. Whereas the West Europeans have tended to respond to "the Japanese problem" by shutting out the latter's goods, American pressures to open up and transform Japanese society itself have elevated the economic disputes to the political level so that even the political ties between the two nations are threatened.

These American pressures have placed Japan in a serious dilemma. On the one hand, meeting these demands would require that the Japanese change many of their cherished social values and traditional ways, traditions regarded by many Japanese as crucial to domestic social harmony and political stability. Liberalization would threaten high unemployment in many sectors and necessitate major structural changes in the economy. As one Japanese business executive vehemently stated, "foreign requests concerning Japan's nontariff barriers [to imports] are tantamount to raising objections to Japan's social structure." He went on to assert that "there is little possibility that those requests will be met."[2]

Can a liberal international economy long survive if it is not composed primarily of liberal societies as defined in the West, that is, societies with an emphasis on the price system, markets open to all, and limited interventionism on the part of the state? Liberal economists conceive of societies as black boxes connected by exchange rates; as long as exchange rates are correct, what goes on inside the black box is regarded as not very important. With the increasing integration of national economies, however, what states do inside the black box to affect economic relations has become much more important. Although in the 1980s this issue is most immediately relevant to Japan and the clash between its Confucian social order and the American Lockean order, the issue also applies to the NICs, to the socialist Eastern bloc economies, and to the growth of nationalized industries in Western Europe and throughout the world. The advent of industrial policy, new modes of state interventionism, and the existence of domestic institutions that act in themselves as nontariff barriers have become formidable challenges to the liberal international economic order.

In a highly interdependent world composed of powerful illiberal economies, the GATT principles of nondiscrimination, National Treatment, and

Most-Favored Nation may no longer be appropriate. If a greater harmonization among national economic practices and domestic societies does not occur, liberal societies may be forced in their own defense to adopt industrial and other countervailing practices. The question of whether statist societies should become more liberal, liberal societies should become more statist, or, as most economists aver, domestic structures do not really matter has become central to an evaluation of the problem posed by the inherent conflict between domestic autonomy and international norms.

A MIXED SYSTEM: MERCANTILISTIC COMPETITION, ECONOMIC REGIONALISM, AND SECTORAL PROTECTIONISM

In the mid-1980s, the liberal international economy established at the end of the Second World War has been significantly transformed. The trend toward liberalization of trade has been reversed and the Bretton Woods principles of multilateralism and unconditional Most-Favored Nation status are being displaced by bilateralism and discrimination. With the collapse of the system of fixed exchange rates, conflicting interests gave rise to intense clashes over exchange values and other monetary issues among the advanced economies. The displacement of the United States by Japan as the dominant financial power and the global debt problem have raised troubling questions about the leadership and stability of the world financial system.

Although few doubt the reality of these changes, opinion differs greatly over their significance. Some believe that these developments reflect "norm-governed change" and the continuity of common purposes among the dominant economic powers. Less sanguine observers, including myself, believe these changes are responses to hegemonic decline and are caused by diverging national interests among the advanced countries. As a consequence of profound structural changes in the international distribution of power, in supply conditions, and in the effectiveness of demand management, the liberal international economic order is rapidly receding.

Certain significant trends or developments can be observed. Growing mercantilistic competition threatens to increase economic nationalism; thus far the vestiges of American leadership, the forces of historical inertia, and the common interest in avoiding conflict have moderated the consequences of this situation. There is also a tendency toward regionalization of the world economy; the closure of Western Europe, the economic consolidation of North America, and the rise of the Pacific Basin point in that direction. Furthermore, sectoral protectionism has gained strength; the conflicting desires of nations both to protect particular sectors and to acquire foreign markets in these same industries strongly encourage this New Protectionism. Although the relative importance of each cannot be determined, a mixed system of nationalism, regionalism, and sectoral protectionism is replacing the Bretton Woods system of multilateral liberalization.

Intensified Mercantilistic Competition

The first factor suggesting an intensification of mercantilistic competition is the increasing role of the state and of economic power in international economic relations. States (especially large states) have begun to use political and economic leverage extensively to increase their relative gains from international economic activities. The clash between economic interdependence and domestic autonomy is more frequently resolved in favor of autonomy than interdependence, even though nations want the benefits of interdependence at the same time that they seek to limit its effects on national autonomy. They want the collective goods of liberalized trade and a stabilized monetary order without sacrificing their capacity to manage their own economy as they see fit. The result has been an expanding competition among states to maximize their own benefits from and to minimize the costs of global interdependence.

The second factor promoting mercantilistic conflict is the growing struggle for world markets. Due to such factors as domestic limits on economic growth in the form of high wages and inflationary pressures, the global debt problem, and the continuing need of most countries to import energy, almost every nation pursues export-led growth and aggressive export-expansion policies. These pressures on export markets will intensify due to the reversal of the American financial position and the fact that for the first time in the postwar era the United States must achieve an export surplus to repay its massive debt. This classical mercantilistic conflict over market shares is reflected in clashes over trade and macroeconomic and other policies.

Third, the challenge and example of Japan and the NICs also stimulate mercantilism. The structure of Japanese trade and the unprecedented rate of change of Japan's comparative advantage increase pressures on other economies. As Japan and the NICs move rapidly up the technological ladder, they impose heavy adjustment costs on other economies, thereby stimulating strong resistance and demands for protectionism. Japanese success reflects an adroit interventionist and mercantilist state that has been able to manage social consensus, establish economic objectives, and increase the overall competitiveness of the economy. This success encourages other states to emulate the Japanese and develop interventionist policies of their own.

The mercantilism generated by these developments promises to be different in purpose and method from its eighteenth- and nineteenth-century predecessors. During the first mercantilist era, the objective was to acquire specie for military purposes, and the means employed was an export surplus. The purpose of nineteenth-century mercantilism was to speed industrialization through protectionism and other policies. In the closing decades of the present century, the goal is at least survival in world markets and, optimally, the achievement of economic supremacy. Pursuing this goal, the Japanese and their imitators have implemented . . . a strategy of competitive development.

The success and example of Japan and the NICs thus carry one step further to its logical conclusion, the transformation in the relationship of state and market that Schumpeter predicted would result from the First World War;

through its control over economic levers, the modern state attempts to direct and shape the economy to achieve its primary objective whether it be the prosecution of war, the promotion of domestic welfare, or, as in the case of Japan, the industrial and technological superiority of the society. As a result of this change in the relationship of state and economy a new form of mercantilistic competition . . . has become important.

At the end of the twentieth century, there is a powerful incentive for governments to manipulate economic policies in order to advance their economic, political, and related interests. The Japanese tactic of "preemptive investment," the American retreat to earlier ideas of "conditional reciprocity," and the temptation of all nations to move toward strategic trade policy are examples of such competitive policies. Developments in the 1980s such as the rise of the New Protectionism, the spread of industrial policies, and governmental support of their own multinationals illustrate this predilection of individual states to adopt policies that benefit themselves at the expense of other economies.

How will mercantilism as a new form of inter-state competition affect international economic and political relations? Will nations compete, for example, on an individual basis, or will what Giersch has called "policy cartels" arise?[3] If nations coordinate their economic policies and form economic alliances, who will participate and to what end? The rise of economic regionalism resulting from the erosion of a liberal international economic order may provide some answers to these questions.

Loose Regional Blocs

The difficulties of pluralist leadership, the resistance of many advanced economies to economic adjustment, and domestic priorities threaten further dissolution of the unity of the liberal international economic order. Loose regional blocs are likely to result. In the 1980s, the world economy is coalescing along three axes. Debt, monetary, and trade matters as well as changing security concerns will surely pull the regions of the world economy further apart but should not cause a complete break.

The European Economic Community constitutes one focus for regionalization of the world economy. A Europe-centered system would include the enlarged Community, peripheral European states, and many of the former European colonies. It would no doubt form close ties to the Eastern bloc and certain of the Middle East oil exporters. As has been noted earlier, this region could be relatively self-sufficient except for energy and certain commodities; by the early 1980s, it had already achieved a high degree of monetary unity and policy coordination. In a world of increasing uncertainty and politicized economic relations, a more closely integrated Western Europe would be able to confront the United States, Japan, and the emergent centers of economic power more effectively.

The United States has begun to draw its northern and southern neighbors into closer interdependence, as both the Canadian and Mexican economies have become increasingly integrated with that of the United States. Although not much attention is given to the fact, Canada is the largest trading partner of the United States, and these ties are increasing with Canada's dramatic loss of its European markets in the postwar period. The United States is the largest importer of Mexican oil, and American multinationals have made the area along the southern Rio Grande one of the principal locales of "off-shore" production. A growing percentage of Mexico's exports are sent north of the border. The Caribbean Basin Initiative has also bound that region, including parts of Central and northern South America, more closely to the United States. It should be noted that, in addition, the United States has established loose economic arrangements with its political and security dependencies: Israel, South Korea, Taiwan, and, for the moment, Saudi Arabia. Shifts in trading patterns, foreign investment, and financial flows also have reinforced the regionalizing tendencies, and the debt problem has further strengthened the polarizing forces. For economic and security reasons the United States is giving increased and special attention to its own hemisphere and to a larger economic orbit that is yet to be defined.

The third and most amorphous emerging region is that of the Pacific Basin or the Asian Pacific. Centered principally upon Japan and its East Asian trading partners, this region includes ASEAN (Indonesia, the Philippines, Malaysia, Singapore, and Thailand), Australia, Canada, New Zealand, the Asian NICs (South Korea, Hong Kong, Taiwan, and, again, Singapore), and parts of Latin America. The United States, especially the West Coast, has also become a major participant in this economic region. American trade with the nations of the Pacific overtook U.S. Atlantic trade in the mid-1970s and subsequently has expanded much more rapidly than U.S. trade with the rest of the world.

The Pacific Basin in the 1980s became the fastest growing and fore-most trading region of the world. Between 1960 and 1982, the ratio of its exports to world exports doubled; this expansion was even more remarkable in manufactured goods.[4] The region is the most nearly self-sufficient one of the three in commodities, manufactures, and investable capital. But the most notable development of all was that trade *within* the region grew even faster than trade with the rest of the world. This regionalization was a function of domestic economic growth, complementarities of the economies, and the relative openness of the economies. Moreover, this intraregional trade was shifting from a series of bilateral relationships to a more truly multilateral trading network.

The size and dynamism of the Pacific region are indicative of its increased importance in shaping the future of the international political economy. The ratio of Pacific gross product to Atlantic gross product increased from about 40 percent in 1960 to about 60 percent in 1982. The region's share of global gross product rose in this same period from 16 to almost 25 percent and its ratio to the U.S. GNP shot up from 18 to more than 50 percent.[5] In the 1980s Northeast Asia (Japan, Taiwan, and South Korea) became the electronics capital of the world; partially reflecting this development, a substantial portion of both American and Japanese foreign direct investment was in that region. . . . As with prior major shifts in the locus of global economic activities, the political consequences of this development will be profound.

The shape and internal relationships of the region, however, remain unclear, and several important questions have yet to be answered. The first and most critical is whether its two economic giants—the United States and Japan—can continue to be close partners or will become antagonistic rivals. The second is how the tension between the complementarity and the competitiveness of the East Asian economies will be resolved; although the complementary factor endowments of Japan, the Asian NICs, and ASEAN could lead to a relatively self-sufficient division of labor in the region, these economies are also increasingly competitive with one another in commodities and manufactured goods in the American and other markets. The third question is whether Japan will exercise economic leadership through such measures as opening its markets to the manufactured goods of its neighbors or exporting its hugh capital surplus to China and other regional economies. The answers to these and similar questions will significantly affect the place of this region in the larger world economy.

The developing pattern of trading and investment relations is creating a regional division of labor with Japan and the United States as the two anchors. Japan is the foremost exporter of consumer goods and importer of raw materials, and the American market is a vital element tying the region together; American exports of capital and high technology goods to the developing countries of the Pacific Basin and Latin America are also becoming increasingly important. Between 1980 and 1985, LDC exports to the United States increased from 40 to 60 percent of total U.S. imports, and in 1985, the LDCs took one-third of American exports.[6] Also, American exports to the Pacific region nearly doubled between 1960 and 1983 from about 13 percent to about 25 percent of total exports.[7]

The Pacific region has a number of potential problems that could thwart its development. The first is the tendency toward bipolarization between the industrialized economies of northeast Asia and the commodity-exporters of ASEAN countries; the former is pulling ahead of the latter in exports and growth (Nomura Research Institute, 1986a, p. 19). The second is the overdependence of the Asian members of the region on the American market as their engine of economic growth; they do not yet constitute a self-sustaining bloc and the decline of the American rate of growth, as occurred in 1986, has a depressing effect on the region. And, third, the political stability of East Asia since the end of the Vietnam War may not last; many domestic regimes are unstable and the Pacific is increasingly a focus of superpower confrontation. Thus, although the Pacific Basin holds great promise, its serious difficulties must not be overlooked.

The boundaries of these three partially coalesced regions are unclear and porous; the membership of the regions overlap. The trading, financial, and other commercial relations among the regions and especially among the major powers remain strong, yet the lines of demarcation among the regions are discernible and becoming more pronounced with the spread of protectionism and other changes in the world economy. In the mid-1980s the pattern of international trade is strongly characterized by regional constellations.

This tendency toward greater regionalization means that large segments of the human race will undoubtedly be excluded from the world economy. The

Soviet Union lies outside these regions, and a number of the Eastern European countries, with the failure of the debt-financed industrialization strategy of the 1970s and under the pressure of the Soviet Union, will be only partially integrated. The Southern Cone (Argentina, Chile, Peru, etc.) and other Latin American countries that had become integrated into the world economy in the nineteenth century appear to be falling out of the system. Much of black Africa has become marginalized and is sinking into economic and political despair. Where China, India, and Brazil, nations with immense potential, will eventually fit is not yet determined. There is a great danger that a more regionalized world economy will be composed of a few islands of relative prosperity in a turbulent sea of global poverty and alienated societies.

A greater regionalization of the world economy also poses a threat to the economic health of the dominant economic powers themselves. As this book has argued, if a market or capitalist system is to grow and be prosperous, it must be outwardly expansive. In a closed system, the operation of what the Marxists call the "laws of motion of capitalism" threaten in time to lead to economic and technological stagnation. Considered from this perspective, the growth potential of the emergent high technology industries of the future can probably be fully achieved only in a truly global economy. The cost of their development and the scale of these technologies necessitate the generation of a level of demand that is possible only in an integrated world market.

This clash between the static gains from trade that would be possible in a regionalized world economy and the dynamic gains from technological advance in a larger international economy has been well described by William Cline:

> There is another, potentially dangerous, implication of the line of analysis developed in this appendix [i.e., the shift to arbitrary comparative advantage and intra-industry trade]. To the extent that a wide group of countries has endowments of resources, factors, and technology that are broadly indistinguishable, the traditional grounds for welfare benefits from trade are eroded. After all, gains from trade accrue to both parties because of the difference between their respective relative costs of the products. With similar factor endowments, resources, and technology, these differences are not likely to be great, and neither would the losses from reduction of trade. This consideration would suggest that the welfare costs of limiting trade of this sort would not be high. But this inference is dangerous not only because it issues an open invitation to protectionist interests but also because it may overlook important economic welfare effects associated with economies of scale and competitive pressure for technological change even if the static welfare costs associated with comparative costs are limited.[8]

Sectoral Protectionism

The dynamic advantages to be gained from economies of scale, corporate alliances across national boundaries, and the sharing of technology suggested in the 1980s that sectoral protectionism, that is, international cartelization, particularly in high-technology and service industries, will also be a distinctive feature of the emergent international economy. In place of multilateral tariff reductions, governments will increasingly negotiate bilateral arrangements regarding market shares in specific economic sectors, arrangements that reflect the shift away from multilateralism and unconditional reciprocity to bilateralism and conditional reciprocity.

Sectoral protectionism, cartelization, or . . . "liberal protectionism" is, of course, nothing new. Nations have long protected particular economic sectors such as European and Japanese agriculture. The new element is the increasing importance, as signified by the rise of the New Protectionism, of negotiating market shares on a sector-by-sector basis. In contrast, the various rounds of the GATT succeeded by negotiating tradeoffs across industrial sectors based on considerations of revealed comparative advantage; for example, concessions by a country in one sector might be matched by another country in another sector. The purpose of sectoral protectionism, on the other hand, is to divide up or cartelize individual sectors among various producers.

American and Japanese trade negotiations have become the foremost expression of this move toward sectoral protectionism. In the so-called MOSS (Market-Oriented, Sector-Selective) discussions, which have taken place over several years in Tokyo and Washington, the United States tried to decrease Japanese regulatory, tariff, and other import barriers in the sectors of telecommunications, medical equipment and pharmaceuticals, electronics, and forest products. The decision of Japan and the United States in 1986 to cartelize the semiconductor industry was the most significant outcome of these discussions; it was the first extension of the New Protectionismism from traditional industries like steel and automobiles to high-technology products. Whatever the merits of this particular action, because of the economic importance and political sensitivity of these service and high technology sectors, any other approach than that of the MOSS discussions would undoubtedly be exceptionally difficult.

An important cause of the increasing importance of sectoral protectionism has been that the new technologies associated with the contemporary technological revolution such as the laser, the computer, and bioengineering can never achieve their potential in a fragmented world economy of restricted demand. Just as the technologies of the Second Industrial Revolution (steel, electricity, the automobile, other consumer durables, etc.) could only be fully developed in the continental mass market of the United States, the exploitation of the technologies of the Third Industrial Revolution will also require the existence of a hugh global market. A regionalized world economy composed of relatively impervious national and regional markets could thwart this possibility.

The nature of the contemporary technological revolution also suggests that sectoral protectionism will be prevalent. The role of basic science has become increasingly important to the generation and the diffusion of these technologies, and these new technologies are frequently neither sector-specific nor merely a new product; instead they constitute novel processes, are ubiquitous in their effects, and cut across the economy, affecting traditional as well as modern industries. The computer, for example, is transforming all aspects of economic life from agriculture to manufacturing to office management.

These newer technologies are also very costly to develop, involve large economies of scale, and will require mass markets to amortize development costs. This means that there is unlikely to be any clear technological leader as in the past; instead there will be many centers of innovation and the technology will diffuse rapidly. The importance of these technologies to the wealth, power, and autonomy of national societies means that every state will want to maintain a presence in the technology.

The rise of sectoral protectionism is associated with the New Multinationalism . . . the tendency of multinational corporations to invade one another's home market. A major reason for this cross or reciprocal foreign direct investment has been set forth by Kenichi Ohmae: "In such high-tech industries as computers, consumer electronics, and communications, the rapid pace of product innovation and development no longer allows firms the luxury of testing the home market before probing abroad. Moreover, because consumer preferences vary subtly by culture and are in constant flux, companies must intimately understand local tastes—and react instantly to changing market trends and prices."[9] He also points out that direct investment will continue to be necessary because insiders have greater immunity from protectionism; further, unless a corporation operates in all three of the regional centers of the world economy, it will not be able to "achieve the economies of scale world-class automated plants demand in order to pay for themselves." The New Protectionism, the rise of joint ventures across national boundaries, and the like are reflections of the movement toward sectoral protectionism.

Under these conditions, sectoral protectionism has become attractive to governments. It enables them to keep foreign markets open while they retain some control over their own internal markets and establish a national presence in the sector. Intra-industry rather than interindustry trade will thus be encouraged. They thereby gain some of the benefits of economic interdependence without the attendant costs of a fully liberalized trading regime.

Although secotral protectionism departs from the liberal emphasis on economic efficiency and nondiscrimination, it appears to be the only way to satisfy both the need for economies of scale and the desire of governments to possess what they consider to be high-employment and strategic industries. Those economies with bargaining leverage, that is, with large internal markets, capital availability, or technological monopolies, would be the major winners through sectoral protectionism.

In the mid-1980s, it is not possible to determine the nature and extent of the industries that will propel economic growth in the advanced economies in the forthcoming era or to project which country or countries will be the winners or the losers. Will there be, as in the past, a clear technological leader such as Great Britain or the United States or, as has been suggested, will this leadership role be shared by two or more economies? Whatever the answer to this question, sectoral protectionism, along with mercantilism and regionalism, is a crucial feature of the transformed economic order. In a substantial number of economic sectors, world markets are characterized in the mid-1980s by voluntary export restraints, orderly marketing agreements, and reciprocal foreign direct investment. Bilateralism and conditional reciprocity are increasingly important determinants of economic relations.

An international economy based on sectoral protectionism might help resolve the inherent tension between a liberal world economy and a decentralized state system. Through encouraging international joint ventures, establishing linkages among multinationals of different nationalities, and creating crosscutting interests among the three major centers of economic power, sectoral protectionism promises to counter the inherent tendencies in a regionalized system toward destabilizing conflict.

In the emergent configuration of the world economy, what portion of international economic transactions will be governed by mercantilistic competition, by economic regionalism, or by sectoral protectionism? At the moment it is too early to determine which tendency will predominate. What can be said is that unless these three elements can be successfully balanced, the danger of severe mercantilistic conflict and destabilizing economic nationalism will surely increase.

I have written elsewhere that one should make a distinction between benign and malevolent mercantilism.[10] Benign mercantilism entails a degree of protectionism that safeguards the values and interests of a society; it enables a society to retain domestic autonomy and possess valued industries in a world characterized by the internationalization of production, global integration of financial markets, and the diminution of national control. Malevolent mercantilism, on the other hand, refers to the economic clashes of nations characteristic of the eighteenth century and the interwar period of the 1930s; its purpose is to triumph over other states. The first is defensive; the second is the conduct of interstate warfare by economic means. Thus, as John Ruggie has observed, the difference between the two forms of mercantilism is one of social purpose. The former serves domestic economic and social objectives such as employment, the control of macroeconomic policy, and the preservation of key industries; the latter's objective is the accumulation of national power and domination of other states.[11]

Although there can be no guarantee that a world economy based on benign mercantilism would not degenerate into the malevolent form, in the words of Barry Buzan, "a benign mercantilist system would have a better chance of containing peacefully states with different organizing ideologies. Liberal systems force a polarization between capitalist and centrally-planned states, and malign mercantilism encourages a general alienation of each from all. Benign mercantilism perhaps offers a middle way in which divergent actors can relate to each other on more equal terms over the whole system."[12] In an era of spreading economic nationalism, one could hardly hope for more than this benign mercantilist solution to the problem posed by the decline of economic leadership.

However, the dangers inherent in the tendencies toward mercantilistic competition, economic regionalism, and sectoral protectionism should not be minimized. Liberalism and the principles embodied in it depoliticize international economic relations and can protect the weak against the strong. The Most-Favored Nation principle, nondiscrimination, and unconditional reciprocity provide as close to an objective basis of judging the legitimacy of economic behavior as may be possible; they place a constraint on arbitrary actions. In a world of policy competition, regional alliances, and bilateralism, what will be the norms guiding and limiting more managed economic relations? For example, will there be increasing demands that certain economies become more like those of other nations, similar to the American demands on the Japanese for reciprocity and greater harmonization of domestic structures?

The attempts of the United States to open foreign markets, privatize other economies, and preserve a liberal economic order, all in the name of liberal principles and domestic harmonization, could prove to be counterproductive. The exertion of political pressures on the Japanese to harmonize domestic structures with those of the West and the aggressive demand for reciprocity could inhibit the search for solutions more in keeping with the new economic and political realities. It would be far better for the United States to follow the European emphasis on sectoral protectionism than to attempt to force open the Japanese economy. . . . A sectoral protectionism has always been something with which the Japanese could more easily learn to live. If governments fail to heed this advice, then the present global movement toward benign mercantilism could degenerate into malevolent mercantilism. Uncompromising economic nationalism might become the new international norm, replacing state efforts to work out their economic differences with due regard to both market efficiency and national concerns.

Over the past three centuries the modern world has witnessed a parallel evolution of the scale of technology and the scope of the international market. At the same time that the cost of technology and the need for economies of scale have increased, national and international markets have adjusted and have enlarged, thereby increasing the level of global demand. But as Eugene Staley observed during the global economic and political collapse of the 1930s, markets and politics need not ultimately adjust to technology. Many times in the past, technology and economics have ultimately adjusted to politics: "In the 'Dark Ages' following the collapse of the Roman Empire, technology adjusted itself to politics. The magnificent Roman roads fell into disrepair, the baths and aqueducts and amphitheatres and villas into ruins. Society lapsed back to localism in production and distribution, forgot much of the learning and the technology and the governmental systems of earlier days."[13] The transition to the growth technologies of the contemporary industrial revolution will not be achieved without the establishment of a more stable political framework for economic activities.

CONCLUSION

The transition to a new international economic order from the declining era of American hegemony is and will continue to be difficult. Among the many factors that make a return to the halcyon days of the first decades of the postwar era virtually impossible is the decline of clearly defined political leadership. Conflict-ing economic and political objectives make the achievement of international cooperation and pluralist leadership of the world economy unlikely. National economies are inclined to resist adjustment to changes in comparative advantage and in the global distribution of economic activities. There is little likelihood of a return to high rates of economic growth unless market forces are permitted to relocate economic activities on the basis of shifts in competitive advantage. Fur-thermore, the tendency of states to place domestic priorities above international norms has serious implications for the continuation of a highly interdependent international economy. A return to the path of economic liberalization is impossi-ble unless governments are willing to subordinate short-term parochial interests to the larger goal of a stable international economy and to carry out extensive harmonization of domestic institutions and business practices.

The diffusion of economic power and the reemergence of economic national-ism necessitate a very different international economic order from that of the Bretton Woods system. The reassertion of the state in economic affairs means a slowing, if not a reversal, of the postwar primacy of the market as the means of organizing global economic relations. Although it is impossible to predict the nature of state and market interaction in the new environment, certain develop-ments seem likely. There has been and will be growing politicization of the international economic order and an increase in policy competition. Govern-ment intervention in the areas of trade, money, and production has grown immensely despite the revival of neoconservatism and a rediscovery of the market in many countries. Deregulation at home appears to be accompanied frequently by increased protection of domestic markets and policy initiatives designed to promote nationalistic goals. It is significant that at the same time the Reagan Administration was deregulating the American economy, it was also raising protectionist barriers more rapidly than any other postwar American administration and fashioning policy instruments to gain greater leverage over other economies.

There is also an increasing regionalization of the world economy as global economic activities cluster around the several poles of the world economy. The increased closure of the European Common Market, the continued separation of the Soviet bloc from the world economy, and the perceptible shift of the United States toward the Pacific Basin as well as the increasing importance of Japan and the newly industrializing countries are all elements in this retreat from the postwar ideal of a multilateral liberal system. The debt problem, the disorders of the international monetary system, and the cartelization of a sub-stantial fraction of world trade are pushing the world more and more in this direction. Although it is highly unlikely that increased fragmentation will lead to a collapse of the global system as serious as that of the 1930s, regionalism will surely become a more prominent feature of international economic and political relations.

A system of sectoral protectionism or, perhaps, sectoral regimes is emerg-ing. In many economic sectors national shares of international markets and the international location of economic activities will be as much a function of bilateral negotiations among governments and economic actors as of the operation of the "laws" of comparative advantage. The New Protectionism, the emergence of industrial and strategic trade policies, and the increasing role of imperfect competition are forces moving the world economy toward sectoral protectionism. Cartelization, voluntary export restraints, and similar mechanisms to divide markets or encourage domestic production by foreign firms are becoming an integral, albeit a regrettable, feature of the international political economy. It is possible that a world economy composed of a more protectionist United States, an increasingly autarkic Western Europe, and a Japan determined to preserve its traditional culture can be held together only through such devices. In a world of "arbitrary" comparative advantage, states will wish to ensure a strong national presence in emergent high-technology industries and the growth sectors of the future. Thus, although the relative balance of political and market determinants of economic activities will differ from one economic sector to another and from time to time, market shares and the global location of economic activities will be strongly influenced by bargaining among nation-states and multinational corporations.

It is paradoxical that governments have responded to the growth of global economic interdependence by enhancing their authority over economic activities. Both global market forces and state interventionism have become more important determinants of international economic relations than in the recent past. In this new environment, bilateralism or minilateralism has largely displaced the multilateralism of the GATT and political considerations have become increasingly important in the determination of economic relations and economic policy.

The new international economic order of the mid-1980s raises profound issues of economic equity for the conscience of mankind. Many societies will suffer from the closure of world markets and will require massive economic assistance if they are to have any chance to escape from their poverty. The liberal world economy based on nondiscrimination and multilateralism had defects; however, it did at least provide economic opportunities that will shrink in a more nationalistic world economy.

The mixed system of multilateral, regional, and protectionist arrangements may or may not prove stable over the long run. Yet this politicized economic world need not mean a return either to the malevolent mercantilism and economic warfare of the 1930s or to the expanding and relatively benevolent interdependence of the 1960s. The postwar age of multilateral liberalization is over and the world's best hope for economic stability is some form of benign mercantilism. The continuing residue of American power and leadership, the security ties of the major economic actors, and the promise of high technology as a source of economic growth provide support for moderate optimism. Nevertheless, at this juncture in the trasition from one economic order to another, the only certainty is that a new international political economy is emerging. It is not clear who will gain, who will lose, or what the consequences will be for global prosperity and world peace.

NOTES

1. Gary Saxonhouse, "Comparative Advantage and Structural Adaptation," Department of Economics, University of Michigan, unpublished (undated).
2. Quoted in Murray Sayle, "Victory for Japan," *New York Review of Books*, vol. 32 (1985), p. 39.
3. Herbert Giersch, "The Age of Schumpeter," *American Economic Review*, vol. 74 (May 1984), pp. 103–109.
4. Staffan Buvenstam Linden, *The Pacific Century* (Stanford: Stanford University Press, 1986), p. 14.
5. Ibid., p. 10.
6. *The New York Times*, October 4, 1985, p. D1.
7. Linden, p. 78.
8. William R. Cline, *"Reciprocity: A New Approach to World Trade Policy?"* (Washington, DC: Institute for International Economics, 1982), p. 40.
9. Kenichi Ohmae, *Triad Power: The Coming Shape of Global Competition* (New York: The Free Press, 1985).
10. Robert Gilpin, *U.S. Power and the Multinational Corporation* (New York: Basic Books, 1975), pp. 234–35.
11. John Gerard Ruggie, "Embedded Liberalism in The Postwar Order," *International organization*, vol. 36 (1982), p. 382.
12. Barry Buzan, *People, States, and Fear: The National Security Problem in International Relations* (Chapel Hill: University of North Carolina Press, 1983), p. 141.
13. Eugene Staley, *World Economy in Transition* (New York: Council on Foreign Relations, 1939), p. 52.

The Trading State– Then and Now

Richard Rosecrance

The Second World War initially strengthened both the military-political world and the trading world, but the second impetus was more enduring. After most major conflicts in Western history, peacetime brought a respite, a period of consolidation and agreement. This period did not last long after World War I when the victors concentrated on keeping Germany down, economically and militarily. After World War II, a peace of reconciliation was effected with the defeated powers, Germany and Japan, in part because the Cold War with the Soviet Union broke out at its close. As a new enemy emerged, the Western victors effected a rapprochement with the reformed ex-enemy states. The new trading system might have been undermined at the outset as political hostility and the threat of war overshadowed all other events. It was not, because despite the antagonism between Soviet and Western camps neither side wanted another round of war. Both Western Europe and the Soviet Union needed time to rebuild their economies and restore their devastated homelands. On the Western side there was a much greater understanding of the means by which liberal economies with convertible currencies could contribute to the rebuilding process. Part of the pressure for open economies came from the United States, no doubt desirous of extending her export markets. Part was based on conclusions reached in the 1930s that when financial collapse cuts the commercial links between societies, all nations will suffer, and some will move to seize what they cannot acquire through trade. Economic crisis and depression had been the fare that nourished domestic desperation and brought radical and nationalist leaders to power in more than one state. Prosperity, on the other hand, contributed to stable governments and to a more relaxed foreign policy stance.

The 1930s had also witnessed a transformation in domestic politics in a series of states. The Great Depression of 1929–37 convinced both peoples and governments that employment and social welfare were major national responsibilities: they were too important to be left to the private market and the workings of free enterprise. Henceforth governments in democratic countries—indeed in many others—would act to ensure basic levels of social and economic living. They could do this not only through domestic pump-priming or Keynesian deficit financing: the economic outcomes in one country were likely to be affected by policies in other nations. Depression could easily be communicated from America to Europe as had in fact happened in 1929–31. Depression could partly be avoided by holding export markets open to countries in need. But it was even more important to provide the international funds that would temporarily solve their balance of payments deficits. They would then not have to place restrictions upon their own trade or capital movements, restrictions which would hurt other nations. "Exporting one's unemployment" was a recipe for disaster for the developed world, and it could be avoided by mutual agreement.

The creation of the International Monetary Fund at Bretton Woods in 1944 was a giant step toward a trading system of international relations. The new regime called for an open world economy with low tariffs and strictly limited depreciation of currencies. Tariff hikes and competitive devaluation of currencies were to be restricted by the General Agreement on Tariffs and Trade (GATT) and by the Fund. Unlike the situation after World War I, nations were to be persuaded not to institute controls by offering them liquid funds to float over any period of imbalance in international payments. They would then have a grace period to get their economies in order, after which they could repay the loans.

The plethora of small nations created after the war by the decolonization process in Africa, Asia, the Middle East, and Oceania were generally not large or strong enough to rely on domestic resources, industry, agriculture, and markets for all their needs. Unless they could trade, they could not live. This meant that the markets of the major Western and industrial economies had to take their exports and they in return would need manufacturing exports from the developed countries. The open international economy was critical to their growth and stability. This is not to say that there were no other factors which supported the independence of new nations in the post-World War II period. Military factors and superpower rivalries made the reconquest of colonial areas very costly; ethnic and cultural differences limited the success of attempts to subdue one country or another. But political and military viability were not enough. Small states could not continue to exist as independent entities unless they could earn an economic livelihood. To some degree economic assistance from developed nations or from multilateral agencies met this need. If tariffs and restrictions had inhibited the trade of new nations, however, they would not have been able to function as independent units.

But the open economy of the trading world did not benefit only small nations. The growth of world trade, which increased faster than gross national product until 1980, attracted larger states as well. As the cost of using force increased and its benefits declined, other means of gaining national welfare had to be found. The Federal Republic of Germany, following Hanseatic precedents, became more dependent on international trade than the old united Germany had been. The United Kingdom, France, Italy, Norway, Switzerland, Germany, Belgium, Holland, and Denmark had imports and exports which equalled 30 percent or more of their gross national product, nearly three times the proportion attained in the United States. Japan's huge economy was fueled by foreign trade, which amounted to 20 percent of her GNP total.

The role of Japan and Germany in the trading world is exceedingly interesting because it represents a reversal of past policies in both the nineteenth century and the 1930s. It is correct to say that the two countries experimented with foreign trade because they had been disabused of military expansion by World War II. For a time they were incapable of fighting war on a major scale; their endorsement of the trading system was merely an adoption of the remaining policy alternative. But that endorsement did not change even when the economic strength of the two nations might have sustained a much more nationalistic and militaristic policy. Given the choice between military expansion to achieve self-sufficiency (a choice made more difficult by modern conventional and nuclear weapons in the hands of other powers) and the procurement of necessary markets and raw materials through international commerce, Japan and Germany chose the latter.

It was not until the nineteenth century that this choice became available. During the mecantilist period (1500–1775) commerce was hobbled by restrictions, and any power that relied on it was at the mercy of the tariffs and imperial expansion of other nations. Until the late eighteenth century internal economic development was slow, and there seemed few means of adding to national wealth and power except by conquering territories which contained more peasants and grain. With the Industrial Revolution the link between territory and power was broken; it then became possible to gain economic strength without conquering new lands.[1] New sources of power could be developed within a society, simply by mobilizing them industrially. When combined with peaceful international trade, the Industrial Revolution allowed manufactured goods to find markets in faraway countries. The extra demand would lengthen production runs and increase both industrial efficiency (through economies of scale) and financial return. Such a strategy, if adhered to by all nations, could put an end to war. There was no sense in using military force to acquire power and wealth when they could be obtained more efficiently through peaceful economic development and trade.

The increasing prevalence of the trading option since 1945 raises peaceful possibilities that were neglected during the late nineteenth century and the 1930s. It seems safe to say that an international system composed of more than 160 states cannot continute to exist unless trade remains the primary vocation of most of its members. Were military and territorial orientations to dominate the scene, the trend to greater numbers of smaller states would be reversed, and larger states would conquer small and weak nations.

The possibility of such amalgamations cannot be entirely ruled out. Industrialization had two possible impacts: it allowed a nation to develop its wealth peacefully through internal economic growth, but it also knit new sinews of strength that could coerce other states. Industrialization made territorial expansion easier but also less necessary. In the mid-nineteenth century the Continental states pursued the expansion of their territories while Britain expanded her industry. The industrialization of Prussia and the development of her rail network enabled her armies to defeat Denmark, Austria, and France. Russia also used her new industrial technology to strengthen her military. In the last quarter of the century, even Britain returned to a parimarily military and imperialist policy. In his book on imperialism Lenin declared that the drive for colonies was an imminent tendency of the capitalist system. Raw materials would run short and investment capital would pile up at home. The remedy was imperialism with colonies providing new sources for the former and outlets for the latter. But Lenin did not fully understand that an open international economy and intensive economic development at home obviated the need for colonies even under a capitalist, trading system.

The basic effect of World War II was to create much higher world interdependence as the average size of countries declined. The reversal of past trends toward a consolidation of states created instead a multitude of states that could not depend on themselves alone. They needed ties with other nations to prosper and remain viable as small entities. The trading system, as a result, was visible in defense relations as well as international commerce. Nations that could not stand on their own sought alliances or assistance from other powers, and they offered special defense contributions in fighting contingents, regional experience, or particular types of defense hardware. Dutch electronics, French aircraft, German guns and tanks, and British ships all made their independent contribution to an alliance in which no single power might be able to meet its defense needs on a self-sufficient basis. Israel developed a powerful and efficient small arms industry, as well as a great fund of experience combating terrorism. Israeli intelligence added considerably to the information available from Western sources, partly because of its understanding of Soviet weapons systems accumulated in several Arab-Israeli wars.

Defense interdependencies, however, are only one means of sharing the burdens placed upon the modern state. Perhaps more important is economic interdependence among countries. One should not place too much emphasis upon the existence of interdependence per se. European nations in 1913 relied upon the trade and investment that flowed between them; that did not prevent the political crisis which led to a breakdown of the international system and to World War I. Interdependence only constrains national policy if leaders accept and agree to work within its limits. In 1914 Lloyds of London had insured the German merchant marine but that did not stop Germany attacking Belgium, a neutral nation, or England from joining the war against Berlin.[2] The United States was Japan's best customer and source of raw materials in the 1930s, but that did not deter the Japanese attack on Pearl Harbor.

At least among the developed and liberal countries, interdependent ties since 1945 have come to be accepted as a fundamental and unchangeable feature of the situation. This recognition dawned gradually, and the United States may perhaps have been the last to acknowledge it, which was not surprising.

The most powerful economy is ready to make fewer adjustments, and America tried initially to pursue its domestic economic policies without taking into account the effect on others, on itself, and on the international financial system as a whole. Presidents Kennedy and Lyndon B. Johnson tried to detach American domestic growth strategies from the deteriorating United States balance of payments, but they left a legacy of needed economic change to their successors. Finally, in the 1980s two American administrations accepted lower United States growth in order to control inflation and began to focus on the international impact of United States policies. The delay in fashioning a strategy of adjustment to international economic realities almost certainly made it more difficult. Smaller countries actively sought to find a niche in the structure of international comparative advantage and in the demand for their goods. Larger countries with large internal markets postponed that reckoning as long as they could. By the 1980s, however, such change could no longer be avoided, and United States leaders embarked upon new industrial and tax policies designed to increase economic growth and enable America to compete more effectively abroad.

The acceptance of new approaches was a reflection of the decline in economic sovereignty. As long as governments could control all the forces impinging upon their economies, welfare states would have no difficulty in implementing domestic planning for social ends. But as trade, investment, corporations, and to some degree labor moved from one national jurisdiction to another, no government could insulate and direct its economy without instituting the extreme protectionist and "beggar thy neighbor" policies of the 1930s. Rather than do this, the flow of goods and capital was allowed to proceed, and in recent years it has become a torrent. In some cases the flow of capital has increased to compensate for barriers or rigidities to the movement of goods.

In both cases the outcome is the result of modern developments in transportation and communications. Railway and high-speed highway networks now allow previously landlocked areas to participate in the international trading network that once depended on rivers and access to the sea. Modern communications and computers allow funds to be instantaneously transferred from one market to another, so that they may earn interest twenty-four hours a day. Transportation costs for a variety of goods have reached a new low, owing to container shipping and handling. For the major industrial countries, (member countries of the Organization for Economic Cooperation and Development, which include the European community, Austria, Finland, Iceland, Portugal, Norway, Spain, Sweden, Switzerland, Turkey, Australia, Canada, Japan, New Zealand, and the United States) exports have risen much faster than either industrial production or gross domestic product since 1965, with the growth of GDP (in constant prices) at 4 percent and that of exports at 7.7 percent.[3] Only Japan's domestic growth has been able to keep pace with the increase in exports (see Table 1).

Foreign trade (the sum of exports and imports) percentages were roughly twice as large as these figures in each case. The explosion of foreign trade since 1945 has, if anything, been exceeded by the enormous movement of capital.

Table 1   EXPORTS OF GOODS AND SERVICES (as a Percentage of GDP)

Country	1965	1979
United States	5	9
Japan	11	12
Germany	18	26
United Kingdom	20	29
France	14	22

Source: Michael Stewart, *The Age of Interdependence* (Cambridge, Mass.: MIT Press, 1981), p. 21 (derived from United Nations *Yearbook of National Accounts Statistics,* 1980, vol. 2, table 2A).

In 1950 the value of the stock of direct foreign investment held by U.S. companies was $11.8 billions, compared with $7.2 billions in 1935, $7.6 billions in 1929 and $3.9 billions in 1914. In the following decade, these investments increased by $22.4 billions, and at the end of 1967 their total value stood at $59 billions.[4]

In 1983, it had reached $226 billions.[5] And direct investment (that portion of investment which buys a significant stake in a foreign firm) was only one part of total United States investment overseas. In 1983 United States private assets abroad totaled $774 billion, or about three times as much.

The amounts, although very large, were not significant in themselves. In 1913, England's foreign investments, equaled one and one-half times her GNP as compared to present American totals of one-quarter of United States GNP. England's foreign trade was more than 40 percent of her national income as compared with contemporary American totals of 15–17 percent. England's pre-World War I involvement in international economic activities was greater than America's today.

Part of what must be explained in the evolution of interdependence is not the high level reached post-1945, but how even higher levels in 1913 could have fallen in the interim. Here the role of industrialization is paramount. As Karl Deutsch, following the work of Werner Sombart, has shown, in the early stages of industrial growth nations must import much of their needed machinery: rail and transportation networks are constructed with equipment and materials from abroad. Once new industries have been created, in a variety of fields, ranging from textiles to heavy industry, the national economy can begin to provide the goods that previously were imported.[6] The United States, the Scandinavian countries, and Japan reached this stage only after the turn of the century, and it was then that the gasoline-powered automobile industry and the manufacturing of electric motors and appliances began to develop rapidly and flourish. The further refinement of agricultural technology also rested on these innovations. Thus, even without restrictions and disruptions of trade, the 1920s would not have seen a rehabilitation of the old interdependent world economy of the 1890s. The further barriers erected in the 1930s confirmed and extended this outcome. If new industrial countries had less need for manufacturing imports, the growth and maintenance of general trade would then come to depend upon an increase in some other category of commerce than the traditional exchange of raw materials for finished goods. In the 1920s, as Albert Hirschman shows, the reciprocal exchange of industrial goods increased briefly, but fell again in the 1930s.[7] That decrease was only made up after 1945 when there was a striking and continuing growth in the trade of manufactured goods among industrial countries.[8] Some will say that this trade is distinctly expendable because countries could produce the goods they import on their own. None of the trade that the United States has today with Western Europe or Japan could really be dubbed "critical" in that the United States could not get along without it. American alternatives exist to almost all industrial products from other developed economies. Thus if interdependence means a trading link which "is costly to break,"[9] there is a sense that the sheer physical dependence of one country upon another, or upon international trade as a whole, has declined since the nineteenth century.

But to measure interdependence in this way misses the essence of the concept. Individuals in a state of nature can be quite independent if they are willing to live at a low standard of living and gather herbs, nuts, and fruits. They are not forced to depend on others but decide to do so to increase their total amount of food and security. Countries in an international state of nature (anarchy) can equally decide to depend only on themselves. They can limit what they consume to what they can produce at home, but they will thereby live less well than they might with specialization and extensive trade and interchange with other nations.

There is no shortage of energy in the world, for example, and all energy needs that previously have been satisfied by imported petroleum might be met by a great increase in coal and natural gas production, fission, and hydropower. But coal-generated electric power produces acid rain, and coal liquification (to procude fuel for automobiles) is expensive. Nuclear power leaves radioactive wastes which have to be contained. Importing oil is a cheaper and cleaner alternative. Thus even though a particular country, like the United States, might become energy self-sufficient if it wanted to, there is reason for dependence on the energy supplies of other nations. Does this mean creating a "tie that is costly to break"? Yes, in the sense that we live less well if we break the tie; but that doesn't mean that the tie could not be broken. Any tie can be broken. In this respect, all ties create "vulnerability interdependence" if they are in the interest of those who form them. One could get along without Japanese cars or European fashions, but eliminating them from the market restricts consumer choice and in fact raises opportunity costs. In this manner, trade between industrial countries may be equally important as trade linking industrial and raw material producing countries.

There are other ways in which interdependence has increased since the nineteenth century. Precisely because industrial countries imported agricultural commodities and sold their manufactured goods to less developed states, their dependence upon each other was much less in the nineteenth century and the 1920s than it is today. Toward the end of the nineteenth century Britain increasingly came to depend upon her empire for markets, food, and raw

materials or upon countries in the early stages of industrialization. As Conti-
nential tariffs increased, Britain turned to her colonies, the United States, and
Latin America to find markets for her exports. These markets provided

> ready receptacles for British goods when other areas became too competitive or
> unattractive; for example, Australia, India, Brazil and Argentina took the cotton,
> railways, steel and machinery that could not be sold in European markets. In the
> same way, whilst British capital exports to the latter dropped from 52 percent in
> the 1860s to 25 percent in the few years before 1914, those to the empire rose
> from 36 percent to 46 percent, and those to Latin America from 10.5 percent to 22
> percent.[10]

The British foreign trade which totalled 43.5 percent of GNP in 1913 went
increasingly to the empire; thus, if one takes Britain and the colonies as a single
economic unit, that unit was much less dependent upon the outside world than,
say, Britain is today with a smaller (30.4 percent) ratio of trade to GNP. And
Britain alone had much less stake in Germany, France, and the Continental
countries' economies than she does today as a member of the European Common Market.

In the nineteenth century trade was primarily vertical in character, taking
place between countries at different stages of industrial development, and involving an exchange of manufactured goods on the one hand for food and raw materials on the other. But trade was not the only element in vertical interdependence.

British investment was also vertical in that it proceeded from the developed
center, London, to less developed capitals in the Western Hemisphere, Oceania, and the Far East. Such ties might contribute to community feeling in the
British Empire, later the Commonwealth of Nations, but it would not restrain
conflicts among the countries of Western Europe. Three-quarters of foreign
investment of all European countries in 1914 was lodged outside of Europe. In
1913, in the British case 66 percent of her foreign investment went to North and
South America and Australia, 28 percent to the Middle and Far East, and only 6
percent to Europe.

In addition, about 90 percent of foreign investment in 1913 was portfolio
investment, that is, it represented small holdings of foreign shares that could
easily be disposed of on the stock exchange. Direct investment, or investment
which represented more than a 10 percent share of the total ownership of a
foreign firm was only one-tenth of the total. Today the corresponding figure for
the United States is nearly 30 percent. The growth of direct foreign investment
since 1945 is a reflection of the greater stake that countries have in each other's
well-being in the contemporary period.

In this respect international interdependence has been fostered by a growing interpenetration of economies, in the sense that one economy owns part of
another, sends part of its population to live and work in it, and becomes increasingly dependent upon the progress of the latter.[11] The multinational corporation
which originates in one national jurisdiction, but operates in others as well, is
the primary vehicle for such investment ownership. Stimulated by the demands
and incentives of the product life cycle, the multinational corporation invests

and produces abroad to make sure of retaining its market share. That market may be in the host country, or it may be in the home country, once the foreign production is imported back into the home economy. Foreign trade has grown enormously since 1945. But its necessary growth has been reduced by the operation of multinational companies in foreign jurisdictions: production abroad reduces the need for exports. In this way an interpenetrative stake has increased between developed economies even when tariffs and other restrictions might appear to have stunted the growth of exports. The application of a common external tariff to the European Economic Community in the 1960s greatly stimulated American foreign investment in Europe, which became such a massive tide that Europeans reacted against the "American challenge," worrying that their prized national economic assets might be preempted by the United States.

They need not have worried. The reverse flow of European and Japanese investment in the United States is reaching such enormous proportions that America has become a net debtor nation: A country that has fewer assets overseas than foreigners have in the United States. The threatened imposition of higher American tariffs and quotas on imports led foreign companies to invest in the United States in gigantic amounts, thereby obviating the need to send exports from their home nation. Such direct investment represents a much more permanent stake in the economic welfare of the host nation than exports to that market could ever be. Foreign production is a more permanent economic commitment than foreign sales, because large shares of a foreign company or subsidiary could not be sold on a stock exchange. The attempt to market such large holdings would only have the effect of depressing the value of the stock. Direct investment is thus illiquid, as opposed to the traditional portfolio investment of the nineteenth century.

After 1945 one country slowly developed a stake in another, but the process was not initially reciprocal. Until the beginning of the 1970s, the trend was largely for Americans to invest abroad, in Europe, Latin America, and East Asia. As the American dollar cheapened after 1973, however, a reverse flow began, with Europeans and Japanese placing large blocs of capital in American firms and acquiring international companies. Third World multinationals, from Hong Kong, the OPEC countries, and East Asia also began to invest in the United States. By the end of the 1970s world investment was much more balanced, with the European stake in the American economy nearly offsetting the American investment in Europe. Japan also moved to diversify her export offensive in the American market by starting to produce in the United States. But Japan did not benefit from a reciprocal stake in her own economy. Since foreign investors have either been kept out of the Japanese market or have been forced to accept cumbersome joint ventures with Japanese firms, few multinationals have a major commitment to the Japanese market. Japan imports the smallest percentage of manufactured goods of any leading industrial nation. Thus when economic policy makers in America and Europe formulate growth strategies, they are not forced to consider the Japanese economy on a par with their own because Americans and Europeans have little to lose if Japan does not prosper. In her own self-interest Japan will almost certainly have to open her capital market and economy to foreign penetration if she wishes to enjoy corresponding access to economies of other nations. Greater Japanese foreign direct investment will only partly mitigate the pressures on Tokyo in this respect.

It is nonetheless true that interpenetration of investment in industrial economies provides a mutual stake in each other's success that did not exist in the nineteenth century or before World War I. Then Germany cared little if France progressed and the only important loan or investment stake between major powers was that between France and Russia, a factor that could hardly restrain conflict in 1914. It is very important at the moment that the Arab oil countries have substantial investments in Europe and North America because their profitability will be influenced by changes in the oil price. Too high oil prices, throwing the industrial West into depression, would have the effect of cutting returns on Arab overseas investments. It would therefore restrain OPEC from precipitate price increases. American business interests with a large stake in Europe would hardly encourage their government to take steps to export American unemployment to other industrial economies for this would only depress their own holdings abroad. A recognition of the degree to which all industrial economies are in the same boat has led to a series of economic summit meetings of seven developed nations in hopes that policies of multilateral growth could be agreed upon to benefit all. These have not solved economic problems, but they have contributed to much greater understanding of the difficulties and policies of other states and perhaps to a greater tolerance for them.

Between the developed countries and the Third World, energy and mineral interdependence fostered a more equal relationship (see Table 2). Australia was the leading producer of bauxite and a huge provider of iron ore in 1982. South Africa was an important source of manganese. Otherwise many of the world's minerals were found in developing nations like Zimbabwe (chromium), Zaire (cobalt), Malaysia (tin), Guinea and Jamaica (bauxite), Zambia (cobalt), Brazil and India (iron ore), and Gabon (manganese). Indian production of iron ore exceeds that of the United States, and Brazilian output is nearly three times as much as America's. In 1982 the twenty-four OECD countries imported eighteen million barrels of oil per day from the OPEC countries and Mexico. Only the United Kingdom and Norway, among Western industrial countries, were virtually self-sufficient in oil supplies. In this way the Third World obtained a considerable leverage in Western industrial economies, and they were bound to obtain more as industrial dependence on imported minerals and oil increased with time.

Yet the great dependence of industrial economies upon each other for markets and the need for Third World minerals and oil would not produce political interdependence between countries in all circumstances. If governments were committed to reducing or eliminating their interdependence with others, the network of economic ties could actually be a factor for conflict. One of the fundamental differences between the Western and democratic industrial countries in 1914 and today—was the lack of commitment to maintain the

Table 2 DEPENDENCE ON FOREIGN MINERALS (50 Percent or More)

Country/region	Bauxite	Copper	Nickel	Zinc	Tin	Cobalt	Iron ore	Manganese	Chromium
United States	X	—	X	X	X	X	—	X	X
Japan	X	X	X	X	X	X	X	X	X
European Economic Community	X	X	X	X	X	X	X	X	X

Source: Directorate of Intelligence, *Handbook of Economic Statistics*, 1983 (Washington, D.C., Sept. 1983), p. 13.

structure of international economic relations prior to World War I. War between such economies was accepted as a natural outcome of the balance of power system. No pre-1914 statesman or financier was fully aware of the damage that war would do to the European body economic because of the belief that it would be over very quickly. Few bankers or finance ministers interceded with their foreign office brethren to seek to reduce the probability of war.

But the economic interdependence of 1913 had little restraining effect in another respect. Depression and economic disturbances were believed to be natural events like earthquakes and floods; they were not expected to be mediated by governmental intercession or economic policy. It was not until the 1930s that one of the chief functions of the modern democratic state became the achievement of domestic welfare with full employment and an avoidance of inflation. Because it was not the business of government in 1914 to prevent economic disruption and dislocation, little effort was made to minimize the effect of a prolonged war upon society, and no effort to prevent war altogether. Between Western industrial countries and Japan today, war is virtually unthinkable. Even if economic interdependence was lower after 1945 than it had been in 1913 (and this is not the case), the political significance of interdependence is still much greater today. Governments in the present era cannot achieve the objectives of high employment without inflation except by working together.

NOTES

1. It is true that the greatest imperial edifices were constructed after the start of the Industrial Revolution. It was precisely that revolution, however, which prepared the groundwork for their demise.
2. Paul Kennedy, *Strategy and Diplomacy 1870–1945* (London: Fontana Paperbacks 1984), pp. 95-96.
3. Michael Stewart, *The Age of Interdependence* (Cambridge, Mass.: MIT Press, 1984), p. 20.
4. John H. Dunning, *Studies in International Investment* (London: George Allen and Unwin, 1970), p. 1.
5. "International Investment Position of the United States at Year End" in *Survey of Current Business* (Washington, D.C.: Department of Commerce, June 1984).
6. Karl W. Deutsch and Alexander Eckstein, "National Industrialization and the Declining Share of the International Economic Sector, 1890–1959" in *World Politics,* 13 (January 1961), pp. 267–99.
7. *National Power and the Structure of Foreign Trade* (Berkeley: University of California Press, 1980), pp. 129–43.
8. Richard Rosecrance and Arthur Stein, "Interdependence: Myth or Reality" in *World Politics* (July 1973), pp. 7–8.
9. Kenneth Waltz, "The Myth of National Interdependence" in Charles Kindleberger, ed., *The International Corporation* (Cambridge, Mass.: MIT Press, 1970), p. 206.
10. Paul Kennedy, *The Rise and Fall of British Naval Mastery* (London: Allen Lace, 1976), pp. 187–88.

11. Nothing could be more misleading than to equate these interrelations with those of nineteenth-century imperialism. The imperial dictates went in one direction—military, economic, and social. The metropole dominated the colony. Today, does North America become a colony when Chicanos and Hispanics move to it in increasing numbers or England a tributary of the West Indies? Does Chinese or Korean investment in the United States render it a peripheral member of the system? The point is that influence goes in both directions just as does investment and trade in manufactured goods.

The Changed World Economy

Peter F. Drucker

The talk today is of the "changing world economy." I wish to argue that the world economy is not "changing"; it has *already changed*—in its foundations and in its structure—and in all probability the change is irreversible.

Within the last decade or so, three fundamental changes have occurred in the very fabric of the world economy:

- The primary-products economy has come "uncoupled" from the industrial economy.
- In the industrial economy itself, production has come "uncoupled" from employment.
- Capital movements rather than trade (in both goods and services) have become the driving force of the world economy. The two have not quite come uncoupled, but the link has become loose, and worse, unpredictable.

These changes are permanent rather than cyclical. We may never understand what caused them—the causes of economic change are rarely simple. It may be a long time before economic theorists accept that there have been fundamental changes, and longer still before they adapt their theories to account for them. Above all, they will surely be most reluctant to accept that it is the world economy in control, rather than the macroeconomics of the nation-state on which most economic theory still exclusively focuses. Yet this is the clear lesson of the success stories of the last 20 years—of Japan and South Korea; of West Germany (actually a more impressive though far less flamboyant example than Japan); and of the one great success within the United States, the turnaround and rapid rise of an industrial New England, which only 20 years ago was widely considered moribund.

Practitioners, whether in government or in business, cannot wait until

From "The Changed World Economy" by Peter F. Drucker, from *Foreign Affairs* (Spring 1986). Copyright © 1986 by the Council on Foreign Relations, Inc. Reprinted by permission of *Foreign Affairs*, (Spring 1986). Portions of the text and some footnotes have been omitted.

there is a new theory. They have to act. And their actions will be more likely to succeed the more they are based on the new realities of a changed world economy.

First, consider the primary-products economy. The collapse of non-oil commodity prices began in 1977 and has continued, interrupted only once (right after the 1979 petroleum panic), by a speculative burst that lasted less than six months; it was followed by the fastest drop in commodity prices ever registered. By early 1986 raw material prices were at their lowest levels in recorded history in relation to the prices of manufactured goods and services—in general as low as at the depths of the Great Depression, and in some cases (e.g., lead and copper) lower than their 1932 levels.[1]

This collapse of prices and the slowdown of demand stand in startling contrast to what had been confidently predicted. Ten years ago the Club of Rome declared that desperate shortages for *all* raw materials were an absolute certainty by the year 1985. In 1980 the Carter Administration's *Global 2000 Report to the President: Entering the Twenty-First Century* concluded that world demand for food would increase steadily for at least 20 years; that worldwide food production would fall except in developed countries; and that real food prices would double. This forecast helps to explain why American farmers bought up all available farmland, thus loading on themselves the debt burden that now so threatens them.

Contrary to all these expectations, global agricultural output actually rose almost one-third between 1972 and 1985 to reach an all-time high. It rose the fastest in less-developed countries. Similarly, production of practically all forest products, metals and minerals has gone up between 20 and 35 percent in the last ten years—again with the greatest increases in less-developed countries. There is not the slightest reason to believe that the growth rates will slacken, despite the collapse of commodity prices. Indeed, as far as farm products are concerned, the biggest increase—at an almost exponential rate of growth—may still be ahead.[2]

Perhaps even more amazing than the contrast between such predictions and what has happened is that the collapse in the raw materials economy seems to have had almost no impact on the world industrial economy. If there was one thing considered "proven" beyond doubt in business cycle theory, it is that a sharp and prolonged drop in raw material prices inevitably, and within 18 to 30 months, brings on a worldwide depression in the industrial economy.[3] While the industrial economy of the world today is not "normal" by any definition of the term, it is surely not in a depression. Indeed, industrial production in the developed non-communist countries has continued to grow steadily, albeit at a somewhat slower rate in Western Europe.

Of course, a depression in the industrial economy may only have been postponed and may still be triggered by a banking crisis caused by massive defaults on the part of commodity-producing debtors, whether in the Third World or in Iowa. But for almost ten years the industrial world has run along as though there were no raw material crisis at all. The only explanation is that for the developed countries—excepting only the Soviet Union—the primary-products sector has become marginal where before it had always been central.

In the late 1920s, before the Great Depression, farmers still constituted nearly one-third of the U.S. population and farm income accounted for almost a quarter of the gross national product. Today they account for less than 5 percent of population and even less of GNP. Even adding the contribution that foreign raw material and farm producers make to the American economy through their purchases of American industrial goods, the total contribution of the raw material and food producing economies of the world to the American GNP is, at most, one-eighth. In most other developed countries, the share of the raw materials sector is even lower. Only in the Soviet Union is the farm still a major employer, with almost a quarter of the labor force working on the land.

The raw material economy has thus come uncoupled from the industrial economy. This is a major structural change in the world economy, with tremendous implications for economic and social policy as well as economic theory, in developed and developing countries alike.

For example, if the ratio between the prices of manufactured goods and the prices of non-oil primary products (that is, foods, forest products, metals and minerals) had been the same in 1985 as it had been in 1973, the 1985 U.S. trade deficit might have been a full one-third less—$100 billion as against an actual $150 billion. Even the U.S. trade deficit with Japan might have been almost one-third lower, some $35 billion as against $50 billion. American farm exports would have bought almost twice as much. And industrial exports to a major U.S. customer, Latin America, would have held; their near-collapse alone accounts for a full one-sixth of the deterioration in the U.S. foreign trade over the past five years. If primary-product prices had not collapsed, America's balance of payments might even have shown a substantial surplus.

Conversely, Japan's trade surplus with the world might have been a full 20 percent lower. And Brazil in the last few years would have had an export surplus almost 50 percent higher than its current level. Brazil would then have had little difficulty meeting the interest on its foreign debt and would not have had to endanger its economic growth by drastically curtailing imports as it did. Altogether, if raw material prices in relationship to manufactured goods prices had remained at the 1973 or even the 1979 level, there would be no crisis for most debtor countries, especially in Latin America.[4]

What accounts for this change?

Demand for food has actually grown almost as fast as the Club of Rome and the *Global 2000 Report* anticipated. But the supply has grown much faster; it not only has kept pace with population growth, it has steadily outrun it. One cause of this, paradoxically, is surely the fear of worldwide food shortages, if not world famine, which resulted in tremendous efforts to increase food output. The United States led the parade with a farm policy of subsidizing increased food production. The European Economic Community followed suit, and even more successfully. The greatest increases, both in absolute and in relative terms, however, have been in developing countries: in India, in post-Mao China and in the rice-growing countries of Southeast Asia.

And there is also the tremendous cut in waste. In the 1950s, up to 80 percent of the grain harvest of India fed rats and insects rather than human beings. Today in most parts of India the wastage is down to 20 percent. This is largely the result of unspectacular but effective "infrastructure innovations" such as small concrete storage bins, insecticides and three-wheeled motorized carts that take the harvest straight to a processing plant instead of letting it sit in the open for weeks.

It is not fanciful to expect that the true "revolution" on the farm is still ahead. Vast tracts of land that hitherto were practically barren are being made fertile, either through new methods of cultivation or through adding trace minerals to the soil. The sour clays of the Brazilian highlands or the aluminum-contaminated soils of neighboring Peru, for example, which never produced anything before, now produce substantial quantities of high-quality rice. Even greater advances have been registered in biotechnology, both in preventing diseases of plants and animals and in increasing yields.

In other words, just as the population growth of the world is slowing down quite dramatically in many regions, food production is likely to increase sharply.

Import markets for food have all but disappeared. As a result of its agricultural drive, Western Europe has become a substantial food exporter plagued increasingly by unsalable surpluses of all kinds of foods, from dairy products to wine, from wheat to beef. China, some observers predict, will have become a food exporter by the year 2000. India is about at that stage, especially with wheat and coarse grains. Of all major non-communist countries only Japan is still a substantial food importer, buying abroad about one-third of its food needs. Today most of this comes from the United States. Within five or ten years, however, South Korea, Thailand and Indonesia—low-cost producers that are fast increasing food output—are likely to try to become Japan's major suppliers.

The only remaining major food buyer on the world market may then be the Soviet Union—and its food needs are likely to grow.[5] However, the food surpluses in the world are so large—maybe five to eight times what the Soviet Union would ever need to buy—that its food needs are not by themselves enough to put upward pressure on world prices. On the contrary, the competition for access to the Soviet market among the surplus producers—the United States, Europe, Argentina, Australia, New Zealand (and probably India within a few years)—is already so intense as to depress world food prices.

For practically all non-farm commodities, whether forest products, minerals or metals, world demand is shrinking—in sharp contrast to what the Club of Rome so confidently predicted. Indeed, the amount of raw material needed for a given unit of economic output has been dropping for the entire century, except in wartime. A recent study by the International Monetary Fund calculates the decline as one and one-quarter percent a year (compounded) since 1900.[6] This would mean that the amount of industrial raw materials needed for one unit of industrial production is now no more than two-fifths of what is was in 1900. And the decline is accelerating. The Japanese experience is particularly striking. In 1984, for every unit of industrial production, Japan consumed only 60 percent of the raw materials consumed for the same volume of industrial production in 1973, 11 years earlier.

Why this decline in demand? It is not that industrial production is fading in importance as the service sector grows—a common myth for which there is not the slightest evidence. What is happening is much more significant. Industrial production is steadily switching away from heavily material-intensive products and processes. One of the reasons for this is the new high-technology industries. The raw materials in a semiconductor microchip account for 1 to 3 percent of total production cost; in an automobile their share is 40 percent, and in pots and pans 60 percent. But also in older industries the same scaling down of raw material needs goes on, and with respect to old products as well as new ones. Fifty to 100 pounds of fiberglass cable transmit as many telephone messages as does one ton of copper wire.

This steady drop in the raw material intensity of manufacturing processes and manufacturing products extends to energy as well, and especially to petroleum. To produce 100 pounds of fiberglass cable requires no more than 5 percent of the energy needed to produce one ton of copper wire. Similarly, plastics, which are increasingly replacing steel in automobile bodies, represent a raw material cost, including energy, of less than half that of steel.

Thus it is quite unlikely that raw material prices will ever rise substantially as compared to the prices of manufactured goods (or high-knowledge services such as information, education or health care) except in the event of a major prolonged war.

One implication of this sharp shift in the terms of trade of primary products concerns the developed countries, both major raw material exporters like the United States and major raw material importing countries such as Japan. For two centuries the United States has made maintenance of open markets for its farm products and raw materials central to its international trade policy. This is what it has always meant by an "open world economy" and by "free trade."

Does this still make sense, or does the United States instead have to accept that foreign markets for its foodstuffs and raw materials are in a long-term and irreversible decline? Conversely, does it still make sense for Japan to base its international economic policy on the need to earn enough foreign exchange to pay for imports of raw materials and foodstuffs? Since Japan opened to the outside world 120 years ago, preoccupation—amounting almost to a national obsession—with its dependence on raw material and food imports has been the driving force of Japan's policy, and not in economics alone. Now Japan might well start out with the assumption—a far more realistic one in today's world—that foodstuffs and raw materials are in permanent oversupply.

Taken to their logical conclusion, these developments might mean that some variant of the traditional Japanese policy—highly mercantilist with a strong de-emphasis of domestic consumption in favor of an equally strong emphasis on capital formation, and protection of infant industries—might suit the United States better than its own tradition. The Japanese might be better served by some variant of America's traditional policies, especially a shifting from favoring savings and capital formation to favoring consumption. Is such a radical break with more than a century of political convictions and commitments likely? From now on the fundamentals of economic policy are certain to come under increasing criticism in these two countries—and in all other developed countries as well.

These fundamentals will, moreover, come under the increasingly intense scrutiny of major Third World nations. For if primary products are becoming of marginal importance to the economies of the developed world, traditional development theories and policies are losing their foundations.[7] They are based on the assumption—historically a perfectly valid one—that developing countries pay for imports of capital goods by exporting primary materials—farm and forest products, minerals, metals. All development theories, however much they differ otherwise, further assume that raw material purchases by the industrially developed countries must rise at least as fast as industrial production in these countries. This in turn implies that, over any extended period of time, any raw material producer becomes a better credit risk and shows a more favorable balance of trade. These premises have become highly doubtful. On what foundation, then, can economic development be based, especially in countries that do not have a large enough population to develop an industrial economy based on the home market? As we shall presently see, these countries can no longer base their economic development on low labor costs.

The second major change in the world economy is the uncoupling of manufacturing production from manufacturing employment. Increased manufacturing production in developed countries has actually come to mean *decreasing* blue-collar employment. As a consequence, labor costs are becoming less and less important as a "comparative cost" and as a factor in competition.

There is a great deal of talk these days about the "de-industrialization" of America. In fact, manufacturing production has risen steadily in absolute volume and has remained unchanged as a percentage of the total economy. Since the end of the Korean War, that is, for more than 30 years, it has held steady at 23–24 percent of America's total GNP. It has similarly remained at its traditional level in all of the other major industrial countries.

It is not even true that American industry is doing poorly as an exporter. To be sure, the United States is importing from both Japan and Germany many more manufactured goods than even before. But it is also exporting more, despite the heavy disadvantages of an expensive dollar, increasing labor costs and the near-collapse of a major industrial market, Latin America. In 1984—the year the dollar soared—exports of American manufactured goods rose by 8.3 percent; and they went up again in 1985. The share of U.S.-manufactured exports in world exports was 17 percent in 1978. By 1985 it had risen to 20 percent—while West Germany accounted for 18 percent and Japan 16. The three countries together thus account for more than half of the total.

Thus it is not the American economy that is being "de-industrialized." It is the American labor force.

Between 1973 and 1985, manufacturing production (measured in constant dollars) in the United States rose by almost 40 percent. Yet manufacturing employment during that period went down steadily. There are now five million fewer people employed in blue-collar work in American manufacturing industry than there were in 1975.

Yet in the last 12 years total employment in the United States grew faster than at any time in the peacetime history of any country—from 82 to 110 million between 1973 and 1985—that is, by a full one-third. The entire growth, however, was in non-manufacturing, and especially in non-blue-collar jobs.

The trend itself is not new. In the 1920s one out of every three Americans in the labor force was a blue-collar worker in manufacturing. In the 1950s the figure was one in four. It now is down to one in every six—and dropping. While the trend has been running for a long time, it has lately accelerated to the point where—in peacetime at least—no increase in manufacturing production, no matter how large, is likely to reverse the long-term decline in the number of blue-collar jobs in manufacturing or in their proportion of the labor force.

This trend is the same in all developed countries, and is, indeed, even more pronounced in Japan. It is therefore highly probable that in 25 years developed countries such as the United States and Japan will employ no larger a proportion of the labor force in manufacturing than developed countries now employ in farming—at most, 10 percent. Today the United States employs around 18 million people in blue-collar jobs in manufacturing industries. By 2010, the number is likely to be no more than 12 million. In some major industries the drop will be even sharper. It is quite unrealistic, for instance, to expect that the American automobile industry will employ more than one-third of its present blue-collar force 25 years hence, even though production might be 50 percent higher.

If a company, an industry or a country does not in the next quarter century sharply increase manufacturing production and at the same time sharply reduce the blue-collar work force, it cannot hope to remain competitive—or even to remain "developed." It would decline fairly fast. Britain has been in industrial decline for the last 25 years, largely because the number of blue-collar workers per unit manufacturing production went down far more slowly than in all other non-communist developed countries. Even so, Britain has the highest unemployment rate among non-communist developed countries—more than 13 percent.

The British example indicates a new and critical economic equation: a country, an industry or a company that puts the preservation of blue-collar manufacturing jobs ahead of international competitiveness (which implies a steady shrinkage of such jobs) will soon have neither production nor jobs. The attempt to preserve such blue-collar jobs is actually a prescription for unemployment.

So far, this concept has achieved broad national acceptance only in Japan.[8] Indeed, Japanese planners, whether in government or private business, start out with the assumption of a doubling of production within 15 to 20 years based on a cut in blue-collar employment of 25 to 40 percent. A good many large American companies such as IBM, General Electric and the big automobile companies have similar forecasts. Implicit in this is the conclusion that a country will have less overall unemployment the faster it shrinks blue-collar employment in manufacturing.

This is not a conclusion that American politicians, labor leaders or indeed the general public can easily understand or accept. What confuses the issue even more is that the United States is experiencing several separate and different shifts in the manufacturing economy. One is the acceleration of the substitution of knowledge and capital for manual labor. Where we spoke of mechanization a few decades ago, we now speak of "robotization" or "automation." This is actually more a change in terminology than a change in reality. When Henry Ford introduced the assembly line in 1909, he cut the number of man-hours required to produce a motor car by some 80 percent in two or three years—far more than anyone expects to result from even the most complete robotization. But there is no doubt that we are facing a new, sharp acceleration in the replacement of manual workers by machines—that is, by the products of knowledge.

A second development—and in the long run this may be even more important—is the shift from industries that were primarily labor-intensive to industries that, from the beginning, are knowledge-intensive. The manufacturing costs of the semiconductor microchip are about 70 percent knowledge—that is, research, development and testing—and no more than 12 percent labor. Similarly with prescription drugs, labor represents no more than 15 percent, with knowledge representing almost 50 percent. By contrast, in the most fully robotized automobile plant labor would still account for 20 to 25 percent of the costs.

Another perplexing development in manufacturing is the reversal of the dynamics of size. Since the early years of this century, the trend in all developed countries has been toward ever larger manufacturing plants. The economies of scale greatly favored them. Perhaps equally important, what one might call the "economies of management" favored them. Until recently, modern management techniques seemed applicable only to fairly large units.

This has been reversed with a vengeance over the last 15 to 20 years. The entire shrinkage in manufacturing jobs in the United States has occured in large companies, beginning with the giants in steel and automobiles. Small and especially medium-sized manufacturers have either held their own or actually added employees. In respect to market standing, exports and profitability too, smaller and middle-sized businesses have done remarkably better than big ones. The reversal of the dynamics of size is occurring in the other developed countries as well, even in Japan where bigger was always better and biggest meant best. The trend has reversed itself even in old industries. The most profitable automobile company these last years has not been one of the giants, but a medium-sized manufacturer in Germany—BMW. The only profitable steel companies, whether in the United States, Sweden or Japan, have been medium-sized makers of specialty products such as oil drilling pipe.

In part, especially in the United States, this is a result of a resurgence of entrepreneurship.[9] But perhaps equally important, we have learned in the last 30 years how to manage the small and medium-sized enterprise to the point where the advantages of smaller size, e.g., ease of communications and nearness to market and customer, increasingly outweigh what had been forbidding management limitations. Thus in the United States, but increasingly in the other leading manufacturing nations such as Japan and West Germany as well, the dynamism in the economy has shifted from the very big companies that dominated the world's industrial economy for 30 years after World War II to companies that, while much smaller, are professionally managed and largely publicly financed.

Two distinct kinds of "manufacturing industry" are emerging. One is material-based, represented by the industries that provided economic growth in the first three-quarters of this century. The other is information- and knowledge-based: pharmaceuticals, telecommunications, analytical instruments and information processing such as computers. It is largely the information-based manufacturing industries that are growing.

These two groups differ not only in their economic characteristics but especially in their position in the international economy. The products of material-based industries have to be exported or imported as "products." They appear in the balance of trade. The products of information-based industries can be exported or imported both as "products" and as "services," which may not appear accurately in the overall trade balance.

An old example is the printed book. For one major scientific publishing company, "foreign earnings" account for two-thirds of total revenues. Yet the company exports few, if any, actual books—books are heavy. It sells "rights," and the "product" is produced abroad. Similarly, the most profitable computer "export sales" may actually show up in trade statistics as an "import." This is the fee some of the world's leading banks, multinationals and Japanese trading companies get for processing in their home office data arriving electronically from their branches and customers around the world.

In all developed countries, "knowledge" workers have already become the center of gravity of the labor force. Even in manufacturing they will outnumber blue-collar workers within ten years. Exporting knowledge so that it produces license income, service fees and royalties may actually create substantially more jobs than exporting goods.

This in turn requires—as official Washington seems to have realized—far greater emphasis in trade policy on "invisible trade" and on abolishing the barriers to the trade in services. Traditionally, economists have treated invisible trade as a stepchild, if they noted it at all. Increasingly, it will become central. Within 20 years major developed countries may find that their income from invisible trade is larger than their income from exports.

Another implication of the "uncoupling" of manufacturing production from manufacturing employment is, however, that the choice between an industrial policy that favors industrial *production* and one that favors industrial *employment* is going to be a singularly contentious political issue for the rest of this century. Historically these have always been considered two sides of the same coin. From now on the two will increasingly pull in different directions; they are indeed already becoming alternatives, it not incompatible.

Benign neglect—the policy of the Reagan Administration these last few years—may be the best policy one can hope for, and the only one with a chance of success. It is probably not an accident that the United States has, after Japan, by far the lowest unemployment rate of any industrially developed country. Still, there is surely need also for systematic efforts to retrain and to place redundant blue-collar workers—something no one as yet knows how to do successfully.

Finally, low labor costs are likely to become less of an advantage in international trade simply because in the developed countries they are going to account for less of total costs. Moreover, the total costs of automated processes are lower than even those of traditional plants with low labor costs; this is mainly because automation eliminates the hidden but high costs of "not working," such as the expense of poor quality and rejects, and the costs of shutting down the machinery to change from one model of a product to another. Consider two automated American producers of televisions, Motorola and RCA. Both were almost driven out of the market by imports from countries with much lower labor costs. Both subsequently automated, with the result that these American-made products now successfully compete with foreign imports. Similarly, some highly automated textile mills in the Carolinas can underbid imports from countries with very low labor costs such as Thailand. On the other hand, although some American semiconductor companies have lower labor costs because they do the labor-intensive work offshore, e.g., in West Africa, they are still the high-cost producers and easily underbid by the heavily automated Japanese.

The cost of capital will thus become increasingly important in international competition. And this is where, in the last ten years, the United States has become the highest-cost country—and Japan the lowest. A reversal of the U.S. policy of high interest rates and costly equity capital should thus be a priority for American decision-makers. This demands that reduction of the government deficit, rather than high interest rates, becomes the first defense against inflation.

For developed countries, especially the United States, the steady downgrading of labor costs as a major competitive factor could be a positive development. For the Third World, especially rapidly industrializing countries such as Brazil, South Korea or Mexico, it is, however, bad news.

In the rapid industrialization of the nineteenth century, one country, Japan, developed by exporting raw materials, mainly silk and tea, at steadily rising prices. Another, Germany, developed by leap-frogging into the "high-tech" industries of its time, mainly electricity, chemicals and optics. A third, the United States, did both. Both routes are blocked for today's rapidly industrializing countries—the first because of the deterioration of the terms of trade for primary products, the second because it requires an infrastructure of knowledge and education far beyond the reach of a poor country (although South Korea is reaching for it). Competition based on lower labor costs seemed to be the only alternative; is this also going to be blocked?

The third major change that has occurred in the world economy is the emergence of the "symbol" economy—capital movements, exchange rates and credit flows—as the flywheel of the world economy, in place of the "real" economy—the flow of goods and services. The two economies seem to be operating increasingly independently. This is both the most visible and the least understood of the changes.

World trade in goods is larger, much larger, than it has ever been before. And so is the "invisible trade," the trade in services. Together, the two amount to around $2.5 trillion to $3 trillion a year. But the London Eurodollar market, in which the world's financial institutions borrow from and lend to each other, turns over $300 billion each working day, or $75 trillion a year, a volume at least 25 times that of world trade.[10]

In addition, there are the foreign exchange transactions in the world's main money centers, in which one currency is traded against another. These run around $150 billion a day, or about $35 trillion a year—12 times the worldwide trade in goods and services.

Of course, many of these Eurodollars, yen and Swiss francs are just being moved from one pocket to another and may be counted more than once. A massive discrepancy still exists, and there is only one conclusion: capital movements unconnected to trade—and indeed largely independent of it—greatly exceed trade finance.

There is no one explanation for this explosion of international—or more accurately, transnational—money flows. The shift from fixed to floating exchange rates in 1971 may have given an initial impetus (though, ironically, it was meant to do the exact opposite) by inviting currency speculation. The surge in liquid funds flowing to petroleum producers after the two oil shocks of 1973 and 1979 was surely a major factor.

But there can be little doubt that the U.S. government deficit also plays a big role. The American budget has become a financial "black hole," sucking in liquid funds from all over the world, making the United States the world's major debtor country.[11] Indeed, it can be argued that it is the budget deficit that underlies the American trade and payments deficit. A trade and payments deficit is, in effect, a loan from the seller of goods and services to the buyer, that is, to the United States. Without it Washington could not finance its budget deficit, at least not without the risk of explosive inflation.

The way major countries have learned to use the internationl economy to avoid tackling disagreeable domestic problems is unprecedented: The United States has used high interest rates to attract foreign capital and avoid confronting its domestic deficit; the Japanese have pushed exports to maintain employment despite a sluggish domestic economy. This politicization of the international economy is surely also a factor in the extreme volatility and instability of capital flows and exchange rates.

Whichever of these causes is judged the most important, together they have produced a basic change: In the world economy of today, the "real" economy of goods and services and the "symbol" economy of money, credit and capital are no longer bound tightly to each other; they are, indeed, moving further and further apart. . . .

Traditional international economic theory is still neoclassical, holding that trade in goods and services determines international capital flows and foreign exchange rates. Capital flows and foreign exchange rates since the first half of the 1970s have, however, moved quite independently of foreign trade, and indeed (e.g., in the rise of the dollar in 1984–85) have run counter to it. . . .

From now on exchange rates between major currencies will have to be treated in economic theory and business policy alike as a "comparative-advantage" factor, and a major one.

Economic theory teaches that the comparative-advantage factors of the "real" economy—comparative labor costs and labor productivity, raw material costs, energy costs, transportation costs and the like—determine exchange rates. Practically all businesses base their policies on this notion. Increasingly, however, it is exchange rates that decide how labor costs in country A compare to labor costs in country B. Exchange rates are thus a major "comparative cost" and one totally beyond business control. Any firm exposed to the international economy has to realize that it is in two businesses at the same time. It is both a maker of goods (or a supplier of services) and a "financial" business. It cannot disregard either.

Specifically, the business that sells abroad—whether as an exporter or through a subsidiary—will have to protect itself against three foreign exchange exposures: proceeds from sales, working capital devoted to manufacturing for overseas markets, and investments abroad. This will have to be done whether the business expects the value of its own currency to go up or down. Businesses that buy abroad will have to do likewise. Indeed, even purely domestic businesses that face foreign competition in their home market will have to learn to hedge against the currency in which their main competitors produce. If American businesses had been run this way during the years of the overvalued dollar, from 1982 through 1985, most of the losses in market standing abroad and in foreign earnings might have been prevented. They were management failures, not acts of God. Surely stockholders, but also the public in general, have every right to expect management to do better the next time around. . . .

We are left with one conclusion: economic dynamics have decisively shifted from the national economy to the world economy.

Prevailing economic theory—whether Keynesian, monetarist or supply-side—considers the national economy, especially that of the large developed countries, to be autonomous and the unit of both economic analysis and economic policy. The international economy may be a restraint and a limitation, but it is not central, let alone determining. This "macroeconomic axiom" of the modern economist has become increasingly shaky. The two major subscribers to this axiom, Britain and the United States, have done least well economically in the last 30 years, and have also had the most economic instability.

West Germany and Japan never accepted the "macroeconomic axiom." Their universities teach it, of course, but their policymakers, both in government and in business, reject it. Instead, both countries all along have based their economic policies on the world economy, have systematically tried to anticipate its trends and exploit its changes as opportunities. Above all, both make the country's competitive position in the world economy the first priority in their policies—economic, fiscal, monetary, even social—to which domestic considerations are normally subordinated. And these two countries have done far better—economically and socially—than Britain and the United States these last 30 years. In fact, their focus on the world economy and the priority they give it may be the real "secret" of their success.

Similarly the "secret" of successful businesses in the developed world—the Japanese, the German carmakers like Mercedes and BMW, Asea and Erickson in Sweden, IBM and Citibank in the United States, but equally of a host of medium-sized specialists in manufacturing and in all kinds of services—has been that they base their plans and their policies on exploiting the world economy's changes as opportunities.

From now on any country—but also any business, especially a large one—that wants to prosper will have to accept that it is the world economy that leads and that domestic economic policies will succeed only if they strengthen, or at least do not impair, the country's international competitive position. This may be the most important—it surely is the most striking—feature of the changed world economy.

NOTES

1. When the price of petroleum dropped to $15 a barrel in February 1986, it was actually below its 1933 price (adjusted for the change in the purchasing power of the dollar). It was still, however, substantially higher than its all-time low in 1972–73, which in 1986 dollars amounted to $7–$8 a barrel.
2. On this see two quite different discussions by Dennis Avery, "U.S. Farm Dilemma: The Global Bad News Is Wrong," *Science*, Oct. 25, 1985; and Barbara Insel, "A World Awash in Grain," *Foreign Affairs*, Spring 1985.
3. The business cycle theory was developed just before World War I by the Russian mathematical economist, Nikolai Kondratieff, who made comprehensive studies of raw material price cycles and their impacts all the way back to 1797.
4. These conclusions are based on static analysis, which presumes that which products are bought and sold is not affected by changes in price. This is of course unrealistic, but the flaw should not materially affect the conclusions.
5. Although the African famine looms large in our consciousness, the total population of the affected areas is far too small to make any dent in world food surpluses.
6. David Sapsford, *Real Primary Commodity Prices: An Analysis of Long-Run Movements*, International Monetary Fund Internal Memorandum, May 17, 1985, (unpublished).
7. This was asserted as early as 1950 by the South American economist Raúl Prebisch in *The Economic Development of Latin America and its Principal Problems* (E/CN.12/89/REV.1), United Nations Economic Commission for Latin America. But then no one, including myself, believed him.
8. The Japanese government, for example, sponsors a finance company that makes long-term, low interest loans to small manufacturers to enable them to automate rapidly.

9. On this see my book, *Innovation and Entrepreneurship: Practice and Principles*, New York: Harper & Row, 1985.

10. A Eurodollar is a U.S. dollar held outside the United States.

11. This is cogently argued by Stephen Marris, for almost 30 years economic adviser to the Organization for Economic Cooperation and Development (OECD), in his *Deficits and the Dollar: The World Economy at Risk*, Washington: Institute of International Economics, December 1985.

Who Is Us?

Robert B. Reich

Who is "us"? Is it IBM, Motorola, Whirlpool, and General Motors? Or is it Sony, Thomson, Philips, and Honda?

Consider two successful corporations:

- Corporation A is headquartered north of New York City. Most of its top managers are citizens of the United States. All of its directors are American citizens, and a majority of its shares are held by American investors. But most of Corporation A's employees are non-Americans. Indeed, the company undertakes much of its R&D and product design, and most of its complex manufacturing, outside the borders of the United States in Asia, Latin America, and Europe. Within the American market, an increasing amount of the company's product comes from its laboratories and factories abroad.

- Corporation B is headquartered abroad, in another industrialized nation. Most of its top managers and directors are citizens of that nation, and a majority of its shares are held by citizens of that nation. But most of Corporation B's employees are Americans. Indeed, Corporation B undertakes much of its R&D and new product design in the United States. And it does most of its manufacturing in the United States. The company exports an increasing proportion of its American-based production, some of it even back to the nation where Corporation B is headquartered.

Now, who is "us"? Between these two corporations, which is the American corporation, which the foreign corporation? Which is more important to the economic future of the United States?

As the American economy becomes more globalized, examples of both Corporation A and B are increasing. At the same time, American concern for the competitiveness of the United States is increasing. Typically, the assumed vehicle for improving the competitive performance of the United States is the American corporation—by which most people would mean Corporation A. But today, the competitiveness of American-owned corporations is no longer the same as American competitiveness. Indeed, American ownership of the corporation is profoundly less relevant to America's economic future than the skills, training, and knowledge commanded by American workers—workers who are increasingly employed within the United States by foreign-owned corporations.

So who is us? The answer is, the American work force, the American people, but not particularly the American corporation. The implications of this new answer are clear: If we hope to revitalize the competitive performance of the United States economy, we must invest in people, not in nationally defined corporations. We must open our borders to investors from around the world rather than favoring companies that may simply fly the U.S. flag. And government policies should promote human capital in this country rather than assuming that American corporations will invest on "our" behalf. The American corporation is simply no longer "us."

GLOBAL COMPANIES

American corporations have been abroad for years, even decades. So in one sense, the multinational identity of American companies is nothing new. What is new is that American-owned multinationals are beginning to employ large numbers of foreigners relative to their American work forces, are beginning to rely on foreign facilities to do many of their most technologically complex activites, and are beginning to export from their foreign facilities—including bringing products back to the United States.

Around the world, the numbers are already large—and still growing. Take IBM—often considered the thoroughbred of competitive American corporations. Forty percent of IBM's world employees are foreign, and the percentage is increasing. IBM Japan boasts 18,000 Japanese employees and annual sales of more than $6 billion, making it one of Japan's major exporters of computers.

Or consider Whirlpool. After cutting its American work force by 10 percent and buying Philips's appliance business, Whirlpool now employs 43,500 people around the world in 45 countries—most of them non-Americans. Another example is Texas Instruments, which now does most of its research, development, design, and manufacturing in East Asia. TI employs over 5,000 people in Japan alone, making advanced semiconductors—almost half of which are exported, many of them back to the United States.

American corporations now employ 11 percent of the industrial work force of Northern Ireland, making everything from cigarettes to computer software, much of which comes back to the United States. More than 100,000 Singaporians work for more than 200 U.S. corporations, most of them fabricating and assembling electronic components for export to the United States. Singapore's largest private employer is General Electric, which also accounts for a big share of that nation's growing exports. Taiwan counts AT&T, RCA, and Texas Instruments among its largest exporters. In fact, more than one-third of Taiwan's notorious trade surplus with the United States comes from U.S. corporations making or buying things there, then selling or using them back in the United States. The same corporate sourcing practice accounts for a substantial share of the U.S. trade imbalance with Singapore, South Korea, and Mexico—raising a question as to whom complaints about trade imbalances should be directed.

The pattern is not confined to America's largest companies. Molex, a suburban Chicago maker of connectors used to link wires in cars and computer boards, with revenues of about $300 million in 1988, has 38 overseas factories, five in Japan. Loctite, a midsize company with sales in 1988 of $457 million, headquartered in Newington, Connecticut, makes and sells adhesives and sealants all over the world. It has 3,500 employees—only 1,200 of whom are Americans. These companies are just part of a much larger trend: according to a 1987 McKinsey & Company study, America's most profitable midsize companies increased their investments in overseas production at an annual rate of 20 percent between 1981 and 1986.

Overall, the evidence suggests that U.S. companies have not lost their competitive edge over the last 20 years—they've just moved their base of operations. In 1966, American-based multinationals accounted for about 17 percent of world exports; since then their share has remained almost unchanged. But over the same period, the share of exports from the United States in the world's total trade in manufactures fell from 16 percent to 14 percent. In other words, while Americans exported less, the overseas affiliates of U.S.-owned corporations exported more than enough to offset the drop.

The old trend of overseas capital investment is accelerating: U.S. companies increased foreign capital spending by 24 percent in 1988, 13 percent in 1989. But even more important, U.S. businesses are now putting substantial sums of money into foreign countries to do R&D work. According to National Science Foundation figures, American corporations increased their overseas R&D spending by 33 percent between 1986 and 1988, compared with a 6 percent increase in R&D spending in the United States. Since 1987, Eastman Kodak, W.R. Grace, Du Pont, Merck, and Upjohn have all opened new R&D facilities in Japan. At Du Pont's Yokohama laboratory, more than 180 Japanese scientists and technicians are working at developing new materials technologies. IBM's Tokyo Research Lab, tucked away behind the far side of the Imperial Palace in downtown Tokyo, houses a small army of Japanese engineers who are perfecting image-processing technology. Another IBM laboratory, the Kanagawa arm of its Yamato Development Laboratory, houses 1,500 researchers who are developing hardware and software. Nor does IBM confine its pioneering work to Japan: Recently, two European researchers at IBM's Zurich laboratory announced major breakthroughs into superconductivity and microscopy—earning them both Nobel Prizes.

An even more dramatic development is the arrival of foreign corporations in the United States at a rapidly increasing price. As recently as 1977, only about 3.5 percent of the value added and the employment of American manufacturing originated in companies controlled by foreign parents. By 1987, the number had grown to almost 8 percent. In just the last two years, with the faster pace of foreign acquisitions and investments, the figure is now almost 11 percent. Foreign-owned companies now employ 3 million Americans, roughly 10 percent of our manufacturing workers. In fact, in 1989, affiliates of foreign manufacturers created more jobs in the United States than American-owned manufacturing companies.

And these non-U.S. companies are vigorously exporting from the United States. Sony now exports audio- and videotapes to Europe from its Dothan, Alabama factory and ships audio recorders from its Fort Lauderdale, Florida plant. Sharp exports 100,000 microwave ovens a year from its factory in Memphis, Tennessee. Last year, Dutch-owned Philips Consumer Electronics Company exported 1,500 color televisions from its Greenville, Tennessee plant to Japan. Its 1990 target is 30,000 televisions; by 1991, it plans to export 50,000 sets. Toshiba America is sending projection televisions from its Wayne, New Jersey plant to Japan. And by the early 1990s, when Honda annually exports 50,000 cars to Japan from its Ohio production base, it will actually be making more cars in the United States than in Japan.

THE NEW AMERICAN CORPORATION

In an economy of increasing global investment, foreign-owned Corporation B, with its R&D and manufacturing presence in the United States and its reliance on American workers, is far more important to America's economic future than American-owned Corporation A, with its platoons of foreign workers. Corporation A may fly the American flag, but Corporation B invests in Americans. Increasingly, the competitiveness of American workers is a more important definition of "American competitiveness" than the competitiveness of American companies. Issues of ownership, control, and national origin are less important factors in thinking through the logic of "who is us" and the implications of the answer for national policy and direction.

Ownership Is Less Important

Those who favor American-owned Corporation A (that produces overseas) over foreign-owned Corporation B (that produces here) might argue that American ownership generates a stream of earnings for the nation's citizens. This argument is correct, as far as it goes. American shareholders do, of course, benefit from the global successes of American corporations to the extent that such successes are reflected in higher share prices. And the entire U.S. economy benefits to the extent that the overseas profits of American companies are remitted to the United States.

But American investors also benefit from the successes of non-American companies in which Americans own a minority interest—just as foreign citizens benefit from the successes of American companies in which they own a minority interest, and such cross-ownership is on the increase as national restrictions on foreign ownership fall by the wayside. In 1989, cross-border equity investments by Americans, British, Japanese, and West Germans increased 20 percent, by value, over 1988.

The point is that in today's global economy, the total return to Americans from their equity investments is not solely a matter of the success of particular companies in which Americans happen to have a controlling interest. The return depends on the total amount of American savings invested in global portfolios comprising both American and foreign-owned companies—and on the care and wisdom with which American investors select such portfolios. Already Americans invest 10 percent of their portfolios in foreign securities; a recent study by Salomon Brothers predicts that it will be 15 percent in a few years. U.S. pension managers surveyed said that they predict 25 percent of their portfolios will be in foreign-owned companies within 10 years.

Control Is Less Important

Another argument marshaled in favor of Corporation A might be that because Corporation A is controlled by Americans, it will act in the best interests of the United States. Corporation B, a foreign national, might not do so—indeed, it might act in the best interests of its nation of origin. The argument might go something like this: Even if Corporation B is now hiring more Americans and giving them better jobs than Corporation A, we can't be assured that it will continue to do so. It might bias its strategy to reduce American competitiveness; it might even suddenly withdraw its investment from the United States and leave us stranded.

But this argument makes a false assumption about American companies—namely, that they are in a position to put national interests ahead of company or shareholder interests. To the contrary: Managers of American-owned companies who sacrificed profits for the sake of national goals would make themselves vulnerable to a takeover or liable for a breach of fiduciary responsibility to their shareholders. American managers are among the loudest in the world to declare that their job is to maximize shareholder returns—not to advance national goals.

Apart from wartime or other national emergencies, American-owned companies are under no special obligation to serve national goals. Nor does our system alert American managers to the existence of such goals, impose on American managers unique requirements to meet them, offer special incentives to achieve them, or create measures to keep American managers accountable for accomplishing them. Were American managers knowingly to sacrifice profits for the sake of presumed national goals, they would be acting without authority, on the basis of their own views of what such goals might be, and without accountability to shareholders or to the public.

Obviously, this does not preclude American-owned companies from displaying their good corporate citizenship or having a sense of social responsibility. Sensible managers recognize that acting "in the public interest" can boost the company's image; charitable or patriotic acts can be good business if they promote long-term profitability. But in this regard, American companies have no particular edge over foreign-owned companies doing business in the United

States. In fact, there is every reason to believe that a foreign-owned company would be even more eager to demonstrate to the American public its good citizenship in America than would the average American company. The American subsidiaries of Hitachi, Matsushita, Siemens, Thomson, and many other foreign-owned companies lose no opportunity to contribute funds to American charities, sponsor community events, and support public libraries, universities, schools, and other institutions. (In 1988, for example, Japanese companies operating in the United States donated an estimated $200 million to American charities; by 1994, it is estimated that their contributions will total $1 billion.)[1]

By the same token, American-owned businesses operating abroad feel a similar compulsion to act as good citizens in their host countries. They cannot afford to be seen as promoting American interests; otherwise they would jeopardize their relationships with foreign workers, consumers, and governments. Some of America's top managers have been quite explicit on this point. "IBM cannot be a net exporter from every nation in which it does business," said Jack Kuehler, IBM's new president. "We have to be a good citizen everywhere." Robert W. Galvin, chairman of Motorola, is even more blunt: should it become necessary for Motorola to close some of its factories, it would not close its Southeast Asian plants before it closed its American ones. "We need our Far Eastern customers," says Galvin, " and we cannot alienate the Malaysians. We must treat our employees all over the world equally." In fact, when it becomes necessary to reduce global capacity, we might expect American-owned businesses to slash more jobs in the United States than in Europe (where labor laws often prohibit precipitous layoffs) or in Japan (where national norms discourage it).

Just as empty is the concern that a foreign-owned company might leave the United States stranded by suddenly abandoning its U.S. operation. The typical argument suggests that a foreign-owned company might withdraw for either profit or foreign policy motives. But either way, the bricks and mortar would still be here. So would the equipment. So too would be the accumulated learning among American workers. Under such circumstances, capital from another source would fill the void; an American (or other foreign) company would simply purchase the empty facilities. And most important, the American work force would remain, with the critical skills and capabilities, ready to go back to work.

After all, the American government and the American people maintain jurisdiction—political control—over assets within the United States. Unlike foreign assets held by American-owned companies that are subject to foreign political control and, occasionally, foreign expropriation, foreign-owned assets in the United States are secure against sudden changes in foreign governments' policies. This not only serves as an attraction for foreign capital looking for a secure haven; it also benefits the American work force.

Work Force Skills Are Critical

As every advanced economy becomes global, a nation's most important competitive asset becomes the skills and cumulative learning of its work force. Consequently, the most important issue with regard to global corporations is whether and to what extent they provide Americans with the training and experience that enable them to add greater value to the world economy. Whether the company happens to be headquartered in the United States or the United Kingdom is fundamentally unimportant. The company is a good "American" corporation if it equips its American work force to compete in the global economy.

Globalization, almost by definition, makes this true. Every factor of production other than work force skills can be duplicated anywhere around the world. Capital now sloshes freely across international boundaries, so much so that the cost of capital in different countries is rapidly converging. State-of-the-art factories can be erected anywhere. The latest technologies flow from computers in one nation, up to satellites parked in space, then back down to computers in another nation—all at the speed of electronic impulses. It is all fungible: capital, technology, raw materials, information—all, except for one thing, the most critical part, the one element that is unique about a nation: its work force.

In fact, because all of the other factors can move so easily any place on earth, a work force that is knowledgeable and skilled at doing complex things attracts foreign investment. The relationship forms a virtuous circle: Well-trained workers attract global corporations, which invest and give the workers good jobs; the good jobs, in turn, generate additional training and experience. As skills move upward and experience accumulates, a nation's citizens add greater and greater value to the world—and command greater and greater compensation from the world, improving the country's standard of living.

Foreign-Owned Corporations Help American Workers Add Value

When foreign-owned companies come to the United States, they frequently bring with them approaches to doing business that improve American productivity and allow American workers to add more value to the world economy. In fact, the come here primarily because they can be more productive in the United States than can other American rivals. It is not solely America's mounting external indebtedness and relatively low dollar that account for the rising level of foreign investment in the United States. Actual growth of foreign investment in the United States dates from the mid-1970s rather than from the onset of the large current account deficit in 1982. Moreover, the two leading foreign investors in the United States are the British and the Dutch—not the Japanese and the West Germans, whose enormous surpluses are the counterparts of our current account deficit.

For example, after Japan's Bridgestone tire company took over Firestone, productivity increased dramatically. The joint venture between Toyota and General Motors at Fremont, California, is a similar story: Toyota's managerial system took many of the same workers from what had been a deeply troubled GM plant and turned it into a model facility, with upgraded productivity and skill levels.

In case after case, foreign companies set up or buy up operations in the

United States to utilize their corporate assets with the American work force. Foreign-owned businesses with better design capabilities, production techniques, or managerial skills are able to displace American companies on American soil precisely because those businesses are more productive. And in the process of supplanting the American company, the foreign-owned operation can transfer the superior know-how to its American work force—giving American workers the tools they need to be more productive, more skilled, and more competitive. Thus foreign companies create good jobs in the United States. In 1986 (the last date for which such data are available), the average American employee of a foreign-owned manufacturing company earned $32,887, while the average American employee of an American-owned manufacturer earned $28,954.[2]

This process is precisely what happened in Europe in the 1950s and 1960s. Europeans publicly fretted about the invasion of American-owned multinationals and the onset of "the American challenge." But the net result of these operations in Europe has been to make Europeans more productive, upgrade European skills, and thus enhance the standard of living of Europeans.

NOW WHO IS US?

American competitiveness can best be defined as the capacity of Americans to add value to the world economy and thereby gain a higher standard of living in the future without going into ever deeper debt. American competitiveness is not the profitability or market share of American-owned corporations. In fact, because the American-owned corporation is coming to have no special relationship with Americans, it makes no sense for Americans to entrust our national competitiveness to it. The interests of American-owned corporations may or may not coincide with those of the American people.

Does this mean that we should simply entrust our national competitiveness to any corporation that employs Americans, regardless of the nationality of corporate ownership? Not entirely. Some foreign-owned corporations are closely tied to their nation's economic development—either through direct public ownership (for example, Airbus Industrie, a joint product of Britain, France, West Germany, and Spain, created to compete in the commercial airline industry) or through financial intermediaries within the nation that, in turn, are tied to central banks and ministries of finance (in particular the model used by many Korean and Japanese corporations). The primary goals of such corporations are to enhance the wealth of their nations, and the standard of living of their nations' citizens, rather than to enrich their shareholders. Thus, even though they might employ American citizens in their world-wide operations, they may employ fewer Americans—or give Americans lower value-added jobs—than they would if these corporations were intent simply on maximizing their own profits.[3]

On the other hand, it seems doubtful that we could ever shift the goals and orientations of American-owned corporations in this same direction—away from profit maximization and toward the development of the American work force. There is no reason to suppose that American managers and shareholders would accept new regulations and oversight mechanisms that forced them to sacrifice proftis for the sake of building human capital in the United States. Nor is it clear that the American system of government would be capable of such detailed oversight.

The only practical answer lies in developing national policies that reward *any* global corporation that invests in the American work force. In a whole set of public policy areas, involving trade, publicly supported R&D, antitrust, foreign direct investment, and public and private investment, the overriding goal should be to induce global corporations to build human capital in America.

Trade Policy

We should be less interested in opening foreign markets to American-owned companies (which may in fact be doing much of their production overseas) than in opening those markets to companies that employ Americans—even if they happen to be foreign-owned. But so far, American trade policy experts have focused on representing the interests of companies that happen to carry the American flag—without regard to where the actual production is being done. For example, the United States recently accused Japan of excluding Motorola from the lucrative Tokyo market for cellular telephones and hinted at retaliation. But Motorola designs and makes many of its cellular telephones in Kuala Lumpur, while most of the Americans who make cellular telephone equipment in the United States for export to Japan happen to work for Japanese-owned companies. Thus we are wasting our scarce political capital pushing foreign governments to reduce barriers to American-owned companies that are seeking to sell or produce in their market.

Once we acknowledge that foreign-owned Corporation B may offer more to American competitiveness than American-owned Corporation A, it is easy to design a preferable trade policy—one that accords more directly with our true national interests. The highest priority for American trade policy should be to discourage other governments from invoking domestic content rules—which have the effect of forcing global corporations, American and foreign-owned alike, to locate production facilities in those countries rather than in the United States.

The objection here to local content rules is not that they may jeopardize the competitiveness of American companies operating abroad. Rather, it is that these requirements, by their very nature, deprive the American work force of the opportunity to compete for jobs, and with those jobs, for valuable skills, knowledge, and experience. Take, for example, the recently promulgated European Community nonbinding rule on television-program production, which urges European television stations to devote a majority of their air time to programs made in Europe. Or consider the European allegations of Japanese dumping of office machines containing semiconductors, which has forced Japan to put at least 45 percent European content into machines sold in Europe (and thus fewer American-made semiconductor chips).

Obviously, U.S.-owned companies are already inside the EC producing both semiconductors and television programs. So if we were to adopt American-owned Corporation A as the model for America's competitive self-interest, our trade policy might simply ignore these EC initiatives. But through the lens of a trade policy focused on the American work force, it is clear how the EC thwarts the abilities of Americans to excel in semiconductor fabrication and filmmaking—two areas where our work force already enjoys a substantial competitive advantage.

Lack of access by American-owned corporations to foreign markets is, of course, a problem. But it only becomes a crucial problem for America to the extent that both American and foreign-owned companies must make products within the foreign market—products that they otherwise would have made in the United States. Protection that acts as a domestic content requirement skews investment away from the United States—and away from U.S. workers. Fighting against that should be among the highest priorities of U.S. trade policy.

Publicly Supported R&D

Increased global competition, the high costs of research, the rapid rate of change in science and technology, the model of Japan with its government-supported commercial technology investments—all of these factors have combined to make this area particularly critical for thoughtful public policy. But there is no reason why preference should be given to American-owned companies. Dominated by our preoccupation with American-owned Corporation A, current public policy in this area limits U.S. government-funded research grants, guaranteed loans, or access to the fruits of U.S. government-funded research to American-owned companies. For example, membership in Sematech, the research consortium started two years ago with $100 billion annual support payments by the Department of Defense to help American corporations fabricate complex memory chips, is limited to American-owned companies. More recently, a government effort to create a consortium of companies to catapult the United States into the HDTV competition has drawn a narrow circle of eligibility, ruling out companies such as Sony, Philips, and Thomson that do R&D and production in the United States but are foreign-owned. More generally, long-standing regulations covering the more than 600 government laboratories and research centers that are spread around the United States ban all but American-owned companies from licensing inventions developed at these sites.

Of course, the problem with this policy approach is that it ignores the reality of global American corporations. Most U.S.-owned companies are quite happy to receive special advantages from the U.S. government—and then spread the technological benefits to their affiliates all over the world. As Sematech gets under way, its members are busily going global: Texas Instruments is building a new $250 million semiconductor fabrication plant in Taiwan; by 1992, the facility will produce four-megabit memory chips and custom-made, application-specific integrated circuits—some of the most advanced chips made anywhere. TI has also joined with Hitachi to design and produce a super chip that will store 16 million bits of data. Motorola, meanwhile, has paired with Toshiba to research and produce a similar generation of futurist chips. Not to be outdone, AT&T has a commitment to build a state-of-the-art chip-making plant in Spain. So who will be making advanced chips in the United States? In June 1989, Japanese-owned NEC announced plans to build a $400 million facility in Rosedale, California for making four-megabit memory chips and other advanced devices not yet in production anywhere.

The same situation applies to HDTV. Zenith Electronics is the only remaining American-owned television manufacturer, and thus the only one eligible for a government subsidy. Zenith employs 2,500 Americans. But there are over 15,000 Americans employed in the television industry who do not work for Zenith—undertaking R&D, engineering, and high-quality manufacturing. They work in the United States for foreign-owned companies: Sony, Philips, Thomson, and others (see Table 1). Of course, none of these companies is presently eligible

Table 1   U.S. TV SET PRODUCTION, 1988

Company name	Plant type	Location	Employees	Annual production
Bang & Olufsen	Assembly	Compton, Calif.	n.a.†	n.a.
Goldstar	Total*	Huntsville, Ala.	400	1,000,000
Harvey Industries	Assembly	Athens, Tex.	900	600,000
Hitachi	Total	Anaheim, Calif.	900	360,000
JVC	Total	Elmwood Park, N.J.	100	480,000
Matsushita	Assembly	Franklin Park, Ill.	800	1,000,000
American Kotobuki (Matsushita)	Assembly	Vancouver, Wash.	200	n.a.
Mitsubishi	Assembly	Santa Ana, Calif.	550	400,000
Mitsubishi	Total	Braselton, Ga.	300	285,000
NEC	Assembly	McDonough, Ga.	400	240,000
Orion	Assembly	Princeton, Ind.	250	n.a.
Philips	Total	Greenville, Tenn.	3,200	2,000,000+
Samsung	Total	Saddle Brook, N.J.	250	1,000,000
Sanyo	Assembly	Forrest City, Ark.	400	1,000,000
Sharp	Assembly	Memphis, Tenn.	770	1,100,000
Sony	Total	San Diego, Calif.	1,500	1,000,000
Tatung	Assembly	Long Beach, Calif.	130	17,500
Thomson	Total	Bloomington, Ind.	1,766	3,000,000+
Thomson	Components	Indianapolis, Ind.	1,604	n.a.
Toshiba	Assembly	Lebanon, Tenn.	600	900,000
Zenith	Total	Springfield, Mo.	2,500	n.a.

Source: Electronic Industries Association, HDTV Information Center, Washington, D.C.

*Total manufacturing involves more than the assembling of knocked-down kits. Plants that manufacture just the television cabinets are not included in this list.

†Not available.

to participate in the United States's HDTV consortium—nor are their American employees.

Again, if we follow the logic of Corporation B as the more "American" company, it suggests a straightforward principle for publicly supported R&D: We should be less interested in helping *American-owned companies* become technologically sophisticated than in helping *Americans* become technologically sophisticated. Government-financed help for research and development should be available to any corporation, regardless of the nationality of its owners, as long as the company undertakes the R&D in the United States—using American scientists, engineers, and technicians. To make the link more explicit, there could even be a relationship between the number of Americans involved in the R&D and the amount of government aid forthcoming. It is important to note that this kind of public-private bargain is far different from protectionist domestic content requirements. In this case, the government is participating with direct funding and thus can legitimately exact a quid pro quo from the private sector.

Antitrust Policy

The Justice Department is now in the process of responding to the inevitability of globalization; it recognizes that North American market share alone means less and less in a global economy. Consequently, the Justice Department is about to relax antitrust policy—for American-owned companies only. American-owned companies that previously kept each other at arm's length for fear of prompting an inquiry into whether they were colluding are now cozying up to one another. Current anti-trust policy permits research joint ventures; the attorney general is on the verge of recommending that antitrust policy permit joint production agreements as well, when there may be significant economies of scale and where competition is global—again, among American-owned companies.

But here again, American policy seems myopic. We should be less interested in helping American-owned companies gain economies of scale in research, production, and other key areas, and more interested in helping corporations engaged in research or production within the United States achieve economies of scale—regardless of their nationality. U.S. antitrust policy should allow research or production joint ventures among any companies doing R&D or production within the United States, as long as they can meet three tests: They could not gain such scale efficiencies on their own, simply by enlarging their investment in the United States; such a combination of companies would allow higher levels of productivity within the United States; and the combination would not substantially diminish global competition. National origin should not be a factor.

Foreign Direct Investment

Foreign direct investment has been climbing dramatically in the United States: last year it reached $329 billion, exceeding total American investment abroad for the first time since World War I (but be careful with these figures, since investments are valued at cost and this substantially understates the worth of older investments). How should we respond to this influx of foreign capital?

Clearly, the choice between Corporation A and Corporation B has important implications. If we are most concerned about the viability of American-owned corporations, then we should put obstacles in the way of foreigners seeking to buy controlling shares in American-owned companies, or looking to build American production facilities that would compete with American-owned companies.

Indeed, current policies tilt in this direction. For example, under the so-called Exon-Florio Amendment of the Omnibus Trade and Competitiveness Act of 1988, foreign investors must get formal approval from the high-level Committee on Foreign Investments in the United States, comprising the heads of eight federal agencies and chaired by the secretary of the treasury, before they can purchase an American company. The expressed purpose of the law is to make sure that a careful check is done to keep "national security" industries from passing into the hands of foreigners. But the law does not define what "national security" means: Thus it invites all sorts of potential delays and challenges. The actual effect is to send a message that we do not look with favor on the purchase of American-owned assets by foreigners. Other would-be pieces of legislation send the same signal. In July 1989, for instance, the House Ways and Means Committee voted to apply a withholding capital gains tax to foreigners who own more than 10 percent of a company's shares. Another provision of the committee would scrap tax deductibility for interest on loans made by foreign parents to their American subsidiaries. A third measure would limit R&D tax credits for foreign subsidiaries. More recently, Congress is becoming increasingly concerned about foreign takeovers of American airlines. A subcommittee of the House Commerce Committee has voted to give the Transportation Department authority to block foreign acquisitions.

These policies make little sense—in fact, they are counterproductive. Our primary concern should be the training and development of the American work force, not the protection of the American-owned corporation. Thus we should encourage, not discourage, foreign direct investment. Experience shows that foreign-owned companies usually displace American-owned companies in just those industries where the foreign businesses are simply more productive. No wonder America's governors spend a lot of time and energy promoting their states to foreign investors and offer big subsidies to foreign companies to locate in their states, even if they compete head-on with existing American-owned businesses.

Public and Private Investment

The current obsession with the federal budget deficit obscures a final, crucial aspect of the choice between Corporation A and Corporation B. Conventional wisdom holds that government expenditures "crowd out" private investment, making it more difficult and costly for American-owned companies to get the capital they need. According to this logic, we may have to cut back on public expenditures in order to provide American-owned companies with the necessary capital to make investments in plant and equipment.

But the reverse may actually be the case—particularly if Corporation B is really more in America's competitive interests than Corporation A. There are a number of reasons why this is true.

First, in the global economy, America's public expenditures don't reduce the amount of money left over for private investment in the United States. Today capital flows freely across the national borders—including a disproportionately large inflow to the United States. Not only are foreign savings coming to the United States, but America's private savings are finding their way all over the world. Sometimes the vehicle is the far-flung operations of a global American-owned company, sometimes a company in which foreigners own a majority stake. But the old notion of national boundaries is becoming obsolete. Moreover, as I have stressed, it is a mistake to associate these foreign investments by American-owned companies with any result that improves the competitiveness of the United States. There is simply no necessary connection between the two.

There is, however, a connection between the kinds of investments that the public sector makes and the competitiveness of the American work force. Remember: A work force that is knowledgeable and skilled at doing complex things attracts foreign investment in good jobs, which in turn generates additional training and experience. A good infrastructure of transportation and communication makes a skilled work force even more attractive. The public sector often is in the best position to make these sorts of "pump priming" investments—in education, training and retraining, research and development, and in all of the infrastructure that moves people and goods and facilitates communication. These are the investments that distinguish one nation from another—they are the relatively nonmobile factors in the global competition. Ironically, we do not ordinarily think of these expenditures as investments; the federal budget fails to distinguish between a capital and an operating budget, and the national income accounts treat all government expenditures as consumption. But without doubt, these are precisely the investments that most directly affect our future capacity to compete.

During the 1980s, we allowed the level of these public investments either to remain stable or, in some cases, to decline. As America enters the 1990s, if we hope to launch a new campaign for American competitiveness, we must substantially increase public funding in the following areas:

- *Government spending on commerical R&D.* Current spending in this critical area has declined 95 percent from its level two decades ago. Even as late as 1980, it comprised 0.8 percent of gross national product; today it comprises only 0.4 percent—a much smaller percentage than in any other advanced economy.
- *Government spending to upgrade and expand the nation's infrastructure.*

Public investment in critical highways, roads, bridges, ports, airports, and waterways dropped from 2.3 percent of GNP two decades ago to 1.3 percent in the 1980s. Thus many of our bridges are unsafe, and our highways are crumbling.

- *Expenditures on public elementary and secondary education.* These have increased, to be sure. But in inflation-adjusted terms, per pupil spending has shown little gain. Between 1959 and 1971, spending per student grew at a brisk 4.7 percent in real terms—more than a full percentage point above the increase in the GNP—and teachers' salaries increased almost 3 percent a year. But since then, growth has slowed. Worse, this has happened during an era when the demands on public education have significantly increased, due to the growing incidence of broken homes, unwed mothers, and a rising population of the poor. Teachers' salaries, adjusted for inflation, are only a bit higher than they were in 1971. Despite the rhetoric, the federal government has all but retreated from the field of education. In fact, George Bush's 1990 education budget is actually smaller than Ronald Reagan's in 1989. States and municipalities, already staggering under the weight of social services that have been shifted onto them from the federal government, simply cannot carry this additional load. The result of this policy gap is a national education crisis: One out of five American 18-year-olds is illiterate, and in test after test, American schoolchildren rank at the bottom of international scores. Investing more money here may not be a cure-all—but money is at least necessary.

- *College opportunity for all Americans.* Because of government cutbacks, many young people in the United States with enough talent to go to college cannot afford it. During the 1980s, college tuitions rose 26 percent; family incomes rose a scant 5 percent. Instead of filling the gap, the federal government created a vacuum: Guaranteed student loans have fallen by 13 percent in real terms since 1980.

- *Worker training and retraining.* Young people who cannot or do not wish to attend college need training for jobs that are becoming more complex. Older workers need retraining to keep up with the demands of a rapidly changing, technologically advanced workplace. But over the last eight years, federal investments in worker training have dropped by more than 50 percent.

These are the priorities of an American strategy for national competitiveness—a strategy based more on the value of human capital and less on the value of financial capital. The simple fact of American ownership has lost its relevance to America's economic future. Corporations that invest in the United States, that build the value of the American work force, are more critical to our future standard of living than are American-owned corporations investing abroad. To attract and keep them, we need public investments that make America a good place for any global corporation seeking talented workers to set up shop.

NOTES

1. Craig Smith, editor of *Corporate Philanthropy Report*, quoted in *Chronicle of Higher Education*, November 8, 1989, p.A-34.
2. Bureau of Economic Analysis, *Foreign Direct Investment in the U.S.: Operations of U.S. Affiliates, Preliminary 1986 Estimates* (Washington, D.C.: U.S. Department of Commerce, 1988) for data on foreign companies; Bureau of the Census, *Annual Survey of Manufacturers: Statistics for Industry Groups and Industries, 1986* (Washington, D.C., 1987) for U.S. companies.
3. Robert B. Reich and Eric D. Mankin, "Joint Ventures with Japan Give Away Our Future," *Harvard Business Review* (March–April 1986)p.78.

PART
Four

PERSPECTIVES ON DECISION-MAKING

W e talk about states acting and having policies, but obviously this is an abstraction; and one that can mislead. States are not concrete entities. Actions must be taken and decisions must be made by individuals, usually those who hold high-level positions in their governments. The distinction between a state and its leaders would be academic if the behavior of the latter were completely determined by a rational reaction to the external environment. Were this the case, we would not have to look within the decision-making processes of the government and at its bureaucratic factions; nor would we need to pay attention to leaders' personalities and the ways in which statesmen perceive the actions of others.

To the extent that statesmen react only to the objective situations confronting them, we can fruitfully conceive of state behavior as the product of a "rational, unitary actor," to use Graham Allison's phrase. Such a view implies that all states would usually behave the same way in the same situation because the external context is such a compelling one. This view denies much freedom of choice in international behavior, largely because of the impact of international anarchy. People may be less than fully rational; leaders may have different personalities; bureaucratic feuds may prosper. But it can be argued that all these factors will be overridden by the objective situation the state faces and by the need to reach generally accepted goals such as security, autonomy, and prosperity.

In many cases, the assumption that the state acts like a unitary rational actor is a fruitful one. Even though the state is not actually personified by a rational individual, much national behavior can be explained by the fact that the processes of decision-making lead to the same outcome that would have been produced by an individual acting rationally. Many lines of argument in international relations have made progress by adopting this premise, progress similar to that made by the economists' assumption that people behave according to the postulates of a self-interested, rational, maximizing "economic man." This is, however, not the only way to proceed. It cannot explain all national behavior and can lead to inaccurate predictions. It can overestimate the power of the external environment and underestimate the impact of domestic concerns, bureaucracies, and personalities. As a consequence, it can undervalue the degree of freedom of choice that decision-makers have.

This obviously is not an either/or matter. The degree of determinism varies in complex ways that depend heavily on the specifics of the situation, the nature of the domestic scene, and the views and strengths of individual leaders. To deal with this question and gain a more balanced picture of the causes and consequences of national behavior, we need to examine how policies are developed and carried out.

LEADERS VERSUS BUREAUCRATS

One key question to ask is: How determinative a role can the national leader, whether he be an elected president, a prime minister, or a dictator, play? Although most national elections are taken in the name of the leader, he rarely acts alone. For example, on any given issue, little information directly reaches the President. Only on a few occasions can he "see for himself." He talks to some foreign diplomats and a few foreign leaders, but in almost all cases the information he relies on must be filtered through his advisors and their supporting bureaucracies. Similarly, only on occasion does he design his own policy alternatives. Most of the time they are the product of staffs in the White House and government agencies, such as the State Department and the Department of Defense. Moreover, although the President makes the final decision in these cases, what he decides is almost never self-implementing. The policy chosen must be carried out by the bureaucracy.

At every step in this process, middle level bureaucrats and heads of departments can exercise influence. Strong and diverse bureaucratic biases enter the process as information flows upward to the President and as post-decisional orders proceed downward from him. Bureaucratic organizations have "standard operating procedures" that affect the options they offer and limit the range of actions they are able to take. Their interests can differ from those of the President. The responsibilities people have and the training they have undergone influence the way they see problems. As Lord Salsbury, a leading nineteenth-century British statesman, put it: "If you believe doctors, nothing is wholesome; if you believe theologians, nothing is innocent; if you believe the soldiers, nothing is safe."

The State Department, Defense Department, and Treasury will often given quite different reports about the same issue. Indeed, different parts of the same department often have different perspectives. As information and alternatives move up the hierarchy, then, they are subject both to the bureaucrats' organizational perspectives and to tactics that strengthen the bureaucrats' positions by putting matters in a light most favorable to their views. "Spontaneous" reports from American diplomats or military missions in the field are sometimes crafted with the object of influencing more than informing. Collusion is also possible: Bureaucrats in Washington may tell their colleagues in the field exactly what it is that they want to hear.

When the statesman's decisions are not self-implementing, the state's foreign policy makes itself felt through the myriad decisions taken at lower levels in the government. Even with the best will in the world, this task is not easy. Decisions made at the highest level are general in nature. What top leaders want done is often a puzzle to those below. The circumstances in which the policy is to be carried out have their own peculiarities that require adaptation of any general rule. In implementing policies and in conveying information, government departments have interests and biases that may differ from those of the President. Two consequences follow. First, the implementation of the policy may skew it in a direction consistent with the preferences of the bureaucrats but contrary to those of the President. Second, because most policies are carried out not by one department of the government but by many, the policy is likely to be implemented in conflicting ways. The State Department, for example, is likely to stress those parts of Presidential decision calling for bargaining and diplomacy; the Defense Department, to implement with greater vigor the call for the country to be ready to counter all military threats.

The resulting policy can then be inconsistent and self-contradictory. Halperin and Kanter argue that presidential decisions often are not implemented as the President intended and expected. Perhaps the most important example occurred in the summer of 1941. In response to the Japanese takeover of southern Indo-China, the United States cut off sales of oil to Japan. That country then faced the choice between political capitulation and seizure of the oil in the Dutch East Indies (now Indonesia). She chose the latter, which required a war with Britain and the United States. The result for America was Pearl Harbor. What is less commonly known, however, is that the decision Roosevelt made in July 1941 was not to cut off all oil sales, but rather to set up a complex system of controls that would allow the United States carefully to regulate the amount of oil Japan could buy. Not Roosevelt but a committee of sub-cabinet officials subsequently developed implementing regulations so tight and complex that they effectively constituted an embargo. This clearly was not what Roosevelt had decided.

This example raises some important questions. Why can the President (or any other leader) not see that policies are carried out as he wants? Why can he not obtain useful and unbiased information? After all, he is the head of the executive branch, can give orders, and fire those who fail to obey. In practice, the President is under constraints, both political and practical. To start with the latter, there are simply too many issues for him to be able to monitor more than a few closely. Even very important issues, like limiting sales of oil to Japan, may not be of high enough priority to gain the detailed and sustained Presidential attention that would be needed to ensure that what is done fits with his preferences. In the summer of 1941, Roosevelt had his hands full preparing for the summit meeting with Churchill, trying to speed aid to Russia, and worrying about the clashes between American destroyers and German submarines in the Atlantic. Other constraints are political: To override strongly-held bureaucratic preferences is likely to lead to unpleasant political disputes and undesired newspaper stories about the administration's disarray. The problems will be especially great in those cases, which are frequent, in which there are close ties between the bureaucracies and certain segments of Congress.

This is not to say that the President is powerless. Robert Art argues that excessive stress on the role of bureaucracies can lead us to overlook the fact that, on the most important issues, it is the President who makes the crucial decisions. Although much of the information reaching him is biased, the fact that information comes from different organizations with differing biases gives the President a wide range of perspectives and options. The bureaucracy may attempt to keep some significant issues from reaching him, but he can take steps to influence his own agenda and decrease the likelihood that his options will be prematurely foreclosed. When one looks at the central issues of American foreign policy—the basic stance toward the Soviet Union, policy towards restructuring the world economy, military intervention in other countries—one finds that while a President is not the only relevant actor, he almost always is the most important one. This is probably true for executive leaders in other countries, although we know much less about them than we do about the United States.

RATIONALITY AND MISPERCEPTION

The articles in the first section talk about whether states can fruitfully be conceived as unitary actors. Those in the second deal with the rationality of individuals. It is apparent that statesmen, like people in their everyday lives, do not make decisions in accord with the rules of strict rationality. They do not examine all information, search for all possible policy alternatives, consider how each possible policy is likely to affect all of their goals, and choose the policy that maximizes their expected gain. The world is too complicated and the capacity of our brains too limited to allow us to perform all the calculation that would be called for. Instead, statesmen adopt a number of short-cuts to rationality to reduce the intellectual burdens on them.

First of all, people simplify their processing of complex information by permitting their established framework of beliefs to guide them. They can then assimilate incoming information to what they already believe. Although people will change their minds when confronted with sufficiently dramatic and important information, these cases are rare. Information is usually ambiguous enough so that people can see it as consistent with the views that they already hold. In most cases, how a person interprets an event will be determined largely by such factors as his general beliefs about international politics and his images of the countries involved. Two people with different views are likely to see the same event differently.

Beliefs and images act as at least a proximate cause of the statesman's behavior. That is, rather than reacting directly to the external environment, the environment affects him only as he perceives it. These perceptions may differ from one statesman to another. To understand or predict a statesman's policies, one must first delve into his images of other countries and his beliefs about what policies will be efficacious.

If people's beliefs are resistant to discrepant information, it is important to know how they are formed. Unfortunately, our knowledge on this matter is sharply limited. Personality may play a role. . . . History is also important. Statemen's images of other countries are strongly influenced by important, recent events. Although they know that history cannot be expected to repeat itself, they tend to see current situations as resembling past ones. For example, the British appeasement policy of the 1930s can be explained in part by the statesmen's retrospective beliefs about the causes of World War I. Most of them saw the war as a mistake and believed that the Kaiser's Germany was not out to dominate Europe. They concluded that a more conciliatory policy toward Germany could have prevented war. Because they carried these beliefs with them, they were slow to recognize Hitler's true nature and aims. Similarly, the experience of Hitler led post-war Western statesmen to be quick to see Russia as fitting the mold of Nazi Germany.

People are less than fully rational, not only in the way they process information, but also in the way they choose among alternatives. Statesmen, like ordinary individuals, rarely search for the best possible policy. Instead, they "satisfice," to use Herbert Simon's term, one that combines the notions of "suffice" and "satisfy." This means that they usually take the first acceptable alternative policy they find rather than continue their search in the hope of discovering the best. The reason is that the search process is expensive in terms of time, energy, and political resources. A second deviation from complete rationality is that people often avoid value trade-offs. Whenever possible, they tend to minimize the extent to which a policy that favorably affects one of their values harms the others. For example, most of those who opposed the war in Vietnam believed both that the war could not be won at acceptable cost and that withdrawl would not lead to very bad consequences. By contrast, those who supported the war felt that it could be won if we continued our effort a bit longer and believed that defeat would lead to the fall of many other non-communist countries. People thereby minimized the cost entailed by the policies they favored, irrespective of what those policies were.

The readings in Part Four are designed to sample the range of factors that can influence the way statesmen select policies. Determining how these factors interact with each other and with the influences of the external environment is, of course, the crucial next step. All of us—teachers and students alike—can ponder that step but firm answers now elude us.

Leaders and Bureaucrats

The Bureaucratic Perspective

Morton H. Halperin and Arnold Kanter

We call our approach a *bureaucratic perspective* because it emphasizes the centrality of those individuals who are members of the national security bureaucracy. In the United States this means the President and that portion of the executive branch directly involved in decisions and actions affecting foreign policy and national security. We proceed on the assumption that the international environment permits a state to pursue a wide variety of goals and on the assumption that the predominant sources of a nation's behavior in the international arena are the organizations and individuals in the executive branch who are responding to opportunities for, and threats to, the maximization of their diverse interests and objectives. We believe that membership in the bureaucracy substantially determines the participants' perceptions and goals and directs their attention away from the international arena to intra-national, and especially intra-bureaucratic, concerns. Accordingly, we argue that a focus on the international objectives of a state is essentially misleading, in that the participants' attention primarily is focused on domestic objectives. Events in international affairs, according to this perspective, are most often the reflection of these internal concerns; the scholar requires an understanding of a nation's domestic political structure and of its national security bureaucracy in order to explain or predict the foreign policy actions it will take.

The bureaucratic perspective in this special sense implies (1) that change in the international environment is only one of several stimuli to which participants in the foreign policy process are responding (possibly among the weakest and least important) and (2) that events involving the actions of two or more nations can best be explained and predicted in terms of the actions of two or more *national bureaucracies* whose actions affect the domestic interests and objectives of the other bureaucracies involved. Both implications represent significant departures from the conventional wisdom of studies of foreign policy and international policies. . . .

NATIONAL SECURITY AS A DECISION MAKING GUIDE

Participants in the national security policy process believe that the policies and actions they should (and do) support promote the national security interest. Their perception of what constitutes that interest is in turn affected by their view of the world. In the postwar period a widely shared set of images of the functioning of the international system and the U.S. role in the world shaped the prevailing consensus on the requirements of American security.

These images combined perceptions of reality with preferences and objectives in an often conflicting set of beliefs. For example, it was widely held that in self-defense the United States had to maintain military superiority over the Soviet Union because the Soviet Union (because of Communism and/or Russian nationalism) was an aggressive nation. Any expansion of the area under Communist control was deemed to represent a serious challenge and had to be resisted because it would cast doubt on the credibility of American commitments. At the same time, these images of the respective roles of the Soviet Union and the United States were accompanied by a deep commitment to avoid a nuclear war.

Where a proposed course of action can be shown to be unambiguously necessary to preserve a shared objective, there is usually unanimous agreement. By the same token, widely shared images often lead to agreement on basic objectives and therefore to the exclusion of some options. Thus, in response to the Soviet launching in 1957 of the first Sputnik satellite, no one suggested that the United States simply yield leadership in strategic weapons and technology to the Soviet Union.

However, when the consequences of an action are ambiguous, which is most often the case, there is rarely agreement on what action to take, in spite of the shared images. For example, despite the general consensus that the United States needed to preserve its strategic deterrent and maintain its technological advantage over the Soviet Union after the Sputnik launching, President Eisenhower, Congressional leaders and the heads of the military services all had very different notions of what course of action would achieve these objectives. . . .

The set of shared images which has prevailed since World War II has established only very broad limits for policy deliberations: Mutually incompatible policies and actions can and do fall within the limits set by common conceptions of the national security interest. Each participant is relatively free to give operational meaning to those conceptions, and, at any one time, there is a wide divergence among the members of the national security bureaucracy regarding what, in specific cases, the national security requires. Thus it is not enough to say that a nation's foreign policies seek to protect and enhance its national security. Such a statement has very little predictive power and offers a poor guide for policy advice. If we are to explain a nation's foreign policy decision and actions, and if we are to be able to predict future decisions and actions, we must first identify the various participants of the national security bureaucracy, discover the sources of their particular perceptions of the national security, and seek to understand the process of interaction among them which yields the decisions and actions we observe.

Participants and Interests

Many discussions of American foreign policy assume either that officials in the government share a set of interests and work to accomplish an agreed set of goals or that the President determines policy and others seek to implement his decisions. Descriptions of "American" interests in Europe, for example, are often based on the assumption that actions by the American government affecting Europe are the result of unanimous "policy." Indeed, given the available data, such explanations may be the best we can provide in some cases.

However . . . the reality is quite different. The individuals involved in decisionmaking do not see the problem in the same way, nor do they have the same interests. Each participant, because of his background and his particular role in the government, has access to different information and has different concerns. Each sees a different *face* of the issue. What is a budget issue to one participant will be a foreign relations issue to a second or a Congressional relations issue to a third. . . .

Participants   The President stands at the center of the foreign policy process in the United States. His role and influence over decisions are qualitatively different from those of any other participants. In any foreign policy decision widely perceived at the time to be important, the President will be a principal if not the principal figure determining the *general* direction of actions. It was President John F. Kennedy who made the decision to blockade Cuba, and President Lyndon B. Johnson who decided to oppose the defeat of the South Vietnamese government by committing U.S. combat troops.

Although the President is the principal decisionmaker on important foreign policy matters, he does not act alone. He is surrounded, on the one hand, by a large number of participants with whom he is more or less required to statute or tradition to consult (obligatory consultation) and on the other hand, by those with whom he chooses to consult (discretionary consultation).

Regardless of who is President, Cabinet officers and heads of relevant agencies will be consulted because of their formal responsibilities and access to information. Law and custom dictate that among the Cabinet officers involved in foreign policy decisions almost always will be included the Secretary of State, the Secretary of Defense, the Director of Central Intelligence, and in economic matters the Secretary of the Treasury. The Joint Chiefs of Staff will be consulted on defense budget issues and matters concerning the possible use of force. Officials from agencies such as AID and USIA and departments such as Agriculture and Commerce may become involved in economic decisions. In many cases American ambassadors and military commanders in the field are brought into the process for consultation.

Depending on the particular preferences of the incumbent President, certain members of the White House staff may also be consulted—specialists on national security or foreign policy, political advisers, speechwriters and managers of the President's legislative program. President Eisenhower relied less on these advisers than did other Presidents. President Johnson drew on them for general foreign policy matters but not often for defense budget issues. President Nixon . . . [leaned] heavily on his adviser for national security affairs in all matters of foreign policy and national security.

Classifying Participants (I)

The participants from the national security bureaucracy can be arrayed around the President at varying distances depending on the probability that they will be consulted by him. In detailed analyses of particular decisions it is useful to distinguish those participants who are regularly consulted (*senior* participants) and those who have access to the President only very infrequently or only through a senior participant (*junior* participants). It is important to note that whether a particular participant is senior or junior is only imperfectly related to the formal hierarchy of organization. Thus President Nixon's adviser for national security affairs clearly [was] a very senior participant but [held] an office whose position in the formal hierarchy [was], at best, unclear. More generally, a President's discretionary advisers are not necessarily located in formally high-ranking positions.

Although not formal members of the national security bureaucracy, individuals outside the executive branch have frequently been consulted by the President and have had significant influence on the shape of national security decisions and actions. Some Congressmen and Senators are senior participants, i.e., they are routinely contacted by the President for advice and support. These men are most often influential members or chairmen of the Congressional committees with direct responsibility for national security affairs (e.g., Armed Services, Foreign Relations, Appropriations, Atomic Energy). To the extent that Congress is the focus of the President's domestic political concerns, Congressmen and Senators who hold positions of leadership in their respective houses will be important participants even without direct legislative responsibilities for national security policy.

Individuals outside the government sometimes are participants in the national security policy process. Ostensibly private citizens who are the close personal confidants of the President are included in this category. Private interest groups, such as defense contractors, whose concerns are affected by foreign policy decisions will seek to influence the direction of policy. These groups may be consulted by the President from time to time but in any case are involved routinely through their contacts with the Congress. Other outsiders may be formally invited to participate in the process, although for limited periods of time and with narrowly defined responsibilities. The various Presidential commissions and study groups are examples.

The farther removed the outside participants are from routine involvement in the national security bureaucracy, the weaker their independent sources of bargaining power. This is especially striking in the case of ad hoc commissions and study groups. For example, neither the Gaither Committee nor the Rand study group on strategic bases was sufficiently influential to achieve its objectives without substantial assistance from regular members of the bureaucracy.

The relative success of the Rand group and failure of the Gaither Committee can be attributed, in large measure, to their respective skills in forging alliances with important participants from the executive branch.

Guides to Interests

Since national security interests per se are essentially non-operational and therefore inadequate guides for action, most participants in the national security policy process turn to other sources for clues to the requirements of security and the best means to protect and enhance it. Other concerns and other interests become synonymous with the national security interest. These other interests may stem from the participant's organizational affiliation, his personal ambitions, and/or his evaluation of the domestic political climate.

Classifying Participants (II)

Participants may be classified not only in terms of whether they are junior or senior but also in terms of how accurately their stands on a wide range of national security issues can be predicted from a knowledge of their organizational affiliation.

Career officials come naturally to believe that the health of their organization is vital to the nation's security. So also do certain individuals who are appointed by the President to senior posts in the Washington national security bureaucracy. . . .

The tendency of a Presidential appointee to identify his agency's success with the national security will depend on the individual, the strength of his prior convictions, and his definition of his role. However, the nature of the organization he heads will be of special importance: Organizations vary in the extent to which positions of equivalent seniority constrain the behavior of role-occupants. For example, a Secretary of one of the military services usually will be strongly guided by the organizational interests of his service, since they ordinarily provide clear and coherent standards against which to measure success and failure. A Secretary of State, on the other hand, is likely to be less influenced by the organizational interests of his department and the foreign service, since these provide guidelines that are less clearcut and in many cases offer conflicting guides to the nation's security interest. . . .

Participants whose stands on issues can be predicted with high reliability from a knowledge of their organizational affiliation will be termed *organizational participants,* and those for whom organizational membership is not a good predictor will be termed *players.* Thus an individual in the national security bureaucracy may be classified as either relatively junior or relatively senior and as an organizational participant or a player.

The higher the formal position occupied by the participant, the more likely it is that he will be classified as a senior participant and that he will behave like a player. There is not a perfect relationship, however, since the Chiefs of Staff of the military services and the Chairman of the Joint Chiefs are more usefully classified as senior organizational participants, and members of planning staffs who ordinarily occupy lower-ranking positions in the bureaucracy often should be classified as junior players.

Organizational Interests

Bureaucrats will examine any policy proposal, at least in part, to determine whether it will increase the effectiveness with which the mission of their particular organization can be carried out; their organizational responsibilities will help to define the face of the issue they see. For example, in examining a proposal for a new security commitment, the Office of Management and Budget (formerly the Budget Bureau) and the Comptroller's Office in the Pentagon gauge how it will affect their ability to keep down the defense budget. Treasury asks how its ability to maintain the U.S. balance of payments in equilibrium will be affected. State Department officials may assess the possible impact of the security arrangement on political relations with the country in question and its neighbors. The military services will weigh the possible effect of the proposal on their existing commitments. . . .

All organizations seek *influence;* many also have a specific *mission* to perform; and some organizations need to maintain expensive *capabilities* in order to perform their mission effectively. Organizations with missions seek influence to promote their missions. Those that also have large operational capabilities— like the armed forces—seek influence on decisions in part to maintain the capability necessary to perform their mission. They will see the face of an issue that affects their ability to justify the maintenance of these capabilities. Other organizations, such as the Office of International Security Affairs (ISA) in the Office of the Secretary of Defense and the Policy Planning Staff in the State Department, have neither large capabilities nor stable, organizationally defined missions. Hence their only constant organizational interest is in enhancing their influence for its own sake, because individuals in such organizations share with those in other organizations the belief that they can best judge the nation's security interests.

Organizations with missions strive to maintain or to improve their (1) essential role, (2) domain, (3) autonomy, and (4) morale. Organizations with high-cost capabilities are also concerned with maintaining or increasing their (5) budgets. These organizational objectives are the source of the stakes and stands of organizational participants.

1. Organizational "essence" refers to the notion held by members of an organization as to what the main capabilities and primary mission of the organization should be. For example, European cavalry commanders had great difficulty in adapting to technological advances in weaponry because, in their view, the essence of their mission permitted them to fight only while mounted on horseback. The American horse cavalry did not confront similar problems of adaptation because its doctrine allowed

the cavalry to engage the enemy while dismounted. In some organizations, a view of the essence is shared by all of those in the same promotion and career structure. In other cases there is a difference of view. A large proportion of the Air Force officers believe that the essence of their service involves flying aircraft in combat, either to bomb targets behind enemy lines or to engage enemy aircraft. The strenuous efforts to extend the life of the manned bomber, as reflected in the Skybolt missile and B-70 bomber programs, is an indication of their view of the Air Force's essence and their unwillingness to see the same strategic function performed by different weapons (the intercontinental ballistic missile, or ICBM) even though their service would retain major responsibility for the mission.

2. Concern about "domain" (or "roles and missions" when referring to the military services) arises from uncertainty about where the operations of one organization end and those of another begin. The conflict between the Air Force and Navy regarding responsibility for the strategic nuclear mission was intensified by the Navy's efforts in the 1940s to develop carrier-launched aircraft capable of dropping atomic bombs. Such disputes also can occur within organizations. For example, the TFX (now F-111) aircraft had its origins in the attempt by the Air Force Tactical Air Command to take over some of the responsibility for strategic bombing which had been the preserve of the Air Force Strategic Air Command.

3. Autonomy refers to the desire of an organization to have control over its own resources in order to preserve what it views as its essence and to protect its domain from encroachment. Thus the military services opposed the Gaither Committee's report because they feared that, although implementing its recommendations might mean larger budgets for their organizations, it would change the decisionmaking process in a way which would reduce their ability to control their own operations. . . .

4. Organizational morale encompasses those things which organizations come to believe are necessary to preserve the loyalty of all members. For example, the other branches of the Air Force supported the Strategic Air Command on the Skybolt issue in order to minimize intraservice conflict, even though a favorable decision on Skybolt implied reduced funds for their own programs. Considerations of morale require, among other things, that what the organization is doing must look important in its own estimation, and it also means that serious attention must be given to problems of promotion.

5. Insofar as it is consistent with protecting and promoting their essence, organizations wish to maximize their budgets, both absolutely and in relation to the organizations with which they are in budgetary competition (e.g., each military service seeks to maximize its respective share of the Pentagon budget). Adequate budgets are needed to provide the resources necessary to accomplish the organization's mission and permit it to remain autonomous, independent of any of its bureaucratic competi-

tors or its nominal superiors. Success in budgetary competition also contributes to an organization's reputation for influence.

Organizations with large and expensive capabilities (notably the military services) will be particularly concerned about budget decisions and about the budgetary implications of policy decisions. Organizations with missions but low-cost capabilities will be primarily concerned with policy decisions and their implications for missions. Thus the British Royal Navy opposed the substitution of Polaris missiles for Skybolt because it feared that the missile-firing submarines would be financed at the expense of programs with a higher Royal Navy priority. By contrast, the bureaucrats in ISA with responsibility for the Military Assistance Program were willing, and even eager, to see funds for that program reduced.

Domestic Interests

There is no doubt that domestic interests affect foreign policy decisions and actions. Nevertheless the view persists that such interests are and should be ignored in the shaping of foreign policy. The perception that such calculations are illegitimate in the foreign policy sphere leads to a reluctance to put forward explicit domestic political arguments in favor of a particular policy. Except for a single note passed between two of its members, the upcoming Congressional elections were not mentioned in the meetings of ExCom (the ad hoc Executive Committee of the National Security Council) during the 1962 Cuban missile crisis. Yet, outside the national security bureaucracy, the announcement that missiles had been discovered was greeted with suspicion of political motivations. Similarly, the debates over the Chinese Offshore Islands did not include an explicit discussion of how the American political environment, which included wide support for the Nationalist regime, would be affected by a serious challenge to Chiang Kai-shek. For the incumbent Conservative government in Britain, the cancellation of Skybolt represented a serious threat to Tory prospects for re-election, but the party's political future did not enter into the dialogue with the American government.

Domestic political concerns differ in their impact on Presidents and on the bureaucracy. They are much more likely to be included in the President's calculations as well as those of his senior political appointees (particularly the White House staff) than in those of career civil servants. Three kinds of domestic interests come to be interpreted by Presidents and their senior political appointees as serving the national security.

1. The first is getting and keeping office. Presidents easily come to believe that their re-election is in the national interest and that their ability to be re-elected could be adversely affected by a controversial foreign policy decision. For example, a President may be concerned about denying an opponent a key political issue such as a "missile gap." Alternatively a President may see a particular foreign policy decision as an

effective appeal to a particular group of potential supporters such as textile manufacturers in the South or Jewish voters in New York. Contractors and labor unions frequently are affected by defense budget decisions, the TFX being a notable example.

2. Presidents and those who support them share with other bureaucratic participants a concern about maintaining their effectiveness—the ability to get things done. Stands on issues are affected in part by the desire to display influence—building a reputation for "winning" and avoiding a reputation for "losing." Thus a President and his supporters need to ask how a particular decision or action will affect his power. The desire to maintain and enhance influence leads to three rules:

   (a) Avoid the appearance of failure. Presidents and their associates are reluctant to take on efforts that probably cannot succeed, for each defeat tarnishes their reputation for success and, consequently, diminishes the probability of success in the future.

   (b) Avoid rows with Congress, the press or the public. Even if the President is successful in the present instance, he may have paid too great a price in his own time as well as in antagonism, bitterness and resentment. This was President Kennedy's assessment of his fight with Congress over the B-70 manned bomber.

   (c) Develop a consensus of support for a particular policy. In seeking this wide support, Presidents may feel the need to maintain consistency. A particular decision should appear to be consistent with other decisions made by the administration. The decision by President Truman to defend Taiwan in 1950 was made because he felt that he could not get the public's support for his defense of Korea if, at the same time, he permitted Taiwan to be overrun. This was particularly the case because leading Congressional Republicans, as well as the Joint Chiefs of Staff, were more concerned about Taiwan than they were about Korea. Officials also feel bound by the precedents they inherit from their predecessors in office. The consistency in United States policy toward Vietnam or the Offshore Islands through successive administrations had been attributed to pressures on Presidents for continuity of policy.

   The desire for consensus may also lead the President to placate the bureaucracy or to appoint an administrator trusted by his opponents. Thus Harry Truman appointed a Republican to head the Marshall Plan.

3. Finally, domestic interests and foreign policy interact in the clash over the use of scarce resources. Although domestic political calculations may make him reluctant to do so in particular situations (for example, when such economizing implies reduced aerospace procurement or military base closings), the President usually desires to hold down spending on defense and foreign policy in order to avoid inflation and to have funds for other purposes.

Personal Interests

Participants have a variety of personal interests which they come to identify with national security and which shape their perception of what should be done. One can distinguish, as Anthony Downs has suggested, two groups among those individuals who are dominated by their personal interests and who come to see national security in these terms.[1] In one group are the "climbers" interested mainly in getting ahead and becoming more powerful. In the other are the "conservers" interested in maintaining what they have. A career bureaucrat primarily interested in job security will tend to be a "conserver." An appointed official for whom present participation in the national security bureaucracy is a means to a more ambitious end will probably be a "climber." Knowing whether a man is one or the other provides a clue to the personal interests that will color his view of national security.

Many "climbers," particularly those who come into the government for limited periods of time, have a desire to be effective, to be involved, and to be powerful. Others are concerned about being promoted and increasing their prestige. Still other officials, particularly those in high positions, may be concerned about the impact of decisions or actions on their own ability to gain elective office in the future or even about how they will look in the history books. This makes them anxious to accomplish any particular mission which they are given. It also leads them to seek the confidence and support of the President, to avoid "making waves," and to avoid standing alone against a developing consensus within the government.

"Conservers" are more concerned with keeping what they have. They are interested in convenience—that is, in avoiding decisions that would threaten their jobs, increase their workload, or upset their routine. . . .

Faces, Stakes and Stands

In any specific case it is difficult to predict the exact mix of interests which will determine the face of a national security issue seen by the participant, his stake in its resolution and his stand on it. However, a few simplifying generalizations can be offered.

Few career participants see any conflict between their personal interests and the objectives of the organization with which they are affiliated. A career official's view of what is in the national security interest is determined in large part by the shared images held within the organization in which he seeks promotion, as well as in the larger bureaucracies with which he comes in contact. He recognizes that if his organization prospers, he is more likely to be promoted and that his promotion may depend on his appearing to fight for the interests of his organization. . . . [T]here was a widespread but probably only tacit agreement within the Air Force to overestimate the effectiveness of bombing North Vietnam: The organizational interests of the service required that interdiction appear to be effective, and the personal interests of its members required that the Air Force's organizational objectives be served. The absence of conflict among these sets of interests resulted in a highly—if spontaneously—coordinated effort to exaggerate bombing reports.

A participant less calculating and more selfless nevertheless may turn to his organization's interests and objectives for guides to stands on national security issues. Organizational interests tend to be more concrete and operational than general perceptions of national security and hence come to dominate the judgments of most career officials. . . . [M]ost members of the national security bureaucracy may be classified as organizational participants for the purposes of predicting their stands on issues.

However, non-career officials, particularly senior officials, in the national security bureaucracy are more likely to be players—that is, participants whose stands on issues cannot be reliably predicted from a knowledge of their organizational affiliation. Their perceptions of the national security interest are more likely to be dominated by images shared with society, their own experiences and their historical memories. The position of senior officials in the bureaucracy nevertheless will affect the information which is called to their attention by subordinates and the faces of an issue they see. Their dependence on the organization that they manage for information and for definitions of interests and stakes will depend on the extent of operational responsibility they have and on their degree of contact with other individuals and organizations. A noncareer official's definition of interests also will be affected by his conception of his role and of his relation to the President.

DECISIONS

Thus far, we have presented an image of numerous participants with divergent interests seeing differing faces of any issue. In examining any particular case, we need to understand not only what each participant wanted but also how these individuals sought what they desired. This leads to a consideration of *when* a participant may seek to change the pattern of governmental actions, the *constraints* within which the game is played, the strategies designed and implemented to effect the desired change, and the *bargaining advantages* which may be available.

The Impetus of Change

Given their interests and perspectives, participants are prone to believe that a large number of governmental actions ought to be altered. They also recognize, however, that the national security policy process would lapse into chaos and that they would fail if they sought to change everything they found undesirable. Thus mere preference does not determine which current policies and decisions will be challenged.

Participants will act to change decisions when (a) the expected probability of success increases and/or (b) the expected positive or negative payoffs shift substantially. For the purposes of the discussion, we will assume that the desired change requires a Presidential decision.

In a relatively few instances, the President, in his own interest and on his own initiative, raises an issue in order to make a decision. However, in general, Presidents do not address an issue unless one participant or a coalition makes a sustained effort to get him to do so.

For participants other than the President, the first problem is that a situation must occur which reopens an issue for a new decision. For certain classes of issues, this condition occurs *routinely*. The annual preparation of the defense budget, for example, virtually guarantees that, even in the absence of special efforts by any of the participants, a wide range of national security issues will receive Presidential scrutiny at least once a year.

A variety of less routine events may also create the necessary circumstances. Dramatic changes in the *actions of other nations* frequently create a situation in which new decisions appear feasible or even necessary. Sometimes the decision is closely related to those actions. For example, Communist Chinese pressures against the Offshore Islands forced a decision about whether or not the United States would defend those islands and, if so, whether it would use nuclear weapons. The relation between another nation's actions and the issues reopened for new decisions may be less direct. For example, when the Soviets detonated an atomic bomb in 1949, the debate over the pace of the American H-bomb program was reopened. At the extreme, the decision may be only peripherally related to the event. Thus the Joint Chiefs of Staff used the 1968 Tet offensive to press for a Presidential decision to mobilize reserve forces, a decision which they long had sought, less to increase the level of United States forces in Vietnam than to replenish the strategic reserves. . . .

In other cases, changes in *domestic mood* which affect participant's calculations of the domestic political consequences of a foreign policy decision may lead them to press for a particular decision. Also, changes in *personnel*, notably changes in administration, may lead to efforts to change a decision. This may be occasioned by the entrance of a new participant who is strongly committed to a different pattern of action, or it may occur because a participant who has effectively blocked a decision leaves the government. Accordingly, a change in Presidential administrations presents the opportunity to seek new decisions on a wide range of issues. When Kennedy replaced Eisenhower, the military services took advantage of the situation to renew their pressure for programs such as Skybolt and the nuclear-powered airplane which had been cancelled by the Republicans.

The Decision to Participate

Once an issue is raised, other participants in the process may recognize that an important individual or coalition is seeking a (Presidential) decision or that the President himself is prepared to make a decision. They then have to make a number of strategic estimates. The first calculation is to determine how their interests might be affected by the issue as they see it—to estimate their stakes in the outcome. They must consider what the range of decisions and changes in actions is likely to be. They must consider whether, if they become involved, they would be able to affect the decision and at what cost. In short, they must determine the intensity of their commitment and the scope of their involvement.

Some participants have no choice but to become involved. Because of their responsibilities they are directly concerned and find it impossible to opt out. The military services were inevitably involved in giving advice on whether the Offshore Islands could be defended and on whether the recommendations of the Gaither Committee made sense. Other officials are able to choose, since they will find it relatively easy either to become involved or to stay out. For example, because he saw it primarily as a choice among weapons systems and a defense budget issue, Secretary of State Dean Rusk played a minor role in the Skybolt decision and the ensuing crisis in Anglo-American relations. Perhaps more surprising, he chose not to become involved in most of the ExCom meetings during the Cuban missile crisis.

Where there is a choice, a participant's determination of whether to get involved depends on his calculation of the risks to his own personal interests and position, as well as his perception of national security interests. He is concerned about the time and energy involved in getting caught up in an issue, as well as the consequences to his reputation for effectiveness if he loses.

If a participant decides to get involved, he may plan a strategy—that is, a set of moves designed to produce the desired decision. Participants in the American government vary enormously in the degree to which they plan strategies. Many participants never plan, a few always plan, and the rest plan to a degree depending on the issue. In general, planning of this type is more likely to occur at lower levels. . . .

If they do plan, the participants' first step is to define their operational goal. They need to determine what decisions they hope to get made, by whom, and in what sequence. Next they must classify the other participants according to who has power with the President, who is likely to be neutral, who is an ally, and who is an opponent. It is then necessary to consider the kinds of arguments, the kinds of bargaining, and the kinds of coercive efforts that are required to achieve the desired decision. The resulting plans usually involve a series of *maneuvers* and *arguments* designed to influence the outcome. The maneuvers are directed first at determining the procedure by which an issue is raised, who should be involved, and how high up the ladder of organization the issue will go. Second, they are designed to influence the information presented to senior players. In each case, however, the range of choice is limited.

Constraints and Maneuvers

The national security policy process does not occur in an unstructured environment. In devising strategies to achieve desired outcomes, participants must take cognizance of the fact that they are *constrained* by a variety of factors, some of which derive from the laws and customs which govern the operation of the bureaucracy, others whose source lies in the images of international reality widely shared by members of the bureaucracy and/or the electorate, and still others which are attributes of any large and complex organization. Astute participants will design *maneuvers* which either seek to exploit an existing set of constraints for their advantage or try to modify constraints in order to increase the probability of success.

Two important classes of constraints which will be discussed in this section are (a) the rules of the game and (b) widely shared images of international reality. The corresponding maneuvers will describe (a) moves designed to exploit or alter the rules of the game, and (b) the arguments intended to maximize support on behalf of the desired decision. A third class of constraint—the limited performance of large and complex organizations—will also be addressed.

Rules of the Games The rules of the game are the constitutional provisions, statutes, regulations, procedures, customs, traditions, etc., which organize the government and structure the process by which decisions are made and actions are undertaken: They are a device for arranging minds to work on a problem. The rules determine who has the "action"—who will be responsible for raising the issue and carrying the necessary papers through the government, whose concurrence will be needed before a decision is made, the alternate channels through which a piece of paper can be moved, and how high up in those channels one may (or must) go to get a decision on a particular issue.

In seeking to get the decision they want, participants engage in maneuvers within the limits imposed by the rules of the game. They recognize that the way the decision is made will affect the results—e.g., whether and in what form the issue gets to the President. Among the key variables to be considered are who is involved in the process, whose views are reported to the President, and who is informed in advance that a decision is to be made. . . .

The rules of the game impose more or less narrow limits on participants who seek to change governmental actions. They always will permit some choice of behavior which defines the scope of potential maneuvers. Yet, the rules will necessarily have an important influence by affecting the decision to participate, i.e., who becomes involved, and whether he enters the game as an ally, opponent or neutral. . . . [C]ertain rules of the game based on custom affected policymaking on Vietnam: As issues are perceived to be increasingly important, they are handled by bureaucrats of increasing rank. Consequently, as Vietnam became a salient issue, it was removed from the jursidiction of relatively low-ranking experts on the area and made the responsibility of senior political appointees who had few specialized qualifications for the assignment.

The rules of the game vary in their permanence and in their application to particular cases: Various administrations have applied different sets of rules to similar cases, and the same administration frequently varies certain rules under its control, depending upon the circumstances. One set of rules stems from Presidential directives, such as those that established the new National Security Council system under President Nixon in 1969. Still others come from directives issued by Cabinet officers. The customs and traditions of the bureaucracy, the participants' personal perceptions of their roles and the nature of their personal relationships with the President are other sources of rules.

Some rules, such as those deriving from the American constitutional system, persist regardless of the particular incumbents. Most notable perhaps is the separation of powers which permits the Congress to constrain certain Presidential actions. Congressional legislation also helps to shape the rules of the game by requiring a specific subordinate official to make one or another kind of determination, by attempting to stipulate whom the President shall consult, or by specifying that the President personally must make a particular decision. For example, Congress has established a statutory membership for the National Security Council. While Presidents have been and are free to consult with other more informal bodies, the formal stipulation of membership affects who is consulted and when. Similarly, the formal procedures established by Congress for processing military assistance grants and sales dictate that several different organizations within the bureaucracy participate in each decision and must give their concurrence.

The more informal the rules, the more likely they are to be challenged or changed: Acts of Congress are relatively permanent, whereas procedures imposed by a personal style of decisionmaking are relatively ephemeral. During the course of administration, participants seek to change the rules if they feel that the current set of rules is strongly biased against the kinds of decisions and actions that they seek. Usually the changes they desire are ones which would bring about either greater involvement on their own part in the decisionmaking process or reduced involvement by participants whose views they oppose. . . .

Getting to the President   A fundamental choice which participants may be able to make is whether or not an issue should be sent to the President. Participants frequently calculate that their prospects for success are enhanced if the President can be excluded or, at least, if Presidential involvement can be postponed to a more opportune time. . . .

Participants have a tendency to compromise an issue among themselves rather than to submit it to the President. They do so in the belief that they can better protect their own organizational interest by getting a compromise which leaves other participants and themselves free to pursue their respective goals than by submitting the issue to unpredictable Presidential arbitration.

An issue will go to the President when (a) participants are unable to agree among themselves, (b) a senior participant believes he can secure a more favorable decision by taking the issue to the President, (c) the rules of the game require Presidential attention, or (d) the President has a strong personal interest in the issue.

Those who seek a Presidential decision face two problems. How and in what form shall they get the issue to the President? How shall they get him to make a decision?

The way in which an issue comes before the President—the face of the issue he sees—affects the decision that he makes. The rules of the game permit some choice: The same basic issue might come to the President in the form of a budget issue, or in the form of a sentence in a speech, or in the form of clearing a cable. The way it is raised will influence who in the White House is involved and whether the President sees it as a question of money, a question of policy, or a question of his relationship to a particular Cabinet officer.

There are a number of different maneuvers available to participants for bringing an issue to the President's attention. They may, for example, simply use existing formal channels, involving either consideration by the National Security Council or memoranda from the principal Cabinet officers to the President. In other cases, they may use more informal methods. For example, White House staff members, whether involved in foreign policy or not, are frequently used as channels to bring issues to the attention of the President. Sometimes this will be done informally before the issue comes up in formal channels; in other cases it will be a substitute for formal movement of the issue to the President. Other means used to bring issues to the President involve providing information to an allied country so that it will make a request which requires Presidential consideration, leaking information to the press or to the Congress, or simply making a public statement on an issue which then forces the matter to Presidential attention.

Once the issue gets to the President, the problem is not merely to get him to choose correctly, but to get him to choose at all. . . . Presidents are notoriously reluctant to make binding decisions and tend to deal only with those problems which have a critical deadline. Thus the question for those who seek a Presidential decision is how to impose a deadline on the President or how to make the issue part of an existing Presidential deadline. Those who oppose a Presidential decision, on the other hand, will seek a delay by proposing additional clearances, or additional study, or the appointment of a commission to make a thorough study. As the history of the Gaither Committee suggests, Presidents themselves frequently resort to the tactic of appointing special commissions in order to postpone or avoid the necessity of making substantive decisions.

When the issue involves a budget item or when it is a matter of major concern, getting the President to act is no problem—he is routinely and unavoidably involved in the decisionmaking. By contrast, issues without built-in deadlines have difficulty gaining Presidential attention. In the case of the Offshore Islands, those favoring American withdrawal were able to get the issue to the President on only one occasion and even then had difficulty establishing a deadline.

Arguments   Thus far we have discussed maneuvers which exploit or modify the rules of the game with a view toward influencing the decision to participate and affecting the face of the issue perceived. These maneuvers logically (and usually temporally) precede another set of maneuvers designed primarily to affect the perceived stakes of those officials who participate. The latter class of maneuvers depend crucially upon controlling the substance and dissemination of information. Since the ostensible purpose of these maneuvers is, in one sense or another, to persuade other participants to support (or not oppose) the preferred stand, the information usually is presented in the form of rationales for action which we call *arguments.*

Participants may seek to maximize support on behalf of their position in basically three ways. First they may seek to persuade someone that he has a stake in the issue. To do this, they stress information that will appeal either to the other party's sense of what is in the national security interest or to that party's more particular organizational, domestic or personal interests.

Second, they may seek a bargain which will persuade a participant to give his support. They may, for example, offer to compromise: to alter the proposal in a way which reduces its cost to the interests of a particular participant. In other cases, the bargaining will involve logrolling: trade-offs between different issues.

Finally, participants may resort to coercion. They may try to convince an opposing participant that to make a substantial effort to alter the decision would affect his ability to accomplish things on other issues. By seeking to convince another participant that they have the power or ability to hurt his interests on other questions, they may persuade opponents to exit from the game (or reduce the probability that opponents initially will become involved).

Arguments also perform another function, closely related to that of persuasion. Particularly through . . . the formal communications channel within a bureaucracy, arguments are offered not only to persuade but also to communicate the stakes and stands of various participants. Since arguments designed to persuade are more familiar, we will concentrate our attention on the other purposes for which arguments are offered.

One of these is simply to fill in the blank. That is, under the rules of the game, proposals for new decisions must be accompanied by an explanatory memorandum presenting justifications. More specifically, in some cases the purpose of advancing arguments simply will be to demonstrate that there is a national security rationale for this proposal. Officials whose other interests incline them to support a proposal will need to be convinced that a responsible and reputable case can also be made for the national interest. The basic stakes of the participants in the Skybolt decision were obscured by focusing the public debate on technical feasibility and cost-effectiveness.

Another purpose of putting forward arguments is to signal strongly what one's policy preferences are. For example, when Eisenhower's principal advisers told him in 1958 that the loss of the Offshore Islands would have consequences greater than those which followed the capture of the Chinese mainland by the Communists, they were indicating to him not only what they thought he should do but also the strength of their commitment to the position being recommended.

Finally, arguments may be designed to present the appearance of a consensus not only on what decisions should be made but on the purpose. The Departments of State and Defense both supported an accelerated H-bomb program, but they did so for quite different reasons. However, these differences were not made clear to the President. Since participants will feel that the President is more likely to go along with their position if they appear to favor it, they also are likely to seek agreement on a set of general arguments to which they can all subscribe. Participants advocating United States defense of the Offshore Islands did so for diverse reasons and could not agree on a set of specific arguments. As a result, a prediction of vague "dire consequences" was presented to the President.

In many cases a gap develops between the arguments put forward at one level and the arguments which actually persuade participants at another. Junior participants in the process are likely to focus on their conceptions of national security interest, as shaped by the organizational concerns of their agency. Presidents and senior participants are likely to have in mind a different notion of national security, more influenced by domestic politics and the history book, and by their relationships with other senior officials. Thus, in internal Air Force debates, the case for intensified bombing of North Vietnam was argued in terms of the Air Force's competition with the Navy for the deep interdiction mission after the war. However, when pressing senior civilian participants for an expanded bombing role, the Air Force argued in terms of the bombing's effectiveness.

Just as maneuvers intended to influence the decision to participate and to affect the face of the issue perceived are limited by the rules of the game, arguments also are constrained. The most important constraints on arguments derive from widely shared images of international and domestic reality and commonly accepted standards which determine legitimate and unacceptable lines of argument.

Shared images provide an important constraint on what participants see and on what conclusions they draw from the evidence presented. Whatever their own beliefs, moreover, participants must shape their arguments for any particular case according to the shared images of the bureaucracy and society at the time. This reluctance to challenge unstated assumptions and conventional wisdom is related to . . . the "effectiveness trap": participants will not question the prevailing images lest they no longer be taken seriously, either in the present discussion or on future unrelated matters. For example, in the early 1950s, those in the Department of State who advocated forcing the Chinese Nationalists off Quemoy and Matsu could not support their case by advancing the argument that this would result in a substantial improvement of relations between the United States and Communist China. Since improved relations between the two countries was not a widely shared goal, such an argument would have been counterproductive. Similarly, during the Cuban missile crisis Secretary of Defense McNamara quickly retreated from his initial recommendation that the United States do nothing about the Soviet missiles, for he recognized that he was in danger of being excluded from further effective participation in the decision.

A participant may, from time to time, seek to change the shared images in order to expand the range of arguments that can be used. However, images are so resistant to modification that he is likely to do so only when he feels that there is no other way to challenge decisions of importance to him and only if he feels that he has built a record of reasonableness and credibility sufficient to avoid his being dismissed as eccentric. . . .

To this point, we have implicitly assumed that the participants who offer arguments have relatively complete and accurate information, particularly regarding the intentions and behavior of foreign countries. Of course, such intelligence in reality is rarely if ever either complete or accurate. An important constraint on the content of arguments as well as their effectiveness derives from the fact that most of the information about the world used by the national security bureaucracy is developed by large and complex organizations. How organizations operate greatly affects what information is made available to senior participants, when it comes to their attention, and in what context. . . .

Decisions as System Outputs

Given participants with different interests who see different faces of an issue, given their maneuvering to affect what information is available to other participants and how the issue is decided, what determines which decisions are made? How does the process affect what is to be done and who is to do it?

Biases of the System   In part, decisions are biased by the constraints of the system. Even if all the participants were equal in the bargaining skills, the set of constraints which exist at any given time tends to skew the distribution of possible decisions, making some more likely than others. Thus some arguments will be more persuasive than others, particular options will be consistently offered and regularly selected, and the rules of the game will confer added bargaining advantages on certain participants.

A set of shared images determines what sort of actions participants will come to believe are in the national security interest and what kinds of arguments can be used in favor of these decisions. In the postwar United States the fact that there was a set of shared images about the need to contain Communist aggression, about the indivisibility of security, about the need to avoid appeasement, and about the need for military force to oppose Communist military expansion shaped the decisions made by Presidents on major issues. The system was biased in favor of decisions which could be supported by these kinds of arguments and against stands which were perceived to be counter to these doctrines.

The existing organizations and their procedures also shape what is to be done. The fact that the United States has a large Navy with aircraft carriers, that it has an Agency for International Development to give out aid, and that these and other organizations are structured in particular ways leads to support for particular policies and to capabilities for carrying out particular decisions. The system is heavily biased toward doing what its large organizations are eager and prepared to do.

The influence of individuals within the policy process consists of a blend of bargaining advantages conferred by the rules of the game, skill and will in using these advantages, and others' perceptions both of one's bargaining advantages and one's skill and will in using them.

The rules of the game are an important bias in the system because they result in an unequal distribution of bargaining advantages. An official who the rules stipulate must be consulted on a decision has greater influence than one who has to fight his way into the process. A rule which gives important powers to the Congress affects what can be accomplished in the executive branch as well. The different rules established by each President affect who has influence and access and how decisions are made. The rules also determine who has control over information and options and may, in some cases, provide a monopoly of expertise to certain participants.

Another form of bargaining advantage is the responsibility for implementing a decision. A participant who is to carry out a Presidential decision must be consulted and must be prepared to certify that the proposed action is feasible. Presidents find it difficult to order someone to do something that the latter said is infeasible or dangerous. This is particularly true for the armed forces, in that Presidents are reluctant to order combat operations which the responsible military commanders say are dangerous or unduly threaten American lives. Those responsible for implementation will also have the important bargaining advantage, at least in some cases, of being able to control deadlines.

The domestic political reality, as perceived by the particpants in the process, also plays a major role in affecting the kind of decisions which emerge. All of the participants have a sense of what the society's shared imgaes are. In addition, they are concerned about and dependent upon different groups within the society. Presidents will be concerned about political supporters and interest groups of importance in key states; members of the bureaucracy will be concerned about those interest groups within the society with which they have rapport. In the case of the Offshore Islands, for example, those who resisted any change of policy were able to bring to bear the weight of large, important groups that opposed any change in American China policy, while there were no comparable groups pressing for change.

Consequently, a key bargaining advantage conferred by the rules of the game in the United States is the ability to threaten to go beyond the executive branch, to appeal to the Congress, interest groups, or the general public in a way which may affect elections. Such a bargaining advantage manifests itself in the implicit threat to leak particular information or to resign from office. . . . [T]he role of outsiders is less to introduce new information or ideas into the bureaucracy than to strengthen the position of some of the participants by giving their stand the stamp of approval of disinterested experts. This is one of the ways in which a Presidential commission can become a Presidential headache. Once the President has appointed a group of prestigious outside experts to make recommendations, he can ignore their advice only at great political peril.

Not every bargaining advantage derives from the rules of the game. Certain bargaining resources can be created and exploited by the participants themselves. For example, in making the choice about what to do, Presidents are also deciding who should do it. Accordingly, one form of bargaining advantage comes from a reputation for competence and willingness to obey orders. Staff skills, including the ability to draft effective memoranda, are also important in determining one's influence. In many cases Presidents in the postwar period have accepted Defense Department national security proposals because of the belief that this part of the government was more likely than was the State Department to be responsive to their needs.

A major set of bargaining advantages comes from personal attributes of particular participants. Perhaps the most important is the confidence of the President. Secretary of State Dean Acheson's principal advantage during the Truman administration was the knowledge that he had Truman's confidence and that the President was almost certain to support him on any issue. This resulted, in part, from Truman's perceptions that in order to enable his Secretary of State to operate effectively he had to support him and, in part, from the fact that Acheson was likely to be persuasive with the President on the merits of the issue. . . .

Another personal attribute of considerable importance is the willingness and ability to assert one's prerogatives, even if doing so involves a certain amount of unpleasantness—including raising voices and banging tables. . . . Participants who do not assert their prerogatives may well find that they are bypassed; others may be able to establish their right to involvement in particular decisions by making clear that, if they are not consulted or if their wishes are ignored, they are prepared to be nasty.

Finally, time, determination, and the willingness to seek responsibility and to act are important attributes affecting the influence of a participant in any particular case. Participants who do not have major ongoing responsibility, such as members of planning staffs, can pick a single issue and devote substantial time and determination to it. Many observers believe that the proposal for multi-national ship crews drawn from a number of NATO countries—the Multilateral Force (MLF)—got as far as it did because the State Department's Policy Planning Council was able to devote considerable time and effort to guiding the project through the bureaucracy while its opponents were preoccupied with other, more pressing responsibilities.

By virtue of the rules of the game, the President himself has the major advantage of formal responsibility and authority for most of the decisions to be made in the executive branch. On foreign policy questions the problem, from his perspective, is to get the issue to him in time and with the necessary information and options so that he can make a sensible choice, given his own interests. He must therefore create additional bargaining advantages for himself. These depend on his own skill in establishing rules to increase the probability that the issue will get to him in the way that he wants. He may, for example, deliberately assign overlapping responsibilities. They also depend on his willingness to assert his authority by hiring or firing people and by acting tough if necessary.

Decisions as Guides to Action

Our discussion of the national security bureaucracy has left the term "decision" deliberately undefined. From the context it is clear that "decision" has been used to mean "an authoritative determination that the stipulated member(s) should act in a specified manner." Conventional discussions of the policymaking process frequently concentrate on the manner in which decisions are reached and virtually exclude consideration of their subsequent implementation. Yet, most participants and analysts primarily are interested in the *actions* or outputs of governments and in the consequences or *outcomes* of those actions. Presumably the decisionmaking process is studied in the belief that decisions substantially determine actions and outcomes. However, this belief is frequently mistaken. Decisions are often imperfect predictors of governmental outputs, and actions can occur in the absence of decisions.

Although foreign policy decisions stipulate that someone should act in a specified manner, there usually is a wide range in the specificity of the directive. A significant proportion of foreign policy decisions do not explicitly direct well-defined actions. It might be useful to think of decisions arrayed along a continuum from least specific (with regard to directing actions) to most specific. At the one end of the continuum fall *policy decisions*, which in effect are statements of aspirations. At the opposite end fall *action decisions*, which explicitly direct particular participants to engage in a detailed set of activities. . . .

Despite the enormous time and effort which goes into the struggle over the decisions the President will make, in most cases the decisions which emerge are in no sense definitive. Often they are very general. They may be only statements of aspiration—vague policy decisions—or they may be somewhat more specific in that they assign a general action to a particular organization or individual. Even then, they are likely to leave considerable leeway as to who should act, what precisely they should do, and when they should do it. This is true for a number of reasons.

First, policymakers tend to assume that detailed instructions from them are unnecessary. Presidents, especially at the beginning of their terms, incline to think that what they order will be obeyed and obeyed faithfully. Hence, they believe, one needs only to give general direction and the decisions will be translated into effective actions. Even when Presidents learn that this is not true, they tend to feel that details are unimportant and that what really counts is the general thrust of policy.

Moreover, Presidents find that they lack the time and the expertise to draft detailed plans. When Kennedy ordered the blockade of Cuba in 1962, he left most of the details of implementation to the Navy. Until the British ambassador drew his attention to the fact, the President did not realize that the blockade had a much larger radius than he had intended, resulting in a sharp reduction of the time interval before Soviet vessels encountered United States ships.

Presidents also find that the legitimacy of providing great detail is questioned by operating agencies. These organizations assert that it is their responsibility to provide the detail, and they resist efforts by the President and by Cabinet officers to provide specifics. This is particularly true for the conduct of diplomatic negotiations and military operations. The Navy deeply resented Secretary McNamara's detailed questioning of its blockade procedures during the Cuban missile crisis and virtually expelled him from the Pentagon command post where the operation was being coordinated.

In some cases, generality and vagueness are used deliberately by the President. He may not want to be committed in great detail. He may see his decisions essentially as giving a hunting license to particular individuals to pursue a policy without having to commit himself to its effective implementation. In other cases, a President's compromise with his subordinates may prohibit him from spelling out in detail what he has decided. The compromise may be designed to gain adherence to a particular policy and to avoid harming the strongly felt interests of certain participants.

Presidents, as a rule, are likely to delay decisions on non-urgent matters in order to concentrate on pressing issues. They are also likely to decide as little as possible, leaving open the possibility of changing their position later. In many cases, this leads them to make narrow individual decisions on a number of different issues which come to them separately, even though an observer might feel that the decisions contradicted each other (or at least were not mutually supporting). Such a series of incremental, "minimal" decisions may culminate in what amounts to a major policy decision although no one of the decisions was made with this in view. The decision to support a crash program to develop and produce the hydrogen bomb is one such example. Similarly, the separate decisions taken in the days following the crossing of the 38th Parallel yielded an American commitment to defend South Korea although no single one of them necessarily implied that commitment.

Finally, Presidents frequently fear "leaks" and recognize that the more detail they give and the more they appear to be committed to a specific policy, the more likely somebody is to leak it. In international relations this reluctance to be explicit can lead to serious complications. For example, the Kennedy administration feared a serious adverse reaction from influential Congressmen if and when it announced the cancellation of Skybolt. This fear led the administration to be publicly vague and ambivalent about the program and prevented it from giving clear and explicit signals to the British regarding the missile's prospects. When cancellation finally was announced, many of the British felt they had been misled.

ACTIONS

Regardless of the motivation which leads to ambiguous decisions, the lack of complete specificity permits and often requires subordinates to exercise considerable discretion. To the extent that decisions allow discretion, they are poor predictors of governmental output; any analysis of the policy-making process that stops with decisions is incomplete. If we are to understand why a government behaves as it does, we must analyze what happens in the aftermath (or absence) of a Presidential decision.

Self-Executing Decisions

In most cases, once a President decides that some part of his government should do something, this decision is conveyed orally or in writing (in a non-public manner) to the official concerned, on occasion by the President himself, but more likely by some member of the White House staff. This official in turn must draft implementing instructions to those who will actually do the work. Frequently this includes embassies and military commanders outside of Washington as well as subordinate officials in the major departments. Receipt of these instructions should theoretically result in the implementation of the actions which the President has decided upon. But at each stage of the process there are occasions for misunderstandings and mistakes and opportunities for discretion and non-compliance.

Opportunities for subordinate discretion are minimized and governmental outputs are most likely to resemble the President's intentions only in the severely restricted set of circumstances that permit the President to issue what Neustadt has called a "self-executing" order.[2] Such conditions require that the President's involvement in the process be unambiguous, that the decision which he makes be unambiguous, that his orders be widely publicized, that the men who receive them have control over everything and everyone needed to carry them out, and that they stand in no doubt of his authority to issue these orders.

Even in the absence of these ideal circumstances, other factors may induce an attempt at faithful compliance. The extent to which the government's actions implement Presidential decisions depends both on the willingness and ability of subordinates to fulfill the President's wishes and on the ability of the White House to check on subordinates' actions. Faithful compliance is most likely if it is relatively easy for the President to monitor actions or if there are known to be lower-ranking enthusiasts for the policy who are likely to monitor. The President's reputation for pressing for compliance and for punishing those who fail to obey is important in determining whether his decisions are loyally implemented. However, where those responsible for implementing the decision favor it and share the President's reasons for wanting to carry it out, they are likely to execute it faithfully regardless of the President's ability to detect and to punish disobedience.

The Struggle over Implementation

But complete and faithful implementation of a Presidential decision remains the exception rather than the rule. More often than not, governmental outputs noticeably diverge from the President's expectations regarding the implementation of his decision. The gap between decision and follow-through results in part from the fact that compliance is not routinely forthcoming, particularly in cases where subordinates feel strongly about their positions and have a reasonable expectation of escaping detection and/or punishment. The gap results also in part from the fact that organizations are relatively inflexible instruments and that decisions frequently provide little or no guidance for action: Even when there is a substantial effort to comply faithfully with a Presidential decision, there will be severe limits on "faithful compliance." Both forms of non-compliance—deliberate and inadvertent—derive from the fact that decisions are much more likely to be vague, ambiguous policy decisions than explicit, well-defined, self-executing action decisions.

One source of inadvertent non-compliance stems from the fact that the President himself may not know exactly what he wants done. A Presidential decision to consider seriously and sympathetically the recommendations of the Gaither Committee does not provide much guidance to his subordinates on how to react to its individual proposals. Moreover, those seeking to carry out the decision may not be aware of why and in what context the President decided as he did. In some cases, Presidents seek to keep this secret for fear of leaks or overcommitment. In other cases, a compromise may prevent him from making it known. But in any case, the gap between how the President looks at problems and how junior participants who are likely to carry out a decision see them produces a great divergence in their perceptions of the necessary details. In many cases, there simply will be confusion. Orders can be misinterpreted, misread, or not sent out; they can go to the wrong officials or to officials who will simply not understand that they are supposed to implement them.

In some cases, decisions may be conveyed to officials who have in the past been informed of other decisions which they see as incompatible. Hence their desire for faithful compliance with two directives may lead to a conflict causing them to alter what they have been told to do in one or both cases.

Finally, there will be important organizational constraints. When the action directed is a complicated one, it is carried out by an organization in ways that conform to one of the organization's existing plans of action. . . . [L]arge organizations tend to be rigid, inflexible instruments incapable either of appreciating or implementing subtleties. As a result, execution may differ a good deal from what a President thought was going to be done.

Deliberate non-compliance derives from the fact that a Presidential decision does not end the conflict about what actions the United States should take. Participants still have very different interests, see different faces of the issues, have different stakes, and therefore have different notions as to what should be done. Because they see different aspects of the issue, they will interpret the decision differently and continue to fight the President's purpose, as well as his specific decisions. President Eisenhower discovered that his decision to cancel the atomic-powered airplane had little impact on the progress of the program. Indeed, he found himself making several decisions to terminate the project in the course of his administration. Nevertheless, when Kennedy entered office in 1961, he was confronted with a program to develop a nuclear-powered aircraft.

Action games repeat many features of decision games. The action phase can become simply a new round in the process in which participants plan strategies, decide to opt in or out, and seek to find allies and overcome potential opponents. Those who favor the decision move to have it implemented as they want; those who oppose it try to block implementation. However, in this case, participants with responsibility for implementing the decision—primarily organizational participants—play a key role.

If deliberate non-compliance is possible, the key variable determining the degree of congruence between decision and action is whether or not the executors favor implementation. Albert Wohlstetter and the Rand study group on strategic bases apparently appreciated this fact. Since the Air Force would be responsible for implementation of the decisions the group favored, they made great efforts to win Air Force confidence and support for their recommendations. In fact, they did not go outside the Air Force to those officials formally responsible for approving the recommendations until the Air Force had adopted their report as its own. The Gaither Committee, on the other hand, seemingly gave only passing attention to designing its report to stimulate support among those participants who would be responsible for implementation.

In many cases, some or all of those who are supposed to implement a decision do not feel obliged to strive for faithful implementation. As Kennedy discovered during the Cuban missile crisis, his order that American IRBM's be removed from Turkey did not even lead to negotiations on their removal. In some cases, implementation may be overly zealous; those who receive a Presidential hunting license may carry the action further than the President intended. In other cases, those opposed to a policy fight back and seek a change in the Presidential decision or at least an exception for their organization. They may demand a meeting with the President; they may try to persuade other governments to protest the proposed action; or they may leak the information to the Congress or the press—all in the hope of reversing the decision. . . .

Action in the Field

Although non-compliance occurs throughout the national security bureaucracy, a gap between decisions and actions is especially likely to be opened up by officials in the field—removed in time and distance from the President and senior participants in Washington. In general, compared with participants in Washington, officials in the field are even less willing to obey orders and less able to obey them faithfully, even when they choose to do so. They understand less of what the President wants and are less willing to respond. Not only do the actions of these participants highlight certain features of the process, but they often are the officials whose actions are most visible and most salient to foreign governments.

Officials in the field, particularly ambassadors and military commanders, tend to have a different perspective on issues than officials in Washington. They see these issues in terms of accomplishing their objectives—maintaining good relations with the local country or meeting their military responsibilities. They also tend to believe that Washington does not understand the problem, is out of touch with the realities of the situation in the local area, and does not respond properly to their suggestions, initiatives, and requests. . . .

Participants in the field often have been only peripherally involved in the Washington decisions which they are asked to implement. Thus they are not fully informed about why the President decided what he did and the context in which he made the decision. In many cases, they are not sure whether indeed it was a Presidential decision, a Cabinet officer's decision, or a lower-level decision, since all cables come to them signed by the Secretary of State or the Secretary of Defense.

When confronted with decisions from Washington with which they do not agree, officials in the field engage in a number of different maneuvers. They may object to the proposed action, arguing that now is not the time to carry it out, or they may assert that it would be infeasible or counterproductive to do so. Alternatively, they may fail to do what they are ordered to do, in hope that Washington will not notice. In many cases this hope is justified. If they do feel the need to carry out the order, they may nevertheless depart from their instructions in a number of significant ways. . . .

Actions need not be preceded by either policy decisions or action decisions. At times, officials in the field maneuver to accomplish their purposes in the absence of decisions from Washington. Instead of sending an issue to Washington for a decision, they may act without instructions. Alternatively, they may commit Washington to a policy by doing something in the field which forecloses the President's options. They may exploit visits to the area by high-level officials to get them to support their position, and then act as if there were now a commitment by the United States government. When they do consult Washington, they are likely to formulate messages along the lines of "Unless I hear to the contrary by a certain date, I will take a certain action." They count on the fact that Washington may be too busy or too preoccupied or too much in disagreement to send out a cable stopping them from taking the action that they propose to take.

Actions as System Outputs

The dominant bias in the American system is continuity. In the absence of some major disturbance which causes or allows them to change, officials, whether in the field or in Washington, will continue to do what they have been doing. Since continuity is the rule, our objective is to explain discontinuities.

Formal authority has some impact on what actions are taken, but even more important is control over resources and actual responsibility for implementation, as well as control over information regarding whether actions have in fact been carried out.

In those cases where a President does make a decision, the main thrust of what is done is generally in line with what the President orders. But the details stem largely from a combination of the objectives of the implementors and the constraints imposed by their organizations' repertoire of operating procedures. Where the line is drawn between general direction and specific detail will depend, not only on organizational constraints, but also on the President's interest and his willingness to commit his time and his public prestige.

A President has several options in seeking to increase the probability of compliance. He can, for example, utilize that organization or entity he thinks most likely to faithfully implement the decision. In many cases Presidents will send a White House official or private emissary to carry out diplomatic negotiations which they fear the State Department may not carry out faithfully or promptly. In other cases, they may create a whole new organization. Or they may create competition among existing organizations by assigning responsibility to more than one. In some cases, they will keep decisions or their reasons secret from those who might oppose the policy and who might leak the information to the press or Congress. However, in this case there is the dilemma that those who are not told of the policy are incapable of taking actions which will reinforce it.

The most effective Presidential weapon is personal involvement which demonstrates a willingness to be forceful and, if necessary, nasty. This personal involvement shows that the President cares, making it much harder for officials to resist doing what he has ordered. He can make an authoritative decision and, with the assistance of the White House staff, can monitor actions for compliance. When decisions are made in the name of senior participants other than the President, the frequency and degree of non-compliance will increase. . . .

INTERACTION AMONG NATIONS

Thus far, we have attempted to explain the process by which the American government makes foreign policy decisions and how this affects the actions of American officials. These foreign policy actions are designed to advance the national security interests of the United States as viewed by the participants. In some cases the actions are aimed at affecting the decisions and actions of other goverments and hence are intended to affect outcomes—what happens in the world.

As was suggested in discussing interests, many of the objectives of each of the participants can be satisfied only at home. Political leaders of a nation rise and fall depending on whether they satisfy domestic needs. Individuals advance in the bureaucracy when they meet the standards set by political leaders or by career ladders. Organizations prosper or decline depending on the strength of their support in the bureaucracy and elsewhere within the nation. Such matters preoccupy participants in the foreign policy process. Perhaps because they are more immediate, threats to interests from rival organizations or from leading political groups seem much more real than threats from abroad.

Participants, of course, also bear national security interests in mind. No leader wnats to see his nation attacked, and few desire to send their soldiers off to fight in distant wars. Some leaders are committed to a conception of world order. Several paticipants may have a wide range of interests beyond the borders of their nation. But whatever participants are concerned about, they are likely to see the battles as being won or lost mainly at home. This became obvious in the case of the Vietnam War.

It is not that actions of other nations do not matter, but rather that they matter mainly if and when they influence domestic and especially bureaucratic struggles. A participant's efforts to accomplish his objectives—whether to advance domestic political interests, organizational interests, personal interests or national security interests—are sometimes affected by what he and other participants come to believe about the actions of other nations. A German Chancellor whose domestic position depends on his reputation for being able to get what the Federal Republic wants from the United States will be concerned about American actions that lead his colleagues and opponents to conclude that Washington no longer listens to him. An American President or Secretary of Defense who wishes to reduce defense spending will see that his position requires Soviet actions which permit him to argue that the nation's security can be protected with reduced forces. The Skybolt program was so crucial to the British government primarily because it was the heart of the Conservative Party's election pledge to maintain an independent nuclear deterrent.

Since actions by other nations can affect the stands that participants take, and thereby affect both decisions and outputs, we must consider how actions of other nations enter into the process of bargaining over decisions and actions. Therefore this . . . section . . . outlines briefly the way in which the actions of officials in one nation are likely to affect the actions of officials in another.

In considering how actions of American officials affect the decisions and actions of foreign governments, we begin with the fact that other governments are, in at least one important aspect, no different from the American government. They too consist of different participants with different interests and responsibilities who see different faces of an issue and struggle to get the decisions and actions they desire. . . . [T]he relevant participants in other national security bureaucracies are not necessarily those officials with the same formal titles—function does not necessarily follow structure. But the communication between governments is not, as it is frequently painted, a dialogue between two rational individuals. Rather, actions of one government are simply one of the many elements that affect the struggle within the other over decisions and actions.

Nations affect the actions of one another less by physically compelling changes in behavior than by acting on one another's perceptions and expectations: interaction among nations is primarily a matter of threats, promises, and warnings designed to influence behavior by persuasion. Accordingly, the primary vehicle for the exercise of international influence takes the form of "signals" among international actors. Actions—the outputs of the national security bureaucracy—are the "signals," designed to persuade another nation to alter its behavior in the preferred direction. The bureaucratic perspective highlights the process of communication among nations. . . .

NOTES

1. See Anthony Downs, *Inside Bureaucracy* (1967), pp.92–101.
2. Richard E. Neustadt, *Presidential Power* (1960), p. 19.

A Critique of Bureaucratic Politics

Robert J. Art

Bureaucracies, we are told, have become central to the forging and welding of American foreign policy, but with consequences adverse to the substance of that policy. In the words of a past critic and present practitioner of American foreign policy: "The nightmare of the modern state is the hugeness of bureaucracy, and the problem is how to get coherence and design in it."[1] That bureaucracies are crucial to our foreign policy and that they can make life difficult for Presidents are two propositions with which any analyst of American foreign policy could scarcely disagree. But what precisely do these propositions mean? Do they mean that bureaucracies largely determine our foreign policy through their ability to select the information presented to top political leaders and through the control they exert over the details of implementing policy? Do they mean that Congress has little effect on foreign policy because Congress as an institution plays a small role in formulating policy and virtually none in implementing it? do they mean that the systemic perspective on international politics is of no use, or that Presidential assumptions, perspectives, and decisions are not the controlling factors in our foreign policy? Do they mean that bureaucracies, if they are powerful, are equally powerful in all areas of foreign policy? Do these propositions mean that we must concentrate primarily on the mechanics of the foreign policy bureaucracy in order to understand or adduce the substance of policy? Must we look to the nuts and bolts of bureaucracy to explain the thrust of policy? Should we now adopt as the most fruitful method of analysis what is variously called "the governmental politics model," "the bureaucratic politics paradigm," or "the bureaucratic perspective"? What, in short, are we now being told; and how does it differ from what we have known or assumed for a long time?[2]

From "Bureaucratic Politics and American Foreign Policy—A Critique" by Robert J. Art, published in *Policy Sciences*, Vol.4 (1973), pp. 467–490. Reprinted by permission of Kluwer Academic Publishers. Portions of the text and some footnotes have been omitted.

THE FIRST WAVE—POLICY VIA POLITICS

What we have known for the last 10 years has been a result of the "first wave" of theorists who applied a bureaucratic, but essentially a political perspective to foreign policy making. In the works of the early sixties of Roger Hilsman, Samuel Huntington, Richard Neustadt, and Warner Schilling,[3] we were given some crucial insights into the ways that process affects the content of policy—how the manner in which we make decisions influences the types of decisions that we do make. Five distinct propositions that bear on a bureaucratic perspective can be extracted from their works.[4] The first four propositions specify the internal structural conditions or constraints under which foreign policy is made in our system of government; the fifth derives the content of policy—the outcome of the process—from the first four constraints:

(1) Political power (the ability to get someone to do something he would otherwise not do) is widely dispersed at the national governmental level. There is no sovereign power in Washington; rather there are a series of sovereign powers. No one figure has a monopoly of power; all the important ones possess a veto power. It is easier to block the policy initiatives of others than it is to get your own initiatives translated into action. In Neustadt's famous phrase, we have "separated institutions *sharing* powers."[5] Diffusion of power is thus the structural starting point from which actors and analysts must begin their respective tasks.

(2) Within these institutions, which Schilling termed "quasi-sovereign powers,"[6] sit participants in the policy process with differing views on what they would like done on any given issue. The basis of their differences in view stems *partly* from their differences in position. With position comes responsibility, but different institutional positions bring with them a different cluster of responsibilities. Participants who have different roles to perform will see different issues as of consequence to them, but even when they do focus on the same issue, they will almost invariably emphasize different aspects of it. Participants can look at the same issue but see it differently. Differing institutional perspectives can thus partially account for differing policy stances.

(3) Political leadership within or across these institutions is exercised primarily through persuasion, but with persuasion dependent upon the skill with which a figure makes use of the limited power that his position gives him. With no figure having a monopoly of power and with the most important possessing a blocking power, the task of a participant who wants to get something done is to convince others that what he wants them to do for him is what they would or should do for their own interests.[7]

(4) Foreign policy making is thus a political process of building consensus and support for a policy among those participants who have the power to affect the outcome and who often disagree over what they think the outcome should be. As Hilsman said in 1959, "the making of policy in government . . . is essentially a political process, even when it takes place entirely inside the government, screened from the voter's view, or even when it takes place entirely within one agency of the government."[8] The aspects of this process that

make it political, then, are: first, that there are divergences among participants over the ends and means of policy; second, that these participants can influence, though in varying degree, the choices that are made; and, third, that the forging of a policy consensus is achieved through the standard techniques of negotiation, bargaining, and compromise. In what probably remains the best analytical discussion of the foreign policy process, Schilling captures the essence of its political nature:

> The general character of conflict among such "powers" is in many respects comparable to the diplomatic struggle among contending nations. Each endeavors to isolate the other, to secure "allies" for itself, and to gain the favorable opinion of "neutrals"—activities of great importance given the dispersion of power among elite groups. Discussions between the contending parties are negotiatory rather than analytical in nature. The object is to persuade the opponent that his position is unreasonable (either by arguments designed to show that it will not really serve his interest or by appeals to other interests alleged to be both common and more important), or, failing that, to search for grounds on which a satisfactory settlement can be made. This may take the form of a direct compromise on the issue concerned (where the incentive to accommodate stems from the desire to avoid the costs of even winning a fight) or of a bargain reached by bringing into negotiation another issue in dispute and thereby permitting each (provided they evaluate the two issues disproportionately) to give up something of less value than that which it receives.[9]

(5) The outcome or resultant of such a process is clear. The content of any particular policy reflects as much the necessities of the conditions in which it is forged—what is required to obtain agreement—as it does the substantive merits of that policy. How we go about making decisions does affect the kinds of decisions we make. Process influences content. Hilsman put it nicely:

> . . . in a political process the relative power of these participating groups is as relevant to the final decisions as the cogency and wisdom of the arguments used in support of the policy adopted. Who advocates a particular policy may be as important as what he advocates. . . . The test of policy is not that it will most effectively accomplish an agreed-upon value but that a wider number of people decide to endorse it. . . .[10]

These are important insights. They alert us to the effects of process on substance. They tell us that "organization is politics by other means." They remind us that we cannot look solely to the impact of other nations' actions on the United States in order to explain America's reactions to what they do to us. Above all, they impress upon us the political aspects of our foreign policy: that conflicts over goals and the means appropriate to attain them are reconciled in a domestic arena of bargaining, negotiation, compromise, and consensus building. In foreign policy, politics may "stop at the water's edge"; but there certainly is a lot of it before we reach the coast lines.

Notice, however, what these theorists have *not* told us about what characterizes this political process. First, they have not told us to ignore the effects that Congress has on foreign policy. To the contrary, they have emphasized Congress's reactive role to Executive initiative, with the attendant stress on the lobbyist and anticipatory functions that it performs in the policy process. Huntington stresses Congress's lobbyist function in framing military policy:

> The unwillingness of Congress to exercise a veto over strategic programs does not mean that Congress has no role in the formulation of those programs. . . . The most prominent congressional role is that of prodder or goad of the Adminstration on behalf of specific programs or activities. With the executive the decision-maker, Congress becomes the lobbyist.[11]

Hilsman accentuates the anticipatory function and the general constraints that Congress puts on Executive action:

> Congress participates only fitfully in the actual formulation of foreign policy. . . . Yet it is equally clear that Congress—subtly and indirectly, but, nevertheless, effectively—sets the tone of many policies and limits on many others. . . . It seems obvious that Executive proposals are shaped by estimates of how Congress and individual congressmen will react, the mood of Congress, and the probability, circumstances, and possible means they may use in reprisal.[12]

Second, the first wave never said that the perspectives of participants, the stances they take on issues, and the resulting conflicts over policy stem *solely* from the institutional positions these participants occupy. To the contrary, what emerges from a close reading of their work is the crucial significance of the fundamental assumptions (what I appropriately think should be called "mindsets") that participants bring to their jobs in determining their perspectives and subsequent stances. In characterizing the conflicts inherent in the foreign policy process, Schilling tells us something quite important:

> . . . there are two basic causes for policy conflict among government elites and . . . these conflicts lead to two different kinds of groupings among them. Many of these conflicts simply reflect the diversity of opinion Americans are likely to hold in the absence of sanctions to the contrary, regarding the state of the world and what America should do in it. *The groups that coalesce in support of one or another of these views appear, for the most part, to cut across formal institutional and organizational lines* (Congress, Executive, State, Defense).
>
> In contrast, some policy conflicts are "institutionally grounded." These are differences that result from the peculiar responsibilities (with respect either to values or to skills) of various government institutions and organizations. Not sharing the same responsibilities (or, put the other way, not charged with the representation of the same values or skills), government organizations will necessarily bring divergent interests and approaches to common problems. When conflicts of this order occur, the lines of battle are more likely to conform to the boundaries of the organizations involved. These are also the more enduring of the two kinds of group conflict. Specific ideas about what to do in the world will change, and with them the ad hoc groupings that once espoused them. But divergent responsibilities are built into the structure of government. The allocation of responsibility may be changed, but the effect is usually to shift the location of battle rather than to bring it to an end.[13]

Allison's summary of Schilling's work accurately states that the budgetary process is characterized in part by "participants whose policy differences stem from *both intellectual and institutional differences.* . . . "[14] Organizational role (or institutional responsibility) is a component of a participant's outlook, but often only a component and often not even the overriding one.

Third, and integrally related to the second point, the first wave theorists have not emphasized the nature of the policy process over the images that participants have of the international environment when they assess the relative weights of each on the substance of policy. To the contrary, the images are primary, the process secondary, though not inconsequential, in the framing of policy. In prefacing his analysis of the politics of the fiscal 1950 defense budget, an area where one would expect the process to be more significant than the mind-sets,[15] Schilling cautions us thus:

> The kind of defenses a budget provides will be *primarily a reflection of the kinds of ideas people have about the political-military world in which they are living*. . . . But the influence exercised on the content of the budget by the character of the political process, *while definitely subordinate*, is not insignificant.[16]

If Schilling is representative of the first wave, then pre-existing mind-sets tell us more about the direction and character of our foreign policy than the nature of the governmental political process in which it is forged.

Fourth, the first wave never told us that the resultant of the political process, the *compromised* nature of the policy that emerges from the pulling and hauling of the participants, was one unintended by many or most of them. To the contrary, the spirit, if not the substance of their work, is to assert the reverse: participants frame their actions with a view towards what is required to get a policy adopted. Initial positions are so framed, negotiations are undertaken, compromises are entered into precisely because participants are aware of what it takes to get a particular proposal accepted. In our system, the cost of consensus is compromise; but the participants know that before they begin their policy battles. Initial positions are taken with a view towards the negotiations and compromises that will be necessary in order to obtain agreement. What participants want and what they know they are likely to get are two different things. What they ask for will not always, nor perhaps even usually, reflect what they ideally would like or what they know they can get. The need to "anticipate" the probable reactions of others to one's initiatives requires that participants frame their positions with these "anticipated reactions" in mind. In a bargaining situation, never ask for what you know you can get; if you do so, you will not get it. This need to anticipate reactions and to get others to go along is what Hilsman meant when he said: "The test of a policy is that a wider number of people decide to endorse it." This is what Schilling meant when he said, "Discussions between contending parites are negotiatory rather than analytical in nature." This is what Huntington meant when he said, "In strategy, as elsewhere, meaningful policy requires both content and consensus. . . . Consensus is a cost to each participant in the policy-making process, but it is a prerequisite to any policy."[17] The point, then, is that the compromise that results from the pulling and hauling was deliberately intended by the participants. The *exact nature* of the compromise that results may be unintended or unforeseen, but not the *initial intent* to achieve some sort of a compromise.

Fifth and last, the first wave has not allowed us to neglect the influence of domestic politics on foreign policy—not the politics of executive legislative relations, not the politics of executive pulling and hauling, but the politics of getting elected, staying in office, and carrying constituents along in support of particular foreign policies. This theme emerges most conspicuously from Huntington's study of national security policy from 1945 through 1960:

> If this book has any distinctive message, it is that military policy can only be understood as the responses of the government to conflicting pressures from its foreign and domestic environments. . . . Military policy cannot be separated from foreign policy, fiscal policy, and domestic policy. *It is part of the warp and woof of American politics.* [18]

In assessing the effects of domestic politics on military policy, Huntington's study stresses two general points: First, that major shifts in strategic policy by Administrations and major criticisms by the party out of power were as much partisan and political as they were reactions to external threats or refinements due to strategic analysis[19]; second, although the public's opinions only loosely constrained executive choice in framing military policy, nevertheless, these opinions affected executive action, not because of the nature of those opinions per se, but because elites were responsive to the images that they had in their heads of what the public wanted, demanded, or merely would tolerate.[20]

THE SECOND WAVE—POLICY VIA BUREAUCRATIC POLITICS

Why discuss the first wave theorists in so much detail? Why quote copiously from their works? Why retread ground so familiar to all of us? The answer is simple: to build a record in order to determine whether the "second wave" is saying something different from the first and, if so, in what respects it differs. If the second wave theorists are not merely rehashing in another guise the significant insights of the first wave, then we must compare what they are saying to what has been said before. Stating the latter, however, is easier than specifying the former. The second wave theorists have engaged in considerable "waffling" (ambiguity and backtracking) on precisely those propositions that would merit calling their approach something new. If we are sufficiently severe about their waffling, we could conclude that the bureaucratic approach is in fact "old (but extremely) fine wine in new bottles." That is, unless we can tighten up their argument, the bureaucratic politics paradigm rapidly decays into the political process approach of the first wave. By tightening up their central propositions, we can form a clear picture of what the bureaucratic approach *should* be and then determine its merits. Therefore, if a *bureaucratic* politics approach is to claim any distinctness, much less validity, it must at the least assert the following propositions:

Proposition One: Organizational position determines policy stance, or, "where you stand depends on where you sit."[21] The first wave theorists never specified under what precise circumstances or in which particular issue areas this proposition held, but because most of their work centered on national security policy and particularly on issues that had immediate budgetary implications (especially for the military services), by inference one could assume this proposition applied primarily to decisions having clear, immediate budgetary effects. Hence Allison asserts "for large classes of issues—e.g., budgets and procurement decisions—the stance of a particular player can be predicted with high reliability from information about his seat."[22] So far we have not gone too far. . . . But the second wave has as yet not gone any further with this proposition, and they have, moreover, surrounded it with so many qualifiers and such ambiguity that its reliability (and hence predictive power) must be seriously questioned. Witness the following:

> Each participant sits in a seat that confers separate responsibilities. Each man is committed to fulfilling his responsibilities *as he see them.*[23]

> Thus propensities and priorities stemming from position are sufficient to allow analysts to make reliable predictions about a player's stand *in many cases.* But these propensities are filtered through the baggage that players bring to positions. *Some knowledge of both the pressures and the baggage is thus required for sound predictions.*[24]

> We believe that membership in the bureaucracy *substantially determines the participants' perceptions and goals.* . . .[25]

> Participants whose stands on issues can be predicted with high reliability from a knowledge of their organizational affiliation will be termed organizational participants and those for whom organizational membership is not a good predicter will be termed players. . . . *The higher the formal position occupied by the participant, the more likely it is that he will behave like a player.*[26]

> Their [senior players'] perceptions of the national security interest are more likely to be dominated *by images shared with society, their own experiences, and their historical memories.*[27]

> *In any specific case it is difficult to predict the exact mix of interests which will determine* the face of a national security issue seen by the participant, his stake in its resolution, and *his stand on it.*[28]

The left hand taketh away what the right hand giveth! If each man is "committed to fulfilling his responsibilities as he sees them," do different men who occupy the *same* seat over time see the responsibilities of the office in the same way? If not, then what is the relative weight of position in policy stance? How constraining are the top positions in our governmental bureaucracy for the roles that senior participants who fill these positions choose to play? If "senior players" are the most powerful participants in the policy process, but if their stances on issues are not correlated with their organizational affiliations, then of what use is the first proposition for analysis and prediction? If you cannot specify stance from position for these players in most issue areas, then why bother with their *bureaucratic* position? If "shared images" (or mind-sets) are far more important for determining the policy stance of senior players, then again why disaggregate them by *bureaucratic* position? If senior officials actually *share* mind-sets, then how do the mechanics of pulling and hauling explain the thrust of our foreign policy; or, better yet, do we in fact *have* pulling and hauling?[29] If you cannot specify in what issue areas other than budgetary and procurement decisions stance correlates highly with position, instead merely stating that this works "in many cases," then why claim something for your paradigm that your own analysis does not bear out? By asking these questions of the position-perception proposition, we begin to see in microcosm one of the central difficulties with the bureaucratic politics paradigm: we must qualify it with so many amendments before it begins to work that when it does, we may not be left with a bureaucratic paradigm, but may in reality be using another one quite different.

Proposition Two: In foreign policy, governmental decision and actions do not represent the intent of any one figure, but are rather the unintended resultant of bargaining, pulling, and hauling among the principal participants. Allison puts the case this way:

> The decisions and actions of governments are intranational political *resultants:* resultants in the sense that what happens is not chosen as a solution to a problem but rather results from compromise, conflict and confusion of officials with diverse interests and unequal influence; *political* in the sense that the activity from which decisions and actions emerge is best characterized as bargaining along regularized channels among individual members of the government.
>
> *The sum of behavior of representatives of a government relevant to an issue is rarely intended by any individual or group.* Rather, in the typical case, separate individuals with different intentions contribute pieces to a resultant (italics added).
>
> Equally often however, different groups pulling in different directions produce a result, or better a restraint . . . distinct from what any person or group intended.
>
> If a nation performed an action, that action was the *resultant* of bargaining among individuals and groups within the government.[30]

In one fundamental sense this proposition is descriptive of what goes on in our governmental machinery. No analyst could deny that there is pulling, hauling and bargaining by the principal participants involved in a given issue. As the first wave told us, in a system of government where power is dispersed, all have "to give a little to get a litte."[31] But in another fundamental sense, proposition two begs the issue because it does not specify for us *how much difference all the pulling and hauling and bargaining actually makes;* or, to put the matter more carefully, under what circumstances and in what issue areas does all the commotion make a significant difference? If, for example, the resultant of governmental mechanics was a decision to buy three nuclear-powered aircraft carriers instead of two conventionally-powered ones initially intended, is this to be considered a resultant significantly different from that which anyone intended? In short, if there is pulling, hauling and bargaining (and there often is), what are the precise effects on the decisions made and the actions taken?

To ask the question this way is not to nitpick, but rather to raise the central question about bureaucratic politics paradigm: in foreign policy formulation (the act of making a choice), how much does the pulling, hauling and bargaining below the President affect Presidential choice? How much does he have to give in order to get? If there is no direction or control from the top, then obviously a bureaucratic paradigm is essential for analyzing the foreign policy process; then, decisions are truly the resultants of governmental mechanics. But if there is central control from the top, then how much of a difference do the mechanics make? How far do they deflect Presidential decisions from Presidential intent? Are the mechanics only marginally important, or do they cause significant deflection? When do Presidential perspectives override bureaucrats' preferences, or do they at all?[32]

The second wave theorists have not ignored the role the President plays, but they have not helped us answer the deflection question. They appear to want to have their cake (assert the resultant effect of the bureaucratic perspective) and yet eat it too (acknowledge the President's signal importance in foreign policy formulation). Again,

> . . . action . . . [is] a resultant of political bargaining among a number of independent players, *the President being* only a "superpower" among many lesser but considerable powers.[33]

> The details of the action are therefore not chosen by any individual (and are rarely identical with what any of the players would have chosen if he had confronted the issue as a matter of simple, detached choice). *Nevertheless, resultants can be roughly consistent with some group's preference in the context of the political game.*[34]

> Where an outcome was for the most part the triumph of an individual (e.g., the President) or group (e.g., the President's men or a cabal) *this model attempts to specify the details of the game that made the victory possible.*[35]

> The President stands at the center of the foreign policy process in the United States. *His role and influence over decisions are qualitatively different than those of any other participants.* In any foreign policy decision widely perceived at the time to be important, the President will be a principal if not the principal figure determining the *general* direction of actions.[36]

> As the ABM decision illustrates, *the President is qualitatively different—not simply a very powerful player among less powerful players.*[37]

> . . . the diplomatic and defense spheres yield our man [the President] *authority for binding judgments on behalf of the whole government.* Although he rarely gets unquestioning obedience and often pays a price, *his personal choices are authoritative,* for he himself is heir to royal prerogatives.[38]

The bureaucratic paradigm will explain a great deal about foreign policy formulation if we assume that Presidential preferences do not significantly constrain senior executive players in what they can do. But the paradigm will explain very little if we accept the amendments about the Presidency that the second wave has made to proposition two. When we accept the amendments, moreover, we are forced by inference to adopt two corollaries that bring into doubt the usefulness of proposition two:

Corollary One: When senior executive players are split on their policy stances, the President, by virtue of the division, has considerable leeway to choose that which he wishes to do, or that which he thinks he ought to do, or that which he reasons he must do.

Corollary Two: When senior executive players are split on their policy stances, the President, to the extent that he reasons he must take account of bureaucrats' pressures, will respond to those demands that he thinks will damage him politically if he does not respond.

Corollary one reminds us of the old divide-and-conquer adage. If we press it to its extreme, then we might very well conclude that it is the very divisions which arise in the executive branch that preserve Presidential flexibility in foreign policy. Corollary two reminds us that we must not lose sight of the forest by concentrating on the quirks of each and every tree: the preferences of senior players per se are not what count, but rather Presidential estimation of who outside the executive branch, which members of Congress, for example, will back these players. A close look at proposition two thus forces us away from the nuts and bolts of executive wrangling to the truisms of American government. It is Presidential anticipation of Congressional and public response that causes him to heed those bureaucrats' demands he chooses to accede to. By reminding us of the power that Presidents derive from executive decisions, corollary one makes us dubious of the *resultant* aspects of proposition two. By reminding us of the President's need to anticipate the Congressional reactions that stem from the sharing of powers, corollary two makes us dubious of the *unintended* aspect of proposition two. Each requires that we focus on what Neustadt ten years ago told us was crucial to Presidential power—the choices that Presidents make. Both force us to concentrate on the conscious act of Presidential choice and thereby refresh our memory about Presidential predominance in foreign policy. Where, then, are we? What shall we conclude from proposition two: Presidential preferences and decisions are (check one)—always,—usually,—often,—sometimes,—not usually,—rarely,—not at all, decisive in the foreign policy choices we make?

If this were not enough, let us open one more can of worms about proposition two, one that forces us to look at the perceived external constraints, not the internal mechanics of government. How often and over what issues do participants disagree in their policy stances? Does it ever happen that participants are unanimously opposed to Presidential preferences? How often and over what issues do participants *not* disagree over the thrust of action to be taken? These queries raise again the significance of mind-sets in foreign policy formulation. If shared images dominate senior players' outlooks and if they are truly *shared*, then what is the merit in asserting that governmental actions are the resultants of pulling, hauling and bargaining? If organizational responsibilities do not pull players apart and if the images they share draw them together, then are we not talking about what Allison calls the nation-state as a "unitary purposive actor"?[39] In this case, governmental action does not represent the intent of any one figure but the intent of most, if not all. Finally, have not the cases of shared mind-sets occurred on precisely the pivotal decisions of American foreign policy since 1945? And if that be so, why not spend time on the mind-sets of the senior players rather than on the mechanics of their position in order to explain the thrust of our foreign policy? Thus, if both of these criticisms are valid—that Presidents have predominated in our postwar foreign policy and that similar or shared mind-sets have characterized decisions on pivotal issues—then the result is to give much more weight to the nation-state-as-unitary-actor view than the bureaucratic paradigm would lead us to believe.

Proposition Three: Organizational routine, standard operating procedures, and vested interests can affect the Presidential implementation of policy much more than they can its formulating. The first two propositions are aimed at showing how bureaucratic politics affect the formulation of policy, but they apply there the least. Where the bureaucratic paradigm finds its forte is with the implementation of policy. As Allison puts it:

> . . . making sure that the government does what is decided is more difficult than selecting the preferred solution.
>
> Detail and nuance of actions by organizations are determined chiefly by organizational routines, not government leaders' directions.
>
> A considerable gap separates what leaders choose . . . and what organizations implement.[40]

Practitioners agree with parts of this proposition and with the distinction between policy formulation and policy implementation. The most recent expression of agreement is by Henry Kissinger:

> Making foreign policy is easy; what is difficult is its coordination and implementation. . . . [t]he outsider believes a Presidential order is consistently followed out. Nonsense. I have to spend considerable time seeing that it is carried out and in the spirit the President intended.[41]

That making decisions is easier for Presidents than getting them implemented is no accident. Presidents have been ingenious at developing sources of information outside of bureaucratic channels and hence have reduced their dependence on standard information operating procedures. The deference that Congress and the public have given to Presidential lead in foreign affairs in the postwar era accounts for the predominance of Presidential perspectives and preferences. The primacy and immediacy of foreign policy since 1945 have turned all Presidents into activists in the realm of foreign policy, even if they have wished otherwise, with the consequent Presidential attention and energy directed to these matters. Almost all of our Presidents, moreover, have come into office with clear and fixed ideas on what they wished to do, or not wished to do, in foreign policy. With the necessary information, political deference, will and determination, Presidents have been able to make decisions tailored to their own desires. But when Presidents and their personal staffs have had to implement these decisions, necessity has forced them to delegate. The limits of their collective physical capabilities and of the time they can devote to any single issue require that Presidents rely largely on existing bureaucratic machinery in order to implement the decisions they make. When the organizational machinery is engaged, then the standard operating procedures begin to take their toll. Presidential monitoring and oversight of bureaucratic motion can mitigate, if not remedy, the distorting effects of bureaucratic momentum; but the opportunity costs of too much time spent on any one issue can be quite high due to the pressure of other issues that require resolution. Unless Presidents carefully follow up the decisions they make, there is *some* slippage between Presidential intent and organizational output.

Where, then, does this proposition leave us? If Presidential intent can be subverted by bureaucratic implementation, then what difference does the initial decision make? If bureaucracies determine the "detail and nuance" of policy, then does not the bureaucratic paradigm work even if its validity with respect to policy formulation is close to nil? Does acceptance of proposition three nullify the criticisms of propositions one and two? What we make of proposition three hangs heavily on how we answer three additional questions. First, how important are the initial acts of Presidential choice? Second, how much slippage is there between intent and output? Third, how detrimental is the slippage to the success of policy?

Unfortunately, these questions are not easy to answer in the abstract. The answers, especially to the last two, depend largely on the particular circumstances attendant to the decision at issue. There are, however, three general points to be made that put the significance of proposition three into its proper perspective. First, the initial act of choice is crucial, no matter how the choice is implemented. As Alexander George remarks: ". . . the fact that any Presidential decision has to be effectively implemented cannot be used to down-grade the importance of choices which the President makes."[42] Analytically, there are two types of choices—to do something, or not to do something. In cases where the President decides not to do something—not to intervene some place with military force, not to buy new bombers, not to conclude an alliance, not to negotiate an arms control agreement, not to recognize a country, not to extend foreign aid to some nation—implementing the decision is irrelevant to its success. In acts of negative choice, Presidential decisions obviate the need to implement them. The case is not so sharp with acts of positive choice, but even here the choices themselves are nevertheless critical. We may wish to know, for example, how organizational interests affected the air war and ground strategy in Vietnam,[43] but we still would want to know why we had an air war over North Vietnam and American combat troops in South Vietnam, that is, why we intervened in the first place. We may wish to know how standard operating procedures influenced the way our troops were deployed in the Dominican Republic in 1965, but we would not want to forget why we put them there in the first place.[44] We may wish to know how MacArthur made life difficult for Truman in the Korean War, but we would still wish to know why MacArthur was there leading troops in the first place.[45] We may be interested in why we chose to blockade Cuba in October of 1962 instead of launching an air strike in order to get Soviet missiles out of Cuba, but we would not want to ignore the reasons why Kennedy decided that we had to get the missiles out in the first place.[46] To state the matter in this fashion is to show the critical importance of Presidential decisions to do something. The details of implementation will, of course, influence the likelihood of success of a policy; but they become operative only after an act of positive choice. And while slippage can affect success, it cannot explain why the policy was launched. The "detail and nuance" of actions by organizations cannot be used to denigrate the signal importance of the act of Presidential choice.

Second, the slippage between Presidential intent and organizational output is greatest on those issues that Presidents consider least important and smallest on those that they deem most important. This point is a logical consequence of proposition three: organizational procedures can cause slippage, but they do not automatically or mechanistically do so. Whether they do so depends on the President's degree of determination *not* to permit them to do so. Slippage is inversely correlated with a Presidential commitment to make his decision stick. Allison himself confirms this inverse correlation in his study of Presidential control of the Cuban missile crisis blockade:

> Thus the governmental leaders had both the capability and the incentive to reach out beyond the traditional limits of their control. Maps in the "Situation Room" in the basement of the White House tracked the movement of all Soviet ships. The members of the Ex. Com. knew each of the ships by name and argued extensively about which should be stopped first, at what point, and how. Sorenson records, "The President's personal direction of the quarantine's operation . . . his determination not to let needless incidents or reckless subordinates escalate so dangerous and delicate a crisis beyond control. *Thus, for the first time in U.S. military history, local commanders received repeated orders about the details of their military operations directly from political leaders.. . . .*[47]

Nor is this an isolated case. Lyndon Johnson's personal conduct of the air war over North Vietnam and Richard Nixon's personal conduct of negotiations to "end" the war are but two recent examples. Therefore, not only do the pivotal issues find their way up to the President for resolution; but once he deems them to be so, the President finds ways to reach down into the bureaucracy so as to ensure that his intent will be realized. This requires considerable time and effort, and Presidents are thereby forced to be selective.[48] Thus, on issues the President deems pivotal, the bureaucratic paradigm will alert us to the exertions that a President must go through in order to get the executive bureaucracies to give them what he wants; but it will err if it tells us that Presidents do not get substantially what they want. The paradigm will account for the effort required, but it will not predict the result of that effort.

Third, slippage is not equally detrimental on all types of policy issues.[49] For one type of decision, all that matters to the President is that the positive choice be made. The details of implementation are not of consequence from his perspective, and slippage is irrelevant. For example, for Lyndon Johnson in 1967, what mattered was that a decision be made to deploy *an* ABM system, never mind the details of what kind of system. He cared most about avoiding an "ABM gap" in the 1968 election and about getting arms control talks started with the

Soviet Union. From his vantage point almost any kind of initial ABM deployment served his purposes. What mattered least to him (and most to McNamara) were the details—whether the ABM would be designed as thick or thin, whether it would appear to be directed against the Chinese or the Russians, what contractor would build it, which service would "own" it.[50] For another type of decision, one where slippage can hurt it, it will, unless Presidential commitment is there. If it is, then, as we saw above, the slippage is least likely to occur. Finally, for a third type of issue, slippage may be desirable from the President's perspective; or, perhaps a clearer way to put it is that the President wants to communicate ambiguity over what decision has been made, not only to his subordinates, but to foreigners. The MLF is a good case in point. Kennedy and Johnson gave enough of a commitment to enable the bureaucratic partisans to go "hunting," but not so much of a commitment that they could not discount it if it proved a disaster. Their intent was to see whether the Europeans would buy the idea of a MLF. The ambiguity over what it would look like and how fully the President was committed served Presidential purposes of testing European reactions and of killing it (as Johnson did) if they proved too hostile.[51]

The thrust of the above three points is not to deny that slippage between Presidential intent and executive output can result from the mediating impact of organizational procedures. Such slippage does occur, sometimes even on issues Presidents deem vital. The above points, however, do tell us, first, that the slippage is neither as automatic nor always as crucial as the second wave would have us believe; second, that the probability of slippage is lowest on those issues Presidents fully commit themselves to and wholly invest their prestige in; and third, therefore, that when the detail and the nuance of action are critical in implementing a decision Presidents deem vital, more often that not "the directions of government leaders," not organizational routine, will determine them. Presidents are not omnipotent, but neither, then, are they impotent. No President can control everything, but that does not mean he cannot control a great many things. His capacity to get what he wants from his executive subordinates should not be underestimated. The constraints he works under should not blind us to the constraints he can and does make them work under. In short, the gap is not always, nor even usually, considerable between "what leaders choose and organizations implement." Precisely because the size of the gap is correlated with the degree of Presidential commitment, Presidential intent becomes all the more significant. It is the key variable for determining the degree of applicability of the bureaucratic paradigm. Thus, a close look at what the paradigm says about policy implementation drives us inexorably back to policy formulation—to the act of Presidential choice, to the area where the paradigm works weakly, if at all.

EVIDENCE VIA ISSUE AREA

The arguments presented thus far have by no means invalidated propositions two and three of the bureaucratic paradigm.[52] These arguments have, however, raised serious doubts about the internal consistency and logical implications of the approach. If the arguments have any teeth to them, the paradigm has been found wanting on both counts: it is neither consistent, nor do inferences drawn from it lead us where the paradigm's supporters want us to go. What clearly needs to be done next—and what the second wave theorists have not yet done—is to examine the record of American foreign policy by issue area in order to determine the fit of the paradigm to the record. No attempt to do this comprehensively will be made here.[53] Instead, three issue categories have been chosen: (1) decisions to intervene with military force; (2) decisions marking major policy shifts; and (3) decisions revolving primarily around institutionally-grounded matters. These categories are not perfect. They are not inclusive of all types of foreign policy decisions; there is some overlap among them; they are not necessarily the best for building theory. Nevertheless, they do have rough analytic validity because they enable us to separate out past decisions and to determine what factors weighed most heavily for the choices made in each category. In short, the categories serve well as a preliminary issue-area test of the bureaucratic paradigm. A very brief look at some pivotal or significant decisions in each category suggests that with respect to policy formulation, in two out of three issue areas, three inescapable conclusions emerge. First, Presidential preferences were of overriding importance for the types of decisions made. Second, like mind-sets among the top executive decisions-makers characterized their perspectives on nearly all of the pivotal and significant decisions. Third, domestic political pressures, much more so than any exigencies of bureaucratic politics, affected the substance of the decisions made, or shaped the manner in which they were presented to the public, or both, with domestic political pressures understood in three distinct senses—as Presidential anticipation of likely Congressional and public reaction to one of his comtemplated decisions, as Presidential constraint due to his past campaign oratory, or as Presidential maneuvering for reelection. Not to bureaucratic politics, but to Presidents, mind-sets, and domestic politics—these are where we must look if we are to understand why decisions were made the way they were.

1. Decisions to Intervene with Military Force. The decisions to intervene with military force in Korea in June of 1950, in South Vietnam from 1961 through 1965, around Cuba in October of 1962, and in the Dominican Republic in April of 1965 all illustrate, not only the importance of Presidents, but also of like mind-sets to the decisions made. In a fundamental sense each of them was a "non-decision"[54]: because of either Presidential preferences or identical mind-sets, almost none of the top executive decision-makers questioned the need to resort to military force. For Korea and the Dominican Republic, there was unanimity on the need to use military force, once the principals involved realized that nothing short of that would achieve American objectives. These two cases are all the more remarkable because in the former we did a complete about-face on our previous policy, while in the latter no one wanted, nor initially contemplated, the use of force. For Cuba and Vietnam, the need to use force was questioned by one or two principal advisors; but they were clearly out of the mainstream of the President's thinking and his advisors' outlooks. Two passages are worth quoting here because they demonstrate by specific example the importance of mind-sets and Presidential preferences to military intervention decisions. The first is from Truman's memoirs recounting his reactions to the North Korean attack; the second, from Sorenson's account of the Cuban missile crisis:

> The plane left the Kansas City Municipal Airport at two o'clock, and it took just a little over three hours to make the trip to Washington. [After being informed of the North Korean attack] I had time to think aboard the plane. In my generation, this was not the first occasion when the strong had attacked the weak. I recalled some earlier instances: Manchuria, Ethiopia, Austria. I remembered how each time that the democracies had failed to act it had encouraged the aggressors to keep going ahead. Communism was acting in Korea just as Hitler, Mussolini, and the Japanese had acted ten, fifteen, and twenty years earlier. I felt certain that if South Korea was allowed to fall Communist leaders would be emboldened to override nations closer to our own shores. If the Communists were permitted to force their way into the Republic of Korea without opposition from the free world, no small nation would have the courage to resist threats and aggression by stronger Communist neighbors. If this was allowed to go unchallenged, it would mean a third world war, just as similar incidents had brought on the second world war. It was also clear to me that the foundations and the principles of the United Nations were at stake unless this unprovoked attack on Korea could be stopped.[55]

> Choice No. 1—doing nothing— . . . [was] seriously considered. . . . But the President had rejected this course from the outset. He was concerned less about the missiles' military implications than with their effect on the global political balance. The Soviet move had been undertaken so swiftly, so secretly and with so much deliberate deception—it was so sudden a departure from Soviet practice—that it represented a provocative change in the delicate status quo. Missiles on Soviet territory or submarines were very different from missiles in the Western Hemisphere, particularly in their political and psychological effect on Latin America. . . . Such a step, if accepted, would be followed by more; and the President's September pledges of action clearly called this step unacceptable. While he desired to combine diplomatic moves with military action, he was not willing to let the UN debate and Khrushchev equivocate while the missiles became operational. . . . The President increasingly felt that we should not avoid the fact that this was a confrontation of the great powers—that the missiles had been placed there by the Soviets, were manned and guarded by the Soviets, and would have to be removed by the Soviets in response to direct American action.[56]

2. Decisions Marking Major Policy Shifts. Category two includes the class of decisions that brought a fundamental re-orientation of American foreign policy and hence that signified that a major departure from the past had occurred. Decisions like the Truman Doctrine, the Marshall Plan, the NATO alliance, massive retaliation, flexible response, the 1972 detente with Russia and China, and the SALT I treaty fall into this category. Each of these decisions once again illustrates either the importance of Presidential preferences, or the workings of like mind-sets, or both. The decision to give economic and military aid to Greece and Turkey in the spring of 1947 is a good example of where identical mind-sets in the executive branch characterized the perspectives of the participants. Note the words of a man who participated in the formulation of the Truman Doctrine:

> [Secretary of State] Marshall's reaction was similar to that of all the others in the Department who had heard the news [that the British could no longer meet their responsibilities in Greece and Turkey]. Without any exception known to the writer, everyone in the executive branch recognized what this meant, and saw that if Russian expansion was to be checked, the United States must move into the defaulted position in the Middle East.
>
> The instant recognition of this, the virtual unanimity of view, made it possible, within a single week beginning February 21, for the staff of the State Department to prepare a documented statement of position and recommendations, for this to be approved by Acheson, Marshall, the Secretaries of War and of the Navy, and the President, for it to be cleared by the President with congressional leaders, and for a State Department working party to start preparing a detailed program of action. The singleness of reaction grew from accumulating facts that had been shouting for recognition for a long time. One more fact was added, and the situation no longer shouted, but commanded, and was obeyed. History took a new course.[57]

The decision to pursue detente with China that materialized in 1972 is a good example of a Presidentially imposed, Presidentially initiated policy. There was no hue and cry from the Congress or the American public in 1972 for Nixon to seek better relations with Communist China, though segments from each had previously argued that we should. There were bureaucrats who had for twelve years prior to Nixon's move argued the case for reversing the policy we had set toward China in late 1949 and early 1950 and had pursued since. But as one participant has written, the bureaucrats who urged a moderation of our China policy before the Nixon move were generally unsuccessful and achieved a limited degree of success only when the President was receptive to such a course.[58] Kennedy was not receptive:

> The political climate, then, of January 1961 was not one that encouraged China policy innovation at the White House. The electoral margin was too narrow. The Republican leadership stood ready and waiting for telltale signs of Democratic "appeasement." The bitter charges of the early fifties still echoed. As Kennedy was to confide with regret to more than one White House aide and visitor, China was a matter that would probably have to await his second term in office.[59]

Johnson was more receptive, but for reasons that tell much about the impact of a President's personal outlook on policy making:

> White House private polls corroborated the Steele-Michigan results: a considerable degree of public tolerance on most China questions; and the data were passed on to a restless President.
>
> Why restless? It would be foolish to attempt any firsthand insight into Johnson's personal views on the China problem at the time. One can only report that those who dealt with him sensed a lack of ideological rigidity on the subject, a desire for Sino-American friendship, and most notably a grouping for some presidential act of trans-Pacific statecraft that might somehow envelop and mute the Vietnam un-

pleasantness. . . . [Hence] on 12 July 1966, . . . Lyndon Johnson became the first president since China's "loss" to speak of the Peking regime in conciliatory terms . . . he set as the central objective of U.S.–China policy the concept of reconciliation.[60]

Nixon's opening to China was dictated by his desire to gain flexibility vis à vis the Soviet Union, once she had achieved nuclear parity with us, and by his wish to obtain China's help in ending America's involvement in the Vietnam War. Latent public support for detente with China may have been there, but certainly manifest public clamor for it was not. Nixon's move was dictated by his calculations of the necessities of *haute politique*.[61] It was a decision that came from the top. We moderated our policy toward China only after our President made that policy his own.

The decision to adopt and pursue a strategy of flexible response based in part on large numbers of missiles invulnerable to a first strike is a good example of the effects that not only Presidential preferences but also domestic political pressures can have on policy formulations.[62] Kennedy came into office after having consistently and vociferously charged the Republicans with endangering America's security by allowing a missile gap vis à vis the Russians to materilize. Once in office, he quickly discovered that there was indeed a significant missile gap, but overwhelmingly in America's favor. Why, then, did he go ahead with a missile building program that his Secretary of Defense several years later stated was far more than our security needs at the time required?[63] Three reasons seem significant. First, there was the belief prevalent at the time that "the more the better." In the era of the cold war, our leaders thought that superiority in numbers of nuclear forces could somehow be translated into political leverage vis à vis the Russians. Second, there was the need to plan on the basis of Russian capability, not her then present intentions. Capability planning always leads to larger required forces.[64] Third, and most important for our purposes here, there was the need to consider the alliance between the hawks who dominated military affairs in Congress and the military services who always wanted more. Whether by scuttlebutt or literal quotation, David Halberstam captures Kennedy's perceived need to appease Congressional hawks:

> In early 1961 some of the White House people like Science Advisor Jerome Wiesner and Carl Kaysen of the National Security Council were trying to slow down the arms race, or at least were in favor of a good deal more talking with the Soviets before speeding ahead. At that point the United States had 450 missiles; McNamara was asking for 950, and the Joint Chiefs of Staff were asking for 3,000. The White House people had quietly checked around and found that in effectiveness, in sheer military terms, the 450 were the same as McNamara's 950. Thus a rare moment existed, a chance to make a new start, if not turn around the arms race, at least give it a temporary freeze.
> "What about it, Bob?" Kennedy asked.
> "Well, they're right," McNamara answered.
> "Well, then, why the nine hundred and fifty, Bob?" Kennedy asked.
> "Because that's the smallest number we can take up on the Hill without getting murdered," he answered.[65]

3. Decisions Revolving Primarily Around Institutionally Grounded Issues. On decisions in the first two issue areas, remarkably little pulling and hauling among the President's principal executive advisors occurred. Not widespread division and conflict, but rather a consensus approaching a unanimity of outlook characterized the manner in which most of the decisions were made. The resultant of policy formulation was not something unintended by the principal executive participants, but rather a course of action consciously chosen by most or all of them with little or no debate. If the above examples are representative of decisions in these two categories, then, on the pivotal decisions of the past, our executive branch looked like a unitary purposive actor, not a bunch of bureaucrats tugging at one another. If we had adopted the bureaucratic perspective, we would have spent a lot of time looking for something that was not there. What pulling and hauling did occur was between the President and the Congress, not between the President and his executive advisors, nor among them.

Is this the case for category three decisions, those that have direct, immediate, clearly predictable results for the structural set-up of institutions and for their long-term prosperity—those decisions which we may call the "bread and butter choices" that determine the long-term competitive position of an institution, decisions such as those regarding the roles and missions of the military services, decisions regarding career advancement in the foreign service or in the uniformed military, budgetary allocation decisions, or those regulating the instruments by which situations will carry out the tasks assigned to them (like weapon systems for the services)? On this type of issue is there more pulling and hauling; and if so, are the resultants clearly unintended by the participants doing the tugging? Our answers to these questions must be quite precise, for, otherwise, we can end up either mindlessly accepting or rejecting the fit of the bureaucratic paradigm to policy formulation in the third issue area.

We can devise three analytically distinct cases for the institutional bread and butter issues in order to give a tentative answer to the above questions. First is the case where the President does not get his way because of a Congressional committee–Executive bureaucratic alliance that he cannot break, or chooses not to fight because of the opportunity costs involved and because of Presidential reading of the political climate. Second is the case where resource deployment questions engage Presidential interest and where Presidential energy is committed because the President perceives that such questions spill over, with important ramifications, to his *haute politique* strategies, either domestic or foreign or both. Third is the case where neither the President nor the relevant Congressional figures are particularly interested in what the bureaucrats want, or where the two former are in accord with what the latter want. In this case, as in the first, the bureaucrats will likely get their way. In the second case, they are less likely to do so. In all three cases, however, what is clearly predictable is that lower-level bureaucrats will assume policy stances that stem from their estimate of what will best serve the long-term interests of the institutions to which they belong. Whether they succeed depends primarily on three factors: how strong are their allies in Congress, how willing the senior players attached to their institutions are to fight for these interests, and how committed a President is to getting his way, that is, how the President perceives bread and butter issues affecting his domestic program and foreign policies.

The merit of these three distinct subcases is not that they enable us to predict *a priori* what will be the outcome for any particular example in category three, but rather that they show the situation to be more fluid, less categorical, for category three than for category one and two issues. The situation is more fluid precisely because personal factors and short-term, variable political climates are involved. Too much depends on Presidential predispositions, on senior players' conceptions of the institutional responsibilities that they must meet and of the roles they should perform, and on the Congressional climate for any analyst to state what the probable outcome will be before someone specifies to him the personal and situational constraints. In general, for policy formulation, the bureaucratic paradigm is more likely to apply to category three than to category one and two issues. But whether it does apply for any given case in category three depends upon the presence or absence of, and the nature of, the *nonbureaucratic* constraints at work. The latter are of first-order importance because they will determine the degree of applicability of the bureaucratic paradigm.

An example will illustrate, though not prove, the point.[66] Reorganization of the Defense Department has been a continuing preoccupation of all of our post World War II Presidents. So too has it been for the military services because the lines of authority and the structure of the units within the Department will affect the long-term competitive position of each service.[67] With varying degrees of commitment and success, all our Presidents have pushed for more centralized civilian control over the services, for more functional integration by the services, and for less duplication among them. Their continuing inability to achieve these ends fully testifies to the power of the services to resist organizational changes that they consider inimical to their interests. But from whence comes this power? The ability of the services to obstruct has stemmed primarily from Congress's desire to keep the Defense Department open to Congressional scrutiny and control and from the general aura of sanctity that Congress until very recently has accorded to national security matters. Congress has been the major impediment to military unification because of its calculation of how it can best fulfill its oversight role. From its view, the more centralized is the Defense Department, the less will Congress's ability be to influence military affairs. What applies for Congressional committees in their relations with their respective Houses also applies for executive agencies in their relations with Congress as a whole: the more unified the front the agency or the committee presents, the more likely they are to get their way with Congress.

The importance of Congressional attitude to military reorganization becomes even clearer if we ask ourselves why Eisenhower was more successful in 1959 in obtaining legislation from Congress on military unification than Truman had been in 1947. Certainly part of the answer must lie with the difference in the prestige of the two Presidents on military matters. But much of the answer lies in changed Congressional attitudes. In 1947 everyone thought some kind of unification desirable, but no one could agree on how to operationalize the term.

The major reason the Navy succeeded in watering down the Army plan for a truly unified military establishment was because of its ability to muster its core of pro-Navy allies in Congress and to add to that core a large bloc of uncommitted Congressmen and Senators who reasoned that separate service autonomy would preserve Congressional influence in military matters. The need for civilian-control-over-the-military argument, specifically the need to have a strong Secretary of Defense, never carried much weight with the bulk of Congress in 1947.[68] It did, however, in 1958; and the reason is not hard to find. The effects of service autonomy had proved too patent and costly for Congress to ignore any longer. Duplication of function and the consequent waste of national resources, added to the calculation that some reorganization was required in order to meet the Russian technological challenge, convinced Congress to strengthen the Secretary of Defense in ways that for the first time since 1947 provided him with the formal authority to run the Pentagon. But even, for example, in giving him legal discretionary authority to alter the combat functions and missions of the services, Congress retained its right to veto any proposed changes. During the 1958 Reorganization hearings, Senator Richard Russell put the Congressional perspective well:

> I must say I am intrigued with, but not convinced by, the argument that Congress ought to resolve all its troubles by just delegating all of its powers to the executive branch. . . .
>
> If that argument is good with respect to the Department of Defense, it is good with respect to any other department. If we do, it is just a confession that Congress has outlived its usefulness. . . .
>
> I want to give the Secretary any authority that is necessary in this bill. But I cannot accept the basic argument that Congress, because it might be criticized for the manner of carrying out its constitutional responsibilities, ought to delegate all of them to any executive officer.[69]

CONCLUSION

Where are we? Have we shown by argument and example that the bureaucratic paradigm is of limited utility for analyzing the formulation of American foreign policy? Does the case for its limited utility also hold for policy implementation? Why does the paradigm work better with institutional issues than with military interventions and major policy shifts? Are these three the best issue areas by which to categorize American foreign policy? Are there better examples than the ones cited above for weighing the merits of the bureaucratic approach?

More questions have obviously been raised in this essay than can be answered here.[70] But enough has been said to raise severe doubts about the merits of the bureaucratic paradigm as an approach for analyzing American foreign policy. These doubts point the way to two fundamental weaknesses of the paradigm: First, it undervalues the influence (or weight) of both generational mindsets and domestic politics on the manner in which top decision-makers approach foreign policy; second, it is too sloppy, vague, and imprecise as presently constituted to make its use worthwhile. Both of these weaknesses boil down into one central complaint: too many constraints of a non-bureaucratic nature must be set before the paradigm works, and more often than not, once we set the constraints, the paradigm will account for very little, if anything. That complaint, however, does not constitute a good case against ever using a bureaucratic paradigm. Rather it is an argument for keeping the proper perspective. Once we have specified the external and internal constraints—once we have adopted the systemic perspective—the paradigm may tell us some things that we would otherwise overlook. But we need the systemic perspective in order to avoid the opposite dangers that an uncritical acceptance of the paradigm would bring—looking for things that are not there and seeing things that we should overlook.

NOTES

1. Henry A. Kissinger, quoted in I.M. Destler, *Presidents, Bureaucrats, and Foreign Policy* (Princeton: Princeton University Press, 1972), p.3.
2. The best statements on what the "second wave" thinks the bureaucratic policies paradigm is and on what we should expect from it can be found in the following works: Graham T. Allison, *Essence of Decision: Explaining the Cuban Missile Crisis* (Boston: Little, Brown, 1971), especially chapters 5 and 6; Graham T. Allison and Morton H. Halperin, "Bureaucratic Politics: A Paradigm and Some Policy Implications," *World Politics*, Vol. 24 (Spring 1972), pp. 40–80, Supplement; *Theory and Policy in International Relations*, edited by Raymond Tanter and Richard H. Ullman; Morton H. Halperin, *Bureaucratic Politics and Foreign Policy* (Washington, D.C.: The Brookings Institution, 1974); Morton H. Halperin and Arnold Kanter, "The Bureaucratic Perspective: A Preliminary Framework," in Halperin and Kanter, *Readings in American Foreign Policy* (Boston: Little, Brown, 1973), pp. 1–42; Richard E. Neustadt, *Alliance Politics* (New York: Columbia University Press, 1970), especially chapters 5 and 6; Morton H. Halperin, "The Decision to Deploy the ABM: Bureaucratic and Domestic Politics in the Johnson Administration," *World Politics*, Vol. 25 (October, 1972), 62–96; and Morton H. Halperin, "Why Bureaucrats Play Games," *Foreign Policy*, Spring 1971.
3. See Richard E. Neustadt, *Presidential Power: The Politics of Leadership* (New York: John Wiley, 1960); Warner R. Schilling, "The Politics of National Defense: Fiscal 1950," in Warner R. Schilling, Paul T. Hammond, and Glenn H. Snyder, *Strategy, Politics and Defense Budgets* (New York: Columbia University Press, 1962), pp. 1–267; Samuel P. Huntington, *The Common Defense: Strategic Programs in National Politics* (New York: Columbia University Press, 1961); Roger Hilsman, "The Foreign-Policy Consensus: An Interim Report," *Journal of Conflict Resolution*, Vol. 3 (December, 1959), pp. 361–382 and his *To Move A Nation* (Garden City: Doubleday and Company, 1967), especially Parts 1, 2, and 10.
4. In chapter 5 of *Essence of Decision*, Allison has carefully catalogued the insights of these scholars. The list that follows does not parallel Allison's but rather reflects my estimation of what we should select from the "first wave" in order to be better able to analyze and evaluate the contribution of the "second wave." Why I have selected these five and not others will become clear shortly.
5. Neustadt, *Presidential Power*, p. 33.

6. Schilling, "The Politics of National Defense," p. 22.

7. A paraphrase of Neustadt, *Presidential Power*, p. 34.

8. Hilsman, "The Foreign-Policy Consensus," p. 365.

9. See pp. 5–27 of Schilling's "The Politics of National Defense." The quotation comes from p. 22.

10. "The Foreign-Policy Consensus," pp. 365 and 364.

11. Huntington, *The Common Defense*, p. 135.

12. Hilsman, "The Foreign Policy Consensus," p. 369. See also his "Congressional-Executive Relations and the Foreign Policy Consensus," *American Political Science Review*, Vol. 52 (September, 1958), pp. 725–744.

13. Schilling, "The Politics of National Defense," pp. 21–22 (italics added).

14. Allison, *Essence of Decision*, pp. 154–55 (italics added).

15. I shall discuss why this should be so later.

16. Schilling, "The Politics of National Defense," p. 15 (italics added).

17. Huntington, *The Common Defense*, p. 167.

18. *Ibid.*, pp. x–xi (italics added).

19. *Ibid.*, chapter 4.

20. *Ibid.*, p. 251.

21. Attributed to Don K. Price; quoted in Allison, *Essence of Decision*, p. 176.

22. *Ibid.*, p. 176.

23. *Ibid.*, p. 148 (italics added).

24. *Ibid.*, p. 167 (italics added).

25. Halperin and Kanter, "The Bureaucratic Perspective," p. 3.

26. *Ibid.*, pp. 9–10 (italics added).

27. *Ibid.*, p. 16 (italics added).

28. *Ibid.*, p. 15 (italics added).

29. I shall amplify this point below, for it is crucial in assessing the merits of the "rational actor" vs. the bureaucratic politics paradigm.

30. Allison, *Essence of Decision*, pp. 162, 175, 145 and 173.

31. A phrase attributed to former speaker of the House of Representatives, Sam Rayburn.

32. In his "The Politics of National Defense," Schilling, for example, found that Truman had to give very little. He details marvelously the bargaining among the chiefs and between them and Secretary of Defense Forrestal and the extensive maneuvers Forrestal went through in order to get the Chiefs something above the $15 billion figure that Truman had set for the services. Schilling concludes thus (p. 199):

> Finally, the day for which Forrestal had been seven months in preparation arrived. On December 9 he and Webb [Director of the Budget Bureau] met with the President at the White House, together with the Chiefs, the service Secretaries, Gruenther, Webb and Souers. With maps and charts the military briefed Truman on the difference between what they could accomplish with a $14.4 billion budget and a $16.9 billion budget. The President listened. When the presentation was over he thanked them and then announced that the ceiling still stood.
>
> Forrestal's defeat on December 9 was complete and final. "In the person of Harry Truman," he concluded, "I have seen the most rocklike example of civilian control that the world has ever witnessed."

33. Allison, *Essence of Decision*, p. 162 (italics added).

34. *Ibid.*, p. 175 (italics added).

35. *Ibid.*, p. 173 (italics added).

36. Halperin and Kanter, "The Bureaucratic Perspective," pp. 6 and 7 (italics added).

37. Halperin, "The Decision to Deploy the ABM," p. 91.

38. Neustadt, "White House and Whitehall," *The Public Interest*, No. 2 (1966), pp. 50–69; reprinted in Halperin and Kanter, *Readings in American Foreign Policy*, p. 40 (italics added).

39. Allison, *Essence of Decision*, chapter 1.

40. *Ibid.*, pp. 146, 89, 93.

41. Quoted in John P. Leacacos, "Kissinger's Apparat," and I.M. Destler, "Can One Man Do?"; both in *Foreign Policy*, No. 5 (Winter, 1971–72), pp. 5 and 2.

42. "The Case for Multiple Advocacy in Making Foreign Policy," *American Political Science Review*, Vol. 66 (September, 1972), p. 792.

43. See Robert Gallucci, "U.S. Military Policy in Vietnam: A View from the Bureaucratic Perspective," unpublished Ph.D. dissertation, Brandeis University, 1973.

44. See Abraham F. Lowenthal, *The Dominican Intervention* (Cambridge: Harvard University Press, 1972).

45. See Neustadt, *Presidential Power*, chapters 2 and 6.

46. Allison, *Essence of Decision*, chapters 2, 4 and 6.

47. *Ibid.*, p. 128 (italics added).

48. See I.M. Destler's *Presidents, Bureaucrats, and Foreign Policy* for a prescription of how a President can increase the range of issues on which he can make his will felt, especially chapter 9.

49. I have not been able to devise suitable analytical categories, by policy issue, for which slippage is more or less important, and have therefore resorted to listing the three possible cases. Someone else should try to do so.

50. Halperin, "The Decision to Deploy the ABM."

51. See John Steinbrunner, *The Cybernetic Theory of Decision: New Dimensions of Political Analysis* (Princeton: Princeton University Press, 1974); and also Philip Geyelin, *LBJ and the World* (New York: Praeger, 1966), chapter 7.

52. Because the second wave theorists have admitted that organizational position does not determine policy stance for senior decision-makers, there is no reason to dwell on proposition one any further, except to state that the evidence clearly supports the view that proposition one is generally invalid for senior players on most issue areas.

53. See my forthcoming monograph that will deal with the question of issue areas for both formulation and implementation more thoroughly than space here permits.

54. The term is that of Peter Bachrach and Morton S. Baratz. See their "Two Faces of Power," *American Political Science Review*, LVI (1962), pp. 947–952.

55. Harry S. Truman, *Years of Trial and Hope* (Garden City: Doubleday, 1956), pp. 332–333.

56. Theodore Sorensen, *Kennedy* (New York: Harper and Row, 1965), pp. 682–683. See also Stephen D. Krasner, "Are Bureaucracies Important?" *Foreign Policy*, Summer, 1972, pp. 159–179 for a critical analysis of Allison's work on the Cuban missile crisis.

57. Joseph Jones, *The Fifteen Weeks* (New York: Harcourt, Brace and World, 1955), p. 130.

58. James C. Thompson, Jr., "On the Making of U.S. China Policy, 1961–1969: A Study in Bureaucratic Politics," *The China Quarterly*, 50 (April–June, 1972), pp. 220–243. The title of the article is a misnomer. If anything, Thompson's account shows how powerless were the middle-rank bureaucrats with an unreceptive Kennedy, and how powerful only with a receptive Johnson. The significance of the President for policy initiatives is clear.

59. *Ibid.*, p. 221.

60. *Ibid.*, pp. 239–241.

61. See Henry Brandon, *The Retreat from Power* (Garden City: Doubleday, 1973), for more on this point.

62. For Kennedy and Johnson, our China policy also demonstrates this third facet of policy formulation for category two issues. By Thompson's own account, these two Presidents clearly considered public receptiveness in calculating their contemplated moves (or non-moves) toward China.

63. See Robert S. McNamara, *The Essence of Security* (New York: Harper and Row, 1968), pp. 57–58.

64. This is how McNamara justifies our large build-up in the early sixties. See his *Essence of Security*, chapter 4.

65. David Halberstam, *The Best and the Brightest* (New York: Random House, 1972), p. 72. See also D.J. Ball, "The Strategic Missile Programme of the Kennedy Administration, 1961–1963," unpublished Ph.D. dissertation, Australian National University, 1972. Ball and Halberstam agree on the crucial importance of the Administration's anticipated reactions of Congressional response in determining the size of the missile force. My own interviewing accords with this conclusion.

66. I shall develop category three issues, as well as those of one and two, more fully in my forthcoming monograph on bureaucratic politics.

67. For more on this issue, consult Demetrios Caraley, *The Politics of Military Unification* (New York: Columbia University Press, 1966); Michael H. Armacost, *The Politics of Weapons Innovation* (New York: Columbia University Press, 1969); John C. Reis, *The Management of Defense* (Baltimore: John Hopkins Press, 1964); Paul Y. Hammond, *Organizing for Defense* (Princeton: Princeton University Press, 1961); Samuel P. Huntington, *The Common Defense;* William W. Kaufman, *The McNamara Strategy* (New York: Harper and Row, 1964); Robert J. Art, *The TFX Decision* (Boston: Little, Brown, 1968); and Alain C. Enthoven and K. Wayne Smith, *How Much Is Enough?* (New York: Harper and Row, 1971).

68. See Caraley, *Politics of Military Unification*, pp. 255 and 260 and Parts 3 and 4, for an extensive analysis of these points.

69. Quoted in Reis, *Management of Defense*, p. 176.

70. My forthcoming monograph will treat these questions and others more fully in an attempt to specify more precisely where the paradigm works, where it does not, and why it does and does not work.

Rationality and Cognition

Adapting to Constraints on Rational Decisionmaking

Alexander L. George

Much of foreign policymaking consists of efforts to calculate the utility of alternative courses of action.[1] Rational calculation of this kind requires (1) *information* about the situation; (2) *substantive knowledge* of cause-and-effect relationships that is relevant for assessing the expected consequences of alternative courses of action; and (3) a way of applying the *values* and interests engaged by the problem at hand in order to judge which course of action is "best" and/or least costly and which, therefore, should be chosen.

These three requirements are imperfectly met by the way in which most foreign-policy issues present themselves. As a result, the policymaker must proceed under the handicap of severe constraints on the possibility of meeting these requirements of rational decisionmaking. These constraints are often referred to as the problems of "value-complexity" and "uncertainty."

Considerable psychological stress—in the form of anxiety, fear, shame, or guilt—can be evoked in a decisionmaker who struggles to cope with these two types of constraints on his ability to work out a good solution to the policy problem that confronts him. It is a central thesis . . . that a policymaker often experiences decisional conflicts in attempting to deal with the value complexity and uncertainty imbedded in a problem and that the resulting psychological stress, depending on how the decisionmaker copes with it, can impair adaptive responses to policy issues.[2]

The policymaker can deal with the psychological stress of decision-making in either of two ways: (1) by utilizing *analytical* modes of coping with value-complexity and uncertainty or (2) by resorting to *defensive* modes of coping with the malaise they engender. This chapter discusses these different modes of coping with value-complexity and uncertainty and calls attention to their implications for the quality of information processing and appraisal. . . .

Reprinted by permission of the publishers, Westview Press, Inc., from *Presidential Decisionmaking in Foreign Policy: The Effective Use of Information and Advice* by Alexander L. George, pp. 25–55. Copyright © 1980 by Alexander L. George. Portions of the text and some footnotes have been omitted.

VALUE-COMPLEXITY AND UNCERTAINTY: SOME DEFINITIONS

A brief statement of what is meant by "value-complexity" and by "uncertainty" is useful at the outset. *"Value-complexity" refers to the presence of multiple, competing values and interests that are imbedded in a single issue.* When this is the case, it is difficult, if not impossible, for the decisionmaker to formulate a single yardstick that encompasses and aggregates all of the competing values and interests. Lacking a single criterion of utility, the decisionmaker may experience great difficulty judging which course of action is "best" on an overall basis. He is confronted instead by a value-tradeoff problem which can be extremely difficult and painful to deal with. In order to do so he may attempt to order his value priorities and decide which of the competing values and interests to pursue in the given situation at the expense of the other values and interests that are also at stake. Value tradeoff decisions of this kind are often extremely stressful for the decisionmaker. Neither the analytical nor the defensive modes of coping with value-complexity adopted by the decisionmaker may be conducive to sound policy even though they may be successful in relieving or reducing the malaise he experiences. . . .

Finally, we take note of the fact that the effect of value-complexity on decision-making can be considerably accentuated by what has been referred to as "value extension,"[3] i.e., the all too familiar tendency of policy issues to arouse a variety of motives and interests that are extraneous to values associated with even a very broad conception of the "national interest." Thus, foreign-policy issues and the circumstances in which they arise may arouse the policymaker's personal motives and values, his political interests, or those of the administration or political party to which he belongs. This is not surprising since the way in which a policymaker deals with a particular foreign-policy problem can indeed have important consequences for his personal well-being and political fortunes: thus, it can:

- satisfy or frustrate personal values held by the policymaker;
- provide an outlet for expressing his deep-seated motives and impulses;
- obtain approval or disapproval from those who are significant figures in his life;
- enhance or damage his self-esteem;
- advance or set back his career prospects;
- strengthen or weaken his bureaucratic resources.

At times the policymaker's personal stakes in a foreign-policy issue may lead him in the same direction as his objective conception of where the national interest lies. But often, whether he is aware of his personal motives and interests or attempts to repress such awareness, they add to the problem of value-complexity and exacerbate his value conflicts. As a result, the dilemma of choice the decisionmaker experiences can become accentuated, and the value trade-off problem he faces in trying to decide what to do may become even more difficult. Finally, the decisionmaker may be willing or unwilling, able or unable, to prevent his personal motives and interests from affecting his perception of the policy problem and his judgment in dealing with it.

"Uncertainty," as the term is used here, refers to the lack of adequate information about the situation at hand and/or the inadequacy of available general knowledge needed for assessing the expected outcomes of different courses of action. Uncertainty complicates the task of making good assessments of the problem facing the decisionmaker and the additional task of deciding how to deal with it. In the face of uncertainty the decisionmaker has difficulty in making reliable cost-benefit appraisals of the alternative courses of action under consideration. He is faced with the necessity of choosing from among the options without a firm basis for confidence in his judgment. Uncertainty of this kind adds to the stress of decisionmaking. This is an important consideration to keep in mind when focusing upon emotional and psychological factors that can affect decisionmaking. Some of the ways available to individuals and organizations for coping with stress induced by uncertainty can seriously degrade the quality and effectiveness of the decisions that emerge.

Together, the presence of value-complexity and uncertainty impose severe limits on the possibility of raising policymaking to the level of rationality associate with models of "pure" rationality in decision theory.[4] Very often, both value-complexity and uncertainty are present in a problem which the policymaker is trying to decide. For purposes of analysis and presentation, however, we shall deal with them separately in this chapter.

DEALING WITH VALUE-COMPLEXITY

There are, as decision theorists have emphasized, analytical ways of dealing with value-complexity in choice situations in order to strive for as "efficient" and acceptable a solution to such problems as possible. We shall not review this technical literature here, nor attempt to judge how germane it is for different types of foreign-policy problems. Such analytical techniques may be relevant in principle but, for various reasons, difficult to apply in practice in the settings in which foreign-policy decisions are made.

Precisely because it is so difficult to employ objective analysis to deal with value-complexity, the top executive is expected by others in the policymaking group to reconcile competing values and interests by going through an "internal debate." The hope is that a subjective ordering and aggregation of the competing values by the executive will enable him to offer a satisfactory solution to what would otherwise be left to be settled entirely via conflict and bargaining among the actors within the policymaking system. To the extent that the top executive accepts and discharges this unique task of leadership, he may be able to make a decisive contribution to lessening the social-political tensions and costs associated with making policy in a highly pluralistic political system. As Dean Pruitt has noted, the executive is in a better position to deal with value conflict than a small group or an organization because his own intrapersonal tensions are "more easily resolved, since [he] can better subordinate one value to another."[5] . . .

Internal debate and subjective aggregation of competing values and interests do not always work. The top executive may search for but be unable to find a course of action that promises to safeguard all of the multiple stakes aroused for him by that issue. Faced with this dilemma, he may attempt to deal with it strategically as, for example, by assigning higher priority to achieving some of the values and interests at stake and by utilizing available information and analytical skills as best he can for this purpose. But even a strategic approach for dealing with difficult value trade-offs may not be wholly successful and may result in the decisionmaker experiencing considerable frustration, anxiety, self-doubts, etc. To cope with the ensuing emotional stress, he may react defensively in ways that may further prejudice the possibilities for a more satisfactory response to the policy problem. In sum, the decisionmaker may deal with value-complexity analytically and strategically; or he may resort to defensive psychological modes of coping with the emotional stress of being faced by difficult value trade-off problems. It is also possible that his response will include elements of both analytical-strategic and defensive modes of coping.

It is useful to distinguish three different ways in which a policymaker may attempt to deal with the malaise associated with value-complexity. First, he may *resolve* the value conflict, at least in his own mind, by devising a course of action that constitutes either a genuinely creative analytical solution to the problem or a spurious and illusory resolution of it that may also be psychologically comforting even though analytically defective. A second way is to *accept* the value conflict as unavoidable and to face up to the need to make the difficult trade-off choice as part of one's role requirements as a decisionmaker. This, too, can be psychologically comforting; but whether the decisionmaker is correct in perceiving the value conflict as unavoidable and whether he deals adequately with the trade-off is another matter. Finally, the decisionmaker may seek to *avoid* a value conflict by denying its existence or playing down its importance. This strictly defensive mode of coping may succeed in reducing or banishing psychological stress, but it may do so only at the cost of markedly impairing information processing and appraisal. Let us examine these three models of dealing with value-complexity more closely.

Value-Conflict Resolution

This way of dealing with value-complexity takes the form of attempting to satisfy, to some extent at least, all of the competing values and interests of which one is aware. This is usually a formidable task, if not an impossible one. But, if the policymaker is successful in doing so, the rewards are considerable; not only does he achieve a high-quality decision, he derives inner psychological satisfaction from doing so and may also expect political benefits from satisfying many different constituencies. Particularly in a democracy or in a pluralistic policymaking system the executive is under strong temptation and indeed often under strong political pressure to try to reconcile conflicting values imbedded in an issue he must decide. In these circumstances, the inventive executive may indeed come up with a creative, novel option that genuinely resolves the apparent value conflict, demonstrating thereby that the values in question were really congruent. More often, the best that can be done is the lesser, but still significant achievement of reconciling the value conflict through some kind of compromise. The weaker solution of value compromise may result in a policy that sacrifices the quality of the decision for greater acceptability.[6]

The resolution of value conflict may be attained in one of two ways: (1) by inventing a single policy that yields some satisfaction for each of the multiple interests and values at stake; or (2) by staging or scheduling satisfaction for these values/interests via a series of separate actions or policies over a longer period of time. In the latter case, the policymaker realizes that the value trade-off problem cannot be avoided entirely. His initial action is designed to promote only some of the competing values/interests; he may try to promote the remaining values/interests damaged or neglected by his initial policy by additional actions shortly thereafter. This type of "scheduling" may prove to be beneficial or damaging to foreign policy objectives, depending on circumstances and the perspicacity of the policymaker. Inept "scheduling," of course, may produce a policy that is incoherent and inconsistent.

We have to recognize that, however effective in relieving the policymaker's psyhological stress, efforts to resolve value conflicts may in fact be unrealistic, spurious, and illusory. Some value conflicts simply cannot be resolved. Efforts to do so may actually impede the search for effective policies, resulting in highly questionable compromises of all or most of the values imbedded in the issue. A decisionmaker who impulsively or rigidly strives to resolve or reconcile value conflicts shirks thereby his responsibility to determine value priorities and to make reasoned trade-off choices. Thus, while value-conflict resolution, is the best strategy when it is possible and skillfully done, it is often not feasible, and other strategies for dealing with the problem posed by conflicting values are then preferable.

Value-Conflict Acceptance

In this way of dealing with a complex mix of values the decisionmaker faces up to the fact that a difficult choice among them must be made. It is important, however, that he should not determine value priorities *prematurely;* rather, he should maintain unimpaired receptivity to information that illuminates the full range of values imbedded in the issue. Only then should he proceed to make a reasoned, conscientious determination of value priorities in order to resolve the trade-off problem that confronts him.

To do so requires the policymaker to accept the fact that he has to put aside or give lesser weight to some salient values and interests in order to advance those judged to be of greater importance or, at least, those with the greatest chance of being realized in the situation at hand. Ideally, he does so without engaging in a fruitless effort to achieve a genuine, full resolution of the value conflict or resorting to defensive psychological mechanisms of denying or minimizing the conflict. . . .

By identifying with the role of executive and viewing oneself as being a role player, the individual may find it possible to make difficult decisions with greater detachment and also with greater sensitivity to priorities among competing interests and values. At the same time, being a good role player may enable the individual to experience less stress and less personal damage when he is obliged to make a decision that sacrifices some interests. For then he may see these losses as an unavoidable consequence of fulfilling his role requirements, which oblige him to make the best possible decision that focuses on the most important of the various stakes at issue. Finally, by fulfilling difficult role requirements of this kind, as Truman did, the individual may in fact derive personal satisfaction—if not also the respect and praise of others—that bolsters and protects his self-esteem.

But, as with the first mode of dealing with the analytical difficulty and psychological stress of value-complexity which has already been discussed, this second mode, too, may be performed ineptly so far as its impact on foreign policy is concerned. Critical in this respect is whether the decisionmaker is correct in perceiving a value conflict as being unavoidable. As a matter of fact, he may arrive at this conclusion *prematurely* without adequate information or analysis of the policy problem. Being a good role player, insofar as concerns fulfilling the requirement to make difficult decisions when necessary, does not guarantee good judgment. . . .

Value-Conflict Avoidance

To avoid or minimize the psychological malaise created for him by perception of important value conflicts an individual may resort to the tactics of ignoring or playing down some of the competing values and interests that are imbedded in the decisional problem. Defensive maneuvers of this kind have received considerable attention in psychological studies of decisional stress. A variety of psychological devices are available to any individual for reducing his perception of a value conflict that would otherwise create severe stress. These mechanisms are described in various psychological theories of balance, consistency, dissonance, and conflict. The two which seem of greatest importance here are "cognitive restructuring" and "devaluation."

In the first of these, cognitive restructuring, the individual finds a way of turning aside incoming information that calls attention to or heightens a value conflict. Thus, he may ignore, discount, deny, forget, or unintentionally misinterpret information about some of the competing values. In "devaluation," on the other hand, the individual downgrades one of the values or interests that he or others close to him hold. Doing so minimizes the value conflict he would otherwise experience and makes it more manageable, psychologically and analytically. Devaluation may lead the individual to reduce or abandon his identification with significant others who are going to be damaged as a result of his ignoring their interests or values. The decisionmaker may cut out of his consultations those holding the devalued values, or refuse to credit the information they put before him, or even denigrate them before others.

Avoiding value conflicts in these two ways is more likely to impede information processing than other mechanisms that may also be utilized for the same purpose.[7] Thus, cognitive restructuring and devaluation are likely to distort the decisionmaker's perception of the full range of values imbedded in the issue and hamper appraisal of options that best deal with the multiplicity of values and interests at stake.

Cognitive restructuring exemplifies a more general tendency displayed by individuals and organizations to see what they expect to see and to assimilate incoming information to preexisting images, beliefs, hypotheses, and theories. . . .

Choices are indeed easier when there is no need to consider value trade-offs. Avoidance of value complexity is particularly likely . . . when a decisionmaker initially considers only one or two of the values involved in the problem at hand and comes to favor a particular policy for dealing with it because it seems appropriate for safeguarding or enhancing those particular values. Later, when he becomes aware that other important values and interests are also imbedded in the problem, he may proceed to bolster his premature adherence to a favored policy option by finding questionable or ill-considered arguments for believing that the same action will also somehow safeguard, or at least not seriously damage, the other values and interests. As a result, the process of information "search" and "appraisal" is inhibited and cut short before the decisionmaker has examined the range of values at stake more fully and weighed the evidence of a conflict among them more carefully.

Psychological avoidance of hard choices may be detected also in instances when foreign-policymakers fail to recognize that the set of goals they are pursuing are in fact likely to be inconsistent with one another. Thus, for example, as World War II drew to an end American policymakers were disposed to agree that the Soviet Union's security requirements made it necessary for her to have friendly regimes on its borders in Eastern Europe; but, at the same time, American leaders also strongly embraced the idea of free elections in Eastern Europe. President Roosevelt appears to have avoided a clear recognition of the likely incompatibility of these two goals—and hence a dilemma for U.S. policy—by embracing the optimistic but highly questionable expectation, which he stated at the Yalta Conference, that free elections in Eastern Europe would result in governments "thoroughly friendly to the Soviet [Union] for years to come." Roosevelt's unwillingness to contemplate that Eastern European governments formed via free elections might be hostile to the Soviet Union made it possible for U.S. foreign policy to embrace what were in fact mutually incompatible objectives, thus laying the groundwork for further exacerbation of Soviet-American relations later on.[8]

As this case illustrates, the failure of policymakers to perceive an admittedly difficult value trade-off spawns unrealistic policies that can prove damaging to the realization of either of the conflicting objectives. It is well to recognize that excessive consistency-striving is often abetted, as in the case just cited, by the *political* constraints under which policymakers operate. To face up to the necessity for choice can sometimes entail severe political costs, whichever way the value trade-off is resolved. Perception of value conflicts can be blurred, moreover, when—as is often the case when policymakers attempt to assess the "national interest"—the values in question are vague or ill-defined. Perception of value trade-offs can be muted also when the impact of the policy chosen upon the values in question will not be felt immediately and when the longer-term consequences of the policy cannot be reliably predicted.

DEALING WITH UNCERTAINTY

When the information and knowledge needed for making an important decision are inadequate, this, too, can create emotional stress for the executive.[9] Thus, in a pioneering essay on political decisionmaking many years ago, three political scientists called attention to the need to look for the "devices" employed by decisionmakers to minimize "the psychological tensions which accompany decisionmaking under circumstances of uncertainty and lack of complete information." Continuing, they asked: "How do decisionmakers learn to live with the possibility of 'unacceptable error'? And what effects do the devices used to cope with uncertainty have on their deliberations?"[10] We shall list and discuss briefly a number of well-known ways in which individuals deal with uncertainty in making decisions. Some of these devices serve to minimize psychological tension for the decisionmaker without necessarily helping him to deal effectively with the situation.

Calculated Procrastination

It is understandable that in the face of stress induced by uncertainty executives often find it difficult to act. Indeed, some leaders go so far as to conclude that the best strategy of leadership is to do as little as possible, hoping that the problems that seem to require their attention will go away or find some other solution.

Of the many executives in political life or in other sectors of society who have adopted this philosophy as a strategy for dealing with decisional uncertainty, it will suffice to take note of Calvin Coolidge's well-known principle of "calculated inactivity." As one political scientist has put it, Coolidge's strategy in the presidency "was to 'sit down and keep still' in the face of problems rather than to confront them, to 'remain silent until an issue is reduced to its lowest terms, until it boils down to something like a moral issue.' 'If you see ten troubles coming down the road, you can be sure that nine will run down into the ditch before they reach you and you have to battle with only one.' "[11]

The philosophy of "calculated procrastination" may be surprisingly effective under some circumstances, but it carries with it the risk that the executive will be confronted by acute crises more often than would otherwise have been the case had he taken action on a timely basis to deal with emerging problems.

Defensive Procrastination

While some executives adopt the general *strategy* of "calculated procrastination" to deal with uncertainty in a variety of situations, many more executives will resort to the *tactic* of procrastination only on occasion.[12] It is useful in this connection to distinguish between "rational (or calculated) procrastination" and "defensive procrastination." When the relative merits of alternative courses of action for dealing with a particular problem are clouded by uncertainty, it may be quite rational to postpone making a decision if (a) there is no time pressure to do so, or (b) there is reason to hope that more information and a better appraisal of the problem and of the options may be available later on; or (c) there is reason to believe that the situation itself may improve.

"Defensive procrastination" occurs, on the other hand, when a person seizes upon the fact that there is no immediate necessity for a decision to escape from the decisional conflict that the uncertainty has created by putting the problem out of his mind and turning his attention to other matters. (Delegating the problem to an assistant or to a committee, in effect for "burial," can facilitate defensive procrastination.) A person who engages in "defensive procrastination" displays lack of interest in the issue thereafter, with the consequence that he foregoes further information search, appraisal, and contingency planning. In contrast, the person who engages in "rational procrastination" sees to it that active search, appraisal, and contingency planning continue.

In brief, whereas the defensive procrastinator "leaves the field" in order to escape the unpleasantness of uncertainty, the rational procrastinator *uses* the time the lack of a deadline offers, taking steps to reduce the uncertainty that plagues the decision he will have to make.

Examples of both kinds of procrastination can be found in the conduct of foreign policy. In the management of conflict relations with other states, decisionmaking is often geared to externally imposed time pressure, by deadlines implicit in rapidaly developing situations or deliberately created by other actors in the international arena. Viewed from this standpoint, international crises may have a necessary and useful catalytic function in forcing foreign-policymakers to come to grips with and to decide difficult issues on which they would rather procrastinate. A similar function may be performed, of course, by a variety of other events—for example, congressional budget hearings, summit meetings, press conferences, etc. . . .

Dealing with Uncertainty Under Time Pressure

We have noted that in the face of uncertainty imbedded in complex issues executives often find it difficult to act. How *does* a leader overcome such inhibitions? There are, after all, many situations in which the policymaker has to decide what to do even when the relative merits of alternative options are by no means clear and when he perceives serious risks in any course of action. Self-imposed deadlines and time pressures facilitate choice in such situations, but they do not by themselves make it easier for the decisionmaker to cope with the malaise of having to make an important decision in a matter that is laden with uncertainty.[13] What, we may ask, does forced choice under these circumstances do to the quality of search and appraisal?

Social psychologists who have studied decisionmaking under circumstances of this kind have noted two different ways in which information processing and appraisal can be impaired. One type of impairment results from "hypervigilance"; the other from "defensive avoidance." The first refers to a paniclike state of mind that is accompanied by a marked loss of cognitive efficiency. The second refers to psychological devices used to escape from current worrying about a decision by not exposing oneself to cues that evoke awareness of a decisional conflict or dilemma that is fraught with potential losses. While hypervigilance is relatively rare, defensive avoidance is a highly pervasive tendency that is encountered in many different types of decisions, whether in business, family affairs, or in politics.[14]

We have already discussed one type of defensive avoidance, namely, "defensive procrastination." Another manifestation of defensive avoidance is what is sometimes called "bolstering," a phenomenon that occupies a prominent role in the theory of cognitive dissonance and in related social psychological theories.[15]

"Bolstering"

"Bolstering" refers to the psychological tendency under certain conditions of decisional stress to increase the attractiveness of a preferred (or chosen) option and doing the opposite for options which one is inclined to reject (or has rejected). Thus, the expected gains from the preferred alternative are magnified and its expected costs/risks are minimized. Similarly, the expected gains from rejected alternatives are downgraded; their expected costs/risks are magnified.

It is important to note that bolstering makes the decisionmaker's task of choosing what to do easier; it reduces the malaise of making a decision that is clouded by uncertainty.[16] It does so by *"spreading the alternatives,"* i.e., making one option seem more attractive than the alternative options. Thus, bolstering is accompanied by *distorted information-processing and appraisal.*

Bolstering can occur before a decision is made as well as, perhaps more often, afterwards.[17] Predecisional bolstering occurs when the decisionmaker believes that a firm deadline for decision is approaching and when he believes that he will not obtain additional relevant information of much consequence. He will then move towards closure by selecting what he regards as the least objectionable alternative and then consolidate his choice by reinterpreting the uncertainties to make it appear more attractive than it has seemed to be earlier.

It should be noted that the decisionmaker's belief that there is little time left to make the decision and his belief that no additional useful information can be expected may both be in error. In order to cut short the stress and malaise of decisional dilemma he may rush his decision, thereby foregoing the possibility of using the remaining time to obtain still additional information and advice. In other words, anxiety and stress may push the decisionmaker towards premature closure, cutting off search and appraisal in the interest of resolving his decisional dilemma via bolstering. Supportive bolstering by sycophantic (or equally troubled) subordinates can aggravate this danger.[18]

It has to be recognized, of course, that bolstering can be of positive value to the decisionmaker if it is preceded by search and appraisal that is as thorough as circumstances permit. Then a last-minute bolstering—one that does not cut short search and appraisal—can help the decisionmaker to avoid suffering gnawing self-doubts that can further drain his time and energy. Of course, if carried too far in this respect, last-mintue bolstering may render the decisionmaker less capable of monitoring the consequences of his decision and less inclined to reconsider his policy on the basis of evidence that is not working.

A variety of rationalizations and other psychological devices may be utilized by the decisionmaker who resorts to bolstering in order to achieve the comforting feeling that the action he is taking is likely to lead to a successful outcome. An *incomplete* list includes the following:

1. He may convert the genuine uncertainty that exists as to the likelihood of different outcomes into spuriously calculated risks to which he assigns probabilities.
2. He may distort the estimate of the probability of future events, exaggerating the likelihood that his action will lead to a favorable outcome and minimizing the likelihood of an unfavorable outcome.
3. He may exaggerate in his own mind possibilities open to him for reversing his decision, should it turn out badly, or for limiting or correcting whatever undesirable effects it may have.
4. He may reevaluate some of the negative consequences his decision may entail by attributing certain long-range benefits to them.
5. He may engage in wishful thinking as to the likelihood that the risks of his policy will materialize, if at all, only in the long-run whereas its benefits will emerge more quickly.
6. He may attempt to convince himself that if his policy fails, its failure will at least not be highly and widely visible or that he will not in any case be held personally responsible for its failure.
7. He may believe that even if his policy fails in the end, it will have done enough good to have been worthwhile.[19]

The Use of Aids to Decision and Simple Decision Rules

In addition to "bolstering," which provides *psychological* assistance for enabling the policymaker to come to a decision, there are a variety of *cognitive aids* that enable him to cope with the intellectual problem of deciding what to do in the face of uncertainty.[20]

Most individuals have learned to diagnose new situations even when the available information is ambiguous or incomplete. And most individuals have also acquired ways of choosing among alternative courses of action even when limitations of knowledge and information exclude the possibility of assessing the expected outcomes by applying a comprehensive, rigorous, analytic model. Let us review quickly some of the major decision rules and strategies employed to cope with decisional uncertainty.

The Use of a "Satisficing" Rather than an "Optimizing" Decision Rule Because the search for a course of action that will yield the highest possible payoff is often impractical, most people settle for a course that is "good enough," one that offers a sufficient rather than a maximum payoff.[21] Not only does the use of "satisficing" as a decision rule fit the severe limitations of man's capacity to process information—and, only to a lesser extent, that of organizations as well—it is also an appropriate way of adjusting to the fact that to apply an "optimizing" decision rule requires enormous quantities of information and analytical resources such as are often simply not available or could be obtained only at great cost.

A distinction needs to be made between the most limited application of the "satisficing" criterion, in which the decisionmaker selects the first option coming to his attention that offers some degree of improvement over the present state of affairs, and "satisficing" after a more persistent search for an option that does better than the others that have been considered.

The Strategy of "Incrementalism" Incrementalism converts the "satisficing" decision rule for dealing with uncertainty for any single decision problem into a strategy convering a whole sequence of decisions aimed at improving the present state of affairs gradually by means of small steps.[22] The incremental approach recommends itself to leaders when they find it difficult to obtain agreement on longer-range objectives and when the knowledge and information needed to devise more comprehensive plans to achieve them is in any case lacking. Under these circumstances, a decisionmaker employing the incremental strategy will consider a narrow range of policy alternatives that differ only slightly from existing policies and aim at securing marginal rather than dramatic improvements. The strategy relies on feedback as part of a "remedial," "serial," "exploratory" attack on the problem at issue—hence, the description of incrementalist strategy as "the art of muddling through."

While the incrementalist approach may recommend itself to the policymaker as a way of hedging against uncertainty and as a conservative strategy that avoids the risks of seeking more far-reaching changes, it nonetheless entails risks of its own that are not always recognized. The marginal improvements sought may be proven illusory or grossly insufficient. Incrementalism may degenerate into a costly series of trial-and-error actions that fail to secure a cumulative improvement in the situation. Reliance upon incrementalism may encourage policies that attack symptoms and offer marginal relief rather than deal with root causes. There is, in brief, no guarantee that the decisionmaker will somehow muddle through successfully. And, by focusing on securing marginal improvements in the near future, the policymaker may fail to see opportunities for larger gains by means of strategies geared to longer-range objectives. Further, particularly in foreign policy but also in domestic policy, incrementalism can be dangerously myopic insofar as the actions taken to achieve short-term gains, as in U.S. policy in Vietnam, may turn out to be steps on a slippery slope to highly unfavorable outcomes. . . .

The Strategy of Sequential Decisionmaking   This strategy attempts to bring incremental decisionmaking into a framework of sophisticated policy planning, thereby giving policymakers an opportunity to avoid or minimize the worst consequences of sloppy, myopic incrementalism.[23] It does so in two ways: (1) by breaking up a big policy decision into a series of smaller-step decisions over time and (2) by attempting to deal with different uncertainties at optimal points in the sequence of interrelated decisions.

In developing an appropriate decision strategy for dealing with a complex policy problem, it is important for the policymaker to determine what has to be decided now and what can be left for decision later. Making the component decisions seriatim in this way often enables the policymaker to develop options that did not exist at the outset and to obtain better inputs from his analysts and experts for some aspects of the evolving policy later on.

This strategy attempts to turn to account the fact that the informational and analytical requirements differ for different parts of an evolving policy. By breaking up a big decision into smaller component decisions, the strategy uses the available time to improve the quality of some of the analytical inputs needed for later component decisions. For the policymaker to deal intelligently with uncertainties imbedded in the problem, it is useful, as systems analysts have emphasized, to distinguish among the various types of uncertainty. In addition to statistical uncertainty, there are technological and economic uncertainties as well as uncertainties with regard to human behavior and future environments. Stratagems for dealing with one type of uncertainty are not appropriate for coping with other types of uncertainty.[24]

One should not ignore the possible risks and costs of attempting to create a variety of options and to retain as much policy flexibility as possible. The policymaker who employs this decision strategy may find that the options he has created for planning purposes often create or attract support from influential actors in the policymaking system and the public, thereby achieving a momentum that may force the policymaker's hand.[25] But while the practice of "flexible options" may have been oversold or misapplied on occasion in the past, the strategy of sequential decisionmaking with which it is associated nonetheless constitutes a more sophisticated variant of the strategy of incrementalism in that it attempts to find a way of coping with and avoiding the worst consequences of "muddling through."

"Consensus Politics"   The policymaker may decide what to do on the basis of what enough people want and will support rather than attempt to master the cognitive complexity of the problem by means of analysis. In the search for an effective decision there is often a potential trade-off between the substantive "quality" of a decision and its "acceptability" to those whose support the decisionmaker feels he would like to have or, indeed, must have. When the search for a "quality" option is handicapped by the difficulty of calculating expected outcomes, the policymaker may fall back on the decision rule of "consensus." In effect, then, the decisionmaker bypasses the thorny trade-off dilemma between "quality" and "acceptability" by making the criterion of "acceptability" a substitute for that of "quality."

Use of Historical Analogies   Many thoughtful observers have remarked about the universal human tendency to force the present into constructs of the past. Thus, "history does not repeat itself in the real world but it does repeat itself in the 'reality world' of the mind. . . . "26

Our purpose here is not to call attention once more to the lessons of an earlier historical case or of misapplying the correct lessons of that case to a new situation which differs from it in important respects. Rather, attention is drawn to the fact that policymakers often cope with the difficulty of comprehending and dealing with new situations by resorting to historical analogies. Thus, an earlier historical case that had made a particularly strong impression on the policymaker becomes an aid to diagnosing the present situation and for deciding what is the best or necessary way with which to respond to it. Very often it is relatively recent history—events that the statesman personally experienced earlier in his life or which he experienced vicariously through contact with significant figures in his intellectual development—that provides the models or analogies to which the decisionmaker turns most readily. Very often, too, it is the "remembered history" of his generation on which he draws. Thus, as World War II began to draw to a close and Franklin Roosevelt addressed himself to the peace that would follow, he was influenced particularly by a desire to avoid the mistakes Woodrow Wilson had made at the end of World War I. As for Harry Truman, when the Korean War unexpectedly broke out in late June of 1950, he quickly oriented himself by viewing it in terms of its presumed parallel with the events of the 1930s, when the democracies had failed to act in the face of totalitarian aggression against Manchuria, Ethiopia, and Austria, thus encouraging the totalitarian powers to go further until World War II broke out. . . . [27]

Ideology and General Principles as Guides to Action   Other sources of relatively simple decision rules for coping with decisional complexity and the uncertainties that hamper calculation of outcomes are to be found in the ideological beliefs and moral principles of the policymaker. They provide a generalized, deductive belief system which, applied to a particular situation, can help the decisionmaker to cut through its complexity to illuminate whether, when, and how he should respond to it.

Thus, for example, Cordell Hull, secretary of state under Franklin D. Roosevelt, had memorized as a youth a set of maxims from Jefferson and Gladstone. "As I faced the stupendous problems to be dealt with abroad," Hull wrote of his first month in office, "it gave me some relief and greater confidence to feel that I was strongly grounded on the fundamental propositions that should govern relations among nations. I proceeded to assemble and classify these principles, all of which the President, too, believed in strongly, and to make practical application of them at appropriate times.[28]

Hull's principles no doubt served to simplify and structure the problem of action he faced repeatedly as secretary of state. Whether they also enabled him to exercise consistently good judgment in foreign policy is another matter. Arthur Schlesinger, Jr., for one, wrote critically of the use to which Hull put his "principles": "often . . . they served as a means of avoiding problems until he could find an aspect reducible to his set of principles, or of disguising, even from himself, some of his less creditable impulses. . . . Hull's moral world was bounded, in other words, not by the facts or by original moral convictions, but by the copybook maxims into which he absorbed both the facts and his emotions."[29]

Beliefs About Correct Strategy and Tactics   The problem of action in the face of uncertainty is eased for the decisionmaker by fundamental beliefs he holds about (a) the nature of international politics and conflict; (b) the extent to which historical developments can be shaped by intelligent or misguided action; (c) axioms regarding correct strategy and tactics for dealing with friendly and unfriendly actors in domestic and world political arenas. Most political actors have developed relatively stable views on many of these matters. These beliefs are part of the "cognitive map" which enables them to process information and engage in appraisals of alternative courses of action.

The term "operational code" has been employed in referring to beliefs of this kind held by a particular statesman or policy elite. But the term is somewhat a misnomer insofar as it implies or permits the inference that a leader's "operational code" consists of a set of recipes or rules for action that he applies mechanically in his decisionmaking. Rather, beliefs of this kind serve as a prism or filter that influences the actor's perception and diagnosis of political situations and that provides norms and standards to guide and channel his choices of action in specific situations. The function of an operational code belief system in decisionmaking, then, is to provide the actor with "diagnostic propensities" and "choice propensities." Neither his diagnosis of situations nor his choice of action for dealing with them is rigidly prescribed and determined by these beliefs. Rather, their function is to *simplify* and *channel* the task of processing information, inventing and appraising options, and choosing the action that seems best in the circumstances. Stated in another way, these beliefs serve to adopt the actor's effort to engage in optimal informational processing and in rational calculation to the complexity and uncertainty that are characteristic of so much political decisionmaking. . . .

Each of the seven cognitive aids to decisionmaking that have now been discussed can enable the policymaker to cope in some way with the intellectual problem he faces when the decision he must make is clouded with uncertainty. The substantive quality of the decision is, of course, another matter. Leaving aside a direct answer to this question, let us consider instead the implications of the policymaker's use of these cognitive aids and simple decision rules for his ability to benefit from the contribution that close advisers and the organizational information-processing system can make to his search for an effective decision.

The first thing to be noted is the danger that the executive will resort *prematurely* to one of his favored cognitive aids or simple decision rules—for example, a historical analogy or a maxim of correct strategy, "satisficing" or a "consensus" decision rule—or *rely too heavily* on it in making his decision. The result may well be to cut himself off from the possibility of benefiting from a broader or in-depth analysis of the problem that advisers or the organizational information-processing system can provide. Cognitive aids and decision rules may be indispensable, but they carry the risk of serving as filters that screen, channel, or block the executive's receptivity to information and advice from others. The cognitive aid or decision rule an executive leans on in order to reach a decision can easily serve to define in a narrow way his informational needs in that situation. He will tend to pay less attention or give less weight to available information and advice that is not directly relevant and usable with respect to the cognitive aid or decision rule he utilizes in order to cut through the intellectual complexity and "confusion" surrounding the problem at hand. This has important implications for the design and management of advisory relationships and organizational information-processing systems.

INTERNATIONAL CRISES AS A SOURCE OF STRESS

Diplomatic confrontations and military crises can be extremely stressful for policymakers and, depending on how policymakers cope with the emotions aroused, can impair information processing and performance of the cognitive tasks associated with policymaking.[30]

Let us consider first the characteristics of crises and confrontations that can generate high levels of stress:

First, stress is generated by the fact that an international crisis typically entails *a strong threat to major values and interests* that top officials are responsible for safeguarding.

A second source of stress is present when, as is so often the case, the crisis comes as a *surprise* to policymakers—that is, with little warning. Even crises that have been anticipated to some extent can have quite a shock effect insofar as they present novel features that were not foreseen.

A third source of stress stems from the fact that crises often require *quick decisions*. Short response time is typical of many international crises, and it imposes an additional psychological burden on decisionmakers.

Finally, a fourth source of stress is the cumulative *emotional and physical fatigue* that an international crisis often imposes on top policymakers and their staffs. In a crisis, minutes seem like hours, hours like days, days like weeks. The demands on one's energies and emotions are intense; at the same time, opportunities for rest and recuperation are limited. Robert Kennedy's memoir of the Cuban missile crisis makes it clear that tensions during some days reached an almost unbearable intensity: "that kind of [crisis-induced] pressure does strange things to a human being, even to brilliant, self-confident, mature, experienced men. For some it brings out characteristics and strengths that perhaps even they never knew they had, and for others the pressure is too overwhelming."[31] Theodore Sorensen, also a participant in the policymaking group during the missile crisis, reports that he saw firsthand, "during the long days and nights of the Cuban crisis, how brutally physical and mental fatigue can numb the good sense as well as the senses of normally articulate men."[32]

What, then, can be said about the effects of crisis-induced stress on performance of policymaking tasks? Only a brief summary of laboratory and field studies will be presented here. It is true that *mild* levels of stress often facilitate and may actually improve performance, especially if the responses required by the situational task are relatively uncomplicated. But as stress increases to higher levels, performance worsens. This general relationship between stress and peformance—often referred to as an "inverted U" curve—is well supported by research findings for a variety of tasks and conditions. At some point, every individual reaches a "threshold" or crossover point at which increased stress no longer improves performance but leads to a more or less rapid decline in performance. However, the point at which the "threshold" is reached varies for different individuals so that, fortunately, one would expect some members of a decisionmaking group to be functioning effectively even though the performance of others has sharply deteriorated. Moreover, the threshold for any given individual varies depending on the nature of the task and the setting in which he or she is experiencing the stress.

While stress affects the performance of a variety of tasks, we are interested here in its effects on the types of complex cognitive tasks associated with foreign-policy decisionmaking. The following is a brief summary of major types of effects that have been noted:

1. *Impaired attention and perception:* (a) important aspects of the crisis situation may escape scrutiny; (b) conflicting values may be overlooked; (c) the range of perceived alternatives is likely to narrow but not necessarily to the best alternatives; and (d) "search" for relevant information and options tends to be dominated by past experience, with a tendency to fall back on familiar solutions that have worked in the past whether or not they are appropriate to the present situation.

2. *Increased cognitive rigidity:* (a) impaired ability to improvise and reduced creativity; (b) reduced receptivity to information that challenges existing beliefs; (c) increased stereotypic thinking; and (d) reduced tolerance for ambiguity, which results in a tendency to cut off information search and evaluation and make decisions prematurely.

3. *Shortened and narrowed perspective:* (a) less attention to longer-range consequences of options; (b) less attention to side effects of options.

4. *Shifting the burden to the opponent:* the belief that one's own options are quite limited and that only the other side has it within its power to prevent an impending disaster.

Many other events and situations that arise in the conduct of foreign policy share some of the same characteristics of threat, surprise, and short response time associated with international crises and, hence, can have similar effects on performance. This is the case, for example, when decisionmakers must meet deadlines on important matters. It is also the case at times when decisionmakers experience role conflicts and role overload. The effects of situationally aroused stress upon performance, therefore, are not confined to international crises. The fundamental constraints of value-complexity and uncertainty that are imbedded in so many foreign-policy problems are themselves capable of generating psychological stress in policymakers that can impair their judgment.

NOTES

1. In preparing this chapter, I have drawn on my earlier discussion of some of these problems in A.L. George, "Adaptation to Stress in Political Decision Making," in George V. Coelho, David A. Hamburg, and John E. Adams, eds., *Coping and Adaptation* (New York: Basic Books, 1974).

2. A similar postulate underlies the "conflict theory" developed by Janis and Mann. The desire to avoid the stress of decisional conflicts, they emphasize, is a more general motivation than the consistency-striving postulated in early cognitive dissonance theory. Janis and Mann note, further, that neo-dissonance theory has moved in the direction of this more general motivational concept (I.L. Janis and L. Mann, *Decision Making: A Psychological Analysis of Conflict, Choice, and Commitment* [New York: Free Press, 1977], pp. 17, 420).

3. The concept of "value extension" is taken from the valuable discussion of constraints on rational decisionmaking in John D. Steinbruner, *The Cybernetic Theory of Decision* (Princeton: N.J.: Princeton University Press, 1974), p. 145.

4. For useful discussions of these cognitive limits on rational choice and some of their implications in the arena of political decisionmaking, *see*, for example, James G. March and Herbert A. Simon, *Organizations* (New York: Wiley, 1958); and Charles E. Lindblom, "The Science of 'Muddling Through,' " *Public Administration Quarterly* 29 (Spring 1959):79–88. An incisive discussion of these issues is provided in Chapter 2, "The Analytic Paradigm," in Steinbruner, *Cybernetic Theory.*

5. Dean Pruitt, *Problem Solving in the Department of State*, Monograph Series in World Affairs, no. 2 (Denver: University of Denver, 1965), p. 62; *see also* John McDonald, "How the Man at the Top Avoids Crises," *Fortune* 81 (1970):121–22, 152–55.

6. On the trade-off between "quality" and "acceptability" of a decision *see Introduction* to this book.

7. For example, after having made a decision that ignores or gives insufficient weight to some values, the policymaker may attempt to convince those damaged by his action that it was the right or necessary thing to do, or to demonstrate that he is a worthwhile person who is still identified with their interests and welfare, or to resort to acts of expiation or asceticism in order to relieve the self-disapproval or guilt that he experiences as a result of having acted contrary to their interests and values (*see* Janis and Mann, *Decision Making*, pp. 144–47).

8. This example is taken from Jervis, *Perception and Misperception* (Princeton: Princeton University Press, 1977) p. 140. Of course, we cannot be certain of the psychological explanation advanced here for Roosevelt's policy. It is possible that Roosevelt

was well aware that the Eastern European governments might prove to be hostile to the USSR but accepted that possibility as a calculated risk.

9. A particularly vivid example of the stress produced for an executive by his inability to cope with decisional complexity is provided by President Warren G. Harding. On one occasion, Harding unburdened himself to a friend: "John, I can't make a damn thing out of this tax problem. I listen to one side and they seem right, and then God! I talk to the other side and they seem just as right, and there I am where I started. I know somewhere there is a book that would give me the truth, but hell, I couldn't read the book. I know somewhere there is an economist who knows the truth, but I don't know where to find him and haven't the sense to know him and trust him when I did find him. God, what a job!" (Quoted by Richard Fenno, *The President's Cabinet* [Cambridge, Mass: Harvard University Press, 1959], pp. 40–41).

10. R.C. Snyder, H.W. Bruck, and B. Sapin, *Foreign Policy Decisionmaking* (New York: Free Press, 1962), p. 167.

11. Fenno, *President's Cabinet*, pp. 40–41.

12. The discussion of "defensive procrastination" here and the discussion of "hypervigilance," "defensive avoidance," and "bolstering" draw in part on the work of Irving L. Janis. *See* particularly Janis and Mann, *Decision Making*.

13. The importance of deadlines and the functions they serve has been stressed in the work of a number of specialists on organizational decisionmaking. For a summary of research findings, *see* Lennart A. Arvedson, *Deadlines and Organizational Behavior* (Ph.D. diss., Stanford University, July 1974).

14. As Janis notes (in a personal communication), defensive avoidance is probably rare when different persons at different levels of an organization work independently on a policy problem, insofar as this increases the likelihood that flimsy rationalizations entertained by any one person or group will be challenged by others. The absence of such conditions, on the other hand, is likely to increase the incidence of defensive avoidance. For a fuller discussion, *see* Janis and Mann, *Decision Making*.

15. Janis and Mann also discuss a third type of defensive avoidance—the familiar practice of "buck-passing" (*Decision Making*, pp. 58, 312–14).

16. Bolstering also occurs when the decisionmaker resorts to consistency-striving devices to avoid value trade-off problems; the present discussion focuses on its use in dealing with uncertainty, as defined here.

17. This is still something of a controversial issue among social psychologists, with some of those associated with cognitive dissonance theory holding that bolstering or dissonance reduction occurs only *after* a decision is made. However, Janis and Mann present evidence that under certain conditions bolstering occurs *before* a decision is made.

18. I am indebted for the last point to Lincoln Bloomfield (personal communication).

19. This seventh type of rationalization is suggested by Jervis, *Perception and Misperception*, p. 135, who gives as an example the argument of the type made by McGeorge Bundy in February 1965 for the bombing of North Vietnam.

20. The following discussion draws upon and elaborates the ideas presented earlier in George, "Adaptation to Stress."

21. This simple (and widely used) distinction between seeking a satisfactory (i.e., sufficient and good enough) as against an optimal outcome was made by Herbert A. Simon, "A Behavorial Model of Rational Choice," *Quarterly Journal of Economics* 69 (February 1955). *See also* James G. March and Herbert A. Simon, *Organizations* (New York: Wiley, 1958), pp. 140–41; and Richard M. Cyert and James G. March, *A Behavioral Theory of the Firm* (Englewood Cliffs, N.J.: Prentice-Hall, 1964).

22. Charles E. Lindblom is perhaps the foremost expositor and exponent of incremental decisionmaking. *See* "The Science of 'Muddling Through,'" which appeared originally in *Public Administration Review* 29 (1959):79–88 and has been widely reprinted. For a fuller development of his views, in which he doubted that incrementalism was an appropriate strategy in foreign policy, *see* C.E. Lindblom and D. Braybrooke, *A Strategy of Decision* (New York: Free Press, 1963), and C.E. Lindblom, *The Policy-making Process* (Englewood Cliffs, N.J.: Prentice-Hall, 1968). For an important reformulation of incrementalism, *see* Steinbruner, *Cybernetic Paradigm*, Chapter 3.

23. This section draws upon A.L. George, "Problem-oriented Forecasting," in Nazli Choucri and Thomas W. Robinson, eds. *Forecasting in International Relations* (San Francisco: W.H. Freeman & Co., 1978), pp. 329–36.

24. *See,* for example, the discussion of uncertainties in Edward Quade and Wayne Boucher, eds., *Systems Analysis and Policy Planning* (New York: American Elsevier Co., 1968), pp. 39–40, 312, 355–57, 371–72, 384–85. *See also* Edward Quade, ed., *Analysis for Military Decisions* (Santa Monica: The Rand Corporation, 1964), pp. 136, 170–72, 228ff. 232. 235.

25. The emphasis of this strategy on creating options and maintaining policy flexibility encounters other criticisms as well, among them that there are often hidden costs to avoiding clear-cut and timely policy commitments. *See,* for example, Thomas L. Hughes, "Relativity in Foreign Policy," *Foreign Affairs,* July 1967.

26. Davis Bobrow, "The Chinese Communist Conflict System," *Orbis* 9 (Winter 1966):931. *See also* Jervis, *Perception and Misperception,* chapter 6.

27. For a useful discussion, *see* Ernest R. May. *"Lessons" of the Past: The Uses and Misuses of History in American Foreign Policy* (New York: Oxford University Press, 1972), p. 161.

28. Cordell Hull, *Memoirs* (New York: Macmillan, 1948), vol. 1, p. 173.

29. Arthur Schlesinger, "The Roosevelt Era: Stimson and Hull." *The Nation* (June 5, 1948). As Schlesinger's essay indicates, historians often employ cognitive psychology to interpret the behavior of historical actors. Available historical materials contain considerable data relevant for such analysis, but they are seldom studied systematically and with a more explicit theoretical framework.

30. Pioneering research of a systematic kind on the stress-inducing effects of international crises on decisionmaking has been done by Charles F. Hermann in *Crises in Foreign Policy: A Simulation Analysis* (Indianapolis: Bobbs-Merrill, 1969) and in a later book which he edited: *International Crises: Insights from Behavioral Research* (New York: Free Press, 1972). Important pioneering work on the effects of stress on policymakers during the events leading to World War I was undertaken by Robert North and his associates at Stanford University; the fullest account is Ole R. Holsti, *Crisis, Escalation, War* (Montreal and London: McGill-Queen's University Press, 1972).

An important synthesis of the effects of crisis-induced stress on foreign-policy decisionmaking, together with suggestions for monitoring and dealing with these effects, was presented by Margaret G. Hermann and Charles F. Hermann, "Maintaining the Quality of Decision-making in Foreign Policy Crises: A Proposal," in A.L. George et al., *Towards A More Soundly Based Foreign Policy: Making Better Use of Information,* vol. 2, Appendices, Commission on the Organization of the Government for the Conduct of Foreign Policy, June 1975 (Washington, D.C.: U.S. Government Printing Office, 1976). A broader summary of research findings of the effects of stress from a variety of sources, including crises, was presented by Ole R.

Holsti and Alexander L. George, "The Effects of Stress on the Performance of Foreign Policy-makers," in Cornelius P. Cotter, ed., *Political Science Annual,* vol. 6, 1975 (Indianapolis: Bobbs-Merrill, 1976), pp. 255–319.

31. Robert F. Kennedy, *Thirteen Days* (New York: W.W. Norton & Co., 1969), p. 22.

32. Theodore C. Sorensen, *Decision-Making in the White House* (New York: Columbia University Press, 1964), p. 76.

Hypotheses on Misperception

Robert Jervis

In determining how he will behave, an actor must try to predict how others will act and how their actions will affect his values. The actor must therefore develop an image of others and of their intentions. This image may, however, turn out to be an accurate one; the actor may, for a number of reasons, misperceive both others' actions and their intentions. In this research note I wish to discuss the types of misperceptions of other states' intentions which states tend to make. The concept of intention is complex, but here we can consider it to comprise the ways in which the state feels it will act in a wide range of future contingencies. These ways of acting usually are not specific and well-developed plans. For many reasons a national or individual actor may not know how he will act under given conditions, but this problem cannot be dealt with here. . . .

THEORIES—NECESSARY AND DANGEROUS

. . . . [Past] writers have touched on a vital problem that has not been given systematic treatment by theorists of international relations. The evidence from both psychology and history overwhelmingly supports the view (which may be labeled Hypothesis I) that decision-makers tend to fit incoming information into their existing theories and images. Indeed, their theories and images play a large part in determining what they notice. In other words, actors tend to perceive what they expect. Furthermore (Hypothesis Ia), a theory will have greater impact on an actor's interpretation of data (a) the greater the ambiguity of the data and (b) the higher the degree of confidence with which the actor holds the theory.[1]

For many purposes we can use the concept of differing levels of perceptual thresholds to deal with the fact that it takes more, and more unambiguous,

Excerpt from "Hypotheses on Misperception" by Robert Jervis, from *World Politics* (April, 1968). Copyright © 1968 by Johns Hopkins University Press. Reprinted by permission of Johns Hopkins University Press. Portions of the text and some footnotes have been omitted.

information for an actor to recognize an unexpected phenomena than an expected one. . . .

However, we should not assume . . . that it is necessarily irrational for actors to adjust incoming information to fit more closely their existing beliefs and images. ("Irrational" here describes acting under pressures that the actor would not admit as legitimate if he were conscious of them.) Abelson and Rosenberg label as "psycho-logic" the pressure to create a "balanced" cognitive structure—i.e., one in which "all relations among 'good elements' [in one's attitude structure] are positive (or null), all relations among 'bad elements' are positive (or null), and all relations between good and bad elements are negative (or null)." They correctly show that the "reasoning [this involves] would mortify a logician."[2] But those who have tried to apply this and similar cognitive theories to international relations have usually overlooked the fact that in many cases there are important logical links between the elements and the processes they describe which cannot be called "psycho-logic." (I am here using the term "logical" not in the narrow sense of drawing only those conclusions that follow necessarily from the premises, but rather in the sense of conforming to generally agreed-upon rules for the treating of evidence.) . . . When we say that a decision-maker "dislikes" another state this usually means that he believes that the other state has policies conflicting with those of his nation. Reasoning and experience indicate to the decision-maker that the "disliked" state is apt to harm his state's interests. Thus in these cases there is no need to invoke "psycho-logic," and it cannot be claimed that the cases demonstrate the substitution of "emotional consistency for rational consistency."[3]

The question of the relations among particular beliefs and cognitions can often be seen as a part of the general topic of the relation of incoming bits of information to the receivers' already-established images. The need to fit data into a wider framework of beliefs, even if doing so does not seem to do justice to individual facts, is not, or at least is not only, a psychological drive that decreases the accuracy of our perceptions of the world, but is "essential to the logic of inquiry."[4] Facts can be interpreted, and indeed identified, only with the aid of hypotheses and theories. Pure empiricism is impossible, and it would be unwise to revise theories in the light of every bit of information that does not easily conform to them.[5] No hypothesis can be expected to account for all the evidence, and if a prevailing view is supported by many theories and by a large pool of findings it should not be quickly altered. Too little rigidity can be as bad as too much.

This is as true in the building of social and physical science as it is in policy-making.[6] While it is terribly difficult to know when a finding throws serious doubt on accepted theories and should be followed up and when instead it was caused by experimental mistakes or minor errors in the theory, it is clear that scientists would make no progress if they followed Thomas Huxley's injunction to "sit down before fact as a mere child, be prepared to give up every preconceived notion, follow humbly wherever nature leads, or you will learn nothing."[7]

Thomas Kuhn has noted, "There is no such thing as research without counter-instances."[8] If a set of basic theories—what Kuhn calls a paradigm—

has been able to account for a mass of data, it should not be lightly trifled with. As Kuhn puts it: "Lifelong resistance, particularly from those whose productive careers have committed them to an older tradition of normal science [i.e., science within the accepted paradigm], is not a violation of scientific standards but an index to the nature of scientific research itself. The source of resistance is the assurance that the older paradigm will ultimately solve all its problems, that nature can be shoved into the box the paradigm provides. Inevitably, at times of revolution, that assurance seems stubborn and pig-headed as indeed it sometimes becomes. But it is also something more. That assurance is what makes normal science or puzzle-solving science possible."[9]

Thus it is important to see that the dilemma of how "open" to be to new information is one that inevitably plagues any attempt at understanding in any field. Instances in which evidence seems to be ignored or twisted to fit the existing theory can often be explained by this dilemma instead of by illogical or nonlogical psychological pressures toward consistency. This is especially true of decision-maker's attempts to estimate the intentions of other states, since they must constantly take account of the danger that the other state is trying to deceive them.

The theoretical framework discussed thus far, together with an examination of many cases, suggests Hypothesis 2: Scholars and decision-makers are apt to err by being too wedded to the established view and too closed to new information, as opposed to being too willing to alter their theories.[10] Another way of making this point is to argue that actors tend to establish their theories and expectations prematurely. In politics, of course, this is often necessary because of the need for action. But experimental evidence indicates that the same tendency also occurs on the unconscious level. Bruner and Postman found that "perhaps the greatest single barrier to the recognition of incongruous stimuli is the tendency for perceptual hypotheses to fixate after receiving a minimum of confirmation. . . . Once there had occurred in these cases a partial confirmation of the hypothesis . . . it seemed that nothing could change the subject's report."[11]

However, when we apply these and other findings to politics and discuss kinds of misperception, we should not quickly apply the label of cognitive distortion. We should proceed cautiously for two related reasons. The first is that the evidence available to decision-makers almost always permits several interpretations. It should be noted that there are cases of visual perception in which different stimuli can produce exactly the same pattern on an observer's retina. Thus, for an observer using one eye the same pattern would be produced by a sphere the size of a golf ball which was quite close to the observer, by a baseball-sized sphere that was further away, or by a basketball-sized sphere still further away. Without other clues, the observer cannot possibly determine which of these stimuli he is presented with, and we would not want to call his incorrect perceptions examples of distortion. Such cases, relatively rare in visual perception, are frequent in international relations. The evidence available to decision-makers is almost always very ambiguous since accurate clues to others' intentions are surrounded by noise[12] and deception. In most cases, no matter how long, deeply, and "objectively" the evidence is analyzed, people can differ in their interpretations, and there are no general rules to indicate who is correct.

The second reason to avoid the label of cognitive distortion is that the distinction between perception and judgment, obscure enough in individual psychology, is almost absent in the making of inferences in international politics. Decision-makers who reject information that contradicts their views—or who develop complex interpretations of it—often do so consciously and explicitly. Since the evidence available contains contradictory information, to make any inferences requires that much information be ignored or given interpretations that will seem tortuous to those who hold a different position.

Indeed, if we consider only the evidence available to a decision-maker at the time of decision, the view later proved incorrect may be supported by as much evidence as the correct one—or even by more. Scholars have often been too unsympathetic with the people who were proved wrong. On closer examination, it is frequently difficult to point to differences between those who were right and those who were wrong with respect to their openness to new information and willingness to modify their views. Winston Churchill, for example, did not openmindedly view each Nazi action to see if the explanations provided by the appeasers accounted for the data better than his own beliefs. Instead, like Chamberlain, he fitted each bit of ambiguous information into his own hypotheses. That he was correct should not lead us to overlook the fact that his methods of analysis and use of theory to produce cognitive consistency did not basically differ from those of the appeasers.[13]

A consideration of the importance of expectations in influencing perception also indicates that the widespread belief in the prevalence of "wishful thinking" may be incorrect, or at least may be based on inadequate data. The psychological literature on the interaction between affect and perception is immense and cannot be treated here, but it should be noted that phenomena that at first were considered strong evidence for the impact of affect on perception often can be better treated as demonstrating the influence of expectations.[14] Thus, in international relations, cases like the United States' misestimation of the political climate in Cuba in April 1961, which may seem at first glance to have been instances of wishful thinking, may instead be more adequately explained by the theories held by the decision-makers (e.g., Communist governments are unpopular). Of course, desires may have an impact on perception by influencing expectations, but since so many other factors affect expectations, the net influence of desires may not be great.

There is evidence from both psychology[15] and international relations that when expectations and desires clash, expectations seem to be more important. . . . Actors are apt to be especially sensitive to evidence of grave danger if they think they can take action to protect themselves against the menace once it has been detected.

II. SAFEGUARDS

Can anything then be said to scholars and decision-makers other than "Avoid being either too open or too closed, but be especially aware of the latter danger"? Although decision-makers will always be faced with ambiguous and confusing evidence and will be forced to make inferences about others which will often be inaccurate, a number of safeguards may be suggested which could enable them to minimize their errors. First, and most obvious, decision-makers should be aware that they do not make "unbiased" interpretations of each new bit of incoming information, but rather are inevitably heavily influenced by the theories they expect to be verified. They should know that what may appear to them as a self-evident and unambiguous inference often seems so only because of their preexisting beliefs. To someone with a different theory the same data may appear to be unimportant or to support another explanation. Thus many events provide less independent support for the decision-makers' images than they may at first realize. Knowledge of this should lead decision-makers to examine more closely evidence that others believe contradicts their views.

Second, decision-makers should see if their attitudes contain consistent or supporting beliefs that are not logically linked. These may be examples of true psycho-logic. While it is not logically surprising nor is it evidence of psychological pressures to find that people who believe that Russia is aggressive are very suspicious of any Soviet move, other kinds of consistency are more suspect. . . . [I]n Finland in the winter of 1939, those who felt that grave consequences would follow Finnish agreement to give Russia a military base also believed that the Soviets would withdraw their demand if Finland stood firm. And those who felt that concessions would not lead to loss of major values also believed that Russia would fight if need be.[16] In this country, those who favored a nuclear test ban tended to argue that fallout was very harmful, that only limited improvements in technology would flow from further testing, and that a test ban would increase the chances for peace and security. Those who opposed the test ban were apt to disagree on all three points. This does not mean, of course, that the people holding such sets of supporting views were necessarily wrong in any one element. The Finns who wanted to make concessions to the USSR were probably correct in both parts of their argument. But decision-makers should be suspicious if they hold a position in which elements that are not logically connected support the same conclusion. This condition is psychologically comfortable and makes decisions easier to reach (since competing values do not have to be balanced off against each other). The chances are thus considerable that at least part of the reason why a person holds some of these views is related to psychology and not to the substance of the evidence.

Decision-makers should also be aware that actors who suddenly find themselves having an important shared interest with other actors have a tendency to overestimate the degree of common interest involved. This tendency is especially strong for those actors (e.g., the United States, at least before 1950) whose beliefs about international relations and morality imply that they can cooperate only with "good" states and that with those states there will be no major conflicts. On the other hand, states that have either a tradition of limited cooperation with others (e.g., Britain) or a strongly held theory that differentiates occasional from permanent allies[17] (e.g., the Soviet Union) find it easier to resist this tendency and need not devote special efforts to combating its danger.

A third safeguard for decision-makers would be to make their assumptions, beliefs, and the predictions that follow from them as explicit as possible. An actor should try to determine, before events occur, what evidence would count for and against his theories. By knowing what to expect he would know what to be surprised by, and surprise could indicate to that actor that his beliefs needed reevaluation.[18]

A fourth safeguard is more complex. The decision-maker should try to prevent individuals and organizations from letting their main task, political future, and identity become tied to specific theories and images of other actors.[19] If this occurs, subgoals originally sought for their contribution to higher ends will take on value of their own, and information indicating possible alternative routes to the original goals will not be carefully considered. For example, the U.S. Forest Service was unable to carry out its original purpose as effectively when it began to see its distinctive competence not in promoting the best use of lands and forests but rather in preventing all types of forest fires.[20] . . .

Fifth, decision-makers should realize the validity and implications of Roberta Wohlstetter's argument that "a willingness to play with material from different angles and in the context of unpopular as well as popular hypotheses is an essential ingredient of a good detective, whether the end is the solution of a crime or an intelligence estimate."[21] However, it is often difficult, psychologically and politically, for any one person to do this. Since a decision-maker usually cannot get "unbiased" treatments of data, he should instead seek to structure conflicting biases into the decision-making process. The decision-maker, in other words, should have devil's advocates around. Just as, as Neustadt points out,[22] the decision-maker will want to create conflicts among his subordinates in order to make appropriate choices, so he will also want to ensure that incoming information is examined from many different perspectives with many different hypotheses in mind. To some extent this kind of examination will be done automatically through the divergence of goals, training, experience, and information that exists in any large organization. But in many cases this divergence will not be sufficient. The views of those analyzing the data will still be too homogeneous, and the decision-maker will have to go out of his way not only to cultivate but to create differing viewpoints. . . .

Of course all these safeguards involve costs. They would divert resources from other tasks and would increase internal dissension. Determining whether these costs would be worth the gains would depend on a detailed analysis of how the suggested safeguards might be implemented. Even if they were adopted by a government, of course, they would not eliminate the chance of misperception. However, the safeguards would make it more likely that national decision-makers would make conscious choices about the way data were interpreted rather than merely assuming that they can be seen in only one way and can mean only one thing. Statesmen would thus be reminded of alternative images of others just as they are constantly reminded of alternative policies.

These safeguards are partly based on Hypothesis 3: Actors can more easily assimilate into their established image of another actor information contradicting that image if the information is transmitted and considered bit by bit than if it comes all at once. In the former case, each piece of discrepant data can be coped with as it arrives and each of the conflicts with the prevailing view will be small enough to go unnoticed, to be dismissed as unimportant, or to necessitate at most a slight modification of the image (e.g., addition of exceptions to the rule). When the information arrives in a block, the contradiction between it and the prevailing view is apt to be much clearer and the probability of major cognitive reorganization will be higher.

III. SOURCES OF CONCEPTS

An actor's perceptual thresholds—and thus the images that ambiguous information is apt to produce—are influenced by what he has experienced and learned about.[23] If one actor is to perceive that another fits in a given category he must first have, or develop, a concept for that category. We can usefully distinguish three levels at which a concept can be present or absent. First, the concept can be completely missing. The actor's cognitive structure may not include anything corresponding to the phenomenon he is encountering. This situation can occur not only in science fiction, but also in a world of rapid change or in the meeting of two dissimilar systems. Thus China's image of the Western world was extremely inaccurate in the mid-nineteenth century, her learning was very slow, and her responses were woefully inadequate. The West was spared a similar struggle only because it had the power to reshape the system it encountered. Once the actor clearly sees one instance of the new phenomenon, he is apt to recognize it much more quickly in the future.[24] Second, the actor can know about a concept but not believe that it reflects an actual phenomenon. Thus Communist and Western decision-makers are each aware of the other's explanation of how his system functions, but do not think that the concept corresponds to reality. Communist elites, furthermore, deny that anything *could* correspond to the democracies' description of themselves. Third, the actor may hold a concept, but not believe that another actor fills it at the present moment. Thus the British and French statesmen of the 1930's held a concept of states with unlimited ambitions. They realized that Napoleons were possible, but they did not think Hitler belonged in that category. Hypothesis 4 distinguishes these three cases: Misperception is most difficult to correct in the case of a missing concept and least difficult to correct in the case of a recognized but presumably unfilled concept. All other things being equal (e.g., the degree to which the concept is central to the actor's cognitive structure), the first case requires more cognitive reorganization than does the second, and the second requires more reorganization than the third.

However, this hypothesis does not mean that learning will necessarily be slowest in the first case, for if the phenomena are totally new the actor may make such grossly inappropriate responses that he will quickly acquire information clearly indicating that he is faced with something he does not understand. And the sooner the actor realizes that things are not—or may not be—what they seem, the sooner he is apt to correct his image.[25]

Three main sources contribute to decision-makers' concepts of international relations and of other states and influence the level of their perceptual thresholds for various phenomena. First, an actor's beliefs about his own domestic political system are apt to be important. In some cases, like that of the USSR, the decision-makers' concepts are tied to an ideology that explicitly provides a frame of reference for viewing foreign affairs. Even where this is not the case, experience with his own system will partly determine what the actor is familiar with and what he is apt to perceive in others. Louis Hartz claims, "It is the absence of the experience of social revolution which is at the heart of the whole American dilemma. . . . In a whole series of specific ways it enters into our difficulty of communication with the rest of the world. We find it difficult to understand Europe's 'social question'. . . . We are not familiar with the deeper social struggles of Asia and hence tend to interpret even reactionary regimes as 'democratic.' "[26] Similarly, George Kennan argues that in World War I the Allied powers, and especially America, could not understand the bitterness and violence of others' internal conflicts: ". . . The inability of the Allied statesmen to picture to themselves the passions of the Russian civil war [was partly caused by the fact that] we represent . . . a society in which the manifestations of evil have been carefully buried and sublimarted in the social behavior of people, as in their very consciousness. For this reason, probably, despite our widely traveled and outwardly cosmopolitan lives, the mainsprings of political behavior in such a country as Russia tend to remain concealed from our vision."[27]

Second, concepts will be supplied by the actor's previous experience. An experiment from another field illustrates this. Dearborn and Simon presented business executives from various divisions (e.g., sales, accounting, production) with the same hypothetical data and asked them for an analysis and recommendations from the standpoint of what would be best for the company as a whole. The executives' views heavily reflected their departmental perspectives.[28] William W. Kaufmann shows how the perceptions of Ambassador Joseph Kennedy were affected by his past: "As befitted a former chairman of the Securities Exchange and Maritime Commissions, his primary interest lay in economic matters. . . . The revolutionary character of the Nazi regime was not a phenomenon that he could easily grasp. . . . It was far simpler, and more in accord with his own premises, to explain German aggressiveness in economic terms. The Third Reich was dissatisfied, authoritarian, and expansive largely because her economy was unsound."[29] . . . Since members of the diplomatic corps are responsible for meeting threats to the nation's security before these grow to major proportions and since they have learned about cases in which aggressive states were not recognized as such until very late, they may be prone to interpret ambiguous data as showing that others are aggressive. It should be stressed that we cannot say that the professionals of the 1930's were more apt to make accurate judgments of other states. Rather, they may have been more sensitive to the chance that others were aggressive. They would then rarely take an aggressor for a status-quo power, but would more often make the opposite error.[30] Thus in the years before World War I the permanent officials in the British Foreign Office overestimated German aggressiveness.[31] . . .

A third source of concepts, which frequently will be the most directly relevant to a decision-maker's perception of international relations, is international history. As Henry Kissinger points out, one reason why statesmen were so slow to recognize the threat posed by Napoleon was that previous events had accustomed them only to actors who wanted to modify the existing system, not overthrow it.[32] The other side of the coin is even more striking: Historical traumas can heavily influence future perceptions. They can either establish a state's image of the other state involved or can be used as analogies. An example of the former case is provided by the fact that for at least ten years after the Franco-Prussian War most of Europe's statesmen felt that Bismarck had aggressive plans when in fact his main goal was to protect the status quo. Of course the evidence was ambiguous. The post-1871 Bismarckian maneuvers, which were designed to keep peace, looked not unlike the pre-1871 maneuvers designed to set the stage for war. But that the post-1871 maneuvers were seen as indicating aggressive plans is largely attributable to the impact of Bismarck's earlier actions on the statesmen's image of him.

A state's previous unfortunate experience with a type of danger can sensitize it to other examples of that danger. While this sensitivity may lead the state to avoid the mistake it committed in the past, it may also lead it mistakenly to believe that the present situation is like the past one. Santayana's maxim could be turned around: "Those who remember the past are condemned to make the opposite mistakes." As Paul Kecskemeti shows, both defenders and critics of the unconditional surrender plan of the Second World War thought in terms of the conditions of World War I.[33] Annette Baker Fox found that the Scandinavian countries' neutrality policies in World War II were strongly influenced by their experiences in the previous war, even though vital aspects of the two situations were different. Thus "Norway's success [during the First World War] in remaining non-belligerent though pro-Allied gave the Norwegians confidence that their country could again stay out of war."[34] And the lesson drawn from the unfortunate results of this policy was an important factor in Norway's decision to join NATO.

The application of the Munich analogy to various contemporary events has been much commented on, and I do not wish to argue the substantive points at stake. But it seems clear that the probabilities that any state is facing an aggressor who has to be met by force are not altered by the career of Hitler and the history of the 1930's. Similarly the probability of an aggressor's announcing his plans is not increased (if anything, it is decreased) by the fact that Hitler wrote *Mein Kampf.* Yet decision-makers are more sensitive to these possibilities, and thus more apt to perceive ambiguous evidence as indicating they apply to a given case, than they would have been had there been no Nazi Germany.

Historical analogies often precede, rather than follow, a careful analysis of a situation (e.g., Truman's initial reaction to the news of the invasion of South Korea was to think of the Japanese invasion of Manchuria). Noting this precedence, however, does not show us which of many analogies will come to a decision-maker's mind. Truman could have thought of nineteenth-century European wars that were of no interest to the United States. Several factors having nothing to do with the event under consideration influence what analogies a decision-maker is apt to make. One factor is the number of cases similar to the analogy with which the decision-maker is familiar. Another is the importance of the past event to the political system of which the decision-maker is a part. The more times such an event occurred and the greater its consequences were, the more a decision-maker will be sensitive to the particular danger involved and the more he will be apt to see ambiguous stimuli as indicating another instance of this kind of event. A third factor is the degree of the decision-maker's personal involvement in the past case—in time, energy, ego, and position. The last-mentioned variable will affect not only the event's impact on the decision-maker's cognitive structure, but also the way he perceives the event and the lesson he draws. Someone who was involved in getting troops into South Korea after the attack will remember the Korean War differently from someone who was involved in considering the possible use of nuclear weapons or in deciding what messages should be sent to the Chinese. Greater personal involvement will usually give the event greater impact, especially if the decision-maker's own views were validated by the event. One need not accept a total application of learning theory to nations to believe that "nothing fails like success."[35] It also seems likely that if many critics argued at the time that the decision-maker was wrong, he will be even more apt to see other situations in terms of the original event. For example, because Anthony Eden left the government on account of his views and was later shown to have been correct, he probably was more apt to see as Hitlers other leaders with whom he had conflicts (e.g., Nasser). A fourth factor is the degree to which the analogy is compatible with the rest of his belief system. A fifth is the absence of alternative concepts and analogies. Individuals and states vary in the amount of direct or indirect political experience they have had which can provide different ways of interpreting data. Decision-makers who are aware of multiple possibilities of states' intentions may be less likely to seize on an analogy prematurely. The perception of citizens of nations like the United States which have relatively little history of international politics may be more apt to be heavily influenced by the few major international events that have been important to their country.

The first three factors indicate that an event is more apt to shape present perceptions if it occurred in the recent rather than the remote past. If it occurred recently, the statesman will then know about it at first hand even if he was not involved in the making of policy at the time. Thus if generals are prepared to fight the last war, diplomats may be prepared to avoid the last war. Part of the Anglo-French reaction to Hitler can be explained by the prevailing beliefs that the First World War was to a large extent caused by misunderstandings and could have been avoided by farsighted and nonbelligerent diplomacy. And part of the Western perception of Russia and China can be explained by the view that appeasement was an inappropriate response to Hitler.[36]

IV. THE EVOKED SET

The way people perceive data is influenced not only by their cognitive structure and theories about other actors but also by what they are concerned with at the time they receive the information. Information is evaluated in light of the small part of the person's memory that is presently active—the "evoked set." My perceptions of the dark streets I pass walking home from the movies will be different if the film I saw had dealt with spies than if it had been a comedy. If I am working on aiding a country's education system and I hear someone talk about the need for economic development in that state, I am apt to think he is concerned with education, whereas if I had been working on, say, trying to achieve political stability in that country, I would have placed his remarks in that framework.[37]

Thus Hypothesis 5 states that when messages are sent from a different background of concerns and information than is possessed by the receiver, misunderstanding is likely. Person A and person B will read the same message quite differently if A has seen several related messages that B does not know about. This difference will be compounded if, as is frequently the case, A and B each assume that the other has the same background he does. This means that misperception can occur even when deception is neither intended nor expected. Thus Roberta Wohlstetter found not only that different parts of the United States government had different perceptions of data about Japan's intentions and messages partly because they saw the incoming information in very different contexts, but also that officers in the field misunderstood warnings from Washington: "Washington advised General Short [in Pearl Harbor] on November 27 to expect 'hostile action' and any moment, by which it meant 'attack on American possessions from without,' but General Short understood this phrase to mean 'sabotage.' "[38] Washington did not realize the extent to which Pearl Harbor considered the danger of sabotage to be primary, and furthermore it incorrectly believed that General Short had received the intercepts of the secret Japanese diplomatic messages available in Washington which indicated that surprise attack was a distinct possibility. Another implication of this hypothesis is that if important information is known to only part of the government of State A and part of the government of state B, international messages may be misunderstood by those parts of the receiver's government that do not match, in the information they have, the part of the sender's government that dispatched the message.[39]

Two additional hypotheses can be drawn from the problems of those sending messages. Hypothesis 6 states that when people spend a great deal of time drawing up a plan or making a decision, they tend to think that the message about it they wish to convey will be clear to the receiver.[40] Since they are aware of what is to them the important pattern in their actions, they often feel that the pattern will be equally obvious to others, and they overlook the degree to which the message is apparent to them only because they know what to look for. Those who have not participated in the endless meetings may not understand what information the sender is trying to convey. George Quester has shown how the German and, to a lesser extent, the British desire to maintain target limits on bombing in the first eighteen months of World War II was undermined partly by the fact that each side knew the limits it was seeking and its own reasons for any apparent "exceptions" (e.g., the German attack on Rotterdam) and incorrectly felt that these limits and reasons were equally clear to the other side.[41]

Hypothesis 7 holds that actors often do not realize that actions intended to project a given image may not have the desired effect because the actions themselves do not turn out as planned. Thus even without appreciable impact of different cognitive structures and backgrounds, an action may convey an unwanted message. For example, a country's representatives may not follow instructions and so may give others impressions contrary to those the home government wished to convey. The efforts of Washington and Berlin to settle their dispute over Samoa in the late 1880's were complicated by the provocative behavior of their agents on the spot. These agents not only increased the intensity of the local conflict, but led the decision-makers to become more suspicious of the other state because they tended to assume that their agents were obeying instructions and that the actions of the other side represented official policy. In such cases both sides will believe that the other is reading hostility into a policy of theirs which is friendly. Similarly, Quester's study shows that the attempt to limit bombing referred to above failed partly because neither side was able to bomb as accurately as it thought it could and thus did not realize the physical effects of its actions.[42]

V. FURTHER HYPOTHESES FROM THE PERSPECTIVE OF THE PERCEIVER

From the perspective of the perceiver several other hypotheses seem to hold. Hypothesis 8 is that there is an overall tendency for decision-makers to see other states as more hostile than they are.[43] There seem to be more cases of statesmen incorrectly believing others are planning major acts against their interest than of statesmen being lulled by a potential aggressor. There are many reasons for this which are too complex to be treated here (e.g., some parts of the bureaucracy feel it is their responsibility to be suspicious of all other states; decision-makers often feel they are "playing it safe" to believe and act as though the other state were hostile in questionable cases; and often, when people do not feel they are a threat to others, they find it difficult to believe that others may see them as a threat). It should be noted, however, that decision-makers whose perceptions are described by this hypothesis would not necessarily further their own values by trying to correct for this tendency. The values of possible outcomes as well as their probabilities must be considered, and it may be that the probability of an unnecessary arms-tension cycle arising out of misperceptions, multiplied by the costs of such a cycle, may seem less to decision-makers than the probability of incorrectly believing another state is friendly, multiplied by the costs of this eventuality.

Hypothesis 9 states that actors tend to see the behavior of others as more centralized, disciplined, and coordinated than it is. This hypothesis holds true in related ways. Frequently, too many complex events are squeezed into a perceived pattern. Actors are hesitant to admit or even see that particular incidents cannot be explained by their theories.[44] Those events not caused by factors that are important parts of the perceiver's image are often seen as though they were. Further, actors see others as more internally united than they in fact are and generally overestimate the degree to which others are following a coherent policy. The degree to which the other side's policies are the product of internal bargaining,[45] internal misunderstandings, or subordinates' not following instructions is underestimated. This is the case partly because actors tend to be unfamiliar with the details of another state's policy-making processes. Seeing only the finished product, they find it simpler to try to construct a rational explanation for the policies, even though they know that such an analysis could not explain their own policies.

Familiarity also accounts for Hypothesis 10: because a state gets most of its information about the other state's policies from the other's foreign office, it tends to take the foreign office's position for the stand of the other government as a whole. In many cases this perception will be an accurate one, but when the other government is divided or when the other foreign office is acting without specific authorization, misperception may result. . . . America's NATO allies may have gained an inaccurate picture of the degree to which the American government was committed to the MLF because they had greatest contact with parts of the government that strongly favored the MLF. And states that tried to get information about Nazi foreign policy from German diplomats were often misled because these officials were generally ignorant of or out of sympathy with Hitler's plans. The Germans and the Japanese sometimes purposely misinformed their own ambassadors in order to deceive their enemies more effectively.

Hypothesis 11 states that actors tend to overestimate the degree to which others are acting in response to what they themselves do when the others behave in accordance with the actor's desires; but when the behavior of the other is undesired, it is usually seen as derived from internal forces. If the *effect* of another's action is to injure or threaten the first side, the first side is apt to believe that such was the other's *purpose.* An example of the first part of the hypothesis is provided by Kennan's account of the activities of official and unofficial American representatives who protested to the new Bolshevik government agains several of its actions. When the Soviets changed their position, these representatives felt it was largely because of their influence.[46] This sort of interpretation can be explained not only by the fact that it is gratifying to the individual making it, but also, taking the other side of the coin mentioned in Hypothesis 9, by the fact that the actor is most familiar with his own input into the other's decision and has less knowledge of other influences. The second part of Hypothesis II is illustrated by the tendency of actors to believe that the hostile behavior of others is to be explained by the other side's motives and not by its reaction to the first side. Thus Chamberlain did not see that Hitler's behavior was related in part to his belief that the British were weak. More common is the failure to see that the other side is reacting out of fear of the first side, which can lead to self-fulfilling prophecies and spirals of misperception and hostility.

This difficulty is often compounded by an implication of Hypothesis 12: When actors have intentions that they do not try to conceal from others, they tend to assume that others accurately perceive these intentions. Only rarely do they believe that others may be reacting to a much less favorable image of themselves than they think they are projecting.[47]

For state A to understand how state B perceives A's policy is often difficult because such understanding may involve a conflict with A's image of itself. Raymond Sontag argues that Anglo-German relations before World War I deteriorated partly because "the British did not like to think of themselves as selfish, or unwilling to tolerate 'legitimate' German expansion. The Germans did not like to think of themselves as aggressive, or unwilling to recognize 'legitimate' British vested interest."[48]

Hypothesis 13 suggests that if it is hard for an actor to believe that the other can see him as a menace, it is often even harder for him to see that issues important to him are not important to others. While he may know that another actor is on an opposing team, it may be more difficult for him to realize that the other is playing an entirely different game. This is especially true when the game he is playing seems vital to him.[49]

The final hypothesis, Hypothesis 14, follows: Actors tend to overlook the fact that evidence consistent with their theories may also be consistent with other views. When choosing between two theories we have to pay attention only to data that cannot be accounted for by one of the theories. But it is common to find people claiming as proof of their theories data that could also support alternative views. This phenomenon is related to the point made earlier that any single bit of information can be interpreted only within a framework of hypotheses and theories. And while it is true that "we may without a vicious circularity accept some datum as a fact because it conforms to the very law for which it counts as another confirming instance, and reject an allegation of fact because it is already excluded by law,"[50] we should be careful lest we forget that a piece of information seems in many cases to confirm a certain hypothesis only because we already believe that hypothesis to be correct and that the information can with as much validity support a different hypothesis. For example, one of the reasons why the German attack on Norway took both that country and England by surprise, even though they had detected German ships moving toward Norway, was that they expected not an attack but an attempt by the Germans to break through the British blockade and reach the Atlantic. The initial course of the ships was consistent with either plan, but the British and Norwegians took this course to mean that their predictions were being borne out.[51] This is not to imply that the interpretation made was foolish, but only that the decision-makers should have been aware that the evidence was also consistent with an invasion and should have had a bit less confidence in their views.

The longer the ships would have to travel the same route whether they were going to one or another of two destinations, the more information would be needed to determine their plans. Taken as a metaphor, this incident applies generally to the treatment of evidence. Thus as long as Hitler made demands for control only of ethnically German areas, his actions could be explained either by the hypothesis that he had unlimited ambitions or by the hypothesis that he wanted to unite all the Germans. But actions against non-Germans (e.g., the takeover of Czechoslovakia in March 1939) could not be accounted for by the latter hypothesis. And it was this action that convinced the appeasers that Hitler had to be stopped. It is interesting to speculate on what the British reaction would have been had Hitler left Czechoslovakia alone for a while and instead made demands on Poland similar to those he eventually made in the summer of 1939. The two paths would then still not have diverged, and further misperception could have occurred.

NOTES

1. Floyd Allport, *Theories of Perception and the Concept of Structure* (New York 1955), 382; Ole Holsti, "Cognitive Dynamics and Images of the Enemy," in David Finlay, Ole Holsti, and Richard Fagen, *Enemies in Politics* (Chicago 1967), 70.
2. Robert Abelson and Milton Rosenberg, "Symbolic Psycho-logic," *Behavioral Science,* III (January 1958), 4–5.
3. *Ibid.*, 26.
4. I have borrowed this phrase from Abraham Kaplan, who uses it in a different but related context in *The Conduct of Inquiry* (San Francisco 1964), 86.
5. The spiral theorists are not the only ones to ignore the limits of empiricism. Roger Hilsman found that most consumers and producers of intelligence felt that intelligence should not deal with hypotheses, but should only provide the policy-makers with "all the facts" (*Strategic Intelligence and National Decisions* [Glencoe 1956], 46). The close interdependence between hypotheses and facts is overlooked partly because of the tendency to identify "hypotheses" with "policy preferences."
6. Raymond Bauer, "Problems of Perception and the Relations Between the U.S. and the Soviet Union," *Journal of Conflict Resolution,* v (September 1961), 223–29.
7. Quoted in W.I.B. Beveridge, *The Art of Scientific Investigation,* 3rd ed. (London 1957), 50.
8. *The Structure of Scientific Revolution* (Chicago 1964), 79.
9. *Ibid.*, 150–51.
10. Requirements of effective political leadership may lead decision-makers to voice fewer doubts than they have about existing policies and images, but this constraint can only partially explain this phenomenon. Similar calculations of political strategy may contribute to several of the hypotheses discussed below.
11. P. 221.
12. For a use of this concept in political communication, see Roberta Wohlstetter, *Pearl Harbor* (Stanford 1962).
13. Similarly, Robert Coulondre, the French ambassador to Berlin in 1939, was one of the few diplomats to appreciate the Nazi threat. Partly because of his earlier service in the USSR, "he was painfully sensitive to the threat of a Berlin-Moscow agreement. He noted with foreboding that Hitler had not attacked Russia in his *Reichstag* address of April 28. . . . So it went all spring and summer, the ambassador relaying each new evidence of the impending diplomatic revolution and adding to his admonitions his pleas for decisive counteraction" (Franklin Ford and Carl Schorske, "The Voice in the Wilderness: Robert Coulondre," in Gordon Craig and Felix Gilbert, eds., *The Diplomats,* Vol. II [New York 1963] 573–74). His hypotheses were correct, but it is difficult to detect differences between the way he and those ambassadors who were incorrect, like Neville Henderson, selectively noted and interpreted information. However, to the extent that the fear of war influenced the appeasers'

perceptions of Hitler's intentions, the appeasers' views did have an element of psycho-logic that was not present in their opponents' position.

14. See, for example, Donald Campbell, "Systematic Error on the Part of Human Links in Communications Systems," *Information and Control*, I (1958), 346–50; and Leo Postman, "The Experimental Analysis of Motivational Factors in Perception," in Judson S. Brown, ed., *Current Theory and Research in Motivation* (Lincoln, Neb., 1953), 59–108.

15. Dale Wyatt and Donald Campbell, "A Study of Interviewer Bias as Related to Interviewer's Expectations and Own Opinions," *International Journal of Opinion and Attitude Research*, IV (Spring 1950), 77–83.

16. Max Jakobson, *The Diplomacy of the Winter War* (Cambridge, Mass., 1961), 136–39.

17. Raymond Aron, *Peace and War* (Garden City 1966), 29.

18. Cf. Thomas Kuhn, *The Structure of Scientific Revolutions* (Chicago 1964), 65. A fairly high degree of knowledge is needed before one can state precise expectations. One indication of the lack of international relations theory is that most of us are not sure what "naturally" flows from our theories and what constitutes either "puzzles" to be further explored with the paradigm or "anomalies" that cast doubt on the basic theories.

19. See Philip Selznick, *Leadership in Administration* (Evanston 1957).

20. Ashley Schiff, *Fire and Water: Scientific Heresy in the Forest Service* (Cambridge, Mass., 1962). Despite its title, this book is a fascinating and valuable study.

21. P. 302. See Beveridge, 93, for a discussion of the idea that the scientist should keep in mind as many hypotheses as possible when conducting and analyzing experiments.

22. *Presidential Power* (New York 1960).

23. Most psychologists argue that this influence also holds for perception of shapes. For data showing that people in different societies differ in respect to their predisposition to experience certain optical illusions and for a convincing argument that this difference can be explained by the societies' different physical environments, which have led their people to develop different patterns of drawing inferences from ambiguous visual cues, see Marshall Segall, Donald Campbell, and Melville Herskovits, *The Influence of Culture on Visual Perceptions* (Indianapolis 1966).

24. Thus when Bruner and Postman's subjects first were presented with incongruous playing cards (i.e., cards in which symbols and colors of the suits were not matching, producing red spades or black diamonds), long exposure times were necessary for correct identification. But once a subject correctly perceived the card and added this type of card to his repertoire of categories, he was able to identify other incongruous cards much more quickly. For an analogous example—in this case, changes in the analysis of aerial reconnaissance photographs of an enemy's secret weapons-testing facilities produced by the belief that a previously unknown object may be present—see David Irving, *The Mare's Nest* (Boston 1964), 66–67, 274–75.

25. Bruner and Postman, 220.

26. *The Liberal Tradition in America* (New York 1955), 306.

27. *Russia and the West Under Lenin and Stalin* (New York 1962), 142–43.

28. DeWitt Dearborn and Herbert Simon, "Selective Perception: A Note on the Departmental Identification of Executives," *Sociometry*, XXI (June 1958), 140–44.

29. "Two American Ambassadors: Bullitt and Kennedy," in Craig and Gilbert, 358–59.

30. During a debate on appeasement in the House of Commons, Harold Nicolson declared, "I know that those of use who believe in the traditions of our policy, . . . who believe that one great function of this country is to maintain moral standards in Europe, to maintain a settled pattern of international relations, not to make friends

with people who are demonstrably evil . . . —I know that those who hold such beliefs are accused of possessing the Foreign Office mind. I thank God that I possess the Foreign Office mind" (quoted in Martin Gilbert, *The Roots of Appeasement* [New York 1966], 187). But the qualities Nicolson mentions and applauds may be related to a more basic attribute of "the Foreign Office mind"—suspiciousness.

31. George Monger, *The End of Isolation* (London 1963). I am also indebted to Frederick Collingnon for his unpublished manuscript and several conversations on this point.
32. *A World Restored* (New York 1964), 2–3.
33. *Strategic Surrender* (New York 1964), 215–41.
34. *The Power of Small States* (Chicago 1959), 81.
35. William Inge, *Outspoken Essays*, First Series (London 1923), 88.
36. Of course, analogies themselves are not "unmoved movers." The interpretation of past events is not automatic and is informed by general views of international relations and complex judgments. And just as beliefs about the past influence the present, views about the present influence interpretations of history. It is difficult to determine the degree to which the United States' interpretation of the reasons it went to war in 1917 influenced American foreign policy in the 1920's and 1930's and how much the isolationism of that period influenced the histories of the war.
37. For some psychological experiments on this subject, see Jerome Bruner and A. Leigh Minturn, "Perceptual Identification and Perceptual Organization" *Journal of General Psychology*, LIII (July 1955), 22–28; Seymour Feshbach and Robert Singer, "The Effects of Fear Arousal and Suppression of Fear Upon Social Perception," *Journal of Abnormal and Social Psychology*, LV (November 1957), 283–88; and Elsa Sippoal, "A Group Study of Some Effects of Preparatory Sets," *Psychology Monographs*, XLVI, No. 210 (1935), 27–28. For a general discussion of the importance of the perceiver's evoked set, see Postman, 87.
38. Pp. 73–74.
39. For example, Roger Hilsman points out, "Those who knew of the peripheral reconnaissance flights that probed Soviet air defenses during the Eisenhower administration and the U-2 flights over the Soviet Union itself . . . were better able to understand some of the things the Soviets were saying and doing than people who did not know of these activities" (*To Move a Nation* [Garden City 1967], 66). But it is also possible that those who knew about the U-2 flights at times misinterpreted Soviet messages by incorrectly believing that the sender was influenced by, or at least knew of, these flights.
40. I am grateful to Thomas Schelling for discussion on this point.
41. *Deterrence Before Hiroshima* (New York 1966), 105–22.
42. *Ibid.*
43. For a slightly different formulation of this view, see Holsti, 27.
44. The Soviets consciously hold an extreme version of this view and seem to believe that nothing is accidental. See the discussion in Nathan Leites, *A Study of Bolshevism* (Glencoe 1953), 67–73.
45. A. W. Marshall criticizes Western explanations of Soviet military posture for failing to take this into account. See his "Problems of Estimating Military Power," a paper presented at the 1966 Annual Meeting of the American Political Science Association, 16.
46. George Kennan, *Russia Leaves the War* (New York 1967), 404, 408, 500.
47. Herbert Butterfield notes that these assumptions can contribute to the spiral of "Hobbesian fear. . . . You yourself may vividly feel the terrible fear that you have of

the other party, but you cannot enter into the other man's counter-fear, or even understand why he should be particularly nervous. For you know that you yourself mean him no harm, and that you want nothing from him save guarantees for your own safety; and it is never possible for you to realize or remember properly that since he cannot see the inside of your mind, he can never have the same assurance of your intentions that you have" (*History and Human Conflict* [London 1951], 20).

48. *European Diplomatic History 1871–1932* (New York 1933), 125. It takes great mental effort to realize that actions which seem only the natural consequence of defending your vital interests can look to others as though you are refusing them any chance of increasing their influence. In rebutting the famous Crowe "balance of power" memorandum of 1907, which justified a policy of "containing" Germany on the grounds that she was a threat to British national security, Sanderson, a former permanent undersecretary in the Foreign Office, wrote, "It has sometimes seemed to me that to a foreigner reading our press the British Empire must appear in the light of some huge giant sprawling all over the globe, with gouty fingers and toes stretching in every direction, which cannot be approached without eliciting a scream" (quoted in Monger, 315). But few other Englishmen could be convinced that others might see them this way.

49. George Kennan makes clear that in 1918 this kind of difficulty was partly responsible for the inability of either the Allies or the new Bolshevik government to understand the motivations of the other side: "There is . . . nothing in nature more egocentric than the embattled democracy. . . . It . . . tends to attach to its own cause an absolute value which distorts its own vision of everything else. . . . It will readily be seen that people who have got themselves into this frame of mind have little understanding for the issues of any contest other than the one in which they are involved. The idea of people wasting time and substance on any *other* issue seems to them preposterous" (*Russia and the West*, 11–12).

50. Kaplan, 89.

51. Johan Jorgen Holst, "Surprise, Signals, and Reaction: The Attack on Norway," *Cooperation and Conflict*, No. I (1966), 34. The Germans made a similar mistake in November 1942 when they interpreted the presence of an Allied convoy in the Mediterranean as confirming their belief that Malta would be resupplied. They thus were taken by surprise when landings took place in North Africa (William Langer, *Our Vichy Gamble* [New York 1966], 365).

Five

JUSTICE, HUMAN RIGHTS, AND THE GLOBAL ENVIRONMENT

*T*he selections in Part Five deal with two issues that go well beyond a focus on individual states: the role of justice and human rights in international politics and the emerging threat to the global environment. The first has been a long-standing preoccupation of political theorists, foreign policy analysts, and statesmen; the second is a product of a broadening and deepening international concern about the degradation of the global environment that a century of industrialization has brought about. Both sets of issues transcend the concerns of individual states and their jockeying for relative advantage with one another and instead require that states somehow collectively take into account the interests of all individuals, even those not yet born.

In dealing with the issue of distributive justice in international relations, Stanley Hoffmann asks two fundamental questions: (1) What do we mean by international justice?; and (2) having defined that, what are our obligations? He surveys three possible responses to the first question and argues that there is no definitive answer to the second question. It is easier to find a consensus within a state on what constitutes justice than it is in the relations among states. Because there is no consensus on what constitutes justice internationally, the agreement over what are our obligations to individuals in other states is, in his words, "flickering."

Rhoda E. Howard and Jack Donnelly, however, take a more definitive view on the subject of human rights. Such rights, they argue, are clear and universal in their application. Individual human beings have a set of rights by virtue of being humans beings. As a consequence, they reject the position of cultural relativism: that the definition of what human beings are entitled to varies with the culture in which they live. For Howard and Donnelly, the difficulty of injecting human rights into state action, therefore, is not that such rights are disputed, not that states reject the view that such rights are binding on all states, but rather that the implementation of those rights is left to the states themselves. In the absence of an effective international government, there is no choice but to rely on states for enforcement. This, then, raises three difficult issues: (1) What specific set of rights will a nation decide to pursue?; (2) under what conditions do states have a right to intervene in the affairs of other states to enforce universal human rights?; and (3) how can human rights concerns be integrated into the myriad other foreign policy concerns that every state legitimately holds?

Justice and human rights issues deal with the duties and responsibilities that individuals owe one another. So, too, does the protection of the global environment. But in this case there is the added difficulty of how to concert action among states. Protection of the global environment is a classic collective action problem: No single state owns the global environment, but all use it (and abuse it), and none can be prevented from so using and abusing it. A commons (or a public) good is one that no single individual or entity owns, but that all can utilize. For such commons resources, no individual or state has an incentive to minimize its degradating effects unless it is persuaded that all others will act in similar fashion. There is little incentive for India to reduce its carbon-dioxide emissions into the atmosphere unless it is convinced that the United States and the other industrialized nations will do so. The three central tasks for solving international collective action problems are: first, to obtain agreement that there are serious problems; second, to reach consensus on how to solve the problems; and third, to devise institutional agreements for monitoring compliance and for punishing offenders.

The four selections by Wijkman, Mathews, Simon, and Rathjens deal with these issues. Per Magnus Wijkman lays out the problem of dealing with abuses of the global commons, sets forth the nature of the institutional arrangements that must be devised to deal with them, and surveys how states have dealt with selected commons issues. Jessica Tuchman Mathews calls for a new definition of state security. The next decade will require that states focus their intellectual and financial resources less on armaments and more on the environment. Environmental degradation is at war with the traditional assumptions and practices of international relations. Environmental problems know no borders; solutions based on customary views of national sovereignty are no longer appropriate to deal with them. Cross-national environmental challenges will require transnational institutions.

Julian Simon challenges the view that mankind must husband its natural resources because he argues that the supply of natural resources is infinite, or at least not finite in an economic sense. He challenges us to think like an economist: to consider not just the absolute supply of a good, but rather how much of it is available at a given price. In this sense, no resource is finite because substitutes are always available if the price of a good rises too high compared to other goods that can be substituted for it. In short, the market will solve the problem of the availability of resources. And, by extension, the market can deal with the degradation of the environment if the costs of cleaning it up are included in the price of those goods that contribute to its degradation.

Finally, George Rathjens takes a similar tack with regard to the control of carbon-dioxide emissions that appear to be enhancing the greenhouse effect. The increasing use of fossil fuels, so those who hold to global warming argue, has lead to an increase in the average global temperature and will continue to do so unless the nations of the world cut back on the use of fossil fuels. Rathjens, however, is skeptical that international action will be taken to reduce fossil fuel use if the only rationale is to retard global warming. The reason is that some nations will actually benefit from global warming. To surmount this problem, he argues that the most effective solution to global warming lies in national action taken on other grounds. Increasing energy efficiency is such a rationale because it is a productive goal for nations to pursue in its own right. It saves on energy imports, makes nations more competitive in the international market, and frees up resources to be used for other pursuits. But by increasing its energy efficiency, each state, acting in its own self-interest, will contribute to the common good of all: reducing the emissions of carbon dioxide that are contributing to global warming.

The selections in the section on the global environment thus present two different perspectives on how to deal with environmental degradation. Wijkman and Tuchman argue for international institutional solutions because the problems spill across national boundaries. Simon and Rathjens argue for national and market solutions because of their skepticism about governmental solutions and concerted international action. Which approach is taken will greatly affect our futures.

Justice and Human Rights

Duties Beyond Borders
Stanley Hoffmann

INTERNATIONAL INJUSTICE

The issue of justice in international relations is broader than that of distributive justice, which deals with "the proper distribution of the benefits and burdens of social cooperation"[1] and particularly with the proper distribution of economic resources;[2] but the problems of international distributive justice are by far the most troublesome. . . .

There are two versions of what constitutes international injustice. It is a debate about whether the distributive injustice we are worried about concerns states or concerns peoples. The first version could be called classical. It asserts that the problem lies in the inequality of states. The supporters of this view spin out a whole series of contradictions. The first one is the contradiction between the formal and well-known principle of sovereignty, which belongs to all states, and the absence of what one legal philosopher, Julius Stone, in a slightly convoluted way calls "the absence of inequality in the quantum of rights . . . conferred"[3] to states by international law. There is, in other words, a contrast between the fact that all states are supposed to be sovereign, and the fact that the rights which are at the disposal of some states are inferior to those at the disposal of others. This is at the root of the demand which many of the states, and in particular the new ones, have been making for the last twenty or thirty years, for changes in international law—for instance, for the abolition of uneven treaties, or for a change in the law which used to govern expropriations (I am thinking of the 1974 UN Charter on the Economic Rights and Duties of States which grants them "full permanent sovereignty" over all their wealth, natural resources and economic activities). Secondly, there is another contradiction between even the notion of an equal quantum of rights, were it granted, and the material inequality which empties equality of rights of any meaning. It is argued that states require not just equal rights but equal possibilities of development. The famous demands for a new international economic order which have been made by the countries of the Third World for the last years include many

From "Duties Beyond Borders," by Stanley Hoffman (Syracuse University Press, 1981), pp. 141, 144–151, 156–165. By permission of the publisher. Portions of the text and some footnotes have been omitted.

which relate to equal chances of development—for instance, those which concern the international exploitation of ocean seabeds (instead of a laissez faire
system that would favor the technologically advanced nations), or the terms of
trade, or commodity agreements, or the flows of aid, or the reform of the
monetary system, or debt relief, or technology transfers. Finally, in this view
there is also a contradiction between even a formal egalitarian system of rights
and opportunities, were it established, and a highly concentrated system of
power. If all uneven treaties were abolished, if all states had exactly the same
rights, and even if they were somehow provided with equal possibilities of
development, this would still be a world in which power and decisions about
international regimes are heavily concentrated in the hands of a few; this is at
the root of the demand for power-sharing in international institutions, or of the
claim that the poorer states have the right to exercise collectively whatever
power they have to change the rules of the game, since those rules are stacked
against them—for instance by forming cartels such as OPEC.

Where does this view originate? The people who present it are mostly
representatives of the governments of underdeveloped countries, and their
case is accepted, at least rhetorically, by several Western governments (the
Scandinavian ones in particular). What is the significance of this view? In one
sense, as Robert W. Tucker says in his argumentative and incisive book, *The
Inequality of Nations*,[4]—a fine critique that leads nowhere—it looks like a
demand for a radical redistribution of power and wealth in the international
system; but on the other hand it is a rather conservative view of what constitutes international injustice, defined as injustice to the less privileged states,
whereas the well-being of individuals is seen as a concern not for outsiders, but
only for the state to which the citizens belong. International injustice is a matter
of relations between states, like traditional international law. Internal injustice
is a domestic matter for each government. There is an assumption here: If only
there were a more equal distribution of power and wealth among sates, somehow the lot of individuals in the poorer states would improve. This is, of course,
no more than an assumption: "greater equality among states may facilitate the
promotion of domestic equalities; the former may be a ncessary condition, but it
is far from sufficient."[5] But it explains (and the fact that this view is largely
offered by representatives of Third World governments is highly relevant) why
these governments and some of the spokesmen for Third World states are
extremely resistant to the idea that the richer states might make their aid
conditional on performance criteria to be met by the recipient countries, if
those performance criteria should concern the treatment of individuals. As soon
as spokesmen of or writers in the developed countries ask "What are you doing
with all this aid? Are you not perhaps making inequality even worse, or confirming it?", the answer is, "We are sovereign states; it is sovereignty we are talking
about; we want equal rights and power, and for you to look at what we do to our
citizens is a violation of our sovereignty."

Not so paradoxically, Third World statesmen have not endorsed the idea—
adopted by the U.S. Congress—that aid should be directed at basic human
needs (defined by the donor), or the suggestion—made by the International

Labor Organization—of basic social norms to improve the condition of low wage workers in developing countries: many of these countries, eager to industrialize, rely on their comparative advantage in labor costs to reach this goal,[6] and they fear that a "basic human needs" strategy would condemn "them to the status of permanent welfare clients, with no prospect for developing to high consumption levels."[7] So this first view, while it looks like a radical demand for change, really amounts to a reinforcement of the state system, as Tucker points out. This is not without a paradox, since after all the "advanced" states, to use that shorthand, are being summoned to assist, to share, and to divest, by developing states which, for their part, say that they have absolute rights of sovereignty over their natural resources. To use Mr. Kennedy's famous description of what Mr. Khrushchev said to him in Vienna, what is ours is ours, and what is yours should be negotiable. There is also a paradox within the paradox: It is representatives of the underdogs, of the hundreds of millions of poor people, who are the most ardent defenders of what Charles Beitz, in his book, calls the "morality of states," the view that in international affairs states, not persons, are the subjects of moral and legal rights and duties.

There is of course another view, not the classical but the radical one, for which international injustice resides not in uneven distribution of power and wealth among states, but in the fate of individuals. When we begin again by looking at the substance of this view, we find that it divides into two different formulations which should not be confused. Both are radical by comparison with the interstate view, but one is more radical than the other; We could call them the moderately radical version and the extremely radical one. The moderately radical view argues that the scandal, international injustice, lies in the poverty of a great part of mankind, of hundreds of millions of people. This is what Richard Fagen calls "equality as non-poverty."[8] In this view, which is shared by Julius Stone, international distributive justice should be concerned with the achievement of minimal rights by individuals. It should go beyond interstate relations, but insofar as individuals are in question it should just be concerned with these minimal rights. This moderately radical formulation essentially says that international justice means providing what in the previous chapter I called basic human rights in the economic and social realm.

On the other hand, the more extreme radical version asserts that the scandal does not just lie in the fact that hundreds of millions of people—40 percent of mankind—are poor. The scandal lies in the causes of that phenomena, not in the phenomenon itself—in the unequal distribution of wealth, not just among states (because the unequal distribution of wealth among states is an abstract matter of statistics, GNP, trade figures, etc.) but among individuals in most states. It is not enough to be concerned with the problem of poverty in the Third World. It is not enough to humanize poverty or to ennoble it, by trying to provide a minimum level of subsistence, so as to raise, so to speak, the floor of poverty to this point. One should, as Tucker puts it, provide course-of-life needs to all: Go beyond the mere relief of suffering and try to provide an equal start for all, which is a rather ambitious program.

What is the significance of this view—in either version? Clearly it blurs the distinction between states and individuals, and even deems the distinction illegitimate. It states that problems of distributive justice in international affairs are problems of duties to individuals, and it suggests that the problems of state inequality, which the first view stressed, are either irrelevant or subordinate. What really matters is not that my state has less power or fewer actual rights or chances that yours; it is that the people in my state are poorer than they should be, or more unequal than they should be. Where does this view come from? Here we meet certain surprises. First of all, the Marxists, whom one would expect somehow to find here, have one foot in this camp and one foot elsewhere. Of course they stress the problem of extreme inequality among individuals in the Third World; however, the individuals are not really their units of concern. They are concerned with classes; and they see in the state—if it has the right class basis—an instrument of progress and change that needs to be protected from outside intrusion and onslaught. The body which stresses the problem of individual inequality or individual poverty most is composed above all of Western political and economic writers—philosophers, social scientists, social democrats, and some (but far from all) Third World writers.

One last surprise—the view that justice is a matter of duty to individuals is also held by some Western writers who use the radical moral definition as a splendid way of denying in fact any obligation, of escaping any debt or duty. Thus one of the most brilliant and logical political economists of our day, Richard Cooper, argues that the only moral scandal is the scandal of individual inequality, the only moral obligation is to individuals, because "all of the main lines of ethical thought apply to individuals (or families), not to collectives such as nations."[9] The real horror, thus, is the violation of their basic rights as individuals. However, international relations, alas, only deals with states, and in interstate affairs the only considerations are prudential ones, not moral ones (or else "a new set of ethical principles applicable to nations must be developed"). Let us combine these two ideas. The result is complex. On the one hand, there are, on prudential grounds, areas of mutual gain to developed and developing states that should be explored; on the other hand, in interstate dealings, the only resource transfers justified on ethical grounds are those which would ultimately help individuals. What does this really mean? It is a very roundabout way of saying one of three things. It could be a way of saying, "Let us not, on liberal grounds, give Third World states any assistance at all, since many of them are corrupt, all of them object to externally imposed performance criteria, and the money will therefore not go to individuals." Or else it could be a way of saying, as Cooper does, that we should not give them any large or automatic package of assistance, since we cannot control whether it will really help individuals, and since (on prudential grounds) most of the assistance is likely to be given to the better-off developing countries, in exchange for political services, and with no direct relation to poverty. Or else it may be a way of saying: Let us give them only the kind of assistance which is supposed theoretically to reach individuals. We cannot see whether it reaches them or not, because that would violate the states' sovereignty, but there is a theory which assures us that it ordinarily will: It is classical liberalism, it is the "trickle down" theory. But the only "assistance" it justifies is liberal trade. These are, then, three different ways of minimizing the response to the problem, while starting with a very radical formulation. This shows already something we are going to find throughout this chapter: that the diagnosis is often tailored to the desired prescriptions rather than the other way around. And it also shows that the analysis of the nature of international injustice leads into that of our obligations.

OBLIGATIONS

The problem of international injustice could have been described as states vs. people. The question of the nature of our obligation is different. What do we owe whom, and why? There are two debates: one about the scope of our obligation, and one about its foundation. In other words, how wide is it? How deep is it? . . .

One can adopt neither the interstate nor the interindividual framework exclusively. First, international justice is a matter both of rights of states and of rights of individuals. Secondly, there are obligations of justice to other states. The claims of those states are not only claims for power and for status. Insofar as they are claims for wealth, they must be considered for the sake of distributive justice. Thirdly, however, one has to keep in mind that states exist only as communities of people; states are not divinities, their rights are rooted in the presumption of fit between them and their people; and this does put a kind of damper on the demands of the Third World governments for absolute sovereignty, for impermeable state rights. We may feel that we have a duty to share some of our wealth with them, but only if that wealth is used toward justice for those communities of people. This also means that all equity claims presented by Third World states are in a sense conditional on their doing something for their people. Fourth, when it comes to the issue of how much we actually owe the Bantus, my position is close to Julius Stone's. International justice by now should *at least* be concerned with the minimal rights of all people, the first formulation of the radical vision. One cannot say that we have already an obligation to full equality for everybody, everywhere for two reasons. One is that there is as of now no way in which we could meet such an obligation. After all, it is not possible, in helping others, to go beyond what can be consented to domestically. You cannot violate your own public opinion in this matter. You should educate it; you should make it less parochial or selfish; but you cannot go so far ahead as to be rejected. The second reason is the possibility of a moral conflict between making subsistence available to all, and starting with the poorest in one's own nation—between the practical consequences of the most radical formulation, which treats mankind as an undifferentiated entity, and those of the view that stresses the moral priority of the nation. Each view stands on strong moral grounds; neither one is acceptable if one insists on excluding consideration of the other. And therefore I end up somewhat inevitably with the philosophically untidy and politically elastic notion, that the scope of our obligation to individuals in other societies varies in time and in space. There was none of it perhaps sixty or fifty years ago (or rather, very few people acknowledged one). There is some now, more widely recognized. If all goes well, and states-men, writers, and so on, press on, it may grow in the future. Our sense of obligation is of course strongest in our own community, but it also exists within larger groups, communities intermediate between the national one and man-kind (let us say, the European community, for West Europeans), and it gets weaker as one goes farther away.

To sum up, our obligation of justice is not just to our own people; when it comes to obligations to other individuals we are acknowledging obligations of mutual aid to states in order to improve the lot of their people, and particularly of their poorest people, but the scope of these duties is somehow still in an evolving position in time and in space—except, I would say, insofar as there are violations of the most elementary human rights of other individuals.

The second question about what we owe others entails a debate about the foundations of obligation. How deep is the sense of duty that we have toward others in other societies? And what does it stem from? Here there are other difficulties. In the literature on this subject, first we find the argument that we must feel obliged because we are all guilty. Our obligation as citizens of rich states derives from our misbehavior in the past; we owe reparations to the poor states and their people. It is a kind of tribute. This I reject for a number of reasons. Psychologically, I think it is the most counterproductive argument; the only result of trying to inject a sense of collective guilt is the generalization of resentment, not a feeling of obligation. Just think of what has happened in history each time such a guilt clause has been imposed, or think about the history of reparations—what it did to Franco-German relations after 1871, or to Germany's relations with the rest of the world after 1919. Also, historically, this is Pandora's Box. Let us assume that our ancestors have indeed harmed millions of people. How far back in time do you have to go? When did malfeasance begin? Who is supposed to pay? Is it just the descendants of the people who went and exploited them, is it all of us? We are dealing most of the time now with what Karl Deutsch would call "socially mobilized publics," or "democratic publics," even if the regimes are not always democratic. Now, one of the princi-ples of democratic publics is that they do not accept responsibility for the sins of their ancestors. As Tocqueville put it, each generation believes it begins anew. And you will never be able to convince people in this country or in England or in France that the aid which they feel a duty to give, they must provide because their ancestors were brigands and exploiters and murderers. It is not a suitable basis of obligation.

Finally, scientifically, the argument of exploitation is quite unprovable. We cannot prove what would have happened to India or Bangladesh or Pakistan or Africa if colonialism had never occurred. After all, there have been considerable variations there. Some countries which were never colonial powers did not do any better than those that were colonized. Some colonized countries did far better than others. Nor do I know how one assesses the evils of colonialism as a yardstick for present duties, because one would have to calculate intangibles. On the one scale, as the defenders of colonialism always do, one puts law and order, and what figure do you give to this? On the other scale one must indeed put the disintegration of existing communities, or the forced mergers of communities which explode later on, or the destruction of native institutions, or the lack of self-respect, or the feeling of being exploited even when it goes far beyond the actual provable economic exploitation. How do you weigh that?

If one says that it is not just a matter of colonialism; that exploitation is the result of what the rich did to the poor, whether the rich took colonies or not, alas, there are enormous disagreements about what constitutes exploitation. It is a fundamentally unscientific and subjective notion. In the case of Latin America, Tony Smith has recently demolished standard arguments about "decapitalization" and "denationalization";[10] and Richard Cooper has argued that the greater profitability of overseas investment is in doubt.[11] But for Johan Galtung, practically any kind of trade, except the barter of simple objects, is a nucleus of imperialism.[12] Again, all attempts at measuring what would be due in restitution have failed, for the best of reasons. What would constitute a good quantitative index? James Caporaso's attempt to use terms of trade as a "ready measure of exploitation"[13] foundered on a variety of empirical and conceptual arguments. How could the sum be converted in current prices? Nor is there any agreement about the effects of exploitation, between those who stress evident possibilities of resistance, and those like Johan Galtung who find it at the root of practically all institutions and forms of conduct.

A second foundation of obligation is suggested by the absolutist argument that like all other moral obligations it comes from our consciences. Here we are in a difficult area too. On one point Richard Cooper is right. Conscience is matter of relations between individuals, or between individuals in families or in voluntary groups. When we talk of obligation to other states, then is this really a matter of conscience? Is it not an obligation that is conditional on their performance, and no longer a categorical imperative (and therefore often resented by the recipients)? Furthermore, it is fairly clear that our sense of moral obligation is far from universal because, within a given country, those who recognize such duties beyond borders are often not even the majority. The people whose consciences are so strong that they feel, as citizens of the rich countries, that they have duties both to the states and to the individuals of the Third World are, as Julius Stone puts it, enclaves, and normally small enclaves, of liberals—I do not say guilt-ridden liberals because I do not like the rhetoric or the clichés of the conservatives and neoconservatives. Even the sense of obligation which exists in those enclaves has limits of scope that we have already discussed. They do not feel a duty to promote full equality at severe costs for the living standards of their own people, and, to go back to an earlier argument, they do not feel a duty to give aid to states that may be aggressive, or totally chaotic, or totally ineffective. As usual in moral politics, pure conscience is not enough.

Do we encounter here what is normally behind obligation in international affairs a combination of conscience—at least incipient conscience—and calculation of interest, or moral sense and prudence? There are more difficulties. What kinds of interests are in evidence? The literature offers many arguments about mutual benefits, and they are most important for persuading the publics of advanced countries—pure moral appeals would not suffice. A commission headed by Willy Brandt has just produced one more report on North-South relations, and it lists once more a whole series of possible mutual gains—in commodities, in trade, with respect to multinational corporations and to the international monetary system, etc.[14] These are mutual economic benefits. The mutual political benefit is our joint interest in orderly change. It all sounds very good on paper. However, orderly change is not the goal of all states and is far from certain to happen even if one transfers resources and provides all kinds of assistance. And as for economic interests, there are many important mutual gains, but unfortunately they are often long term. Moreover, those long-term mutual interests exist primarily with the wealthiest of the poor nations, because they are the ones with whom we deal most. It is the least needy with whom we have the most mutual interests. The neediest either we do not need, or else— in those cases where we *do* need their raw materials—they are too weak either to absorb enough of our exports or of our surplus investment capacity, or to be much of a bother. In the short term, aid costs a great deal. In the long run, the huge potential market of the developing nations may serve as an engine of growth for the industrial ones, but in the short run there are all the costs of adapting to the competition from the imports of the manufactured or agricultural products from the developing countries. In the short run, as we can see from looking at the story of OPEC in the last six years, our interests are very often antagonistic. The question raised by the interest argument is: "Can long-term, diffuse mutual interests prevail over short-term intense national ones?" And the answer which the democratic publics also very often give is: "No, the priorities should be our immediate interest."

There is another kind of interest argument which is not in terms of mutual benefits. It is an uglier one. It is interest derived from fear. We should give them something, because they can do an enormous amount of harm to us. That is the argument made by C. Fred Bergsten.[15] Economically they can harm us greatly by cartelization or by just falling into chaos. And politically they can harm us by refusing to cooperate in the establishment of international regimes, or by promoting nuclear proliferation, or by siding with our chief rival. The trouble with this argument is that it does not work to reenforce a sense of obligation, for all kinds of reasons. First of all, the number of possibly successful cartels is limited. Most products do not lend themselves to cartelization, unlike oil, and many raw materials are produced by the developed nations. Secondly, the greatest risks of economic chaos happen to exist in those countries which are least linked to the wealthy. If Bangladesh or some of the other really poor countries sank into chaos, we could afford to be extraordinarily indifferent. Politically, it is true that even they can do harm, for instance by turning to Moscow or by throwing us out; but they might do that same harm if we aided them economically but without resolving their formidable internal problems (think of Iran, or Egypt). It is not a one-to-one connection. Finally, like guilt, fear—in those cases where it is justified, as in our relations with OPEC or with other Third World states wealthy or advanced enough to foster nuclear proliferation or to spread political chaos—is an extraordinarily bad and shaky psychological foundation for obligation. Moral obligations must come from within (as they do even when we find a calculation of interest behind them). Fear constrains and coerces, it does not oblige. Within a nation, fear can be effective because it is the fear of superior power: the police, the judge. In international affairs, fear is more likely to breed resentment, to provoke reaction and backlash.

Does this mean that there is really no foundation, and that all we have toward the poor is a kind of duty of charity? There is one school of thought which says just this; that is the school of thought represented by *Commentary and the Wall Street Journal.* (One name is common to the two: Irving Kristol.) All we owe the poor is charity, because we are good Christians, or good Jews, or out of prudence, but we have no obligation of justice really. Indeed, to say that we have an obligation to the poor is very bad for us and for them, for us because it could lead them into extortion—into reverse imperialism[16]—and for them because they would be self-indulgent, they would sit on their poverty and just wait until we fulfill our obligation. Charity of course is conditional on their behaving like good dependents. In other words, nothing is due to them anymore if, to quote Kristol, "the poor should start Mau-Mauing their benefactors."[17] This is clearly totally insulting to the poor abroad (just like the argument that welfare is not in the interests of the poor at home, since it damages their self-esteem). And it is most unacceptable insofar as basic human rights, such as the right to food, are concerned. Charity denies the structural roots of radical inequalities. And if it cannot be said that it has been as entirely superseded in international affairs as its has been in the domestic realm, there are enough doubts about the legitimacy of the international distribution of resources—whatever the disagreements on causes and remedies—to have blown away the good conscience of simple charity.[18]

Where do we end? With a question mark, which is not the first time, about how deep our sense of obligation is. This is not so surprising. We are dealing with something inconclusive, because it is of an intermediate and complex nature. Our duty is partly to states, partly to individuals. And our state of conscience is somewhere in-between the argument that we owe nothing, except a dole, outside of our community and the argument that we owe the same thing, full justice, to all mankind. So it is not shocking to find that the foundations of obligation are still shaky. It does not mean that we should not work at making them stronger and firmer. And yet, it is a discouraging conclusion, but "I never promised you a rose garden," either in analyzing where we are, or in suggesting how far we can travel on the road we ought to follow. We must never forget that the problem of distributive justice, like that of force, looks fundamentally different in the context of the state and in that of the world. Within the national community, either through the work of political and intellectual leaders, or through the efforts of the state, we usually find a consensus on what constitutes justice—a consensus that can evolve dramatically, as the American New Deal and the post–World War II West European welfare state show. And it is through the state that the common standards of justice get refined and enforced. In the international milieu, there is a cacophony of standards—Marxist ideas of social justice conflict with social-democratic and with laissez faire notions—and the instruments of enforcement are the separate states;

which means, unhappily, either that justice becomes a matter of sheer force—carried at the point of a sword—or, when force does not prevail, a matter of fleeting bargains and tests of fear or strength. In the absence of a "world market" of opinion, and of supranational institutions, how could the sense of obligation be anything but flickering?

NOTES

1. John Rawls, *A Theory of Justice* (Cambridge, Mass.: Harvard University Press, 1971), p. 5.
2. For other kinds of justice see Hedley Bull, *The Anarchical Society* (New York: Columbia University Press, 1977), Chapter 4.
3. "Approaches to the Notion of International Justice," in *The Future of the International Legal Order*, ed. Cyril Black and Richard Falk (Princeton: Princeton University Press) I: 409.
4. Robert W. Tucker, *The Inequality of Nations* (New York: Basic Books, 1977).
5. Fouad Ajami, "The Global Logic of the Neoconservatives," *World Politics* 30, no. 3 (April 1978): 462.
6. See remarks by Albert Bressand, "Six dialogues en quête d'auteur," *Politique Etrangère* (June 1980), pp. 308ff.
7. Nathaniel H. Leff, "Changes in the American Climate Affecting the NIEO Proposals," *The World Economy* (1979), p. 96.
8. In "Equity in the South in the Context of North-South Relations," in Albert Fishlow et al., *Rich and Poor Nations in the World Economy* (New York: McGraw Hill, 1978), pp. 173ff.
9. In Jagdish N. Bhagwati, ed., *The New International Economic Order: The North-South Debate* (Cambridge, Mass.: MIT Press, 1977), p. 355.
10. Tony Smith, "The Underdevelopment of Development Literature," *World Politics* 21, no. 2 (January 1979): 247–88.
11. Richard Cooper, "A New International Economic Order for Mutual Gain," *Foreign Policy*, no. 26 (Spring 1977), pp. 87ff.
12. Johan Galtung, *The True Worlds* (New York: Free Press, 1980), pp. 113ff.
13. James Caporaso, "Methodological Issues in the Measurement of Inequality, Dependence and Exploitation," in Steven J. Rosen and James R. Kurth, *Testing Theories of Economic Imperialism* (Lexington: Lexington Books, 1974), pp. 108–110.
14. Willy Brandt et al., *North-South* (Cambridge, Mass.: MIT Press, 1980).
15. Cf. C. Fred Bergsten, "The Threat from the Third World," *Foreign Policy* 2 (Summer 1973): 102–124.
16. Harry G. Johnson in Bhagwati, *New International Economic Order*, p. 360.
12. Quoted in Roger Hansen, *Beyond the North-South Stalemate* (New York: McGraw Hill, 1979), p. 61.
18. Cf. Thomas Nagel, "Poverty and Food: Why Charity is Not Enough, " in Brown and Shue, *Food Policy*, pp. 54ff.

Human Rights in World Politics

Rhoda E. Howard and Jack Donnelly

WHAT ARE HUMAN RIGHTS?

The International Human Rights Covenants[1] note that human rights "derive from the inherent dignity of the human person." But while the struggle to assure a life of dignity is probably as old as human society itself, reliance on human rights as a mechanism to realize that dignity is a relatively recent development.

Human rights are, by definition, the rights one has simply because one is a human being. This simple and relatively uncontroversial definition, though, is more complicated than it may appear on the surface. It identifies human rights as *rights*, in the strict and strong sense of that term, and it establishes that they are held simply by virtue of being human.

The term "right" in English has a variety of meanings, but two are of special moral importance. On the one hand, "right" may refer to something that is (morally) correct or demanded, the fact of something being right. In this sense, "right" refers to conformity with moral standards; righteousness; moral rectitude. On the other hand, "right" may refer to the entitlement of a person, the special title one has to a good or opportunity. Such titles ground special and particularly strong claims against those who would deny the right; as Ronald Dworkin[2] puts it, rights in ordinary circumstances "trump" other moral and political considerations. It is in this sense that one *has* a right. And it is in this sense that one has human rights.

The sense of moral standards, must be as old as the notion of moral standards themselves. In the Western tradition of moral and political discourse there have been a variety of theories resting on this sense of right, but perhaps the most popular has been the theory of natural law. Natural law theories hold that there is an objective moral law (given by God and/or grasped by human reason). This natural law binds all men and women and provides a standard for evaluating human practices, including political practices. A regime that transgresses the natural law is guilty of serious crimes and, in severe instances, loses its moral and political legitimacy.

Perhaps the most highly developed theory of natural law was that of St. Thomas Aquinas (1225–1274), who sought to combine Christian doctrine with the philosophical ideas of classical antiquity, especially those of Aristotle. For Aquinas, all law is the expression of divine reason, which is made available to mankind in two principal forms: "divine law," or the revelation of the Bible, and "natural law," the imprint of divine reason, directly available to all though the exercise of reason. What Aquinas calls "human law," the ordinary sorts of law made by legislators, is legitimate to the extent that it conforms to the natural law, of which it ought to be merely a practical political expression.[3]

Such theories in the Western world go back explicitly at least as far as Cicero (106–43 B.C.), and they may be seen as implicit in the writings of Plato and Aristotle. They also extend well into the modern era; even John Locke, one of the most important early modern natural rights theorists, has an explicit theory of natural law.[4] Today, natual law ideas still receive the support of a number of respected philosophers and have considerable popular appeal, particularly, but not entirely, in certain religious circles.

Furthermore, such ideas have been the norm in most premodern or preindustrial societies throughout the world. For example, the Chinese emperor was held to rule through a mandate from heaven, and thus was held to be accountable to heaven for his actions. Similarly, Islam provides a very detailed set of substantive norms, expressed in the Koran and in Sharia law, to which rulers are required to conform. In very few societies have rulers been conceived of as truly absolute and unconstrained; even the Ancien Régime monarchs of France who claimed to rule by divine right acknowledged an obligation to conform their rule to the dictates of divine justice. Whatever the deviations in practice, almost all rulers in preindustrial societies ruled under what in the West was usually referred to as natural law. Most traditional societies, Western and non-Western alike, have conceived of justice primarily in terms of conformity with substantive principles of right (although usually known through tradition, not apprehended directly by reason).

The political leverage that natural law provides citizens against the state—that is, the ability to indict a violator of natural law as one who transgresses objective principles of justice, not merely the preferences or interests of a particular person or group—should not be denigrated. For example, a tyrannical ruler in medieval Europe or imperial China would stand condemned in the eyes of God and the objective principles of law and justice; a ruler could be held accountable to objective standards. But the difference between natural *law* and natural or human *right* indictments is quite important, both theoretically and practically.

A state that violates the natural law is guilty of moral crimes, but it has not necessarily violated the rights of its citizens. Natural law does not necessarily give rise to natural rights, one has "by nature," simply as a human being. In fact, while some recent natural law theorists (most prominently, Jacques Maritain[5]) link natural law with natural or human rights, historically such a linkage is quite rare; it certainly is not made by figures such as Cicero, Aquinas, and Richard Hooker. Typically, regimes that stand condemned by the natural law do not face citizens whose natural *rights* have been violated, and thus the kinds of actions that are justified to remedy the injustice are quite different.

In particular, without natural (or legal) rights against the government, citizens are not *entitled* to seek redress; natural law by itself gives no one any right to enforce its injunctions. For that they must have natural or human (or legal) *rights* in the strong sense of entitlements that ground claims that have a special force. If the state violates their rights, citizens may claim not only that injustice is perpetrated against them but that their rights have been violated. This gives considerable additional force to these claims. In addition, and no less important, it puts the process of redress under their control, as rights-holders who are entitled to press claims of rights. When those rights are natural or human rights, rights one has simply because one is a human being, the moral offense is of the greatest magnitude.

This understanding of states being constrained by the *rights* of citizens, which are morally prior to and above the state, is historically of relatively recent date, distinctively "modern." Thomas Hobbes, in *Leviathan* (1655), speaks of the "right of nature," a precursor of our conception of natural rights, but he explicitly denies that such rights limit the sovereign's power.[6] By the time of Locke's *Second Treatise of Government* (1688),[7] a clear and explicit theory of natural rights exists side by side with a fairly traditional theory of natural law. By the time of the American and French revolutions, ideas of natural rights—or, in the language of the era, the rights of man—are not only politically central but have replaced natural law both in popular revolutionary discourse and in the writings of figures such as Thomas Jefferson and Thomas Paine.[8]

As is clear from the authors already cited, the human rights tradition is, in its inception at least, closely tied to contractarian political thought. In the social contract tradition, individuals are seen as possessors of natural rights entirely independent of the state; their basic rights derive "from (human) nature," not from the state, politics, God, or tradition. In fact, the state (and society) are seen as products of a contract among individuals to protect natural rights and provide the social and political conditions that will allow individuals to realize them. As such, the state is letigimate only if it respects, enforces, and permits the fuller realization of natural rights. And if it fails to discharge its part of the contract—if it grossly and systematically violates human rights—citizens, either individually or collectively, are entitled to revolt. For example, Locke recognizes and defends a right to revolution held by society against governments that systematically violate natural rights; Jefferson in the American Declaration of Independence justifies the revolution by the British denial of natural rights; and the French Declaration of the Rights and the Citizen explicitly includes a right to revolution.

Natural law and other (nonhuman rights) theories of justice certainly are capable of denying the legitimacy of corrupt or vicious governments. The grounds of the denial, however, and the position in the fact of such a government, are quite different in the absence of natural rights.

For example, Aquinas holds that tyrants are illegitimate because they have grossly and systematically violated the natural law. But citizens, lacking natural *rights* that this law be respected, are not entitled to revolt or even press rights-claims against the tyrant.[9] When, however, it is considered legitimate for citizens to react not only against the injustice of violations of the natural law but also in defense of their natural rights, the state is guilty of additional and particularly severe affronts to human dignity. Not only are its practices unjust, but they also violate human rights. And citizens are entitled to act to restore their rights. A natural or human rights conception of politics places individual citizens and their rights at the heart of politics, which is viewed as ultimately a device for the vindication of natural rights.

As we have already indicated, there is nothing necessary about such a conception of persons or politics. Elsewhere we have argued in some detail that most societies at most times (including Western society in previous eras) have had quite different views.[10] But this is what is entailed by a human rights conception. And the nearly universal acceptance of the idea (if not the practice) of human rights by virtually all states in all areas of the contemporary world gives this conception a validity that cannot be ignored. . . .

WHAT RIGHTS DO WE HAVE?

The definition of human or natural rights as the rights of each person simply as a human being specifies their character; they are rights. The definition also specifies their source: (human) nature. We have already talked briefly about human rights as rights. A few words are necessary about the claim that human *nature* gives rise to human rights, as well as the particular list that results.

What is it in human nature that gives rise to human rights? There are two basic answers to this question. On the one hand, many people argue that human rights arise from human needs, from the naturally given requisites for physical and mental health and well-being. On the other hand, many argue that human rights reflect the minimum requirements for human dignity or *moral* personality.[11] These latter arguments derive from essentially philosophical theories of human "nature," dignity, or moral personality.

Needs theories of human rights run into the problem of empirical confirmations; the simple fact is that there is sound scientific evidence only for a very narrow list of human needs. But if we use "needs" in a broader, in part nonscientific, sense, then the two theories overlap. We can thus say that people have human rights to those things "needed" for a life of dignity, for the full development of their moral personality. The "nature" that gives rise to human rights is thus *moral* nature.

This moral nature is, in part, a social creation. Human nature, in the relevant sense, is an amalgam consisting both of psycho-biological facts (constraints and possibilities) and of the social structures and experiences that are no less a part of the essential nature of men and women. Human beings are not isolated individuals, but rather individuals who are essentially social creatures, in part even social creations. Therefore, a theory of human rights must recognize both the essential universality of human nature and the no less essential particularity arising from cultural and socioeconomic traditions and institutions.

Human rights are, by their nature, universal; it is not coincidental that we have a *Universal* Declaration of Human Rights, for human rights are the rights of all men and women. Therefore, in its basic outlines a list of human rights must apply at least more or less "across the board." But the nature of human beings is also shaped by the particular societies in which they live. Thus the universality of human rights must be qualified in at least two important ways.

First, the forms in which universal rights are institutionalized are subject to some legitimate cultural and political variation. For example, what counts as popular participation in government may vary, within a certain range, from society to society. Both multiparty and single-party regimes may reflect legitimate notions of political participation. Although the ruling party cannot be removed from power, in some one-party states individual representatives can be changed and electoral pressure may result in significant policy changes.

Second, and no less important, the universality (in principle) of human rights is qualified by the obvious fact that any particular list, no matter how broad its cross-cultural and international acceptance, reflects the necessarily contingent understandings of a particular era. For example, in the seventeenth and eighteenth centuries, the rights of man were indeed the rights of men, not women, and social and economic rights (other than the right to private property) were unheard of. Thus we must expect a gradual evolution of even a consensual list of human rights, as collective understandings of the essential elements of human dignity, the conditions of moral personality, evolve in response to changing ideas and material circumstances.

In other words, human rights are by their essential nature universal in form. They are, by definition, the rights held by each (and every) person simply as a human being. But any universal list of human rights is subject to a variety of justifiable implementations.

In our time, the Universal Declaration of Human Rights (1948) is a minimum list that is nearly universally accepted, although additional rights have been added (e.g., self-determination) and further new rights (e.g., the right to nondiscrimination on the grounds of sexual orientation or the right to peace) may be added in the future. We are in no position to offer a philosophical defense of the list of rights in the Universal Declaration. To do so would require an account of the source of human rights—human nature—that would certainly exceed the space available to us. Nonetheless, the Universal Declaration is nearly universally accepted by states. For practical political purposes we can treat it as authoritative. All the contributors to this volume have agreed to do precisely that. Therefore a brief review of the list of rights contained in the Universal Declaration . . . is appropriate here.

It is conventional to divide human rights into two major classes, civil and political rights, and economic, social, and cultural rights. Such a division is rather crude and unenlightening. It also has too often been the basis for partisan arguments, by left and right alike, for granting priority to one category or the other, arguments that often simply attempt to cloak the abuse of rights. Nevertheless, it is a common and convenient categorization.

The civil and political rights enumerated in the Universal Declaration include rights to life; nationality; recognition before the law; protection against cruel, degrading, or inhuman treatment or punishment; and protection against racial, ethnic, sexual, or religious discrimination. They also include such legal rights as access to remedies for violations of basic rights; the presumption of innocence; the guarantee of fair and impartial public trials; prohibition of ex post facto laws; and protections against arbitrary arrest, detention or exile, and arbitrary interference with one's family, home, or reputation. Civil liberties enumerated include rights to freedom of thought, conscience and religion, opinion and expression, movement and residence, and peaceful assembly and association. Finally, political rights include the rights to take part in government and to periodic and genuine elections with universal and equal suffrage. Economic, social, and cultural rights recognized in the Declaration include the rights to food and a standard of living adequate for the health and well-being of oneself and one's family; the rights to work, rest and leisure, and social security; and rights to education and to participation in the cultural life of the community.

There are occasional claims still made, especially by political conservatives in the West, that only civil and political rights are really rights.[12] Likewise, one still runs across no less one-sided arguments, made principally by Soviet bloc and Third World politicians and scholars, that economic and social rights have priority over civil and political rights.[13] But virtually all states are explicitly committed to the view that all the rights recognized in the Universal Declaration are interdependent and indivisible. . . .

INTERNATIONAL HUMAN RIGHTS INSTITUTIONS

The international context of national practices deserves some attention.[14] There are, as we have already noted, international human rights standards that are widely accepted—in principle at least—by states. Thus the discussion and evaluation of national practices take place within an overarching set of international standards to which virtually all states have explicitly committed themselves. Whatever the force of claims of national sovereignty, with its attendant legal immunity from international action, the evaluation of national human rights practices from the perspective of the international standards of the Universal Declaration thus is certainly appropriate, even if one is uncomfortable with the moral claim sketched above that such universalistic scrutiny is demanded by the very idea of human rights.

In the literature on international relations it has recently become fashionable to talk of "international regimes," that is, norms and decision-making procedures accepted by states in a given issue area. National human rights practices do take place within the broader context of an international human rights regime centered on the United Nations.

We have already sketched the principal norms of this regime—the list of rights in the Universal Declaration. These norms/rights are further elaborated in two major treaties, the International Covenant on Economic, Social and Cultural Rights and the International Covenant on Civil and Political Rights, which were opened for signature and ratification in 1966 and came into force in 1976. Almost all of the countries studied in this volume have ratified (become a party to) both the Covenant on Civil and Political Rights and the Covenant on Economic, Social and Cultural Rights. . . . Even the countries that are not parties to the Covenants often accept the principles of the Universal Declaration. In addition, there are a variety of single-issue treaties that have been formulated under UN auspices on topics such as racial discrimination, the rights of women, and torture. These later Covenants and Conventions go into much greater detail than the Universal Declaration and include a few important changes. For example, the Covenants prominently include a right to national self-determination, which is absent in the Universal Declaration, but do not include a right to private property. Nevertheless, for the most part they can be seen simply as elaborations on the Universal Declaration, which remains the central normative document in the international human rights regime.

What is the legal and political force of these norms? The Universal Declaration of Human Rights was proclaimed in 1948 by the United Nations General Assembly. As such, it has no force of law. Resolutions of the General Assembly, even solemn declarations, are merely recommendations to states; the General Assembly has no international legislative powers. Over the years, however, the Universal Declaration has come to be something more than a mere recommendation.

There are two principal sources of international law, namely, treaty and custom. Although today we tend to think first of treaty, historically custom is at least as important. A rule or principle attains the force of customary international law when it can meet two tests. First, the principle or rule must reflect the general practice of the overwhelming majority of states. Second, what lawyers call *opinio juris*, the sense of obligation, must be taken into account. Is the customary practice seen by states as an obligation, rather than a mere convenience or courtesy? Today it is a common view of international lawyers that the Universal Declaration has attained something of the status of customary international law, so that the rights it contains are in some important sense binding on states.

Furthermore, the International Human Rights Covenants are treaties and as such do have the force of international law, but only for the parties to the treaties, that is, those states that have (voluntarily) ratified or acceded to the treaties. The same is true of the single-issue treaties that round out the regime's norms. It is perhaps possible that the norms of the Covenants are coming to acquire the force of customary international law even for states that are not parties. But in either case, the fundamental weakness of international law is underscored: Virtually all international legal obligations are voluntarily accepted.

This is obviously the case for treaties; states are free to become parties or not entirely as they choose. It is no less true, though, of custom, where the tests of state practice and *opinio juris* likewise assure that international legal obligation is only voluntarily acquired. In fact, a state that explicitly rejects a practice during the process of custom formation is exempt even from customary international legal obligations. For example, Saudi Arabia's objection to the provisions on the equal rights of women during the drafting of the Universal Declaration might be held to exempt it from such a norm, even if the norm is accepted internationally as customarily binding. Such considerations are particularly important when we ask what force there is to international law and what mechanisms exist to implement and enforce the rights specified in the Universal Declaration and the Covenants.

Acceptance of an obligation by states does not carry with it acceptance of any method of international enforcement. Quite the contrary. Unless there is an explicit enforcement mechanism attached to the obligation, its enforcement rests simply on the good faith of the parties. The Universal Declaration contains no enforcement mechanisms of any sort. Even if we accept it as having the force of international law, its implementation is left entirely in the hands of individual states. The Covenants do have some implementation machinery, but the machinery's practical weakness is perhaps its most striking feature.

Under the provisions of the International Covenant on Civil and Political Rights, a Human Rights Committee of independent experts was created in the United Nations to supervise the Covenant's implementation.[15] The Committee's principal function, however, is simply to review periodic reports submitted by the different states who are party to the Covenant concerning their practices with respect to the enumerated rights. While the reports of states are examined in public, the most the Committee can do is raise questions and request further information. It is powerless to compel more than pro forma compliance with the requirement of periodic reporting, and even that sometimes cannot be achieved. Furthermore, even this minimal international scrutiny applies only to the parties to the Covenant, which numbered only eighty— about half the countries of the world—in 1985.

An Optional Protocol to the Civil/Political Covenant permits the Human Rights Committee to receive and examine complaints from individuals. The Committee receives about two dozen complaints a year, about half of which are admissible and receive substantive scrutiny. But even here the most that the Committee can do is state its views on whether a violation has occurred. In other words, even in this, probably the strongest procedure in the international human rights regime, there is only international monitoring of state practice. Enforcement remains entirely national. And by 1985 only thirty-five countries had accepted the provisions of the Optional Protocol. Not surprisingly, almost none of those covered are major human rights violators. Thus relatively strong procedures apply primarily where they are least needed—which is not at all surprising given that participation in these procedures is entirely voluntary.

The procedures under the International Covenant on Economic, Social and Cultural Rights are even weaker. Periodic reports are reviewed not by an independent committee of experts but by a working group of the UN Economic and Social Council (ECOSOC), a body of political delegates representing the views of their governments. (A new committee of experts was established in

1986, but it has yet to meet.) In addition, there is no individual complaint procedure.

The single-issue treaties on racial discrimination, torture and women's rights also contain periodic reporting procedures, as well as various complaint procedures, but the coverage of the first two is narrow and their provisions not significantly stronger than those of the Civil and Political Covenant. The International Labour Organization, which provided the model for the reporting procedures adopted in the field of human rights, also has similar powers for the workers' rights issues within its purview, but once more the furthest the system goes is voluntarily accepted monitoring of voluntarily accepted obligations. There is no real international enforcement of any sort.[16]

The one other major locus of activity in the international human rights regime is the UN Commission on Human Rights. In addition to being the body that played the principal role in the formulation of the Universal Declaration, the Covenants, and most of the major single-issue human rights treaties, it has some weak implementation powers. Its public discussion of human rights situations in various countries can help to mobilize international public opinion, which is not always utterly useless in helping to reform national practice. For example, in the 1970s the Commission played a major role in publicizing the human rights conditions in Chile, Israel, and South Africa. Furthermore, it is empowered by ECOSOC resolution 1503 (1970) to investigate communications (complaints) from individuals and groups that "appear to reveal a consistent pattern of gross and reliably attested violations of human rights."

The 1503 procedure, however, is at least as thoroughly hemmed in by constraints as are the other enforcement mechanisms that we have considered.[17] Although individuals may communicate grievances, the 1503 procedure deals only with *"situations"* of gross and systematic violations, not the particular cases of individuals. Individuals cannot even obtain an international judgment in their particular case, let alone international enforcement of the human rights obligations of their government. Furthermore, the entire procedure remains confidential until a case is concluded, although the Commission does publicly announce a "blacklist" of countries being studied. In only four cases (Equatorial Guinea, Haiti, Malawi, and Uruguay) has the Commission gone public with a 1503 case. Its most forceful conclusion was a 1980 resolution provoked by the plight of Jehovah's Witnesses in Malawi, which merely expressed the hope that all human rights were being respected in Malawi.

In addition to this global human rights regime, there are regional regimes.[18] The 1981 African Charter of Human and Peoples' Rights, drawn up by the Organization of African Unity, provides for a Human Rights Commission, but it is not yet functioning. In Europe and the Americas there are highly developed systems involving both commissions with very strong investigatory powers and regional human rights courts with the authority to make legally binding decisions on complaints by individuals (although only eight states have accepted the jurisdiction of the Inter-American Court of Human Rights).

Even in Europe and the Americas, however, implementation and enforcement remain primarily national. In nearly thirty years the European Commission of Human Rights has considered only about 350 cases, while the European Court of Human Rights has handled only one-fifth that number. Such regional powers certainly should not be ignored or denigrated. They provide authoritative interpretations in cases of genuine disagreements and a powerful check on backsliding and occasional deviations by states. But the real force of even the European regime lies in the voluntary acceptance of human rights by the states in question, which has infinitely more to do with domestic politics than with international procedures.

In sum, at the international level there are comprehensive, authoritative human rights norms that are widely accepted as binding on all states. Implementation and enforcement of these norms, however, both in theory and in practice, are left to states. The international context of national human rights practices certainly cannot be ignored. Furthermore, international norms may have an important socializing effect on national leaders and be useful to national advocates of improved domestic human rights practices. But the real work of implementing and enforcing human rights takes place at the national level. . . . Before the level of the nation-state is discussed, however, one final element of the international context needs to be considered, namely, human rights as an issue in national foreign policies.

HUMAN RIGHTS AND FOREIGN POLICY

Beyond the human rights related activities of states in international institutions such as those discussed in the preceding section, many states have chosen to make human rights a concern in their bilateral foreign relations.[19] In fact, much of the surge of interest in human rights in the last decade can be traced to the catalyzing effect of President Jimmy Carter's (1977–1981) efforts to make international human rights an objective of U.S. foreign policy.

In a discussion of human rights as an issue in national foreign policy, at least three problems need to be considered. First, a nation must select a particular set of rights to pursue. Second, the legal and moral issues raised by intervention on behalf of human rights abroad need to be explored. Third, human rights concerns must be integrated into the nation's broader foreign policy, since human rights are at best only one of several foreign policy objectives.

The international normative consensus on human rights noted above largely solves the problem of the choice of a set of rights to pursue, for unless a state chooses a list very similar to that of the Universal Declaration, its efforts are almost certain to be dismissed as fatally flawed by partisan or ideological bias. Thus, for example, claims by officials of the Reagan administration that economic and social rights are not really true human rights are almost universally denounced. By the same token, the Carter administration's serious attention to economic and social rights, even if it was ultimately subordinate to a concern for civil and political rights, greatly contributed to the international perception of its policy as genuinely concerned with human rights, not just a new rhetoric for the Cold War or neo-colonialism. Such an international perception is almost a necessary condition—although by no means a sufficient condition—for an effective international human rights policy.

A state is, of course, free to pursue any objectives it wishes in its foreign policy. If it wishes its human rights policy to be taken seriously, however, the policy must at least be enunciate in terms consistent with the international consensus that has been forged around the Universal Declaration. In practice, some rights must be given particular prominence in a nation's foreign policy, given the limited material resources and international political capital of even the most powerful state, but the basic contours of policy must be set by the Universal Declaration.

After the rights to be pursued have been selected, the second problem, that of intervention on behalf of human rights, arises. When state A pursues human rights in its relations with state B, A usually will be seeking to alter the way that B treats its own citizens. This is, by definition, a matter essentially within the domestic jurisdiction of B and thus outside the legitimate jurisdiction of A. A's action, therefore, is vulnerable to the charge of intervention, a charge that carries considerable legal, moral, and political force in a world, such as ours, that is structured at the international level around sovereign nation-states.

The legal problems raised by foreign policy action on behalf of human rights abroad are probably the most troubling. Sovereignty entails the principle of nonintervention; to say that A has sovereign jurisdiction over X is essentially equivalent to saying that no one else may intervene in A with respect to X. Because sovereignty is the foundation of international law, any foreign policy action that amounts to intervention is prohibited by international law. On the face of it at least, this prohibition applies to action on behalf of human rights as much as any other activity.

It might be suggested that we can circumvent the legal proscription of intervention in the case of human rights by reference to particular treaties or even the general international normative consensus discussed above. International norms per se, however, do not authorize even international organizations, let alone individual states acting independently, to enforce those norms. Even if all states are legally bound to implement the rights enumerated in the Universal Declaration, it simply does not follow, in logic or in law, that any particular state or group of states is entitled to enforce that obligation. States are perfectly free to accept international legal obligations that have no enforcement mechanisms attached.

This does not imply, though, that for a state to comply with international law it must stand by idly in the face of human rights violations abroad. International law prohibits intervention. It does, however, leave considerable room for *action*—perhaps even interference—on behalf of human rights.

Intervention is most often defined as coercive interference (especially by the threat or use of force) in the internal affairs of another country. But there are many kinds of noncoercive "interference," which is the stuff of foreign policy. For example, barring explicit treaty commitments to the contrary, no state is under an international legal obligation to deal with any other state. Should state

A choose to deny B the benefits of its friendly relations, A is perfectly free, as a matter of international law, to reduce or eliminate its relations with B. And should A decide to do so on the basis of B's human rights performance, A is legally within its rights.

Scrupulously avoiding intervention (coercive interference) thus still leaves considerable room for international action at improving the human rights performance of a foreign country. Quiet diplomacy, public protests or condemnations, downgrading or breaking diplomatic relations, reducing or halting foreign aid, and selective or comprehensive restrictions of trade and other forms of interation are all actions that fall short of intervention. Thus in most circumstances they will be legally permissible actions on behalf of human rights abroad.

An international legal perspective on humanitarian intervention, however, does not exhaust the subject. Recently, several authors have argued, strongly and we believe convincingly, that moral considerations in at least some circumstances justify humanitarian intervention on behalf of human rights.[20] Michael Walzer, whose book *Just and Unjust Wars* has provoked much of the recent moral discussion of humanitarian intervention, can be taken as illustrative of such arguments.

Walzer presents a strong defense of the morality of the general international principle of nonintervention, arguing that it gives force to the basic right of peoples to self-determination, which in turn rests on the rights of individuals, acting in concert as a community, to choose their own government. Walzer has been criticized for interpreting this principle in a way that is excessively favorable to states by arguing that the presumption of legitimacy (and thus against intervention) should hold in all but the most extreme circumstances. Nonetheless, even Walzer allows that intervention must be permitted "when the violation of human rights is so terrible that it makes talk of community or self-determination . . . seem cynical and irrelevant."[21] when gross, persistent, and systematic violations of human rights shock the moral conscience of mankind.

The idea underlying such arguments is that human rights are of such paramount moral importance that gross and systematic violations present a moral justification for remedial international action. If the international community as a whole cannot or will not act—and above we have shown that an effective collective international response will usually be impossible—then one or more states may be morally justified in acting ad hoc on behalf of the international community.

International law and morality thus lead to different and conflicting conclusions in at least some cases. One of the functions of international politics is to help to resolve such a conflict; political considerations will play a substantial role in determining how a state will respond in its foreign policy to the competing moral and legal demands placed on it. But the political dimensions of such decisions point to the practical dangers by moral arguments in favor of humanitarian intervention.

If we search the historical record it is very hard to find a clear example of humanitarian intervention in practice. In the last twenty-five years, the two leading candidates are the 1971 Indian intervention in East Pakistan (which soon became Bangladesh) in response to the massacre of Bengalis by the government, and the 1979 Tanzanian intervention in Uganda to topple Amin. But even here it must be noted that India intervened so as to partition its archenemy, Pakistan, and Tanzania intervened only after almost a decade of extremely poor Ugandan-Tanzanian relations, and close on the heels of a failed Ugandan invasion of Tanzanian territory. By contrast, the use of the language of humanitarian intervention to cloak partisan political adventurism—for example, in the U.S. interventions in the Dominican Republic in 1965, Grenada in 1983, and Nicaragua in the mid-1980s—is distressingly common.

Reasonable people may disagree on whether the danger of abuse outweighs the benefits of openly acknowledging and advocating a right to coercive humanitarian intervention. At the very least it should be noted that such a right is at best a very dangerous double-edged sword. Our preference would be to keep that particular sword sheathed and focus the pursuit of human rights in national foreign policy instead on actions short of military intervention. Such nonmilitary actions are legally and morally relatively unproblematic, and far less subject to catastrophic political abuse.

Having selected the rights to be pursued and satisfied itself that the means to be employed in that pursuit are, all things considered, acceptable, a state still faces the fact that human rights are only one part of its foreign policy, and a part that is not always consistent with other parts of the national interest. The relationship between human rights and the rest of the national interest, however, is neither as clear nor as simple as critics often make it out to be. In fact, a concern for human rights may enhance the national security, as a few examples from recent U.S. foreign policy clearly indicate.

In the late seventies, the United States "lost" Nicaragua and Iran in large measure as a result of its support of repressive rulers who managed to alienate virtually their entire populations and provoke genuine popular revolutions. A few years earlier, Angola was "lost" because of the colonial policy and human rights abuses of the U.S.-backed Portuguese regime. More recently, the cost of supporting dictators has been underscored by the fall of Marcos in the Philippines: Any problems faced by the United States in this strategically important country are not only almost entirely of its own making but also largely the result of a misguided subordination of human rights concerns.

Human rights may be moral concerns, but often they are not *merely* moral concerns. Morality and realism are not necessarily incompatible, and to treat them as if they always were can harm not only a state's human rights policy but its broader foreign policy as well.

Sometimes a country can afford to act on its human rights concerns; other times it cannot. Politics involves compromise, as a result of multiple and not always compatible goals that are pursued and the resistance of a world that more often than not is unsupportive of the particular objectives being sought. Human rights, like other goals of foreign policy, must at times be compromised. In some instances there is little that a country can afford to do even in the face of major human rights violations. . . .

If such variations in the treatment of human rights violators are to be part of a consistent policy, human rights concerns need to be explicitly and coherently integrated into the broader framework of foreign policy. A human rights policy must be an integral part of, not just something tacked on to, a country's overall foreign policy.

Difficult decisions have to be made about the relative weights to be given to human rights, as well as other foreign policy goals, and at least rough rules for making trade-offs need to be formulated. Furthermore, such decisions need to be made early in the process of working out a policy, and as a matter of principle. Ad hoc responses to immediate problems and crises, which have been the rule in the human rights policies of countries such as Canada and the United States, are almost sure to lead to inconsistencies and incoherence, both in appearance and in fact. Without such efforts to integrate human rights into the structure of national foreign policy, any trade-offs that are made will remain, literally, unprincipled.

Standards will be undeniably difficult to formulate, and their application will raise no less severe problems. Hard cases and exceptions are unavoidable. So are gray areas and fuzzy boundaries. Unless such efforts are seriously undertaken, however, the resulting policy is likely to appear baseless or inconsistent, and probably will be so in fact as well.

There are many opportunities for foreign policy action on behalf of human rights in foreign countries, but effective action requires the same sort of care and attention required for success in any area of foreign policy. . . .

Culture and Human Rights

This view of the creation of the individual, with individual needs for human rights, is criticized by many advocates of the "cultural relativist" school of human rights. They present the argument that human rights are a "Western construct with limited [universal] applicability."[22] But cultural relativism, as applied to human rights, fails to grasp the nature of culture. A number of erroneous assumptions underlie this viewpoint.

Criticism of the universality of human rights often stems from erroneous perceptions of the persistence of traditional societies, societies in which principles of social justice are based not on rights but on status and on the intermixture of privilege and responsibility. Often anthropologically anachronistic pictures are presented of premodern societies, taking no account whatsoever of the social changes we have described above. It is assumed that culture is a static entity. But culture—like the individual—is adaptive. One can accept the principle that customs, values, and norms do indeed glue society together, and that they will endure, without assuming cultural stasis. Even though elements of culture have a strong hold on people's individual psyches, cultures can and do change. Individuals are actors who can influence their own fate, even if their range of choice is circumscribed by the prevalent social structure, culture, or ideology.

Cultural relativist arguments also often assume that culture is a unitary and unique whole; that is, that one is born into, and will always be, a part of a distinctive, comprehensive, and integrated set of cultural values and institutions that cannot be changed incrementally or only in part. Since in each culture the social norms and roles vary, so, it is argued, human rights must vary. The norms of each society are held to be both valuable in and of their own right, and so firmly rooted as to be impervious to challenge. Therefore, such arguments are applicable only to certain Western societies; to impose them on other societies from which they did not originally arise would do serious and irreparable damage to those cultures. In fact, though, people are quite adept cultural accommodationists; they are able to choose which aspects of a "new" culture they wish to adopt and which aspects of the "old" they wish to retain. For example, the marabouts (priests), who lead Senegal's traditional Muslim brotherhoods, have become leading political figures and have acquired considerable wealth and power through the peanut trade.

Still another assumption of the cultural relativism school is that culture is unaffected by social structure. But structure does affect culture. To a significant extent cultures and values reflect the basic economic and political organization of a society. For example, a society such as Tokugawa Japan, that moves from a feudal structure to an organized bureaucratic state is bound to experience changes in values. Or the amalgamation of many different ethnic groups into one nation-state inevitably changes the way that individuals view themselves: For example, state-sponsored retention of ethnic customs, as under Canada's multicultural policy of preserving ethnic communities, cannot mask the fact that most of those communities are merging into the larger Canadian society.

A final assumption of the cultural relativist view of human rights is that cultural practices are neutral in their impact on different individuals and groups. Yet very few social practices, whether cultural or otherwise, distribute the same benefits to each member of a group. In considering any cultural practice it is useful to ask, who benefits from its retention? Those who speak for the group are usually those most capable of articulating the group's values to the outside world. But such spokesmen are likely to stress, in their articulation of "group" values, those particular values that are most to their own advantage. Both those who choose to adopt "new" ideals, such as political democracy or atheism, and those who choose to retain "old" ideals, such as a God-fearing political consensus, may be doing so in their own interests. Culture is both influenced by, and an instrument of, conflict among individuals or social groups. Just as those who attempt to modify or change customs may have personal interests in so doing, so also do those who attempt to preserve them. Quite often, relativist arguments are adopted principally to protect the interests of those in power.

Thus the notion that human rights cannot be applied across cultures violates both the principle of human rights and its practice. Human rights mean precisely that: rights held by virtue of being human. Human rights do not mean human dignity, nor do they represent the sum of personal resources (material, moral, or spiritual) that an individual might hold. Cultural variances that do not violate basic human rights undoubtedly enrich the world. But to permit the interests of the powerful to masquerade behind spurious defenses of cultural relativity is merely to lessen the chance that the victims of their policies will be able to complain. In the modern world, concepts such as cultural relativity, which deny to individuals the moral right to make comparisons and to insist on universal standards of right and wrong, are happily adopted by those who control the state.

THIRD WORLD CRITICISMS

In recent years a number of commentators from the Third World have criticized the concept of universal human rights. Frequently, the intention of the criticisms appears to be to exempt some Third World governments from the standard of judgment generated by the concept of universal human rights. Much of the criticism in fact serves to cover abuses of human rights by state corporatist, developmental dictatorship, or allegedly "socialist" regimes.

A common criticism of the concept of universal human rights is that since it is Western in origin, it must be limited in its applicability to the Western world. Both logically and empirically, this criticism is invalid. Knowledge is not limited in its applicability to its place or people of origin—one does not assume, for example, that medicines discovered in the developed Western world will cure only people of European origin. Nor is it reasonable to state that knowledge or thought of a certain kind—about social arrangements instead of about human biology or natural science—is limited to its place of origin. Those same Third World critics who reject universal concepts of human rights often happily accept Marxist socialism, which also originated in the Western world, in the mind of a German Jew.

The fact that human rights is originally a liberal notion, rooted in the rise of a class of bourgeois citizens in Europe who demanded individual rights against the power of kings and nobility, does not make human rights inapplicable to the rest of the world. As we argue above, all over the world there are now formal states, whose citizens are increasingly individualized. All over the world, therefore, there are people who need protections against the depradations of class-ruled governments.

Moreover, whatever the liberal origins of human rights, the list now accepted as universal includes a wide range of economic and social rights that were first advocated by socialist and social-democratic critics of liberalism. Although eighteenth-century liberals stressed the right to private property, the 1966 International Human Rights Covenants do not mention it, substituting instead the right to sovereignty over national resources. . . . To attribute the idea of universal human rights to an outdated liberalism, unaffected by later notions of welfare democracy and uninfluenced by socialist concerns with economic rights, is simply incorrect.

The absence of a right to private property in the Covenants indicates a sensitivity to the legitimate preoccupations of socialist and postcolonial Third World governments. Conservative critics of recent trends in international human rights in fact deplore the right to national sovereignty over resources, as some of them also deplore any attention to the economic rights of the individual. We certainly do not share this view of rights; we believe that the economic rights of the individual are as important as civil and political rights. But it is the individual we are concerned with. We would like to see a world in which *every individual* has enough to eat, not merely a world in which every *state* has the right to economic sovereignty.

We are skeptical, therefore, of the radical Third Worldist assertion that "group" rights ought to be more important than individual rights. Too often, the "group" in question proves to be the state. Why allocate rights to a social institution that is already the chief violator of individuals' rights? Similarly, we fear the expression "peoples' rights." The communal rights of individuals to practice their own religion, speak their own language, and indulge in their own ancestral customs are protected in the Covenant on Civil and Political Rights. Individuals are free to come together in groups to engage in those cultural practices which are meaningful to them. On the other hand, often a "group" right can simply mean that the individual is subordinate to the group—for example, that the individual Christian fundamentalist in the Soviet Union risks arrest because of the desire of the larger "group" to enforce official atheism.

The one compelling use that we can envisage for the term "group rights" is in protection of native peoples, usually hunter-gatherers, pastoralists, or subsistence agriculturalists, whose property rights as collectivities are being violated by the larger state societies that encroach upon them. Such groups are fighting a battle against the forces of modernization and the state's accumulative tendencies. For example, native peoples in Canada began in the 1970s to object to state development projects, such as the James Bay Hydroelectric project in Quebec, which deprived them of their traditional lands. At the moment, there is no international human rights protection for such groups or their "way of life."

One way to protect such group rights would be to incorporate the group as a legal entity in order to preserve their land claims. However, even if the law protects such group rights, individual members of the group may prefer to move into the larger society in response to the processes of modernization discussed above. Both opinions must be protected.

If the purpose of group rights is to protect large, established groups of people who share the same territory, customs, language, religion, and ancestry, then such protection could only occur at the expense of states' rights. These groups, under international human rights law, do not have the right to withdraw from the states that enfold them. Moreover, it is clearly not the intention of Third World defenders of group rights to allow such a right to secession. A first principle of the Organization of African Unity, for example, is to preserve the sovereignty of all its member states not only against outside attack but also against internal attempts at secession. Group rights appear to mean, in practice, states' rights. But the rights of states are the rights of the individuals and classes who control the state.

Many Third World and socialist regimes also argue that rights ought to be tied to duties. A citizen's rights, it is argued, ought to be contingent upon his duties toward the society at large—privilege is contingent on responsibility. Such a view of rights made sense in nonstate societies in which each "person" fulfilled his roles along with others, all of the roles together creating a close-knit, tradition-bound group. But in modern state societies, to tie rights to duties is to risk the former's complete disappearance. All duties will be aimed toward the preservation of the state and of the interests of those who control it.

It is true that no human rights are absolute; even in societies that adhere in principle to the liberal ethos, individuals are frequently deprived of rights, especially in wartime or if they are convicted of criminal acts. However, such deprivations can legitimately be made only after the most scrupulous protection of civil and political rights under the rule of law. The difficulty with tying rights to duties without the intermediate step of scrutiny by a genuinely independent judiciary is the likelihood of wholesale cancellation of rights by the ruling class. But if one has rights merely because one is human, and for no other reason, then it is much more difficult, in principle, for the state to cancel them. It cannot legitimate the denial of rights by saying that only certain types of human beings, exhibiting certain kinds of behavior, are entitled to them.

One final criticism of the view of universal human rights embedded in the International Covenants is that an undue stress is laid on civil and political rights, whereas the overriding rights priority in the Third World is economic rights. In this view, the state as the agent of economic development—and hence, presumably, of eventual distribution of economic goods or "rights" to the masses—should not be bothered with problems of guaranteeing political participation in decision making, or of protecting people's basic civil rights. These rights, it is argued, come "after" development is completed. The empirical basis for this argument is weak. . . . Economic development per se will not guarantee future human rights, whether of an economic or any other kind. Often, development means economic growth, but without equitable distributive measures. Moreover, development strategies often fail because of insufficient attention to citizens' needs and views. Finally, development plans are often a cover for the continued violations of citizens' rights by the ruling class.

Thus we return to where we started: the rights of all men and women against all governments to treatment as free, equal, materially and physically secure persons. This is what human dignity means and requires in our era. And the individual human rights of the Universal Declaration and the Covenants are the means by which individuals today carry out the struggle to achieve their dignity. . . .

NOTES

1. The International Bill of Human Rights includes the Universal Declaration of Human Rights (1948; reprinted below as appendix 1), the International Covenant on Economic, Social and Cultural Rights (1966), the International Covenant on Civil and Political Rights (1966), and the Optional Protocol to the latter Covenant.

2. Ronald Dworkin, *Taking Rights Seriously* (Cambridge: Harvard University Press, 1977), pp. xi, 90.

3. Thomas Aquinas, *The Political Ideas of St. Thomas Aquinas*, ed. Dino Bigongiari (New York: Hafner Press, 1953).

4. John Locke, *Essays on the Law of Nature* (Oxford: Clarendon Press, 1954); *Two Treatises of Government* (Cambridge: Cambridge University Press, 1967), *Second Treatise*, para. 6, 12, 16, 57, 59, 60, 118, 124, 135, 172.

5. Jacques Maritain, *The Rights of Man and Natural Law* (New York: Charles Scribner's Sons, 1947); *Man and the State* (Chicago: University of Chicago Press, 1951).

6. Thomas Hobbes, *Leviathan* (Baltimore: Penguin Books, 1971).

7. Locke, *Second Treatise*.

8. Thomas Jefferson, *The Life and Selected Writings of Thomas Jefferson*, ed. Adrienne Koch and William Peden (New York: Modern Library, 1944); Thomas Paine, *Rights of Man* (New York: Penguin Books, 1984).

9. See Jack Donnelly, "Natural Law and Right in Aquinas' Political Thought," *Western Political Quarterly* 33 (December 1980); 520–35.

10. Rhoda E. Howard and Jack Donnelly, "Human Dignity, Human Rights and Political Regimes," *American Political Science Review* 80 (September 1986); 51–63; Jack Donnelly, "Human Rights and Human Dignity: An Analytic Critique of Non-Western Human Rights Conceptions," *American Political Science Review* 76 (June 1982); 303–16; Rhoda E. Howard, *Human Rights in Commonwealth Africa* (Totowa, N.J.: Rowman and Littlefield, 1986), chap. 2.

11. See Jack Donnelly, *The Concept of Human Rights* (London: Croom Helm; New York: St. Martin's, 1985), chap. 3 and the sources cited therein.

12. See, for example, Marc F. Plattner, ed., *Human Rights in Our Time: Essays in Memory of Victor Baras* (Boulder, Col.: Westview Press, 1984); Maurice Cranston, "Are There Any Human Rights?" *Daedalus* 112 (Fall 1983); 1–17; Jeane J. Kirkpatrick, "Establishing a Viable Human Rights Policy," in *Human Rights and U.S. Human Rights Policy*, Howard J. Wiarda, ed. (Washington, D.C.: American Enterprise Institute, 1982).

13. See, for example, H. Klenner, "Freedom and Human Rights," *GDR Committee for Human Rights Bulletin* 10, no. 1 (1984); 13–21; A. G. Egorov, "Socialism and the Individual: Rights and Freedoms," *Soviet Studies in Philosophy* 18 (Fall 1979); 3–51; and UN document number A/C.3/32/SR.51.

14. This section is a very much abbreviated version of Jack Donnelly, "International Human Rights: A Regime Analysis," *International Organization* 40 (Summer 1986); 599–642.

15. See Farrokh Jhabvala, "The Practice of the Covenant's Human Rights Committee, 1976–82; Review of State Party Reports," *Human Rights Quarterly* 6 (February 1984); 81–106; Dana D. Fischer, "Reporting under the Covenant on Civil and Political Rights: The First Five Years of the Human Rights Committee," *American Journal of International Law* 76 (January 1982); 142–53; and Donnelly "International Human Rights," pp. 609–11.

16. See Donnelly, "International Human Rights," pp. 628–33 and the works cited there.

17. Howard Tolley, "The Concealed Crack in the Citadel: The United Nations Commission on Human Rights' Response to Confidential Communications," *Human Rights Quarterly* 6 (November 1984); 420–62.

18. See Donnelly, "International Human Rights," pp. 620–28 and the works cited there.

19. This section draws heavily on Jack Donnelly, "Human Rights and Foreign Policy," *World Politics* 34 (July 1982); 574–95, and "Human Rights, Humanitarian Intervention and American Foreign Policy: Law, Morality and Politics," *Journal of International Affairs* 37 (Winter 1984); 311–28.

20. See, for example, Jerome Slater and Terry Nardin, "Nonintervention and Human Rights," *Journal of Politics* 48 (February 1986); 86–96; Charles R. Beitz, "Nonintervention and Communal Integrity," *Philosophy and Public Affairs* 9 (Summer 1980); 385–91; and Robert Matthews and Cranford Pratt, "Human Rights and Foreign Policy: Principles and Canadian Practice," *Human Rights Quarterly* 7 (May 1985); 159–88.

21. Michael Walzer, *Just and Unjust Wars* (New York: Basic Books, 1977), p. 90. For criticisms of Walzer see Slater and Nardin, "Nonintervention;" Beitz, "Nonintervention"; and David Luban, "The Romance of the Nation State," *Philosophy and Public Affairs* 9 (Summer 1980); 392–97.

22. Adamantia Pollis and Peter Schwab, "Human Rights: A Western Concept with Limited Applicability," in *Human Rights: Cultural and Ideological Perspectives* Pollis and Schwab, ed. (New York: Praeger, 1979), pp. 1–18.

Protecting the Global Environment

Managing the Global Commons

Per Magnus Wijkman

Our planet contains some natural resources over which no single nation has a generally recognized exclusive jurisdiction. Familiar examples are the resources of the continental margin and the deep seabed, the water column beyond territorial seas, celestial bodies and orbits in outer space, the electromagnetic frequency spectrum, and the Antarctic. Less familiar but ultimately more important resources are the planet's ozone layer and carbon dioxide balance.

These resources have long been a global commons, free of national or international regulations. With growing world population and improving technology, however, the absence of exclusive property rights and well-defined management rights is leading inevitably to economic inefficiency and to international contention. Garrett Hardin's "tragedy of the commons" is enacted through depletion of fishing stocks and the ozone layer, congestion of orbital slots by satellites, and overheating of the atmosphere.[1] Once theoretical possibilities, these are now acute problems.

Increasing awareness of the need to manage the global commons has led to attempts to redefine property rights. The effect of these ongoing negotiations within and without the United Nations Organization has been to award some resources to the international community and others to nation states.[2]

This development evokes several major questions. Will national jurisdiction over resources that traditionally have been open to all increase or decrease the efficiency of exploitation? How will extension of national jurisdiction over previously shared resources redistribute income between countries? Should national or international organizations manage these resources?[3]

This article considers these fundamental policy issues. Section I considers why firms or individuals may prefer communal ownership to private ownership, while Section II considers why governments may favor internationally shared jurisdiction over national jurisdiction. In both cases, joint ownership or management confers economic benefits at the price of some elements of sovereignty; and the more extensive are the joint management powers involved, the greater the costs in terms of abrogated sovereignty. Section III outlines an international organization for efficiently managing a common resource (assuming that the parties can agree on the distribution of its benefits). Section IV considers some current proposals for managing internationally shared resources and illustrates the practical problems involved in achieving agreement. It assesses whether the proposed regimes are efficient and pays particular attention to how the new entitlements will redistribute income between countries.

I. WHY COMMONS EXIST

A commons is a resource to which no single decision-making unit holds exclusive title. This can mean that it is owned by no one (*res nullius*) or by everyone (*res communis*). This seems an anomaly in a world of private property and national jurisdiction. Why does it persist?

Traditionally, access to a commons has been free for all, and any individual could exploit the resource independently of others. As long as the resource is plentiful, users are unlikely to interfere with each other. However, when it becomes scarce, uncontrolled access results in congestion and overuse. Access must be limited in some way to prevent use by one from inflicting costs on another. One possibility is to subdivide the resource and award each commoner private property rights to some part of it, leaving to each new owner the decision on how to use his own share. I shall call this procedure "enclosing the commons," in reference to the most famous historical example—enclosure of the village commons.[4]

While private ownership and national appropriation have been usual historically, dissolution of the commons is not the inevitable outcome. Another possibility is for the users or other interested parties to form an organization to manage the resource jointly. Which form of management and ownership is more efficient depends on the relative costs and benefits of extending property rights in each particular case.[5]

If exclusive ownership reduces interference, enclosure should both result in more efficient use and conserve the resource. If these benefits exceed the costs of negotiating, transacting, and policing enclosure, subdivision should be socially profitable. However, these costs are not always included though they are often considerable. In the past, some users excluded others without compensation and some existing users forcibly prevented new entry.[6] Uncompensated appropriation has been frequent historically, and even the Third United Nations Conference on the Law of the Sea (UNCLOS III) does not require coastal states to pay when they extend their resource jurisdiction seaward. Excessive claims result when possibly valuable resources can be obtained for free.

Enclosure will come about through market forces if actual or potential users can buy out others and still be better off. Assume, for instance, that the commons is appropriated by giving all commoners transferable rights to use the resource. Voluntary market transactions may, as a first step, consolidate user rights in the hands of a limited number of users. As a second step, these owners may agree to divide the commons into private lots of sizes proportional to their user rights if the economic benefits of enclosure exceed its costs. Voluntary, informed market transactions will provide the optimal amount of enclosure. Such transactions have the additional advantage that those who give up user rights are adequately compensated by those who gain property rights. Enclosure through markets is a Pareto-sanctioned change; that is, society as a whole benefits from the introduction of private property rights and no single member is worse off as a result.

Unfortunately, the legal nature of communally owned resources usually precludes the existence of marketable user rights. Enclosure must be accomplished by means other than market forces. Unless legislative measures determine whether enclosure occurs, might becomes right and possession becomes nine-tenths of the law. The English enclosure movement provides notable examples during the last half of the nineteenth century of legislative measures designed to ensure that those who lost rights through enclosure were compensated by those who gained.

While a failure to pay adequate compensation stimulates private or state appropriation of the commons, three other factors work to maintain communal ownership: high risks associated with subdividing resources of uncertain value, high costs of defining and policing private property rights or enforcing national jurisdiction, and significant external economies in production. By contrast, prime candidates for enclosure are those resources that are easily subdivided, have a definite value, and lack external economies.

When the value of the resource being divided is uncertain, an individual nation risks obtaining a worthless share. This risk is especially great when the resource consists of heterogeneous parts about which a governments lacks information. It must invest resources in finding out which fishing grounds are richer than others, which orbital slots are more useful than others, or which nodule fields are cheaper to mine than others. Already complex political negotiations to divide a resource become even more difficult to resolve when the value of the resource is also at issue. The key element in these negotiations is determining appropriate compensation upon enclosure. Two basic issues are involved—how to divide the resource and distribute its parts between the new owners, and how to compensate those who lose historical rights. These issues require assessing the value of respective user rights in order to determine how much a user either should pay to acquire property rights or should receive to part with user rights. Of course, a decision *not* to compensate is a possible outcome of negotiations: Only some commoners may receive property rights, those who do may receive their deeds gratis, and losers of historical rights may not be compensated.

Subdividing and distributing in parts of a largely unexplored resource more closely resembles a lottery than a deliberate distribution of wealth. A government averse to risk may prefer to own a share in the whole asset rather than to subdivide an asset the value of whose parts is uncertain, especially if the administrative costs of communal ownership are small. This preference saves both the prospecting cost necessary to reduce risk and the cost of negotiating a subdivision of the commons.

In addition, private ownership of the parts of a commons may be impractical or undesirable when property rights to parts of the resource cannot be economically enforced (the resource is not divisible); when the size of the resource is unknown; and when exploitation of the resource involves external economies. Resources possessing these characteristics are sometimes called common property resources.[7] Considerations of economic efficiency caution against enclosing such common property resources and argue for communal ownership and joint management. Consider some examples of this important group of resources.

Many oil or water pools and fishing stocks are shared by several owners or are under the jurisdiction of several nations. Enclosing part of an oil or water pool . . . or a fishing ground . . . common to several parties may be prohibitively expensive. Fluid flows among sections of the pool indiscriminately; fishing stocks migrate among different areas of the shared habitat in the course of their life cycles.

When a habitat cannot be enclosed at reasonable cost, it is necessary to enforce property rights to the individual animals. Sometimes this is feasible; large animals with a tendency to move in herds (such as reindeer, cattle, and goats) can be rounded up, caught, and marked at little cost relative to their value. If property rights can be enforced in the face of poaching and rustling, the animals can graze on the common habitat. In other cases, as with most fish and fowl, the costs of acquiring and enforcing property rights to individual animals are too high.[8] Even such large animals as whales are prohibitively expensive to mark. In these cases, the animals themselves are a common property resource.

An important consequence for public resource policy follows from failure to define and enforce property rights. When several owners have overlapping rights to a resource, it is rational for each to attempt to exploit the resource before the others. Such competition depletes stocks, and fisheries provide many familiar examples of this process. To maintain the resource, whether grazing ground or herd, at an optimal level, the user rights of commoners must be restricted. Restriction can take the form of a voluntary agreement by the joint owners to exclude new entrants and to limit their own use of the resource. This requires a unanimous decision by all the parties that claim user rights to the resource.

When the precise size of the resource is unknown, harvesting quotas may be difficult to establish.[9] Often the parties sharing a resource cannot agree upon its size due, perhaps, to insufficient prospecting or to imperfect prospecting techniques. For instance, the sampling necessary to estimate the size of fishing stocks is so extensive that an estimate with a normal margin of error is prohibitively expensive to obtain. Thus, policy makers are usually uncertain about the size of individual fish stocks.

Resource size may be uncertain also because it is determined by available production technology and by relative factor and commodity prices; as these change, so does the size of the resource. For instance, the amount of "recoverable oil" in a well depends among other considerations on the price of oil. Similarly, the number of telecommunications that the electromagnetic spectrum can accommodate depends on production technology and on the amount of capital invested in sending and receiving equipment. The size of many important natural resources is thus inherently uncertain because it depends on changing economic and technological factors. Finally, even if the size of the resource can be known accurately, owners may have different views on what size is optimal to maintain because they employ different interest rates to discount future benefits. In theory, the parties can achieve a mutually beneficial solution in these cases if capital movements are free or if side-payments are allowed.[10] But in practice this is not always possible.

Even if the owners could agree both on the actual and on the desired size of the resource, and on each other's share of the harvest, the occurrence of external economies creates problems when each exploits his own share of the resource independently of the others.[11] While the parts of a resource might be legally separated, they are then joined through production effects and can be exploited separately only at extra cost. Assume that a firm from country A is the first to drill an oil or artesian well . . . or to fish the grounds. . . . This exploitation lowers the pressure in the common pool or thins the common fishing stock and raises costs for a firm from country B that arrives later to pump from the pool or to catch fish. The prospect of lower exploitation costs prompts each co-owner of a shared resource to extract his share of the resource first. In this way, external economies lead to an overly rapid rate of harvesting. To prevent this, production quotas must be expressed as a flow (units per time period) rather than as a share of the resource stock.

In summary, the crucial characteristic of common property resources is that property rights to parts of the resource cannot be economically defined and enforced. Additional complications in sharing the resource arise when the size of the resource is unknown and its exploitation involves significant external economies. In such a situation the many small firms of the perfectly competitive model fail to exploit the resource efficiently. Each firm lacks incentives to limit its harvest and strives instead to exploit the resource before its competitors do, thereby harvesting more and faster than is socially efficient. Not only is the resource depleted, but too much capital and labor are employed in the industry. Rational pursuit of private profit by firms is therefore wasteful of capital, labor, and natural resources alike.

II. COOPERATIVE OR COERCIVE MANAGEMENT

Some form of regulation is necessary to realize fully the economic benefits from exploiting common property resources. I shall discuss first the problems of regulation when the participating parties agree to maximize pecuniary benefits and agree on their distribution. The main issue in this case is whether management can be based on voluntary cooperation or requires some coercive power. Thereafter, I shall discuss some of the problems that arise when countries include nonpecuniary or political benefits among their objectives, which makes agreement more difficult.

Regulation can be organized either by the private interests involved in exploiting the resource or by a public authority endowed with coercive powers. Sometimes private interests find it profitable to regulate use of the resource themselves on a voluntary basis. This is likely to occur if only a few owners have overlapping rights to the resource. For instance, if two firms of roughly equal size share the resource . . . and neither can be certain of being the first to exploit it, an awareness of the external economies could influence them to coordinate their exploitation. They could set up a joint venture (i.e., drilling one oil well) if each believes that its share of the larger joint profits available through coordinated effort will exceed what it would get through individual, uncoordinated exploitation (i.e., drilling two independent oil wells). Joint ventures are a way to internalize externalities and to approximate the efficiency of sole ownership.

When firms are few and of equal size, and have similar perceptions of the future, each may find it advantageous to coordinate use of the commons. Thus, voluntary regulation may achieve efficient use.[12]

When many firms exploit the resource . . . and interfere with one another's activities, public regulation is necessary. The task of the manager is to restrict the commoners' rights of access and to coordinate exploitation in order to minimize externalities. The selection of appropriate regulatory tools is a complex issue, not treated here. The basic choices are regulating by means of quotas, by taxes and subsidies, or by a system of liability rules enforced through the courts.

The difficult problems of public regulation are compounded when the common property resource is internationally shared and several governments are involved. A key question is whether these governments will voluntarily cooperate in managing the resource. Failing cooperation, efficient regulation requires use of coercive powers, that is, creation of a management authority with the power to impose its decisions on any uncooperative co-owner of the resource. Few examples of this exist in fact, and in this section I suggest why this is so.

The prospects for voluntary joint management depend critically on how many governments share the resource. If two governments share it equally . . . both may perceive the interdependence of their national harvests. Each government therefore has an incentive to agree to control the rate and the amount of exploitation of the shared resource by its own nationals. It will do this only if it can rely on the other government's willingness and ability to enforce its part of the agreement.[13]

The greater the number of nations sharing resource jurisdiction, the less likely it is that voluntary agreements between governments to manage the resource will work. Each government is a potential free rider on any management regime; each is tempted clandestinely to ignore the system of production controls that it espouses publicly. This occurs when the individual government retains all the benefits of cheating but bears only a small fraction of the costs.[14]

Voluntary agreements among many governments quickly break down—they contain strong incentives to cheat and they lack effective enforcement mechanisms. The history of international fisheries commissions is replete with examples of ineffectual voluntary agreements to limit harvest of the stocks, the best known, perhaps, being the Northeast Atlantic Fisheries Commission. When many governments share a resource, the management authority must be given power to determine harvesting limitations unilaterally and to enforce the observance of national quotas allocated within this general limit. Management of the commons requires, in Garrett Hardin's words, a "system of mutual coercion mutually agreed upon."

Most governments are reluctant on principle to surrender sovereignty even in minor issues. Substantive factors contribute to this reluctance. Sovereignty allows a government greater freedom in formulating its policy goals and a greater choice of instruments with which to pursue these goals. The more a government's goals differ from those of others, the greater the perceived cost of surrendering sovereignty. For instance, a government may want its nationals to participate in production not solely to generate profits but also to ensure security of supply of strategic commodities, to maintain employment in a particular occupation or region, or to increase national prestige. Several governments view deep seabed mining as important for each of these different reasons. No standard exists by which to measure the value of one unit of nonpecuniary benefit: the value of a given level of self-sufficiency or of employment maintenance can only be determined by the government concerned, and it will differ from government to government. Consequently, the distribution of nonpecuniary benefits by an international bureaucracy is inherently arbitrary. If these values are important to a country, it will preserve its freedom to pursue them and will be reluctant to depend on other nations' decisions. This complicates the management of common property resources, since countries have noncomparable objectives.

In summary, economically efficient exploitation of global common property resources requires restrictions on national sovereignty. Governments must abide by decisions made by a supranational authority and accept supranational enforcement of these decisions. The "tragedy of the commons" occurs on the international level because governments are either unable to design appropriate international authorities or unwilling to accept the consequent "stinting" of their national sovereign rights. The basic reason for this reluctance is the absence of a sufficient community of interest among the participating governments. A government that holds minority opinions is unlikely to surrender power to an authority where it may be outvoted consistently, even if this refusal entails an economic loss.

III. A MANAGEMENT PARADIGM

Section I gave some reasons why internationally shared resources may remain under communal ownership and shared jurisdiction in spite of the historical trend to private ownership and national jurisdiction. Defining and enforcing property rights may make subdivision unreasonably expensive; if subdivision is possible, it may reduce efficiency because individual owners cannot exploit their parts independently of each other, or it may increase their risk because of the uncertain value of the parts they receive. Finally, like heirs to an estate, the commoners simply may fail to agree on how to divide the inheritance and none may be inclined to appropriate it unilaterally. When a scarce resource is maintained as a commons for any of the above reasons, open access will result in inefficient use. Section II considered the conditions under which voluntary cooperation between governments was unlikely to occur. When many governments are involved, efficient management requires the creation of a supranational authority. A government will surrender jurisdiction only if it feels it has sufficient common interests with other governments. Inevitably, some governments will not feel that this is the case.

This section presents a paradigm of an international management institution in order to illustrate clearly the different interests involved. Any management regime for common property resources discharges three primary functions. First, it assesses the harvesting or carrying capacity of the commons and determines an annual quota to be harvested. Second, it allocates rights to participate in harvesting this quota. Third, it distributes the benefits derived from exploiting the resource among its co-owners. A condominium designed to exercise separately each of these functions of allocation, distribution, and scientific assessment provides a useful comparison norm when analyzing management problems.[15] I shall use it to distinguish reconcilable from irreconcilable conflicts of interest between parties.

Allocation of User Rights

Deciding who gets to use a scarce common resource is a controversial issue when valuable rights are given away for free. Nonmarket method of allocating rights of access to a resource are inherently discretionary and inevitably arbitrary. An alternative is the market method, whereby the right of access is sold on an open market. For instance, leases to drill on the continental shelf or to log public forest lands in the United States are commonly sold at public auctions. The first task of the condominium is to auction user rights to the resource.

Competitive bidding ensures that the most efficient firms obtain harvesting rights, since normally they outbid less efficient firms. In the absence of monopoly power this minimizes production costs, which benefits consumers, and maximizes rents from the commons, which benefits its owners. A user fee that reflects the scarcity value of the natural resource provides users with the information they need to produce commodities with the least possible expenditure of real resources. Resources are thereby put to the best possible use.[16]

Nonmarket methods mean that an institution other than the market assigns access rights according to some criterion other than the users' willingness to pay. Bureaucratic allocation normally results in less efficient production, since it allows less efficient firms to produce. Discrimination on the grounds of equity rather than of efficiency has been claimed to be justified when granting access to common property resource. Each co-owner, it is claimed, should have "equal" use of the resource. However, this is the case only if economic institutions are imperfect. An efficient allocation results in greater pecuniary benefits and is therefore preferable if social institutions (tax and transfer systems) exist to redistribute those benefits in a generally acceptable manner.

As noted previously, access to a common property resource may provide a government with nonpecuniary benefits. However, this is not an argument for nonmarket methods of allocating user rights—on the contrary. By their nature, nonpecuniary benefits are distributed imperfectly by bureaucracies. Market methods of allocation allow a government that values nonpecuniary benefits highly to reflect its evaluation in a premium on its bid for user rights. Ironically, market methods achieve the most efficient allocation of nonpecuniary benefits. Also, it is just as illogical from a distributional viewpoint for the international community to provide nonpecuniary benefits to a government free of charge as it is for it to provide pecuniary benefits gratis.

The distribution of pecuniary benefits, not the allocation of user rights, is therefore the key to achieving equity.

Distribution of Pecuniary Benefits

A commons generates three forms of pecuniary benefits. Rents from the natural resource normally accrue to its owner; producers' surplus accrues to the firms that use the resource as an input to produce commodities; and, finally, consumers' surplus is enjoyed by those who consume these commodities or their close substitutes. Residents of a country benefit from increased exploitation of a communally owned resource to the extent that they can claim some of the resource rents, and consume or produce commodities (or close substitutes) that use the resource as an input. For instance, low-cost seabed production of nickel lowers its price, benefits consumers, and harms landbased producers, in addition to providing benefits in the form of seabed rents.

The second task of the condominium is to accommodate the conflicting interests of nations as consumers, producers, and *rentiers* by providing a mechanism to distribute rents and to transfer income from consumers to existing producers. I shall treat these functions separately for clarity.

Rents can be distributed by awarding nations shares in the condominium, shares that entitle them to a portion of the revenues generated by auctioning user rights to the highest bidder. The initial distribution of shares between nations must reflect a consensus about the appropriate distribution of rents from the commons. On this political question opinions will inevitably differ; the following factors are bound to enter into the decision. First, it is necessary to identify those who are entitled to claim an ownership interest in the commons. Is a resource the property of a few states, or is it the common heritage of mankind? If the latter, what representative of mankind is the appropriate recipient of shares in the condominium? Shares could be distributed to individuals themselves, to national governments as representatives of individuals, or to the United Nations and its agencies as representatives of national governments.[17]

There is clearly a trade-off between the degree of representativeness of a given distribution and the transaction costs it entails. The most representative alternative—distributing rents directly to each individual—involves high transaction costs. Letting the United Nations Organization receive the rents involves the lowest transaction costs but is less representative. An intermediate solution is to distribute the shares in the condominium to national governments. They could be distributed in proportion to the population subject to each national government, on the assumption that each person has an equal claim on rents from the commons. But there is no *objective* basis for determining the best distribution. The explicit determination of national interests in a commons is probably the most emotionally loaded aspect of management.

Since countries consume and produce in different proportions those commodities that use the communally owned resource as an input, exploitation of the commons will change consumer and producer surplus for most countries. This redistribution of benefits can so be large that the losers demand compensation before they will permit exploitation of the commons (if this is in their power). For instance, the government of a land-based producer of copper and nickel can expect to lose significant amounts of producer surplus and tax revenues when seabed mining starts; a net consuming country will gain a substantial consumer surplus. The condominium may therefore have to set up a compensation fund to effect lump-sum transfers from consumer to producer nations. Ideally, governments of net consumer countries would annually pay into this fund an amount reflecting their gain of consumer surplus, while governments of traditional net producer countries would receive corresponding payments from the fund. These payments and disbursements should be assessed separately from the determination of the international distribution of rents for two reasons. First, national consumption and production patterns change more rapidly than population, requiring more frequent reassessments of compensation payments than of rents. Second, the distribution of rents is a permanent phenomenon while it can be argued that compensation payments should be transitory.

The distribution of shares in the condominium and the establishment of a compensation fund would inevitably be subject to intense controversy. This is desirable, because it would force an explicit discussion of the distribution of benefits and would separate decisions about who gets the rents from decisions about who gets to exploit the resource. This is a major advantage of the proposed condominium: In sum, rents are distributed at the conference table and user rights are allocated in the marketplace. The resource can therefore be managed efficiently while demands for equity can be satisfied through political compromise. The cost of failing to strike a compromise can be measured as the reduced efficiency in exploiting the commons. This cost is likely to materialize when government views on equity consist of mutually inconsistent claims for absolute levels of income or shares in decision-making powers.

Determination of Harvesting Capacity

Decentralized decision making by private firms or individuals who possess perfect information and well-defined property rights, and act on competitive markets, results in efficient allocation of resources among competing present and future uses. This well-known and attractive property of competitive markets is lost in the case of common property resources. Market imperfections caused by external economies and by the absence of effective property rights must be corrected by a central decision maker.

The third task of the condominium, therefore, is to determine the optimal rate at which the resource should be harvested and to ensure that this rate is not exceeded. This is normally a very complex task since the optimal harvesting rate must be determined in spite of imperfect knowledge of the state of the resource, changing costs of production, and difficult time preferences of consumer nations. In addition, the condominium must have the authority and the resources to enforce observance of its rulings. Ideally the scientific council would be independent of national producer and consumer interests. This might be achieved if council members were to be nominated by national academies of science and voted for by governments with votes proportionate to their share in resource rents. This might encourage a decision-making structure that maximizes rents. However, achieving such an institution encounters problems familiar from the theory of regulation and public choice.[18] I shall not deal with this complex issue here.

International resource commissions have seldom been empowered to exercise all three of the above functions. A classic exception is the Interim Convention on the Conservation of North Pacific Fur Seals of 1957, which the U.S. Senate is currently considering extending. The fur seal breeds on North Pacific islands under the sovereignty of the Soviet Union and of the United States, in particular the Pribilof Islands. In the nineteenth century, hunters from these two countries and Japan and Canada caught seals as common property on the high seas and depleted the herd. The 1957 Convention, like its predecessor of 1912, bans open-sea hunting. A North Pacific Fur Seal Commission coordinates research to determine the maximum sustainable yield. Hunting is limited to the breeding islands, where the agreed-upon quota is caught by local hunters employed by Soviet and U.S. government agencies. Profits from the commercial sale of pelts are shared with Japan and Canada, whose citizens must abstain from their traditional high-seas hunting. The Pribilof Treaty contains on a small scale the elements of an efficient management regime for a common property resource: an efficient allocation and enforcement of harvesting rights, an acceptable distribution of the resource rents among the interested parties, and a scientifically determined harvesting quota. The question is whether such a management regime can be duplicated when more countries are involved. . . .

IV. CURRENT MANAGEMENT PROPOSALS

Technical progress has opened previously inaccessible resources for exploitation. As the exploitation of marginal resources becomes worthwhile, prime resources generate more rents. Distrustful of international organizations, nations strive to enclose the resources and to appropriate the rents. The common heritage is thus transformed into national inheritances.

Whether national enclosure is more efficient than managing these resources through a supranational resource regime, and whether it is as fair, must be judged from case to case. It depends on the answers to three questions. First, does the resource possess such common property characteristics that coordination of use provides benefits sufficiently large to offset the management costs? Second, can the voluntary cooperation of co-owners achieve coordinated use more cheaply than a centralized decision-making authority? Third, how do awards of new property rights and the loss of historical rights affect the distribution of wealth? . . .

Fisheries and Antarctic living resources fall in the category of resources that are costly to subdivide. The amount harvested must be limited and harvesting rights allocated. The difficulties of the distributional issue are compounded by efficiency considerations. The resources of the deep seabed and the continental margin constitute a commons that can be partitioned, and its parts individually exploited, without much extra cost. Subdivision poses mainly a question of equity, and the primary function of an international authority should be to negotiate an acceptable initial distribution of private property rights. . . .

Fishing Stocks

Fishing stocks are a classic example of a common property resource. Early in the Third United Nations Conference on the Law of the Sea delegates agreed on the principle of an exclusive economic zone (EEZ), whereby each coastal state would be granted exclusive management and fishing rights within two hundred nautical miles of its coastline. In most cases, this broader includes the continental shelf, in whose shallow waters are located the richest fishing grounds. The world's annual fish catch was worth close to $20 billion in the late seventies, and virtually all of this is caught in the proposed EEZs. Thus, UNCLOS III proposes in effect that eighty coastal states enclose the world's major fishing grounds.[19]

For the purpose of conserving fishing stocks, two hundred-mile EEZs are superior to the current regime of nonexistent or voluntary management, but they probably are inferior to a supranational management regime. National management will result in efficient management of stocks only if the extension of fishing limits brings the fishing stock, and sometimes also the fish it preys upon and those that prey upon it, entirely within the coastal state's jurisdiction. The key question therefore is how often this occurs. Many stocks that migrate along coasts remain transboundary resources even after the outward extension of fishing limits. In Africa, where coastlines tend to be short, fishing stocks pass through the waters of several countries in their seasonal or life-cycle migrations. The waters of both Chile and Peru contain the Pacific anchovy stock; the North Sea remains a common fishing ground for five European countries. Georges Bank is shared by Canada and the United States, even with limits of two hundred nautical miles. With some exceptions—Icelandic cod is notable— major fishing stocks will remain common property resources, though common now to fewer states than before.

The fewer the states, the more willing each government will be to limit the catch in its EEZ and to rely on other governments' promises to do likewise. Will this extension of fishing limits reduce the number of co-owners of fishing stocks sufficiently to induce effective voluntary cooperation? The answer to this requires a detailed study stock by stock, but no such studies were made prior to UNCLOS III. Thus, its Draft Convention proposes dispensing management rights to coastal states without any assurances that management will be effective.

In addition to imperfectly managing stocks, government will be tempted to follow protectionist policies. The political difficulties encountered by a government that attempts to introduce effective management programs should not be underestimated. Programs to control harvesting are unpopular with fishermen, who are extended fishing limits as a means to protect domestic fishermen rather than fishing stocks. The Draft Convention produced by UNCLOS III condones protectionist use of extended fishing limits. It does not require that entry to fishing grounds by controlled in a nondiscriminatory way, for example by requiring domestic and foreign fishermen to pay the same price for fishing licenses. In many of the eighty countries that now claim two hundred nautical mile fishing limits, domestic fishermen have replaced foreign fishermen and domestic political opposition has postponed the introduction of effective controls on total catch. The effect of protectionist policies is to reduce the efficiency of the world's fishing fleet by forcing parts of it to move to new waters and to convert to new types of fishing.

The Draft Convention proposals would also have significant income redistribution effects. The creation of EEZs permits the coastal state to appropriate all the rents from fishing grounds should it wish to.[20] These rents have been estimated to be at least $2 billion annually. Compared with the existing situation, this would redistribute income from nations with long-distance fishing fleets to states with long coasts bordering on rich fishing grounds. Since the richest fishing grounds, like the richest countries, are located in the temperate zones, the benefit go mainly to developed coastal states. One may debate the fairness of this redistribution, but one cannot deny either that it fails to compensate those who lose historical fishing rights or that it favors rich countries more than poor countries.

Hydrocarbon Resources and Manganese Nodules

The continental margin and the deep seabed traditionally have been international commons under the doctrine of the freedom of the high seas. However, since the Truman proclamation in 1945 an increasing number of coastal states have extended their resource jurisdiction over the adjoining continental shelf. UNCLOS III proposes to place the resources of the continental margin and those of the deep seabed under separate regimes. It would confirm the coastal states' jurisdiction over most of the continental margin while placing the remaining area of the seabed under an International Seabed Authority. Do the resource characteristics of these areas justify these different assignments?

The main resources of the deep seabed are currently believed to be manganese nodules, containing most notably manganese, nickel, cobalt, and copper. Deep-seabed mining holds out the prospect of commercial success, especially for prime mine sites in the Pacific. In the absence of limits on production the seabed might provide the major part of world consumption of these minerals in twenty or thirty years.

Hydrocarbons are the main resource of the continental margin. Currently, offshore oil and gas come entirely from the continental shelf (e.g., from the North Sea and the Gulf of Mexico); large areas remain to be exploited—Georges Bank, the Arctic Sea, and the China Sea. The average water depth of the shelf is two hundred meters. Recently, however, deposits have been discovered on the continental slope, which descends down to about two thousand meters. Recovering hydrocarbons from these water depths is already technically possible, and will become commercially feasible as the relative price of oil increases. Today offshore reserves account for about 20 percent of the world's total oil and gas production, a share that may double by the year 2000.[21]

Efficiency considerations do not justify regulating the exploitation of manganese nodules or of hydrocarbons, except in rare cases.

Manganese nodules present none of the characteristics of common property resources that make private ownership or national jurisdiction inefficient. On the contrary, efficient mining requires exclusive rights to mine a well-defined site.[22] The seabed regime proposed by UNCLOS III provides exclusive mining rights, but it also proposes to limit the volume of seabed mineral production. Pollution aside, seabed mining does not exhibit the external economies that require coordination of mining activities. Production limitation, therefore, reduces the economic efficiency of mining.

Hydrocarbon exploitation on the continental margin may provide examples of common pools, which would benefit from coordinated management. Common pools occur in the North Sea and elsewhere (e.g., fields off Newfoundland and the Aleutian Islands). However, it is unlikely that more than two governments, or one government and the International Seabed Authority, will share a pool. This increases the likelihood that the involved parties will be able to negotiate a solution to the common-pool problem on their own. Even if they cannot, this problem is likely to remain no matter where the boundary between national and international jurisdiction over resources is drawn.

In the case of the continental margin and the deep seabed, in contrast to international fisheries, efficiency considerations argue for allowing private property rights but not for imposing central production control. The primary function of an international authority should be to distribute resource rents and consumer surplus, not to regulate production. National enclosure of the deep seabed would award its rents to the new owners unless they paid a maket price for seabed real estate. However, auctioning off large tracts of the seabed would favor large countries and those rich in capital, while allowing coastal states alone to enclose the deep seabed would preclude the possibility of extracting a market price. Consequently, distributional considerations argue against national enclosure of the seabed and in favor of allowing an International Seabed Authority to sell or lease mine sites at market prices and to distribute the resulting revenues among governments.

The Antarctic

The Antarctic is a disputed commons. Seven countries claim sovereignty over parts of the continent. The claims of Argentina, Chile, and the United Kingdom partially overlap; Australia, France, New Zealand, Norway, and the United Kingdom recognize one another's claims. These seven, together with six non-claimant states, are parties to the Antarctic Treaty of 1959.

The treaty is designed to ensure the exclusively peaceful use of the continent—one tenth of the globe's land surface—and to facilitate scientific research by allowing scientists access to the whole area. It sidesteps the issue of territorial claims by freezing existing claims and prohibiting new ones. It does not deal with the issue of the exploitation of Antarctic resources.

The natural resources of the Antarctic consist of onshore and offshore oil and gas reserves estimated to be about one-half of Alaskan offshore reserves.[23] There are also large but currently inaccessible coal and iron ore deposits. The living resources include fur seals, crabs, lobsters, fish, and krill; the last may be the most important. The annual sustainable catch of krill has been estimated at between 50 and 150 million tons, and thus perhaps equivalent to the current annual world catch of all other seafoods.[24]

The Treaty's tenth consultative meeting (1979) initiated negotiation of a convention to regulate the exploitation of living marine animals other than whales and fur seals (which are covered by separate conventions). The treaty, signed by the parties in December 1980, adopts a comprehensive ecosystem management approach. Krill is the base of a complex food web in the Antarctic ecosystem. The amount of krill harvested annually affects the stocks of animals that prey upon it and, in particular, affects the already severely decimated population of Antarctic baleen whales. During the Antartic winter, these whales migrate toward the equator and are caught by countries other than Antarctic claimant states. The amount of krill harvested thus affects a group of countries and interests wider than just the krill fishing nations (USSR, Japan, West Germany) or even the thirteen nations party to the Antarctic Treaty.

Furthermore, the circular flow of ocean currents around the Antarctic continent makes the planktonic krill a common property resource. No single claimant state can by itself control the size of the stocks of krill under its jurisdiction. The governments must agree upon and enforce a common management policy and extend their jurisdiction beyond two hundred nautical miles if they are to manage all krill stocks.

Comprehensive management of the Antarctic's living resources is thus essential, and must cover the major animal groups of the food web and their habitats. It is therefore unfortunate that the harvesting of whales and seals is regulated by separate conventions. Another weakness is that the covention, while establishing a scientific committee, provides no financial support to make it independent of the treaty members; nor does it empower the committee to determine the annual harvesting campacity of the resource. There is no political mechanism to allocate national quotas, since this might prejudge the issue of territorial claims, and consequently there is no enforcement mechanism to ensure that the actual harvest does not exceed the allowable catch. Given the large number of countries involved either as claimant states or as exploiters of the resources, management based on voluntary observance may well prove ineffective. Interests not represented in the decision-making process may be especially reluctant to comply with the committee's recommendations.

The lack of a supranational enforcement mechanism, a serious shortcoming of the convention, may be due to a desire to avoid creating a precedent for the convention on mineral resources on which negotiations started in 1981. These resources also provide examples of external economies. Some oil pools may be common to several Antarctic claims, and the exploitation of offshore oil reserves may affect the living resources of the Southern Ocean. Comprehensive management with supranational enforcement is appropriate here as well. However, enforcement presupposes representation of the interested parties in the decision-making process, and identifying the parties interested in the exploitation of Antarctic resources broaches the question of who owns Antarctica. Rising prices of raw materials, and especially of hydrocarbons, increase the value of territorial claims to the continent and of membership in the Antarctic club. This encourages the members to retain for themselves the right to exploit and otherwise to benefit from Antarctic resources. Not surprisingly, developing countries have suggested that these benefits be shared with a larger group of countries. . . .

V. CONCLUSION

The appropriate organization for managing a commons depends on a variety of factors, the most important being why communal ownership is maintained to begin with and how many co-owners are involved.

When the resource is held as a commons simply because the parties cannot agree on how to subdivide it, the organization serves primarily to pool risks, distributing to co-owners the revenues that result from auctioning user rights.

If communal ownership is maintained because external diseconomies in resource use are significant, the organization in addition must limit production to a level that is socially optimal. When several governments share jurisdiction over the resource, interdependence between the firms exploiting it results in policy interdependence of the governments. In some countries politicians may resent this interdependence, but refusal to recognize it will result in less efficient use of the resource.

When few governments share jurisdiction over the resource, strong economic incentives exist for them to cooperate voluntarily in managing the commons in order to avoid inefficiency. They are more likely to do this if their respective national interests in the resource are roughly equal and if they share common values. On the other hand, when many governments share jurisdiction over the resource, experience shows that effective management requires that the organization have coercive powers, that is, the power to make decisions binding on members and to monitor and enforce compliance.

Sovereign governments are normally reluctant to surrender jurisdiction, although their reluctance may be less in regional organizations than in international organizations with more heterogeneous membership. It is easy to despair, therefore, about the ability of international organizations to deal effectively with the problems posed by transborder fisheries, ozone layer depletion, and atmospheric carbon dioxide accumulation.

Nevertheless, let us hope that governments will be persuaded to pool modest jurisdictional powers before the global commons suffer large and irreversible damage. They may do this if they recognize that the unique physical characteristics of common property resources require governments to coordinate their management powers regardless of any distributional considerations; that distributional goals can be achieved independently of resource use given political willingness to effectuate income transfers; and that the price mechanism can be an effective facilitator of compromise for conflicts over resource use.

NOTES

1. Garrett Hardin, "The Tragedy of the Commons," *Science*, 13 December 1968.
2. In 1970 the General Assembly declared the deep seabed the "common heritage of mankind" and convened UNCLOS III to draft a comprehensive new law of the sea. The Conference holds its eleventh session in March and April 1982. In 1979 the General Assembly declared outer space the "common province of all mankind" and declared its intention to negotiate an international regime for the exploration of outer space resources. The second World Administrative Radio Conference met in 1979 under the auspices of the International Telecommunications Union to allocate radio frequencies and orbital slots for the next 20 years; it reconvenes in 1982. In 1980; the consultative parties of the Antarctic treaty concluded a treaty for the conservation of Antarctic living marine resources and are currently negotiating a treaty for mineral resources.
3. For analysis of these problems leading to different policy conclusions see S. Brown, N. Cornell, L. Fabian, and E. Weiss, *Regimes for the Ocean, Outer Space and Weather* (Washington, D.C.: Brookings, 1977); and R. Eckert, *The Enclosure of Ocean Resources: Economics and the Law of the Sea* (Stanford, Cal.: Hoover Institution Press, 1979). See also the thematic issue entitled "Managing International Commons" of *Journal of International Affairs*, 31, no. 1 (Spring–Summer 1977); Ann Hollick's contribution to R. W. Arad et al., *Sharing Global Resources* (New York: McGraw-Hill, 1979); O. Schachter, *Sharing the World's Resources* (New York: Columbia University Press, 1977).
4. Villages in medieval Europe contained tracts of land, especially pasture and woodland, to which commoners as well as the lord of the manor had access. Their rights were usually clearly specified, allowing them to graze cattle, to gather wood, etc. These user rights were personal, and customarily the produce collected was not sold to others, so there were no markets affiliated with these rights. The rising price of

agricultural produce created incentives to "enclose" the commons by hedge or by fence. When the price of wool rose in 13th century England, for instance, the lord of the manor characteristically attempted to reduce the commons by converting some land to pasture for his exclusive personal use. In response to rising food prices in 19th century Europe, common pasture was enclosed and converted to private farmland. By now enclosure was closely regulated in most countries and included consolidation of private holdings of land and compensation for loss of rights in the commons. For one view see J. S. Cohen and M. L. Weitzman, "A Marxian Model of Enclosures," *Journal of Development Economics* 1 (1975).

5. Ricardo noted the possibility that property rights might be extended to certain "gifts of nature which exist in boundless quantity," such as air and water, once they became sufficiently scarce to generate rents to their owners. "If air, water, the elasticity of steam, and the pressure of the atmosphere were of various qualities; if they could be appropriated, and each quality existed only in moderate abundance, they, as well as the land, would afford a rent, as the successive qualities were brought into use." *The Principles of Political Economy and Taxation*, 3d ed. (1821), chap. 2, "On Rent." Compare this to the reaction of the Indian chief Tecumseh, a contemporary of Ricardo, when the white man offered to buy Indian land: "What! Sell land! As well sell air and water. The Great Spirit gave them in common to all, the air we breathe, the water we drink, and the land we live upon."

6. H. Demsetz, "Toward a Theory of Property Rights," *American Economic Review* 57 (May 1967). Demsetz argues that property rights develop to internalize externalities when the gains exceed the costs of internalization. He illustrates his argument by pointing out that the emergence of property rights among the Indians of the Labrador Peninsula in the 18th century was due to the low cost of enclosing the relatively stationary beaver combined with a high return as foreign trade increased the demand for furs. The absence of property rights to land among the Plains Indians was due to higher costs relative to benefits of enclosing grazing cattle.

7. While a commons is characterized by the legal form of ownership, the term "common property resource" refers to certain physical rather than legal characteristics. High costs of enforcing individual property rights and high returns from coordinated use make it socially inefficient to subdivide the resource. Thus, common property resources are exploited more efficiently if production is coordinated. For other resources, private property rights are socially more efficient than communal ownership when the resource is scarce; a classical proof of this statement is provided by M. L. Weitzman, "Free Access vs. Private Ownership as Alternative Systems for Managing Common Property," *Journal of Economic Theory* 8 (1974).

8. See Cyrille de Klemm, "The Conservation of Migratory Animals through International Law," *Natural Resources Journal* 12, 2 (April 1972). An international convention on the conservation of migratory species of wild animals was signed in June 1978. The text, with comments, is published in *Environmental Policy and Law Journal* no. 5 (1979).

9. Indeed, when the size of the resource is unknown, it may in practice be difficult to convince those who exploit the resource of the need to limit the harvest.

10. See G. R. Munro, "The Optimal Management of Transboundary Renewable Resources," *Canadian Journal of Economics* 12 (August 1979).

11. An external economy occurs if the rate at which A exploits the resource affects the exploitation costs for B, or vice versa, or both. Its occurrence serves to define common property resources, according to Robert Dorfman:" Any economic unit's behavior can affect the welfare or productivity of others in a vast number of different

ways, through altruism, envy, congestion, pollution, and a myriad of other kinds of connection. Sometimes the connection is physical. That is to say, sometimes there is an identifiable physical medium through which the effects of one agent's activities are transmitted to other agents. Such a medium is what I shall mean by a common property resource. . . . [This] means that all problems attributable to the misuse or abuse of common property resources are instances of externalities, and the entire theory of externalities applies to them." See "The Technical Basis for Decision Making," in E. T. Haefele, ed., *The Governance of Common Resources* (Washington, D.C.: Resources for the Future, 1974). I have argued in the text that the infeasibility of defining exclusive property rights and the resulting overlapping of rights is a distinctive feature of common property resources leading to the characteristic depletion of the resource. This is often related to the externality.

12. Some historical examples of voluntary management of a commons are provided by T. L. Anderson and T. J. Hill, "Property Rights as a Common Pool Resource," in J. Baden and R. Stroup, eds., *Bureaucrats vs. Environment* (Ann Arbor: University of Michigan Press, 1981).

13. For instance, an international convention to abate pollution of the Rhine River in Europe has been difficult to achieve because of the many countries involved (five), and because of the asymmetry in the interdependence of "downstream" and "upstream" countries.

14. This is the familiar thesis of M. Olson, *The Logic of Collective Action: Public Goods and the Theory of Groups* (Cambridge: Harvard University Press, 1965). See also his "Increasing the Incentives for International Cooperation," *International Organization* 25, 4 (Autumn 1971). The point is illustrated by H. V. Muhsam in "An Algebraic Theory of the Commons," in G. Hardin and J. Baden, eds., *Managing the Commons* (San Francisco: W. H. Freeman, 1977), pp. 34–37. For a practical illustration of the management problems posed by an internationally shared resource, see P. Bohm, "CFC Emissions Control in an International Perspective," in J. Cumberland, J. Hibbs, and I. Hoch, eds., *The Economics of Managing Chlorofluorocarbons: Stratospheric Ozone and Climate Issues* (Washington, D.C.: Resources for the Future, 1982).

15. Discussions of international resource management would benefit from more explicit application of this distinction, which corresponds to the classical distinction in economics between the allocation, distribution, and stabilization branches of government. It is spelled out clearly by some economists dealing with this subject. See R. D. Tollison and T. D. Willett, "Institutional Mechanisms for Dealing with International Externalities: A Public Choice Perspective," in R. C. Amacher and R. J. Sweeney, *The Law of the Sea: U.S. Interests and Alternatives* (Washington, D.C.: American Enterprise Institute, 1976); F. T. Christy Jr., "Economic Criteria for Rules Governing Exploitation of Deep Sea Minerals," *International Lawyer* 2, 2 (April 1968); *Alternative Arrangements for Marine Fisheries: An Overview* (Washington, D.C.: Resources for the Future, May 1973); and R. Cooper, "An Economist's View of the Oceans," *Journal of World Trade Law* 9, 4 (1975).

16. Demsetz speaks in this connection of the valuation function of the price system: "The Exchange and Enforcement of Property Rights," *Journal of Law and Economics* 7, 1 (October 1964). By guiding resources to their most valuable use, the price mechanism contributes to efficiency. Consequently, free use of the scarce orbit-spectrum frequency means that too much of the spectrum is devoted to satellite communications instead of to other purposes, and that more labor and capital are devoted to constructing and launching satellites than would be required to lay an

equivalent amount of transatlantic cable. Similarly, if the charges levied on seabed mining are in excess of the rent due to the mine site, more capital and labor will be devoted to landbased mining than would be required to mine the same amount of ore from the seabed.

17. For instance, Richard Cooper interprets the concept "common heritage of mankind" to mean that any rents "from use of the oceans or seabed should be used for internationally agreed purposes. That is, the international community as a whole should hold title to the property" and any net revenues be "used for a variety of common purposes: budgetary support for the United Nations, which is frequently strapped for funds; U.N. peace-keeping activities; and most obviously, development assistance to the poor countries of the world." Cooper, "Economist's Vie of Oceans," p. 370. A similar approach has been presented by Tollison and Willett, "Institutional Mechanisms," pp. 91–97.

18. See S. Zamora, "Voting in International Economic Organizations," *American Journal of International Law* 74, 3 (July 1980). For an interesting example see A. Klevorick and G. H. Kramer, "Social Choice on Pollution Management: The Genossenschaften," *Journal of Public Economics* 2 (1973), pp. 101–146; and K. A. Mingst, "The Functionalist and Regime Perspectives: The Case of Rhine River Cooperation," *Journal of Common Market Studies* 20, 2 (December 1981).

19. S. Holt estimates the world marine catch, excluding whales, to have been $15 billion (U.S.) in 1974, or about 0.44% of world GNP. FAO statistics of the value of fish landings have been discontinued since then, but allowance for inflation places the yearly value of the world marine catch at the end of the 1970s at roughly $20 billion. See Holt's "Marine Fisheries," in E. M. Borgese and N. Ginsburg, eds., *Ocean Yearbook 1* (Chicago: University of Chicago Press, 1978), p. 53. J. Gulland notes that only 1% of the total world catch of marine fish is caught beyond 200 nautical miles from shore. This 1% consists mainly of tuna. See his "Developing Countries and the New Law of the Sea," *Oceanus* 22, 1 (Spring 1979), p. 36.

20. The Draft Convention of UNCLOS III allows the coastal state to give domestic fishermen prior claim to the resources of the EEZ, to determine unilaterally if these resources are sufficiently large to permit foreign fishermen to share in harvesting them, and to charge foreigners an entry fee upon admitting them. Such a fee may be larger than that charged domestic fishermen. Noncoastal states and others with an interest or a tradition of fishing in a foreign EEZ are dependent on the host country's permission.

21. See G. J. Mangone, ed., *The Future of Gas and Oil from the Sea* (New York: Van Nostrand, 1982), for an informed survey of current and future technologies for exploring and exploiting offshore hydrocarbon resources. See Wijkman, "UNCLOS," pp. 34–37, for estimates of offshore hydrocarbon wealth and its distribution.

22. Nodule fields are divisible and property rights to sites can be enforced cheaply in the courts once nations have agreed on a legal regime. While one firm's mining costs are not affected by mining conducted on other sites, they are affected if other firms mine the *same* site. This is because of the characteristics of the resource and of the exploitation technology. Nodules will be recovered from about 4000 meters of water depth by complex dredging systems. Unlike wild berries on a commons, they are evenly distributed on certain parts of the seafloor so that harvesting costs are lower when firms systematically comb a given area than where they sweep it randomly. When several firms work the same field, harvesting becomes random and, because of the large sunk costs of the dredging equipment, recovery costs rise signicantly. Thus, exclusive mining rights to a site are important for minimizing costs.

The minimum economic size of a single site may be large. Since processing plans evidence economies of scale and each one is adapted specifically to process nodules possessing the chemical composition characteristic of that site, each site must be large enough to supply three million metric tons annually for 20 to 25 years. It has been estimated that this requires that mine sites be about 40,000 square kilometers in size assuming that profitability requires at least 10 kg of nodules per square meter and nickel and copper content of 2.25% in the nodules. See J.-P. Levy, "Evolution of a Resource Policy," pp. 23–24. Such prime sites may be few and expensive to find and consequently need to be husbanded.

23. This estimate is based on a recent U.S. Geological Survey report quoted in Barbara Mitchell and Lee Kimball, "Conflict over the Cold Continent," *Foreign Policy* no. 35 (Summer 1979). See also Ursula Wassermann, "The Antarctic Treaty and Natural Resources," *Journal of World Trade Law* 12, 2 (March–April 1978).

24. See S. Z. El-Sayed and Mary A. McWhinnie, "Antarctic Krill: Protein of the Last Frontier," *Oceanus* 22, 1 (Spring 1979), p. 13. A resource survey is provided by Inigo Everson, *The Living Resources of the Southern Ocean*, FAO/UNDP, Southern Ocean Fisheries Survey Programme, GLO/SO/77/1 (Rome, September 1977).

Redefining Security

Jessica Tuchman Mathews

The 1990s will demand a redefinition of what constitutes national security. In the 1970s the concept was expanded to include international economics as it became clear that the U.S. economy was no longer the independent force it had once been, but was powerfully affected by economic policies in dozens of other countries. Global developments now suggest the need for another analogous, broadening definition of national security to include resource, environmental and demographic issues.

The assumptions and institutions that have governed international relations in the postwar era are a poor fit with these new realities. Environmental strains that transend national borders are already beginning to break down the sacred boundaries of national sovereignty, previously rendered porous by the information and communication revolutions and the instantaneous global movement of financial capital. The once sharp dividing line between foreign and domestic policy is blurred, forcing governments to grapple in international forums with issues that were contentious enough in the domestic arena.

Despite the headlines of 1988—the polluted coastlines, the climatic extremes, the accelerating deforestation and flooding that plagued the planet—human society has not arrived at the brink of some absolute limit to its growth. The planet may ultimately be able to accommodate the additional five or six billion people projected to be living here by the year 2100. But it seems unlikely that the world will be able to do so unless the means of production change dramatically. Global economic output has quadrupled since 1950 and it must continue to grow rapidly simply to meet basic human needs, to say nothing of the challenge of lifting billions from poverty. But economic growth as we currently know it requires more energy use, more emissions and wastes, more land converted from its natural state, and more need for the products of natural systems. Whether the planet can accommodate all of these demands remains an open question.

Individuals and governments alike are beginning to feel the cost of substituting for (or doing without) the goods and services once freely provided by healthy ecosystems. Nature's bill is presented in many different forms: the cost of commercial fertilizer needed to replenish once naturally fertile soils; the expense of dredging rivers that flood their banks because of soil erosion hundreds of miles upstream; the loss in crop failures due to the indiscriminate use of pesticides that inadvertently kill insect pollinators; or the price of worsening pollution, once filtered from the air by vegetation. Whatever the immediate cause for concern, the value and absolute necessity for human life of functioning ecosystems is finally becoming apparent.

Moreover, for the first time in its history, mankind is rapidly—if inadvertently—altering the basic physiology of the planet. Global changes currently taking place in the chemical composition of the atmosphere, in the genetic diversity of species inhabiting the planet, and in the cycling of vital chemicals through the oceans, atmosphere, biosphere, and geosphere are unprecedented in both their pace and scale. If left unchecked, the consequences will be profound and, unlike familiar types of local damage, irreversible.

Population growth lies at the core of most environmental trends. It took 130 years for world population to grow from one billion to two billion: It will take just a decade to climb from today's five billion to six billion. More than 90 percent of the added billion will live in the developing world, with the result that by the end of the 1990s the developed countries will be home to only 20 percent of the world's people, compared to almost 40 percent at the end of World War II. Sheer numbers do no translate into political power, especially when most of the added billion will be living in poverty. But the demographic shift will thrust the welfare of developing nations further toward the center of international affairs.

The relationship linking population levels and the resource base is complex. Policies, technologies and institutions determine the impact of population growth. These factors can spell the difference between a highly stressed, degraded environment and one that can provide for many more people. At any given level of investment and knowledge, absolute population numbers can be crucial. For example, traditional systems of shifting agriculture—in which land is left fallow for a few years to recover from human use—can sustain people for centuries, only to crumble in a short time when population densities exceed a certain threshold. More important, though, is the *rate* of growth. A government that is fully capable of providing food, housing, jobs and health care for a population growing at one percent per year (therefore doubling its population in 72 years), might be completely overwhelmed by an annual growth rate of 3 percent, which would double the population in 24 years.

Today the United States and the Soviet Union are growing at just under one percent annually (Europe is growing only half that fast). But Africa's population is expanding by almost 3 percent per year. Latin America's by nearly 2 percent and Asia's somewhat less. By 2025 the working-age population in developing countries alone will be larger than the world's current total population. This growth comes at a time when technological advance requires higher levels of education and displaces more labor than ever before. For many developing countries, continued growth at current rates means that available capital is swallowed up in meeting the daily needs of people, rather than invested in resource conservation and job creation. Such policies inescapably lay the foundations of a bleak future.

An important paradox to bear in mind when examining natural resource trends is that so-called nonrenewable resources—such as coal, oil and minerals—are in fact inexhaustible, while so-called renewable resources can be finite. As a nonrenewable resource becomes scarce and more expensive, demand falls, and substitutes and alternative technologies appear. For that reason we will never pump the last barrel of oil or anything close to it. On the other hand, a fishery fished beyond a certain point will not recover, a species driven to extinction will not reappear, and eroded topsoil cannot be replaced (except over geological time). There are, thus, threshold effects for renewable resources that belie the name given them, with unfortunate consequences for policy.

The most serious form of renewable resource decline is the deforestation taking place throughout the tropics. An area the size of Austria is deforested each year. Tropical forests are fragile ecosystems, extremely vulnerable to human disruption. Once disturbed, the entire ecosystem can unravel. The loss of the trees causes the interruption of nutrient cycling above and below the soil, the soil loses fertility, plant and animal species lose their habitats and become extinct, and acute fuelwood shortages appear (especially in the dry tropical forests). The soil erodes without the ground cover provided by trees and plants, and downstream rivers suffer siltation, causing floods and droughts, and damaging expensive irrigation and hydroelectric systems. Traced through its effects on agriculture, energy supply and water resources, tropical deforestation impoverishes about 2 billion people. This pattern is endemic throughout Central America, much of Asia, sub-Saharan Africa and South America.

The planet's evolutionary heritage—its genetic diversity— is heavily concentrated in these same forests. It is thererfore disappearing today on a scale not seen since the age of the dinosaurs, and at an unprecedented pace. Biologists estimate that species are being lost in the tropical forests 1,000–10,000 times faster than the natural rate of extinction.[1] As many as 20 percent of all the species now living may be gone by the year 2000. The loss will be felt aesthetically, scientifically and, above all, economically. These genetic resources are an important source of food, materials for energy and construction, chemicals for pharmaceuticals and industry, vehicles for health and safety testing, natural pest controls and dozens of other uses.

The only reason that species loss is not a front-page issue is that the majority of species have not yet been discovered, much less studied, so that none but a few conservation biologists can even guess at the number and kinds of species that are vanishing. The bitter irony is that genetic diversity is disappearing on a grand scale at the very moment when biotechnology makes it possible to exploit fully this resource for the first time.

Soil degradation is another major concern. Both a cause and a consequence of poverty, desertification, as it is generally called, is causing declining agricultural productivity on nearly two billion hectares, 15 percent of the earth's land area. The causes are overcultivation, overgrazing, erosion, and salinization and waterlogging due to poorly managed irrigation. In countries as diverse as Haiti, Guatemala, Turkey and India, soil erosion has sharply curtailed agricultural production and potential, sometimes destroying it completely. Though the data are uncertain, it is estimated that the amount of land permanently removed from cultivation due to salinization and waterlogging is equal to the amount of land newly irrigated at great expense each year.

Finally, patterns of land tenure, though not strictly an environmental condition, have an immense environmental impact. In 1975, 7 percent of landowners of Latin America possessed 93 percent of all the arable land in this vast region. In Guatemala, a typical case, 2 percent of the population in 1980 owned 80 percent of the land, while 83 percent of farmers lived on plots too small to support a household. At the same time, even in Costa Rica, with its national concern for social equity, 3 percent of landowners held 54 percent of the land. These large holdings generally include the most desirable land. The great mass of the rural population is pushed onto the most damage-prone land, usually dry or highly erodible slopes, and into the forests. Land reform is among the most difficult of all political undertakings, but without it many countries will be unable to create a healthy agricultural sector to fuel economic growth.

Environmental decline occasionally leads directly to conflict, especially when scarce water resources must be shared. Generally, however, its impact on nations' security is felt in the downward pull on economic performance and, therefore, on political stability. The underlying cause of turmoil is often ignored; instead goverments address the poverty and instability that are its results.

In the Philippines, for example, the government regularly granted logging concessions of less than ten years. Since it takes 30–35 years for a second-growth forest to mature, loggers had no incentive to replant. Compounding the error, flat royalties encouraged the loggers to remove only the most valuable species. A horrendous 40 percent of the harvestable lumber never left the forests but, having been damaged in the logging, rotted or was burned in place. The unsurprising result of these and related policies is that out of 17 million hectares of closed forests that flourished early in the century only 1.2 million remain today. Moreover, the Philippine government received a fraction of the revenues it could have collected if it had followed sound resource management policies that would have also preserved the forest capital. This is biological deficit financing writ large.

Similarly, investments in high-technology fishing equipment led to larger harvests but simultaneously depleted the stock. Today, 10 of 50 major Philippine fishing grounds are believed to be overfished; the net result of heavy investment is that the availability of fish per capita has actually dropped. These and other self-destructive environmental policies, combined with rapid population growth, played a significant role in the economic decline that led to the downfall of the Marcos regime. So far, the government of Corazon Aquino has made few changes in the forestry, fishery and other environmental policies it inherited.

Conditions in sub-Saharan Africa, to take another case, have reached catastrophic dimensions. In the first half of this decade export earnings fell by almost one-third, foreign debt soared to 58 percent of GNP, food imports grew rapidly while consumption dropped, and per capita GNP fell by more than 3 percent. A large share of those woes can be traced to Africa's dependence on a fragile, mismanaged and overstressed natural resource base.

Exports of mineral and agricultural commodities alone account for a quarter of the region's GNP, and nearly three-quarters of the population makes its living off the land, which also supplies, as fuelwood, 80 percent of the energy consumed. The land's capacity to produce is ebbing away under the pressure of rapidly growing numbers of people who do not have the wherewithal to put back into the land what they take from it. A vicious cycle of human and resource imporverishment sets in. As the vegetative cover—trees, shrubs and grass— shrinks from deforestation and overgrazing, soil loses its capacity to retain moisture and nourish crops. The decline accelerates as farmers burn dung and crop residues in place of fuelwood, rather than using them to sustain the soil. Agricultural yields then fall further, and the land becomes steadily more vulnerable to the naturally variable rainfall that is the hallmark of arid and semiarid regions, turning dry spells into droughts and periods of food shortage into famines. Ethiopia is only the most familiar case. The sequence is repeated throughout the region with similarly tragic results.

If such resource and population trends are not addressed, as they are not in so much of the world today, the resulting economic decline leads to frustration, resentment, domestic unrest or even civil war. Human suffering and turmoil make countries ripe for authoritarian government or external subversion. Environmental refugees spread the disruption across national borders. Haiti, a classic example, was once so forested and fertile that it was known as the "Pearl of the Antilles." Now deforested, soil erosion in Haiti is so rapid that some farmers believe stones grow in their fields, while bulldozers are needed to clear the streets of Port-au-Prince of topsoil that flows down from the mountains in the rainy season. While many of the boat people who fled to the United States left because of the brutality of the Duvalier regimes, there is no question that—and this is not widely recognized—many Haitians were forced into the boats by the impossible task of farming bare rock. Until Haiti is reforested, it will never be politically stable.

Haitians are by no means the world's only environmental refugees. In Indonesia, Central American and sub-Saharan Africa, millions have been forced to leave their homes in part because the loss of tree cover, the disappearance of soil, and other environmental ills have made it impossible to grow food. Sudan, despite its civil war, has taken in more than a million refugees from Ethiopia, Uganda and Chad. Immigrants from the spreading Sahel make up one-fifth of the total population in the Ivory Coast. Wherever refugees settle, they flood the labor market, add to the local demand for food and put new burdens on the land, thus spreading the environmental stress that originally forced them from their homes. Resource mismanagement is not the only cause of these mass movements, of course. Religious and ethnic conflicts, political repression and other forces are at work. But the environmental causes are an essential factor.

A different kind of environmental concern has arisen from mankind's new ability to alter the environment on a planetary scale. The earth's physiology is shaped by the characteristics of four elements (carbon, nitrogen, phosphorous and sulfur); by its living inhabitants (the biosphere); and by the interactions of the atmosphere and the oceans, which produce our climate.

Mankind is altering both the carbon and nitrogen cycles, having increased the natural carbon dioxide concentration in the atmosphere by 25 percent. This has occurred largely in the last three decades through fossil-fuel use and deforestation. The production of commercial fertilizer has doubled the amount of nitrogen nature makes available to living things. The use of a single, minor class of chemicals, chlorofluorocarbons, has punched a continent-sized "hole" in the ozone layer at the top of the stratosphere over Antarctica, and caused a smaller, but growing loss of ozone all around the planet. Species loss is destroying the work of three billion years of evolution. Together these changes could drastically alter the conditions in which life on earth has evolved.

The greenhouse effect results from the fact that the planet's atmosphere is largely transparent to incoming radiation from the sun but absorbs much of the lower energy radiation reemitted by the earth. This natural phenomenon makes the earth warm enough to support life. But as emissions of greenhouse gases increase, the planet is warmed *un*naturally. Carbon dioxide produced from the combustion of fossil fuels and by deforestation is responsible for about half of the greenhouse effect. A number of other gases, notably methane (natural gas), nitrous oxide, ozone (in the lower atmosphere, as distinguished from the protective ozone layer in the stratosphere) and the man-made chlorofluorocarbons are responsible for the other half.

Despite important uncertainties about aspects of the greenhouse warming, a virtually unanimous scientific consensus exists on its central features. If present emission trends continue, and unless some as yet undocumented phenomenon (possibly increased cloudiness) causes an offsetting cooling, the planet will, on average, get hotter because of the accumulation of these gases. Exactly how large the warming will be, and how fast it will occur, are uncertain. Existing models place the date of commitment to an average global warming of 1.5–4.5°C (3–8°F) in the early 2030s. The earth has not been this hot for two million years, long before human society, and indeed, even Homo sapiens, existed.

Hotter temperatures will be only one result of the continuing greenhouse warming. At some point, perhaps quite soon, precipitation patterns are likely to shift, possibly causing dustbowl-like conditions in the U.S. grain belt. Ocean currents are expected to do the same, dramatically altering the climates of many regions. A diversion of the Gulf Stream, for example, would transform Western Europe's climate, making it far colder than it is today. Sea level will rise due to the expansion of water when it is warmed and to the melting of land-based ice. The oceans are presently rising by one-half inch per decade, enough to cause serious erosion along much of the U.S. coast. The projected rise is one to four feet by the year 2050. Such a large rise in the sea level would inundate vast coastal regions, erode shorelines, destroy coastal marshes and swamps (areas of very high biological productivity), pollute water supplies through the intrusion of salt water, and put at high risk the vastly disproportionate share of the world's economic wealth that is packed along coastlines. The great river deltas, from the Mississippi to the Ganges, would be flooded. Estimates are that a half-meter rise in Egypt would displace 16 percent of the population, while a two-meter rise in Bangladesh would claim 28 percent of the land where 30 million people live today and where more than 59 million are projected to live by 2030.

Positive consequences would be likely as well. Some plants would grow more quickly fertilized by the additional carbon dioxide. (Many of them, however, will be weeds.) Rainfall might rise in what are now arid but potentially fertile regions, such as parts of sub-Saharan Africa. Conditions for agriculture would also improve in those northern areas that have both adequate soils and water supplies. Nonetheless, as the 1988 drought in the United States vividly demonstrated, human societies, industrial no less than rural, depend on the normal, predictable functioning of the climate system. Climate undergoing rapid change will not only be less predictable because it is different, but may be inherently more variable. Many climatologists believe that as accumulating greenhouse gases force the climate out of equilibrium, climate extremes—such as hurricanes, droughts, cold snaps and typhoons—will become more frequent and perhaps more intense.

Since climate change will be felt in every economic sector, adapting to its impact will be extremely expensive. Developing countries with their small reserves of capital, shortages of scientists and engineers, and weak central governments will be the least able to adapt, and the gap between the developed and developing worlds will almost certainly widen. Many of the adaptations needed will be prohibitively costly, and many impacts, notably the effects on wildlife and ecosystems, will be beyond the reach of human correction. A global strategy that relies on future adaption almost certainly means greater economic and human costs, and vastly larger biological losses, than would a strategy that attempts to control the extent and speed of the warming.

Greenhouse change is closely linked to stratospheric ozone depletion, which is also caused by chlorofluorocarbons. The increased ultraviolet radiation resulting from losses in that protective layer will cause an increase in skin cancers and eye damage. It will have many still uncertain impacts on plant and animal life, and may suppress the immune systems of many species.

Serious enough in itself, ozone depletion illustrates a worrisome feature of man's newfound ability to cause global change. It is almost impossible to predict accurately the long-term impact of new chemicals or processes on the environment. Chlorofluorocarbons were thoroughly tested when first introduced, and found to be benign. Their effect on the remote stratosphere was never considered.

Not only is it difficult to anticipate all the possible consequences in a highly interdependent, complex system, the system itself is poorly understood. When

British scientists announced the appearance of a continent-sized "hole" in the ozone layer over Antarctica in 1985, the discovery sent shock waves through the scientific community. Although stratospheric ozone depletion had been the subject of intense study and debate for more than a decade, no one had predicted the Antarctic hole and no theory could account for it.

The lesson is this: Current knowledge of planetary mechanisms is so scanty that the possibility of surprise, perhaps quite nasty surprise, must be rated rather high. The greatest risk may well come from a completely unanticipated direction. We lack both crucial knowledge and early warning systems.

Absent profound change in man's relationship to his environment, the future does not look bright. Consider the planet without such change in the year 2050. Economic growth is projected to have quintupled by then. Energy use could also quintuple; or if post-1973 trends continue, it may grow more slowly, perhaps only doubling or tripling. The human species already consumes or destroys 40 percent of all the energy produced by terrestrial photosynthesis, that is, 40 percent of the food energy potentially available to living things on land. While that fraction may be sustainable, it is doubtful that it could keep pace with the expected doubling of the world's population. Human use of 80 percent of the planet's potential productivity does not seem compatible with the continued functioning of the biosphere as we know it. The expected rate of species loss would have risen from perhaps a few each day to several hundred a day. The pollution and toxic waste burden would likely prove unmanageable. Tropical forests would have largely disappeared, and arable land, a vital resource in a world of ten billion people, would be rapidly decreasing due to soil degradation. In short, sweeping change in economic production systems is not a choice but a necessity.

Happily, this grim sketch of conditions in 2050 is not a prediction, but a projection, based on current trends. Like all projections, it says more about the present and the recent past than it does about the future. The planet is not destined to a slow and painful decline into environmental chaos. There are technical, scientific and economical solutions that are feasible to many current trends, and enough is known about promising new approaches to be confident that the right kinds of research will produce huge payoffs. Embedded in current practices are vast costs in lost opportunities and waste, which, if corrected, would bring massive benefits. Some such steps will require only a reallocation of money, while others will require sizable capital investments. None of the needed steps, however, requires globally unaffordable sums of money. What they do demand is a sizable shift in priorities.

For example, family-planning services cost about $10 per user, a tiny fraction of the cost of the basic human needs that would otherwise have to be met. Already identified opportunities for raising the effiency of energy use in the United States cost one-half to one-seventh the cost of new energy supply. Comparable savings are available in most other countries. Agroforestry techniques, in which carefully selected combinations of trees and shrubs are planted together with crops, can not only replace the need for purchased fertilizer but also improve soil quality, make more water available to crops, hold down weeds, and provide fuelwood and higher agricultural yields all at the same time.

But if the technological opportunities are boundless, the social, political and institutional barriers are huge. Subsidies, pricing policies and economic discount rates encourage resource depletion in the name of economic growth, while delivering only the illusion of sustainable growth. Population growth remains a controversial subject in much of the world. The traditional prerogatives of nation states are poorly matched with the needs for regional cooperation and global decision-making. And ignorance of the biological underpinning of human society blocks a clear view of where the long-term threats to global security lie.

Overcoming these economic and political barriers will require social and institutional inventions comparable in scale and vision to the new arrangements conceived in the decade following World War II. Without the sharp political turning point of a major war, and with threats that are diffuse and long term, the task will be more difficult. But if we are to avoid irreversible damage to the planet and a heavy toll in human suffering, nothing less is likely to suffice. A partial list of the specific changes suggests how demanding a task it will be.

Achieving sustainable economic growth will require the remodeling of agriculture, energy use and industrial production after nature's example—their reinvention, in fact. These economic systems must become circular rather than linear. Industry and manufacturing will need processes that use materials and energy with high efficiency, recycle by-products and produce little waste. Energy demand will have to be met with the highest efficiency consistent with full economic growth. Agriculture will rely heavily upon free ecosystem services instead of nearly exclusive reliance on man-made substitutes. And all systems will have to price goods and services to reflect the environmental costs of their provision.

A vital first step, one that can and should be taken in the very near term, would be to reinvent the national income accounts by which gross national product is measured. GNP is the foundation on which national economic policies are built, yet its calculation does not take into account resource depletion. A country can consume its forests, wildlife and fisheries, its minerals, its clean water and its topsoil, without seeing a reflection of the loss in its GNP. Nor are ecosystem services—sustaining soil fertility, moderating and storing rainfall, filtering air and regulating the climate—valued, though their loss may entail great expense. The result is that economic policymakers are profoundly misled by their chief guide.

A second step would be to invent a set of indicators by which global environmental health could be measured. Economic planning would be adrift without GNP, unemployment rates, and the like, and social planning without demographic indicators—fertility rates, infant mortality, literacy, life expectancy—would be impossible. Yet this is precisely where environmental policymaking stands today.

Development assistance also requires new tools. Bilateral and multilateral donors have found that project success rates climb when nongovernmental organizations distribute funds and direct programs. This is especially true in agriculture, forestry and conservation projects. The reasons are not mysterious. Such projects are more decentralized, more attuned to local needs and desires, and have a much higher degree of local participation in project planning. They are usually quite small in scale, however, and not capable of handling very large amounts of development funding. Often, too, their independent status threatens the national government. Finding ways to make far greater use of the strengths of such groups without weakening national governments is another priority for institutional innovation.

Better ways must also be found to turn the scientific and engineering strengths of the industrialized world to the solution of the developing world's problems. The challenges include learning enough about local constraints and conditions to ask the right questions, making such research professionally rewarding to the individual scientist, and transferring technology more effectively. The international centers for agricultural research, a jointly managed network of thirteen institutions launched in the 1960s, might be improved upon and applied in other areas.

On the political front, the need for a new diplomacy and for new institutions and regulatory regimes to cope with the world's growing environmental interdependence is even more compelling. Put bluntly, our accepted definition of the limits of national sovereignty as coinciding with national borders is obsolete. The government of Bangladesh, no matter how hard it tries, cannot prevent tragic floods, such as it suffered last year. Preventing them requires active cooperation from Nepal and India. The government of Canada cannot protect its water resources from acid rain without collaboration with the United States. Eighteen diverse nations share the heavily polluted Mediterranean Sea. Even the Caribbean Islands, as physically isolated as they are, find themselves affected by others' resource management policies as locusts, inadvertently bred through generations of exposure to pesticides and now strong enough to fly all the way from Africa, infest their shores.

The majority of environmental problems demand regional solutions which encroach upon what we now think of as the prerogatives of national governments. This is because the phenomena themselves are defined by the limits of watershed, ecosystem, or atmospheric transport, not by national borders. Indeed, the costs and benefits of alternative policies cannot often be accurately judged without considering the region rather than the nation.

The developing countries especially will need to pool their efforts in the search for solutions. Three-quarters of the countries in sub-Saharan Africa, for example, have fewer people than live in New York City. National scientific and research capabilities cannot be built on such a small population base. Regional cooperation is required.

Dealing with global change will be more difficult. No one nation or even group of nations can meet these challenges, and no nation can protect itself from the actions—or inaction—of others. No existing institution matches these criteria. It will be necessary to reduce the dominance of the superpower relationship which so often encourages other countries to adopt a wait-and-see attitude (you solve your problems first, then talk to us about change).

The United States, in particular, will have to assign a far greater prominence than it has heretofore to the practice of multilateral diplomacy. This would mean changes that range from the organization of the State Department and the language proficiency of the Foreign Service, to the definition of an international role that allows leadership without primacy, both in the slogging work of negotiation and in adherence to final outcomes. Above all, ways must soon be found to step around the deeply entrenched North-South cleavage and to replace it with a planetary sense of shared destiny. Perhaps the successes of the UN specialized agencies can be built upon for this purpose. But certainly the task of forging a global energy policy in order to control the greenhouse effect, for example, is a very long way from eradicating smallpox or sharing weather information.

The recent Soviet proposal to turn the UN Trusteeship Council, which has outlived the colonies it oversaw, into a trusteeship for managing the global commons (the oceans, the atmosphere, biological diversity and planetary climate) deserves close scrutiny. If a newly defined council could sidestep the U.N.'s political fault lines, and incorporate, rather than supplant, the existing strengths of the United Nations Environment Programme, it might provide a useful forum for reaching global environmental decisions at a far higher political level than anything that exists now.

Today's negotiating models—the Law of the Sea Treaty, the Nuclear Nonproliferation Treaty, even the promising Convention to Protect the Ozone Layer—are inadequate. Typically, such agreements take about 15 years to negotiate and enter into force, and perhaps another ten years before substantial changes in behavior are actually achieved. (The NPT, which required only seven years to complete these steps, is a notable exception.) Far better approaches will be needed.

Among these new approaches, perhaps the most difficult to achieve will be ways to negotiate successfully in the presence of substantial scientific uncertainty. The present model is static: years of negotiation leading to a final product. The new model will have to be fluid, allowing a rolling process of intermediate or self-adjusting agreements that respond quickly to growing scientific understanding. The recent Montreal agreement on the ozone layer supplies a useful precedent by providing that one-third of the parties can reconvene a scientific experts group to consider new evidence as it becomes available. The new model will require new economic methods for assessing risk, especially where the possible outcomes are irreversible. It will depend on a more active political role for biologists and chemists than they have been accustomed to, and far greater technical competence in the natural and planetary sciences among policymakers. Finally, the new model may need to forge a more involved and constructive role for the private sector. Relegating the affected industries to a heel-dragging, adversarial, outsiders role almost guarantees a slow process. The ozone agreement, to cite again this recent example, would not have been reached as quickly, and perhaps not at all, had it not been for the cooperation of the chlorofluorocarbon producers.

International law, broadly speaking, has declined in influence in recent years. With leadership and commitment from the major powers it might regain its lost status. But that will not be sufficient. To be effective, future arrangements will require provisions for monitoring, enforcement and compensation, even when damage cannot be assigned a precise monetary value. These are all areas where international law has traditionally been weak.

This is only a partial agenda for the needed decade of invention. Meanwhile, much can and must be done with existing means. Four steps are most important: prompt revision of the Montreal Treaty, to eliminate completely the production of chlorofluorocarbons no later than the year 2000; full support for and implementation of the global Tropical Forestry Action Plan developed by the World Bank, the UN's Development Programme, the Food and Agricultural Organization, and the World Resources Institute; sufficient support for family planning programs to ensure that all who want contraceptives have affordable access to them at least by the end of the decade; and, for the United States, a ten-year energy policy with the goal of increasing the energy productivity of our economy (i.e., reducing the amount of energy required to produce a dollar of GNP) by about 3 percent each year. While choosing four priorities from dozens of needed initiatives is highly arbitrary, these four stand out as ambitious yet achievable goals on which a broad consensus could be developed, and whose success would bring multiple, long-term global benefits touching every major international environmental concern.

Reflecting on the discovery of atomic energy, Albert Einstein noted "everything changed." And indeed, nuclear fission became the dominant force—military, geopolitical, and even psychological and social—of the ensuing decades. In the same sense, the driving force of the coming decades may well be environmental change. Man is still utterly dependent on the natural world but now has for the first time the ability to alter it, rapidly and on a global scale. Because of that difference, Einstein's verdict that "we shall require a substantially new manner of thinking if mankind is to survive" still seems apt.

NOTES

1. E.O. Wilson, ed., *Biodiversity*, Washington, D.C.: National Academy Press, 1988. pp. 3–18.

The Infinite Supply of
Natural Resources

Julian Simon

Natural resources are not finite. Yes, you read correctly. This chapter shows that the supply of natural resources is not finite in any economic sense, which is why their cost can continue to fall in the future.

On the face of it, even to inquire whether natural resources are finite seems like nonsense. Everyone "knows" that resources are finite, from C.P. Snow to Isaac Asimov to as many other persons as you have time to read about in the newspaper. And this belief has led many persons to draw far-reaching conclusions about the future of our world economy and civilization. A prominent example is the *Limits to Growth* group, who open the preface to their 1974 book, a sequel to the *Limits*, as follows:

> Most people acknowledge that the earth is finite. . . . Policy makers generally assume that growth will provide them tomorrow with the resources required to deal with today's problems. . . . Recently, however, concern about the consequences of population growth, increased environmental pollution, and the depletion of fossil fuels has cast doubt upon the belief that continuous growth is either possible or a panacea.[1]

(Note the rhetorical device embedded in the term "acknowledge" in the first sentence of the quotation. That word suggests that the statement is a fact, and that anyone who does not "acknowledge" it is simply refusing to accept or admit it.)

The idea that resources are finite in supply is so pervasive and influential that the President's 1972 Commission on Population Growth and the American Future based its policy recommendations squarely upon this assumption. Right at the beginning of its report the commission asked, "What does this nation stand for and where is it going? At some point in the future, the finite earth will not satisfactorily accommodate more human beings—nor will the United

States. . . . It is both proper and in our best interest to participate fully in the worldwide search for the good life, which must include the eventual stabilization of our numbers."[2]

The assumption of finiteness is responsible for misleading many scientific forecasters because their conclusions follow inexorably from that assumption. From the *Limits to Growth* team again, this time on food: "The world model is based on the fundamental assumption that there is an upper limit to the total amount of food that can be produced annually by the world's agricultural system."[3]

THE THEORY OF DECREASING
NATURAL-RESOURCE SCARCITY

We shall begin with a far-out example to see what contrasting possibilities there are. (Such an analysis of far-out examples is a useful and favorite trick of economists and mathematicians.) If there is just one person, Alpha Crusoe, on an island, with a single copper mine on his island, it will be harder to get raw copper next year if Alpha makes a lot of copper pots and bronze tools this year. And if he continues to use his mine, his son Beta Crusoe will have a tougher time getting copper than did his daddy.

Recycling could change the outcome. If Alpha decides in the second year to make new tools to replace the old tools he made in the first year, it will be easier for him to get the necessary copper than it was the first year because he can reuse the copper from the old tools without much new mining. And if Alpha adds fewer new pots and tools from year to year, the proportion of copper that can come from recycling can rise year by year. This could mean a progressive decrease in the cost of obtaining copper with each successive year for this reason alone, even while the total amount of copper in pots and tools increases.

But let us be "conservative" for the moment and ignore the possibility of recycling. Another scenario: If there are two people on the island, Alpha Crusoe and Gamma Defoe, copper will be more scarce for each of them this year than if Alpha lived there alone, unless by cooperative efforts they can devise a more complex but more efficient mining operation—say, one man on the surface and one in the shaft. Or, if there are two fellows this year instead of one, and if copper is therefore harder to get and more scarce, both Alpha and Gamma may spend considerable time lookng for new lodes of copper. And they are likely to be successful in their search. This discovery may lower the cost of copper to them somewhat, but on the average the cost will still be higher than if Alpha lived alone on the island.

Alpha and Gamma may follow still other courses of action. Perhaps they will invent better ways of obtaining copper from a given lode, say a better digging tool, or they may develop new materials to substitute for copper, perhaps iron.

The cause of these new discoveries, or the cause of applying ideas that were discovered earlier, is the "shortage" of copper—that is, the increased cost of getting copper. So a "shortage" of copper causes the creation of its own remedy. This has been the key process in the supply and use of natural resources throughout history.

Discovery of an improved mining method or of a substitute product differs, in a manner that affects future generations, from the discovery of a new lode. Even after the discovery of a new lode, on the average it will still be more costly to obtain copper, that is, more costly than if copper had never been used enough to lead to a "shortage." But discoveries of improved mining methods and of substitute products, caused by the shortage of copper, can lead to lower costs of the services people see from copper. Let's see how.

The key point is that a discovery of a substitute process or product by Alpha or Gamma can benefit innumerable future generations. Alpha and Gamma cannot themselves extract nearly the full benefit from their discovery of iron. (You and I still benefit from the discoveries of the uses of iron and methods of processing it that our ancestors made thousands of years ago.) This benefit to later generations is an example of what economists call an "externality" due to Alpha and Gamma's activities, that is, a result of their discovery that does not affect them directly.

So, if the cost of copper to Alpha and Gamma does not increase, they may not be impelled to develop improved methods and substitutes. If the cost of getting copper does rise for them, however, they may then bestir themselves to make a new discovery. The discovery may not immediately lower the cost of copper dramatically, and Alpha and Gamma may still not be as well off as if the cost had never risen. But subsequent generations may be better off because their ancestor suffered from increasing cost and "scarcity."

This sequence of events explains how it can be that people have been using cooking pots for thousands of years, as well as using copper for many other purposes, and yet the cost of a pot today is vastly cheaper by any measure than it was 100 or 1,000 or 10,000 years ago.

It is all-important to recognize that discoveries of improved methods and of substitute products are not just luck. They happen in response to "scarcity"—an increase in cost. Even after a discovery is made, there is a good chance that it will not be put into operation until there is need for it due to rising cost. This point is important: Scarcity and technological advance are not two unrelated competitors in a race; rather, each influences the other.

The last major U.S. governmental inquiry into raw materials was the 1952 President's Materials Policy Commission (Paley Commission), organized in response to fears of raw-material shortages during and just after World War II. The Paley Commission's report is distinguished by having some of the right logic, but exactly the wrong predictions, for its twenty-five year forecast.

> There is no completely satisfactory way to measure the real costs of materials over the long sweep of our history. But clearly the manhours required per unit of output declined heavily from 1900 to 1940, thanks especially to improvements in production technology and the heavier use of energy and capital equipment per worker. This long-term decline in real costs is reflected in the downward drift of

prices of various groups of materials in relation to the general level of prices in the economy.

[But since 1940 the trend has been] soaring demands, shrinking resources, the consequences pressure toward rising real costs, the risk of wartime shortages, the strong possibility of an arrest or decline in the standard of living we cherish and hope to share.[4]

For the quarter century for which the commission predicted, however, costs declined rather than rose.

The two reasons why the Paley Commission's cost predictions were topsy-turvy should help keep us from making the same mistakes. First, the commission reasoned from the notion of finiteness and from a static technological analysis.

A hundred years ago resources sseemed limitless and the struggle upward from meager conditions of life was the struggle to create the means and methods of getting these materials into use. In this struggle we have by now succeeded all too well. . . . The nature of the problem can perhaps be successfully over-simplified by saying that the consumption of almost all materials is expanding at compound rates and is thus pressing harder and harder against resources which whatever else they may be doing are not similarly expanding.[5]

The second reason the Paley Commission went wrong is that it looked at the wrong facts. Its report gave too much emphasis to the trends of costs over the short period from 1940 to 1950, which included World War II and therefore was almost inevitably a period of rising costs, instead of examining the longer period from 1900 to 1940, during which the commission knew that "the man-hours required per unit of output declined heavily."[6]

We must not repeat the same mistakes. We should look at cost trends for the longest period, rather than focus on a historical blip; the OPEC-led price rise in all resources after 1973 is for us as the temporary 1940–50 wartime reversal for the Paley Commission. And the long-run trends make it very clear that the costs of materials, and their scarcity, continuously decline with the growth of income and technology.

RESOURCES AS SERVICES

As economists or as consumers, we are interested in the particular services that resources yield, not in the resources themselves. Examples of such services are an ability to conduct electricity, an ability to support weight, energy to fuel autos, energy to fuel electrical generators, and food calories.

The supply of a service will depend upon (a) which raw materials can supply that service with the present technology; (b) the availabilities of these materials at various qualities; (c) the costs of extracting and processing them; (d) the amounts needed at the present level of technology to supply the services that we want; (e) the extent to which the previously extracted materials can be recycled; (f) the cost of recycling; (g) the cost of transporting the raw materials and services; and (h) the social and institutional arrangements in force. What is relevant to us is not whether we can find any lead in existing lead mines but whether we can have the services of lead batteries at a reasonable price; it does not matter to us whether this is accomplished by recycling lead, by making batteries last forever, or by replacing lead batteries with another contraption. Similarly, we want intercontinental telephone and television communication, and, as long as we got it, we do not care whether this requires 100,000 tons of copper for cables or just a single quarter-ton communications satellite in space that uses no copper at all.[7]

Let us see how this concept of services is crucial to our understanding of natural resources and the economy. To return to Crusoe's cooking pot, we are interested in a utensil that we can put over the fire and cook with. After iron and aluminum were discovered, quite satisfactory cooking pots, perhaps even better than pots of copper, could be made of these materials. The cost that interests us is the cost of providing the cooking service rather than the cost of copper. If we suppose that copper is used only for pots and that iron is quite satisfactory for the same purpose, as long as we have cheap iron it does not matter if the cost of copper rises sky high. (But in fact that has not happened. As we have seen, the prices of the minerals themselves, as well as the prices of the services they perform, have fallen over the years.)

ARE NATURAL RESOURCES FINITE?

Incredible as it may seem at first, the term "finite" is not only inappropriate but is downright misleading when applied to natural resources, from both the practical and philosophical points of view. As with many of the important arguments in this world, the one about "finiteness" is "just semantic." Yet the semantics of resource scarcity muddle public discussion and bring about wrong-headed policy decisions.

The word "finite" originates in mathematics, in which context we all learn it as schoolchildren. But even in mathematics the word's meaning is far from unambiguous. It can have two principal meanings, sometimes with an apparent contradiction between them.[8] For example, the length of a one-inch line is finite in the sense that it is bounded at both ends. But the line within the endpoints contains an infinite number of points; these points cannot be counted, because they have no defined size. Therefore the number of points in that one-inch segment is not finite. Similarly, the quantity of copper that will even be available to us is not finite, because there is no method (even in principle) of making an appropriate count of it, given the problem of the economic definition of "copper," the possibility of creating copper or its economic equivalent from other materials, and thus the lack of boundaries to the sources from which copper might be drawn.

Consider this quote about potential oil and gas from Sheldon Lambert, an energy forecaster. He begins, "It's like trying to guess the number of beans in a jar without knowing how big the jar is." So far so good. But then he adds, "God is the only one who knows—and even He may not be sure."[9] Of course Lambert is speaking lightly. But the notion that some mind might know the "actual" size of the jar is misleading, because it implies that there is a fixed quantity of standard-sized beans. The quantity of a natural resource that might be available to us—and even more important the quantity of the services that can eventually be rendered to us by that natural resource—can never be known even in principle, just as the number of points in a one-inch line can never be counted even in principle. Even if the "jar" were fixed in size, it might yield ever more "beans." Hence resources are not "finite" in any meaningful sense.

To restate: A satisfactory *operational* definition of the quantity of a natural resource, or of the services we now get from it, is the only sort of definition that is of any use in policy decisions. The definition must tell us about the quantities of a resource (or of a particular service) that we can expect to receive in any particular year to come, at each particular price, conditional on other events that we might reasonably expect to know (such as use of the resource in prior years). And there is no reason to believe that at any given moment in the future the available quantity of any natural resource or service at present prices will be much smaller than it is now, or non-existent. Only such one-of-a-kind resources as an Arthur Rubenstein concert or a Julius Erving basketball game, for which there are no close replacements, will disappear in the future and hence are finite in quantity.

Why do we become hypnotized by the word "finite"? That is an interesting question in psychology, education, and philosophy. A first likely reason is that the word "finite" seems to have a precise and unambiguous meaning in any context, even though it does not. Second, we learn the word in the context of mathematics, where all propositions are tautologous definitions and hence can be shown logically to be true or false (at least in principle). But scientific subjects are empirical rather than definitional, as twentieth-century philosophers have been at great pains to emphasize. Mathematics is not a science in the ordinary sense because it does not deal with facts other than the stuff of mathematics itself, and hence such terms as "finite" do not have the same meaning elsewhere that they do in mathematics.

Third, much of our daily life about which we need to make decisions is countable and finite—our weekly or monthly salaries, the number of gallons of gas in a full tank, the width of the backyard, the number of greeting cards you sent out last year, or those you will send out next year. Since these quantities are finite, why shouldn't the world's total possible salary in the future, or the gasoline in the possible tanks in the future, or the number of cards you ought to send out, also be finite? Though the analogy is appealing, it is not sound. And it is in making this incorrect analogy that we go astray in using the term "finite."

A fourth reason that the term "finite" is not meaningful is that we cannot say with any practical surety where the bounds of a relevant resource system lie, or even if there are any bounds. The bounds for the Crusoes are the shores of their island, and so it was for early man. But then the Crusoes found other islands. Mankind traveled farther and farther in search of resources—finally to the bounds of continents, and then to other continents. When America was opened up, the world, which for Europeans had been bounded by Europe and perhaps by Asia too, was suddenly expanded. Each epoch has seen a shift in the bounds of the relevant resource system. Each time, the old ideas about "limits," and the calculations of "finite resources" within those bounds, were thereby falsified. Now we have begun to explore the sea, which contains amounts of metallic and other resources that dwarf any deposits we know about on land. And we have begun to explore the moon. Why shouldn't the boundaries of the system from which we derive resources continue to expand in such directions, just as they have expanded in the past? This is one more reason not to regard resources as "finite" in principle.

You may wonder, however, whether "non-renewable" energy resources such as oil, coal, and natural gas differ from the recyclable minerals in such a fashion that the foregoing arguments do not apply. Energy is particularly important because it is the "master resource"; energy is the key constraint on the availability of all other resources. Even so, our energy supply is non-finite, and oil is an important example. (1) The oil potential of a particular well may be measured, and hence is limited (though it is interesting and relevant that as we develop new ways of extracting hard-to-get oil, the economic capacity of a well increases). But the number of wells that will eventually produce oil, and in what quantities, is not known or measurable at present and probably never will be, and hence is not meaningfully finite. (2) Even if we make the unrealistic assumption that the number of potential wells in the earth might be surveyed completely and that we could arrive at a reasonable estimate of the oil that might be obtained with present technology (or even with technology that will be developed in the next 100 years), we still would have to reckon the future possibilities of shale oil and tar sands—a difficult task. (3) But let us assume that we could reckon the oil potential of shale and tar sands. We would then have to reckon the conversion of coal to oil. That, too, might be done; yet we still could not consider the resulting quantity to be "finite" and "limited." (4) Then there is the oil that we might produce not from fossils but from new crops—palm oil, soybean oil, and so on. Clearly, there is no meaningful limit to this source except the sun's energy. The notion of finiteness does not make sense here, either. (5) If we allow for the substitution of nuclear and solar power for oil, since what we really want are the services of oil, not necessarily oil itself, the notion of a limit makes even less sense. (6) Of course the sun may eventually run down. But even if our sun were not as vast as it is, there may well be other suns elsewhere.

About energy from the sun: The assertion that our resources are ultimately finite seems most relevant to energy but yet is actually more misleading with respect to energy than with respect to other resources. When people say that mineral resources are "finite" they are invariably referring to the earth as a boundary, the "spaceship earth," to which we are apparently confined just as astronauts are confined to their spaceship. But the main source of our energy even now is the sun, no matter how you think of the matter. This goes far beyond the fact that the sun was the prior source of the energy locked into the oil and coal we use. The sun is also the source of the energy in the food we eat, and in the trees that we use for many purposes. In coming years, solar energy may be used to heat homes and water in many parts of the world. (Much of Israel's hot water has been heated by solar devices for years, even when the price of oil was much lower than it is now.) And if the prices of conventional energy supplies were to rise considerably higher than they now are, solar energy could be called on for much more of our needs, though this price rise seems unlikely given present technology. And even if the earth were sometime to run out of sources of energy for nuclear processes—a prospect so distant that it is a waste of time to talk about it—there are energy sources on other planets. Hence the notion that the supply of energy is finite because the earth's fossil fuels even its nuclear fuels are limited is sheer nonsense.

Whether there is an "ultimate" end to all this—that is, whether the energy supply really is "finite" after the sun and all the other planets have been exhausted—is a question so hypothetical that it should be compared with other metaphysical entertainments such as calculating the number of angels that can dance on the head of a pin. As long as we continue to draw energy from the sun, any conclusion about whether energy is "ultimately finite" or not has no bearing upon present policy decisions. . . .

SUMMARY

A conceptual quantity is not finite or infinite in itself. Rather, it is finite or infinite if you make it so—by your own definitions. If you define the subject of discussion suitably, and sufficiently closely so that it can be counted, then it is finite—for example, the money in your wallet or the socks in your top drawer. But without sufficient definition the subject is not finite—for example, the thoughts in your head, the strength of your wish to go to Turkey, your dog's love for you, the number of points in a one-inch line. You can, of course, develop definitions that will make these quantities finite; but that makes it clear that the finiteness inheres in you and in your definitions rather than in the money, love, or one-inch line themselves. There is no necessity either in logic or in historical trends to suggest that the supply of any given resource is "finite."

NOTES

1. Meadows, Dennis L.; William W. Behrens, III; Donella H. Meadows; Roger F. Naill; Jorgen Randers; and Erich K. O. Zahn, *Dynamics of Growth in a Finite World* (Cambridge, Mass.: Wright-Allen, 1974) p. vii.
2. U.S. The White House, Population and the American Future, *The Report of the Commission on Population Growth and the American Future* (New York: Signet, 1972) pp. 2–3.
3. Meadows, Dennis L. et al., op. cit., p. 265.
4. U.S. The White House, The President's Materials Policy Commission (The Paley Commission), *Resources for Freedom*, 4 vols. (Washington, D.C.: GPO, 1952) summary of vol. 1, pp. 12–13; idem, p. 1.

5. Ibid., p. 2.
6. Ibid., p. 1.
7. Fuller, Buckminster, *Utopia or Oblivion: The Prospect for Humanity* (New York: Bantam, 1969) p. 4, quoted by Weber, James A., *Grow or Die!* (New Rochelle, N.Y.: Arlington House, 1977) p. 45.
8. I appreciate a discussion of this point with alvin Roth.
9. Sheldon Lambert, quoted in *Newsweek,* June 27, 1977, p. 71.

Energy and Climate Change

George W. Rathjens

AN INTRODUCTION TO THE GREENHOUSE PROBLEM

With the oil shocks of the 1970s, energy policy became an important issue in the United States and most other developed countries, and there developed an impetus to reduce dependence on imported oil through conservation and emphasis on alternative means of energy supply and use. In the trade-off studies that followed, and in debate and legislation, much attention was given to the undesirable effects of burning coal: the emission of sulfur and nitrogen oxides and their destructive effects on ecology and health. There were also references to the fact that carbon dioxide (CO_2) content of the atmosphere would be increased by such combustion, and that of other carbonaceous materials, and that this could lead to a change in world climate, a global warming. When, during the 1980s, summer temperatures, at least in the United States, were noticeably warmer than people were used to, concern about a causal linkage between energy use and climate change increased. Study efforts accelerated and the results got widespread attention. Most of the serious analytical work and a spate of popular articles suggested that if man's consumption of fossil fuels has not already committed us to significant climatic change, continued use of such fuels and changes in the amounts of some other trace gases in the atmosphere will.

This is not a new thesis. It has long been realized that were the earth not endowed with an atmosphere containing a substantial amount of carbon dioxide it would be covered with ice, and be about 34°C. colder. That it is, on average, as warm as it is, is due to the so-called greenhouse effect. This arises because CO_2 and water vapor, along with some other trace gases in the atmosphere, are nearly transparent to light in the visible part of the electromagnetic spectrum, where solar radiation peaks, but are strongly absorbing in some parts of the infrared spectrum. Because an atmosphere containing these greenhouse gases

Selection "Energy and Climate Change" by George W. Rathjens, from *Preserving the Global Environment*, The Challenge of Shared Leadership, edited by Jessica Tuchman Mathews, is reprinted with the permission of George W. Rathjens and W. W. Norton & Company, Inc. Copyright © 1991 by The American Assembly.

(GHGs) envelopes the earth, absorbing some of the infrared radiation from it, the earth's surface is heated to a significantly higher temperature than would be the case for a planet without such an atmosphere. This is essential for the maintenance of thermal equilibrium,[1] i.e, so that the net outward flux from the earth-atmosphere system will balance the heat flux from the sun.

If the amount of CO_2 in the atmosphere were to change, one would expect the equilibrium temperature of the earth to change with it. Although it is by no means obvious that relatively low CO_2 concentrations led to the ice ages, or were even important causal factors, there is a strong correlation between atmospheric CO_2 levels and global average temperatures in ice ages and interglacial periods[2] (see Figure 1). Measurements of the surface temperature of Venus, where the concentration of CO_2 is much higher than in the case of the earth,

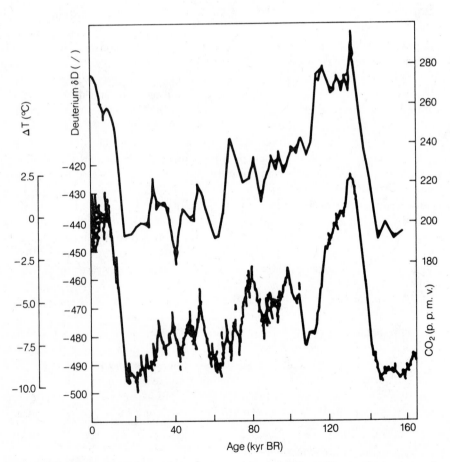

Figure 1 Carbon dioxide levels and temperatures over the last 160,000 years from Vostok 5 Ice Core in Antartica. The temperature scale is for Antartica; the corresponding amplitude of global temperatures swings is thought to be about 5 degrees Centigrade.

also consistent with the greenhouse theory. Even after allowing for the difference in the intensity of radiant energy from the sun due to its different distance from it, Venus is much hotter than would be the case were its atmosphere similar to that enveloping the earth.

But change in average temperatures is only the beginning of the story as regards the impact of GHG loading on climate. The second-order effects—patterns of cloud cover, precipitation, winds, ocean currents, and glaciation—depend sensitively on average surface temperatures and, notably, on seasonal and geographic differences in temperatures.

Until the industrial revolution, the composition of the earth's atmosphere changed slowly—the CO_2 concentration increased from about 195 parts per million (ppm) during the last ice age, 18,000 years ago, to 280 ppm in the late 1700s; but it has been increasing at an accelerating rate since then. It is now about 352 ppm and increasing at about 1.2 ppm per year (see Figure 2). Additionally, other greenhouse gases arising from human industrial and agricultural activities—notably methane, nitrous oxide, tropospheric ozone, and chlorofluorocarbons (CFCs)—are being added to the earth's atmosphere at accelerat-

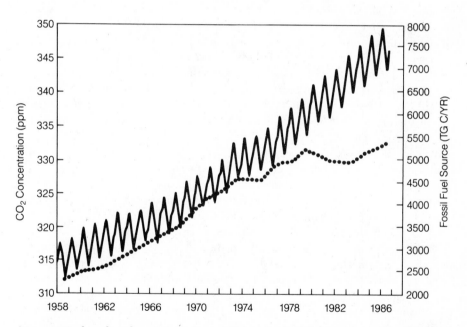

Figure 2 Carbon dioxide concentrations at Mauna Loa and fossil CO_1 emissions. The solid line depicts monthly concentrations of atmospheric CO_2 at Mauna Loa Observatory, Hawaii. The yearly oscillation is explained mainly by the annual cycle of photosynthesis and respiration of plants in the Northern Hemisphere. The steadily increasing concentration of atmospheric CO_2 at Mauna Loa since the 1950s is caused primarily by the CO_2 inputs from fossil fuel combustion (dashed line). Note that CO_2 concentrations have continued to increase since 1979, despite relatively constant emissions; this is because emissions have remained substantially larger than net removal, which is primarily by ocean uptake.

ing rates, and are now estimated to be about as significant in their collective impact on climate as the changes in CO_2 composition that have occurred in the last century.

Most of the change in atmospheric GHG concentrations is directly attributable to energy use. Perhaps 80 percent of the CO_2 increase is due to the burning of fossil fuels (the remainder, mostly to the burning of tropical forests and production of cement); some of the methane increase is due to mining of coal, leakage from gas pipelines, wells, and refineries; the tropospheric ozone is due mainly to the use of internal combustion engines, which are major factors in the creation of photochemical smog; and some of the CFC loading is due to leakage from refrigerating and air conditioning equipment. Thus the "greenhouse problem" is seen as largely one of energy use. And if one is concerned about the possible effects of energy use on *global* climate, the greenhouse issue *is* the problem. (Local climate can be affected by the diversion of rivers and creation of reservoirs for hydroelectric power generation, and by high power output in urban areas.)

What are likely to be the climatic effects of changing GHG loading of the atmosphere? What might be the effects of the consequent climatic changes on humans? What can be done, what is likely to be done, and what should be done to mitigate adverse effects and/or adapt to them? All these questions demand serious attention by scientists and policy makers, now that it seems likely that human activities, including particularly the use of energy, will lead to significant changes in climate some time in the next century.

But there is still considerable doubt about how large and serious the effects might be. Although substantial efforts have been made to model climate, the problems are formidable, and the results so far are anything but definitive. There are many nonlinear processes, competing effects, and feedback loops involved, so that great uncertainty attaches to attempts to estimate the magnitude of effects and, in some instances, even the sign.

The problem is particularly complicated because so much of the earth's surface is covered by water and because, at the temperatures that obtain on the earth, water is present in significant quantities in all three phases: gas, liquid, and solid. The formation, dissipation, and characteristics of clouds are consequently important determinants of climate and so, too, is the transfer of heat and CO_2 within the oceans, and between the oceans and the atmosphere. Unfortunately, some of the processes are poorly understood. For example, it is not yet clear whether clouds have a net heating or cooling effect. They reflect short wave solar radiation, tending to cool the earth, but they also absorb longer wave radiation, thereby acting as GHGs do, warming it. In trying to estimate the effects on climate of clouds, one must they try to estimate the difference between two large quantities, which difference is likely to be much more significant than the *direct* effects of the GHGs. Since the distribution of clouds is likely to depend in very complicated ways on temperatures at the earth's surface and in the atmosphere, there is the possibility of feedback effects of GHG-induced warming being either positive or negative; in fact, of both occurring simultaneously, varying regionally. . . .

From this very limited discussion, it should be clear that the state of the art in modeling climate does not now permit confident prediction of the likely consequences of increases in GHG loading for climate on a global scale, much less on regional bases. Having said this, there is agreement among those engaged in climate modeling on at least two important points, in addition to acceptance of the fact of increasing atmospheric GHG concentrations since the industrial revolution, and of a correlation between atmospheric CO_2 concentration and global temperatures on *geologic* time scales.

a) There is a significant disparity between, on the one hand, the amounts of CO_2 that are released to the atmosphere through combustion of fuels and the burning and decay of vegetation and, on the other, the increases that are measured in the atmosphere. Apparently, about half of the amounts released are removed through photosynthesis and absorption in sea water (and possibly by other mechanisms, unknown).

b) The ocean-atmosphere system is not now at anything like equilibrium. Of major importance is the fact that the heat capacity of the oceans— even of just the upper layers, where mixing time is of the order of a decade or two—is enormous. Accordingly, the oceans can act as a great "sink" for heat, which means that, on a global scale, the full heating effects of increasing levels of GHGs will be much delayed. Additionally, the removal of CO_2 by absorption in the oceans may also be delayed because of the long time constants for mixing of the surface and deeper layers. Because of these phenomena, it could be anywhere from one to several decades before the effects of recent releases of GHGs are reflected in climate change.

There seems, in addition, to be consensus, but by no means unanimity in the community, on the following:

c) Although comparison of satellite and surface-based measurements of temperatures over the last decade raise some doubts about the adequacy of the latter as a basis for reaching conclusions about long-term temperature trends, the average temperature of the earth *appears* to have increased by about 0.5 degrees C. over the last century. . . .

d) It will not likely be possible before the first decade of the next century to make meaningful estimates of regional climatic change with a resolution of better than a few hundred kilometers.

e) It now appears likely that an increase in CO_2 content to twice its preindustrial levels—or the equivalent in total increase in GHG accumulation— will result in an increase in average temperature of 1.5 to 4.5 degrees C. for the earth as a whole. Current trends in emission suggest that this loading may be realized by about 2035. (Dissenters suggest that the range of temperative increase could be an order of magnitude smaller, significantly because changes in cloud cover and characteristics may dwarf the *direct* effects of changes in GHG levels. On the other hand, increases in atmospheric water content with increasing temperature, not fully reflected in most modeling so far, could mean that warming could well be greater than the 1.5–4.5 degree estimate.)

f) It is probable that however great the average increase, it will be several times as large in the polar regions and correspondingly less in the tropics.

g) With a doubling of the GHG loading, average sea level is likely to rise by 0.2 to 0.5 meters.

h) With such doubling, annual precipitation would likely increase overall by a few percent, but there would be marked changes in precipitation patterns. There would likely be increases in high latitudes and the coastal regions of the temperate zones. In the interior regions of the temperate zones, there would be a decrease in moisture content in soils and possibly in precipitation.

PROJECTING ENERGY USE

All this suggests that there is a very broad consensus in the geophysical community that continuing increases in GHG content of the atmosphere will likely lead to climate change that will at least be noticeable sometime in the next century and that may have great impact on humans and their environment, but that there is great uncertainty about the magnitude of change as a function of the level, and the rate of increase, of GHGs. There is also great uncertainty about future patterns of energy use, and other factors that determine GHG levels, and projecting those factors over decades, which is what is desired for policy presciption, turns out to be of about the same order of difficulty and the results, so far, about as uncertain, as attempting to forecast climate as a function of GHG loading.

Until the oil shocks of 1973, one might have had a more sanguine view of energy forecasting, at least as regards the United States. Electricity used increased at a nearly constant rate of 6.9 percent per year from 1920 until the early 1970s (5.5 percent per capita per year), something quite remarkable considering that the period included the Great Depression and World War II. And, utilities came to accept this rate of increase as a basis for planning. More significantly for our purposes, the elasticity of energy use with respect to growth in the gross national product (GNP) was stable from the early 1940s until the early 1970s: With each increase of 1 percent in GNP, energy use increased by about 0.9 percent. From this—and from crossnational comparisons of the ratios of energy use to GNP (see Table 1)—there developed a fairly widespread view that the two were inherently tightly coupled: increase in energy use was seen as essential to economic growth, including notably for societies making the transition from poverty to affluence.

But in all of the Organization for Economic Cooperation and Development (OECD) countries, both the trend in electricity use as a function of time and the correlation between growth in energy use and GNP broke after 1973. The rate of increase in use of electricity in the American economy has been about one-third since then of what it had been (and the rate per capita, about one-quarter);

Table 1   ENERGY INTENSITY
1986 Energy Consumption per $ (1980) of GNP
(kilojoules)

Switzerland	6,389
France	8,719
Sweden	8,871
Japan	9,797
Austria	10,544
Italy	10,989
Germany (Fed Rep)	11,304
United Kingdom	14,591
United States	20,664
USSR	24,400
Canada	24,454
India	26,348
Egypt	34,372
China	43,394
Hungary	49,655
Poland	88,255

and the rate of increase in energy use with increasing GNP has dropped by a factor of about ten. It is noteworthy that corresponding changes did not occur in the centrally planned economies. The energy elasticity to GNP remained at about 1.25 for the Soviet Union, just about the same value that obtained from 1960 to the mid-1970s, and for Eastern Europe, the elasticity actually increased slightly.

Why the energy to GNP elasticity for Western economies has dropped so dramatically is not entirely clear. Three factors, all largely absent in the case of the centrally planned economies, have presumably been important: structural changes, i.e., increases in services relative to energy-intensive industries; legislative and regulatory actions designed to reduce energy use, e.g., the establishment of corporate automobile fuel economy (CAFE) standards; and consumer and industrial responsiveness to increasing costs of energy. (The short-term responsiveness of industry, in particular, seems to have been much greater than many analysts expected.) Whatever the explanation of energy use in Western economies made before about 1975 now seem much inflated. Thus projections for U.S. energy requirements for the year 1985 that were made in 1972 and 1973 generally turned out to be about 60 percent too high; and projections made in 1972–73 for the year 2000 roughly twice those made a decade later.

The dramatic drop in the elasticity of energy use to GNP is especially noteworthy for it lends substantial weight to the thesis of many environmentalists that material well-being need not imply profligate use of energy, and that attempting to reduce energy-related environmental insults through conservation may be less costly than many had thought likely as recently as ten or fifteen years ago. . . .

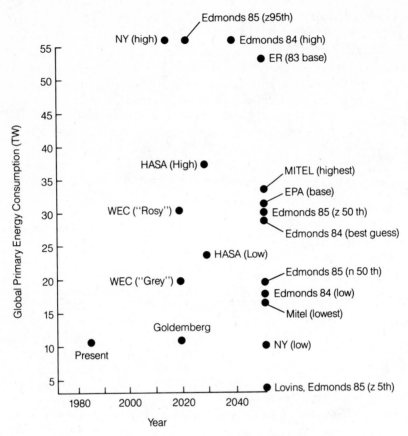

Figure 3 Projections of global primary energy consumption to 2050.

When one compounds the uncertainty [of estimate of future energy use] with that in climate change, *given* a specified level of energy use, it will be apparent that no one should have *any* confidence in a forecast of climate change for say 2020, much less for more remote periods. One should not conclude from this, however, that modeling efforts are worthless. They can be useful for sensitivity analysis, e.g., for estimating how CO_2 emissions, if not climate, might *change* with, say, increased use of nuclear power or electrically powered automobiles. . . .

SPECULATIONS ON THE ECOLOGICAL AND HUMAN CONSEQUENCES OF CLIMATIC CHANGE

With the world probably committed to a more rapid rate of temperature increase than has ever occurred in the past, based on GHG emissions that have occurred during this century and those that can be reasonably projected for the next decade or two,[3] a question arises as to whether humankind, its institutions, and other biological species will be able to adapt readily. A highly differentiated conclusion is almost certainly in order.

Natural species, particularly those unique to particular islands and other isolated regions, may simply die out, and even in the case of those that are found over much larger geographical ranges, there could be massive reductions in, and in some cases increases in populations. Considering the interdependence of biological species, whole ecological systems could be destroyed or transformed, especially with the destruction of wetlands, estuaries, and barrier islands. The possibility of dramatic changes in ocean currents—of which recent variations in El Niño provide an example—could have catastrophic effects on fisheries and local climates.

At the other extreme, many humans, particularly those in modern industrial societies, are not likely to face unusual problems of adjustment. As people have moved from one place to another, they have experienced and adapted to far greater changes in climate than are likely to occur in any one region in a single generation. Particularly in the United States, with it unusually mobile population, people have moved readily in response to economic pressures and opportunities. So has industry; witness the displacement of the textile industry from New England to the South. Moreover, movement has become easier than at an earlier time in our history when a large fraction of our population was engaged in agriculture, or even a generation ago when heavy industry, with its dependence on easy access to raw materials, power, and transportation, played a larger part in our economy. For such industries as information processing and light electronics, location is essentially irrelevant except insofar as the environment, including availability of housing, cultural opportunities, and so on must be attractive to workers.

One can imagine, in the event of gradual warming, movement of both people and industry from regions that become climatically less attractive to those that become more so, at no great *collective*[4] cost. There could well be some reversal, or at least attenuation, of population movement from our northern states to Florida and the Southwest. Presumably fuel bills for most people in the advanced industrial countries would decrease and sales of air conditioners and the cost of running them would increase, including, remotely perhaps, even in northern Europe. We would likely see increased squabbling over water rights in our western states—something that is likely to occur even absent climatic change, given population pressures in the Southwest. But the prospect of such changes is not likely to get most people really very excited about GHG emissions.

For agriculture, adaptation to climatic changes can be expected to be more difficult, but with time scales measured in decades, one can imagine changes in agricultural practices—growing wheat in regions formerly used for corn, developing new strains of plants better adapted to a changed climate, abandoning some farms and opening up other areas to agriculture—that would not seem traumatic, much less impossible, for world agriculture in the aggregate, or even for any of the world's major diversified agricultural producers. It is perhaps worth noting that although the United States is one of the world's great agricultural producers, the direct contribution of its farms to GNP is only 2 percent. Obviously, substantial decreases or increases in its agricultural productivity would have little impact on the standard of living of most Americans.

For many in the developing world, adjustment to climatic change may be much more difficult; indeed, for some, impossible. Poverty implies less mobility and less flexibility to otherwise adapt to change. For the Dutch, building higher dikes as a hedge against rising sea levels and greater frequency of storms is a realistic possibility. Not so for the Bangladeshis. Their choices are likely to be between attempting migration to an already overpopulated, and hence a probably resistant, India or death by drowning or starvation—not all at once or suddenly, for there is no basis for projecting a sudden, dramatic rise in sea level—but as a result of intermittent flooding of increasing severity and perhaps frequency.

But it is perhaps worth noting here that the rates of increase in sea level and of other adverse manifestations of global warming are likely to be very low compared to the rates of population increase for most of the world's nations that are likely to be more vulnerable to climatic change. While ultimately global warming could mean the death of Bangladesh, for many years, for it and most other poor countries, rapid population growth will be a far more serious problem—and one more susceptible of mitigation.

While it is hard—probably impossible—to make much of a case to the effect that the world's present climate is optimal in any absolute sense, it is commonly argued that change would be *generally* undesirable because biological species, agricultural practices, human settlement patterns, and individuals have adapted to what we have. On balance, the benefits of change, it is claimed, would likely be exceeded, indeed perhaps be dwarfed, by the costs.

But it is conceivable that, with improvement in climate modeling capabilities, some nations—and interest groups—will conclude that they will likely be "winners" in the event of global warming, and if this turns out to be the case, they can hardly be expected to do much in support of mitigation efforts. In fact, there are already reports suggesting beneficial effects. Even aside from questions of whether one should have much confidence in such judgments, and the virtual certainty of unanticipated and very possibly offsetting adverse effects,[5] "intuition" about possible advantageous effects may carry some weight in the development of public opinion and in decision making. So too will cultural and experiential factors.

The case of the Soviet Union is perhaps instructive and important. At first blush, one might expect that it could benefit substantially from global warming. Winters would be less severe; it quite possibly would gain more in productive agricultural land than it would lose, particularly since the northern parts of the country were not stripped of top soil by glaciation in the last ice age, as was the case in much of Canada; access to ice-free waters, both ports and the Northeast Passage, would be improved; and any increases in sea level would be proportionately less troublesome than in the case of most other industrial nations. Moreover, although attitudes may be changing after such experiences as

Chernobyl, the pollution of Lake Baikal, and the despoliation of the Aral Sea, the history of the Soviet Union, and of the post–World War II Communist regimes of Eastern Europe, suggests a generally callous and, indeed, shocking disregard for maintenance of environmental quality.

To the extent that the foregoing speculations are borne out, the poor are more likely to suffer, and likely to suffer more, from climatic change than the rich. Inasmuch as a fair case can be made that the latter, including the Soviets, will have been disproportionately responsible, one must expect that climatic change, and even projections of it, will be a source of increased North-South tension. . . .

THE IMPACT OF UNCERTAINTY

Although at some point warming would surely be, on balance, disadvantageous for the world as a whole, there is presently *no solid basis* for believing that a *modest* degree of warming would be so.[6] Moreover, from the earlier commentary on modeling, both of the climatic effects of changes in GHG loading and of growth in energy consumption, it should be clear that it will be at least some years before we can have even modest confidence about whether, and when, the threat might become serious; about the details, e.g., whether, in a given area, precipitation will change, and if so by how much; and about who will be winners and who will be losers.

The fact of enormous uncertainty will, or course, be used by those skeptical about the GHG/global warming thesis to argue against mitigation initiatives that might be costly or socially disruptive. They could be right to the extent that one might compensate for delay by a combination of adaptation and more vigorous mitigation efforts that could be effected beginning at a later date. But proponents of early action can be expected to argue that, in the face of uncertainty, one must act on the basis of worst-case analysis: that if there is a significant possibility of climatic change that would be so severe that no combination of delayed adaptive and mitigative measures could be effectively ameliorative, mitigative measures should be undertaken promptly, the uncertainties not withstanding. They would be right to the extent that such measures were cost-free. But it will turn out that truly effective measures are likely to be costly to at least some people, interest groups, or nations, if not to the world as a whole; and if this is true, one cannot escape having to weigh benefits that are very uncertain (the avoidance of possible catastrophe, the very nature of which may be unforeseeable) against costs that seem certain (although in this case, perhaps not predictable with much precision). The problem is not unlike hedging against some other catastrophes. If one lives in California, one might want to buy insurance against earthquakes or make structural changes in one's home if possible damage might be catastrophic, *provided* the costs were not too high; but if they seemed excessive, or if one felt that he could cope with what he judged to be the worst plausible case, then he would forgo such investment (perhaps until the state of earthquake prediction and/or that of structural response to earthquakes had been refined to the point where better estimates could be made of expected damage).

The fact of uncertainty is likely, then, to greatly reduce the impetus to early and costly mitigation initiatives and tip the argument strongly in favor of adaptation as compared with mitigation. There is surely a case for research to reduce some of the uncertainties in climate modeling and societal responses, and since much can be done at *relatively* modest cost, greater emphasis on this is an obvious meeting ground for those committed to early mitigative action and those favoring delay.

THE "COMMONS" PROBLEM

In the classic version of the "commons" problem, the presumption is that maintenance of the "commons" is in everyone's interest, but in the case of global warming there will almost certainly be some who will benefit from warming, or believe that they are likely to benefit, and so will not have an interest in climate stabilization. Thus, and even putting aside the complicating fact of great uncertainty, getting agreement on some instrumentality to insure that everyone—or at least a significant number—makes an appropriate contribution to a group effort to achieve the benefits of a well-maintained commons will be more difficult than in the usual case.

The global warming problem will differ somewhat from the classic commons problem in another respect. In the latter, it is assumed that no single agent will benefit enough from his own actions to justify a solo effect. In the global warming case, at least some unilateral actions can probably be justified on cost-benefit grounds. Of agents, nations are almost certainly of greatest interest, and of these, the largest merit particular attention, primarily because they are the greatest contributors to the greenhouse problem. To the extent that loss from adverse climatic change might scale with size, they would also have the most to gain from mitigation.

Because it is the largest GHG contributor, the first candidate for unilateral mitigative action would likely be the United States. Moreover, since its GNP is about one-fourth of the world total, one might also argue that it could perhaps capture one-fourth of the total benefits of any unilateral mitigation effort it might undertake. If so, such an effort would be rational on economic grounds if the benefit-to-cost (B/C) ratio for the world as a whole were to exceed four. If one assumes the benefit from mitigating climate change to be proportional to population rather than GNP, the prime candidate for unilateral action would, of course, be China, and with almost a quarter of the world's population, one again arrives at a critical B/C ratio of four. Considering the dubious nature of the underlying assumptions—and that adaptation to change will generally be relatively easier for large nations than for smaller ones, *ceteris paribus*, these ratios should certainly not be taken very seriously. In fact, it is quite plausible that the United States, China, or both might not even be "losers." The fact remains, however, that the United States, China, and maybe the Soviet Union, India, and Japan are so large that unilateral mitigation efforts by one or more of them *might* make good sense. This would hold also for the European Community (EC), assuming a degree of unity that would permit concerted action, and a *fortiori* for, say, the OECD. To an extent, then, the GHG climate problem may differ somewhat from the usual one of the commons.

But even if it could be demonstrated that substantial unilateral mitigative action by one of these entities would make sense, such action would be of exceedingly limited utility, unless there were extensive emulation by others. This is because it must be expected that the benefit-to-cost ratio will drop dramatically with increasing effort. While the United States might, as a result of policy decisions, quite plausibly reduce its GHG emissions by, say, 5 percent below the levels that would otherwise obtain, thereby effecting a delay in the realization of a doubling of GHG loading by perhaps nine months, to "buy" an additional nine months' time would likely be much more costly. If the United States were to *eliminate* its emissions, the cost would be astronomically great and the delay in GHG doubling would only be about twenty years. In fact, of course, elimination of emissions will be politically, if not physically, totally unrealistic, at least for the foreseeable future.

For practical purposes, then, the GHG problem has to be seen essentially as a commons problem, notwithstanding the fact that *at the margin*, the largest actors might logically find some unilateral mitigation initiatives attractive. Some steps already taken, albeit for other reasons, e.g., constraining CFC emissions, may be exemplary,[7] but to effect really major reductions, concerted action by at least most of the major GHG producers will be required.[8]

While many political leaders have expressed concern about global warming, getting concurrence on *broadly based actions* that might result in mitigation is, then, the problem. The degree of motivation and the negotiating leverage available to the interested parties will vary enormously. It may be instructive to speculate on exemplary cases.

The most predictable adverse effect of global warming is probably rising sea level (although there is doubt even about this). This suggests that nations with large populations and/or valuable land at risk from flooding—the United States, the Netherlands, Egypt, Bangladesh, and Maldive Islands—would have especially great interests in the mitigation of GHG emissions. For the United States, the costs of such flooding could well be more or less offset by the costs of mitigation and/or by possible benefits of global warming. But for the others, rising sea level would almost certainly be, on balance, highly undesirable. None of the others would, however, have much bargaining power in a negotiation focused narrowly on the global warming problem since none are significant contributors to it. But their situations would be rather different. With adaptation probably a realistic option for the Netherlands, mitigation would be presumably less important to it; yet it would be in a stronger position to influence the outcome of negotiations because linkages to other issues could be drawn on to elicit support for its views from the European Community as a whole, which would have great bargaining power, and from the other members. And Egypt would be in a stronger bargaining position than Bangladesh because of its key role in the volatile Middle East and because of world concern about stability there. . . .

Then there are the cases of the Soviet Union and China, special because they are such large contributors to the GHG problem (together, their contribution is now about 25 percent of the world total) and because, in the absence of severe constraints on the use of fossil fuels, their contributions will grow disproportionately (to perhaps a third of the world total within the next century). It is not clear that either will see moderate global warming as particularly disadvantageous to it, and both are likely to see restrictions on the use of fossil fuels as costly. This is particularly true of China, which is now more than 50 percent dependent on coal for primary energy (compared with 33 percent and 20 percent for the United States and the Soviet Union, respectively) and which has the world's largest coal reserves by far, and the most expansive plans for its increased use. With other serious demands on resources, and with its population still growing at about 1.5 percent per year, it is hard to see how China might be induced to enter into an international agreement to limit GHG growth if the near-term costs were perceived to be large. Similar arguments would apply to India, which is also a very large producer and consumer of coal.[9]

One concludes that negotiating an effective international agreement to limit global warming by imposing constraints or taxes on the burning of carbonaceous fuels is likely to be exceedingly difficult—*far* more difficult than the Montreal Protocol. Some of the largest contributors to the problems would likely judge the direct benefits, if any, not commensurate with the costs to them, and most of those likely to reach the opposite conclusion on the cost-benefit issue would have little leverage to induce accession by the major actors.

THE PROBLEMS OF TIME DELAY AND DISCOUNTING

Attempting to limit global warming through government intervention (or initiatives by individuals or other entities) is made especially difficult because of the delay in climatic response to interventionary activities. This is in significant measure a consequence of the upper layers of the oceans acting, as has been mentioned, as a great heat sink. This alone can account for a delay in response of a decade or two. More important is the fact that the effects of GHG buildup will be cumulative over a time scale measured in centuries. This follows because at issue is not just the exchange of CO_2 between the atmosphere and the upper layers of the ocean, but also exchange involving the ocean depths and because, with the exception of methane and ozone, the other important greenhouse gases have lives in the range of 50 to 175 years. Accordingly, assuming there are benefits in mitigation of GHG emissions, they may be important over time periods of many generations. The costs of mitigation may also be significant over very long periods—really, until such time as energy (and agricultural and industrial) needs can be met more cheaply through non-GHG emitting processes than through those that produce GHGs. This is also a matter of at least generations, if it can ever be done.

One is confronted, then, with the problem of comparing costs and benefits, with the interval between the imposition of some of the costs and the realization of some of the benefits being measured in many generations.

The usual approach to such problems involves, of course, calculating whether an investment makes sense, depending on whether the discounted value of the benefits exceeds the discounted costs. Determining what discount rate may be appropriate is straightforward in some cases—for industry, it will be the cost of raising money through some combination of borrowing and sale of stock, adjusted to take account of taxes, and perhaps risk—but for public policy decisions, what is appropriate may be more contentious, even aside from the question of how risk factors should be dealt with. What is at issue is how society should allocate resources between current consumption and investment in the future. Those supporting high social discount rates generally contend that past history and the prospect of technological progress suggest that future generations will be so much better off than our own that we need not worry particularly about investment on their behalf. Proponents of low rates, on the other hand, argue that however individuals may feel about saving versus consumption, government has a special responsibility to invest in the future.[10] Some argue, additionally, that while in the past living standards have improved over time, this may not be true as we look to the future, and that the major argument for high discount rates may accordingly no longer be valid. How significant all this is and how sensitive it is to the particular choice of social discount rate is reflected in the fact that at a rate of 3 percent, the benefits of better climate, say, a hundred years hence, get discounted 19-fold but that at a discount rate of 10 percent, more than 13,000-fold. Even over a period as short as twenty-five years, the differences are very significant: twofold discounting at 3 percent versus more than tenfold at 10 percent. Although most economists would presumably settle on a figure of between 3 and 10 percent, in constant dollars, i.e., before making an upward adjustment for inflation, there is no consensus on a preferred value, notwithstanding decades of debate among interested parties.

Perhaps not surprisingly, many argue, with the realization of the implications of such accounting, that discounting at a non-zero rate is simply inappropriate in consideration of protecting the environment.[11] But the fact remains that most, though by no means all, individuals—and governments acting as their surrogates—do heavily discount the future when it comes to laying cash on the line, as distinct from expressing pious concern about, say, the preservation of rare species or the welfare of generations more than, say, two removed (or for that matter, about distant populations now living). . . .

One is forced to the conclusion that when the benefits of an investments are remote in time or space, or particularly both, most individuals and most governments are not likely to be willing to make great sacrifices. We are not likely to see substantial efforts to mitigate global warming by limiting GHG emissions if the costs are perceived to be large and if the adverse consequences of such warming are not likely to be severe for at least another generation. Reluctance to make such efforts is especially likely when adaptation to change would seem to be quite feasible for posterity and, on a discounted cost basis, cheap. Certainly on the record of the last decade, one must be particularly pessimistic about American leadership in respect to these matters.

CONCLUSIONS ABOUT DIRECT MITIGATIVE ACTION

When account is taken of all this, it is hard to escape the conclusion that attempts to slow the rate of global warming and the consequent climatic changes by trying to change patterns of energy use are likely to fail *to the extent that the rationale is mitigation of such change.* This is likely to be the case whether the concern is with just some of the worst "culprits" or about developing a broad international agreement on mitigation. Generally, the hope of reducing GHG emissions, and affecting any other factors that might bear on world climate, probably must lie primarily in "selling" measures—political, institutional, and technical—that are likely to have mitigating effects on climate change, not explicitly on those grounds but on *others*, e.g., on the grounds that they make sense in terms of reducing a nations' dependence of others for energy, that they are attractive because they may have rather immediately palpable environmental benefits, such as reducing smog or acid rain, or that they are likely to benefit powerful special interests.

Is there any reason to believe in—or hope for—more effective action of this kind than would occur in the absence of the possibility of climatic change? Almost certaintly there is. While they are surely not a majority, at least in "Western" cultures, there are many people who are not likely to view climatic change simply from the utilitarian or economic self-interest perspective that has underlain most of the preceding discussion: people who, as noted earlier, attach very special—even spiritual or religious—value to the preservation of biological species, variegated cultures, and the kind of physical environment they have known. It can reasonably be expected that many holding these views will work with greater zeal to implement measures affecting energy use, *which might be perceived to be beneficial on other grounds,* than they otherwise would if they also believe that those measures would be useful in mitigating climatic change that could be destructive of those special values to which they attach such weight.

THE LINKAGE BETWEEN GLOBAL CLIMATIC CHANGE, ENERGY CONSERVATION, AND LOCAL AND REGIONAL ENVIRONMENTAL PROBLEMS

Some energy options raise questions of conflicts between the objectives at issue in this section, economics even aside. Thus increased reliance on coal generally would contribute to energy independence for the United States (and China and India), and its use as feed stock for the production of methanol could lead to reductions in noxious automobile emissions, but all uses of coal would, of course, exacerbate the GHG problem.

Fortunately, though, most measures that might be taken in the interest of realizing any one of the objectives of interest here will have beneficial effects, or no effects at all, in respect to the others. And fortunately, from the perspective of mitigating climatic change, very strong cases can be made for undertaking actions that will conserve energy and/or reduce noxious emissions that are locally or regionally harmful, and which will *also* make global warming less likely.

Very importantly, the three main impediments to action on the climatic change problem either do not apply in respect of these other objectives or are much attenuated.

There can hardly be any qualitiative argument about desirability of energy conservation. It is important because we live in a world of finite resources and because the profligate use of them raises the prospect of future shortages and of conflict over them. And the dispersal of nitric and sulfur oxides is clearly—and, to an extent, calculably—undesirable because of the palpably adverse effects on human health and that of other biological species and, less importantly but nevertheless measurably, on structures. While there may be arguments as to the magnitude of effects and the costs of mitigation, there can be no serious claims—in contrast to the situation as regards global warming—that there will be "winners" in the event of failure to realize these other objectives, and no serious argument to the effect that profligate use of energy and the production of noxious gases from combustion can be dismissed as nonproblems.

The commons issue does arise in trying to deal with these other objectives, but difficult as it may be, it is far more tractable than in the global warming case, in large measure because the problems tend to be regional. Consequently, there are generally more effective instruments for dealing with them than in the global commons case: local governments in many instances, the United States government in disputes between our states, the possibility of the use of EC offices in the case of transfrontier pollution in Europe, and of bilateral negotiations in the case of the United States and its two immediate neighbors. Here the problems of time delay will be much less severe than in the global warming case. The public felt the effects of the oil shocks of the 1970s almost immediately in increased fuel prices and in shortages, and the adverse consequences on human health of noxious gases are felt almost immediately in the event of atmospheric inversions in many cities, and in some areas of Eastern Europe, almost continuously.

All of which is to say that the prospects of doing something to conserve energy and to reduce the emissions of undesirable by-products of its generation are *comparatively* good. Fortunately, there are many options for meeting energy demands and for reducing them in acceptable ways that are attractive on cost effectiveness grounds—some, probably so, even putting externalities aside. It may be appropriate here to do no more than note some that coincidentally offer great promise in reducing GHG emissions.

Foremost on any list must be conservation through greater energy efficiency.

While great price-induced improvements have been realized, especially within the OECD countries, as a response to the oil shocks of the 1970s, the intensity of energy use continues to be uneconomically high in many countries, notably in the United States, Canada, the Soviet Union, Eastern Europe, and many developing countries. The problems are not primarily technical but rather structural: deliberate subsidization of energy use, especially in developing countries; pricing that is unrealistically low—just another form of subsidization—common throughout Eastern Europe and the Soviet Union; and lack of knowledge, incentives, and access to capital at low rates, common everywhere, that might induce consumers and builders of housing to make capital investments that would be demonstrably beneficial in total life cycle costs.

Developments in solar generation of electricity and its possible application to the generation of hydrogen could substitute effectively and beneficially for hydrocarbon fuels. While great progress has been made in reducing the costs of solar-generated electricity, largely through the development of amorphous silicon technology, the point has not yet been reached where these possibilities are likely to have a significant impact on either the greenhouse problem or others of environmental concern.

Nuclear power has had an impact—CO_2 emissions are now less than they would have been without it—and its continued exploitation offers prospects second, in the near term, only to energy efficiency for further reduction in such emissions, but the prospects for its further growth remain decidedly clouded. There is now little doubt that reactors can be built that are "inherently safe," i.e., that are so configured that their ability to dissipate waste heat in the event of an accident or unscheduled shutdown will be sufficient to preclude a "meltdown" and the widespread dispersal of radioactive materials; but the memories of Three Mile Island and Chernobyl, the appalling mismanagement of military nuclear wastes, continuing concerns about the disposal wastes from power reactors, and worry about the possible spread of materials usable for the manufacture of nuclear weapons cannot be lightly dismissed. While the nuclear option will no doubt continue to be pursued in some countries, the choice will be difficult for most, even where the option appears to be economically competitive with fossil fuel generation of electricity.

SUMMARY—A BASIS FOR PLANNING

It is now all but certain that anthropogenic activities will lead to global warming that will be noticeable sometime in the next century. It is also, however, probable that the magnitude and details of the effects on climate and on human welfare will remain highly uncertain until sometime in that century.

Because of the uncertainty, the very long lag-times involved, and the fact that effective mitigative action is likely to require something approaching a global consensus, the prospects for near-term action *directed at reducing global warming* must be seen to be poor. These factors, and particularly the synergism between them, tend to make mitigation a less likely response to the "threat" than delay and eventual adaptation. Public policy would be well advised to face this reality.

This does not mean, however, that it will be either reasonable or desirable to base policy on simple projections of past trends in the emission of GHGs. Actions have been taken, and more are likely—and they should be encouraged—that will mean that such projections are likely to be unrealistically high. The CFC problem is on the way to being solved, mainly because of concern about ozone destruction and because solution seems not likely to be very costly; and desires for energy efficiency and concern about local and regional adverse effects of the combustion of fossil fuels will result in other GHG emissions being less than would be expected in a "business-as-usual" world.

It is clearly desirable that there be a better understanding of the nature and seriousness of the global warming problem, and so further research efforts merit strong support. Perhaps with the results of such research in hand, it will be possible to mobilize support for directed mitigative action, but pending that, betting on measures that can be effectively rationalized on other grounds, and planning on adaptation, will be important and probably more realistic.

NOTES

1. Actually the process is a bit more complex. The earth dissipates heat not only by radiating it away, but also by evaporation of water and convection to the atmosphere. Were it not for these last processes, the earth would be considerably warmer than it is.

2. It is widely believed that changes in the earth's orbital parameters may have been important, if not the dominant, causal factors. Changes in solar luminosity and volcanic activity may also have been contributing factors.

3. It is likely that the rates of change will be at least as great as those that occurred at the end of the medieval warm period and the beginning of the little ice age, and an order of magnitude greater than those that occurred at the end of the last great ice age, approximately 15,000 years ago.

4. This is not to say that many individuals and their families would not suffer. Many did during the exodus from the dust bowl of the 1930s when Nebraska, Kansas, and Oklahoma lost 3.6 percent of their population while the rest of the country grew by 7.8 percent.

5. One cannot help but feel that some analysts, obviously concerned about global warming, "reach" a bit as they argue that beneficial effects of warming may be offset by adverse effects. One analyst, for example, after noting that warming would likely have beneficial first-order effects on agricultural productivity in Japan and Finland, suggests that this could actually be unfortunate because the prices of rice in the former and of agricultural products in general in the latter are maintained at artificially high levels, as matters of governmental policy. The implication is that subsidization would continue in the event of warming to the net disbenefit of Japanese and Finnish taxpayers. Interestingly, in noting that warming might reduce production of American wheat, he does *not* comment on the benefits to American taxpayers of reduced costs of subsidization.

6. One should be cautious, however, about taking comfort in the possibility that such

warming might be tolerable for either the world as a whole or for particular regions. One of the most worrisome aspects of the greenhouse problem arises because of the likelihood—virtual certainty, in the absence of strong mitigative actions—that a realized "modest degree of warming" will foreshadow substantial additional warming because of the aforementioned phenomena of a decade or more's lag-time in the equilibrium of atmospheric and upper ocean level temperatures.

7. As noted earlier, acceptable alternatives to CFCs are likely to be available at relatively low-cost penalties; conceivably even at no penalty at all. Thus the imposition of severe constraints on use by any of the largest countries could well have made sense, even aside from the question of ozone damage and actions by other nations, assuming, of course, that the country in question believed it might be seriously damaged by GHG-induced warming.

8. These points can be perhaps usefully illustrated using some estimates due to W.D. Nordhous, which he emphasizes are very approximate and preliminary, (discussion paper for MIT workshop on energy and environmental modeling, 1989). He calculates damage from GHG-induced warming to the United States by 2050 to be 0.25 ± 2 percent of national income, in the absence of mitigation efforts. If one assumes the central value, i.e., 0.25 percent, one can calculate, using other estimates from his paper, that it would make sense for the United States, acting alone, to reduce its CO_2 emissions by about 5 percent. (Were we to try to go further, on our own, the costs to us would exceed the benefits of additional mitigation.) If, on the other hand, all nations could be induced to reduce their CO_2 emissions proportionally, the optimal reduction would be about 10 percent. If one assumes damage at the upper bound of Nordhaus's estimate, 2.25 percent, it makes sense to go further with CO_2 mitigation. His lower bound, -1.75 percent, implies, of course, that the United States would benefit from GHG-induced warming.

9. In the case of both China and India, the production of coal has been quite heavily subsidized, so there might be some hope that consumption could be reduced in these cases—or at least be expanded less rapidly than is planned—at little, if any, cost.

10. This argument goes back at least to Pigou.

11. While this has been a matter of strong convictions and much argument, there ought to be no conceptual difficulty in accepting non-zero discounting if it is recognized that the fundamental problem lies really in valuing the benefits at issue. What those who would decry discounting perhaps really means is that they attach such a high value to some aspects of environmental protection—say, the preservation of biological diversity—that for them, the benefits of preservation would exceed the costs of prevention of destruction—in our case, the costs of mitigation of climatic change that might lead to such destruction—at *any* discount rate. That discounting should be used in consideration of (at least some of) the implications of climatic change will be apparent if one thinks about the need for water for agricultural purposes. It is usual when contemplating the construction of a dam for irrigation purposes to discount the value of the irrigation water that it might provide. Surely it would be bizarre to discount such benefits from irrigation but then to argue that the benefits from future rainfall that might be realized by an investment in the avoidance of climate alteration should not be discounted.